Sara
Segerson

Communicating through letters and reports

[You learn more by thinking about what you're doing than by simply thinking or simply doing.]

Communicating through letters and reports

J. H. MENNING
Late Professor of Marketing
in Charge of Business Writing Courses
School of Commerce and Business Administration
University of Alabama

C. W. WILKINSON
Professor of Behavioral Studies
Graduate School of Business
College of Commerce and Business Administration
University of Alabama

PETER B. CLARKE
President, Arcus Company

with the assistance of
Dorothy Colby Menning Wilkinson

Sixth Edition 1976

RICHARD D. IRWIN, INC. Homewood, Illinois 60430
Irwin-Dorsey International Arundel, Sussex BN18 9AB
Irwin-Dorsey Limited Georgetown, Ontario L7G 4B3

Sixth Edition

First Printing, May 1976

ISBN 0-256-01819-7
Library of Congress Catalog Card No. 75–39456
Printed in the United States of America

Preface

Note to teachers and students:

THIS SIXTH EDITION of a popular book retains the basic content, spirit, and special teaching and learning aids which met with wide approval in the first five editions.

As before, the central purpose of the book is to help you improve your written business communications. We have retained the original philosophy that the emphasis should be on effective writing; so we stress how to use our remarkably flexible language effectively, with less attention to theories about how communication works. Peter B. Clarke, who after the death of Jack H. Menning was invited to become coauthor of this book, is in full agreement with this approach.

Though this edition is somewhat changed from the previous one, the changes are evolutionary, not revolutionary. Briefly, we have:

1. Updated the text, illustrations, and cases to more closely reflect current conditions and practices in business and industry.
2. Reorganized Parts One and Two, as suggested by a number of users of this textbook.
3. Better adapted the book for use in community colleges.
4. Given fuller treatment to report writing, especially the preparation of short reports in letter or memo form.
5. Revised and supplemented the case materials with many new problems for greater variety and currency.
6. Shortened the presentation wherever we could to help reduce the size of the book, but without hurting its effectiveness.
7. Made numerous editorial changes to increase conciseness, readability, and ease of application (and to avoid sex-indicating words except in contexts referring specifically to one sex or the other).
8. Improved the checklists, especially the reports checklist, to make them more broadly applicable, pointed, and concise—and thus more useful to students as guides and to teachers in marking papers.

Students and teachers of college courses in communicating through letters, through reports, and through combinations of the two will find the book easily adaptable to varying standards and student abilities. By attention to only the major principles and the easier problems, freshmen and sophomores of average ability can use the book effectively. By attention to all the refinements and the more difficult problems, upperclassmen in our best universities will find it among their most challenging texts.

Note to students (in and out of school):

In learning anything as complex as writing superior letters and reports, you need instruction in *principles,* then *illustrations,* and finally *practice* in applying the principles. Accordingly, the first four chapters (Part One) present what we consider to be the basic principles applicable to all business letters. If you go no further, you will have a sound fundamental concept of the language, style, psychology, persuasiveness, tone, and appearance of effective business letters.

For more detailed analysis and application, the next eight chapters (Part Two) show you how to handle your business letters functionally according to three basic plans: good-news, disappointing, and persuasive messages. Though the book presents analyses and examples of inquiries, replies, orders, acknowledgments, claims, adjustments, credits, sales, job applications, requests, and collections, the presentation is not in that order nor is the emphasis on specific letter types. As you read through the book, you will see the fundamentals applied in the many illustrations.

The final four chapters (Part Three) cover all important aspects of writing reports, including their importance, nature, classification, preparation, and appropriate styles of writing.

All of the illustrations are from actual business letters, reports, and memos, or based on actual situations. But because even comparatively good business letters that go through the mail may not serve well as textbook illustrations, we have sometimes edited them beyond merely changing the names of companies, products, and individuals. And in some instances, we have written our own illustrations. We are fully aware, however, that the perfect letter never has been and never will be written.

Having studied the principles and seen them illustrated, you can then make the principles stick in your mind (and thus make their application habitual) by putting them to use in working out selected cases from the many given at the ends of sections. The ample number and variety of cases (many of them in a new, more succinct style) allow selection to fit your interests, abilities, and desired emphasis.

The situations and problems embodied in the cases are drawn from our collective experiences in business and industry, from our reading, and from other sources. We have endeavored to make them as realistic and up-to-date as possible. Indeed, many of them are problems actually faced by real people recently. In a few instances we have the letters these people wrote, and they are included in the *Teacher's Guide.*

Writing *perfect* letters or reports is next to impossible for all of us. Writing even *good* ones does not just come naturally to most. If you are content to write them as many *are* written, instead of as they *should* be, you will gain little or nothing from studying this book (or any other book or course on writing). But with a concentrated effort to improve, you can learn to write superior ones.

Please remember, however, that this book is not a dictionary, formula book, or cookbook to be followed blindly. Your aim should be thoughtful consideration of principles for use in creating your own original writing rather than slavish imitation of textbook models. You should learn and follow the *principles* illustrated, *not the wording* of the illustrations.

Likewise, the checklists (a special feature of this book) are thought starters rather than thought-stopping rules to be followed blindly. They are summary reminders of points about the particular kind of letter under discussion, not formulas for writing or straitjackets on it. They do *not* mean that all the points discussed earlier about a kind of letter and summarized in a checklist are applicable to every letter of that general class. Thoughtful consideration of a point in a checklist will quickly tell you whether the point is applicable to your particular letter problem, but ignoring the lists will frequently lead to omission of important points; and slavish following of a list will often lead to inappropriate contents in a letter. Hence, when used properly, the checklists can help you produce better letters, help teachers to mark student shortcomings quickly, and thus help you to see where you went wrong.

From our own business experience, from the many people in business and industry we have talked and worked with, from thousands of articles in business magazines, from associating with many other teachers on the job, through long and active membership in the American Business Communication Association (including three terms as president), from widely varied consulting work, and from college students and business people we have taught, we have learned much about letters and reports and effective ways for teaching people to write better ones. We have brought together and modified what we have learned from a combined 90 years of experience. And we have contributed our own ideas.

In studying this one book, then, you learn what we think is the best that has been thought and said about letter and report writing through the years. By learning its suggestions, you can improve your letters and reports.

April 1976

C. W. WILKINSON
PETER B. CLARKE

Contents

Checklists

The letter cases in this book are disguised and sometimes slightly modified real situations. Mostly they are from among the more difficult letter-writing situations of business. Most names of firms and individuals are fictitious for obvious reasons.

We have tried to give you the basic information needed without complicating details. You are expected to fill in details from your own imagination. But you are not to go contrary to the statements or implications in the cases, and your imaginary details must be reasonably likely.

The writing in the problems is intentionally not good—nor is the order of points the best—because you would learn nothing from copying from us. So beware of copying sentences and clauses in your letters. Put your ideas in your own words.

Why study letter writing?

THE MAIN REASONS you should study letter writing are:

1. You are almost certain to write many business letters and memos during the rest of your life, regardless of the kind of work you do. Letters and memos are the most common forms of written communication for managing business affairs, and everybody has business affairs to manage.
2. Your degree of failure or success in managing many of those affairs will depend on whether you write ordinary letters and memos or really good ones.
3. All too often the untrained, unthinking business writer writes bad ones. Usually the procedure is to follow the bad writing style, the bad tone, the ineffective psychology, and even the messy or old-hat appearance of bad letters and memos received or read in the files.
4. Through systematic study and practice you can learn to write good letters and memos and thus greatly increase your chances of success in handling your personal business or business affairs on a job.

Other things you learn

In learning to write better letters and memos, you will also learn some principles of practical psychology that will enable you to get along better professionally and socially with other people.

When you improve your ability to write clear, concise, persuasive, and natural English (which *is* the desirable language of business), you gain accuracy and naturalness in phrasing anything else you have to write or speak.

Through your study of letters you will get further insight into the ways of the business world: practices used in getting people to buy; handling orders; gaining and refusing credit; making collections; adjusting claims; and selecting employees.

You will learn how to save time and money on business writing. As a good letter writer, you can often write one letter to settle a business transaction that would require two or three from an untrained writer. By using form letters and form paragraphs, you can cut down on letter costs when the form message will do the job. When, however, you have situations requiring individual letters, you will recognize them and know better than to waste money on forms.

You will also be able to dictate or write the necessary individual letters and memos more rapidly because you will have gained the self-confidence that comes from knowing how to tackle a job. You will write freely and effectively the letters and memos you *have* to write and the many others you *should* write.

Perhaps most important of all, you will realize that every letter and memo you write is an item in your overall public relations—and you will try to make each one win, instead of lose, friends.

Letter volume and costs

If you think letters aren't big business, consider this:

1. In 1975, the average cost of writing and mailing a business letter was $6.74. This figure, compiled by the Dartnell Corp., includes the time of the dictator and typist, stationery, postage, handling, and a portion of the costs of the dictating, transcribing, typing, and mailing equipment. If the letter is written by an upper level executive, the cost can soar to more than $10.00!
2. In the fiscal year ending June 30, 1975, the U.S. Postal Service handled 51,245,846,000 individual pieces of first-class mail.
3. For many years, the percentage of first-class mail that is business rather than personal has stood at 86 percent. The 14 percent that is personal includes Christmas cards, letters to and from your Aunt Susie, and postcards from vacation spots, for example.

A little simple arithmetic tells us that 86 percent of 51,245,846,000 is 44,071,427,560. Multiply this by $6.74 and we have $297,041,421,754.40 spent on business letters in this country in one year.

There's more:

4. In the fiscal year ending June 30, 1975, the U.S. Postal Service handled 21,630,285,000 pieces of third-class mail. This is all business mail and is primarily direct mail, sales efforts made through the mail.
5. Considering the rising costs of postage and printing, an average cost of $.30 to prepare and send a piece of direct mail is a very conservative estimate.

Some more arithmetic, multiplying 21,630,285,000 by $.30, gives us a total figure of $6,489,085,500.00 spent on direct (third-class) mail in one year. Added together, these figures mean that *American business and industry spent more than $303 billion on letters in 1974–75*. That's BIG business—big enough to justify considerable attention to its efficiency!

Letter advantages

When you consider the advantages of doing business by letter, you see why people in business write so many letters and spend so much money on them. Despite the cost of a letter, it is often the most economical way to transact business. You can't go far (not even across town, if you figure your time and traveling expense) or talk much by long distance during business hours or say much in a telex for the cost of a letter. But for that money you can put your message in a letter and send it anywhere in the country and almost anywhere in the world.

Even if you do talk to the other person, you do not have a written record, as you do if you follow the almost universal business practice of making a copy of your letter. Because a letter and its answer can make a written contract, letters often replace personal calls and telephone calls even when the two parties are in the same city.

Telex, Teletype, and facsimile transmission provide written records of communications, and have the added advantage of being virtually immediate. But their cost makes them impractical unless a company can make heavy use of them. This generally restricts their use to large organizations with numerous locations. Another restriction is that only people with access to the system can receive messages.

Still another advantage of letters is that both the writer and reader can handle a letter at their most convenient times. Therefore, it can get by receptionists and secretaries many times when a telephone call or a personal call cannot. Moreover, the reader usually gives it full attention without raising partially considered objections and without interruption. This is a decided psychological advantage.

Emphasis in business

When executives began to realize how much letters cost, how important letters and reports are to the smooth operation of their firms, and how few of their employees were capable writers, many of them started training programs and correspondence control programs. At General Electric, Westinghouse, Southern Pacific, Marshall Field's, the New York Life Insurance Company, and the big mail-order houses (Montgomery Ward, Spiegel's, and Sears, Roebuck), to mention only a few of the leaders, such programs have demonstrated the economy and efficiency resulting from improved correspondence. Even these firms, however, prefer to hire people who can already write rather than train them on company time.

A frequent question in employment interviews and inquiry letters to professors, therefore, concerns the ability of college graduates to do such writing. An applicant who presents evidence of ability to write good letters and reports becomes a favored applicant for nearly any job.

Emphasis in schools

Many of the executives who are aware of the importance of good letters are graduates of the few schools that have taught business writing since early in the 1900s. These business leaders are the main reason why today in the majority of respectable colleges and universities literally thousands of students are studying and practicing how to write more effectively for business. Without exception, surveys by such organizations as Delta Sigma Pi, the American Association of Collegiate Schools of Business, and the American Business Communication Association have confirmed the high regard of former students for the work.

Business letter-writing instructors frequently hear student comments such as "I learned more English in letter writing than in any other course I ever had!" or "*Everybody* should be required to take a course in letter writing!" or "This course is good preparation for living in general."

Common misconceptions

Yet some people—mostly for lack of information—do not respect even university work in business writing. They sometimes think courses in letter writing are merely about letter forms. Although this is a part of the course, it is only a small part (less than 5 percent of this book).

You may even hear the mistaken idea that students of letter writing learn the trite, wordy, and nearly meaningless expressions so common at the beginnings and endings of letters written by some untrained writers. Actually, you learn to write naturally, concisely, and clearly, to take care of the business without beating about the bush, and to end letters when you are through—without wasting first and last sentences saying nothing.

Still others think that in the study of letter writing the emphasis is on high-pressure techniques and tricks and gadgets. Just the opposite is true. In drawing on the findings of psychologists, we are *not* advocating that you attempt to *manipulate* or outsmart your reader in sly, unethical fashion. Use of the findings of psychology is good or bad depending on the intent of the user. The intent of the writer toward a reader should always be morally and ethically proper. Our intent is to help you write acceptable things (determined by you) in an acceptable way (determined by your reader) more likely to convince your reader of the legitimacy and the attractiveness (or soundness) of your proposal or position.

You may hear that letter writing is "just a practical study." It certainly is practical, for the ability to write good business letters is useful. But it is also a cultural study because its primary purposes are the development of (1) your ability to maintain pleasant relations with others and (2) your language effectiveness.

Why the high regard for letter writing?

One of the reasons why courses in business letter writing have found increasing favor with students, executives, and college administrators is that it is a blend of the cultural and the practical.

The business correspondent writes to an individual for a definite, practical purpose—and must write with the same exactness as other good writers. The purpose is not, however, entertainment (or self-expression in purple passages and deathless prose). *Action* is usually the goal. Letter writing is partially a study of probable or estimated human *reaction* as a basis for securing the desired *action*. Since the quality of persuasion is more important to the letter writer than to most writers, a good knowledge of practical psychology is essential.

The good business writer must learn to do more than just sell goods and services. Successful handling of claim, adjustment, credit, and collection letters requires learning tact, patience, consideration of the other person, a necessarily optimistic attitude, and the value of saying things pleasantly and positively instead of negatively. These are the reasons why you can expect more successful social and business relations with other people after a thorough, conscientious, and repeated analysis and application of the principles of good letter writing.

Furthermore, the good letter writer must learn to be concise, interesting, and easy to follow—to hold a reader's attention. For reasons of courtesy a listener will bear with a longwinded, dull, or unclear conversation—maybe even ask for explanations. But the reader of a letter feels no such obligation toward it. The good letter writer therefore edits carefully to phrase ideas more effectively in writing than in talking.

In conversation one can cushion the effect or shade the meaning with the twinkle of an eye, inflection of the voice, or gesture of a hand and can adjust and adapt the presentation according to the listener's reaction. With far less chance of failure a speaker can get along by "doin' what comes naturally." The letter writer has no such chance to observe the effects of the first part of a presentation and adapt the last part accordingly—and therefore must learn to *foresee* the reader's reaction all the way through. This requires more thorough knowledge of practical psychology, more preliminary reader analysis, and more careful planning of messages and phrasing of thoughts than in oral communication.

Such reader analysis, planning, and editing establish good habits of expression—habits which carry over to the spoken message. This is the reason we say that you will learn to talk better if you learn to write better. It is also the reason we say that, in learning to write effective letters, you will learn to do a better job of writing anything else you have to write.

Art, science, or skill?

The use of the language—in clear, concise adaptation to one's readers so that they can absorb the message with the least amount of effort and the greatest amount of pleasant reaction—is an art. Several generations of business writers have shown that the proper language for business in general and for letters in particular is just plain good English. Though it is more concise and more precise, it is neither more nor less formal than the conversational language of people for whom letters are intended.

Good business letters are also the result of a conscious use of principles which have evolved since the turn of the century. No one would claim that business letter writing is an exact and thoroughly developed science, but prominent business writers who have experimented with letters for over 60 years have given us a near-scientific framework of principles as a starting point. Though many of these principles have not been demonstrated with scientific exactness, they have taken a great deal of the speculative out of letter writing. We can therefore approach the writing of business letters with considerable knowledge of what good letter-writing principles are and *when, where,* and *how* to apply them.

Writing good business letters, then, is neither exclusively an art nor exclusively a science. Yet it is certainly more than what we frequently call a skill. It involves thinking of a very complex kind: analyzing both a situation and a reader, and then using good judgment in applying knowledge of English, business, and psychology.

Summary

In studying letter writing, you not only learn how to get the desired results from the many letters you will have to write. You will also get a greater understanding of people and how to influence them, an increased facility in the use of language (both oral and written), a more thorough knowledge of business practices and ethics, and a resultant confidence in yourself.

You may want to make a career of business letters. Correspondence supervisors, letter consultants, and direct-mail specialists have found it highly rewarding. But in *any* business, industry, or profession—as well as in your private life—your ability to write a good letter will be a vital tool and a powerful factor in your eventual success.

PART ONE

How a reader reacts to a letter

[Through your letters you quickly reveal the kind of gentleman or stinker you are.]

chapter 1

Style: What the reader reads

[Transmission of ideas and enthusiasm is essential to great accomplishment.]

JUST ABOUT EVERYBODY has to write business letters and memos. Most people consider themselves "pretty fair" writers, too. Actually, however, the statement "anything done by everybody is seldom done well" is as true of business writing as it is of any other activity.

If you do write good business letters and memos, you can answer yes to these questions:

1. Is your writing style interesting, clear, and inconspicuous?
2. Does your writing follow good persuasion principles?
3. Do your letters and memos reflect basic goodwill?
4. Is the appearance of your letters and memos pleasant and unobtrusive?

You and any other business writer should apply these four tests because

—Your letter or memo may establish a favorable first impression yet fail completely because its language is dull, vague, inaccurate, difficult to follow, unnatural, or full of errors.
—It may be written in natural, clear style yet fail because it does not follow good psychology or does not stress benefits to the reader.
—Even with good style and persuasive presentation, your message can fail if it reflects poor tone and/or fails to reflect a desire to be of service to the reader.
—A pleasant and unobtrusive (undistracting) appearance is also important; it is the first impression the reader has of your letter. If the appearance is bad, you start off with one strike against you.

With all four desirable qualities—good style, appropriate persuasion, goodwill, and good looks—your letters and memos will accomplish their purposes in most instances.

To explain and illustrate these four essentials of any good letter is the function of Part One of this book. To show how the principles apply in all kinds of letters and memos is the main function of Parts Two and Three.

We do not believe you can write the good letters you are capable of without understanding each of these four essentials. For that reason we ask you to read extensively before you start writing; and for the same reason no letter or memo cases appear until the end of Part One.

HOW TO THINK ABOUT YOUR WRITING

For its first test, if your letter is to be considered good, ask yourself: *Is it written in interesting, clear, and inconspicuous style?*

If your letter is so uninteresting that it isn't read, you've obviously wasted your time.

If your letter is interesting enough to be read but is not clear, you've probably confused and annoyed your reader. You may therefore get no response—or have to write again to answer your reader's inquiry.

And if your style is conspicuous because of something unexpected, inappropriate, or incorrect, it distracts your reader from *what* you've said (by calling attention to *how* you've said it) and causes doubt that your facts and reasoning are any more reliable than your writing. Both weaken your message's impact, and your message is what is important in any letter.

To be effective, then, your letter style should be—to your reader—interesting enough to be read, clear when read, and inconspicuous. Its *effect on your reader* is what you should test!

Your first step toward assuring that your style is interesting, clear, and inconspicuous is to think about it. Most people take their style for granted, rarely thinking much about how they say things. When you realize that how you say it vitally affects how your reader gets your message, you are starting to take your first step.

Thinking about your style means not taking anything about it for granted. For example, consider those little elements of English called articles. We generally throw them into whatever we're saying without any thought at all; yet they have considerable effect on what words mean. In fact, most people use too many articles (*a, an* and *the*) and so rob their writing of readability. Too many definite articles make writing complicated and confusing. By making everything specific, they obscure what should be specific and thus turn strong phrases and sentences into weak, generalizing ones.

Next time you write something, go over it and mark every article. Then see how many of them you can omit. If any of your words or phrases can stand alone without articles supporting them, consider omitting those articles. Look at this example:

```
Of all the similar fasteners available today, the Universal is
the one which gives you the most draw strength.
```

This simple statement is adequate—but barely. If we omit some unnecessary articles, we get this:

```
Of all similar fasteners available today, Universal gives you
the most draw strength.
```

Now our statement is concise, more powerful. And notice that without so many articles, you can avoid extra words that don't contribute to meaning.

Please don't misunderstand us. We are not against using articles. Without them, English would be rough and awkward; and it would not adequately communicate specificness. We have made them our example because we want you to begin to *think* about your writing, to consider whether everything you put on paper is really necessary to your message.

Many things in English that most writers take for granted as being essential are not. If you want to take enough time, you can even write fairly well without using articles at all, as we have done so far in this section, except in our example above.

HOW TO WRITE INTERESTINGLY

Depend mainly on content

In writing, you should depend on content, not style, to arouse and hold your reader's interest. Usually you have an inquiry or other indication that your reader is interested in your general subject. A first-class letter will therefore nearly always get a reading. Tricks of style are unnecessary and even distracting. If bare facts have insufficient appeal to gain your reader's attention, you can make them both interesting and persuasive if you *show how those facts point to benefits the reader wants* (**YA** in Appendix C). In writing about a product, for example, a description that merely gives the physical facts (size, shape, color, and/or material) may be pretty dull. But if you interpret the facts as providing reader benefits, the content is much more interesting (psychological description): "Made of aluminum, the Gizmo is light and rust-free—you don't need to paint." And if you write so that the reader imagines successfully using and enjoying the benefits of the product (dramatized copy), the content is even more interesting.

If you have no indication of interest, you may have to work for temporary attention by means of gadgets, tricks of style, and other artificial means at the beginning of your letter. Even then, however, you will have accomplished nothing unless your stunt leads into the message naturally and promptly.

A perfectly good message can become dull, however, if poorly presented. Wordiness, indefiniteness, triteness and pompousness, monotony, and difficult reading are the most common offenders. By replacing these with their opposites, you will speed up your message rather than slow it down or lose it completely—and that's all you can expect style to contribute to making your letters interesting.

Put the emphasis where it belongs (**Emp** and **Sub** in Appendix C)

Since content is the greatest means of gaining interest, the big ideas of your message deserve the major emphasis.

Though you may use minor mechanical means of emphasis (underscoring, capitalizing, itemizing, using two colors), your four primary means of emphasizing an idea are (1) position, (2) space, (3) phrasing, and (4) sentence structure.

The most significant ideas need to be placed in the emphatic beginning and ending positions of the letter, of your paragraphs—even of your sentences.

In addition, you write more about those points you think need stressing. If you write ten lines about the efficiency of a dishwasher and only two lines about its convenience, you emphasize efficiency more than convenience.

As a third major means of emphasis, you should select concrete, specific words and phrases to etch welcome or important ideas in your reader's mind. When an idea is unwelcome or insignificant, choose general words that merely identify, not stress. *Specific:* "Your versatile IBM Selectric typewriter will. . . ." *General:* "The typewriter needs several new parts and. . . ."

Because an independent clause carries more emphasis than a dependent one, you can also stress or subordinate ideas through your choice of sentence structure. An important idea calls for statement in one independent clause (a simple sentence). Sometimes, however, you have two equally important and closely related ideas; so you should put two independent clauses together in a compound sentence. If you have two related ideas of different importance, a complex sentence of one independent and one dependent clause divides the emphasis properly. You may have noticed, for example, that we merely named (parenthetically in a dependent clause) the minor mechanical means of stressing ideas. The four primary means, however, we first itemized; then we gave each a separate paragraph of discussion and thereby emphasized them by independent-clause statement and by means of space.

In messages carrying ideas which the reader will welcome, then, use those ideas to begin and end letters. They usually should begin and end paragraphs. They should take up most of the space of the letter. They should be phrased specifically. And they should enjoy the benefits of independent instead of dependent construction. Conversely, you should embed unwelcome or unimportant ideas in a middle paragraph, cover them just enough to establish their true meaning, and strip them of the emphasis of concrete, specific words.

Controlling the emphasis in your writing is a technique that you can put into immediate successful use—in the next piece of writing you do. We recommend that you work first on emphasis by position, since this is a technique that is easy to use, as well as extremely effective. At first you will have to think about getting important ideas at the beginnings and ends of your letters and paragraphs, but you will be surprised how quickly this becomes an almost automatic procedure . . . and how it will improve the effectiveness of all your writing.

The letter samples throughout this book use these principles for appropriate emphasis and its opposite—subordination. Two special points, however, deserve your attention right here:

1. You may be inclined to write something the reader already knows. If it serves no purpose, of course you should omit it. But if you need to say it (for emphasis or as a basis for something else you want to say), put it subordinately. That is, do *not* put it in an independent clause: *not* "Summer will soon be here . . ." but "Since summer will soon be here, ..."
2. When you need to refer the reader to an enclosure for more information, word your reference to emphasize what he should look for or get from it. *Don't* emphasize that it is enclosed: *not* "Enclosed is (or please find) . . ."

but something like "You'll find further details of construction and users' satisfaction in the enclosed pamphlet."

Write concisely but completely (Conc and Dev in Appendix C)

Every word you can spare without reducing the effectiveness of your writing is wasteful if it remains. Too many words for ideas stretch interest to the breaking point. But if you leave out necessary information and vivid details in trying to achieve brevity, you frequently fail to develop enough interesting ideas to hold or persuade your reader. You therefore face the dilemma of length.

A first step in the solution of that dilemma is a clear distinction between brevity and conciseness. Brevity is mere shortness—which is often overstressed. Sacrificing completeness because of a mistaken notion about the importance of brevity is a common mistake. Writing a letter lacking necessary information (and therefore lacking interest and persuasion) is poor economy. Either the letter is pure waste because it produces no result, or both you and your reader have to write additional letters to fill in the missing links of information. Even those people who say a business letter should be brief do not want to make decisions without all the pertinent information.

What these people who are overly conscious of brevity want—what you want—is conciseness, making every word contribute to your purpose. A 50-word letter is brief; but if you can write the message in 25 words, the 50-word letter is not concise. A 400-word letter is not short; but if all the words contribute to the purpose, it is concise. So if you need three pages to cover all your points adequately and make your letter do what you want it to do, you should use that much space. Conciseness, then, comes not from omitting details that contribute to clearness, persuasiveness, or interest but from writing all you should say in as few words as possible.

Experience may teach you to compose first drafts that are both complete and concise; but while you are gaining that experience, you need to

1. Avoid expressing ideas that don't deserve to be put into words.
2. Revise first drafts to eliminate deadwood.

Besides obviously irrelevant material, *ideas which don't deserve to be put into words are*

Things the reader already knows which you do not wish to emphasize.
Ideas you can imply with sufficient emphasis.

Because it is often insulting as well as wasteful and dull, avoid using an emphatic independent clause for things the reader already knows. For example, a heating engineer's letter to an office manager about the discomfort of workers began as follows:

```
Three days ago you asked us to investigate the problem of
discomfort among your office workers.  [Assumes that the reader
has a short memory.]  We have made our study.  [Obviously,
```

```
since you're reporting results.] Too low humidity is
apparently the main cause of your trouble. Your building is
steam-heated. [Doesn't the reader know?] Therefore your
solution is to. . . .
```

The following revision says or implies everything in that paragraph, avoids the insults, saves most of the words, and is more interesting:

```
Too low humidity is apparently the main cause of your workers'
discomfort. Since your building is steam-heated, your
solution is to. . . .
```

To show the reasoning behind your suggestion, you do need to mention the fact that the building is heated by steam; but the subordinating *since* implies "Of course you and I know this, but it has to go in for the record and for completeness of logic." When you *have* to establish something the reader knows, or when the reader probably knows it but you can't be sure, give the information subordinately—as the "Since . . ." does.

As a general principle, in answering a recent letter from an individual, don't waste words to say "I have your letter of . . ." or to tell what it said. Obviously, you got the letter or you wouldn't be answering it; and starting to discuss the same subject will remind your reader what the letter said. Instead of

```
You asked us to let you know when the new model of the Clarion
radio came on the market. It is obtainable now.
```

you can say the same thing with

```
The new model of the Clarion is now available.
```

That clearly implies that you got the letter and the idea of "You asked us to let you know."

Of course, if the inquiry is not recent, or if somebody other than the original inquirer may read the answer (as often happens in big companies), you may need to make specific reference (by topic and date) to the letter you are answering. But even then you can use a subject line to save words and allow the emphatic first sentence to say something important. Rather than

```
On February 20 you inquired about our experience with Mr.
James H. Johnson. We are glad to tell you about his work
for us.

Johnson was a steady, conscientious worker during the 18
months he kept books for us.
```

you might better write:

```
Mr. James H. Johnson, about whom you inquired on February 20,
was a steady, conscientious bookkeeper here for 18 months.
```

Under no circumstances do you need to waste words as in the following paragraph:

```
Permit me to take this opportunity to thank you for your
letter which I have just received. In reply I wish to state
```

```
that we shall be very glad to exchange the electric water
heater in question for a similar one in a larger size in
accordance with your request.
```

Through implication you can reduce that wordy beginning to

```
We shall be glad to exchange your water heater for a similar
one in a larger size.
```

In most refusals you can save words and your reader's feelings by eliminating the negative statement of what you won't do and concentrating on what you will do. You thus *imply* the negative idea, for economy as well as interest. For illustrations, see "Positive Statement" (p. 46).

If your first draft contains any of the foregoing wasteful expressions, revision should eliminate them and *deadwood phrases* (those which take the long way around or contribute nothing to the ideas expressed).

Consider the following suggestive but far from complete list of offenders, in which a line blocks out the deadwood or the concise statement follows in parentheses:

long ~~period of~~ time
is ~~at this time~~
at ~~a price of~~ $50
~~important~~ essentials
enclosed ~~herewith~~
remember ~~the fact~~ that
held a meeting (met)
main problem is ~~a matter of~~ cost
your ~~order for~~ a cultivator was shipped
~~in the opinion of~~ Mr. Johnson (thinks)
that is the situation ~~at this time~~ (now)
the X plow is quite different ~~in character~~
made the announcement that (announced)
for the purpose of providing (to provide)
all the people who are interested in (interested people)
at an early date (soon, if you have to be indefinite)
decide at a meeting ~~which will be held~~ Monday
eliminate needless words ~~that may be present~~
~~there is~~ only one point ~~that~~ is clear, ~~and that is~~
the price was higher than I expected ~~it to be~~
the workers ~~are in a position to~~ (can) accept or reject
during ~~the course~~ of the
~~engaged in~~ making a survey
~~the color of~~ the X is blue
until ~~such time~~ as you can
in regard to (about or regarding)
in the development of (developing)
in this day and age (today or now)
the soldering process proved ~~to be of an~~ unsatisfactory ~~nature~~
the general consensus of opinion among most businessmen is that (most businessmen think that)
~~the trouble with~~ the light was ~~that it was~~ too dim
in ~~the state of~~ Texas
neat ~~in appearance~~
at ~~the hour of~~ 4
eight ~~in number~~
circular ~~in shape~~
throughout the entire week
~~at a~~ later ~~date~~
during ~~the year of~~ 1976
costs ~~the sum of~~ $10
came ~~at a time~~ when
at all times (always)
in the event that (if)
put in an appearance (came)
during the time that (while)
these facts ~~serve to~~ give an idea
made stronger ~~with a view~~ to
if ~~it is~~ possible, let me have
~~according to~~ Mr. Johnson (says)
arrived at the conclusion (concluded)

Sometimes you can save several words by changing a whole clause to one word. For example:

buying new machines which are expensive—buying expensive new machines
using processes that are outmoded—using outmoded processes
saving work that does not need to be done—saving unnecessary work

Write vividly: Avoid indefiniteness

Even good content concisely stated can be uninteresting if your reader gets only an inactive or fuzzy mental picture. The sharper you can make that picture, the better it will be. You will write vividly if you apply these five techniques:

1. Write about people in action. Make people the subject or object of many sentences.
2. Use active rather than passive voice most of the time.
3. Use concrete rather than abstract language.
4. Use specific rather than general words.
5. Give enough details to make the picture clear.

The most interesting thing in the world is *people in action.* Things happen because people make them happen. The most interesting, the most natural, and the clearest way to write about those happenings is to talk about those people who are the principal actors. That is why we suggest that you make people the subject or object of your sentences.

And since each guy or doll reading a letter is most interested in *that* guy or doll, interest in your letter will depend on how you put that person into the picture as the main actor. "You can save 30 minutes at dinner time with a Pronto pressure cooker" is more vivid than "A Pronto pressure cooker saves 30 minutes at dinner time." (For psychological reasons, if a point is a criticism and hence unpleasant, however, make your actor a third person or your message impersonal.)

Consistent use of people as subjects will help you to write in *active rather than passive voice.* The passive "30 minutes at dinner time can be saved" lacks the vividness of the original illustration because it omits the all-important *who.* Besides, passive constructions are usually longer, weaker, and fuzzier than active ones. Excessive use of "to be" verbs (*be, is, am, are, was, were, been, being*) usually produces flat writing, partly because it leads to a passive style. If the basic verb in more than half your sentences derives from "to be," your style will seem flat instead of lively. "There are" and "It was" beginnings (expletives) delay the real idea of the sentence and frequently force a writer to use the unemphatic passive voice. The sentence "There are 1 million people in Cincinnati" is not so vivid as "One million people live in Cincinnati." "It was felt that . . ." becomes more vivid when the writer rephrases with "We felt. . . ."

You can eliminate most passives and expletives if you will conscientiously try to use action verbs. People live, run, eat, buy—in short, act.

They do not just exist, as indicated by *is, was, were, have been.* The price of a stock *creeps up, rises, jumps, zooms*—or *plummets.* For vividness (and for economy) good writers make their verbs do a big share of the work. Far be it from us to encourage you to coin needless and frivolous words; but *dip, curve, skyrocket, phone, wire,* and many other original nouns are now verbs because people recognized their vividness as verbs. The more action you can pack into your verbs, the more specific and concrete you can make your writing.

When you *use concrete rather than abstract language,* you give your reader sharper mental pictures. When you write *superiority, efficiency,* and *durability* in telling about a product, your words are abstract; they give your reader only hazy ideas. To make the picture sharp and lively, give the evidence back of the abstraction rather than naming the abstraction itself. If you think your product is of highest quality, you must have reasons for thinking so. To establish the idea of superiority in cloth, for instance: Thread count? Number of washings before fraying? Tensile strength? Resistance to shrinkage and fading? Note that answers to these questions also show durability.

In job applications you need to put across the ideas of your sociability, initiative, and dependability, which you can demonstrate by citing activities and organization memberships, ideas and plans you originated, attendance records, and completed projects. Thus you give evidence of these qualities and let your reader draw the abstract conclusions.

You further eliminate haziness and dullness when you use *specific rather than general words.* An investment, for instance, may be a stock, a bond, or a piece of real estate. To illustrate further, stock may be common or preferred. The closer you can come to making your reader visualize the special type of thing named rather than just its general class, the more specific and hence the more vivid your writing is.

Take the verb *walk* as another example. Does a person amble, trudge, skip, or one of the 50 or more other possible ways of walking? When you are inclined to write *contact,* do you mean write, go see, telephone? You present a sharper picture if you name the specific action.

Comparisons help you explain the unknown or variable in terms of the known. *Slowly* becomes sharper if you say "about as fast as you normally walk." "A saving of 2 percent when paid within 10 days" becomes more vivid if you add "$2.80, or two free boxes of Lane's choice chocolates, on your present invoice of $140."

You *can* be specific and concrete in the kind of information you give your reader; but unless you *give enough details to make the picture clear,* you will fail to be vivid. Specifications for a house may call for painting it; but unless they tell the kind of paint, how many coats, and what colors, the painter does not have a clear enough picture to know what to do. You need to flesh out skeletons to bring them to life, even if it means some loss of brevity.

Write naturally to avoid triteness and pomposity (Nat in Appendix C)

All kinds of trite expressions and jargon—usually the result of hazy thinking, or not thinking, by the writer—dull interest and put the reader to sleep. They are even called "bromides" ("flat, commonplace statements," Webster says) because of the use of bromides as sleep-inducing medicines. 

One person meeting another on the street would not say, "I beg to report receipt of your favor of the 29th ult." A good business writer would not write it either, but more likely "Those tonnage figures for April were just what I needed," or "Your suggestions about the committee memberships helped a lot in my decision. Thanks." The first is slow, vague, roundabout, and stilted; the others are clear, direct, and natural.

Bromidic style goes back to the times when people in business first began to have social status enough to write to kings, princes, and others at court. Feeling inferior, they developed a slavish, stilted, and elaborately polite style to flatter the nobility. They "begged to advise" the nobleman that his "kind favor of recent date" was "at hand" and "wished to state" that "this matter" would "receive our prompt attention" and "begged to remain your humble, obedient servant." Today people in business need not be so meek. Unfortunately, however, too many do sheepishly follow somebody else, learn all they know about letter writing from the frequently bad letters they receive, and thus continue an outmoded, inappropriate, and unnatural style. Like parrots, they use expressions unthinkingly.

Pompous writing (puffed-up, roundabout, and using big words) is as dull and confusing as the use of bromides. Why many people write "We will ascertain the facts and advise accordingly," when in conversation they would say quite naturally, "We'll find out and let you know," is a mystery. A Washington blackout order during wartime originally read: "Obscure the fenestration with opaque coverings or terminate the illumination." A high official who wanted the message understood revised it to read: "Pull down the shades or turn out the lights."

A young lawyer was certainly pompous in writing as follows about a husband being sued for divorce:

> The defendant is renowned as a person of intemperate habits. He is known to partake heavily of intoxicating beverages. Further, he cultivates the company of others of the distaff side, and wholly, regularly, and consistently refuses, demurs, and abstains from earnest endeavor to gain remuneration.

The judge summed up that "Mrs. Rigoni's husband drinks, chases other women, and refuses to work."

Stuffed-shirt writers frequently use a phrase or a whole clause when a well-chosen verb would express the idea better. For example: "Smith raises the objection that . . ." instead of "Smith objects that (or objects to). . . ." One writer stretched a simple "Thank you" to "I wish to assure you that it has been a great pleasure to have been the recipient of your gracious generosity."

The good letter writer avoids both bromides and pompous wording to make letters natural. The advice to "write as you talk" can be taken too literally, however. You would have an extremely hard job trying to write just as you talk; and even if you could, the informal style appropriate to letters is more precise and concise than good conversation. What the advisers really mean is that you should not stiffen up, use big words and trite expressions, or get involved in complicated and formal sentences when you write letters. Rather, let the words flow out naturally and informally in phrases and sentences with the general tone and rhythm of the language actually used by people rather than stuffed shirts.

Write like this—	*Not like this—*
Many people	A substantial segment of the population
Know well	Fully cognizant of
Object	Interpose an objection
Wait	Hold in abeyance
Carry out the policy	Effectuate (or implement) the policy
As you requested	Pursuant to your request
Before, after	Prior to, subsequent to
Get the facts	Ascertain (secure) the data
Ask the defendant	Interrogate the defendant
Find it hard to	Encounter difficulty in
Big difference	Marked discrepancy
Begin (or start)	Initiate (or institute)
Complete (or finish)	Consummate
In the first place	In the initial instance
Haste makes waste	Precipitation entails negation of economy
Make unnecessary	Obviate the necessity of

Vary sentence pattern, type, and length to avoid monotony

Unvaried sentence pattern, type, length, or rhythm causes many a reader's mind to wander. Though the necessary variety should come naturally from writing well, revision can sometimes enliven your style by removing a dull sameness.

The normal English sentence pattern is subject-verb-complement (or object). Most of your sentences should follow that sequence; but if all of them do, they produce monotony. Particularly noticeable are series of sentences all beginning the same way. The following list suggests possible variations of sentence beginnings:

With a subject: A simple way to key returns is to use different return envelopes with the several different letters being tested.

With a clause: Because human beings are unpredictable, the sales process cannot be riveted to a formula.

With a phrase: For this reason, no large mailing should be made until tests have proved which letter is best.

With a verb: Should you find that all pull about the same, you have the usual direct-mail dilemma!

With correlative conjunctions: Not only the lack of funds but also the results of continual overcrowding and busing in secondary schools will continue to lower the caliber of work in American colleges.

With an adverb: Ordinarily, students like courses in business letter writing.

With a verbal: Allowing plenty of time, the student started the report early in the semester.

With an infinitive: To be a successful business letter writer, a student must be able to lose selfishness in contemplation of the reader's problem.

With adjectives: Congenial and cooperative, Dorothy worked many nights until midnight when we faced a deadline.

Proper emphasis of ideas (p. 12) is the main reason for varying sentence type, but the variation also avoids monotony and retains interest. Choosing sentence patterns in terms of needed emphasis will nearly always result in enough variety to prevent monotony.

Sameness of sentence length (and to some extent, paragraph length) can be just as monotonous as unvarying sentence pattern and type. Together they produce an interest-killing rhythm characteristic of a childish style. Children's books often put both listener and reader to sleep—but business letters should not.

Although readability specialists have done much good by inducing some people to keep their sentences down to reasonable length, they have done some harm by leading others who have misunderstood them to write too mechanically in trying to average about 16–20 words a sentence. That is an *average*, remember. Nothing could be more monotonous than a series of 14-word sentences—or of 4-word sentences or of 24-word sentences. Lack of variety in sentence length can be just as monotonous as lack of variety in sentence pattern or type.

HOW TO MAKE YOUR WRITING CLEAR

The strongest rebuke a reader can give a writer is "I don't understand; what do you mean?"

Obviously, your message must be clear to your reader, or the interest which induced reading it accounts for nothing. Conciseness helps clarity as well as interest by relieving your reader of the job of separating the important from the unessential, and vividness helps by giving a sharp, clear picture. But other more important aids to clearness are

1. Making your writing easy to read.
2. Planning for unity, coherence, progress, and proper emphasis.
3. Using accurate wording, punctuation, grammar, and sentence structure.

Make it easy to read

Readability is a factor affecting interest, but it relates more intimately to clarity. You have the responsibility as a writer to present ideas so that the reader understands with the least possible effort. As the difficulty of understanding an idea increases, people are more inclined to skip it. Any time your reader has to back up and reread or has to slow down to understand you thoroughly, you are risking the chance of being misunderstood, of arousing disgust, or of being ignored.

Using only those *words which your reader understands* immediately and sharply is a first step in making letters easy to read. You will usually be wise to choose the more commonly known of two words; an uneducated person will understand you, and an educated reader will appreciate your making the reading job easy.

A man well known for his way with words, Arthur Kudner, once said, "Big, long words name little things. All big things have little names, such as life and death, peace and war, or dawn, day, night, hope, love, home. Learn to use little words in a big way; they say what you mean. When you don't know what you mean, use BIG words. . . . That often fools little people."

Short words add force to what we say, for we all know what they mean. Big words can trip us up, for what they mean may be hard to pin down. Small words can say all the things you want to say. Finding the small words you need may take time, but it will be time well spent. Your letters will be easier to read if you use one-syllable words most of the time. If you have 50 percent more syllables than words, your writing requires more reader effort than it should. And the greater number of polysyllabic profundities you use the greater the likelihood that you'll strike your reader as pompous.

Keeping your sentences reasonably short and direct will also help to make your letters easy to read and hence clear. An average of 16–20 words is a healthy one for readability. But you need not avoid sentences of 4 or 5 words—or 40, if necessary for presenting an idea exactly. If the average length is not too much above 20, smooth sequence of thought and directness are more important than the word count. To avoid involved, indirect sentences, look at the punctuation. It cannot make a basically bad sentence into a good one. If you have to punctuate a sentence heavily, you will be wise to rephrase it more directly. Sometimes the best solution is to break it up into two or three sentences.

Paragraph pattern and length influence readability, too. The usual pattern of letter paragraphs is a topic sentence followed by supporting or developing details. But if you write one sentence which says all you need to on the topic, start the next topic—in another paragraph. Padding one with needless stuff or covering two topics in it because some composition books ban single-sentence paragraphs is *baaad* writing.

Frequently a single-sentence paragraph is highly desirable to give an idea the emphasis you want!

Especially in letters, long paragraphs are uninviting and hard to read. First and last paragraphs of more than four lines and others of more than eight are likely candidates for breaking up.

Frequent personal references (names of people and pronouns referring to them) also make your letters more interesting and readable. Since you and your reader are the two persons most directly involved in the actions, desires, and benefits you write about in letters, most of your pronouns will be "you" (or "you" understood) and "I" (or "we").

Itemizations and tabulations may help to make your whole letter or a paragraph clear and easy to read. For instance, if your topic sentence mentions three big advantages in using XYZ wafers, the three will stand out more clearly if you number them and list them on separate lines.

Since *proper pace* also affects the readability of what you write, you will also want to pay some attention to it. (Pace is simply the frequency with which you present ideas.) The physical actions of our eyes in reading have little relation to our mental actions or comprehension. The speed of reading is unlikely to vary much; but if ideas come too fast or too slow, comprehension will drop. A reader will be unable to assimilate the ideas quickly enough or will become bored and inattentive because of a too-slow pace. New writers often make the mistake of presenting snippets of undeveloped ideas too rapidly, one after the other, in an effort to be brief. What they achieve is a loss of comprehension by their readers.

Plan for unity, coherence, progress, and proper emphasis

Later you will study planning for psychological effect as a principle of persuasion, but planning also affects clarity. If you are answering a letter, underscore points in it to be covered. In any case think your answer through before you start to write; you can't plan anything more than a simple letter by just thinking as you write. Clear letters are usually the product of a three-step process which stresses organization and coherence.

1. The preliminary planning step—for completeness, unity, psychological effect, progress, and proper emphasis—requires specific answers to four questions:

a. *What effect do I want the letter to produce?* Decide specifically what you want to happen as a result of your letter. Without keeping this central purpose in mind, you cannot achieve one of the main objectives of organizing —unity. Good organization should result in a oneness by showing how every part relates to the general theme or idea.

b. *Who is the reader?* Until you make a clear estimate of what your reader is like, you cannot hope to apply the principles of adaptation (p. 42).

c. *What facts and ideas must I present to produce the desired effect on this kind of reader?* List not only points of positive interest but probable reader objections to be overcome.

d. *What is the best order of presenting the items listed in answer to Question c?* You will be prepared to answer generally as plan A, B, or C (from your study of "Planned Presentation," pp. 36 ff.). But those are only general plans for the whole letter. Organization includes much more than that.

You can organize well only by answering all four of the questions in preliminary planning. Good organization is the marshaling of statements and supporting details, the orderly procession of paragraphs, the disposition of parts so that each finds its proper place.

Fundamentally, organization is the process of grouping things according to likeness and then putting the groups into an appropriate sequence. For example, if you explain in your letter or report how something is made, you should treat that part fully before going on to explain how it operates. Either of these topics may be just one paragraph, or it may be several. But you do want to group together all the details about how it is made before proceeding. Thus you achieve unity of that topic.

Having grouped according to likenesses, you have several choices of sequence for either a whole letter or a paragraph. Common paragraph sequences are (1) general to specific, (2) cause to effect, (3) order of importance, (4) nearest to farthest (space relations), and (5) order of happening (time relations). All of these may be reversed.

2. In the second step of writing well-organized letters—continuous fast writing for the natural coherence that comes from following a chain of thought straight through—you merely follow your preliminary plan and *keep going.* Write the entire letter without stopping.

3. In the third step—revising for tone (see pp. 52 ff.), conciseness (pp. 14 ff.), coherence, and correctness (pp. 23 ff. and 29 ff.)—you may need to reorganize a bit by shifting words, sentences, or whole paragraphs into better position. But usually the main work on organization through revision will be a few changes in wording for better coherence. You may find that some transitional words are unnecessary because of the natural, logical sequence of the sentence and paragraph; or you may need to strengthen coherence by inserting more transitional words like *and, but, for,* and the variants of each (See **Coh 3** in Appendix C). Although you should not leave out any necessary bridges between parts, the fewer you can use and still make the sequence of thought clear, the better. Try especially to avoid overformal references like *the latter, the above-mentioned,* and *namely.*

Use accurate wording, punctuation, grammar, and sentence structure

Proper usage of words, punctuation, and grammar is established by convention, not rules. The important thing is to use them in writing with the exact significance the reader attaches to them. Words, for example, are mere labels we apply to actions and things. In Great Britain such simple words as *ton* and *gallon* do not mean the same as they do in the United States.

Moreover, words and sentences sometimes change meanings according to what precedes and succeeds them. For instance, a would-be secretary brought laughs when the last two sentences of her ad for a job read "No bad habits. Willing to learn." Similarly, the last two sentences in an ad of a big dog for sale read "Will eat anything. Loves children." (For proper word relations, guard particularly against the errors discussed in **Mod 1** and **2** in Appendix C.)

The difficulties of accurate expression stem partly from the way words pick up related meanings and personal significance from everyday use (connotations, in addition to their denotations or dictionary meanings). Consider the difference between *cheap* and *inexpensive* or between *house* and *home*. And note that *hope, trust* and *if* can suggest doubt. "You claim" or "you say" even suggests doubt of the reader's truthfulness. The accurate user of words will be alert to connotations and implications—if not to avoid confusion, at least to produce effectiveness.

Exceptional cases of failure to follow the conventions have led to readers' getting a completely wrong idea. But rarely does such failure *leave* a reader confused; usually at least the approximate meaning will come—but only after study. Of course, if you say *profit* for what is generally spoken of as the selling price, you will mislead your reader.

Much more frequently, unconventional usage of words confuses a reader temporarily, forces rereading, or leaves the writer's intention uncertain. The words you use should give not only the general idea but the precise idea quickly. If you say *soon* or *later,* your reader doesn't know just when you mean. If you say *checks, notes, stocks, etc.*, nobody can tell whether you mean to include bonds. (In most business letters *etc.* should be used only if its meaning is perfectly clear, as in "I am particularly interested in the odd-numbered questions, 1, 3, 5, etc." But it then becomes unnecessary, as it usually does when what it refers to is clear.) You may be inclined to write *actuarially,* but most readers will get the meaning more quickly if you write *statistically.* The advantage of an extensive vocabulary is that you can choose the precise word to give the exact idea. But if you don't use judgment with a big vocabulary, you sometimes use words that leave the reader in the dark or slow up the pace.

Punctuation marks, like words, mean only what a reader takes them to mean. They can be helpful by breaking your sentences into thought groups if you follow the conventions and use them as they are generally used. But if you use a system of your own which your reader does not understand, you mislead just as if you used words in unfamiliar ways.

For instance, if you put up a sign on a parking lot to mean

No Parking: Reserved for Our Customers

you will certainly mislead people if you write:

No Parking Reserved for Our Customers

Like faulty wording, however, faulty punctuation often confuses only temporarily, if at all, but distracts the reader's mind from the key idea. You've surely seen the laughable highway sign "Slow Men Working."

Fortunately, the system of English punctuation is pretty well established (by convention, not by rules), and most readers know at least the main parts of the conventions. Unfortunately many people who know how to *read* punctuation marks correctly do not know the conventions well enough to use them precisely *in writing*. If you have any doubts about the following main troublesome areas of punctuation, see the symbol **P** in Appendix C for explanation and illustration:

—Semicolon between independent clauses except with strong conjunction (**P** 2).
—Comma after all dependent clauses at the beginnings of sentences and with nonessential ones elsewhere (**P** 3).
—Comma to separate coordinate adjectives (**P** 5).
—Pair of commas around a parenthetical expression unless you want to de-emphasize by parentheses, emphasize by dashes, or avoid confusion with other commas by using parentheses or dashes (**P** 4, 7).
—Hyphen between words used as a single modifier of a following noun (**P** 8).

So-called "errors" in grammar and sentence structure probably mislead readers even less frequently than unconventional uses of words and punctuation; but they, too, slow up reading and produce indefiniteness. Of course, the statement "Strawberries should not be planted where tomatoes have been grown for several years" will mislead readers if you mean "Wait several years before planting strawberries where tomatoes have been grown." And the dangling participle in "Smelling of liquor, the officer arrested the reckless driver" might cause a policeman to be asked why he was drinking on duty. But these are exceptional cases of bad sentence structure. Faulty pronoun references can confuse too, but usually they don't. Most readers will understand perfectly, despite shifts in number like "The Acme Company is located in Chicago. They manufacture. . . ." Wrong verb forms like "He come to my house at 10 P.M." or the wrong choice between *lie* and *lay* are usually definite, quick, and clear. Even this ungrammatical question asked at a state-line roadblock is perfectly clear: "You-all ain't a-totin' no cottonseeds, is ya?"

Indeed, poor grammar and sentence structure so infrequently cause confusion that they hardly need be discussed in connection with clarity. The other factors already discussed are more important influences on clarity; and grammar and sentence structure are more important as factors of reader confidence and the third requirement of good letter style—that it be inconspicuous.

HOW TO KEEP YOUR STYLE INCONSPICUOUS

An obvious striving for "style" is a sign of immaturity. When a reader starts your letter, the point of interest is what you say, not how you say it.

Your style becomes noticeable only if you do something unexpected with it. In reading a well-ordered sentence, a reader will receive no jolt. But consciously noticing an expression as an artificiality is distracting—as the writer you lose attention to your message. Simplicity and naturalness are good guides on the right road.

If you make your style too flowery, formal, or stiff for the situation, or if you make it too flippant and familiar, it will distract the reader from your message and arouse doubts about your sense of appropriateness. If you violate any of the conventions of word choice, spelling, punctuation, sentence structure, or grammar, your unconventional practice will both distract and cause your reader to doubt your general knowledge and ability. For instance, if you cause the reader to say, "Why, that writer can't even spell," the *even* strongly implies "So of course the correspondent can't be depended on to know anything else either."

The two main ways a writer does something unexpected with style and thus draws undue attention to it, then, are

1. Choosing the wrong level of usage for the situation.
2. Violating any of the more common conventions of word choice, spelling, punctuation, grammar, and sentence structure.

Both weaken the impact of the important thing—your message.

Choose the right level of usage for the situation

The appropriate level of language, like proper dress, is a highly variable thing. What is effective in one situation may not be suitable in another. A tuxedo is no better for a day in the office or a weiner roast than blue jeans are for a formal party, or a bathing suit for church.

The first step in choosing the right level of usage is to analyze the situation in the light of the five communication factors (sometimes called the "communication formula"):

1. A writer (or speaker) who has
2. A particular message to communicate through
3. A medium (letter, report, advertisement) to
4. A definite readership (or audience) for
5. A definite purpose.

If any of the factors of communication change, the situation shifts so that a formerly good sentence may become bad, or vice versa. Still, many thoughtless writers almost ignore the last two factors. Only in view of all of them can you classify the situation and choose the appropriate level of usage.

Having classified the communication situation, you can take the second step in choosing the appropriate level of usage by considering the nature of the different levels. Whole books have been written naming and describing them. More concise treatments also appear in some modern college composition books. Some early linguists distinguished as many as seven levels, but a more usual and functional modern classification names three: formal, informal, and illiterate.

Informal English is much the most useful level for letters and for most other kinds of speaking and writing today. In it, the writer's interest is more on content than on style. The emphasis is more on being functional than on being elegant. Its general tone is that of the natural speech of educated people in their usual business and social affairs. In its written form it is more concise and more precise than normal conversation; but its vocabulary, phrasing, sentence structure, grammar, and hence its natural rhythm and tone are essentially the same as in good conversation among educated people. This—rather than a literal interpretation of the words—is the meaning of the often-heard advice that you should write as you talk.

But informal English is a broad category, ranging all the way from a style which verges on formal English to that which verges on the illiterate. When informal English approaches the formal, it does not allow slang, shoptalk, contractions, or omission of relative pronouns and other connecting words. It may use generally understood allusions, figures of speech a little more complex than similes, and words and sentences that are somewhat long. Some writers insist on the highly questionable requirement of impersonal style (no pronouns referring to writer or reader) for reports and research papers at this dignified-informal level of usage.

Near the deep end of the informal level of usage is what we call "familiar-informal." Its whole attention should be on content and to heck with style. It's OK if you're writing to somebody you know pretty well or if the two of you have lots in common. In using it you have to assume that you don't need to show your reader that you know English. Even Churchill and Roosevelt sometimes joshed each other quite a bit in their messages. As in this paragraph, it uses contractions, a light touch, and rather simple sentence structure and words. If you want to use some slang and shoptalk, you just let go. Its value is its freshness, vividness, emphasis, and naturalness. The danger point, which this paragraph flirts with, is that it will be abused in an attempt to be clever and thus will call attention to itself.

Formal English is characterized by precision and elegance of diction, sentence structure, and grammar. Like the man dressed in formal clothes, it often appears stiff and unnatural, more to be admired for its appearance than for any function it may perform. It admits of no contractions, ellipses, or indignities of any kind. Of necessity, it uses many everyday words, but by design it includes many that are not commonly heard. Like the person of high society, it sometimes chooses its associates with more attention to their paternity than to what they are. As a consequence, its words are frequently somewhat rare and long, with histories traceable back to the first word families of Old French or Latin. It is often fraught with abstruse literary and historical allusions, perhaps to impress the reader with the writer's erudition. Rather than concerning itself with facilitating the reader's comprehension, it employs lengthy and labyrinthine sentences more fanciful than functional, more rhythmical than reasoned, more literary than literate, more artificial than accurate, and more absurd than acceptable. Following an unsound belief that they are thereby being more objective, its writers often strive for an impersonal style and bring forth a mountain of words from a molehill of an idea, or a diarrhea of words and a constipation of ideas. Its worst misguided practitioners—some lawyers, doctors, engineers, and politicians, apparently hoping to achieve dignity (and defending their practices by claiming that they achieve precision)—frequently abuse acceptable formal English by carrying it to the ridiculous extremes of the too technical, the pompous, and the flatulent (commonly called "gobbledygook" or "bafflegab").

Abused formal English has no reason for being. Even in its best sense, formal English is nearly always unsuitable for business letters. It would be noticed as inappropriate in all but the most formal occasions.

The illiterate level of usage is the third one of them three we dun named. It ain't got no bizness in letters. Ya see, folks who reads letters spects you ta right right. If'n ya writes wrong, he shore sees ya errors and knows ya ain't eddicated so he thinks ya don't know nuthin else neither if ya cain't get yer rightin right.

An easy way to choose the appropriate level of usage for a situation you have analyzed is to ask yourself which type of dress would be most suitable if you were going to see your reader and talk your message. If the answer is formal dress, choose formal English or dignified-informal. If the answer is an everyday business suit, use the broad middle ground of informal English. If the answer is sport clothes, use familiar-informal. Only if you are the kind of person who goes to church in dirty work clothes should you feel comfortable while revealing your illiteracy by violating the writing conventions expected of educated people.

Follow the conventions

You have already seen how following the conventions of wording, punctuation, sentence structure, and grammar affects clarity. But violations of those and other conventions have an even more important bearing on keeping your style inconspicuous. If you go contrary to the conventions, you do something your reader doesn't expect of an educated writer. You therefore distract attention from your message and lose the reader's respect and faith in you.

After all, if a writer has not even mastered the fundamentals of the native language, knowing anything else of importance or value seems unlikely. This is what enters most readers' minds when they come across letters marred with misspellings and grammatical errors.

Even the following first paragraph in a letter from a hotel manager to an association president is clear. You know what the writer means, despite poor sentence structure, but you are distracted and you can't hold much respect for the manager or the hotel.

```
Your recent convention over with and successful, we are
wondering if since then you have decided on the next year's
meeting city, and you jotting down on the margin of this
letter the city and dates selected, this will be indeed
appreciated.
```

From this, don't you get the impression that the sloppy language probably means the hotel might not be a very well run, clean place to stay?

Spelling is probably the most exactly established convention in the English language. A few words are spelled two ways, but most of them are listed only one way in the dictionary. Because of this definiteness, spelling has acquired much more importance in the minds of most people than it deserves. Although a misspelled word almost never leads to confusion and therefore makes little difference in terms of real communication, most readers (even relatively uneducated ones) will notice your errors and look down on you for them. So unless you prefer to write in other languages (nearly all of which have more systematic and easier-to-learn spelling), you had better accept your fate and learn English spelling.

Because it is so unsystematic, you'll find no easy way. Consider yourself fortunate if you have learned to spell by observing the words you read and by listening closely to how words are pronounced. If you have not used these methods, you should start now; but don't assume that pronunciation is always a safe guide. (You will find some helpful guidelines, however, under **Sp** in Appendix C.)

Poor *word choice* that is close enough to meet the basic requirement of clarity is usually not so noticeable as misspelling, but it may be distracting and even degrading. Among the thousands of possible bad choices, the pairs listed under Diction in Appendix C give the most trouble. If you are unsure of any of the distinctions, look up the words; any educated reader will notice if you confuse them.

Variations from *standard punctuation* may lead to misunderstanding, but more frequently they distract and retard the reader. If you have trouble with punctuation, study the material under **P** in Appendix C.

Grammar and sentence structure are so closely related that they should be considered together. They have a definite bearing on clarity (see discussion on p. 26), but they have more significance in terms of making your style inconspicuous. Most of the troubles come from:

—A writer's having heard uneducated people speak unconventionally, particularly family and fellow workers. (Solution: Observe the skill of other writers and speakers, study writing, practice.)
—Simple carelessness (Solution: Revise).
—Trying to use big words and complicated sentence structures before mastering them. (Solution: Remember that they are unnecessary to dignity; write

simply, at least until you can use more involved structures precisely and clearly.)

In trying to keep your style unnoticed by avoiding violations of the conventions of good English, you would have an easier job if all your readers were modern linguists.

Language scholars know that many of the so-called rules of English are

—Latin rules foisted off on English by early writers who knew Latin and thought English should follow the same system (but it doesn't).
—Rules concocted to systematize English by people who ignored the true nature and history of the language.

Here is a realistic interpretation of some points that language scholars make in contradiction to statements of some less well-informed people:

—A split infinitive is undesirable only if it is awkward or unclear.
—*And, but,* and *so* are good sentence beginnings if they deserve the emphasis they get there. The same applies to *however* and other transitional words, but some people object only to *and, but,* and *so.*
—Prepositions are perfectly good at the ends of sentences if you want them to have the emphasis they would get there.
—One-sentence paragraphs are perfectly good. The ban on them is nonsense. Often a one-sentence paragraph, especially the first or last in a letter, is just what you need.
—Passive voice is usually undesirable because it is weak, wordy, and awkward; but it still exists in the language because it is useful in some situations (to avoid direct accusations, for example). To ban it completely is high-handed.
—What some people still call colloquial expressions and slang are important and useful parts of the language; when the situation calls for the informal level of usage, they can improve language effectiveness.
—Many a word has several possible meanings when used alone; but if the context makes the interpretation readily clear and definite, to ban use of these words or to limit them (*while* or *since,* for example) to one use is unrealistic and lordly.
—The distinctions between *shall* and *will* are almost completely gone except in formal English; *will* is much more widely used.

Unfortunately, not all your readers will have studied courses on the history of the language and modern English usage or have read books on those subjects. Many of them will have been misled by linguistically unsound books and teachers. But they will *think* they know what is right and wrong. If you don't do what they think is right, you will distract them and lose their respect.

If you are writing to someone likely to be linguistically misinformed, we advise you to adhere to the widespread, though unsound, "rules" when you can do so easily. Otherwise, we suggest that you forget unjustifiable restrictions on the language and give your attention to the more important aspects of good style—interest, clarity, and inconspicuousness.

Appendix C covers some common violations of the conventions and gives suggestions for avoiding criticism.

(*All letter cases for the first four chapters are at the end of Part One because we think you should cover all four basic tests of a good business letter before trying to write any kind of letter. We urge you to read the first four chapters quickly but thoroughly so that you can put all the basic principles to use even in your first letter.*)

(*Since you will remember the principles of good style better if you practice them while concentrating on them alone, however, you may profit by working through at least some of the following exercises.*)

EXERCISES

Determine what is not good about the following sentences and rewrite them or be prepared to discuss them, as your teacher directs. Some of them have more than one thing wrong. You may also benefit from finding (in Appendix C) the appropriate symbol(s) for criticism of each sentence and reading the discussion of the symbol(s).

1. (*From an ad.*) Solid oak posture chairs for secretaries with built-in padding.
2. Gadgets can be bought to tell the temperatures and relative humidity at hardware and department stores.
3. The dinner is to honor residents and interns who are leaving the hospital and their wives.
4. We should take steps to eliminate the one sixth of our population which is now in poverty.
5. No lawyer ever learned all the law he or she practices in law school.
6. My own evaluation of Honeywells is the same as that of the engineers and should be installed in our plant.
7. The channel of distribution being utilized most is the use of a traveling sales force.
8. The business district in that area is El Cajon and it has its own police force in it.
9. Not only is this welder useful in the manufacture of products but also in repairing of equipment where replacement of the damaged parts is expensive.
10. It was found that there are 12 main reasons why goods are returned. The most significant of these being entirely or almost entirely customer faults. The 12 reasons are: . . . .
11. According to the journal Trusts and Estates, a greater percentage of common stocks are now included in the investment portfolios of banks.

12. Mr. Richmans recommendation was the Sharpe because he felt it requires the least upkeep of the two machines as well as less shutdowns.
13. The size of the plant and the nature of its hazards determines the fire protection equipment needed.
14. The varied kinds of work we can perform includes: property surveys, staking out substations, taking elevations for contours, and steel inventories.
15. Inside the tube is also placed a tiny drop of mercury and a small amount of argon gas.
16. The evaluation of these problems were made by the department of market research.
17. Thank you for your order and let us know if we can be of service again.
18. There are some manufacturers that I was unable to contact; however, the figures here cover all the major producers.
19. Though the clothing field has a large percentage of returns it is not at all representative of the whole retailing world.
20. In order to understand how this method of distribution would achieve its purpose an analysis of it is necessary.
21. While I worked with the fire crew I was only involved in one run.
22. On first registering all students must pay a $15 deposit to the bursars office which will be returned upon leaving the university.
23. Mr. Johnson insists on neat accurate work.
24. Explaining each type would be a long tiring job.
25. Included in the shipment are three one ounce packages and one sixteen ounce package.
26. The weight of the machines range from 3,000–5,200 pounds.
27. This gives the company that chooses the paper bag more versatility in their packaging line.
28. When buying from an equipment manufacturer the prices might be a bit lower but would not include the shipping charges.
29. While working in Plant 4, fireproof coveralls and protective glasses are issued as a safety measure.
30. Simply check your choice on the return card and immediately upon receiving your preference the typewriter will be sent to you.
31. Common stocks can be classified under three main types. These types are: 1) income stocks, b) cyclical stocks, and c) those stocks which have fast growth.
32. The polyethylene derives two advantages here which are:
    a) Heat sealing made possible by its use speeds up the process.
    b) Economy of eliminating excess material.

33. Arc welding has some advantages over other methods: easier wedge preparation, faster welding speed and it eliminates the use of flux.
34. The report is designed primarily to show the particular need existing in Latin America and recommending a possible solution for it.
35. The problems selected for study were chosen through personal interview with the workers, manager, and my own personal experience.
36. You might also show accounts receivable, long-term accounts and discuss the future outlook.
37. In conformance with our conversation on March 30, the report of the uranium corporation has been reviewed, to determine wherein the operations of the corporation may have been presented inadequately; further, suggested changes in format, illustrations, and treatment of text have been developed, for consideration in the preparation of subsequent reports.
38. Approximately 66 percent had made their most recent hardware purchase in Tulsa. This is an increase over previous findings of 4 percent.
39. It is not unlikely that payment will be received by us within a reasonable length of time and proper form.
40. Unless the Office of Price Administration or an authorized representative thereof shall, by letter mailed to the applicant within 21 days from the date of filing application, disapprove the requested increase in the minimum price, such price increase shall be deemed to have been approved, subject to nonretroactive written disapproval or adjustment at any later time by the Office of Price Administration.

chapter 2

Persuasion: What the reader does

[Knowledge or skill without justice is cunning, not wisdom.]

BECAUSE IN MOST business letters you are trying to produce an action or a reaction which may lead presently to an action, many correspondents maintain that every letter is a sales letter. In the broad sense that you are usually trying to persuade someone that your suggestion (whether it's a product, a service, or an idea) is a good one and/or that yours is a good firm to deal with, that's right.

If you are going to be successful in that mission, you'll want to make conscious use of five principles of persuasion which have proved helpful in getting the desired positive response:

1. Planned presentation in the light of your objective
2. You-viewpoint interpretation
3. Adaptation—even personalization when possible
4. Positive statement
5. Success consciousness

PLANNED PRESENTATION

You can make your job of beginning fairly simple if you will classify your letter according to one of the following three probable reactions of your reader:

A. Will the reader welcome the letter? That is, does it report news or ask action the reader will be glad to hear or at least not unhappy to hear? Does it take action the reader has requested? Does it request action the reader is prepared to take?

B. Will the reader be displeased with the basic message? Does it contain bad news?

C. Or does it request action the reader is probably not already willing to take?

According to subject matter, you can list hundreds of different kinds of business letters; but for predetermining its beginning and the subsequent development of points, all you need to decide upon is whether your letter contains good news or neutral information (A–plan), disappointing information (B–plan), or persuasion intended to motivate the reader to action (C–plan).

Good-news or neutral messages

Most A–plan letters say or imply yes, as in favorable replies to requests, acknowledgments in which you can ship goods as ordered, adjustments fully complying with the reader's request, and credit approvals. Since you are doing what the reader wants you to do, the first sentence should contain the big idea of the letter; that is what the reader most wants to know. Then you follow up with necessary details in order of relative importance or natural sequence. Frequently letters of this kind end with a short punch line recalling the benefits of the good news in the beginning, as suggested by Figure 1.

FIGURE 1 Good-news and routine letters

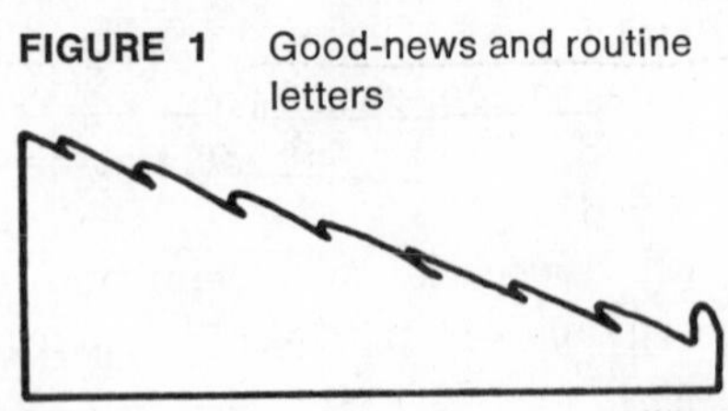

Letters which merely seek or transmit business information follow the same basic order: inquiries and replies about job or credit applicants and explanations or identifications of something about an organization, its personnel, or its products. All these are situations in which your reader is neutral (neither pleased nor displeased), and so the letters are taken for granted. They should be characterized by the same directness and dispatch in their handling as in the following "Yes" letter (replacing a clock ordered for a birthday gift and damaged in transit):

Your new Admiral desk clock was mailed by insured parcel post this morning and should be at your door about January 23.

The same kind of heavy padding carefully protecting your new Admiral in the large corrugated box will be used for all future shipments of fragile articles so that they will arrive in the same perfect condition in which they leave the store.

And now will you take a moment to assist us in recovering for the clock from the Postal Service? Just sign the enclosed notification forms and return them with the original clock.

The recipient of the new Admiral on January 26 will no doubt be pleased with its beauty and practicality. It is an appropriate birthday surprise.

Disappointing messages

B–plan letters, those that say "No" or "Yes, but . . ." (that is, modified refusals), should not be direct. If you have to tell a reader that you can't give the booklet requested, that you can't fill an order as specified, that you can't extend credit, or that you can't make the adjustment desired, you have a situation which is potentially goodwill-killing—especially if you blurt out the disappointing information immediately.

We assume throughout this book that you are a fair-minded person who does not act high-handedly or arbitrarily and that you therefore have good reasons when you refuse anything. We know, too, that in most cases you can show that some of your reasons are beneficial to the other person—as when a mother refuses her child something for the child's good as well as (sometimes even *rather than*) her own. The following psychology of refusing therefore depends on your having good reasons, as does any satisfactory refusal.

You know that when you refuse anybody anything considered due, disappointment and frustration develop unless you give justifying reasons (not just excuses or no explanation at all). You know further that if you begin with the refusal, you will at least disappoint (maybe even anger) your reader. You also know that an angry person is not a logical one. So even if you do give good reasons *after* the refusal, they fall on an illogical mind, where they do not take effect.

But if you start pleasantly and give justifying reasons *before* a refusal, your reader is much more likely to accept your refusal without irritation because you show the justice of it. Thus your logical reasons fall on a logical mind, and the reasons which caused you to feel justified in refusing convince your reader that you *are* justified. This psychology directs you to a rather specific plan for all refusals.

To soften the effect, you try to catch the reader's favorable interest in the opening remarks with something from the situation on which both reader and writer can agree. This is commonly called a "buffer." Writers use it for two reasons: (1) to suggest that the writer is a reasonable person who can see two sides of the question and (2) to set the stage for a review of the facts in the case. A good buffer will therefore be

—Pleasant, usually agreeing with something the reader has said
—Relevant, thus quickly showing the subject of the letter
—Equivocal, avoiding any implication that the answer is yes or no
—Transitional, carefully worded for a natural movement into the explanation

After you establish compatibility, you analyze the circumstances sympathetically and understandingly, giving the reasons why you can't do what the reader wants you to do. Not until you have tactfully prepared the way with these justifying reasons do you want to reveal the disappointing news. You further attempt to soften the blow by embedding the refusal, by giving it minimum space, and by positive statement when you have to state it; but better, when possible, you may be able to make the refusal clear by implication. Certainly you do not want to stress it.

Nor do you want to end your letter on a note of disappointment. To close, select some point of favorable interest to your reader which demonstrates your desire to retain the friend and/or customer relationship.

Graphically, your procedure looks like the line in Figure 2. The following positive refusal illustrates the strategy:

FIGURE 2 Bad-news letters

Your comments, Professor McGinnis, on the effectiveness of the "More Business" series are helpful to those of us at Read's who worked on these practical guides for users of direct mail.

When we first planned the booklets for our customers, we had in mind a checklist for a business using direct mail extensively rather than a thoroughgoing treatment suitable for a textbook. Accordingly, we set our quota for noncommercial users at a low figure—partly because we did not anticipate many requests.

Since the series has proved so popular with our customers, we have for over a month been distributing copies only to commercial users, although we are glad to make available what we can to training institutions.

Perhaps you may be able to use the extra copy—sent to you this morning by parcel post—as a circulating library for your correspondence students. Two or three days' use should be ample for most of them, and they're perfectly welcome to copy anything they care to.

Will you give us the benefit of your suggestions for making the series more extensive after you have had an opportunity to test its teachability more thoroughly?

Persuasive messages

For the third basic letter situation, the C–plan, you start off with something that you can be reasonably sure your reader wants or is interested in. Preferably it will be a promised or implied benefit, thus catching attentive interest from the start. Develop your letter in concrete pictures of that benefit. If you can start off in interested agreement and maintain this agreement as you explain the worth (and reader benefits) of your proposition, you can wind up with the reader doing what you ask.

FIGURE 3 Selling letters

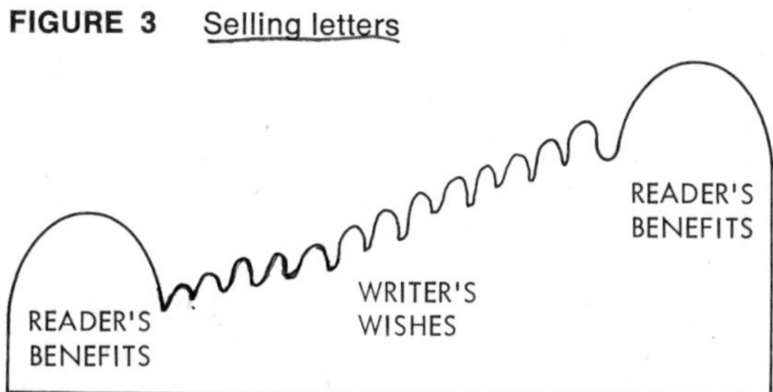

Starting a letter of this kind need not be difficult if you will make your most honest and concrete attempt to figure out something the reader wants (or needs) that you can give. When you have developed the benefits available from complying with your suggestion and have supplied enough evidence for conviction, you are in a psychological position to ask for the action you want.

Prospecting (cold-turkey) sales and application letters, persuasive requests, and some collections follow this pattern, as in the following persuasive request for a confidential manual:

How often have you received—even from well-educated people—letters that are not worth your attention?

As a public relations director and an employer, you are of course interested in this problem. And I, as a teacher of business communication, am too. Here at Harwood we're turning out a thousand students each year who are better trained in writing effective letters than the usual college graduate. We'd like to be sure that we're giving them what business wants.

It's quite likely, you know, that some of these students will some day be writing letters for companies like yours. Wouldn't they be better prepared if we instructors could stress the ideas that you have given special emphasis to in your recent correspondence manual? Both the students and business firms would benefit from your letting us have a copy for our teaching files. Of course, we'd handle the material with whatever confidence you specify. And we'd be most grateful for this practical teaching aid.

But the ones especially benefiting from your sending a copy would be the students and business firms like Southern Atlantic.

Will you send us a copy today?

The planned steps in all selling are here. Whether you want to call them four steps (Attention, Interest, Conviction, and Action; or Promise, Picture, Prove, and Push) or three steps (Attentive Interest, Conviction or Evidence, and Action) or more doesn't matter. But it does matter that you get attentive interest quickly by promising a reader benefit, give evidence backing up that promised benefit, forestall or minimize any objections you can foresee, and confidently ask the reader to do what you want.

YOU-VIEWPOINT

[People wrapped up in themselves are usually small packages.]

The you-viewpoint or you-attitude is a state of mind: always ferreting out and emphasizing the benefits to the reader resulting from your suggestion or decision and subordinating or eliminating (*but not denying*) your own.

Of course, it isn't pure unselfishness. All businesses must be motivated by the profit motive. When you try to sell something, obviously you are trying to make some money; but you don't need to put that idea into words. When you attempt to collect, obviously you want—maybe even need—the money; you don't need to put that idea into words. When you apply for a job, obviously you either want or need work to earn some money; you don't need to put that idea into words. Both reader and writer *assume* all these ideas. Putting them into words merely sounds selfish, wastes words, and helps your cause not one bit.

Nor is the you-attitude a question merely of politeness, courtesy, or good manners. The hard business reason for you-viewpoint presentation is that when you show you are aware of and are doing something about your reader's needs or problems, your suggestion will get a more favorable reaction. In other words, another person will do what you want if—and only if—you show benefits worth the cost and trouble.

Nothing else is so important to your reader as self (and when you're the reader, you'll get the same approach if the other person writing is smart). So by central theme and wording you show that you are thinking of your reader's welfare as you write.

The you-viewpoint requires imagination, certainly. The old story of the village half-wit's answer to how he found the mule is apt ("Why, I just thought, 'If I was a mule, where would I go?' "). The ability to visualize the reader's desires, circumstances, and probable reactions and write in those terms is the answer. When you write to secretaries, you *are* a secretary; when you write to doctors, you *are* a doctor; when you write to merchants, you *are* a merchant. It requires that you be able to play many roles. Without this basic outlook and attitude, you-viewpoint presentation will be superficial.

Phrasing helps, it is true. You are more likely to write in terms of the reader if you use more *you's* and *your's* than the first-person pronouns *I, me, mine, we, us, our.* But if you apply that test alone, the sentence "We want your check" has more you-viewpoint than "We want our check," when obviously neither has any. "Please send your check" is neutral. The reader-dominated sentence might well read, "To keep your account in the preferred-customer class, send your check for $142.63 today," or "Get your account in shape for the heavy Christmas buying coming up by sending your check for $142.63 today." Whether you say "sending *us* your check" or not is immaterial, except that it wastes a word; the *us* is clearly understood. But what is much more significant, the reader-benefit reason—the you-viewpoint—is there.

WE-VIEWPOINT	YOU-VIEWPOINT
We are shipping your order of June 2 this afternoon.	You should receive the Jurgin crosscut saw you ordered June 2 no later than Saturday, June 7.
We have spent 27 years making the Jurgin a fast-selling saw.	Back of your Jurgin blade are 27 years of successful testing and remodeling. Because it is taper-ground alloy steel, it slides through the wood more freely than other models.

Making your reader the subject or object of your sentences will help you keep you-viewpoint interpretation. As you've already seen in the discussion of writing interestingly (p. 12), psychological description and dramatized copy are effective because they keep the reader involved and show that you have the you-viewpoint. The only way to get it in the first place, however, is to subordinate your own reactions to those you estimate are your reader's and then to write in a manner which clearly shows that your reader's interests dominate.

An example of well-intentioned writing that is fundamentally writer-dominated is the conventional thank-you beginning: "Thank you for your order of June 2 for one Jurgin crosscut saw blade" and "We are grateful for. . . ." Even worse is the selfish "We are glad to have your order for. . . ." All three variations have this strike against them: They emphasize the personal reaction of the writer rather than something the reader is interested in knowing.

If you can (or will) make shipment, an opening like the following has more you-viewpoint than any of the three foregoing:

> Your Jurgin crosscut saw blade should arrive by prepaid railway express no later than Friday, June 7.

This is something your reader wants to know! If you can't make shipment, a resale comment is a better example of you-viewpoint than the selfish statement of pleasure upon the receipt of another order or the disappointing statement that the reader is not now getting the ordered goods. If you have to delay shipment only a few days, this is a possibility for retaining positiveness and you-viewpoint:

> The Jurgin crosscut saw blade you ordered will give you long and faithful service.

When the reader has done you a favor, some form of thank you may be one of the best beginnings you could use. In place of the conventional "Dear Mr. Miller," the salutation—

> Thank you, Mr. Miller!

—has directness and enthusiasm which are heartwarming. The first paragraph may then concentrate on a more significant point:

> Those articles about palletization which you suggested contain some of the best information I've been able to uncover.

But doesn't the statement of the significance you attach to your reader's contribution adequately establish your appreciation?

We do not mean to imply that an expression of gratitude is out of place. No one ever offended a reader with a genuine, appropriate thank you. But we do want to stress that you can accomplish the same function with some statement which will place more emphasis on your reader—where it should be!

The preceding remarks concerning planned presentation and you-viewpoint apply whether you're writing a special or a form letter—a sales, credit, collection, application, or simple reply. The closer you can come to making your reader nod in agreement and think, "That's what I want to hear," the greater your possibilities for favorable reception of your letter.

ADAPTATION

When you can make your reader also think "That sure fits me," you have an additional advantage. Successful adaptation makes your reader feel that you wrote your letter with him or her in mind.

Even in a mailing to a large number of people, you will have identifiable common characteristics (of geography, age, educational level, vocation, or income status, for example) that will enable you to adapt the talking points, language, and style of your letter and to make references to circumstances and events recognized as common to each member of the group.

Adapting talking points

In adapting talking points (or theme), you simply seek out and emphasize those reasons you believe will be most influential in causing your reader to act or react as you want. Specifically, you would try to sell a typewriter to a secretary on the basis of ease of operation, to an office manager on ease of maintenance and durability, but to a purchasing agent on the basis of long-range cost. The lawn mower which you would sell to a homeowner because of its ease of handling and maintenance, you would sell to a hardware dealer because of its salability and profit margin. A car may appeal to a man on the basis of economy and dependability of operation; to a woman the appeals of appearance and comfort may be stronger. When a man buys a shirt, he is interested in appearance and fit; his wife may be more interested in launderability and long wear.

Accordingly, you adapt your talking points to your reader(s) for increased persuasiveness. This is a fairly simple procedure when you are writing a single letter and is entirely possible in a mass mailing if you study the characteristics common to all people on your mailing list.

Adapting language and style

You adapt language and style, in general, in the light of your reader's age, educational level, and vocation (which influence social and economic position). As your reader's years, professional and social prestige, and financial status increase, you are safer in using longer sentences, uncommon words, and more formal language. Sometimes you will want to use the specialized terms of vocational classes, such as doctors, lawyers, and insurance people, for instance. Although some of these terms are more technical than you would use in writing to a general audience, to specialized readers they convey the impression that you, the writer, understand their special problems. The application of this suggestion means that when you write to doctors, references to patients, laboratories, diagnoses, and the like help; to a person in insurance, prospects, premiums, and expirations are likely referents.

Referring to common experiences

Better adaptation than language and style, however, are references to common experiences in the reader's life. A reference to vocation, to a geographical factor, to some home and family status—in fact, to any activity or reaction you can be reasonably sure your reader has experienced—rings the bell of recognition and makes the reader feel that very definitely you are writing to and about a person's conditions.

In a letter to college students, for instance, the following reference would almost universally bring positive (and in most cases humorous) recognition:

> When your teacher talks on . . . and on . . . and on . . . (even when it's two minutes past the bell!). . . .

To parents:

> When your child yawns, turns over, and <u>finally</u> goes to sleep.

To doctors:

> . . . for the elimination of dust, smoke, and antiseptic odors from your reception room.

To school superintendents:

> . . . to reduce the necessary and healthy noise of active adolescents when they're changing classes.

To almost any office worker:

> . . . when your files simply won't reveal an important paper.

To anyone who is or has been a secretary:

> An hour's transcription to get in the night's mail—and at five minutes to 5:00!

Any of the preceding phrases could go into a form letter or an individual letter. The more specifically you can phrase these references to make them pinpoint your one reader, the more effective your adaptation will be.

Personalizing

To further the impression that the letter has been prepared for the reader and to heighten the feeling of friendliness, correspondents sometimes use the reader's name or other references so specific as to be individualizing, not only in the inside address and the salutation but also in the letter copy. At about the middle of the letter, much as one uses a friend's name in conversation—or near the end of the letter in the same way you frequently use a person's name in ending a conversation—such references as the following help to give the impression that the letter is for one person rather than a group:

> You'll also appreciate the lightness of the Multimower, Mr. Bowen.
>
> --
>
> Your Atlanta Luminall dealer will be glad to call on you and answer any other questions you may have, Mr. Bowen.

Just check a convenient time on the enclosed card and drop it in the mail today.

In individually typed letters the placement of the name presents no problem; in form letters, try to put the name at the end of a line (as in the preceding examples) so that typing in the reader's name is easy, regardless of length. Unless you can match type and print perfectly, however, you may do more harm than good. (Computerized letters enable a writer to insert special phrasing at any point in a letter. But because of costs this is a process available only to those firms sending out mailings in the thousands, even millions.) In any case use of the reader's name is a more or less mechanical process; it is probably the least effective means of adapting.

You can also increase the feeling of friendliness by the wording of your salutation and complimentary close. *Dear Sir* and *Very truly yours,* although appropriate many times, are somewhat formal and do not reflect the warmth of *Dear Mr. Bowen* and *Sincerely yours* or some other less formal phrasing. The main forms and their order of formality appear in detail on page 72.

Of far greater significance are adaptation of talking points and lifelike references to the reader's activities. The following letter answers the lady's questions in a sound sales presentation and enhances the persuasiveness of the message with special references (such as to the housekeeper and the power failure mentioned in her inquiry) that could apply to no one but the reader:

Dear Mrs. Jackson:

The Stair-Traveler you saw in the June <u>Home and Yard</u> will certainly make daily living easier for you and your faithful old housekeeper. You can make as many trips upstairs and downstairs as you care to <u>every day</u> and still follow your doctor's advice.

Simply sit down on the bench (about the same size as a dressing-table stool) and press the button. Gently and smoothly your Stair-Traveler takes you upstairs at a rate just a little faster than ordinary walking. Should the electricity fail in Greenbriar while you're using your Stair-Traveler, automatic brakes bring it to a gentle stop and hold it in place until the current comes on. Then you just press the button to start it again.

Folded back against the wall when not in use, the Stair-Traveler's simple, straight lines of mahogany will blend in well with your antiques. Your Stair-Traveler will be right at home on your front straight stairway, Mrs. Jackson. It will be more convenient for you there, and the installation is simple and economical. Notice the folded Stair-Traveler on page 3 of the booklet I'm sending; it looks somewhat like a console table.

To explain how simply and economically your Stair-Traveler can be installed, Mr. J. B. Nickle, our Memphis representative,

```
will be glad to call at a time convenient for you.  Will you
use the enclosed postcard to let him know when that will be?
```

Such specialized references do increase letter costs when they mean writing an individualized letter rather than using a form. But many times you must if the letter is to get the job done. Even in form paragraphs and entire form letters, however, you usually can make some adaptation to the reader's situation.

You can find out a great deal about your reader through letters to you, your credit records (including credit reports), sales representatives' reports, and the like. Even a bought or rented mailing list contains the names of people with some common characteristics of vocation, location, age, sex, finances, and buying and living habits. You won't make your letter do all it could do if you don't use your knowledge of these common characteristics to adapt your letter according to talking points and endow it with the marginal pulling power of known references to familiar events, activities, places, or persons.

A word of caution is appropriate here, however: Don't try to be specific beyond the point of likelihood. For example, you may have a mailing list of parents, but you don't know how many children these people have or the sex. A reference to "your child" is safe (even if the reader has more than one); a reference to "your children" is not—and certainly not to "your boy" or "your girl." Obviously, you cannot safely use such tags as "Junior" and "Sister" and certainly not individual names like "Bobby" and "Janie" unless you *know* your reader does have a Bobby or a Janie.

POSITIVE STATEMENT

Your letters have greater prospects for success if you focus on positive ideas because people—most of them, at any rate—respond more favorably to a positive prospect than to a negative one.

Saying the cheerful, positive thing that people want to hear rather than the unpleasant or unhappy, negative thing they do not want to hear is really just an extension of you-viewpoint presentation and tact. It requires, first of all, staying optimistic yourself so that you can see the rosier side of any picture. It comes from constantly superimposing a positive picture on a negative one, thus completely eliminating, or at least subordinating, the negative idea. Translated into letter-writing procedures, it is the result of stressing what something is rather than what it is not, emphasizing what the firm or product can and will do rather than what it cannot, leading with action rather than apology or explanation, and avoiding words that convey basically unpleasant ideas.

Test after test of both advertising copy and letter copy has demonstrated the wisdom of positive statement. That is why nearly 40 years ago successful copywriters warned against the denied negative (and today's writers still issue the same warning). That is why the effective writer will make the following positive statements rather than their negative counterparts:

NEGATIVE	POSITIVE
Penquot sheets are not the skimpy, loosely woven sheets ordinarily in this price class.	Penquot sheets are woven 186 threads to the square inch for durability and, even after 3-inch hems, measure a generous 72 by 108 inches.
We are sorry that we cannot furnish the club chairs by August 16.	After checking with the Production Department, we can definitely assure you your club chairs by August 29.
We cannot ship in lots of less than 12.	To keep down packaging costs and to help customers save on shipping costs, we ship in lots of 12 or more.
I have no experience other than clerking in my father's grocery store.	Clerking in my father's grocery store for three summers taught me the value of serving people courteously and promptly.
If we can help, please do not hesitate to get in touch with us.	Can we help further?

A special form of negativism is the challenging question which invites a negative answer. Although it contains no negative wording, the question "Wouldn't you rather drink Old Judge?" is more likely to bring forth the reply "No, I'd rather drink Colonel Dalton" or maybe "Make mine Dipsi-Cola!" than it is to get a yes answer. "Who wouldn't want a Kreisler Regal?" will bring something like a bristling "Not me, brother; I want a Cabriolet!" from most readers, who will resent the presumptuousness of such a question. "What could be finer than an XYZ dishwasher?" will elicit, among other answers, "A full-time maid!" Such questions, along with the apparently harmless "Why not try a Blank product?" get your reader out of step with you and, because they invite a negative response, are a deterrent to the success of your suggestion.

Keeping your messages positive also means deliberately excluding negative words. You can't be "sorry" about something without recalling the initial unhappy experience. You can't write "unfortunately" without restating some gloomy aspect of a situation. Nor can you write in terms of "delay," "broken," "damages," "unable to," "cannot," "inconvenience," "difficulty," "disappointment," and other negatives without stressing some element of the situation which makes your reader react against you rather than with you. Even a *however,* after you've been talking pleasant things, will surely give a kind of sinking feeling.

For all these reasons the effective writer will write "ABC Dog Biscuits will help keep your dog healthy" instead of "ABC Dog Biscuits will help keep your dog from getting sick." It's just a question of accentuating the positive, eliminating the negative where possible, and otherwise subordinating it (see **Emp** in Appendix C).

SUCCESS CONSCIOUSNESS

Success consciousness is the confident attitude that your reader will do what you ask or accept the decision your letter announces. To reflect this attitude in your letters, guard against any phrasing which suggests that the reader may not take the action you want.

Success consciousness is based on your own conviction that your explanation is adequate, your suggestion legitimate and valuable to your reader, your decision the result of adequate evidence and logical, businesslike reasoning. Thus assured yourself, you are not likely to write something which suggests or even implies that you are unsure of your ground. The sales correspondent who writes

> If you'd like to take advantage of this timesaving piece of equipment, put your check and completed order blank in the enclosed envelope and drop it in the mail today.

would be better off not to remind the reader of the option to reject the proposal. Simply omitting the phrase *if you'd like* establishes a tone of greater confidence. The one word *if* is the most frequent destroyer of success consciousness.

Likewise, when tempted to write

> Why not try a sample order?

the correspondent should remember that the suggestion is stronger with the elimination of *why not*. It has not only the disadvantage of suggesting that the writer is not sure but also the distinct disadvantage of inviting the reader to think of reasons for not doing what the letter suggests. A little mental effort will probably produce several reasons.

Hope and its synonym *trust* are second only to *if* as destroyers of success consciousness. In a letter granting an adjustment, the sentence

> We hope you'll approve of our decision.

has greater success consciousness (and thus more reader response) when revised to read:

> With this extension of your subscription to Vacation you can continue to read each month about the world's most interesting places.

By assumption (implication)—by definitely omitting the doubtful-sounding expression—the writer seems to say, "Of course, you and I realize that this is what you want."

In refusals the following sentence sometimes appears in an otherwise well-written letter:

```
We trust you will understand our position.
```

Usually, however, it appears in a poorly written letter. And it is most frequently the result of inadequate explanation. The writer seems to despair of giving an adequate explanation and to hope that the reader will figure out one. If you find yourself writing or wanting to write such a sentence, go back and see whether your explanation is ample. If it is, omit such a sentence; if it is not, revise your explanation so that it is convincing—and substitute some positive, confident statement for the weak-kneed expression.

Even in simple replies the problem arises with such a sentence as

```
We hope this is the information you wanted.
```

The implications of doubt disappear quickly and easily with

```
We're glad to send you this information.
```

This principle of success consciousness applies in all types of letters, but it is most significant in selling letters—and especially in the action ending.

A word of caution against high-pressure presumptuousness is in order here, however. To omit a reference to a reader's alternative is one thing; to imply that the reader has no alternative is quite another! The application letter writer who so boldly and confidently asks

```
When may I come in to see you?
```

gives the impression that the reader has no alternative but to set up an interview. Such presumptuousness may irritate the reader. Rephrased like the following, a request for an interview would strike most readers favorably:

```
Will you write me a convenient time when I may come in and
tell you more about why I believe I am the aggressive salesman
you're looking for?
```

The proper degree of success consciousness requires careful wording, particularly at the end. Basically, you need to consider what the purpose of the letter is.

Sometimes you want the reader to take no overt action on the topic of the letter—as in most B–plan letters and some A's. In that case you may end with a pleasant comment or further support for something said earlier (thanks or resale, for example), with an off-the-subject comment (usually a pleasant look to the future, perhaps sales promotion material), or with something else pleasant. Certainly you want to avoid suggesting inadequacy of treatment and such jargon as "Please do not hesitate . . ." or "Feel free to. . . ." And in B–plan letters, guard particularly against referring back to the trouble you've supposedly cleared up.

At other times you are asking for action that is simple, easy, and likely —as in most A–plan letters (no strong reader resistance). Here a subtle reference to or suggestion of that action is most appropriate:

—I shall appreciate your answers to. . . .
—You are cordially invited to. . . .
—When you send in your check for the $27.50 now due, please. . . .

In C–plan letters, you are asking for action the reader may be at first reluctant to take. The force of your push for action—to overcome reader resistance—must continue to the end. Here particularly, such words as *if, trust,* and *hope* will show a lack of success consciousness that will be self-defeating.

As you see, each of the three situations requires an ending quite different from what is appropriate for the others. You will do well, therefore, to keep in mind the principle of success consciousness as you study the discussions, illustrations, and checklists for different classes of letters throughout this book.

One important general point deserves your attention here, however: Even though the earlier part of the letter may have indicated a desired action, you need to refer to, suggest, ask for, or push for that action *at the end.*

(*All the cases for the first four chapters are at the end of Part One because we think you should cover all four basic tests of a good business letter before trying to write any kind of letter. We urge you to read the first four chapters quickly but thoroughly so that you can put all the basic principles to use even in your first letter.*)

chapter 3 Goodwill: How the reader feels

[Disagreements come from lost accord.]

Tone
- Acceptable balance of personalities
  - Undue humility
  - Flattery
  - Condescension
  - Preachiness
  - Bragging
- Courtesy
  - Anger
  - Accusations
  - Unflattering implications
  - Sarcasm
  - Curtness
  - Stereotyped language
  - Physical appearance
- Sincerity
  - Effusiveness
  - Exaggeration
  - Undue familiarity

Service attitude
- Resale material
- Sales promotion material
- Special goodwill letters

MOST BUSINESS PEOPLE define goodwill as "the disposition of customers to return to the place where they have been treated well." Look it up in your dictionary, however, and you'll find friendly, positive words like *kindly feeling, benevolence, cheerful consent, heartiness,* and *cordiality.* A business letter helps to produce that positive disposition in the reader by developing a friendly, confident feeling toward the writer.

No business firm or individual intentionally drives away present or potential customers or friends by creating ill will or by seeming indifferent.

For lack of conscious effort to build goodwill, however, many letter writers do drive customers away. Proper *tone* and *service attitude* are the methods of winning the reader's friendliness and confidence—that is, goodwill or disposition to return to you because you treat people well.

TONE

[Beware of those who fall at your feet; they may be reaching for the rug.]

No doubt you have heard someone complain, "It isn't *what* he said—it's the *way* he said it!" Inflections and modulations of voice, facial expressions, hand gestures—all affect the tone or overall impression of a spoken remark almost as much as the words do, sometimes even more. The point applies in writing too—especially in writing letters, the most personal, me-to-you kind of writing. If you want your letters to build goodwill, you *will make a conscious effort to control the tone.*

Basic to a desirable tone in letters is a balance of personalities (writer's and reader's) acceptable to both. Without an attitude of mutual respect, you will have difficulty achieving in your letters the other two qualities necessary for good tone—courtesy and sincerity.

Acceptable balance of personalities

As a writer of good business letters you will need to subordinate your own wishes, reactions, and opinions; the suggestion "Make it *big you* and little me" can be overdone, however. Anything you say that looks up to or down on the reader will throw the relationship off balance.

Undue humility usually backfires. Such a fawning, servile tone as in the following is unwise because it is obviously insincere-sounding; no reader expects a writer to be so humble.

```
I'm sorry to ask a busy person like you to take valuable time
to help me, but without your help I do not know how to
proceed.  Since you are a world authority on . . . , and I
know nothing about it. . . .
```

In addition to the insincere implications, it also suggests an incompetent person whose request for advice is hardly worth considering.

Flattery is another reason why readers question the sincerity of some writers, especially when it is obvious flattery in connection with the writer's attempt to get the reader to do something or to keep buying. The reader, sure that the writer has an ax to grind, discounts such passages as the following:

```
Your keen discrimination in footwear shows in your order of
the ninth.

                          --

Your eminent position in commercial aviation, Mr. Pogue, is the
subject of much admiration.
```

--

```
When an Atlanta girl marries, she immediately thinks of Rich's,
the merchandising cynosure of the South!
```

Flattery also embarrasses many readers and makes them uncomfortable even in the privacy of reading a letter. Instead of gaining favor, the writer loses face and the reader's faith.

Passing deserved compliments or giving credit where credit is due is something else; it is expected of anybody except a boor.

When you want to indicate your sincere awareness of the reader's position or accomplishment, handle the reference subordinately. The writer who began a letter with

```
You are receiving this questionnaire because you are an
authority in retailing
```

got off to a bad start because of the obviousness of the flattery. A supervisor revised the sentence this way:

```
As an authority in retailing, how do you think the passage of
HR-818 will affect co-ops?
```

Before the reader has time to feel irritation or embarrassment over the initial phrase (it's so short and touched so lightly that it may give a faint glow of satisfaction), consideration of the question precludes unfavorable reaction.

Handling a compliment subtly is frequently a question of inserting a complimentary phrase in a statement intended primarily to accomplish something else. The indirect compliments in the following openings imply that the reader's opinion is worth seeking but have no obvious flattery:

```
How, in your opinion, will passage of HR-818 affect co-ops?
```

--

```
After successful experience in the field, would you say that
any single area of preparation is more important than others
for effective public relations work?
```

More frequent than undesirable humility and flattery, however, is a writer's implication of too much self-respect and too little for the reader. Lack of respect usually reflects itself in (1) condescension ("talking down" to the other person), (2) preachiness (*didacticism* is another word for it), and (3) bragging.

Condescension is quick evidence that the writer feels superior to the reader and shows little respect. Almost everybody has a good share of self-respect. No one wants to be considered a nobody and looked down on or talked down to.

Yet, in attempting to be bighearted, a business executive insulted a reader with "It is unlikely that the machine is defective, but a firm of our size and standing can afford to take it back and give you a new one." In the same category go sentences like "I am surprised that you would question the adjustment procedure of a firm like Blank's" and "You are apparently unaware of the long history of satisfactory customer relations at Blank's." The statement "We shall allow you to" has condescending connotations not present in "We shall be glad to" or "Certainly you may."

A particular danger lies in writing to children, who are not lacking in respect for their own ways of looking at things. When the secretary of a boys' club requested that a department store manager contribute some boxing gloves to the club, the manager answered: "When you grow up to have the heavy business responsibilities I have and you're asked for contributions by all kinds of charitable organizations, you'll understand why I cannot make a donation to your club." The boy's vocabulary failed him, but what he tried to express was "That pompous ass!" And to make matters worse, the manager began the next sentence with "You are probably unaware. . . ."

A slightly different form of condescending attitude crops up in application letters in a statement like "You may call me at 743-4601." The implication is that the writer is permitting the reader a privilege when just the opposite is true. An applicant is in no position to appear so aloof.

Repeated use of such phrases as "we think," "we believe," and "we suggest" often appear to be condescension. The writer who reflects such a sense of superiority is almost certain to erect a barrier of incompatibility between writer and reader. Far from attracting a reader, such egocentric talk more likely causes a sputter like "Well Bigshot, I can think for myself!" When this happens, it can virtually destroy the reader's goodwill.

Preachiness (didacticism), which is an extension of condescension, is undesirable because

1. Most people do not like to be bossed.
2. When you tell your reader what ought to be done, you imply reader ignorance or incapability and thus suggest your resented superiority.

The juvenile-sounding marketing lecture some sales writers put into letters to retailers is one of the most frequent offenders (because it is so elementary). The following are typical:

```
The only way for you to make money is by offering your
customers merchandise that has utility, good quality, and an
attractive price.
```

--

```
It's time for all dealers to get in their Christmas stock!
```

A retailer would not remain in business very long without realizing the truth of such statements and acting accordingly. Whether an old-timer or a beginner, a retailer's reaction to such preachy statements will likely be an emphatic negative one like "Don't tell me how to run my business!" or a vigorous "I'll make my own decisions!"

When a statement is flat and obvious (see **Obv** in Appendix C), it is frequently irritating to the reader because it implies stupidity, even though the writer's intent is good:

```
Satisfaction of your customers means turnover and profits to
you.

                              --

You need something new and different to show your customers.
```

You, as a business letter writer, will do well to examine carefully the expressions "you want," "you need," "you should," and their variations, seeking to eliminate them whenever you can without altering the meaning. The following illustration from an application letter is preachy:

```
The business cycle is changing from a seller's market to a
buyer's market.  You are going to need a strong force of good
salespersons.
```

Here is one way it could be improved for the reader's acceptance of the idea without irritation:

```
Now that business is shifting from a seller's market to a
buyer's market, you're probably thinking about the strong
force of good salespersons with which you'll meet competition.
```

The sales writer in the following example is vague, flat, and preachy:

```
Spring will soon be here . . . rain in the morning, cold and
clear in the afternoon.  To be safe, you should carry both a
topcoat and a raincoat with you every day.  But that's a
bother.
```

The writer could have improved the presentation this way (among others):

```
For these early spring days when it's raining in the morning
but clearer and colder in the afternoon, a topcoat which is
also a raincoat will give you protection to and from work—

—and without your having to worry each morning over "Which
shall I take today?"
```

One of the worst kinds of psychological browbeating is this:

```
Do you want Davison's to keep growing and keep getting better?

Of course you do!

Then you should employ only those individuals who want to
move steadily forward and push Davison's on to greater heights.
```

Far more likely to win the reader's approval is the following version, with positive phrasing and a studied attempt *not* to give a management lecture:

```
Good merchandise at the right prices is not the only reason
Davison's has grown as it has in the last five years.  The
team of Davison men and women has been equally influential.
```

Careful phrasing can eliminate most of the irritation due to preachiness. Often the key is to subordinate information that is obvious or known to the reader but must, for a reason, be included. Put it in the middle of a paragraph, preferably in a phrase or dependent clause.

Bragging is another undesirable extension of the writer's ego. It brings to the minds of readers the sometimes comical, sometimes pitiful, sometimes disgusting, chest-pounding would-be caveman. Conscious use of superlative wording ("newest," "latest and greatest," "outstandingly superior," "final word") is a flagrant and obvious way to make your reader not believe you. Even experienced writers sometimes annoy readers with undesirable—and almost always unsupported—references to size of company, efficiency of operations, or quality of product. The following are examples:

```
In a business as large as ours—with literally thousands of
retailers selling our products— . . . .
```

--

```
In a firm as large as Bowen and Bowen, such incidents are
bound to happen.
```

--

```
You are unfortunately a victim of routine made necessary by
the vastness of an institution so well operated as the White
Sands Hotel.
```

The desirable adjustment to both reader and writer (through elimination of servility, flattery, condescension, preachiness, and bragging) will help to improve the tone of your letters; but it will not assure courtesy, the second element in desirable letter tone.

Courtesy

[Kindness is the oil that reduces friction between people.]

Being courteous is being considerate of the other person's feelings through exercising patience and tact. These come only from conscious and determined effort in many cases, because often one's instantaneous, emotional, or unthinking reaction is an impatient or tactless expression. For that reason, one famous lecturer regularly suggests the use of a "soaking drawer"—a special drawer in the desk to put nasty-toned letters overnight, for revision the next day.

Contrary to an oft stated phrase, people are not "born courteous." (If you doubt this, spend an hour talking with almost any child.) Courtesy often requires a conscious effort to be understanding and forgiving, to anticipate the reader's likely reaction, and to avoid offense.

For that reason correspondents need to keep in mind the major causes of discourtesy. An old French proverb applies here: To speak kindly does not hurt the tongue.

Anger displayed is almost certain to cause loss of the reader's friendliness toward you and confidence in you. Most business readers have a good deal of self-respect and confidence in the wisdom of their decisions. An attack on them produces a wave of anger and a consequent necessity for self-defense. The result is two people seriously estranged. Such sentences as the following are almost sure to produce that result:

```
We cannot understand why you are so negligent about paying
bills.
```

--

```
What's going on in the office at your place?
```

--

```
We certainly have no intention of letting you get away with
that!
```

Crude slang or profanity, especially if used in connection with a display of heightened feeling, is likely to be interpreted as anger, whether or not it is intended as such. Don't use either. (And don't try to be coy and cute with quotation marks for questionable slang—or dashes in words that are obviously profanity.)

Petulance (peevishness or fretfulness) is simply anger in a modified degree. It is comparable to the scoldings children often must receive from parents (and unfortunately from teachers too!). Here is how a woman scolded an interior decorator: "When do you expect to return my furniture? You've had it now for more than two weeks. That ought to be long enough to do a little upholstering job." A calm request that the work be finished as soon as possible because of the need for the furniture would probably bring just as quick action, and it would leave the upholsterer in a better mood to do a good job.

Business readers have usually graduated from sandpile psychology too. When they read "We have played fair with you; why don't you play fair with us?" they are likely to regard the writer's whining as unnecessarily and undesirably juvenile.

Both anger and petulance are the result of impatience and unwillingness to accept the responsibilities of successful human relations.

Accusations, on the other hand, are usually the result of insensitivity to how another person will react to a remark. One cannot cultivate tact (skill in dealing with others without giving offense) without a deep and almost constant concern for the feelings of others. The sensitive, thoughtful person knows that people do not like to be reminded of their carelessness or ignorance—*and* that they will be unfriendly to the person who insists upon reminding them of their errors. The customer may not always be right; but if you are going to keep the greatest friendliness (goodwill), you will remember not to call attention to errors if you can avoid doing so, or to do it with the least likely offense (impersonal style or by implication). The writer of the following letter displayed an almost completely insensitive attitude toward the reader:

```
Much as we dislike doing so, we shall have to delay your order
of May 12.

You neglected to specify which shade of sweater you desire.

Kindly check your catalog and this time let us know whether
you want navy, midnight, or powder blue.

We have enclosed an envelope for your convenience.
```

The following revised version has much better tone and is thus more likely to retain the goodwill of the reader. It eliminates the accusation and the unfavorable reminder in the underlined words of the preceding example, the sarcasm the reader would probably read into *kindly*, and the pompous-sounding reference to the enclosure.

```
Since we want you to be entirely satisfied with the blue
sweater you ordered on May 12, will you please let us know
which shade you prefer?

You may obtain the cardigan style in navy, midnight, or
powder blue.  All are popular this spring.

Just check the appropriate blank on the enclosed reply card.
As soon as we receive it, we will mail your sweater.
```

In this revision the reader will no doubt put the blame for carelessness where it belongs but will feel more friendly toward the writer and the firm for the courteous way of asking for additional information without accusing.

Unflattering implications are usually the result of tactlessness combined with suspicion or distrust. The collection correspondent who wrote, "When we sold you these goods, we thought you were honest," implied an idea of much greater impact than the literal statement, an implication which is distinctly unflattering and thus destructive of goodwill.

The adjustment correspondent who writes, "We are investigating shipment of the goods *you claim* you did not receive," need not be surprised to receive a sharp reply. Similarly, "*We are surprised* to receive your report" and "*We cannot understand* why you have had trouble with the Kold-Hold when other people like it so well" establish by implication doubts of the reader's reasonableness, honesty, or intelligence.

And the sales correspondent who begins a message by implying doubts about a reader's alertness can expect few returns from the letter:

```
Alert hardware dealers everywhere are stocking No-Flame, the
fire-resistant liquid which more and more home builders are
including in their specifications.

Are you prepared to meet the demands of your home-building
customers?
```

In similar vein the phrases "Do you realize . . . ?" and "Surely you are . . ." immediately suggest the writer's doubts that the reader measures up on either score.

Such lack of tact is usually unintentional. Most readers, however, do not question whether it is intentional; the result is ill will for the writer and the firm.

Sarcasm, on the other hand, is generally deliberate. And it is usually dangerous in business correspondence. The smile which accompanies friendly sarcastic banter cannot find its way onto paper; unfriendly sarcasm is sheer malice. It is the direct opposite of the attitude necessary for a tone of goodwill because it shows a lack of respect for the other person and a deliberate attempt to belittle. The sales manager sending the following message to a group of employees falling short of their quotas would build no goodwill:

Congratulations on your magnificent showing!

We're only $50,000 short this week.

How do you do it?

The United Fund leader of a community fund drive who included the following in a public report could hardly expect future cooperation from the people indicated:

The ABC employees, with an assigned goal of $800, magnificently responded with $452. Such generosity should not go unmentioned.

Sarcasm should never be used in business correspondence except between people of equal intelligence, of equal station in life, and with highly similar senses of humor. To be safe, do not use it at all. The moment of triumph is short-lived; the loss of the reader's friendship may be permanent.

Curtness, born of impatience and a false sense of what constitutes desirable business brevity, reflects indifference and thus seems discourteous. The manufacturer sending the following letter was promptly labeled a boor by the woman who received it:

We have your request for our booklet and are enclosing same.

Thanking you for your interest, we are. . . .

Better to send no letter than this. Booklets usually do a good job. And experiment after experiment has shown that a good letter accompanying a booklet increases the pulling power. On the other hand, a poor letter like this, reflecting such lack of interest, destroys some of the favorable impression made by the booklet.

This correspondent might very well have helped to convert a casual inquiry into a sale by taking the time to show interest in serving the customer with a letter like the following, which is superior because of the service attitude reflected, the positive and specific resale material, and the action ending (all of which are discussed later):

We're glad to send you Siesta's booklet Color at Mealtime.

When you read it, you'll understand why we say that in Siesta you can now have handsome dinnerware that is sturdy enough for everyday use, yet surprisingly inexpensive.

No photography, however, can do justice to the delicacy of some Siesta shades or to the brilliance of others.

Your friendly local dealer will be glad to show you a selection of Siesta. Unless the stock is complete, the dealer will be glad to order additional colors for your examination.

See your dealer soon and start enjoying Siesta's color at mealtime.

You can find Siesta in Omaha at (name and address of dealer).[1]

---

[1] This letter adapts easily as a form letter with only this one line and the inside address and salutation individually typed.

Stereotyped language is another mark of discourtesy because it suggests indifference. And nobody likes to have his business treated in an indifferent, routine way. Writers of letters like the following jargonistic disgrace can expect little feeling of friendliness from their readers:

```
We have your favor of the 19th and in reply beg to state that
the interest on your mortgage is now $361.66.

We trust this is the information you desired, and if there is
any other way we can oblige, please do not hesitate to call
upon us.
```

Since stereotyped language is primarily a question of style, see p. 19 for fuller discussion.

Physical appearance is one other factor affecting the apparent courtesy of letters, in the eyes of most readers. Sleazy paper, poor placement, strikeovers, messy erasures, dim or clogged type, poorly matched type and processed material, and penciled signatures are like trying to gain admission to an elegant dining room when you're dressed in sweat shirt, dungarees, and sneakers (see Chapter 4).

In putting one's best foot forward through courtesy, however, a correspondent must be careful not to trip up; overdone attempts to be courteous may seem insincere and thus destroy the third element in desirable letter tone.

Sincerity

[Don't stretch the truth; it snaps back.]

When a reader feels the first flashes of doubt, with a resultant reaction of "Well, I'll take that with a grain of salt," confidence in the writer is gone —most likely because of apparent insincerity.

Sincere cordiality is entirely free of hypocrisy. It is unwillingness to exaggerate or fictionalize upon the true state of a situation. Inappropriate cordiality (usually unbelievable and sometimes distasteful) is commonly the result of effusiveness, exaggeration, and undue familiarity. (Flattery and undue humility, it is true, often sound insincere. But in our opinion they relate more closely to the balance of personalities discussed in a preceding section.)

Effusiveness means gushiness. It is excessive politeness which often *is* insincere and always *sounds* insincere. "Overdone" means the same thing. Your letters can sound effusive simply because you've used too many adjectives and adverbs, as in the following examples:

```
We are extremely happy to place your name on our list of
highly valued charge customers, and we sincerely want you to
know that we have hundreds of loyal employees all very eager
and anxious to serve.

--

Your excellent choice of our fine store for the opening of a
charge account we consider a distinct compliment to the superb
```

```
quality of our merchandise and outstanding service.  And we're
genuinely happy about it.
```

--

```
I was exceptionally pleased to note your name on this
morning's list of much-appreciated new charge customers.
```

The plain fact is that in a business relationship such highly charged personal reactions as those suggested in the foregoing examples do not exist—and any reader knows it. No writer and no firm are going to "do everything possible to keep you happy." Rarely will a credit manager be "extremely happy" or "exceptionally pleased" to add a name to a charge list. Phrases like "do all we can" and simply "happy" or "pleased" are appropriate because they are believable.

Furthermore, the coy quality of the following endings is unrealistic in a business situation—and therefore unbelievable:

```
We do hope you'll come in soon.  We can hardly wait!
```

--

```
Don't forget to come in soon.  We'll be looking for you!
```

--

```
Simply note your color choice on the enclosed card, mail it to
us—and then sit back with an air of expectancy.
```

Effusiveness usually shows up as too strong and too many adjectives and adverbs chosen in an attempt to make the reader feel important. You'll do well to watch especially overused words like *very, indeed, genuinely, extremely, really,* and *truly*—which begin to gush in a very short time.

Exaggeration is stronger, and therefore more destructive of sincerity, than effusiveness. The correspondent who wrote, "Work is a pleasure when you use these precision-made tools," appears to be overstating his case to a carpenter-reader. And the writer of the following, if around to overhear, should be prepared for an unrestrained, emphatic "*Bull!*" when his dealer-customer opens the letter and reads:

```
New customers, happy and eager to buy, will surely applaud
your recent selection of 4 dozen Tropical Holiday playsuits
for women.

Especially made for the humidity of Macon, these garments will
lead girls and women for miles around to tell their friends
that "Thompson's has them!"
```

Superlatives and other forms of strong wording are among the most frequent reasons why so many letters sound exaggerated, unbelievable, and therefore insincere. The trite "more than glad" is nearly always an insincere attempt to exaggerate a simple "glad." And "more than happy," if translated literally, could mean only slaphappy. The classic illustration is the misguided "What could be finer than . . . ?" Any reader can and usually does supply at least one quick answer of something which seems finer than the product or service mentioned.

Exaggerated wording is nearly always challenging. Few things are actually *amazing, sensational, revolutionary, ideal, best, finest,* or *perfect.*

Simple, accurate, specific statements of quality and value not only avoid the impression of insincerity; they are often more forceful than the general superlatives made nearly meaningless by years of misuse. If you describe products or services in terms like the following, you are inviting negative responses toward yourself and your firm:

> You'll find that Loomoleum is truly the ideal low-priced floor covering.
>
> --
>
> Want Amazing Protection
> That Can Never Be Canceled?
>
> Here is a really magnificent opportunity. Imagine a health and accident policy that can never be canceled.
>
> --
>
> This new mower is revolutionary in build, style, performance, and customer appeal. Amazing, of course! Here is your golden opportunity!

Whether the reader of such statements feels irritation or disgust is relatively immaterial. What counts is the disbelief aroused. Confidence in the writer and the house, and therefore goodwill, take a sharp downturn.

Undue familiarity also causes a writer to lose favor with the reader in many instances. Sometimes it crops out merely because the writer is uncouth. The reader may feel sympathy for the person who does not know how to act with people—but will not likely have the disposition to return for more uncouthness.

Undue familiarity results from (1) calling the reader by name too frequently or writing in too informal language to a stranger and (2) making references to subjects which are entirely too personal for business discussions. For an obvious purpose the writer pretends a closeness of friendship or an overweening interest which does not exist. It is characteristic of the shyster. Like other forms of pretense, it is resented. In the following letter giving information on home insulation to a college professor, the jocularity doesn't just fall flat; it boomerangs!

> Just set the thermostat and relax. That's all you have to do, Professor Eckberg. Pick up your book and settle down in a cozy chair. The Mrs. won't be continually warning you to get your old sweater, or nagging you to keep turning up the thermostat, or to put another blanket on the cherubs.
>
> Yes, Professor Eckberg, Isotemp will guard over your household. Take a gander at the statistical table in the folder, Modern Insulation for Older Homes. This table shows that out of every 8,000 cases of respiratory diseases, 6,536 occurred in uninsulated homes—over 75 percent from the very type of home you're now living in!
>
> Didn't you say you spent over $400 for fuel last year, Professor Eckberg? That's a lot of money out of a professor's salary; and as you said, "Even then the place wasn't always warm."
>
> If you fill in and return the enclosed card, we will send Mr.

```
Don Diller, our Milwaukee representative, to answer any of
your questions.  Incidentally, Professor Eckberg, Mr. Diller
is a graduate of the University of Wisconsin with a degree in
heating engineering.  He may be the guy who slept through half
your classes six years ago, but somewhere he learned how to
make your home more comfortable and reduce those high fuel
bills.  Then the Mrs. can buy that fur coat she's been nagging
you about for when she goes outside, where it is cold!
```

Such diction as *cherubs, gander,* and *nagging* might be used in breezy conversation with an old friend and perhaps in a letter to the old friend, but certainly not in a letter to someone the writer does not know. Using the reader's name four times in such short space gives the impression of fawning. And the assumptions and references to family relations and activities are typical of familiarity that breeds contempt. These spring from insincerity, but they are discourteous in the truest sense and thus destructive of goodwill.

SERVICE ATTITUDE

In addition to a desirable tone as a means of maintaining goodwill, good letter writers show that their concern extends beyond making a profit or other purely selfish interests. They're like the recently retired business executive who said that success can be summed up in three words—"and then some." He believed that the difference between the average person and the exceptional person usually lies in those three words. The top people, he said, "did what was expected of them—and then some. They met their obligations and responsibilities—and then some. They were good friends to their friends—and then some. They could be depended upon in an emergency—and then some. . . ."

A business organization obviously must make profits if it is to exist; both reader and writer accept that premise. To deny it is to fly under false colors. The answer is neither to deny nor to affirm; just don't talk about it! Instead, let your letters remind readers of your thoughtfulness and genuine desire to be of service—to meet your obligations, and then some—through

1. Resale material on the goods and/or the house
2. Sales promotional material on other goods (in some letters)
3. Special-occasion letters

Resale material

Often a writer needs to assure a reader of the wisdom of an earlier choice of goods and services—or of the house chosen to do business with—and thus stress satisfaction. In *keeping the goods sold,* resale material helps keep unfilled orders on the books, fosters repeat orders, and forestalls complaints. It is an effective device in meeting competition.

As the phrase is most frequently applied by correspondents to goods and services, "resale" means favorable talk about something the reader has already "bought"—that is by purchase, practice, or approval, although it may not yet be delivered. Most buyers would feel better about the product upon reading the following resale idea woven into an acknowledgment letter:

> The Henshaw electric boudoir clocks (eight at $12) you ordered on March 1 are our fastest-selling models in this price range. Because they are accurate as well as beautiful, they make excellent gifts.

The woman receiving the following would most likely feel much more secure in her choice of a dress—and thus happier with the dress as well as the company that sold it to her:

> Your new princess styled dress with portrait neckline by Meredith Parnis will give you equal pleasure and comfort at church services, luncheons, or parties.

Such material is *most effective when it is relatively short and when it is specific.* Tell a reader buying a shirt, for instance, that

> It will launder rapidly and easily because of the no-iron polyester.

or

> The seams are double-lockstitched for long life.

or

> Made from long-staple California cotton, your Pallcraft shirt will give you the wear you expect from a shirt of this quality.

But don't try to tell your reader *all* these points in a resale passage. And for your own greatest effectiveness as a writer, don't try just to get by with a lame "Pallcraft shirts are a good buy."

Used most frequently in acknowledgments, resale material on the goods may also appear in certain credit, collection, and adjustment letters, as you'll see later.

Resale material on the house consists of pointing out reader-oriented policies, procedures, guarantees, and special services sometimes called "the little extras" (the "and then some's") a good firm does for its customers. Resale is especially helpful in the beginning of a business relationship. But any time you add a new service, improve an old one, or expand a line is an appropriate occasion to tell customers about the firm's continued attempt to give satisfaction. You want to tell your dealer readers about services you render—sales assistance, advertising aids, and the like. Retail stores often write their consumer customers about lounges, lunchrooms, and personal shoppers, to mention only a few. The following excerpt from a letter to a dealer is typical:

> Along with your shipment of Lane candies are some display cards and window stickers which you'll find valuable aids in

```
bringing these delicious candies to the attention of your
customers.  Our Advertising Department will regularly furnish
you with seasonal displays and will be glad to help you on any
special display problem in connection with the sale of Lane's.
```

And this—from a retail store to a new charge customer—is also a good sample of resale on the house:

```
You are welcome to use Rosen's air-conditioned lounging and
rest rooms on the mezzanine, the fountain luncheonette on the
first floor, or the spacious parking lot right behind the
store.  It is absolutely free to customers shopping at
Rosen's, even if your purchase amounts to only a spool of
thread.
```

Also from a retail department store to a new customer:

```
When you cannot come to the store, call or write Lola Lane,
our personal shopper, who will gladly do your shopping for
you.  Most of the time she can have your merchandise on the
delivery truck or in the mail the same day she receives your
order.
```

Resale passages are the writer's attempts to confirm or increase the reader's faith in goods, services, or the firm in which committed interest already exists. Sales promotion material (on new and different goods or services) seeks to promote interest in something *else* the firm can supply.

Sales promotion material

For a number of reasons, sales material about related products is desirable in some acknowledgment, credit, collection, and even adjustment letters. The most obvious business reason is that regardless of what you try to market, you must constantly seek to sell more of it to more customers all the time. In letters, however, *the most significant reason is the concrete demonstration that the firm desires to be of further service.* A third function of sales promotion material is that it can end a letter naturally and easily, with emphasis on further service. The following example illustrates the point:

```
          Your carpenter's tools, as itemized on the enclosed
          invoice, were shipped this morning by parcel post;
          they should reach you by October 15.  Thank you for
          your check, which covers all charges.

          The Crossman level with aluminum frame is stronger
          and weighs less than wooden ones, and it will remain
Resale    bright and true.  The true-tempered steel used in the
          Flex-Line tape is permanently oiled; so you can be
          sure it will easily and rapidly unwind and rewind
          every time you use it.

          When you receive the fall and winter catalog we're
          sending separately, turn to page 126 and read the
          description of the Bradford 6½-inch electric handsaw.
```

```
Sales      This is the lowest price at which it has ever been
Promotion  offered.  To enjoy the savings in time and energy
           this efficient piece of equipment offers, use the
           handy order blank at the back of the catalog.
```

You'll need to observe a few precautions in the use of sales promotion material. Above all, it should reflect *the desire to be of service* rather than the desire to sell more goods. It is low-pressure sales effort, comparable to the way a salesclerk, after selling a woman a pair of shoes, will casually pick up a matching or complementary purse and say, "Perhaps you'd like to examine this purse, which goes with your shoes so well." Only after the customer displays an interest in the suggested item does the salesclerk begin a real sales talk. If another sale results, that's good. But if not, it's still good: most customers are pleased because of the demonstrated interest in their welfare or happiness.

If, however, the insatiable sales appetite of "I want to sell you more" shows through selfish, greedy terminology, you neither promote sales nor please the customer. When emphasis is on *what we want* rather than *what you get,* the effect is unfavorable, maybe even repellent, as in the following:

```
More than 8,000 of these Multimowers have been sold through
our factory!

And now that a large demand has been built up for our product,
we want to sell it through dealers.
```

When emphasis is on *order* instead of *service,* Greedy Gus overtones are almost inevitable:

```
We also sell attractive summer purses, silk and nylon hosiery,
and costume jewelry to complete your excellent line of goods.
We are sending you our catalog.  And we hope to fill many more
orders for you.
```

In terms of customer goodwill, this correspondent would have made a better impression by rephrasing the foregoing passage somewhat like this:

```
The summer purses and costume jewelry shown on pages 29 to 32
of the accompanying catalog have also sold well for many of
our other customers.  We'll be glad to handle your order for
these items on the same terms as this one.  Use the handy
order blank and reply envelope in the back of the catalog.
```

Appropriateness is also a factor. When a woman buys a suit, a natural item to call to her attention is a blouse; a man buying a suit may be interested in matching or blending shirts, ties, hats, or shoes. But to tell a purchaser of heavy-duty truck tires about the good buy you now have in refrigerators or the buyer of a washing machine about your special on tires would be questionable most of the time. Such suggestions appear to be dictated by the greedy desire to further sales rather than by an eagerness to render service. Almost always, *sales promotion material should be on items related to those under consideration.*

Before using sales promotion material, consider also the kind of letter you are writing and what it is supposed to do. A letter requiring further action on the reader's part needs final emphasis on that action, not on sales material. In acknowledgment letters, for example, you can use sales promotion material endings to good purpose when you are sending the goods as requested, but not when additional action by the customer is necessary. Also, although you might use such material in an early collection letter to a good customer, it is decidedly inappropriate as soon as your letter reflects concern over the account. And in adjustments you may safely use sales promotion material to end a letter making full reparation, because you can be fairly sure the customer is going to be pleased with the results; but its use in a compromise or a refusal is usually questionable.

Both resale and sales promotion material help to sell more merchandise, but they are even more effective as goodwill builders because they imply positively and emphatically the general statement "We are eager to serve you well."

Special goodwill letters

Also, to demonstrate continuing interest in the customer and the desire to serve, special goodwill letters subtly use resale material on the goods and the house, and sales promotion material. They have often been called the "letters you don't have to write—but should." Since the customer does not expect them, since they usually bring something pleasant, and since your reader knows you do not have to write them, they are doubly welcome and thus greater builders of goodwill than some other types. Because they are of great variety in function and occasion, and because you can write them with greater understanding and skill after studying some other kinds of letters, we treat them in greater detail in Chapter 6.

Suffice it to say here—before we take up some other kinds of letters—that your study of special goodwill letters will reinforce the central theme of the preceding chapters: consideration for the other person.

(*All the letter cases for the first four chapters are at the end of Part One because we think you should cover all four basic tests of a good business letter before trying to write any kind of letter. We urge you to read the first four chapters quickly but thoroughly so that you can put all the basic principles to use even in your first letter.*)

chapter 4

Appearance: What the reader sees

[Appropriate dress is usually the first indication of competence.]

THE APPEARANCE of an individualized letter is like the appearance of a person: Since it is not the most important thing, the less it attracts attention to itself, the better. The wording, the persuasive qualities, and a desirable tone reflecting goodwill are more influential than the looks of the letter in determining its success or failure. But just as some listeners will reject the messages of speakers who do not come up to expected standards of appearance, so will many readers reject the written message that calls attention to the format and distracts from the ideas.

A personalized (individualized) letter sent by first-class mail will nearly always get a reading. Flashy designs and lavish colors in it are like yelling at a person whose attention you already have. Even worse, if your letter is either too messy or too gaudy, or if it violates the conventions of letter form, the appearance distracts the reader's attention from the important feature—your message.

Direct mail sales letters are sometimes justifiable exceptions. Because they are often unpersonalized mass mailings, they often must struggle to get read at all. In striving to capture attention, their writers may use cartoons, gadgets, bright colors, important-seeming messages on the envelopes, and other gimmicks. Except for such direct mail, however, the physical letter should serve only as a vehicle for your message. The reader should not notice it since it would distract attention from the message, and thus weaken it.

STATIONERY

The first thing noticed if it is inappropriate is your stationery. The most common business stationery—and therefore the least noticed—is 20-pound white bond with some rag content in 8½- by 11-inch sheets. Variations acceptable under appropriate circumstances include heavier and lighter paper, different sizes, and various colors and shades.

Paper heavier than 20-pound is more expensive, too stiff for easy folding, and too thick for clear carbons; and lighter than 16-pound is too flimsy and transparent for letters. (If used, carbon copies are usually on lighter paper, both because it is cheaper and because you can make a greater number of clear copies with it.)

The main off-standard sizes are Executive or Monarch letterheads (7½ by 10½ or 11 inches, used mainly by top executives) and half sheets (8½ by 5½ inches, used most frequently in intracompany notes but also often for short replies). A common objection to any odd size is that it does not fit standard files and envelopes.

Though white is the standard, only the rainbow and your sense of appropriateness to your kind of business set the limits for color variations. Numerous tests have shown that colored papers sometimes produce better results in sales mailings. But existing test results do not prove that any one color will always work best for any one kind of letter. If you are sending out large mailings, you may be wise to run your own test on a small sample to see what color works best for that particular situation.

Paper with some rag content is more expensive than all-pulp paper, but it gives the advantages of pleasant feel, durability, and resistance to yellowing. The new plasticized papers have all these advantages, and may be more economical, but may also be somewhat transparent.

Whatever your choice of paper for the letter sheets, you should use the same quality and color for envelopes and second pages.

The acceptable variations in stationery allow you to reflect the personality of your business, just as you select clothes appropriate to your personality. A back-alley repair shop would not use pink-tinted 24-pound bond in the Monarch size. Nor would a bank president select paper that looks and feels cheap. The big points are appropriateness and inconspicuousness. In selecting the paper for your letterheads, then, you should have a good reason before choosing something other than 20-pound white bond, 8½ by 11 inches. Anything else may distract the reader's attention from the message of the letter.

LETTERHEAD

Designing letterheads is a job for specialists who know paper stocks, color, and design. Most paper suppliers provide such specialists to their customers, at least as consultants. Any business writer, however, should know something of the main principles and trends.

The main trend in letterheads for many years has been toward simplicity. Letterheads once took up a good part of the sheet with slogans, names of officers, and pictures of the firm's plant and product. Good modern letterheads usually take no more than two inches at the top, and may occupy just a corner. They use wording, design, color, and graphic techniques to convey the necessary information and communicate an atmosphere symbolic of the firm represented. The minimum content is the name, address, and telephone number of the firm, including area and ZIP codes. Sometimes an added trademark or slogan indicates the nature of the business. Firms doing much international business frequently give a code address for cablegrams.

The past ten years have shown a marked movement toward the use of color in both stationery and letterheads. This trend is partly the result of increased acceptance of colored paper and color printing, and partly from heightened awareness of the role of letterheads as representatives of a company. Firms wishing to present a modern image are turning to carefully designed graphics, such as the imaginative use of special colors and blind embossing. Good designers, however, are careful to avoid garish combinations and tasteless designs.

PLACEMENT ON THE PAGE

Even with appropriate paper and a well-designed letterhead, you can still spoil the appearance (and thus distract from the message) unless you place the letter on the page properly. Two methods are in common use: the picture-frame and the standard-line plans.

Picture-frame plan

Typing a letter so that it looks like a picture framed by the white space around it is one plan. It takes a little more time than the standard-line method because you have to set the typewriter's marginal stops according to your estimate of each letter's length, but it enables you to fit long and short letters to the page in more conventional fashion. Also, you can sometimes save time by increasing the line length and thus getting on one page material that would require two pages by the standard-line plan.

The idea is that a rectangle drawn around the letter (not including a printed letterhead) should look like a picture framed in the marginal white space. You determine the width of side margins according to your letter length and make the top margin about the same. The bottom margin will take care of itself automatically. It should be about one and a half times as long (deep) as the other margins.

In gaining experience, a typist soon learns where to set a typewriter's marginal stops for letters of varied lengths. If you're just starting to gain the experience, however, you might well try this general plan. For short letters (100 words or less) leave about 2-inch margins at the top and sides. For long letters (over 200 words) leave at least 1-inch margins. Split the difference for middle-length letters.

Standard-line plan

The standard-line plan of placing a letter on the page saves time because the typist does not have to reset marginal stops for letters of varied length. Typewriters are set to the company's standard line (usually six inches); thus all letters have the same side margins. The top margin is about the same as the side margins, and the bottom margin is about one and a half times as wide. By varying from the standard spacing between letter parts (more or less between the date and inside address, for example, or three spaces instead of two between paragraphs), the typist can adjust letters of differing lengths for proper height.

POSITION AND SPACING OF LETTER PARTS

Standard parts

The usual business letter has six standard parts. As a general rule, single space within parts and double space between parts. But note exceptions as they come up in the following explanation.

The *heading* or first part of a letter on paper with no letterhead must include the sender's address (but not name) and the date. It establishes both top and side margins because it is the first thing on the page, and the end of the line going farthest to the right sets the margin. It may appear on the left, too, in a pure block form. Such a heading is usually three lines but often more. Thus it affects the number of words you can fit into a given typewriter setting.

On printed stationery you can write the dateline as a unit with the letterhead or as a separate part. As a unit with the letterhead, place the typed-in date for best appearance according to the design of the printed part. Usually it retains the balance by appearing directly under the center of a symmetrical letterhead; often it rounds out one that is off balance. Frequently it is a separate part because of the difference between print and type. As a separate part, it fixes the upper right or left corner of the letter. That is, it leaves the top margin (equal to the side margins) between itself and the letterhead, and its end sets the right margin (or its beginning the left margin). Thus it is the first exception to the general rule of double spacing between letter parts.

The *inside address* includes the title, name, and address of the person to receive the letter, including the ZIP code. The beginning of the address establishes the upper left corner of the letter if the date is a unit with a printed letterhead. Otherwise, it begins at the left margin, two to six spaces lower than the dateline. So it is the second exception to double spacing between letter parts. (*Warning:* Be careful to spell names right and to use the proper title; people do not like to have their names misspelled or to be given the wrong title. And *always* put some form of title—professional, honorary, or courtesy—in *front* of *other* people's names, even when a professional or position title follows.)

The *salutation* or friendly greeting, the third standard part, begins at the left margin a double space below the inside address and ends with a colon (:) or no punctuation whatsoever. The wording must match the first line of the address. If you address an individual, the salutation must fit (usually *Dear* plus title and name); if you address a firm or other group, you must choose an appropriate salutation.

Since a salutation is the first indication of the formality of a letter, you should give some thought to the implications of how you greet your reader and how you match the tone of your salutation in the complimentary close. The main forms listed below are for letters addressed to persons, in descending order of formality with appropriate complimentary closes:

My dear Sir (or Madam)	Respectfully yours or Yours truly
My dear Mr. (Mrs. or Ms.) White	Yours truly or Sincerely yours
Dear (appropriate title plus surname)	Sincerely yours or Yours truly
Dear (surname or given name)	Sincerely yours or Cordially yours
Dear (given name, nickname, or such more familiar term as originality can produce and good taste will allow)	Cordially or Regards or some more familiar phrasing, as long as it remains in good taste

"Gentlemen" is the proper salutation for letters addressed to a company, regardless of formality and regardless of an attention line (even when some of the "gentlemen" are ladies). In line with the trend toward informal friendliness of business letters, most business writers use the person's name in the salutation when they can and match the friendly tone with some form of *sincerely* or *cordially.*

The *body* or message of the letter begins a double space below the salutation. Usually single-space within paragraphs and double-space between, though in very short letters you may use double spacing within and triple spacing between paragraphs. Since the body is all one part, regardless of the number of paragraphs, the standard double spacing between paragraphs is a third exception to the general rule of spacing. The number of paragraphs therefore affects the fit of a letter to a given typewriter setting. A letter of 250 words in seven paragraphs, for example, will take at least four more lines than the same number of words in three paragraphs. Yet you should not overlook the chance to improve readability by keeping paragraphs short and itemizing points.

The *complimentary close* (worded appropriately according to the descending scale of formality illustrated above) goes a double space below the last line of the body. It may begin at the center of the page, or in line with the beginning of a typed heading, or in line with the dateline used as a separate part, or at a point to space it evenly between the center and right margin of the letter. As you've seen, the most common forms employ one of four key words—*cordially*, *sincerely*, *truly*, and *respectfully*—each ordinarily used with *yours*. Juggling the order of the key word and *yours* or adding *very*—as *Yours truly, Yours very truly, Very truly yours*—makes little difference. The key word is the main consideration.

Proper form for the *signature block* depends on whether the letter is about your private affairs or company business where you are an employee. In writing about your own business, you space four times below the complimentary close and type your name. The typed name is important for legibility—and consideration for the reader. You then pen your signature above it.

But if you're writing about company business and the company is to be legally responsible for the letter, the company name should appear above the signature. The fact that the letter is on company stationery makes no difference. So if you want to protect yourself against legal involvement, type the company name *in solid capitals* a double space below the complimentary close; then make the quadruple space for your signature before your typed name. You also give your title on the next line below the typed name or, if there is room, put a comma and your title on the same line with your name. Thus you indicate that you are an agent of the company legally authorized to transact business.

Very truly yours,

ACME PRODUCTS, INC.

John Y. Bowen
Comptroller

Sincerely yours,

LOVEJOY AND LOEB

(Miss) Phyllis Bentley, Treasurer

Because the possibility of legal involvement is usually remote, many writers prefer to omit the company name from the signature block in the hope of gaining a more personal effect through a letter from an individual instead of from a company. If you feel that way and are willing to take the legal risk, you can set up the signature block as follows:

```
Cordially yours,                               Sincerely yours,




H. P. Worthington                              (Mrs.) Phyllis B. Hudson
Assistant Public Relations                            Treasurer
   Manager
```

Before you do, however, we suggest that you (1) get official agreement to bail you out of any legal involvement and (2) remember that some readers will feel greater security in dealing with a company instead of an individual.

Women's signatures bring up a special problem. Note that in all the men's signatures illustrated, no title precedes the names. Without some indication, however, the person who answers a woman's letter would not know whether to address her as Miss or Mrs. You can solve this problem by using Ms., which is becoming widely used (but is not entirely accepted yet). As a matter of consideration, a woman should indicate whether she is Miss or Mrs.—the way Miss Bentley, who became Mrs. Hudson, did in the preceding examples. If she does not, you can take it as an indication that she wishes to be called Ms.

Special parts

Besides the six standard parts of a business letter, you will often find good use for one or more of seven widely used special parts.

You can use an *attention line* in a letter addressed to a company if you want a certain individual in the company to read it. If you don't know the person's name, you may just use the job title. It's equally good form to write "Attention: Purchasing Agent" or "Attention, Purchasing Agent." You may center the attention line, if you prefer, and underscore it for increased emphasis. In either position, flush with the left margin or centered, put it between the inside address and salutation with a double space above and below. Remember, however, that the salutation remains the same as for any letter to a company—"Gentlemen"—even when you use an individual's name in the attention line.

The *subject line* may save words and help you get off to a fast start by telling your reader quickly what the letter is about or referring to former correspondence for necessary background. It usually appears at the left margin a double space below the salutation; it often appears a double space above the salutation; and when space is at a premium, it may appear centered on the same line as the salutation. To make it stand out, either underscore it or use solid capitals. You can save some time by starting it at the left margin and typing it in solid capitals. The old forms "Re" and "In re" have all but disappeared. The informal "About" is increasing in use. And more and more correspondents omit the word *Subject* or its equivalent. The position and wording make clear what the subject line is.

Initials of the dictator and the typist often appear at the left margin a double space below the last line of the signature block. The trend is toward omitting the dictator's initials because of repetition from the signature block; but if used, they come first (usually in unspaced capitals), separated from the typist's by a colon, a diagonal, a dash, or an asterisk. A good method that saves time is to lock the shift and type CRA:MF or just write all in lower case as cra/mf. Some writers place the typed name here and omit it from the signature block.

An *enclosure notation,* a single or double space below the identifying initials (or in their place), is a reminder to the person putting up the mail to actually make the enclosure. Sometimes offices use an asterisk in the left margin at the line in the body referring to the enclosure. The word *Enclosure* may be spelled out or abbreviated *Encl.* or *Enc.*, followed by a number indicating how many enclosures or by a colon and words indicating what the enclosures are.

Carbon-copy designations are useful when persons other than the addressee should be informed of the contents of the letter. The names of people to receive copies are usually listed after *CC* (or *Cc* or *cc* or just *Copy to*) at the left margin, a single or double space below either the initials or the enclosure notation if it is used.

Postscripts are rare in business today in the original sense of afterthoughts. Rather than arouse a reader's resentment by poor planning, the modern business writer would have the letter typed over, or in informal correspondence might add a handwritten note. (Incidentally, some research evidence suggests that such notes actually increase the pulling power of letters—probably because they give the letter a more personal touch.)

The main use of postscripts now is as punch lines. Since they have the advantage of the emphatic end position, writers often plan them from the beginning to emphasize an important point. The well-planned postscript that ties in with the development of the whole letter and stresses an important point is effective.

When you do decide to use a postscript, it should be the last thing on the page, a double space below the last of the preceding parts. The "P.S." is optional; position and wording clearly indicate what it is.

Second-page headings are essential for filing and for reassembling multipage letters that become separated (especially true when a letter runs to three or more pages). Since pages after the first should be on plain paper, even when the first page has a printed letterhead, for identification they should carry something like one of the following, typed down from the top the distance of the side margins:

Mr. C. R. Jeans -2- March 21, 19—

or

Mr. C. R. Jeans
March 21, 19—
Page 2

or (for speed and equal acceptability)

Mr. C. R. Jeans, March 21, 19—, page 2

The body of the letter continues a quadruple space below this.

FORMS OF INDENTION AND PUNCTUATION

The main letter forms in use today are semiblock and block with mixed or open punctuation. The example letter on page 77 and its enclosure (p. 78) explain and illustrate them as well as some outmoded and less popular forms. Those two pages are integral parts of the explanation; so you should read them thoroughly as well as look at them.

As you read and observe them, points you should keep in mind are:

1. The two big trends continue to be toward simplicity and time-saving.
2. All consistent forms are "correct," but the outmoded indented form and closed punctuation and the ultramodern NOMA Simplified form tend to call attention to themselves and characterize their users.
3. In studying letter writing, you should learn all widely used current forms, with their advantages, disadvantages, and dangers; but you should realize that if you go to work for a company, you should use your employer's preferred form unless and until you can persuade the company to change.

INTEROFFICE MEMORANDUMS

The business letter is the conventional form of written communication *between companies* and individuals and other companies. But interoffice memorandums (or memos as they are commonly called) now replace many letters as message carriers *within* companies.

Memos first came into widespread use largely to combat the high costs of producing the more formal business letters. Since the major cost of a letter or memo is the time spent in composing and dictating it, however, about the only cost savings in memos today come from not using an envelope and postage and from the easier job of typing them (despite the simplified letter forms discussed above).

Two other good reasons underlie the proliferation of interoffice memos in business today. Firms use them to transmit information that is too complex for oral transmission and—more important—to have a written record of what was said and when, if either writer or reader wants one.

For anyone in a medium or large company, memos will be the most common form of written communication with other people in the firm, especially those in other locations. What they know about you and how they think of you will be governed by how you communicate with them;

THE UNIVERSITY OF ALABAMA
GRADUATE SCHOOL OF BUSINESS
COLLEGE OF COMMERCE AND BUSINESS ADMINISTRATION
UNIVERSITY, ALABAMA 35486

FACULTY OF BEHAVIORAL STUDIES

TELEPHONE: 205/348-6183
MARKETING
PHYSICAL DISTRIBUTION

TELEPHONE: 205/348-6090
BUSINESS COMMUNICATION
BUSINESS POLICY
INTERNATIONAL BUSINESS
MANPOWER AND INDUSTRIAL RELATIONS
ORGANIZATIONAL BEHAVIOR

February 7, 19--

Miss Louise Steele
1328 Waukegan Street
Grand Rapids, Michigan 49504

Dear Miss Steele: FORMS OF LETTER INDENTION AND PUNCTUATION

Both you and your employer are right. Since your employer has the right to her preference, however, you should type her letters as she likes.

Of course if she welcomes suggestions, you can tell her that indented form with closed punctuation strikes most modern readers as behind the times and costs her money by slowing you up. That form was the style until one day a bright secretary decided to quit wasting time indenting and end-punctuating the lines of headings and inside addresses. She started a continuing trend toward efficiency and simplicity in letter form.

Since she still indented for paragraphs and used a colon after the salutation and a comma after the complimentary close, the form she used is called semiblock with mixed punctuation. Later dropping the paragraph indention and omitting the useless colon and comma produced block form with open punctuation, as explained in the enclosure.

Semiblock and block are more widely used today than any other forms; and the order of frequency in punctuation style is mixed, open, and closed.

You may show your employer this semiblock, mixed-punctuation letter as probably the most widely used form; but don't lose your job over such a small matter. The content, style, psychology, and tone of letters are all more important.

Sincerely yours,

C. W. Wilkinson

C. W. Wilkinson, Professor

ENCLOSURE: Other Forms of Letter Indentation and Punctuation

In block form all typed lines start at the left margin. The now outmoded, but not "incorrect," indented form looked like this (shown here, as it usually was, with nonletterhead paper and closed punctuation):

46 Guild's Woods,
Tuscaloosa, Alabama 35401,
February 7, 19--.

Miss Louise Steele,
1328 Waukegan Street,
Grand Rapids, Michigan 49504.

Successive lines of the complimentary close and signature block were indented as you have just seen in the heading and inside address.

Open punctuation means that you use no punctuation at the ends of lines in the heading or inside address (except periods after standard abbreviations) and no punctuation after the salutation or complimentary close.

Hanging indention (the first line of each paragraph extending five or more spaces to the left beyond the other lines) is also an accepted form, though not common because of the increased chance of typing errors.

The NOMA Simplified letter form, promoted for years by the National Office Management Association (NOMA), is acceptable but not widely used. It is full block and open punctuation, but with some special characteristics that still seem like quirks to some people:

1. Label no parts (like subject line, attention line, carbon copy indication, and P. S.). They are all clear by position and nature.
2. Use no salutation or complimentary close (often insincere anyway). Subject line goes in salutation position, in SOLID CAPITALS. Use reader's name as appositive early in first line.
3. Indent and itemize, as here, wherever helpful to the reader.

in short, by your memos. This is true, too, for upper management. Early in your career, especially, your contacts with higher echelons in your company will likely be the reports and memos you send up. Further, as you progress in your career, you will have to demonstrate your abilities as a manager—often by the memos you send down to your subordinates directing their activities. And finally, in dealing with your peers, you will find memos are important tools in establishing and maintaining your position. A current saying in business about them has an uncomfortable amount of truth in it: "You can know people by their memos."

Memos vary widely in format, from simple handwritten "From the desk of . . ." notes to carefully designed forms with interleaved carbon copies and provisions for assuring an answer and proper filing. But since they usually go from one person to another in the same organization, memo messages are less formal than letters. But whether handwritten or typed, they share with letters the single purpose of communicating information in writing so as to effect an action.

Memos and letters also both have conventional, stylized headings. For memos, the universal elements are a date line, a "To" line (addressee's name—and title unless very informal), a "From" line (writer's name—and identifying position title unless known), and a "Subject" line. (Leaving plenty of room to make the subject clear and precise is a good idea. The more comprehensively you describe the subject here, the less you will have to say in the body to introduce it and identify it before you can say anything of significance.)

The body begins right under the subject line and continues until you've said what you need to, which may take three lines or three pages. Usually that's all there is to a basic memo. No salutation or complimentary close appears, though when needed three other items may. When the memo needs authentication, the writer signs or initials it next to the "From" line, or underneath the body, following personal or company preference. Also, a typist's initials may appear at the bottom as on a letter. If carbon copies are to go to other people, the typist may also type a carbon copy designation and the names of receivers.

Because memos are less formal than letters, in both format and language usually used, some writers give them inadequate attention. That is a mistake, and it can be a very bad one. *Just about everything we say in this book about letters also applies to memos.* Whether your memos will accomplish their purpose depends on the writing style, their organization, the principles of successful business communication we discuss in the next part of the book, and even their appearance. Memos deserve care in preparation just as letters do, for they are important to your company's success, and yours.

Though the interoffice memos we discuss here are not exactly the same as the memo reports discussed in Chapter 16, the similarities may make it worth your while to look there. You will find more details on form, some illustrations, and a checklist.

Applications of part-one principles

1. Select the better in each pair and tell why:

   a) So that we can make immediate shipment, please fill in the enclosed card telling us where you wish your gift of Waynecross stationery sent.

   b) Your order mentioned below could not be shipped because we did not have sufficient or correct information.

   a) Thank you for your recent inquiry about Swissewn Bedspreads. We do not sell directly at retail, so would like to refer you to the store in your city, or nearest you, listed below.

   b) Robinson's Department store, 900 Congress, Austin, is the nearest retailer for SWISSEWN BEDSPREADS.

   a) Please fill in the information requested on the enclosed forms, so that we can help you recover on your insurance for the accident June 10.

   b) Please be good enough to fill in the information requested on the enclosed forms. We are trying to help you recover for damages you claim you received as the result of an accident dated June 10.

   a) We regret to advise the fact that we do not make the large tray holders anymore.

   b) For trays measuring 12″ × 18″, we suggest you write Montgomery Speciality Shop, 1190 Greenview Road, Canoga Park, California 91503, and ask for extra-strong tray hangers.

   a) We are indeed sorry that we failed to send the casters for your bed with your shipment. They were mailed UPS this morning.

   b) Your casters for your bed are on their way by UPS.

   a) Because the top-rated Penncrest iron has the self-cleaning feature, we are now stocking it exclusively.

   b) We regret that we do not carry the Beach Hamilton iron. We do have the Penncrest which has a true self-cleaning feature.

   a) You should have your C8245 curtains in about ten days.

   b) I only wish we could send your entire order to you right now, but we are out of stock of C8245 curtains. They should be here in a few days.

   a) We had a difficult time in evaluating the many splendid applicants we have interviewed, and our task of selecting successful applicants has not been an easy one. We feel that, for the time being, we are unable to take further action. We will be back in contact with you if our situation changes.

b) Thank you for your letter of September 14, with the enclosed résumé. In view of our present commitments to interview other third-year law students, I do not think that an interview would be mutually beneficial now. I am taking the liberty, however, of retaining your résumé and will be in touch with you if circumstances change.
Thanks for thinking of Muff and Scott. I wish you the best of luck in your future endeavors.

2. In answer to an inquiry about Rockwell Electric/Gas Heating Cooling unit, which opening is better?

a) Another Rockwell first! A revolutionary new breakthrough in heating technology, with many advantages not found in most conventional heating systems. It is developed for practical home and commercial use and *only* Rockwell *has it!*

b) Thank you for your interest in the new Rockwell Electric/Gas Heating and Cooling Unit featuring the exclusive Rockwell two-stage heating. Your home can be heated with only ⅔ capacity on mild days. That saves you fuel. When you need more heat, it automatically goes to full capacity.

3. Which closing do you think is best for the Rockell letter?

a) We know you will be interested in not only the "how" the HTM Heat Exchanger works, but "what" it can do for your home. We are asking the Rockwell wholesale distributor in your area to contact you.

b) So that you will learn more about the HTM Heat Exchanger and know what it can do for your home, we are asking Spencer Morton, wholesale distributor in your area, to call you.

4. Which is the better for a microwave oven mailing?

a) We appreciate your interest in our product and look forward with pleasure to serving you.

b) You'll cut operating costs by over one-half and cooking time to a fraction when you use a Hotcenter Microwave oven.

a) The Hotcenter Microwave oven is described on page 4 of the enclosed folder.

b) Turn to page 4 of the enclosed folder and read how Microwave can save you time and money.

5. Compare Letter A and Letter B considering reader interest (social studies department heads), style, general plan. (The letter intends to get action.)

Letter A

Dear Dean:

The Urban Study Center of Eisenhower University is pleased to announce the second year of a unique Urban Studies Program. The program consists of three components: an URBAN EXPLORERS component, an URBAN SEMESTER component, and a SUMMER INSTITUTE component. The program was developed with the primary aim of providing students from many institutions with a variety of exposures designed to narrow the gap between traditional classroom study and field experience. This allows for a meaningful integration of theory and practice.

Enrollment in the program is not limited to individuals who are currently enrolled in a university program. The URBAN EXPLORERS component is perceived as being beneficial especially for concerned individuals who are active in their community. Because of Eisenhower University's unique access to many of the physical, cultural, business, political, and social institutions of New York, we are able to realize the goals outlined in the enclosed brochure describing the URBAN EXPLORERS component.

In the near future, another mailing describing the URBAN SEMESTER and the SUMMER INSTITUTE components will be sent to you. We cordially invite you to participate in all three components. Thank you for your time and consideration.

Letter B
Urban Study field trips now open
for your students at reasonable cost

An important part of the Urban Studies program at Eisenhower University is for students to see for themselves how urban institutions operate.

This is the purpose of the URBAN EXPLORERS program—twenty or more students devoting a day or two examining New York in action. With the help of experienced faculty and community resource people, we take a close look at New York's physical, cultural, business, political, and social institutions.

Your students are invited to come along. Cost is low, $10 a day or less. Hotel accommodations can be arranged at very reasonable cost. See the enclosed folder for details of the tours now being planned.

Field trips for social study groups usually involve much faculty time and concern with detail. Here is an opportunity for your students to get behind the facade, to see what makes a huge city function, and why.

You set your own dates. One- or two-day tours for any size group, investigating the specific study areas that interest you, can be arranged.

Having the URBAN EXPLORERS program available is like operating your own field tour department, but without faculty time or other overhead cost. Isn't this worth investigating?

Return the enclosed card today for specifics on a tour for your students. We welcome your participation.

Sincerely,

P. S. Tours are not limited to students. Any concerned citizens interested in community structure and functions are welcome.

6. Assume that you are a librarian. Which of the following letters (A or B) do you feel has the best tone and does the best selling job (you are looking for magazines that will be read).

Letter A
The daily papers, TV and other communication channels
say that women's participation in sports
is exploding, nationwide!

The trend was just beginning two years ago when THE SPORTSWOMAN magazine was launched.

Today it is 48 pages per issue of action photos and interviews—the kind of reporting that is pulling more young women into tennis, basketball, swimming—and even into such newer fields as soaring, rodeo, race walking, aerobatics and, yes, even ear pulling.

We cover all school levels from grade school through college, and all sports that interest women—even some sports that do not interest them yet, but will very soon.

Pro sports and sports scholarships for women get special attention, to show today's young women that there are cash rewards and a satisfying professional career for women sports enthusiasts.

Active young sports women in your community will be looking to you for information about opportunities in sports journalism, photography, and scholarships. You can give them helpful answers and the inspiration to push their interests further with current issues of THE SPORTSWOMAN.

Library subscriptions are $4.50 a year, $4.00 each for four or more, and $3.50 each for eight or more.

May we enter your subscription now? Watch the reaction to THE SPORTSWOMAN from your young enthusiasts when they see the first copy. An exploding interest in sports among young women all over the country is what makes THE SPORTSWOMAN today's fastest growing sports magazine.

Put a few copies in your display racks and watch the excitement. Send your subscription today.

Letter B

Why should your library subscribe to THE SPORTSWOMAN magazine?

The number of periodicals grows daily and the library budget can stretch only so far. So we think it is only fair that we be asked to come up with some very good reasons why you should include our magazine on your shelves. We don't mind—we've got good reasons.

*Sports are a quickly growing area of interest to girls and women—and as of now we are the *only* magazine which deals with all women's sports.

*Not just a general consumer magazine—THE SPORTSWOMAN has educational and career-oriented reporting. We discuss careers in sports, from being a P.E. teacher or an athletic trainer to becoming a sports journalist or photographer. We discuss new opportunities for women as journalists or photographers. We discuss new opportunities for women in pro sports, and how to apply for sports scholarships. We discuss the laws currently affecting collegiate sports programs, and what they mean to women. We give names and addresses of organizations that will be of help and how to contact them. Our readers' forum features letters from women actively involved in sports programs. They discuss problems they have encountered and how they have solved them.

*Young girls considering careers not only need role models (which we provide) but concrete ideas on what they can expect should they decide to enter sports.

*We're economical for your budget! At $4.50 a year ($8.00 for two years) we're not going to put you financially out on a limb. You can think big with us too. If you have four to eight branches that each need a subscription, we'll let you cut 50¢ off the price of each one. Over eight and you can cut off a dollar.

If you're not yet convinced, send us 25¢ to cover postage and mailing and we will send you a free sample issue. Our publication belongs in your library. We're sure you'll agree.

7. Evaluate Letters A and B and give your reasons for selecting one of them over the other one.

Letter A

The enclosed brochure describes a system that, when applied to the collection of payroll information and information on the distribution of labor in your hospital, could save your facility considerable time and money. With the system described, nursing supervisors can be relieved of much of their clerical duties pertaining to those two areas.

If you are interested in specifics of how this could be applied to your hospital, we would be most pleased to discuss the matter with you and assist you in the configuration of the system and provide assistance and counseling on the software to do your job.

Please call or write for additional information.

Letter B

Does your hospital payroll preparation make clerical workers of your skilled employees?

Hospitals have unusual payroll problems—such as

—random arrival and departure times.

—special call-in work after normal shift service.

—many "arrive one day, leave the next" employees.

—around-the-clock, seven-day week.

—and many technically skilled employees.

The East Electric Data and Security system eliminates nearly all payroll paperwork. A small plastic badge, which normally serves as employee on-the-job identification, also serves as "in" and "out" payroll data generator.

> This small card, inserted in a self-contained reader station, gathers all necessary data for each employee's work shift and records it on a standard cassette cartridge. The cartridge then serves as computer input to produce all payroll records, including checks.

Reader stations can also serve to identify and record arrivals and departures, activate turnstyles, unlock doors, and keep a tally on those remaining in a building.

Many other time-saving advantages and security features in this proven system simplify your hospital payroll controls.

May we tell you more? The enclosed card, mailed today, will bring you more information and the opportunity to examine, at your convenience, a DCS system in operation.

8. Evaluate Letters A and B on the product, a facsimile transmitter. The letters go to presidents of banks.

Letter A

What do you do

when you need a signature verification in a hurry . . .

. . . or when you want fast approval on a loan application, or quick security clearance.

You could phone for the information, of course. But you can't show a signature over the phone, or get a written O. K.

You can't, that is,

. . . unless you have Dex Facsimile Equipment. With Dex equipment and a telephone you can transfer printed or written documents, drawings, reports, financial statements and signatures over your telephone to another department, to a branch miles away, or even across the country.

With a Dex Facsimile unit you can, in three minutes or less, transmit your document and get written approvals. It will drastically reduce your messenger staff and cut your cost of intraoffice document transfers.

Worth investigating? We have an Idea Folder that suggests dozens of ways to speed up document transfer, while maintaining 100 percent accuracy. It shows how Bankers Trust, Bank of America, Chase Manhattan, Wells Fargo and many smaller banks are saving money with Dex Facsimile Equipment.

May we mail you a copy? Just complete and mail the enclosed card and we'll send your Idea Folder at once.

Letter B

Are you looking for ideas
to speed up bank communications
with absolute accuracy?

You'll find more than a few suggestions in an idea package I'm planning to mail to you. And it's yours without cost or obligation.

If you've ever needed a fast decision . . . but the mails were too slow and you couldn't take chances with the accuracy of verbal communications . . . you'll find this idea package and our Dex Facsimile products of particular interest. And if your bank could benefit by sending loan applications and approvals, signature verifications, security clearance instructions, or daily branch summary reports between various departments in your bank, across town, or even across country in three minutes or less, then I'm certain you'd want to know more about our Dex family.

Our idea package contains a complete description of our products and their value to bank communications as well as a list of banks, including among others, Bankers Trust, Bank of America, Chase Manhattan, and Wells Fargo that are successfully using our Dex systems. This package can be yours without obligation. Just complete the enclosed postage-paid reply card and drop it in the mail. The idea package will be mailed to you promptly.

9. Rewrite.

a) I am disturbed by the prolonged delay in receiving the special equipment ordered from your fine, big firm five months ago. Since costly penalties will be assessed against us if construction is not completed on time, I should like to have you investigate the details surrounding our urgently needed order and let me have your personal determination of its status.

b) Thank you for your order of September 16. As you may know, our production workers have been on strike for the past five weeks and we only resumed production yesterday. For this reason, we anticipate a delay of approximately three weeks in filling your order. We regret that we are not able to provide our customary prompt service at this time and hope that the delay will not inconvenience you.

c) Upon receipt of our order October the tenth via Blue and Gray Line, there was no external evidence of any damage. However, when the box was opened, it was found that a number of pieces were broken. It is our opinion that the breakage was caused by improper packing by the manufacturer. By cannibalizing the sets in which breakage occurred, we were able to assemble 19 complete sets. Enclosed you will find a list of the pieces necessary to complete the remaining sets. Ship the pieces necessary to complete our order as soon as possible. We will hold the broken pieces until we receive further instructions from you.

10. Rewrite.

a) Ref. the return of the Rustrak recorder and motors.

The error of the motors was ours. Credit will be issued for the incorrect motor. We will ship the correct 12VDC motors shortly.

We will also issue credit for the material portion of the recorder proper. However, we cannot issue credit for the labor to calibrate this recorder. Mainley credit for $100.00 will be issued. You will be billed for $35.00.

When we ship the correct recorder, you will be billed for that recorder in total.

b) I am in receipt of your check No. 17638, in the amount of $674.00, which was presented to me today, to be used by our clients here at Sunland Training Center.

We plan to use these funds for Summertime Fun, such as camping, picnics, etc. Things that cannot be reasonably asked for in our budget. This is a welcomed donation, without it a good many clients would go without any summer fun.

We hope that you will pass the word that this generous donation is appreciated by all here at Sunland and we trust it will be possible to do the same for another year.

Thanking you with kindest regards.

c) Your delay in shipping 500 theater-type chairs promised six weeks ago under Order #9805-J has seriously impaired our performance schedule for the Civic Assembly Hall Project. Please indicate immediately when we may expect the balance of our order.

11. Rewrite.

a) Read the Book-of-the-Month Club quick-reply form, page 123. Now rewrite the following copy to go with the form in the little folder:

We note with regret that you received a shipment* which was not in perfect condition. In spite of the utmost care on our part, this sometimes happens. We shall make replacement as soon as possible.

* RIMSKY-KORSAKOV: SCHEHERAZADE

Enclosed is a label and postage for your convenience in returning the defective record. Please return via fourth class mail—educational material.

b) The City National Bank holds a 90-day certificate of deposit in the name of Lota M. Spell and Lota Rea Wilson (who is her married daughter). It is at 5½ percent interest and matures one month from today. The bank decided today, however, that it will start (tomorrow) paying 6 percent on all new and renewed 90-day certificates of deposit. So, within the next three months the bank must write all holders of certificates to bring in their CD's on maturity for renewal at the new rate. As the correspondence specialist for the bank, revise the following letter (addressed Lota M. and Lora Rae Wilson, 2108 Hartford Road, Gainesville, Florida) submitted by the secretary to your vice president A. J. Maloney as a fill-in form for notifying all CD holders:

Effective at the close of business (today's date) the new rate paid by City National Bank on Certificates of Deposit will be 6% for ninety day certificates. This note will effect all existing Certificates of Deposit held by the City National Bank for you; consequently, upon the next maturing date of your Certificates, the rate will be adjusted to 6%. This action will necessitate your bringing into the Bank your Certificate upon maturity and it will be reissued at the new rate. All new 90 day Certificates of Deposit will be compounded quarterly and be automatically renewed as they have been in the past. We deeply appreciate your continued good relationship with our Bank.

Very truly yours,
J. A. Maloney
Senior Vice President

12. Rewrite.

a) *MEMORANDUM* October 14, 197–
TO: English Faculty Members
FROM: Bankhead Kelly
English Department Faculty Members

Attached is a copy of a letter sent to the three public high schools, T. M. Sullivan Laboratory School, and the two private high schools. I am writing to ask your assistance in carrying out the program described in paragraph three. Many of you, I am sure, could and would put together a 45 minutes to an hour talk that would stimulate and challenge these bright high school English students. All I ask at this point is your tentative agreement, subject to your availability, to present one lecture-discussion as a part of the program.

Thank you,
Bankhead Kelly

b) I am in receipt of your recent letter in which you claim that you had not received a check for dividends due June 1.

We immediately asked our records division to check into this. Today we received their reply.

Attached is a photostat of the check issued June 1 showing your endorsement on the back. Please examine this photo and return it to our office with your reply.

I am enclosing a stamped, self-addressed envelope for your convenience.

13. Rewrite.

a) We are in receipt of your Proxy Card, but you failed to sign it.

In order for your Proxy to be voted, it is necessary that it be signed. Therefore, we are returning your Proxy and would appreciate if you would sign and date it and return it in the enclosed self-addressed and stamped envelope.

Thank you for your cooperation in this matter.

b) *Letterhead:* Saint John's Episcopal Church, 41 Crockett Avenue, Roanoke, Virginia 24012: *Inside Address:* Jerry Sands, Sand's Real Estate, 409 Brunswick, Roanoke 24015. *Signature Block:* Loyally, Father Raymond Bowers. *Body:* I want to take this opportunity to thank you for heading up our Every-Member Canvas this year. It was great the way you got the teams organized and furthered the spirit of working together. I feel we are off to a good start for Saint John's Episcopal Church. Our dreams of having a daycare center are now reality. I wish I could shake the hand of each person who gave his time and money to our drive.

c) We regret very much that your order No. B-42987 for special components has been delayed. A strike at the plant of one of our major suppliers halted our production for a period of three days and forced us to seek another source of supply. Your order is now in process and will be shipped to you within the next few days. We shall pay the additional costs involved in shipping your order by air express. We hope that the delay in filling your order will not seriously inconvenience you.

14. As your teacher, assume that the chairman of the nominating committee (referred to in the letter below) asked for your suggestions on revising the letter. The letter goes to all faculty members of the college. Rewrite the letter.

Dear Colleague:

As you are aware, Dean X is retiring at the end of June, having served the University as Dean of the College since 1955.

You have elected a faculty committee to serve in an advisory capacity and consult with Vice-President Y regarding the nomination of Dean X's replacement. Your committee held its first meeting with Vice-President Y on (date). It is now undertaking the task of securing nominees for this position.

You are invited to submit your suggestions to any of the members of the advisory committee whose names and campus addresses are listed below. Such suggestions should be in writing. It would be a great help to the committee if, at the time you submit names, you would also furnish any information you may have about your nominees. Additional details may be requested at a later date. Those responsible for bringing about the appointment of a new Dean are faced with a very critical question of timing. There are only a few months available.

The committee, therefore, needs to have your nomination in hand by no later than the first of next month.
All concerned thank you for your cooperation in this matter.

15. Assume that you are the editor of a widely distributed free-subscription magazine put out by some branch of your state or school and that you suspect that many copies are going to people who do not really want them. Write a letter to clean up your mailing list.

Unless you provide some motivation and make the action easy, many of them will simply ignore you. You may include benefits to yourself, but emphasize benefits to your readers.

Make clear that you are not interested in cutting off anybody who really wants the magazine. Also, invite them to send you the names and addresses of people who might be interested in receiving it. Check to be sure that you have the correct names and addresses of those who do want to continue on the mailing list.

16. As an *Appearance Practice Exercise,* set up any one of the following letters in acceptable format as directed by your instructor:

a) *Letterhead:* University of Washington, Seattle, Washington 98195. August 18, 19—. *Inside address:* Dr. Paul R. Gregory, 1125 Northwest 61st Place, Gainesville, Florida 32603. *Signature block:* Cordially yours, Bertha P. Mullins. *Body:* Probably you're wondering why you're hearing from me today during your summer vacation. The main reason is that I respect your good judgment—and will appreciate a bit of information from you. Do you recall that in our brief chat at the American Business Communication Association Convention in Philadelphia you mentioned that your graduate students, in comparing business communications textbooks, had narrowed the field down to two—yours and ours? You added that they had some likes and dislikes about both books. Ever since then my curiosity has been tormenting me. The questionnaire responses I have received so far are gentle and mainly complimentary, though they do reveal some helpful suggestions. Above them all, I'd value *your* comments. Will you be good enough to jot down—*in general*—what your students (and you too if you wish) consider the strong and weak parts of our book? Because I'll make a major decision about the second edition in a few days, I'll be most grateful for your reply this week. The enclosed airmail envelope will help speed your reply. I look forward to seeing you in Houston in December, and hope to find a way to show you how much I appreciate your good deed. In the meantime, have a happy summer and autumn.

b) *Letterhead:* Florida Farm Bureau Insurance Companies, Post Office Box 730, Gainesville, Florida 32601. Use current date. *Inside address:* Dr. Paul R. Gregory, 1125 Northwest 61st Place, Gainesville, Florida 32603. *Signature block:* Sincerely yours, Harold McCallister, Vice President. *Body:* Your Better Letters Course was excellent. Just how much practical application is being used by our graduates remains to be seen. At your convenience, please review the enclosed letters. We would appreciate your evaluation of them, and your comments on improvement, or the lack of it.

c) No letterhead, but instead use a *heading* that includes the sender's address (606 Queens Road, Indianapolis, Indiana 46220) and the current date. *Inside address:* Mr. Andrew Blackweld, Teacher of Vocational Agriculture, Newberry High School, Newberry, Indiana 44714. *Signature block:* Sincerely, Joseph M. Knight. *Body:* Are you finding it is hard to get enough money to operate your land laboratories effectively? Even with the high cost of agricultural products and the country's constant requests for explanations, many agricultural teachers feel that their school boards do not allocate enough funds to operate their labs. I feel that most board members simply do not know very accurately either the costs of operating a good school lab for vocational agriculture or the educational values that can come from one. By answering the enclosed short questionnaire, and having your students do the same, you may help me relieve this problem. The questionnaires will help me to write a better report to the county school board concerning the value of land laboratories relative to their cost. Only I will see the returned questionnaires. You can be certain that what you say will be held in the strictest of confidence. But, if you have no objections, I would like to be able to quote you. Please answer the questionnaire and add any other thoughts you may have. When finished, just put them in the enclosed stamped envelope and drop it in the mailbox. You will be doing yourself, your fellow teachers, and your students a great service. Since the final report is due the last week of May, the information would be most helpful if you would return it by May 12.

d) *Letterhead:* Lyon's Building Supplies, Berry Road, Olathe, Kansas 66061. *Inside address:* George P. White, Chattahoochee Brick Company, Atlanta, Georgia 30305. *Signature block:* Sincerely yours, Joseph Morrison Young, President. *Subject:* Requested confidential information about Paul Rhodes. *Body:* Since Rhodes came here as an accountant and assistant business manager 18 months ago, he has advanced until he is now plant manager. Paul is a hard worker and very eager to succeed in everything he attempts. Sometimes he drives himself into a tense condition, but he always seems to thrive on the challenge his job offers him, and I am sure that in a larger plant like Chattahoochee he would be confronted with enough challenge to satisfy him. Also Paul and his wife want to live in a larger city where they can enjoy all the cultural opportunities a city has to offer. Although at Lyon's Paul has no opportunity to sell, saleswork probably wouldn't be hard for him because he does enjoy people, is impressive looking, and is persistent. All of our employees like Paul—even our truck drivers, for whom he has to plan very strict budgets. In many ways I would hate to lose Paul, but I know he wants larger horizons.

e) *Letterhead:* Brownell Electro Inc., 307 27th Street, Orlando, Florida 32806. *Inside address:* Department of Nuclear Engineering Sciences,

202 Nuclear Sciences Center, University of Florida, Gainesville, Florida 32611. *Attention:* Harvey Andrews, SR Reactor Operator. *Subject:* Your letter of August 22, 19—. *Body:* In our previous letter we meant to type "recorder proper" instead of "recorder paper." The figures that you have in your letter are correct. The credit we are referring to is that which will be written for the incorrect material shipped and returned. We will rebill when we ship the correct material. *Signature block:* Very truly yours, Bill May, Product Specialist.

f) *Letterhead: Tempo,* 1234 Rockefeller Center, New York, N.Y. 10032. (No complimentary close, no date, and no salutation.) *Inside address:* Marion Baker, 874 Walnut Grove, Grand Rapids, Michigan 49507. *Signature block:* David J. Cook, circulation credit manager. *Body:* If the attached bill for your past year's reading of *Tempo,* the magazine that makes news clear and exciting at the same time, were just a little individual matter between the two of us, I certainly wouldn't mention it, any more than I'd make an issue of who would take the check if you and I were eating together.

But if 5,000 of the men and I happened to fall in together for a meal, I couldn't very well take all the checks . . . any more than you could.

Tempo's subscriptions are like that. Somebody has to take the numerous checks. Since it was, after all, a dutch-treat arrangement, I know you won't mind my reminding you of the original agreement: we furnish the magazine—each person at the feast picks up a check. Here's yours.

Use the handy return envelope today, please.

17. Correct the obvious violations of good usage and form. *Letterhead:* Green Light Hospital Service, 301 Troy Drive, Madison, Wisconsin 53701. *Inside address:* Mr. and Mrs. Troy Adams, Rt. 4, Box 241, Madison 53704. *Signature block:* Sincerely yours, Herman Alston, Executive Director. Congradulations! Green Light Hospital Service are glad to share in the program of welcoming the new air. So that you will know the exact hospital service benfits that were provided we are furnishing a copy of the hospitals bill.

Naturally youll want your baby to have Green Light insurance service too, so please dont overlook the necessity of filling in the supplimental application and sending it to us right away. As soon as the application is recorded in this office benefits will be available to your baby as explained in the notation at the bottom of the application.

Constructive criticism and helpful suggestions from our members has been an invaluable aide in the constant advancement of our program. Your Green LIGHT is eager for your comments on the services and charges which may be made on the enclosed form and returned with the supplimental application for including the baby in insurance. Use the convient return self addressed envelop.

PART TWO

How to win the reader's approval and motivate action

chapter 5

Neutral and good-news messages

- **Direct inquiries**
- **Favorable replies**
  - Replies without sales possibilities
    - Direct beginning
    - Completeness of coverage
    - Resale
  - Replies with sales possibilities
    - Getting started positively
    - Answering all questions
    - Subordinating unfavorable information
    - Handling price
    - Securing action
- **Routine transmittal messages**
- **Form enclosures and letters**
- **Short note reply**
- **Orders**
- **Standard acknowledgments**
- **Credit approvals**
  - Establishing the basis for credit
  - Explanation of terms
  - Stimulating sales
  - Making the customer welcome
- **Simple claims and adjustment approvals**
  - Direct claims
  - Adjustment approvals
    - Adjustment policies
    - Analysis and classification of adjustments
    - Attitude of the adjuster
    - Adjustment tools and techniques
      - Using resale
      - Making positive explanations
      - Handling inherent negatives
    - Letters approving the adjustment

As you learned back in Chapter 2, messages that give what the reader wants should do so in the opening phrases. The emphasis should be on speed, specificness, completeness, and conciseness. Inquiries, favorable replies, credit approvals, and adjustment approvals are typical of A–plan, direct-style letters.

Routine claims also should be direct, since they are reports most firms welcome as means for improving service.

Similarly, in courtesy exchanges of information about job and credit applicants—where regardless of whether the information is favorable or unfavorable to the *applicant,* it *is* what the reader wants to know—the message should begin directly with a key point.

DIRECT INQUIRIES

Any firm that wants to stay in business welcomes inquiries about products, services, operations, and personnel. The possibility of making a sale will motivate a reply to an inquiry concerning the products or services the firm sells. An inquiry about routine operations will get a reply out of simple business friendship. Requests for information about job and credit applicants get ready answers because giving such information for business purposes is established business courtesy based on the principle of reciprocity.

In no case would the reader's attitude toward such inquiries be negative; and, if it is not one of eagerness to comply, at least it is willingness. You therefore have no problem of motivating a response; your problem is that of letting your reader know exactly what you want, so that the willing reader can give you the necessary information with as little expenditure of time and energy as possible. Resolve this problem by beginning directly and by being specific and concise.

About products. Requests for catalogs, price lists, descriptive folders, and other information about products and services should be written with the same directness, specificness, and brevity as the following:

```
What choice of colors does a buyer have in the shower curtains
you advertised in the November Ladies' Home Journal?

At what store(s) are they available in Mobile?
```

This example gets right down to brass tacks with a direct question and the specific phrase "choice of color" rather than the vague, stereotyped request for "more information." And the pinpointing phrase "in Mobile" further helps the replier to send exactly the information needed.

The following letter to a resort hotel is another good example of desirable directness and specificness:

```
Please send me descriptive material about your accommodations,
recreational facilities, and rates.

My wife, 16-year-old daughter, and I are planning a two- or
three-weeks' stay in the South this fall and are considering
the Edgewater Gulf.
```

Without the second paragraph, the writer would get the most necessary information in general terms. (He would probably get much more than needed because the hotel employee, not knowing just what to tell, would tell everything and thus waste everyone's time.) With the second paragraph, however, the hotel can give the necessary general information and only the special information that would be of interest to this family group.

A specific paragraph indicating special interest would help even more:

```
My wife and I are primarily interested in the golf facilities
and in dinner dancing; our daughter insists that she be able
to ride horseback every day.
```

In most cases, as in the inquiry to the hotel, the questions require detailed answers for satisfaction. Some are out-of-the-ordinary questions involving special conditions. Because they require explanation before the reader can get a clear picture of exactly what the writer wants to know, they are better set out in expository paragraph form, as in the following letter about a dishwasher:

```
SUBJECT:  INQUIRY ABOUT THE $149.50 DISHWHISK

How complex—and expensive—is installation of the Dishwhisk
you advertised on page 69 of the September Better Homes and
Gardens?

I am attracted by your price, but can your unit be installed
without carpentering or plumbing changes where the present unit
is?  The under-the-counter place for my dishwasher measures
25" x 27" x 34".  What are the outside dimensions of the
Dishwhisk?  Will it fit in my space or would I have to have a
carpenter make changes?

My present connections are soldered ½" flexible copper tubing
to the hot and cold cut-offs under the sink.  Would the
Dishwhisk connect easily to that set-up?

Will low water pressure reduce the cleansing effectiveness of
the Dishwhisk?  Because low water pressure is the rule rather
than the exception in this community, this is an important
consideration.

I would appreciate your answers to these questions, the name
and address of a local owner of a Dishwhisk, and the name of a
local dealer.
```

An inquiry should start with a direct question or identification of the subject. The beginning question (the preferable form) should come before explanations of why you ask or should be interwoven with these explanations because (1) a question commands more attention than a statement, (2) the reader sees the reason for the explanation, and (3) such an arrangement nearly always saves words.

About people. Similarly, *personnel inquiries* should begin with the key question to be answered and follow with necessary explanations and specific questions:

SUBJECT: REQUEST FOR INFORMATION ABOUT JAMES R. SULLIVAN

While Mr. Sullivan worked under you as a part-time instructor in marketing, did he show an aptitude for selling? Was he naturally friendly and able to get along with faculty and students alike?

We are considering him for the job of head salesman in the Georgia, North Carolina, and South Carolina territory. Since he listed you as a former supervisor, we would welcome your comments in light of the following explanation.

The job will take much time and energy and will also require that he be away from his family a great deal. Do you think he will do his best work under these conditions? And has he demonstrated physical stamina and willingness, suggesting that he can stand up under the strain of much traveling for long periods?

As head salesman he would have to supervise the work of two junior salesmen in this territory. We are interested, therefore, in your evaluation of his leadership ability.

Naturally we are looking for someone who will be permanent since our men need to know their territories and customers quite well before they can sell enough to suit themselves or us. Do you believe Sullivan will remain in the business world for any length of time, or do you expect him to return to school to continue his graduate work?

We would appreciate your giving us this and any other confidential information that will help us come to a decision and shall be glad to help you in the same way when we can.

Direct credit applications—those written when no question exists about the desirability of the account—are just as simple and concise as other direct inquiries.

Since requests are welcomed, a visit to the credit department of the business, a telephone call, or a direct-style letter immediately phrasing the request and giving the necessary information is appropriate:

Will you please open a charge account in the name of

Mr. or Mrs. J. T. Holloway
76 Idlewild Drive
Dallas, Texas 75221

We have just moved here from 27 Crescent Drive, Denver 80202.

Stores with which we have had accounts for about five years in Denver are the White House, Foley's, J. P. Price & Co., and the Town and Country Shop.

I am employed as a supervisor at the L. B. Price Distributing Company where I earn about $15,500 annually; Mrs. Holloway is not employed.

The Merchants National Bank handled our checking account in Denver. Our local bank is the First National.

Despite having given enough information of the kind usually required as a basis for the extension or refusal of credit, the writer of the foregoing letter need not be surprised to receive an application form from the store.

Most stores have standard forms which they require all charge customers to fill in and sign.

Requests from business firms of national reputation, with solid capitalization and unquestioned ratings, are also perfunctory. Information about such firms is readily available from any number of credit sources. The acceptability of their credit is assumed; so the application for it is only by implication. Signed by an authorized agent (usually a purchasing agent), the letter might contain no more than the following:

> Please ship subject to your usual terms 6 dozen Samson 10-inch locking plier wrenches.

If the company name might not be recognized at once, adding a note would be proper:

> We are listed in Dun & Bradstreet.

If the company is not listed in any usual sources, the addition might be

> We have done credit business with
>
> L. B. Price Company, Dallas, Texas 75212
> Vendo Company, Chicago, Illinois 60618
> T. L. Painter & Co., Kansas City, Missouri 66109
>
> Our most recent certified statement is enclosed.

Credit inquiries from one business house to another are as routine as those about products. Both should be direct, concise, and specific. And because they ask for the same kind of information over and over again (detailed under "Credit Approvals," p. 131), in most instances they should be forms. The following form inquiry is a typical example, with a time-saving provision for putting the answer(s) on the inquiring letter.

> Gentlemen:
>
> Will you please give us the confidential information requested below?
>
> In applying for credit with us, the applicant gave us your name as a reference.
>
> We would appreciate the courtesy. Any time we can return the favor, please call on us.
>
> Very truly yours,
>
> Credit Manager
>
> Applicant: John Y. Bowen
> Length of time sold on credit ________________
> Credit limit (if any) __________ Credit terms ________
> Current amount due __________ Past due ________
> Highest credit extended __________ Most recent credit ________
> Paying habits ________________
> Remarks ________________

When, however, special circumstances arise which the form letter does not cover, you'll need to write a special letter. Like any direct request, it should get right down to business:

SUBJECT: CREDIT INQUIRY ABOUT MR. H. F. GREEN,
GROCER, VINITA, OKLAHOMA

Will you please send us a confidential summary of your credit experience with Mr. Green?

Naturally we'd like to have the usual items which reveal his buying and paying habits.

But since we learned from one of the companies here in McAlester that Mr. Green buys a large amount of his supplies from you and that he has given your name as a credit reference very recently, we'd like to have your explanation of why he did not list your firm when he applied for credit with us.

We shall appreciate your help and shall be glad to assist you in the same way any time we can.

When you ask your reader to give information about people, as in the two preceding letters, both of you face a special problem—*compliance with the libel and other laws.* You have a duty to help protect your reader as far as possible. Of course, truth is the most important protection, but truth alone is not complete protection in some states.

You can help by making the informative letter what lawyers call a privileged communication. You show that you have an interest to protect, and you promise to keep the information confidential.[1] As a matter of courtesy but with no legal significance, you say that the inquiry was authorized (if true). Otherwise, inquiries and replies about people are the same as those about other things.

Perhaps you noticed that the preceding letters expressed appreciation and offered to return the favor. Especially when asking people to do things without any obvious benefit to themselves, courtesy demands just that. Usually the best way is in connection with your request for specific reader action (generally the last paragraph). But don't be presumptuous or jargonistic about it by using the lazy "Thank you in advance." Instead, express it in first person, future tense—as those writers did. And if *shall* or *will* (the declarative mood) sounds too presumptuous or imperious, change to *should* or *would* (the subjunctive).

You can increase your chances of getting an answer, or a faster answer, if you can justifiably ask for it by a certain date. (People are inclined to put things off—especially if the benefit is not obvious and immediate.) Therefore you should consider justifying and end-dating:

---

1 You go ahead and promise confidentiality despite the fact that you can't keep the information confidential under certain conditions. The Fair Credit Reporting Act (effective April, 1971) empowers the subject of such a report to see what was said to whom and by whom if the information bears on a turndown for credit, insurance, or employment.

Direct Inquiry Checklist

1. Get this letter under way quickly.
   a) A subject line may help by showing the nature of the inquiry.
   b) Start the key question in the first line of the letter.
   c) Make your question(s) specific (not just "some information" but "what colors . . .").
   d) For a fast opening, imply ideas or refer to them subordinately.
      Slow, plodding:
      Will you please give us some information about Travis Brannon? He reports that. . . .
      Fast-moving:
      What would be your reaction if Travis Brannon, your former assistant, walked into your office trying to sell you . . . ?
   e) When you use a subject line, don't depend on it for coherence in the letter or as the antecedent for any pronoun.
2. Cover at least the basic questions to which you want answers.
   a) Ask the minimum number of questions to get the information.
   b) Arrange questions in the most appropriate order.
   c) Provide explanations the reader needs for pointed answers.
3. Be careful about the form and wording of the questions.
   a) Ask directly for information; don't hint. "I should like to know if . . ." is wordy and slow. "What does the . . ." is better and faster.
   b) Word questions to get what you want—not just "yes" or "no" when you need explanation. Avoid questions phrased to suggest a certain answer, too broad questions (". . . any information you have"), and double-barreled questions (". . . whether . . . and, if so, . . . ?").
   c) If you want to run a series of questions, itemize (tabulate).
4. Express gratitude cordially in first person, future tense: "I would be grateful (or appreciate)" eliminates the awkwardness and wordiness of "It will be appreciated if . . ." and the presumptuousness of "Thank you in advance." If appropriate, offer to reciprocate.
5. At the end, confident and positive references to the reader's next action makes a coherent summary to the entire message, leaves your reader clear as to what you want done, and stimulates action. For a surer, faster response, justify and ask for an answer by a certain date.
6. In inquiries about people, establish the privileged aspects.
   a) Be sure your explanation shows you have an interest to protect.
   b) Promise confidential treatment of the information.
   c) If the inquiry is authorized, say so (for courtesy, not legal reasons).

```
Because Mr. Sullivan wants our decision by the end of the
month, we would especially appreciate your answer by the 25th.
```

The most important considerations to keep in mind about direct inquiries, however, are to get started in a hurry, to be as specific in your questions as you can, and to explain enough (but only enough) for your reader to answer well and easily. The direct inquiry checklist of suggestions (p. 101) will help you with most of your inquiry problems, although it is not a prescription, a cover-all, or a cure-all.

None of the checklists in this book are. And they are especially *not* outlines. If you attempt to use them as outlines for constructing letters, you will fail in the attempt. Each case, whether from this book or in real life, demands individual treatment. If you try to use the appropriate checklist as an outline, you will simply not be able to come up with a letter to handle that particular situation. Instead, use the checklists for what we designed them for. First, draft your letter. *Then* use the checklist to make sure you have not neglected anything you should have done, or said something inappropriately, though we realize that not all points apply to every letter.

FAVORABLE REPLIES

Any company or person desiring the goodwill of others replies to all reasonable inquiries—and does so promptly. If a delay is necessary, some explanation should go quickly to the inquirer indicating the reason and approximately when you can give a complete answer, as in this note:

```
Your request for information about palletization is one for
Mr. J. S. McConnough, our materials-handling specialist, who
will be in California for another 10 days.

Shortly after he returns to the office, he will write you.
```

Here is another sample:

```
We shall send your copy of Color Counts about March 15,
when we expect the revision from the printers.

This new edition will show the true colors and will picture in
detail all the popular patterns of Siesta ware, including the
ones introduced just this year.

You will enjoy it when you receive it.
```

The first situation appears to contain no possibilities of sales but, as in the case of any inquiry, represents a good opportunity to make a friend for the firm. The second situation obviously represents someone with an active interest in the product sold by the firm. Proper handling might well lead to a sale.

Because some incoming letters ask only for assistance, whereas others readily indicate a potential customer (and a quite different replying letter), we divide this discussion into (1) replies to inquiries without apparent sales possibilities (including reports dealing with personnel and credit applicants) and (2) replies to inquiries with sales possibilities (often called invited sales letters).

Replies without sales possibilities

When someone asks you something, you say either yes or no—in an A–plan letter or a B–plan letter. For all practical purposes an undecided, noncommittal response like "Well, I'll think it over" is a refusal and needs to be handled in the inductive style (reasons before conclusion) of a B–plan letter. This discussion therefore concerns itself only with letters complying with the request. Refusals and modified refusals come later.

In letters which say yes, particular points to watch are the direct beginning, completeness of coverage, and (when appropriate) resale.

Direct beginning. The fundamental principle in all A–plan replies is to say yes immediately and thus gain increased goodwill, as well as save time and words. When you can do what the reader has asked you to do, begin your letter by doing it or with a statement indicating that you will do it. Your compliance with the reader's request is the point of greatest interest—of far greater interest than any expressions of your gratitude or gladness. And from the standpoint of economical writing the direct beginning cuts through and establishes many ideas by implication, thus shortening your letter copy considerably. Often the letter need contain no more than the notification of compliance, as in this example:

> We are glad to send you with this letter the last three annual reports of National Reaper, Inc. and to add your name to our mailing list to receive future copies as they are released around March 1 each year.

The direct beginning also establishes a cheerful, ungrudging tone for the letter and eliminates pompousness—at least from the all-important beginning. Observe the difference between the following slow, grudging, jargonistic original and the revision:

INDIRECT, WORDY, GRUDGING	DIRECT, COMPACT, CHEERFUL
We have your request for our <u>HOW</u> book.	Here is the <u>HOW</u> book you asked for.
It was prepared primarily for material-handling engineers, and so we were not prepared for the numerous requests we have received from schools. We are sending you one, however, and hope you will find it helpful.	We prepared it after extensive research by our own material-handling engineers with the assistance of outside consultants and plant men who specialize in material-handling methods and procedures. We're sure you'll find it useful in the classroom.
If there is any other way we can be of assistance, please do not hesitate to call on us.	Call on us again when you think we can help you.

In response to a request for material on palletization, one specialist wrote:

> Although there seems to be a dearth of palletization material in textbooks, here are two you may want to study if you haven't already:
>
> Harry E. Stocker, Materials Handling, Prentice-Hall, New York, 1975.
>
> Mathew W. Potts, Materials Handling Equipment, Pitman, New York, 1974.
>
> The following magazines have market research departments and may supply reprints of articles if you'll write them explaining just what information you wish:
>
> Handling & Shipping, 614 Superior Avenue West, Cleveland, Ohio 44113.
>
> Industrial Engineering, 25 Technology Park/Atlanta, Norcross, Georgia 30071.
>
> Material Handling Engineering, 614 Superior Avenue West, Cleveland, Ohio 44113.
>
> Modern Materials Handling, 221 Columbus Avenue, Boston, Massachusetts 02116.
>
> Plant Engineering, 1301 South Grove Avenue, Barrington, Illinois 60010.
>
> In the attached envelope I am sending you a copy of our latest catalog and the last four issues of our company magazine, Material Handling News.
>
> We're glad to pass these suggestions and materials on to you; we realize that today's students are tomorrow's material-handling engineers.
>
> Good luck on the thesis.

You will note that not one of the approved foregoing letters wasted any words referring to receipt of the inquiry. The direct beginning makes such references unnecessary and saves space better used for worthwhile information.

Completeness of coverage. Obviously, you need to take up every question in an inquiring letter; when you fail to do so, extra correspondence results (or your reader marks you as careless, indifferent, or ignorant). At times, of course, you can't answer—because you don't know, or because you can't reveal the information. In either case simply tell your reader so, but don't ignore the question.

When questions call for strictly factual answers, when the requesting letter tabulates questions and leaves space for answering on the letter, your job is easy. When the necessary answers are evaluative and expository in form, your job is sometimes not so easy.

The following personnel report is in answer to an inquiry about the subject's selling ability, personality, cultural background, character, and integrity. Note that the negative information the writer felt necessary to establish appears embedded in the letter and interpreted along with a positive characteristic of the applicant. Note, too, that the letter is *not* a "recommendation" but a *personnel report* of the writer's experience with and evaluation of the applicant—as it should be.

SUBJECT: CONFIDENTIAL REPORT BY REQUEST ON TRAVIS BRANNON

Mr. Brannon is a careful, accurate worker with lots of initiative. And he makes friends readily.

I got to know Travis quite well while he made two A's in my courses, Sales Management and Public Relations, and later when he graded papers, had conferences with students, and did clerical jobs as a student assistant in my office fall semester last year. His questions in class and in conferences showed a keen understanding of business problems and a calm, practical approach to their solution. And his term reports in both cases showed solid, serious, yet original business thinking.

Impressed with his scholastic performance, his friendliness and ability to get along with people, and his obvious wide range of interests in many things, I asked Travis to be my assistant. I particularly liked the quickness with which he caught on to assigned jobs and the willingness and accuracy with which he did a job every time it came up after I had explained it to him only once. On many small jobs and some not so small he went ahead and did what was needed without being told.

As he demontsrated ability, I let him do more and more. And he accepted the added responsibility and authority with obvious delight. As a result of such unbridled enthusiasm, I occasionally had to change a grade or contradict what he had told a student in conference. When that happened, he was noticeably silent for a few days; then he apparently forgot the incident and became his cheerfully helpful self again.

I must say, Mr. Parks, that I never had to lower a grade Travis gave a student. And he was hardest on his friends. I never had one single reason to suspect that any student had an inside track with him. He was completely trustworthy with examinations, grade records, and the like.

Perhaps the most noticeable things about Travis are his eagerness to do his job, his efficiency in making use of all his time, and his general alertness. These qualities, though they sometimes made him officious in interrupting my conferences with students and colleagues, stood him in good stead with students and faculty alike.

I feel sure that if Travis walked into the office of a college professor on almost any campus, the reaction toward him and your company would be favorable.

In most cases requesting information about an applicant for credit, all you'll probably need to do is look at your customer's record and fill in the blanks provided on the inquiring letter. But when some atypical factor presents itself (or when the inquiring firm does not provide blanks), you'll need to write a special letter.

We do not mean to imply here that all credit reports are letters, for most of them are not; the bulk of credit information goes out in special report forms. This is a small point, however, for in report form or letter form the useful credit summary covers essentially the same material:

—Age of account (how long on the books)
—Credit or trading limit (maximum allowed; sometimes labeled "highest credit extended")
—Buying habits (typical or average purchase, annual volume)
—Paying habits *in relation to terms* (identify the terms and show how the customer meets or does not meet them)
—Present status of the account (amount now on the books, what part is overdue, and how long overdue).

In addition to the foregoing information, you may need to incorporate explanations of the effects of local conditions on the size and timing of purchases or on paying habits. And of course, any unusual question—like the one about Mr. Green (p. 100)—requires special attention. Since it is usually the reason for the special letter, it often merits the beginning position, like this:

SUBJECT: CREDIT REPORT ON MR. H. F. GREEN, VINITA, OKLAHOMA

I suspect that Mr. Green did not list us as a reference for fear we would retaliate. About a month ago he was a little miffed when we guessed wrong on one of his vague orders—and he told us so.

Our relations have always been satisfactory, however, from our point of view. Since we started doing business with Mr. Green in August, 1967, we've been safe in allowing him credit up to $700 several times. He has a yearly account of about $4,000; his monthly purchases vary from $30 in the summer to $700 in the fall. When crop money in the fall spurs payments, Mr. Green generally takes advantage of our 2/10 EOM discount. With only a few exceptions, he has paid his net bill by the 30th. On the two occasions that we had to press him for collection, he paid up promptly.

Right now is the slack season in the farming regions; so Mr. Green has let ride his May and June accounts totaling $700.30. Of this amount, only the May bill of $382.40 is now overdue. Since, on June 16, he sent in his $366.60 check in payment of his April account, we know that Mr. Green pays his bills as soon as he gets his money. A retired farmer who still owns three farms, he is the sole owner of his modest store.

I am glad to send you, at your request, this confidential letter about Mr. Green.

Completeness of coverage does *not,* however, mean recommendation. Note that neither the preceding personnel report nor the credit report recommends the applicant—and hence such letters should *not* be misnamed "letters of recommendation."

But in replying about people, completeness *does* require covering the legal aspects. You could get into a peck of trouble by sending damaging information without meeting the obligations of doing so. Conversely, if you play it straight you need have no fear.

Legally and morally you are on safe ground only if your letter meets the requirements of a *privileged* communication. First, don't volunteer information; send it only if *requested by somebody with an interest to protect,* and incidentally make that clear. Beyond that you owe the inquirer, the person reported on, and the state *the truth as you see it (including your evaluations and opinions), good faith to avoid misleading or malice, and reasonable care to be right about facts.*

Resale. Perhaps our suggestion to incorporate resale material in a reply to an inquiry without sales possibilities may strike you as unnecessary —even odd. But look back a moment at the contrasting examples (p. 103) relating to the HOW book and note the different impressions created. The revised version makes comments on the book in such a way as to make the reader realize that it is something special. Furthermore, it enhances the cordiality established by the direct beginning and eliminates any impression of curtness and abruptness of a one-sentence letter.

Note how in the following letter the writer not only applies resale on the requested booklet but goes a step further by sending something additional and offering to do more (real service attitude):

> Of course you may have copies of our booklet; four of them are enclosed with this letter. They'll certainly help to show those future business leaders you spoke of something about how a direct-mail agency operates.
>
> We're also sending you a dividend: a copy of the speech Mr. Ray made at the DMAA meeting in Detroit last month. Some folks have said that it makes some pretty arresting statements about the uses and limitations of direct mail. You and your students will get something from this too, we think.
>
> Call on us again; we're always glad to do what we can.

Certainly you can't use resale in every reply. But in situations where you send information (especially in the form of booklets, brochures, or leaflets) you have every reason to enhance the desirability of what you've done and to offer to help out again (unless you specifically do not want to).

The reminder checklist on page 109 summarizes the more important points to keep in mind as you write replies complying with a reader's request which has no sales possibilities.

Replies with sales possibilities

Failure to answer inquiries and requests of the types we have been discussing will mark you as an uncooperative boor and probably lose you a good many sales in the long run. But failure to answer inquiries with direct sales possibilities is sooner or later business suicide.

When someone sends you an inquiry about your goods or services, clearly an unsatisfied need or desire exists and the inquiry implies that your product might satisfy it. Whether the request is for manufacturing data, a price list, a catalog or descriptive folder, or the name of your nearest dealer, you have an *interested*, potential customer—in other words, a prospect. *If* you give satisfactory information and treatment, you'll probably have a real customer.

Your selling job here is certainly much easier than making a sale through the usual sales letter that has to start from scratch with a "cold" prospect (as discussed in Chapter 8) because the inquirer is already interested and has practically invited you to send a sales letter. You probably spend a lot on advertising to get people into this mood. So don't just sit there!

Although you will be able to write better invited sales letters after studying special sales techniques, we take them up here because they are the most significant kind of reply any business firm sends. They are more than goodwill builders; they are sales builders. Accordingly, they draw heavily on the principles discussed in Chapter 2.

In answering an inquiry with sales possibilities, you have no problem securing attentive interest; your problem is to tell enough to overcome reluctance, to tell it interestingly and convincingly, and to get the reader to take the appropriate steps that lead to a sale. Your effort, then, must go toward starting favorably, answering all questions, subordinating unfavorable information, handling price positively, and stimulating action.

Getting started positively. When a prospective customer writes you the equivalent of "Tell me more," an indifferent reply like this is going to feel like a dash of cold water in the face.

```
Two Endurtone outlets operate in your locality.  Kindly contact
them with your problem.
```

Such unconcern will send most readers to other sources for their needs. This, of course, is an extreme example, but it happens often enough to merit special warning.

The thing the reader most wants to know is the information requested —as specifically as you can give it. That is far more interesting than any of your expressions of pleasure or gratitude.

But in most cases involving a detailed inquiry, you will want to check the order of your reader's questions before framing your reply. Some you can answer with more positiveness than others; one of these is what you should start with:

```
With your Pow-R-Pac you will feel safe even when traveling
alone at night on the country roads you spoke of.
```

--

```
The Rover bicycle you saw advertised in U.S. Youth is made of
lightweight, high-grade steel of the same quality used in
motor bikes.
```

Favorable Reply Checklist

1. Make your opening show that you are doing as asked.
   a) When you are saying yes, sending something, or giving information, do so immediately!
   b) The most effective way to show that you're glad to do something is to do it immediately: not "I am very glad to tell you . . ." but "Henry Benton, about whom you inquired, has served us well as. . . ."
   c) Don't emphasize the obvious: "This is an answer to . . ."; "Concerning your inquiry . . ."; "We have received. . . ."
   d) Consider using a subject line to get you off to a fast start.
2. Completeness, specificness, and correctness are essential.
   a) Answer every question—direct or implied—of the inquiry. Scant, skimpy treatment implies that you are unwilling to extend an ordinary courtesy or that you are dubious.
   b) You want to evaluate when evaluation will be helpful. But do more than editorialize with "fine," "splendid," "excellent." Give specific evidence. In a personnel report, for instance, tell things the applicant did, work habits, personality.
   c) Be careful of the facts; avoid malice or carelessness.
3. Tone is all-important.
   a) In a personnel report:
      (1) Remember that you are reporting, not recommending.
      (2) Beware of superlatives, for accuracy and believability.
   b) Don't do anything grudgingly or parade your generosity.
4. You often have negative material to handle.
   a) Be honest; don't ignore the shortcomings and mislead.
   b) Watch space, word choice, and position to avoid overemphasis on either favorable or unfavorable points.
   c) When you must restrict the use of what you give, be definite —but place the negative in the middle of the letter.
5. Remember the libel laws (p. 107) when writing about a person.
   a) Label the letter confidential.
   b) Indicate that it has been requested.
   c) Subordinate these ideas in the beginning or ending statements.
6. When sending something tangible, add a few words of resale.
   a) Make them short.
   b) Make them as specific as you can.
7. End graciously and confidently.
   a) Your expression of willingness—more appropriate here than in the beginning—nullifies any possible curt impression.
   b) Don't suggest inadequacy: "I hope" or "If this is not. . . ."
   c) Omit bromides: "Please do not hesitate" or "Feel free to."

Yes, the base and standard of the Roanoke lamp you saw in Home and Yard are of solid brass. They will blend in tastefully with almost any style of 18th-century furnishings.

When you can answer yes to an important question, that is the information you should choose for your opening. Such positiveness stimulates enthusiasm and increases the desire to read further.

Answering all questions. In some instances you cannot give the information your reader has asked of you. For example, the letter about the Stair-Traveler (p. 45) could not give cost details because installation varies according to the placement of the machine in a particular home. The visit of the representative (clearly referred to) would have to clear up that point. If you cannot supply an answer, do not ignore it. Such action only leads to suspicion, irritation, or disgust. Indicate that you are supplying the information some other way or that you are getting it.

Most of the time you can give all the information the reader has requested, even though it runs to considerable length. The following reply to a request for more information about reconditioned Lektrasweeps is a good letter and not only because of good you-viewpoint and positiveness but also because it answers every question asked. (Questions about at least a 1-hp. motor, repairs in the home, and a trial period could not be answered fully yes.)

The reconditioned Lektrasweep you asked about has the following attachments: a 6-inch upholstery brush, a 6-inch lampshade brush, a 12-inch prober, and a plastic blower attachment, in addition to the standard 12-inch rug brush.

These are the same attachments that come with vacuum cleaners costing $40 to $80 more. Were we to include a 1-hp. motor (necessary only for spraying attachments), the price would have to be considerably increased. Since most users want their Lektrasweeps for cleaning purposes only, we eliminate the spray attachments and thus are able to give you a good low-cost cleaner operating efficiently on a ½-hp. motor.

I believe we have the machine you'll find convenient for your cleaning. The quiet operation of the motor is especially desirable in small living quarters, and the brown crackle finish will resist nicks and scratches and clean easily. Another convenience is the 20-foot cord, which enables you to clean an entire room from one wall plug.

The Lektrasweep guarantee protects you against mechanical failures of the vacuum cleaner for a full two years. If any parts fail because of defective workmanship, specially trained servicemen at the central plant in Cleveland will put your Lektrasweep in service again and return it to you within a week. Although we consider all sales final (another of the economies resulting in the low price of your Lektrasweep), as long as the machine shows evidence of proper care, as explained on the written guarantee, we absorb the charges for servicing and new parts, and return your Lektrasweep charges prepaid. The few returns to the central plant have been handled to the customers' satisfaction.

```
Next time you're in Birmingham, come in and let us demonstrate
a Lektrasweep.  After a thorough test of its effectiveness in
picking up dust, lint, and other particles from rugs,
upholstery, and walls, you'll see why we are so confident
of the Lektrasweep.

To get your Lektrasweep before you can come to Birmingham, use
the enclosed order blank and reply envelope to send us your
payment and instructions.  You can be enjoying easy
Lektrasweeping the day after we hear from you.
```

This was a particularly difficult letter to write because so many of the questions had to be answered with limitations, reservations, or an implied no.

To get full value out of the replies about Lektrasweeps and Roanoke lamps (next section), you need to look at each a second time. Both effectively illustrate two aspects of you-viewpoint especially important in all sales writing—including the answers to the questions of a product inquiry:

1. *Psychological description.*—Except in the first paragraph of the Lektrasweep letter, every time the writers give a physical fact about the product, they *tell* and *emphasize* a resultant benefit. As you look again, see how many more pieces of psychological description you can find like the italicized part of ". . . 20-foot cord, *which enables you to clean an entire room from one wall plug.*"
2. *Dramatization.*—The most effective kind of sales writing gets the reader to imagine actually using and enjoying the benefits of the product. Where else in the two letters can you find dramatized copy like "You and Mrs. Baines will agree that the Roanoke is a handsome, efficient lamp when you place a pair in your own living room"?

For further help on answering all questions, see the second group of form enclosures, pp. 117–18.

Subordinating unfavorable information. Only a very poor sales writer would have started the Lektrasweep letter with

```
No, the Lektrasweep does not have a 1-hp motor.
```

or even with

```
The Lektrasweep is equipped with a ½-hp. motor.
```

Another case will more firmly implant the reasons for positive handling of unfavorable information in invited sales. The inquiry asked whether

1. the Roanoke lamp was three-way,
2. the shade was of parchment or paper,
3. the shade was available in a design,
4. the lamp was weighted to prevent tipping,
5. the base was real brass or an alloy,
6. a pair could be returned for full refund if they didn't fit in with the 18th-century living room.

Answers to all but question 5 contained negative information. Here is one way of handling this inquiry to turn it into a sale despite the unfavorable circumstances:

> Yes, the base and standard of the Roanoke lamp you saw in Home and Yard are of solid brass, which will blend in tastefully with almost any style of 18th-century furnishings.
>
> For durability and ease in cleaning, the 10-inch shade is lightweight metal. Either the forest green or the royal red shade will contrast effectively with your drapes, and the quarter-inch gold bands around the top and bottom give the Roanoke lamp a distinction which most of our customers prefer to a design.
>
> The white lining of the shade and the milk-white bone china reflector enable the single 150-watt bulb to give you good reading light—10 foot-candles within a radius of 8 feet, which is more than the minimum recommended by the American Institute of Lighting. Then, too, the indirect lighting reflected from the ceiling is pleasant for conversational groups.
>
> To make the Roanoke more stable than other lamps of this size and shape, our designers put six claw feet instead of the usual four on the base and thus eliminated the necessity for weighting. Claw feet, as you know, are characteristic of much 18th-century design.
>
> You and Mrs. Baines will agree that the Roanoke is a handsome, efficient lamp when you place a pair in your own living room. Should you decide to return them within 10 days of our shipping date, we will refund your money less shipping charges.
>
> Use the enclosed order blank and envelope to tell us your choice of color. Include with the order blank your check or money order for $80 (including shipping charges). Within five days after we hear from you, you will be enjoying your Roanoke lamps, which will give you good lighting at a moderate price and will make appropriately decorative additions to your living room.

The letter wisely begins and ends with positive ideas and, as positively as circumstances permit, establishes the negative answers of "No, the Roanoke is not three-way; no, it is not weighted; no, the shade is not available in a design; no, the shade is not parchment or paper; no, we won't refund *all* your money if you return the lamps." It does so through the usual means available to any writer: embedded position and positive statement.

Handling price. When you have a genuine bargain, a real price reduction—one which the reader will recognize as such—that information may be the best lead you can choose for your message.

Most of the time, however, you are trying to sell at an established price. And most of the time you are writing to someone who wishes the price were less! For these reasons, good sales writers attempt to minimize the effect of price by one or more of several methods:

—Introducing price after presenting most of the sales points.

—Stating price in terms of a unit ("50 cents a wrench" rather than "$6 a dozen").
—Identifying the daily, monthly, or even yearly cost based on an estimated life of the product ("10 cents a night" for a good mattress sounds much easier to pay than "$79").
—Suggesting a series of payments rather than the total (an alumnus is more likely to contribute "$10 a month for the next year" than to contribute "$120 next year").
—Comparing the present price with the cost of some product or activity the reader accepts readily. ("For the price of six cigarettes a day your child can have better schools" was the punch line of an ad promoting a school-bond drive. And an Episcopal bishop drove home a point with "This means 17 cents per week from each communicant—not a large sum for the kingdom of God, when we realize that many of us spend twice that amount *every day* for tobacco." Likewise, a sales writer sells air-conditioned sleep for the price of a daily Coke.)
—Associating the price with a reminder of the benefits to be gained.

The first and the last of the suggestions you can always apply; you may want to use the others as indicated by the following varying factors.

In general, the higher the income bracket of your readers, the less desirability for applying the techniques.

The higher the price of your product or service, the greater the desirability for minimizing price in one or more of these ways. The less familiar your readers are with your product or service, the greater the desirability of justifying price. Such devices are incorporated more frequently in consumer letters than in letters to dealers.

Often you will be able to omit direct price talk because a sales representative will handle it in a face-to-face interview or because you need more information before determining price. Sometimes you can shift the burden of price discussion to an enclosure. But when you are trying to close a sale, you must identify what it is going to cost and help your reader justify the expenditure.

Securing action. Having convinced your reader that your product or service is worth the price, you want to get action before a change of mind, before forgetfulness defeats you, before the money goes for something else —before any of the things that could happen do happen.

A word of caution here, however: The bromidic, high-pressure, general expressions like "Act today!" "Do it now!" "Don't delay!" are more likely to produce reactions ranging from indifference to disgust than the favorable reaction you seek.

As in all persuasive letters, your good action ending

—Makes clear the specific action you want your reader to take
—Clears up any question about how the action is to be taken
—Makes the action easy (and makes it sound as easy as possible)
—Supplies a stimulus to action, preferably immediate action.

On finishing your letter, your reader should know just exactly what you want done—(in invited sales letters) to send in an order or take some step in furthering the order, such as to invite the visit of a sales representative, make a visit to a demonstration or salesroom, or try out the product. The psychological urge is stronger if you name the explicit action rather than resort to the vague "Let us hear from you soon" or any of its equivalents.

At times you may have to name two actions and ask the reader to take one or the other. If you possibly can, avoid doing so. Some folks faced with a choice resolve their dilemma by doing nothing.

Facilitating devices—order blanks, order cards, and postcards or envelopes already addressed and requiring no postage—remove some of the work in taking action. References to them—*preferably directing the reader to use them* (see *enclosures,* pp. 117–18)—reassure your reader that what you are asking is simple, requiring little time or effort.

Moreover, through careful wording, you can further this impression. "Write us your choice" suggests more work than "Check your choice of colors on the enclosed card." "Jot down," "just check," "simply initial," are examples of wording that suggests ease and rapidity in doing something. Wording like this will help to reduce some of your reader's reluctance to take action.

The final suggestion for a good action ending—that of supplying a stimulus to action—is a matter of either threatening your reader or promising something. Remember a stimulus is motivation—a reader benefit! Talk of limited supply, price rises after a certain date, introductory offers for a limited time, premiums, and the like is all very well *provided it is true* and *provided it is specific,* so that the reader is likely to accept your statement as accurately depicting the conditions. Otherwise, readers of average intelligence and experience read such statements with some skepticism.

In many circumstances you have nothing you can use as a stimulus but the desirability of your product or service. You *always* have that, however. In the final analysis your reader buys for what the product contributes to life; when you ask for money, mention *again what benefits will result.* (This is called a "stimulus" or a "clincher." But since many sales writers refer to the four steps of the action ending as the "clincher," we think it's simpler just to call this restatement of benefit the "stimulus.")

Such a stimulus comes appropriately as the ending idea of your letter. This placement has decided psychological value too, for it emphasizes the service attitude—rather than the greed stressed if you end with dollars and cents talk or the mechanics of ordering.

Desirably, the stimulus is short—often only a phrase, at most a short sentence, restating the theme of the letter. The Stair-Traveler letter, for example, could have ended effectively with

```
Mr. J. B. Nickle, our Memphis representative, will be glad to
call at a time convenient for you.  Fill out and mail the
```

Invited Sales Checklist

1. Get started in a hurry!
   a) The direct, specific, favorable answer to one of your reader's main questions is the surest way of maintaining interest.
   b) At least give a good sales point if no answer can be affirmative.
   c) "Thank you for"—while perfectly nice—is slow.
   d) Keep out the selfish sounds like "We're glad to have. . . ."
   e) Do not begin with an answer containing negative information.
   f) You don't need to work for attention: you already have it.
2. Arrange points for natural coherence and favorable information at the beginning and end of your letter (and preferably of paragraphs). Embed touchy points.
3. Answer every question, stated or implied, or explain why.
   a) You need specific statements for conviction.
   b) Avoid denied negatives. If a product isn't something, what is it?
4. Psychological description (you-viewpoint) is good selling.
   a) Put the product to work in the life of the reader right from the start, and let reader-use sentences predominate throughout to give a visual image of benefits.
   b) Depict reader possession and/or participation instead of mere mechanical you-beginnings.
5. Consider using an enclosure for details, economy, and pictures.
   a) Don't mention it too early.
   b) Don't emphasize that you have enclosed it; what the reader is to do with it or get from it is what counts: not "Enclosed you will find a folder," but "Read on page 2 of the enclosed folder the comments of some of the more than 8,000 owners of XXX."
6. Adaptation is easy here; your reader's letter gives you cues.
   a) Maybe use the name a time or two beyond the salutation.
   b) Work in a reference to home town, firm, or organization.
   c) Refer casually to a commonplace action or event characteristic of the reader's job, community, area, or economic status.
   d) Fit your style to the person's way of life.
7. Try to cushion the shock of price when you have to state it.
   a) Use the appropriate method(s) of minimizing price.
   b) Make price and payment method clear, or give a reason.
8. In a full-fledged four-point action ending (what to do, how, aids to easy action, stimulus to promptness) confidently ask the reader to take some appropriate action (preferably order, if fitting).

> enclosed postcard, and he will come to your home and explain how simply and economically your Stair-Traveler can make your daily living more pleasurable.

Another example of the built-in stimulus is this ending from a letter to a farmer about an automatic milking machine:

> And for $77.75—less than you pay for 10 sacks of feed—Farm Master Milker can go to work for you. Just leave the enclosed card for the mail carrier tomorrow morning, and our Philadelphia representative will soon be up to give you a demonstration of how Farm Master Milker will increase your dairy profits.

For other examples, reread the endings of the Roanoke lamp letter and the letter selling the Lektrasweep.

A final reminder: Invited sales are sales letters in the truest sense. You should therefore apply all the points discussed in Chapter 2. The checklist on page 115 summarizes the most significant points to keep in mind for a good invited sales letter.

ROUTINE TRANSMITTAL MESSAGES

A frequent type of written communication is the routine transmittal letter or memo. Often people in a firm send information or material to other people, either with their company or with other companies. This information or material usually has a short cover letter or memo which carries the address, announces the material is being sent, and identifies the sender.

These short notes do not strictly fall into the category of favorable replies, since generally no question arises about your compliance with the request, if there is one. The reason we are talking about this routine type of writing is that for most young people early in their careers, such messages are their primary (and maybe only) contact with upper management. Such writing deserves some care.

The routine transmittal message should be short. Though you may sometimes need to explain what you are sending, you have no need to spout eloquence over simply sending information. In any case, do not be trapped into using the old-fashioned "Enclosed you will find" or "Attached is" beginnings. Much more natural and direct beginnings are "Here is the information on . . ." or "This is the material you asked for. . . ." Custom within your firm will dictate whether you need to mention the date of your reader's request, but any file number or other formal identification should appear in the first sentence or a subject line.

After you have announced that the material is here (which should be pretty evident to your reader), quit unless you have something relevant to say. Simply sign off, assuming that your transmittal letter or memo has done its job.

What your note can go on to say after the initial announcement is that you're sending more information than your reader expected, or that the information is dated, perhaps, or not yet complete, or whatever the situation calls for. Keep this second part of your message short and direct; and resist the temptation to add an ending offering further assistance. If your reader does need more information, you'll hear about it! And anyhow, you should have sent all the information in the first place.

FORM ENCLOSURES AND LETTERS

Invited sales letters (and various other kinds of letters) do take time and therefore money—more than many firms can wisely spend unless the profit may be sizable. Unless a firm has practically unlimited money and trained personnel, it therefore needs to use form messages some of the time for speed and economy in handling inquiries with sales possibilities.

Form enclosures and letters can decrease the cost of correspondence by cutting time needed for dictation, transcription, handling, and filing. The closer you can come to completely eliminating one or more of these steps, the more you can save. The big problem is to determine when you can save enough in costs to justify the loss in effectiveness.

Before you can decide, however, you need to know the potentials of forms.

Enclosures. Three classes of *form enclosures* deserve our attention:

1. Forms which are the basic reason for the mailing;
2. Forms which give supplementary information; and
3. Forms which aid the reader in responding.

Since the *first group* are the key things in the envelopes (checks paying for services, interest, dividends, purchases, and deserved refunds; requested pamphlets, brochures, and the like), they deserve to come to the reader's attention immediately. In some cases they may properly be the only thing necessary. In most situations, however, you should *make something of them* by saying something about them—if for no reason than goodwill. You've already seen earlier in this chapter under "Resale" the reasons and approaches for comment when transmitting requested booklets. Similarly, simple and typical covering letters (often forms themselves) beginning something like the following could hardly help making their readers feel better:

> We're glad to send you the attached quarterly dividend check (our 200th without interruption, raised to 50¢ a share this time) and to thank you for your continued confidence in MMM.
>
> --
>
> The enclosed check paying for your services as consultant carries with it our thanks for the good advice you gave us.
>
> --
>
> The enclosed check will tell you more clearly than words that when we guarantee satisfaction with Acme products or your money back, we mean it.

Unlike the first group of form enclosures, the enclosures in the *second group* are *not* the basic reason for writing but are helpful to give additional details and thus avoid cluttering and lengthening the letter unduly. Most frequently useful in sales letters as brochures and detailed price lists, they also help in application letters (as résumés or data sheets) and in answering various inquiries about products (as installation, operating, and repair guides). As supplements to letters, these informative enclosures do not deserve mention until late in the letter—usually the next-to-last paragraph, *after* the letter has covered the key points and near enough to the end that the reader will finish the letter before turning to the enclosure (perhaps never to return). As with the first group, the important thing to say about these enclosures is *not* their mere existence—NOT "We have enclosed . . . ," and certainly NOT "Enclosed please find . . ." (the reader has probably already found)—but what the reader should get from them.

```
As you'll see from the enclosed brochure, . . .

                          --

The illustrations and explanations on pages 3 and 4 of the
enclosed installation guide will answer, better than I can
explain in this letter, your questions about wiring the two
thermostats in combination.

                          --

All the references listed on the enclosed data sheet have
agreed to answer any inquiry you may want to make about. . . .
```

The *third useful group* of form enclosures (reader aids in replying) naturally deserve mention only in the ending—where you are asking for action. Order blanks and reply or return cards and envelopes (usually stamped and addressed—but NOT properly called "self-addressed," unless you insist on being jargonistic, illogical, and wordy) can often help you get an answer when the reader would not go to the trouble necessary without them. As in referring to other form enclosures, the point to stress is NOT the idea that they are enclosed but the suggestion that the reader use them.

If you'll use the word *enclosed* as an adjective instead of a verb, you'll probably put the emphasis where it belongs in referring to all three classes of form enclosures, like this:

```
By filling out and mailing the enclosed reply card
promptly, . . .

                          --

Sending in your order today on the enclosed form will bring
you. . . .
```

Form letters. Although most readers like the implied extra consideration of the individual letter, few business people will object to a *form letter* because it is a form but only if it seems to give them less attention than they desire. New customers and those writing you about important affairs are most likely to feel that way. Anybody, however, will rightly object to a sloppy form or a form message which does not contain the necessary information. And many people will object to a form which tries to masquerade as an individual letter but fails because of discrepancies in type, faulty alignment, or inept wording. But the undisguised form can successfully carry its message in many situations, especially those involving many similar inquiries to which you can reply somewhat like the following:

```
Here's Your Copy of
The Buying Guide
to Fine Furniture.

You will be delighted with the wealth of information condensed
into this conveniently indexed booklet.

For here, in a comparatively few pages, are guideposts used by
experts with a lifetime of experience in weighing true
furniture values.  Here are features which help such experts
actually judge furniture "upside down" as well as right
side up.

And here are features illustrated and described to guide you
in your purchases of furniture so that the pieces you select
to furnish your home will give you utmost pleasure as the
years roll by.

We're glad you've given us this opportunity to send you this
information, for we love fine furniture . . . take great pride
in making it . . . and enjoy distributing information about it
that may be helpful to you in establishing standards of value.

Even though every piece of furniture bearing the Langston seal
is handcrafted to certified standards of quality, nationwide
popularity makes possible budget prices.  For a pleasant
surprise, see your dealer, whose name is imprinted on the back
page of the booklet.
```

Even the signature of this letter is processed. When an inquiry comes in, the letter and booklet are in an envelope. Addressing the envelope is the only time-consuming step. Thus a reply which could cost $3 or more if individually handled runs to no more than a quarter. And the firm gains extra goodwill by a prompt answer.

You can run off completely processed forms (*strict forms*) by the thousands at very low cost. The only additional expense is for addressing. Thus, *completely* processed messages are the cheapest. And they can be adapted in talking points and references even to a large mailing list. They can indicate the disposition of the inquiry (or order), express gratitude, convey some evidence of service attitude, and look forward to future business relations, as in the following postcard acknowledgment:

```
We are glad to give your recent order our immediate careful
attention and to follow your shipping instructions exactly.

You may be sure we appreciate this opportunity to serve you
and shall be happy to do so when you again decide to order
Wolf's fine confections for yourself or as a gift.
```

But completely processed letters have limitations. Personalizing is impossible. And if you process the body and then insert individual inside addresses and salutations, you have two additional problems: greatly increased costs and likely discrepancies between the two types. Unless you sell only one product or have a different form for each product, you can't include resale talk on the goods, although you can for the firm.

Fill-ins enable you to be more specific than you can be in a strict form. For example, the strict form above could read like this as a fill-in (the filled-in parts being in parentheses):

(January 15, 19—)

We sent a carefully packed (2-pound box of Wolf's famous Texas Chewie Pecan Pralines) today, as you requested, by (parcel post) addressed to (Mr. and Mrs. E. F. Blanton, 2443 Hathaway Road, Syracuse, New York 13247).

When it arrives within the next few days we know (they) will enjoy the rich, nutty flavor of this fine candy.

Many thanks for your order. When you want more of Wolf's fine candies for yourself or for pleasing a friend with an inexpensive gift distinctly different, we shall be glad to serve you again.

But even if you do a good job of matching print and type in a fill-in like this, in most instances the irregular spacing calls attention to the fact that the message is a form fill-in. The first two insertions in the example above extend the line of type far beyond what any typist would do if the letter were individually typed. And see what happens when the recipient's name and address are something as short as "Mr. J. P. Ames, Opp, Iowa"! The line then would be much too short. That is one of the reasons why so many users fill in these forms by hand, with no attempt to disguise.

With proper planning, equipment, and patience, however, fill-ins can appear to be individual letters. The following is a good example, where the necessary insertions are the name of the city (at the end of a line), name of the dealer (displayed attractively with additional spacing all around), and the reader's name (again, at the end of the line and with enough space to allow for a "Miss Rives" or a "Miss Getzendannerich"). In this case you would also use full inside address and dateline.

Dear Miss Rives:

The enclosed literature describes several Phenix models we believe will be of interest to you. Although the literature illustrates and describes the instruments, you cannot fully appreciate the beauty of the cabinetry or their magnificent tone without seeing and hearing them.

Phenix instruments are designed for discriminating buyers—for those who have genuine appreciation for refined furniture styling and truly fine musical tone—and they are sold only through high-grade music dealers and selected quality department stores.

We urge you to see these instruments and have them demonstrated to you. You will be thrilled by the perfection of tone that Phenix has attained.

Phenix instruments are on display in Austin at

J. P. Read Music Company
855 Congress Avenue

```
This dealer will be delighted to have the privilege of
demonstrating Phenix instruments to you without any obligation
whatever, Miss Rives.

Plan to go by for a demonstration.
```

For greatest economy the preceding letter would be printed; then, when an inquiry *that this form would be a satisfactory answer for* came in, a typist would need only to fill in the blanks—a matter of two or three minutes. Addressing and stamping (or metering) the envelope would take another two or three.

But because type is hard to match and exact alignment is difficult, many firms use word processing equipment (automatic typewriters run by magnetically recorded instructions) for multiple correspondence like this. After the letter is composed, an operator types it with the machine in "record mode," putting the letter on magnetic tape or card or into a computer memory, along with the necessary instructions about margins, paragraphing, points at which to stop, and so on.

To type the letter, the operator retrieves the recorded copy and instructions, puts paper in the typewriter, types the date, inside address and salutation, and puts the machine in "play mode." The typewriter automatically types the letter, usually at three or four times the speed even an expert typist can achieve—and without mistakes! Instructions to the machine can stop it at any point so the operator can fill in special wording to individualize or personalize the letter.

Word processing equipment, despite its cost, is economical as long as a machine is kept reasonably busy. With a library of tapes or cards, any number of departments within a company can use such equipment, helping assure that it will be used enough. Word processing equipment is also capable of composing type for sales literature and books (including justifying or aligning the type on the right-hand margin) and of doing accounting work, invoicing, addressing, and many other tasks.

This economy measure can apply to form paragraphs as well as to whole letters. The procedure is to write an excellent paragraph covering each frequently recurring point in the firm's correspondence and assign it a classified code number. Some of the classifications may be by type of letter in which the paragraphs are useful. For instance, most of the collection correspondent's paragraphs would be useless to one acknowledging orders, and vice versa. Usually half a dozen ending paragraphs and a dozen beginnings will cover most situations. Other paragraphs will be about the various products of the company. Each company correspondent and each typist then gets a book of the coded paragraphs, which may be typed manually or recorded for use in word processing equipment.

When the letter writer starts to dictate, a letter may be simply 13, 27, 16, 42. That would mean a four-paragraph letter made up of those standard paragraphs in that order. If no ready-made paragraph covers what should be in the second paragraph, dictation would be 13, special, 16, 42 followed by the wording for the special second paragraph. If the same point comes up frequently enough, the firm will prepare a good paragraph for it and put it into the correspondent's book.

Because the paragraphs get frequent use, they get careful preparation and are therefore better than most correspondents would write quickly under the pressure of dictation. Obviously, the same advantage applies to an entire form letter.

And simple arithmetic shows you that even if you spend 30 to 50 hours on one letter, when you send it to a thousand people, dictation time and transcription time are only a fraction of the time individual letters would require. In a nutshell, this is the whole theory back of form letters. They have to be used to cut correspondence costs, to reduce the burdensome human aspects of the ever-increasing correspondence problems of management, and to expedite replies to people who want information as quickly as they can get it.

Certain dangers exist, however. The greatest is the tendency to use a form when it simply does not apply. When a person asks if Pepperdent has chlorophyll in it, the answer—"Pepperdent will make your smile brighter because of its new secret ingredient urium! Leading stars of stage and screen praise its refreshing cleansing effectiveness"—may all be true but it has nothing to do with the inquiry. One good solution, if a form does not answer one specific question, is to add a postscript. If you cannot answer all questions by adding a little to an existing form, you need to write an individual letter.

Another danger is in broadcasting that the message is a form with such references as

```
To all our customers:

Whether you live in Maine or California. . . .
```

In a broadside (circular) such mass impersonality may be necessary. But in a letter the personal touch pays off. The wording of even a form letter, then, should *give each reader the feeling that it fits.* And remember that in every test ever made, the form letter that makes no pretense of being anything else (like the furniture letter on p. 119) results in more returns than the imperfectly disguised form, whether the slipup is due to poor mechanics or inept wording.

The question of whether to use a form or not depends on the recurring nature of the problem, the degree of expediency necessitated—but most of all, on your own good judgment of whether it will do the particular job. Whether a letter is a form or an individualized letter is not the significant consideration; whether a letter does all it can do to cement goodwill and build sales is what counts.

The suggestions made about form letters in this chapter should help with *any repetitive letter situation, whether it is one involving replies to inquiries, acknowledgments of orders, sales, credit, collections, or adjust-*

ments. So except for occasional incidental references pointing out the ease or wisdom of form treatment in a particular situation, the remainder of this book deals with individualized, personalized letters because

1. You can learn more about letter principles and their application that way.
2. As a result of such specific study and practice, you will write much better form letters when you need to.
3. In most circumstances calling for a letter, an individualized letter will do a more effective job for you than a form.

SHORT NOTE REPLY

In an effort to expedite many day-to-day answers to inquiries (and reduce correspondence costs), many executives turn to the SNR. One leading copying-machine manufacturer in its advertising explains this way:

1. Just jot a personal note on the margin of the letter you received—no wasted time in dictation.
2. Insert the letter and a sheet of copy paper into a copying machine.
3. In just four seconds you have a Short Note Reply copy of the letter ready to mail back to the sender—plus the original for your files.

Certainly most readers will appreciate the thoughtfully fast answer. The practice seems to be gaining favor—rightly so, in our opinion. One question we raise, however: Why doesn't the sender mail the original with handwritten notes and keep the copy to file (unless for contractual/legal reasons)?

One of the big mailers of the United States—Book-of-the-Month Club—uses a slightly different method combining a form and short notes to reduce costs and speed up parts of its correspondence. The front of a neat little 3½″ × 6½″ folder contains the printed name and address of the Club and the typed name, address, and membership number of the reader, followed by

QUICK REPLY FOLDER SEE WITHIN

Inside, the first page contains this form note, signed by the Membership Director:

Dear Member:

You will find enclosed in this folder the answer—or answers—to the questions you raised in your recent letter. We have developed this system of "Quick-Reply-Notes" because we have found it results in much better and more satisfactory service to our members. We receive literally tens of thousands of letters every day, and to dictate and type individual replies would inevitably mean considerable delay in every case. We have found that this is a much faster and more efficient way of answering inquiries than separate individual letters.

The third and fourth pages of the folder are blank. But stapled over the third page is a fitting slip of paper carrying the brief typed message (and, if needed—say to return merchandise—a small envelope containing postage and an addressed sticker). (See Case 11, p. 86, as an example of one of the messages.)

ORDERS

Since 1963, the former huge business of buying and selling by mail has had a series of shots in the arm through repeated editions of a new book, *International Yellow Pages*—multilingual pages listing about 3,000 categories of products available in 136 countries from over half a million suppliers (full addresses given).

Buying and selling by mail never has been just through the big mail-order houses like Sears, Ward's, and Spiegel's, as many people seem to think. It has long included mail sales through large department stores like Macy's, Hudson's, and Field's; the national marketing of seasonal and regional produce like fruit, game, syrup, and candy; and farmers' orders for various supplies, machinery, and replacement parts.

Although the old standbys still account for the main volume of mail sales, today more than ever before you can sit at your desk and buy a variety of products in all the markets of the world. Unless you travel widely, not to use the mail to broaden your market (as buyer or seller) is to build a fence of regionalism around yourself.

Furthermore, to overcome the disadvantage of buying without seeing, feeling, and trying the product, sellers by mail usually provide pictures and fuller, more reliable information than you can get from salesclerks about local goods; and they offer excellent guarantees and return privileges, and provide any necessary installation, operation, and service manuals.

Since sellers by mail usually provide well-designed order blanks and addressed envelopes with their catalogs, the only problems connected with writing an order appear when you do not have the blanks and must write a letter.

An order is probably the easiest kind of letter to write. You have no problem of getting attention or interest, and no conviction or persuasion is necessary in this A–plan letter. The reader is in business to sell goods. If you write clearly enough to specify what you want and make satisfactory plans to pay for it, you'll get an answer. A poor order letter may, however, cause the reader some trouble and bring results different from what you really want.

As a considerate and efficient letter writer, you should write orders that will be easy for a clerk to fill and that will bring you just what you want. The basic requirements, as you can see from almost any order blank, are five (which will serve as a checklist for order letters):

1. Make them orders, not just hints. The *acceptance* of a *definite offer to sell* or

an offer to buy is contractual. The usual beginning for an order is therefore "Please send me. . . ."

2. Describe the goods adequately. Although the catalog number alone usually identifies except for color and size, give four or five clean-cut columns of information, preferably in this sequence:
   a) Quantity desired.
   b) Catalog item number, if any, and page number.
   c) Name of product and as many details as are appropriate, such as model, color, size, material, grade or quality, pattern, finish, monogram initials.
   d) Unit price (sometimes not given as a separate column).
   e) Total price for the designated quantity of the item (column *a* times *d*).

   In the absence of a catalog, your information will likely go into two or three columns: quantity, name and description, and perhaps estimated total price. To supplement the inexact information, then, you may need to explain more fully by telling how the product is to be used, and in some cases by sending exact drawings.

   In ordering replacement parts for machines, be sure to give the name and model number of the machine and the name and number of the part. Frequently, you can find the number on the part itself if you have no parts list.
3. Write a separate, single-spaced paragraph for each item, with double spacing between paragraphs.
4. Make clear how you expect to pay. If you have not established credit but want goods charged, you should provide credit information with the order (see pp. 98 and 131).

   If you want neither credit nor c.o.d. shipment (which costs you more), several methods of remitting are open to you: personal check, money order (postal, express, or telegraph), certified or cashier's check, or bank draft.

   Regardless of how you remit, you should refer to the remittance in the letter and tell its form, amount, and intended application.
5. Be sure the *where* of shipment is clear—and also the *when* and *how* unless you want to leave them to the seller.

The following typical order letter illustrates the five points:

```
Please send me the following items listed in your current
spring and summer catalog:

   1   60 C 6587L  Glass casting rod, Model 162, extra
                   light action, 5 ft. 8 in. ............ $ 8.95

   1   60 CP 6302  Pflueger Summit reel, Model 1993L ....  13.75

   2   60 C 6846   Cortland "Cam-o-flage" nylon
                   casting line, 10-lb. test, 100-yd.
                   lengths @ $2.30 ......................   4.60

         Total .................................... $27.30

The enclosed check for $29.63 covers the price, sales tax, and
parcel post charges.

As I plan to go fishing a week from next Saturday (June 26),
I will want the equipment by that time.
```

The following letter did a much more difficult job of ordering. Test it against the five requirements set up for a good order letter. Note how the writer made the specifications very clear without benefit of a catalog or parts list to give code numbers and prices of the items.

> Please send me the following parts for Little Giant Shallow Well Water System P4/12818. Since I have no catalog, I am describing each part carefully.
>
> 1 Valve rubber, 1¼ inches in diameter with 5/16-inch hole. It is one of four that work under springs on the valve plate.
>
> 1 Crank pin. Apparently this is a steel pin of a highly special design. Its threaded end, 7/16 inch in diameter and 11/16 inch long, screws into the eccentric arm on the end of the drive shaft so that the rest of the pin forms the crankshaft. That is, the big end of the connecting rod fits around it. (See drawings on the attached sheet.) The crankshaft part of this pin is an eccentric ½ inch in diameter and 11/16 inch long.
>
> 1 Connecting rod, as shown on the attached sheet. Apparently it is brass or bronze. Please note the specifications as to size of hole. For other models, I know that the sizes are a little different.
>
> I estimate that these parts will cost approximately $14. I am enclosing my check for $15 to cover all charges, including tax and parcel post. You can send me your regular refund check if the charges are less or send c.o.d. for the difference if they are more.
>
> I'll appreciate your trying to fill the order promptly. My pump, much needed these days, is about to quit on me.

STANDARD ACKNOWLEDGMENTS

Poorly written orders cost their buyer-writers much delay in getting the desired goods, and they cost sellers lots of headaches and money (spent on letters required to get the needed information). But poor acknowledgments, for which the sellers are wholly responsible, cost them much more —in loss of goodwill and customers.

The acknowledgment letter should be an effective means of increasing goodwill and promoting business. A person who orders from you evidently has a favorable attitude toward your firm and its goods. That is a healthful climate for business. Your job in acknowledging the order is to keep it that way by giving satisfaction.

A buyer expects to get the product quickly, and to be appreciated—or to get a prompt and reasonable explanation. To give less is to make a customer for somebody else.

Frequently a correspondent who handles a large volume of orders, however, comes to look upon them as routine matters and to answer accordingly. Doing so overlooks three things: (1) The individual customer usually sends comparatively few orders and does not look on them as routine at all; (2) a routine acknowledgment seems like indifference; and (3) indifference, according to a U.S. Department of Commerce survey, is responsible for at least 67 percent of lost customers.

Justifying reasons (strikes, impossibility of always estimating demand accurately, as well as incomplete orders from the buyer) may prevent a seller from filling some orders promptly, or at all. But no reason justifies not acknowledging orders promptly, as the following fill-in form postcard reply from a large department store does.

```
Dear Customer:

Thank you for your letter ordering a ladder.

We're processing your order now, and you should receive the
shipment promptly.
```

Though a form postcard can reflect a service attitude and thus help to retain goodwill, it cannot do all a letter can.

Least of all can a seller find any reason for not showing appreciation for orders, as in this card reply (underscored words are the fill-in—typed if you can, penned if you're swamped):

```
As you requested, the turntable for Scrabble has been sent to
Mrs. M. W. Colby.

Thank you for calling on us.  We try to make our service
convenient.  Order from us again when we can serve you.
```

Neither does the seller have much excuse for not doing more than the minimum the customer ordinarily expects. Even a small first order is an opportunity to cement a lasting business relationship through a well-written acknowledgment letter.

The most important acknowledgment is the standard—acknowledging an order you can fill immediately. It is an easy letter to write.

Clearly *the standard acknowledgment* is a good-news letter. The beginning should be a direct answer to the biggest question in the reader's mind—what you are doing about the order. You tell immediately the *when* and *how* of shipment, preferably timed and worded to indicate that the goods are on the way. (Filling the order *accepts* it [which was *an offer to buy*] and thus forms a legal contract. But remember that you are sending goods, not an order, which is what you received.) The approximate arrival date is also desirable, not only as a convenience to the customer but also for the psychologically favorable effect of helping the reader imagine actually receiving and using the goods.

In talking about the shipment, of course you need to identify what it includes, the charges, and (right there or later) the financial arrangements. The identification is by date and one or more of order number, exact relisting, or sometimes merely a general naming of the class of goods. When the list is long or the value great, you might best list them on an attached invoice or shipping list and refer to it in the letter. On small orders to customers who have established credit or sent the exact amount with the order, you may omit the financial arrangements because they are already clear to both parties.

If you are acknowledging the first order from a new customer, the acknowledgment will certainly include a hearty welcome and will stress resale and the forward look even more than a letter to an old customer. The welcome may be interwoven or implied in what you are doing about the order; but ordinarily it comes later, frequently combined with an expression of appreciation.

Whether new or old, the customer will probably like you better for expressing appreciation, perhaps even interwoven in the first paragraph. In most cases, however, you can demonstrate gratitude more effectively with statements of how you've handled the order, resale talk, and offers to be of service again.

The middle section of a standard acknowledgment is the place for financial details not already completed, any resale talk of more than phrase length, and explicit evidence of service attitude. For instance in acknowledging dealers' orders, you often need to devote a paragraph to how you help the dealer to sell. You might talk about having your sales representative set up window and counter displays. Perhaps you offer free mats (which the dealer can give to a local newspaper for running ads with pictures of the products). You might provide free envelope stuffers (small promotional pamphlets about your products for the dealer to send to good customers—usually at no extra cost because they are "stuffed" in the envelopes carrying monthly bills). Often you will want to talk about your radio, TV, and magazine ads that call customers' attention to your products and help the dealer sell more.

Encouragement to future ordering in a success-conscious forward look to the future (just preceded by any appropriate sales promotion material) is almost invariably the best ending for the standard acknowledgment.

Heres' an example of how the parts go together for an effective personalized acknowledgment covering all points specifically:

> You should receive your eight cases of Tuff Paper towels in time for Friday afternoon shoppers; they were sent by prepaid express this morning.
>
> The $2.27 voucher attached to this letter is your change after we deducted $44.80 charges and $2.93 express from your $50 check.
>
> Thank you for your order. We're glad to serve you with this first shipment of paper products to you.
>
> You'll find these Tuff Paper Towels have a fast turnover, Mr. Ford, because housewives like the way they soak up grease, dust off spots, and save cloth towels from many dirty jobs. And you'll like their attractive small packaging that takes up a minimum of display and shelf space. Your markup figures out at exactly 29 percent.

For more information about Tuff Paper dishrags and window washers, colorful shelf paper your customers will like for their pantries, and other paper products every household needs, look in the enclosed booklet. Notice that each article carries the usual Tuff Paper margin of profit.

Perhaps you'd like to take advantage of our regular terms of 2/10, n/60 on future orders. If so, we'll be glad to consider your credit application when you fill in and return the enclosed form.

And when you order, if you want window and shelf displays to help you sell, just say so. Then watch Tuff kitchen paper products bring Altoona women into your store for frequent repeat sales.

The trouble with this kind of acknowledgment is that it costs dollars, not cents. To be specific on all points, to adapt the message to an individual, and to make it persuasive require an average-length, individually dictated letter. But when the prospect of numerous future orders depends on the letter, to do less would be foolish. Some situations involve enough to justify spending even more to produce the most effective letter possible rather than risk a customer's unfavorable reaction to a quick brush-off or form reply.

The inability to recognize situations that deserve full treatment and the general inclination to save even a little time and money on correspondence frequently lead to trouble. Pinching pennies by dashing off personalized letters that are just a little too short to be adequate, or resorting to forms that don't do the job, is poor economy. The result is comparable to throwing out *almost* enough rope to reach a drowning person. If you are going to write a personalized letter, make it a good one. Its cost does not increase in proportion to length. A question you should always answer before cheapening your correspondence is whether you lose more in results, including goodwill, than you save on costs.

But in many cases a form card or letter serves admirably as an acknowledgment, as we illustrated in the discussion "Form Letters" (p. 118). The preceding Tuff Paper letter could be handled in a form message like this one (which, incidentally, *could* serve for acknowledging a repeat order):

You should receive the Tuff Paper products you ordered in just a few days; they are already on the way.

Thank you for your order. We are glad to serve you in this way.

You'll find that Tuff Paper products have a fast turnover; housewives like the way they can be used for many messy household cleaning jobs and then be disposed of quickly and easily.

You will like their attractive packaging that takes up a minimum of shelf and display space. And the sizable markup!

Read the enclosed booklet for more information about Tuff

Checklist for Standard Acknowledgment

1. Of greatest interest to the reader is the complete, accurate shipment.
   a) Emphasize the good news (sending the goods) in the first sentence, preferably also indicating arrival.
   b) Clearly identify the order by one or more of date, number, reference to the goods by name—perhaps a complete listing.
   c) If you list, tabulate—in the letter if short; on a referred-to invoice or shipping list if long.
   d) Clear up any confusion about payment details.
   e) Consider whether method of shipment should be identified.
   f) Appreciation (and a welcome to a new customer) may come early in the letter but probably will fit better near the end—if not adequately implied.
2. Resale is part of acknowledgments to reassure the reader.
   a) Make it specific.
   b) Keep it short.
   c) Adapt it to your product and reader (consumer versus dealer).
3. Service attitude, especially important to new customers, may help with others.
   a) For a consumer: personal shopping, delivery schedules, and credit possibilities.
   b) For a dealer: sales and service representatives, manuals, displays, and advertising aids and programs (mats, envelope stuffers, etc.)
   c) If you talk advertising programs, give the names of publications and radio or TV stations, amount of space or time, and schedules; and emphasize how the advertising promotes sales: "Your customers will be asking for . . . because of the full-page ads running. . . ."
   d) If you talk credit, invite application without promising approval.
4. Sales promotion material can indicate service attitude and build sales.
   a) Keep it appropriate—usually on seasonal or allied goods.
   b) You-attitude and specificness are necessary in sales promotion.
   c) Emphasize your service to the customer—how the suggested product might help—not your selfish desire to sell more, as implied by "Our product . . . ," "We also make . . . ," or "We'd also like to sell you. . . ."
   d) Emphasize reader action when referring to enclosures.
5. Look forward to future orders.
   a) If sales promotion is the basis, suggest specific, easy action.
   b) If resale talk is the basis, continue in terms of reader satisfaction rather than suggest that something will go wrong.
   c) Guard against bromides and Greedy Gus wording as you close.

```
Paper dishrags, window washers, colorful shelf paper, and
other paper products every household needs.

Use the handy order blank and business reply envelope in the
back of the booklet when you want to order the additional Tuff
Paper products your customers will be asking for.
                                              (Signature)
```

If the situation is one in which specificness would add to the effectiveness of an acknowledgment, a fill-in rather than a strict form could serve. For instance, you could add a postscript of special material to the preceding letter.

Form letters of any kind, however, can go sour from overuse. If, for instance, the buyer above orders Tuff products weekly, blindly sending the same letter week after week would not only overuse the letter, it would shortly have the undesired opposite effect of convincing the buyer that you take such business for granted. If you have a situation where someone may repeatedly get the same form letter from you, you would be wise to revise it periodically to keep it fresh and effective.

The correspondent writing acknowledgments should study the situation and make the wise choices in (*a*) whether to use forms and, if so (*b*), which kind. Either way can be foolish. Economy may seem to dictate choosing the cheapest that will do the job, but the poorest economy of all is to send a form when the situation requires a carefully prepared and individualized letter.

CREDIT APPROVALS

In Latin, *credo* means "I believe." Woven firmly into the meaning of the English word *credit* are the basic ideas of trust, faith, honor, and integrity. Hence, in naming what is commonly called the four *C*'s of credit —the bases for evaluating credit applicants—credit specialists name character first, followed by capacity, capital, and conditions.

Character is honesty. It is one's good word. In business it is living up to the spirit as well as the letter of the contract. In credit, it is meeting obligations as one promises to do.

Capacity is the ability to produce or to earn and thus furnish the means for payment. For a business firm it is the present or potential profit from a business operation such as manufacturing or marketing; for an individual it is usually wages, salary, fees, or commissions.

Capital is the money behind the debtor. It may be cash, of course; but it is also other assets in the form of land, buildings, securities, patents, and copyrights, to mention the more common forms. It could as a last resort furnish the money for payment in the event of reversals.

Conditions (plural) has two parts. One is general business trends. The other is special or local conditions or the trends of the debtor's business as shown in its comparative financial statements.

Because all these four *C*'s—especially the first two—are reflections of personal qualities of an individual, credit letters are surcharged with negative possibilities. When you question a person's honesty, earning ability, or judgment, you are treading on potentially dangerous ground. Credit letters can be one of a firm's greatest means of killing off the goodwill that sales, advertising, and even adjustment departments work to build up. With tact, patience, and a positive attitude, however, your credit letters can be goodwill builders.

One of the fundamental concepts that will help you to write successful letters about credit is this: The credit privilege is *earned;* it is not handed out indiscriminately, given away—or sold. For that reason your letters should not talk about *granting* credit; more appropriate terminology is *approval* or *extension* of credit.

On the basis of one or more of the four *C*'s an individual or firm merits credit. For many people, character is the primary reason. They earn little, and they have little or no capital, but they pay their bills and thus earn the right to credit. And this is the bedrock of credit extension. Firms or individuals may enjoy high earnings but will not continue to enjoy ordinary credit privileges with a record of not taking care of obligations as promised (although they will be accorded more leniency by most firms than the debtor of low earning power). Most customers in a good capital position rate high on both capacity and character. Certainly this statement is true with respect to business firms (they are usually the discounters). An occasional individual in a favorable capital position may have no earning power and may let bills accumulate, but that does not continue in such lackadaisical fashion very long; the ax inevitably falls.

Anticipating those who may be unable or unwilling to pay is one of the primary functions of the credit manager. To hold down losses from bad debts, the credit officer evaluates applicants' credit records and estimates their financial stability in the light of general business ups and downs, does the same for customers already on the books, and periodically reviews accounts (and for business firms, financial statements) for danger signals.

But approving only gilt-edged applications will seriously curtail sales. The job is to contribute to the profits of the firm, not just to conserve them. Accordingly, a credit manager must be sales-minded, and well informed about the firm's goods, as a means of making letters build customer confidence and increase sales.

Since marginal risks are vital for profitable operations, evaluating and encouraging borderline cases must get careful attention. For both the firm and its customers the credit manager is part counselor, part sales promoter, and part detective. To play these many roles well requires a person who keeps well informed on the general conditions of the economy, trends in customers' lines of business, and even the constantly shifting consumer buying interests.

An efficient credit officer need not want for information about customers, however; many sources are available. The customer is a source. Most Americans are fairly well credit-educated and expect to give evidence of credit responsibility. A consumer applying for credit is usually willing to supply information about means of livelihood, names of firms formerly extending credit, name of bank, ownership of any real estate, and approximate annual income. Most business firms, in seeking credit, furnish financial statements and references, many of them unsolicited (and they keep right on furnishing those statements year after year). If for any reason the customer does not furnish all the information desired—or if you want to verify what the customer has stated—you have several reliable ways of finding out.

Other business firms with which the applicant has done credit business expect to furnish details of their experience when asked—but (for legal reasons) *only* when asked by somebody *with an interest to protect*. Banks supply information about both individuals and businesses. Local and national credit bureaus maintain files on concerns and individuals with whom their members have done credit business, and this information is available (on request) to any member. Credit-rating agencies (like Dun & Bradstreet) publish volumes containing credit reports on business firms; if a firm isn't listed and you are a subscriber to its service, it will furnish a special report. Your sales personnel can help to fill in the picture. And a trade association in many instances can give you pertinent information.

When the information you receive is favorable, you will of course approve the application and set up the account. Because of the sheer weight of numbers, most credit approvals are form messages, especially when no purchase (and shipment) of goods is involved. Many stores do no more than send a printed announcement card like the following:

THE J. P. BOWEN COMPANY

Is pleased to open a charge
account for you and welcome you to
our family of regular patrons

We hope you will make regular use
of your charge account

Such a notification sent promptly is certainly better than nothing. Yet it falls far short of what a good credit letter can do to strengthen the credit relationship, promote goodwill, forestall collection problems, and stimulate sales.

Establishing the basis for credit

In credit approvals you may, as an effective credit device, take advantage of the simple, obvious psychology of praise or approval. If you place a customer on the credit list because of a prompt-pay rating, you should say so. Being told about the good rating encourages effort to maintain that rating. The same is true for some reflections of favorable capacity or capital positions.

The reference should not be lengthy; in fact, it is preferably absorbed subordinately in the extension of credit or the explanation of terms. It is a significant reminder to the customer that credit is an earned privilege which requires care, thought, and effort to maintain. Too, thus established, it may serve as an effective collection appeal to the customer if the account begins to get slow.

So forceful is this device in the opinion of one experienced credit manager that letters to credit applicants with prompt-pay records were often only one sentence:

> We have received from your references the reports of your fine pay habits and shall be very happy to have a regular monthly charge account with you.

Obviously, this letter should accomplish more than it does. But it is a good example of the significance of the credit basis.

Here are two other examples of how you can establish the basis:

> Your excellent credit record in Joplin establishes you as a preferred charge customer at Allen Tilby's. The charge identification plate enclosed will make available to you a wealth of quality merchandise gathered from the four corners of the world.

--

> Because of your good credit standing, earned by your personal honesty and the sizable amount of property you own, we have placed your name on our list of regular credit customers.

Form letters can—and do—through careful wording, employ the strategy; the one-sentence letter to prompt-pay accounts is a good example. You can phrase the credit extension and the basis in broad enough fashion to cover a large number of cases.

Explanation of terms

Unless a firm wants to encourage delayed payments, the initial extension of credit should make unmistakably clear how payments are expected, with the confident assumption that the customer will comply with the terms. Even a form card or letter can easily incorporate a simple statement like one of the following:

> On the first of each month you will receive an itemized statement of your purchases made through the 25th day of the preceding month; purchases made after the 25th appear on the following month's bill. Your payment is expected by the 10th.

--

> Under our system of cycle billing your statement of a month's purchases will be mailed to you on the 17th of each month; settlement is expected within 10 days.

(Under cycle billing, bills are prepared and mailed at various intervals throughout the month: names beginning with *A*, on the 1st; with *B*, on the 2d; with *M*, on the 16th and 17th, etc. Matching names and dates in form mailings is a simple matter.)

In special letters the clear, specific explanation of the terms not only can prevent misunderstanding and delay but can also serve as a stimulus to prompt pay. How far to go with the explanation depends on the reader's credit knowledge and reputation. To those you think know and respect credit practices, you would tell only what the terms are; explaining that 2/10, n/30 means take a deduction of 2 percent if paid in 10 days or pay the whole in 30 days would insult such a reader. To a reader who is new to credit business or just barely passes your credit evaluation, however, you had better make the terms not only clear and emphatic but concrete (i.e., show the prompt-pay benefits as savings in money, what it will buy, and the continued credit privilege):

> Under our regular credit terms of 2/10, n/30, you can save $1.36 on this order alone if your check is in the mail by July 10—which will almost pay for another enamel display tray. Your check for the net of $68 by July 30, however, will keep you in the preferred-customer class.

Such specificness is not possible, of course, except in an individually written letter or special paragraph. But the credit extension, whenever possible, should be an individual letter; it is worth the extra money in its salutary effect on the customer.

To stop with the approval, the basis, and the terms would be foolish, however; a good credit writer can also help to further sales—through resale material on goods, resale on the house, or sales-promotion material on other allied goods. All should focus on repeat sales.

Stimulating sales

In credit approvals, sales-building passages should definitely be low pressure; if the service attitude does not dominate, the greedy overtones can repel the reader. But the writer of the following letter, you will note, is careful to tie in a service-to-you reference to all sales-building passages and thus make the customer feel welcome rather than pounced upon:

> Your excellent credit record in Joplin establishes you as a preferred charge customer at Allen Tilby's.
>
> The charge identification plate enclosed will make available to you a wealth of quality merchandise gathered from the four corners of the world.
>
> On the first of each month you will receive an itemized statement of your purchases made through the 25th day of the preceding month: purchases made after the 25th appear on the following month's bill. You'll be prompt in paying your account on time, we know, for our terms—payment in full by

the 10th—are the same as the terms of the stores with which you've been trading in Joplin.

You'll find that our merchandise is just as close as your telephone when you haven't time for shopping. Ask for Paula Penn, our personal shopper, who will be glad to assist you. We'll have your purchases at your door by 5 o'clock if you order no later than noon.

When you come down to Allen Tilby's, you'll find experienced sales personnel ready to help you select exactly the things you want. For all-day shopping or just for a delightful downtown luncheon you may enjoy the Oval Room on the eighth floor. The spacious parking lot just across the street is available to you when you shop at Allen Tilby's.

Since you have just moved to a new home, you may be especially interested in the Home Furnishings Sale, which will extend through next week. Whatever you need, come in soon and let us serve you.

The same considerations enable you to write good credit approvals to dealers. Two minor differences exist in circumstances (but not as far as writing principles are concerned): One is terms (discounts, datings, and number of days allowed); the other is the identification of the credit limit. Few letters to consumers ever identify a limit (although one may go on the office record); most mercantile credit arrangements include limits as part of the explanation of terms.

To prevent—as much as possible—the limit from appearing to be a penalty, with consequent negative reactions by the customer, a good writer phrases it in positive language, as in the following:

The No-Flame you ordered

20 gallons @ $6 .... $120

was shipped to you freight prepaid this morning by the L & M Railroad; it should arrive in Jackson by the weekend. The amount of this shipment has been debited to your newly opened account, which we are glad to open on the basis of your strong personal capital.

Under our regular terms of 2/10, n/60, your No-Flame will cost you only $117.60 if you send your check by May 2; the full $120 is due on June 21. At any one time you may carry as much as $250 worth of No-Flame or other Bronson products on account.

With the increasing demand for No-Flame you will find it a rapid seller—and a good profit item at the usual markup of $3 a can. With your shipment you will receive attractive window displays which our other dealers have found helpful.

Silentol, a flame-resistant, sound-decreasing plaster, is another item your home-building customers will like. The cost is only a fraction more than for conventional plaster. For a trial shipment, just fill out the enclosed order blank and drop it in the mail; we'll send your Silentol to you—along with display material—within a few days.

Making the customer welcome

Much is said and written in credit circles about making the customer feel appreciated. Indeed, the opening welcoming the customer to the "growing number of satisfied customers" or to the "X, X, & Y family" is standard with so many credit writers that it is stereotyped. The customer is more interested in finding out the decision on the application than in such welcomes or in any of the writer's personal (especially if selfish) expressions of happiness at adding another name to a list. If you approve the credit (implied by sending the goods immediately when the application accompanies an order), establish the basis, explain the terms positively, and then follow with resale and sales promotion material concretely implying the desire to be of service, your reader will not be in doubt over whether you appreciate business. By implication you adequately establish such welcomes and thank-you's.

If, despite these suggestions and illustrations, you feel the necessity for either of these expressions, place it near the end of your letter.

The checklist (p. 138) summarizes our major suggestions about credit approvals, although, as always, you should apply them with discretion. We *know* they don't all apply in all cases.

SIMPLE CLAIMS AND ADJUSTMENT APPROVALS

[When things go wrong, see that you don't go with them.]

Claims offer you as a buyer the opportunity to get adjustments on unsatisfactory goods and services you have bought. If you are a seller and therefore the receiver of claims, you welcome them! They offer you an opportunity to discover and correct defects in your goods and services. And your adjustment letters are excellent opportunities for you to build or destroy goodwill. Whether you make the most of your opportunities in either claims or adjustments depends heavily on your attitude.

Any claim and adjustment situation necessarily involves negatives. Somebody is dissatisfied and unhappy. One of the major jobs in writing either claim or adjustment letters is to keep these emotionally based negatives from stealing the show and making the situation worse. What you have learned about goodwill, resale, and handling of negative material is especially important in adjustment letters.

Direct claims

You will probably write good claim letters if you remember these often-forgotten points (which serve as a checklist for direct claims):

1. *Progressive firms like claims, instead of disliking them, because they suggest ways of improvement. So if you think you have a just claim, go ahead.*

Credit Approval Checklist

1. The direct opening should approve credit quickly.
   a) Inject a cheerful, welcoming, ungrudging tone in approving credit, neither condescending nor preachy.
   b) When you are shipping goods, say so in the first line. Shipping the goods first also implies credit approval.
   c) Name the goods specifically (don't call them an "order"!); state the amount (of goods and dollars, or send an invoice).
   d) In general, you'd better identify the method of shipment.
   e) Choose words that get the goods to the reader; don't stop with just getting them onto a freight car.
   f) A touch of resale (say a favorable adjective) is desirable early, but don't slow up your opening with much resale/goodwill.
   g) Use figures and symbols in order and acknowledgment letters.
   h) Take care of all legal details: item prices, freight charges, total. You may assume an invoice or tabulate here.
2. The credit agreement/relation:
   a) For restraint, explain how the customer earned this credit.
   b) Although you might identify terms incidentally in the opening, later (for people who might not understand or respect them properly) you'd explain by
      1) Attaching your interpretation of the terms to the purchase.
      2) Concretizing the discount with specific savings figures (maybe a free unit of the purchase, a month's phone bill . . .).
      3) Bringing in prompt-pay education, in a tone that implies your confidence that the reader will comply.
   c) With its negative potentialities, any credit-limit talk needs a you-viewpoint introduction and positive statement. You might want to label it temporary.
   d) But you don't want to imply "If you don't like these terms, we'll change them."
3. Your resale or sales promotion material in closing the letter:
   a) Include reassuring comments about the reader's good choice.
   b) Mention your services and selling aids concretely.
   c) Consider selling the reader some allied or seasonal goods.
   d) Regardless of how you close, let it point to future orders.
   e) Be specific, not wooden and dull, as in "We have enjoyed serving you and look forward to supplying your future needs."
4. Your appreciation is best worked in incidentally, subordinately.
5. Transitions are easier with a logical order of points.
6. Watch the tone throughout the letter.
   a) Avoid FBI implications about the credit investigation and condescending, mandatory, or selfish explanation of terms.
   b) Proportion affects your tone too; don't talk terms too much.

Many firms even advertise the request: "If you like our products, tell others; if you don't, tell us." Often they encourage claims by "double-your-money-back" guarantees and the like.

2. *When things go wrong, the firm surely did not intend to mistreat the customer. Almost certainly the reader of your claim letter had nothing to do with the dissatisfaction. So keep your shirt on!*

Very few manufacturers expect every item they manufacture to be perfect. They know that even after careful checking, defects may sometimes show up. Nearly always they expect to replace or repair defective merchandise which is returned. This is a more efficient system than to insist on perfection in manufacturing—and consequently higher prices. The consumer who gets defective merchandise and takes the attitude that the seller tried to cheat, then, is usually wrong. In most cases, to get satisfaction, all that's necessary is to make a simple claim such as the following:

```
When the set of Syracuse dinner dishes I ordered from you on
November 1 arrived the day before Thanksgiving, I found that
one of the coffee cups was cracked and one of the dinner
plates had a defective design.

The excelsior around the cup was thin—evidently too thin to
protect the cup from jars in transit.

I am returning the two imperfect pieces by express.  Will you
please replace them to complete my set?
```

Even though a product is defective, almost certainly the person who reads your claim letter didn't make it, check it, or sell it to you. To be nasty to that person is to be quite unfair and unreasonable, even foolish. Instead of creating a favorable mood that will help you get satisfaction, you turn this possible ally against you if you write a nasty letter.

3. *When you know just what is wrong and what is required to set things right, you should make a definite claim; otherwise, explain and ask for an inspection.*

Sometimes you can be sure that the only fair adjustment is a refund of your money or a complete replacement of the product. On other occasions you can see that replacement of a part or proper adjustment of a machine will correct the trouble. You therefore ask definitely for what is necessary to make things right, as in the preceding letter.

Sometimes, however, the product just isn't right, but you don't know exactly what is wrong. Your claim then should be an explanation of how the product is failing to satisfy you and a request for the necessary action. You can make your own estimate and request that action (as in the illustration on p. 140), call in third parties to estimate (as on automobile insurance claims, like that on p. 141), or ask the firm to investigate and take the indicated action. Here are two examples:

```
I think you will be interested in my experience with XXX
outside white house paint used on my house this past summer.
```

A union painter applied three coats according to directions on the can. About three months later smoky streaks began to appear where water runs from the eaves and valleys.

At first I thought the discoloration was from the green roof paint or the stain of the cedar shingles, but the same thing appears on the garage, which has an unpainted tin roof.

Various theories have been advanced concerning the smutty streaks. Some friends have suggested mildew, but my common sense says no. Some have suggested dirt, but it will not wash off. A chemist friend says that the sulfur in the atmosphere here may combine with the lead of the paint to make a sulfur-lead compound that is a smoky color.

So you see that I don't know what the cause is. But if your paint didn't hold its color, I'm sure that you are interested in knowing why. And I feel sure that if you find your product at fault, you will want to grant me an adjustment.

--

Will you please investigate and let me know your decision?

The Dexter fluorescent desk lamp I purchased at your store October 5 has been satisfactory in every way but one.

When in use, the lamp operates coolly and soundlessly; but as soon as the lamp is switched off, something inside produces a humming sound. Not only is the hum annoying, but I fear that it suggests a fire hazard.

I'm returning the lamp to you for repair or replacement, whichever you find necessary.

Since I've lots of reading to do, will you please rush it back to me?

4. *Sometimes a touch of humor can relieve the pressure in small claims.* Somewhat like the nasty tone (Point 2), another common error in writing claim letters is the writer's becoming deadly serious about small matters. A claim for replacement of a defective $3 item makes the writer look silly when written as if it were a matter of life and death. If the situation is really serious, of course, you would not want to treat it lightly. But to avoid the too-serious tone in small matters and make the reader an ally instead of a critic, you can often use humor effectively. You may inject only a touch or two in the letter, or the whole thing may be humorous.

Several dangers confront you if you decide to be humorous:

1. A failing attempt to be funny is worse than no attempt.
2. Humor may make you write a longer letter than necessary.
3. Humor at the reader's expense will nearly always arouse resentment.
4. Humor which verges on the vulgar or sacrilegious may offend.

The following successful letter, which accompanied photocopies of the check and statement, avoids at least the last two dangers.

Gentlemen:

I remember that many years ago one of the happy occurrences in playing Monopoly was to draw a card that said, "Bank Error in Your Favor—Collect $200."

Your September statement for my account (No. 005 461 6) brought back to me for a moment those memories of long ago, for in it there is a "bank error in my favor." It's for only $10.00, but I can't deny I felt a childish little exultation . . . compounded with a modern adult pleasure in catching a computer "goof."

As you can see from the attached photocopies, my check No. 840 was written for $269.23, but entered into your computerized bookkeeping system as $279.23. So my balance should be $3,189.77.

Would you issue a credit memo for $10.00 to adjust this? Or a card that says, "Bank Error in Your Favor—Collect $10.00?"

If you think bankers don't have a sense of humor, a banker—not the computer, which apparently has no sense of humor—sent back a credit memo for $10.00 carefully made out, "Bank error in your favor."

Usually a firm will grant an adjustment merely on the strength of a customer's explanation of what is wrong and suggestions for a fair settlement. In that case you would be ridiculous to misjudge the situation and write a too-strong claim. Unless you have good reason to believe otherwise, assume that the firm will be cooperative. Your letter should simply explain the specific facts and state your claim. Little or no persuasion seems necessary; hence you use no appeal beyond brief reference to the guarantee, reputation for fair dealing, and the like.

This kind of direct claim (A–plan) may start with the requested action, or it may start with the date and conditions of purchase. Beginning with the history of the case is a little less antagonizing and a little more persuasive. The middle part is a carefully planned, complete, and specific explanation of the facts. A test of the adequacy of the explanation is to ask whether it is all you would want to know if you had to decide on the claim. The ending, then, is a request for action. It should be as specific as the conditions will permit (Point 3, p. 139).

CLAIM FOR DAMAGES DONE TO MY CAR BY YOUR CLIENT
(Mr. K. C. Hall, Gary, Indiana—License CG 3035)

On June 9, about 15 or 20 miles west of Decatur, Illinois, on Highway 48, I was driving 55 m.p.h. when I overtook a car going about 35. When I was almost even with this car, passing it, something bumped my car hard on the left rear fender and door, shoving me hard to the right and damaging my car.

The something that hit my car (a new four-door XXXX, Illinois license 885-009) was a late-model green XXXXXXXX driven by your client, Mr. Hall. I estimated that he was driving at least 70, for he whisked on by me before stopping, just as I went on around the car I had overtaken.

Inspection revealed that his car was damaged on the back part of the right front fender and on the right front door, mine on the left rear fender and door.

Certainly the accident was no fault of mine, for I was driving in an entirely normal and legal manner. Good judgment on his

```
part would have told him that I was going to pass the car
ahead, since I was overtaking it at an estimated difference of
20 m.p.h.  Thus he should have checked his speed and waited.

He probably blew his horn, as he said he did, but I could not
hear it because a diesel train on a nearby parallel track was
blowing very loudly.  He probably realized that I did not hear
when I continued to pull left to pass, but he was driving too
fast to control his car.

Since I consider him completely responsible for the accident
and damages, I hereby make claim for repairs to my car, as
listed on any one of the three enclosed estimates.
```

Adjustment approvals

Adjustment policies. Invariably a claim represents loss of goodwill and of confidence in the goods or in the firm. The adjustment writer's key job is to minimize those losses by satisfying customers as far as possible at a reasonable cost to the company.

Some companies try to dodge the basic problem by almost literally adopting the policy that the customer is always right. They figure that the few unfair claims cost less in adjustment losses than the liberal policy pays in goodwill.

Other firms take the opposite view and make all sales final. Usually they depend on low prices rather than goodwill to attract a type of customer to whom price is the strongest possible appeal.

The great majority take the middle ground between those two extremes: *Treat each claim on its merits, and lean a bit toward giving the customer the benefit of the doubt for the sake of unquestioned fairness and the resulting goodwill.*

This seems to be the most ethical and the most satisfactory policy to most people. Generally a customer will not leave a firm or product after only one disappointment if the firm applies this honest and reasonable policy with finesse. Usually a reasonable person will allow at least a second chance, unless the adjuster loses further goodwill by a poor attitude toward the claim or by bungling techniques in handling it.

Carrying out the recommended policy therefore requires

1. Careful analysis and classification of each claim according to the cause of dissatisfaction and consequently what adjustment is fair.
2. Retaining a reasonable attitude even with testy claimants.
3. Skill in the use of the tools and techniques of adjustment.

Analysis and classification of adjustments. If the evidence in a claim (and from inspection when deemed necessary) shows clearly that the company or the product was at fault, you may replace the article free with a perfect one, repair it free, or take it back and refund the money.

The last is the least desirable for both buyer and seller. The purchase of the article was to get the service it would render. If you take it back, you give the purchaser a problem—to make other arrangements or do without that service. If you replace or repair it, you give the service, regain goodwill, and make a satisfied customer who will perhaps buy from you again and pass on the good word about you and your products to other prospects. Indeed, about the only occasion when you would refund the money is when you see that a perfect specimen of the article will not do the job. And even then, if you have another (perhaps larger or of better quality) which you think will satisfy, you should try to give the service wanted and justify any higher price in terms of advantages.

If responsibility for the dissatisfaction is clearly the buyer's, you will ordinarily refuse the claim. In rare cases you may decide that a compromise or even a full-reparation adjustment will be the wise thing because of the amount of goodwill you can regain at small cost. The weakness in this decision is that it implies your acceptance of responsibility and increases your difficulty in regaining confidence in your goods and service.

Whatever your action, your major job is justifying your decision and (usually) educating the customer. By writing your letter as education to the buyer in the proper use and care of the product, you may establish the responsibility by implication, avoid irritating the claimant, and prevent future trouble.

If responsibility for the dissatisfaction is uncertain or divided between buyer and product, you will suggest a compromise or make a full adjustment. Again the educational function of the letter is usually important.

When you approve the adjustment, the discussion of favorable replies to inquiries and requests prepares you rather well to write full-reparation adjustment letters, which are in fact answers to requests (claims). They are essentially the same in organization and psychology, but with some basic differences. In answering requests you have no legal or moral obligation to do anything against your will; in answering claims, you have a legal and moral obligation to be fair.

Attitude of the adjuster. If a firm's adjuster thinks most claims are dishonest or from chronic gripers, this attitude will eventually reduce the number of claims—and probably the firm's sales too. People won't trade where they are considered dishonest or unreasonable.

But most people are honest. Out of 5 million customers of a big mail order firm, only 2,712, or one twentieth of 1 percent, tried to take advantage of the firm in five years. So an adjuster who thinks every claim is an attempt to defraud the firm is wrong in both fact and attitude.

Claims are an invaluable clue to weaknesses in a company's products, methods, services, or personnel. But the weaknesses won't be corrected if the adjuster considers most claims dishonest.

On the other hand, if you start with the attitude that a claimant may be misinformed but is honest and reasonable, you will be right most of the time, and you will do much better. You will use claims as pointers to improvements in your firm's goods and operations, and your adjustment letters will thank customers for the help they have given. (Even claims where the buyer is completely at fault may point to a need for, say, better instructions to users.) But more important, you create a pleasant climate in which people will buy more freely because they know they can get reasonable adjustments if anything goes wrong.

In addition to this sound attitude, you need a thick skin to be an adjuster. Many claimants are not calm. As a wise adjuster, therefore, you will ignore personal taunts. Remember the old saying, "You can't win an argument with a customer; even when you win you lose." So defend your firm, your products, and yourself insofar as you can by explanations; otherwise accept the claims made. Thus you create a climate of goodwill and good business.

A claim represents customer dissatisfaction all right, but it does not necessarily involve really strong negatives which you cannot almost completely overcome with your fair-minded attitude and skillful use of the adjuster's tools and techniques.

Adjustment tools and techniques. *Using resale.* Since the adjustment writer's main job is to regain goodwill and confidence, you will find resale a highly useful tool. Probably nowhere else in letter writing is it more important. Indeed, the main job of an adjuster is essentially the same as the purpose of resale—to recover or strengthen goodwill and confidence in the integrity and efficiency of a firm and/or the quality of its goods. Naturally, then, resale is the main tool for doing that job.

Making positive explanations. Effective resale is impossible, however, unless you avoid the following special pitfalls which frequently trap the untrained adjustment letter writer:

1. Inadequate or inept explanation that leaves the reader thinking slipshod methods of manufacturing or marketing caused the trouble. Explain how careful you really are.
2. Dwelling on the reader's dissatisfaction or likelihood of being a lost customer.
3. Passing the buck by attributing the difficulty to a new clerk or an act of God.
4. Trying to hide in the bigness of your firm. About the only way you can use bigness as an acceptable explanation is to sell it in terms of reader benefits along with its weakness.
5. Stressing your openhandedness. The reader does not want to be considered a beggar, given things not deserved.
6. Suggesting future trouble. You only put undesirable ideas into the customer's head if you say, "If you have any more difficulty, let us know," or even "I don't believe you'll have any more difficulty." In fact, a big problem in adjustments is what to do about the inherent negative in them.

Handling inherent negatives. As an adjustment writer, you therefore need to be a master of the techniques for dealing with negatives. They will be one of your stumbling blocks, for every adjustment situation is full of them. You'll do well to remember the letter writer's definition of *negative* as anything unpleasant to the reader. Moreover, you should remember that *a letter writer avoids negative material when he can and subordinates it when he can't.* You'll find that you can usually avoid most of the goodwill killers like the following, which creep into the letters of untrained adjustment writers:

you claim	policy	damaged	delay
you say	amazed	broken	inconvenience
you state	fault	defective	regret
you (plus any accusing verb)	surprised	unable	sorry

Such wording need not appear. Prune out the negative wording (and implications). Substitute positive phrasing.

Letters approving the adjustment. Since an adjustment approval is a good-news letter (A–plan), you answer the reader's big question in the first sentence as fast as you can. Not only should this sentence tell that you are approving the adjustment, but it should avoid any grudging tone and refrain from recalling the dissatisfaction any more than necessary. You might as well not approve the adjustment, insofar as goodwill is concerned, as do so in a grudging tone. And of course, reminding your reader of trouble by using negative words would hurt rather than help.

The fact that you have approved the adjustment gives you a natural basis for some resale talk on the house. You should use it by interpreting the approval as evidence that you stand behind guarantees and treat the customer right, or something similar.

Somewhere in the letter, but not necessarily right after the good news and its interpretation, you should express appreciation for the claimant's calling your attention to the situation (because the information helps the firm to keep goods and services up to par). This thank you does several important things quickly: (1) It shows the reader that you are fair-minded and do not take a distrusting or bitter attitude toward claims. (2) It is basically resale in showing that you are interested in retaining (if not improving) your standards for goods and services. (3) It makes the customer feel good because a claim seems welcome and appears to get careful consideration.

Of course, if you are taking any steps to prevent recurrence of claims such as you are answering, you should explain them (to rebuild confidence) and give the customer as much credit as the facts allow. Any reader likes to hear that "On the basis of helpful suggestions like yours, we have decided. . . ."

The biggest part of your letter will be an explanation of the situation. If the product was obviously defective or the firm was at fault and no explanation will put either in a better light, you'd better accept the fact and frankly admit the error or defect rather than make excuses. If you explain specifically how your firm tries to see that everything goes well, most readers will accept it as due precaution and will understand that mistakes do occasionally creep in, despite reasonable care. If you have statistics to show how effective your system is in avoiding mistakes and defective goods, they may be effective in rebuilding the customer's confidence and goodwill. You want to be careful, though, not to present such data in a way that seems to say the reader must be odd to have trouble when nearly all your other customers don't.

Although you can't honestly or safely promise that it will never happen again, you can end pleasantly. Having covered the good news, the explanation, the thanks, and any necessary action of the reader, you can end looking forward, not backward. Apologies or other reminders of past dissatisfaction merely leave a bad taste in the reader's mouth. A light touch of resale—or even sales promotion material, if you have a related article you think would serve well—can provide you with a sincere, success-conscious look forward to future business. The customers so well treated will probably return.

The following letter illustrates most of the points:

> The enclosed credit memorandum for $39.60 is an example of Strong-Arch's continuous effort to satisfy our customers in prices, merchandise, and service. We are glad to make this adjustment, requested in your letter of November 28 on the 2 dozen pairs, assorted sizes, of Cordovan Brogues we shipped you last week.
>
> How your shoes were billed becomes clear from a look at the mechanics of our Billing Department. Whenever our salespeople take an order, they enter a symbol for the particular style, size, and color of shoe. In preparing the invoice, the Billing Department automatically enters the latest price, which in this case was $21.50. At the time Mr. Green took your order, this price had been in effect only two days. He entered the old price of $19.85, which was detected and changed in billing. On future orders any discrepancies between orders and current price lists will go to one individual for special handling.
>
> We are grateful for your first order. As these shoes become popular with your customers, we know you will want to add some other Strong-Arch models and styles to your stock. All give long wear and comfort to the customer and good profit margins to the dealer.
>
> In addition to the Cordovan Brogue, you may want to offer your customers a new style, the Strong-Arch Loafer. It is made of top-grain cowhide, with leather soles and rubber heels, and is double-stitched for longer wear. Page 4 of the enclosed leaflet shows you the Loafer as advertised in this month's <u>Esquire</u>.
>
> When you order these loafers (at only $14.95 a pair), we'll include in the shipment a split sample shoe so you can show your customers the exact structure.

Although the letter below does not actually send the check in the first sentence, as is usually desirable, it does say emphatically that the adjust-

Checklist for Approving Adjustments

1. Make the beginning fast, informative, pleasant, and reassuring.
   a) Open with the full reparation—a specific statement of what you are doing.
   b) Avoid any grudging tone.
   c) Build up the favorable reaction with a few resale words.
   d) Too much resale on defective products before explanation may bring an "Oh yeah?"
2. Throughout the letter, avoid emphasis on the disappointing aspects by avoiding negative words.
3. Explain fully, honestly, and reassuringly any favorable facts.
   a) Include a goodwill-building sentence—either that you're glad to make the adjustment or that you welcome the report as an aid in maintaining quality and service.
   b) Whichever you choose, be sure your facts relate logically to your wording of the adjustment you've made.
   c) Judicially, impartially—and preferably impersonally—establish the reason for the mishap in the minimum number of words. Often you can effectively imply the reason in your explanation of corrective measures taken or the ordinary care taken.
   d) Whether you name or imply the source of error, give concrete evidence of normally correct, safe shipments of high-quality goods, or—if applicable—explain changes you are making to prevent recurrence of the difficulty.
   e) Be quick to admit error; don't appear to be buck-passing.
   f) Avoid suggesting frequency of error.
4. Ask for any necessary cooperation from the customer. For example:
   a) Be definite and polite in asking the customer to sign necessary forms.
   b) Clear up what is to be done with the original article if you're replacing it.
   c) Make the customer's action as easy as possible ("When the driver calls to pick up the original shipment, just have . . .").
5. Close pleasantly with a forward look.
   a) Don't tear up your good positive efforts with a backward look apologizing or otherwise recalling the disappointing aspects.
   b) Do leave the customer with a pleasant reminder of the pleasurable use of the perfect article now in hand, if applicable.
   c) You may end the letter with resale talk, but sales promotional material on an allied article may well suggest your additional thoughtfulness—and just may pick up an extra sale.

ment has been approved. Moreover, this letter (in answer to the claim letter on page 391), gives a clear explanation and strong resale:

> You most certainly will get a refund on the XXX suit you purchased, for we support our salesmen in whatever they promise a customer.
>
> The salesman who told you that we would have no sale on XXX suits was sincere. The XXX manufacturers have never before allowed their suits to be sold at reduced prices. We were notified one week before our summer clothing sale this year that they were permitting a reduction for the first time.
>
> We thank you for calling our attention to this situation, and we are glad to enclose our check for $13.80.
>
> When you again need clothing, see our salesmen in the men's department. You can rely on what they tell you, with full confidence that we will back them up.

Sometimes you will need the customer's help on a few details such as filling out blanks for recovery of damages from a transportation company and returning defective articles. Be sure to cover such points in the one letter to avoid unnecessary correspondence. And in doing so, make the reader's action as easy as possible.

> Your Old South cream and sugar set is being mailed prepaid today so that it will arrive two or three days before the wedding.
>
> Since the Old South set is in keeping with southern traditions, it will attract favorable glances and comments as guests look over the gifts.
>
> The set is being carefully wrapped with plenty of newspaper and shipped in a corrugated box of 3/16-inch thickness. This is thicker than required by freight carriers, but it will be standard packing for all Old South china from now on. Your report has helped us to improve our service. Thank you.
>
> To simplify getting the insurance due from the Postal Service on the first shipment, we are sending a claim form completely filled out except for your signature. Will you please sign it and use the reply envelope for mailing it back to us?
>
> The bride and groom will like the antebellum motif of the Old South set and will attach many pleasant memories to it as the years go by.

The checklist for approving adjustments (p. 147) is a comprehensive enough to cover most situations, but not all points are likely to apply to any one letter.

DIRECT INQUIRY CASES

1. Write the Empire Motor Hotel, P.O. Box 140, North Bay, Ontario, to reserve a room, one bed (preferably queen or king), two people, one night, July 9. Your AAA book lists widely varying prices and says part of the Empire has been renovated and part not. Ask for a room in the new part. You want to guarantee your reservation, so include your Bank Ameri-card number 4367–090–076–876 and date of expiration, and your AAA membership number 09–07–009243. If the Empire can not accommodate you, ask the clerk to make reservations at some comparable place nearby. You will be leaving your city before you can get confirmation.

2. For Linda Kehres, 72 Springbrook Road, Berea, Ohio 45207, write The Southwestern Mutual Life Insurance Company, 875 Texas Avenue, Dallas, Texas 75227, asking for information on policy 5017681 insuring her husband, Kelly P. Kehres. Kelly can not write because of some brain damage resulting from a serious accident. You want to know the current gross cash value, the gross loan value, when it was issued, the plan, and the death benefit.

3. Executive Director, American Business Communication Association, Francis W. Weeks, 317-B David Kinley Hall, University of Illinois, Urbana, Illinois 61801, wants to ask one of your authors, C. W. Wilkinson, Department of Behavioral Studies, University of Alabama, University, Alabama 35486, to write the publisher Richard D. Irwin, Inc. for the Company's mailing list of business writing teachers. Weeks wants to solicit them as possible members for the American Business Communication Association. ABCA has used lists from Ronald Press, South-Western, and Prentice-Hall. Weeks wants the name of the person at Irwin in Homewood, Illinois, to contact. With rising costs, ABCA has to work hard to keep the money coming in, and therefore a good membership campaign is needed in spring and fall. Write the letter for Weeks.

4. As the person in charge of personnel placement with a big chain of discount stores, K-Smart, 8700 Cameron Road, Silver Springs, Maryland 20901, you interview and place in stores (after a management training program of one year) able people first as assistant managers and then as managers. This morning you talked with a volatile but nervous 24-year-old, Charles Arnold. As he is soon to graduate from the University of Maryland, Arnold applied for work in your training program. He seemed to be ambitious, energetic, and determined to please. While working on his business administration degree (majoring in marketing), he clerked 22 hours a week for four years at Switzer's Men's Store, 239 West Second, Rockville, Maryland 20852. Besides waiting on customers, he sometimes helped decorate the windows, move merchandise, and mark goods. As an enlisted man in the Army, he did routine work. The only other work experience he had was checking stock, sweeping out, and carrying out packages in Alpine's Supermarket the summer after he was a junior in high school. As you talked with him, you noticed how much he interrupted you—was this just a nervous habit? Apparently he has plenty of determination. In some ways you felt that he was so busy thinking about his own ambition that

he didn't follow what you were saying. To answer your questions about him, write Daniel Bowman, manager of Switzer's Men's Store. Also find out if Bowman thinks Arnold would irritate customers. Would he be able to direct salespeople?

5. As chairman of the site-selection committee for the annual sales conference of DuMont Associates, Inc., DuMont Plaza, Providence, Rhode Island 02909, you have been examining brochures from three resort hotels selected by your committee as candidates to host the conference. All three hotels, which were selected because of their accessibility to all DuMont divisions, listed "convention facilities" as one of their attractions. What you have to know, however, are the sizes of the auditoriums and conference rooms, whether these rooms are in the hotel or some adjoining area, and what kinds of PA systems they have (if they have them).

Since the conference will be a week long—Monday through Sunday—(use exact dates) and last over a week end (the main banquet will be Saturday evening), you will also want to find out what cultural events are scheduled in each of the three areas for that week, what shows, exhibits, concerts, etc. are available. You would like more information about each hotel's golf course and swimming pool, especially the golf course, since DuMont interdivision doubles golf tournament (the I.M.A. Thacker trophy will be awarded at the Saturday banquet) is always one of the conference highlights.

Write a letter that could be sent to any of three eastern U.S. hotels selected by your committee. You must have the information soon, so that you can firm up the plans for the meeting three months hence.

6. The Louisville, Kentucky, Health Department has recently made a crackdown on substandard housing in the city. When four of your block of six two-bedroom frame houses will be empty in the summer quarter, you plan to remodel and repaint all your units, which you rent to students during the school year. You will move the tenants in the occupied housing into the remodeled units as they are finished. Your most important concern at present is getting rid of the roaches that infest your properties. You tried Kentucky Bug Control, but the roaches grew fat on the stuff used.

As Farley Moody, 809 Caldwell Street, Louisville, Kentucky 40208, write a letter to Bugg-Out Pest Control, Inc., 987 Shawnee, Topeka, Kansas 66601, asking for information about Hurry-X, a cyanide-based extermination bomb which Pest Control's ad in *Better Living* claimed will kill every living thing in the house, from ants to bats. However, you have to find out several things about the product: How to prepare the house and set off the bombs (can anybody do it?); how dangerous to human beings is the stuff; is there any residue that might affect pets and children (some of your tenants will have both); how long will the bugs stay away before you have to do it again; does Bugg-Out guarantee Hurry-X? The price of $15 seems reasonable to you; but before you order the six bombs, you want the above information.

7. You and your spouse have recently set up a typing service in Ann Arbor, Michigan. Your company specializes in theses and dissertations, but you also type letters, short papers, reports, etc. Much to your satisfaction the market for your services is larger than you expected and is rapidly growing. To handle the increased business, you have hired 20 part-time typists. Most of them are student wives, and they cannot afford to buy the large, professional typewriters your company now uses.

To solve this problem, you have rented a storefront; but you now need 15 typewriters with tables and chairs, a $12,000 investment if you buy the equipment new. You noticed in the Flint, Michigan, newspaper that Vulcan Supplies, 986 Lansing Road, Flint 48505, is offering reconditioned ABM typewriters for sale at $200 apiece and reconditioned chairs and tables for $50 a set (set means chair and table). That's a total of about $3,700, considerably less than $12,000. Write to Vulcan asking how long the typewriters had been used, and if they are guaranteed for any defective parts or workmanship in the future. You need to have typewriter tables that will have casters that lock. Since your typists will be sitting long hours, you are interested in padded, comfortable chairs that swivel.

Assume that you are Bobbie Moore, 987 Dobbie Road, Ann Arbor, Michigan 48104.

8. As advertising manager of Lambent Products, 4273 Scintilla St., Chicago, Ill., 60681, you are excited about your new product, "Focal-Photic" taillight lenses and reflectors. The optically innovative reflectors and the convergent lenses reduce loss of light to a minimum and project the maximum amount of light in a "wide-beam" pattern. Your company thinks "Focal-Photic" represents a real advance in safety lighting for road vehicles.

Now you need a way for your company's salesmen to show prospective customers how your new product is different and better than others. Obviously a motion picture or slide presentation would be nice, but your budget won't stand the cost. Besides, your salesmen resist carrying projectors on calls. You've heard that an outfit in California has a cheap, hand-held viewer that uses some sort of film strip. A call to a friend gets you an address: Obscura Co., 556 Meniscus Blvd., Los Angeles, Calif., 96432.

Write Obscura asking about availability of the viewer, a complete description, details on the filmstrip, who makes the filmstrip, what you need to start with (color negatives? slides? what size?), and above all, costs. Do prices vary with quantity? What about different quantities of strips and viewers? Are replacement viewers and filmstrips available should you need them later? And how long will it take you to get them if you place an order? Does Obscura have any special facilities for artwork, etc. that you should use (and at what cost) or can you use your regular suppliers?

9. As entertainment director for the Student Government Spring Sing-Out Festival at your university, one of your jobs is to hire rock bands for the three-day Sing-Out and Stomp that accompanies this spring extravaganza (May 23–25). Write a direct inquiry to Elton Fair of the Finch Booking Agency, 908 East Baltimore Avenue, Baltimore, Md. 43186, in which you request the prices and availability of the Electric Wombats, Lincoln Hubcap, and Rubber Stamp groups for your spring show. Tell Elton that he has to let you know within a week so you can firm up your plans.

10. Your company (Shroud, Weeds & Cerement, Inc., White and Sepulcher Streets, Golgotha, Va., 12713) supplies a complete line of mortuary supplies to funeral homes. You have completely revamped your line for the coming season and are going to company-owned station wagons (black, naturally) for your traveling representatives, who cover the United States east of the Mississippi. These new wagons will be delivered by your local Belchmobile dealer in Golgotha.

To introduce your new line of mortuary supplies to your representatives, you have arranged for a week-long sales meeting at the Wooden Kimono Resort near Orlando, Florida. As Sales Manager, you have the thought that Auto-Train might solve several of your problems. You could fly all your representatives to Golgotha, tour them through the plant, deliver their new automobiles to them, and then have Auto-Train take them and the wagons to Florida for the meeting. After the meeting, they could fan out to their territories and begin introducing the new line. You know Auto-Train will take two people and an automobile from Lorton, Virginia, to Deland, Florida, for about $195.

Ask Auto-Train Corp. (826 K St., N.W., Washington, DC 20008) about group fares (23 people, 14 extra-heavy station wagons), schedules, details of payment, and so on. You would like your people to be together in one section of a railroad car for the trip. Also, can arrangements be made for you all to eat together, assuming meals are served. What different accommodations are available, and is the trip overnight?

11. Acting as your teacher, ask McCraw-Hall Films (607 Boylston Street, Boston 02116) whether it has any films on topics you cover in your three courses (business communication, report writing, technical writing). You received the catalog of films for your department, but it lists none pertinent to your particular courses. You will need to make clear the kind of topics in which you are interested. For instance, films on writing freshman themes or term papers would be useless in these functional writing courses, though treatments of such topics as semantics, sentence construction, organization, charts and graphs, and readability would be appropriate. Besides needing to find titles of appropriate films to order for rental, ask if you would be billed for two rentals or one if you show a film to two classes on the same day.

12. Current date/Mr. Robert Sullivan/Century Plaza Suite/1198 Avenue of the Stars/Century City, California 90024. After you heard Sullivan's inspiring talk entitled "The Brotherhood" at the National Convention of Business People of America last week, you write him and ask for copies of the poem "Outwitted" by Edwin Markham and the philosophical statement entitled "I Believe" by John D. Rockefeller, Jr., which Sullivan promised. Enclose an addressed and stamped envelope with your name, B. V. Watson, Watson and Gregg, 4298 Browndale Avenue, Minneapolis, Minnesota 55416.

13. Now that you are about to graduate with a B.A. in (your major), and because the recent recession has reduced the number of jobs in your field, you want to go on to graduate school (in your major). Write one school a letter that, with some modifications, can be sent to the other schools you wish to apply to. Since competition for entry to graduate school in your major is severe, you will need to do some subtle selling by showing your interest in and knowledge of each school, its faculty, the field of study, and graduate work. What will change from letter to letter besides inside addresses are your particular references to the schools you are writing. What you want to find out is the number of places available in the programs. You will also need such items as catalogs and application forms, not to mention special departmental or language requirements. Ask about the availability of fellowships and assistantships and the cost-of-living rating of the city or town where the school is located.

14. One of your jobs as an engineering consultant for Hollywood, Florida's, Better Business Bureau is to provide the Bureau with information to answer consumer complaints. Recently the BBB has received a large number of letters (31) from consumers who were not satisfied with their 19— WW Armadillo automobiles. The main complaint concerned the malfunction of the WW carburetion system; 26 of the consumer letters reported considerable stalling, especially in the morning. Your reply from the WW distributor in Atlanta, although it was informative and cordial, blamed the "hesitation" in the engine on the new, mandatory antipollution devices.

Since the letter from WW did not furnish you enough information for the BBB, you have decided to write to Ralph Nader's Center for Auto Safety (Box 7250, Ben Franklin Station, Washington, D.C. 20044) to ask for the data that the CFAS has gathered on the 19— WW carburetion systems. You read in a recent newspaper article that Mr. Nader had just returned from a trip to Nurmberg, Germany, where he held a week-long conference with WW executives and engineers.

You are writing for John Parham, 1215 Buchanan Street, Hollywood, Florida 33020, of the Hollywood Better Business Bureau.

15. As Arnold MacMillan, personnel director of Furrow, Harrow, and Plough, Tiller Road, Dibble, Ohio 43812, write a direct inquiry to Gordon Lloyd, Director of Sales for the Granger Farm Equipment Co. (811 Michigan Avenue, Chicago, Illinois 60687). You want to find out his opinion of John Muennink, who gave Granger as a reference when you interviewed him for a sales position with your firm. You liked John's confidence, and you have had several favorable replies from other companies that John worked for over the past ten years. You need to know, in addition to an estimate of his sales ability, such confidential information as whether Muennink would be able to handle your Southeast regional area (Va., N.C., S.C., Ga., Ala., and Fla.) and direct the ten-man sales force in this division. John would have to handle large amounts of cash. You also need to know how he got along with his customers and fellow employees. The job also would include considerable paper work and keeping accurate records. You'll also want to know whether Mr. Lloyd feels that John can handle this part of the job too. Use a subject line.

16. *Letterhead:* First Federal Savings and Loan, 1437 Bannock, Denver, Colorado 80204. *Inside address:* Mr. Walter Oliver, Trust Department, First National Bank, Tombstone, Arizona 85638. *Signature block:* Sincerely yours, William P. Barns, Vice President. Use today's date. *Facts:* This is an inquiry about Larry Snipes, former employee of First National for thirteen months. Graduate with *B* average from School of Commerce, Eastern Michigan University, with a major in banking and finance. Two years in Marines, 26 years old; single; worked in university dining room as a waiter while in school; worked in trust department for 13 months of First National in Tombstone but quit because he wanted a more exciting and sophisticated area to live in. The job you have open requires long hours of tedious study as well as tact and patience in dealing with older people (many widows) whose funds are handled by the trust and savings department. If you hire him, he'll train two years under a competent person. Before you hire him, however, you want to know what Mr. Walter Oliver thinks about Snipes' experience for effective work in your savings and trust department. You wonder if Snipes' temperament is suited for hard work. He seemed to be interested in a full social life.

17. In *Family Weekly,* supplement to your Sunday's paper, you noticed an ad from Zodiac Simplex, 315 West Allegon, Lansing, Michigan 48910, on inflatable boats. The ad said that these Dinghies or Runabouts could be stored in a closet, transported in a car's trunk, set up quickly at a beach, riverbank, or dock. Since you are a roving fisherman, the idea of an inflatable boat appeals to you, but you have some questions. What kind of boat would be best to put your 25-hp motor on? Since your wife and son often like to fish with you, would the boat be big enough to hold the three of you? Also, you often like to use a boat for water skiing fun, so you'd want to know if an inflatable Dinghie or Runabout could be used in this way. Cost, too, is a consideration as well as safety. Write the letter as William and Alice Simpson, 14 Glendale Gardens, Pensacola, Florida 32560.

18. Since you are seldom home to answer your phone, you feel that you need some type of answering service. An ad from James Electronics, Inc., 4050 Rockwell Street, Chicago, Illinois 60618, says that the JAMES PHONE-EX adds new dimension to home or office telephones, but there's no mention of how it works or what it looks like. Cost says only $39.95. You are Marie McKenzie, 4890 Mansfield Avenue, Denver, Colorado 80221, distributor and seller of beauty supplies to beauty shops. Write the company and ask if you can receive important messages while you are gone. Find out what it looks like, how it works, and what other costs there are besides the $39.95 charge. Installation? Required software?

19. While reading through last month's issue of *Person's,* you noted an ad for Pephyr 10-speed bicycles. The price to readers who responded to the ad was $100, if you sent in your check with the order by July 1. But before you invest $100 in a bicycle, which you need to travel the two miles to and from the campus each day, you'll want to find out some facts about it:

1. What is it made out of, and is the frame welded or brazed?
2. Does it come assembled? You're not mechanically inclined and you don't want to have to have it put together. Is there any additional charge for assembling the bike?
3. Is there a Pephyr dealer in town, and can you see a 10-speed there? Will the dealer service the bike when it needs it and honor the warranty even though you bought through the mail?
4. *If so,* why buy by mail anyway?

You'll want to have the bike by the first of September, since you want to use it during the fall semester. Write a direct inquiry to Paul Mason, Sales Director, Pephyr Bicycles, Inc., 659 Alfred Avenue, Atlanta, Ga. 30321.

20. No-Insect Strip works like magic, the ad in *Living* reads. Unique insecticide, Repella, seeks out and kills flies, mosquitoes, and other annoying insects wherever they are flying or hiding in an average-size room. *Just what* other annoying insects does it kill—roaches, for example? And moths? And if No-Insect is so effective in annihilating insects in the kitchen, what does it do to open pots and pans on the stove? And open milk bottles and the like? And dishes set out on which to serve meals? What is the price? Each strip lasts up to three months, according to the ad. A three-month accumulation of insects on a strip would hardly be welcome in the kitchen, family room, or bedroom—or *any* room, for that matter. Even if this question can be answered satisfactorily, there are still the questions of secure attachment to walls and surfaces without damaging them. As Director of the Consumer Organization to Protect Our Users Totally, write an inquiry to get answers to these questions and any others you consider pertinent, addressed to Riley Chemical Company, Knightstown, Indiana 46148.

21. *Request from:* Robert A. Piotte, Regional Information Officer, Canadian Forestry Service, Box 650, Sault Ste. Marie, Ontario, Canada.

To: Professor T. M. Callaway, Department of English, University of Florida, Gainesville 32601, U.S.A.

For: Information regarding any intensive short courses in writing, particularly scientific writing. By short Piotte means a course that lasts from a week to six weeks. He wants particulars as to timing, costs, eligibility, etc. As Mr. Piotte, write the request.

22. To honor the retiring Comptroller, executives of Decker and Decker, 7910 Long Avenue, Morton Grove, Illinois 60053, agreed to have an oil portrait unveiled at a banquet in April. The local photography shop could copy a picture, but it does not have the facilities to do fine oil painting. It suggests sending a picture of the Comptroller and getting information from Portrait Studio, 109 Bernardino Road, Albuquerque, New Mexico 87104. Ask what a 24 × 30 inch oil painting would cost. You need to know details about lighting the frame and about different types of frames. One strand of hair is hanging loosely in the photograph, and you need to find out if this hair can be shaded out. Can the eyes be made clearer?

23. A friend told you about the Cleanamatic Company soil extraction system, which is superior to any other cleaning method for rugs. It is the only cleaning process ever developed that actually extracts deep-down, ground-in dirt and grime. A controlled jet of wet steam solution penetrates deep into fabric . . . soil and residue are suspended and actually extracted in one easy operation. No harmful chemicals or messy powders ever touch the carpets. From your home in Ames, Iowa 50601, write the Cleanamatic Company, 908 Main Street, Des Moines, Iowa 50309, for the cost of cleaning wall-to-wall carpeting in a room 15 × 30 feet. The rug is part wool and part acrylic and you need to know if that type of mixture can be cleaned. For several years there has been a stain from a soft drink. You want to know if the cleaning process will remove that stain. Also, you have a baby grand piano and you do not want the steam to damage the piano; so ask about the possibility of moving the piano or of protecting it from the steam in some way.

24. *Letterhead:* Gurnick, Wells, and Fergo, 709 Monument Circle, Indianapolis, Indiana 46204. *Signature block:* Sincerely yours, Angelo C. Fergo, Director, Customer-Auditor Relations. This is a form letter to Beckwith customers about bills they received from D. C. Beckwith Company. *Information:* As a part of an extensive audit, Gurnick, Wells and Fergo has to check the bills which Beckwith has sent its customers. Because of the volume of transactions involved, it is customary to examine accounts for selected, rather than continuous, periods during the year. You are interested in the amount of the bill recorded as $231.18 which was mailed to this customer (you make up the name and address) on (a specific date about six weeks before you're writing). If the customer received this bill and found it to be correct, the customer may simply discard this letter without replying. If, however, the customer either did not receive the bill or received a bill listing an incorrect amount, inform G. W. and F. the circumstances. Enclose an envelope for easy replying. Explain that any audit involving customer transactions must have the cooperation of the customers contacted in order to be successful. Your clients as well as your team of auditors are counting on the customer to help them to keep the audited company honest and correct.

25. Write the Escondido Home for Senior Citizens, 565 Arastrodero, Palo Alto, California 94301, and ask for details about making arrangements for an 82-year-old relative of yours. Find out what the monthly or yearly charges are, and ask about facilities (single, double, or ward). Ask what down payment is necessary and what the charges cover. Many homes for older people include nursing care. Ask if the Escondido will take care of bed patients or semi-bed patients. Your relative insists she will not live with you but wants to live near her hometown, and that is why you considered this home. She has been a victim of anemia and so will need a liver shot every week or ten days, but otherwise she is in excellent health. You want her to have a comfortable place to live, but the cost of comfort is a real consideration. You have limited funds, and so does she.

26. Clip (or copy) from the pages of any newspaper or magazine an ad featuring a product in which you are interested. Write an inquiry to the manufacturer or distributor asking for details not furnished by the ad. Price and local availability are possibilities. Servicing is another. Ask four significant questions, *at least one of which requires explanation on your part.* Attach the ad or copy to your letter.

27. Ms. Mollie Pratt, 108 Gardendale Road, Abbotstown, Pennsylvania 16820, a shy librarian for the public library, is aware that she has a hearing problem. Rather than take her to a doctor, help Mollie write a letter to Renith Hearing Instrument Corporation, 6510 West Grand Avenue, Chicago, Illinois 60635. She wants to know prices, styles of hearing aids, guarantees, and nearest hearing aid center.

28. In the "What's New" section of the Sunday supplement to your paper you see a small ad for Handy-Power Convertor, an inexpensive, quickly installed plant that delivers 110 Volts AC from your car to your camper or other place needing electric power. Write the Wright Curtis Company, Post Office Box 12377, Tallahassee, Florida 32301, and ask about guarantees, installation, costs, uses (particularly light for the camper), and operation.

FAVORABLE REPLY CASES (NO SALES POSSIBILITIES)

1. Sit in for Dr. Henry Bonham (Case 9, p. 160) and write an acceptance letter to Wallace Fenton to appear as the speaker on the Appraisal Report Writing Seminar, 24th of next month. Ask Bonham for reports for your analysis and suggest that the general topic heading be changed from "Elements of Creative Writing" to "Elements of Effective Report Writing" because the term creative writing in general is thought of as writing fiction, poetry, and plays. Your plans call for your arrival late on the 23d. You appreciate his offer to make a room reservation. You'll prefer a queen-size bed—wife with you. Terms OK—all expenses plus $100.

2. Current date/Write B. V. Watson/Watson and Gregg/4298 Browndale Avenue/Minneapolis, Minnesota 55416. You are Mr. Robert Sullivan/ Century Plaza Suite 1198/Avenue of the Stars/Century City, California 90024. You are glad to send copies of the poem "Outwitted" by Edwin Markham and the philosophical statement "I Believe" by John D. Rockefeller, Jr. (Case 12, p. 153). You are always pleased when you get letters like B. V.'s note and even more pleased when you learn that many persons are working hard to help others help themselves. You think they deserve a big vote of thanks.

3. *From:* Professor T. M. Callaway, Department of English, University of Florida, Gainesville, 32600, U.S.A.

To: Robert A. Piotte, Regional Information Officer, Canadian Forestry Service, Box 650, Sault Ste. Marie, Ontario, Canada (Case 21, p. 156).

Information: English Department, U. of F., offers three regular quarter courses (three months): Basic Technical Writing, Business Communications, Report Writing. No short courses of one to six weeks. The College of Journalism and Communication offers undergraduate and graduate work in public relations. On request from time to time Journalism and Communication runs four-day workshops in public relations for School of Forest Resources and Conservation. School has set-up for local, state, and national information and education officers working in forestry and conservation. Callaway (by carbon) is asking School of Forest Resources and Conservation to send Piotte further information on future programs.

4. The Center for Auto Safety's investigation into the carburetion problems of the 197– WW Armadillo (See Case 14, p. 153) revealed that the stalling was caused by an automatic choke that was designed to function in cooler climates than the Southeast. Since the summer temperatures rarely drop below 70 degrees at night, the WW automatic choke does not completely close, which causes fuel starvation and stalling in the morning when the engine is turned over. WW, however, has redesigned the choke mechanism for warmer climates; and WW owners should receive letters requesting them to bring their new cars to their local dealers to have the new chokes installed. Relay this information to John Parham, 1215 Buchanan Street, Hollywood, Florida 33020, of the Hollywood Better Business Bureau.

5. Sit in for Alva Sherill, director of HUD (Housing Urban Development), Washington, D.C. 20009, and write Marvin Copeland, director of Operation New Columbus, 2299 Saffold Avenue, Columbus, Ohio 43212. Sherill agrees to speak to the ONC group from 7:30 to 8:30 P.M. the 15th of next month and to answer questions for another half hour afterward. The only props needed are a screen and overhead projector. He will arrive by plane at 4 P.M. You will appreciate Copeland's suggestions. Can he meet you on arrival? You will also need a hotel room.

6. The Michigan National Bank, East Lansing, Michigan 48823, each year awards a $1,500 scholarship to an Ingham County high school senior. The winner is a student who writes the best essay on a subject the bank selects and who scores high on achievement and personality tests. The subject this year is "Inflation in the Seventies!" The high schools in Ingham County administer the written achievement and personality tests. As professor of finance at the University of Michigan, Ann Arbor 48105, you have been asked to be one of three final judges to read about 20 essays which will have been selected from all the essays turned in. From these, you and the other two judges will pick the three best. Then in about two weeks you'll need to be in East Lansing to interview the three candidates and decide on the winner. The bank will of course pay all your expenses. It's a time-consuming job but in your opinion a most worthwhile project, and so you are accepting.

7. Answer an inquiry about Jonathan White (the usual questions: personality, dependability, judgment, accuracy, leadership), who has applied for the position of quality control supervisor with Old Dominion Paper Company, 1300 West Hull Street, Petersburg, Virginia 23803. You write to Conrad Meek, Personnel Officer. White worked for you (Canfield Publishing Co.) for almost two years as an assistant purchasing agent. While working he was responsible for establishing specifications and processing purchase requests. During peak periods, he negotiated with vendors for merchandise desired. He was industrious, conscientious, and completely reliable. (You may invent specifics, favorable and unfavorable. Find at least one minor flaw.) He left to go to the university and finish his master's degree in business management.

8. For Mrs. Theodore Gibson, manager of the Escondido Home for Senior Citizens, 565 Arastrodero, Palo Alto, California 94301, answer an inquiry about your home for senior citizens (Case 25, p. 157). The new wing should be finished in two months, and it will accommodate 30 residents. Residents will pay rent 90 days in advance and thereafter pay by the month. The rates depend on the facilities taken and range from $175 for a small room with group bath to $250 a room with private bath. The rent includes room, meals, laundry, and personal help with dressing and hair. Medical attention is furnished by a contract doctor. Meals are served in the rooms of residents unable to go to the dining room. The home does not furnish nursing or hospital care. Each resident must carry private medical and hospital insurance. Upon becoming bedridden or needing hospital care, the resident will be removed from the home and cannot return until the doctor certifies that the patient can take care of needed medication and personal hygiene. Application for admission should be made directly to Mrs. Gibson. Suggest that application for admission be made right away because so many senior citizens want to enter the Escondido Home for Senior Citizens.

9. Assume you are Wallace Fenton, M.A.I. (Member of American Institute of Real Estate Appraisers), 2000 4th Street, North, St. Petersburg, Florida 33704. By phone you induced Dr. Henry Bonham, Professor of Technical Writing, 302 Anderson Building, University of Florida, Gainesville, Florida 32601, to be a Guest Lecturer at the Appraisal Report Writing Seminar sponsored by the American Institute of Real Estate Appraisers at the Port O'Call, the convention inn and resort on the Isle of Tierra Verde, St. Petersburg, Florida on the 23rd and 24th of next month. Dr. Bonham's two-hour part of the program starts at 8:30 on the 24th with a general topic heading of "Elements of Creative Writing" divided into (*A*) Lecture, Writing Style, Vocabulary and Elements of Composition, and (*B*) Criticism of Sample Reports with Suggested Rewriting. Since your Chapter has funds for educational purposes, you can reimburse for travel, hotel, meals, and an honorarium of $100 plus any cost for reproduction of pass-out material. Two weeks before the program you'll mail Bonham sample reports which he can use for criticism. With these facts, write an appropriate letter confirming your telephone conversation (saying what you said originally and in answer to questions) and offering to make a room reservation.

10. Two weeks elapsed from the time you wrote the letter described in the preceding case. In this interim you received a letter of acceptance from Dr. Henry Bonham. Enclose one brochure showing the change of title to "Elements of Effective Report Writing," as his reply suggested, and telling him you have confirmed his reservation at the Port O'Call. You are forwarding the sample reports for his study.

11. Dr. Henry Bonham (see two preceding cases) held the audience captive the 24th at the Appraisal Report Writing Seminar as evidenced by notes taken, questions asked, general discussion, and sure changes to be made in future reports. As Wallace Fenton, write Bonham thanking him for a job well done and attaching a check for $153.40 covering travel, meals, and honorarium. Make up and include a forceful quote from one of the influential members of the group.

12. As Rosemary Koplein, Policyowner Correspondence Division, Policyowner Services Department, The Southwestern Mutual Life Insurance Company, 876 Texas Avenue, Dallas, Texas 75227, send the forms and write a covering letter to Linda Kehres, 72 Springbrook Road, Berea, Ohio 45207 (Case 2, p. 149). Ask her to note the blank space for the relationship of John Kehres and Whitney Kehres Adams. If the two Owners were to predecease her, ownership would revert back to her. When you have received the completed documents, properly completed, and once the change has been recorded on all records, the cash value will be referred to another Division which will send her this information.

13. Again for Rosemary Koplein (preceding case) answer Linda Kehres's request for information on policy 5017681 (Case 2, p. 149). The plan is paid-up life. It was issued June 10, 1958, and has basic face value (death benefit) of $634. The $20 of paid-up dividend additions increases the total face value to $654. Current gross cash value is $460.65, including $14.09 cash value of the paid-up dividend additions. Gross loan value is $444.37, on the same basis. There are no loans on the policy.

Assume that you attach a copy of the policy contract.

14. Yesterday you received a letter from England Potter, personnel director of Growmore Fertilizers, Ordure Road, Guano, Indiana 47708. Potter wanted some information about John Henry Alexander, who used to sell tractors and farm equipment for your company, James Dear and McKinley of Princeton, Ind. John was a good salesman for you. He got along well with his customers, and he always followed up his sales by keeping in contact with his customers and facilitating service on their equipment. His customers showed a high rate of repeat purchasing. John kept a small farm himself and seemed to enjoy working the land. He often brought in baskets of seasonal produce to his fellow workers. In fact, he left your company when he bought the two farms neighboring his, so that he could give all his attention to farming. You were surprised to hear that John was looking for work but expected that the three-year flood, difficulty of getting help at harvest time, and general economic conditions of the times have phased out his farming and forced him back into the more lucrative selling profession.

Write a letter to Potter supporting John's job application. Use a subject line. Remember you are dealing with confidential information.

15. Reply favorably to Arnold MacMillan, Personnel Director of Furrow, Harrow, and Plough (Case 15, p. 154). You remember MacMillan from last year's Farm Equipment Fair in Davenport, Iowa. You also remember John Muennink, who was your top salesman for the three years he worked for your firm. John left your company when he went into business (irrigation equipment) with four of his friends. They were doing well, but five straight years of above average rainfall put them out of business. When John worked for you, he kept accurate and precise records. He always followed up on his sales to make sure his equipment performed as it should and kept his customers happy. He had a high ratio of return business with his customers too. He got along well with his fellow salesmen, often giving them good advice on how to sell more and earn larger commissions. He was the favorite of the office staff too. You were surprised to hear that he was in Florida and would have hired him yourself if he had come to you for a job.

16. Answer Case 16, p. 154. *Letterhead:* First National Bank, Tombstone, Arizona 85638. *Inside address:* Charles Dodson, First Federal Savings and Loans, 1437 Bannock, Denver, Colorado 80204. Use today's date. Subject line should include the name of the applicant, Larry Snipes. *Signature block:* Sincerely, Walter Oliver, Trust Department. *Facts:* Larry worked first in the small-loans department, then in the department appraising real estate loans. He made a good impression, learned fast, and worked accurately. He bothered his supervisors with constant suggestions for changes and showed lack of tact by criticizing the head of the real estate loans in front of a customer. One month after his 12 months of training he told you he was quitting and moving to Denver where he thought he'd have more social life and fun.

Write the letter to Dodson candidly and without rancor. Add any other logical facts.

REPLIES WITH SALES POSSIBILITIES

1. In answer to a request for "The Fisherman's Prayer" (a design to be done in needlepoint), Burger Phillips, Carison, Illinois 25233, does not carry this and does not know of a shop in Illinois that does. Matie Albright of the Needlework Department adds that she has added your name to the special order file, and adds that if she should find the piece at a later date, she will get in touch with you. Sit in for Matie and write the personal letter.

2. Assistant Director of Customer Relations of P. D. Podge, Detroit, Michigan 48228, answer Homer Hocutt, 897 Berry Street, Bessemer, Alabama 35020 (Case 14, p. 182). The red and white van is scheduled for assembly February 14, and should be delivered to H. T. Boyle, dealer in Birmingham, about a week after its assembly. Because Podge did not anticipate the popularity and sales potential of this particular model van, desires to retain its quality standards and has had some labor problems, the production of the vans will be delayed somewhat this year. Workers in the Detroit plants have refused to work overtime to help catch up with the production demand. Add appropriate resale material. Tell Hocutt that a copy of this letter goes along with another asking Boyle to expedite delivery as much as possible.

3. Reply to the inquiry (Case 19, p. 155) from A. L. Mate (Apt. 202, Camelot Road, Bloomington, Indiana 46144). The Pephyr 10-speed bike advertised in *Person's* is lightweight magnesium alloy tubing, brazed to insure permanent, unstressed joints; shipped unassembled (in 3 sections); simply have to attach the fork and handlebar section to the frame (3 nuts and a wrench are included along with illustrated instructions) and put the front wheel on (easy to assemble knock-off hubs). Although no dealer in Bloomington, Mate can see the Pephyr 10-speed at Martin and Snow in Indianapolis. Service and warranty can be handled either by DC&H in Indianapolis or by shipping the bike back to you in Atlanta. Answer all questions, sell the Pephyr 10-speed, and get check for $100, which is about $50 off the retail price. Negative details, the service and warranty arrangement and assembling the bike, you will have to mention and minimize.

4. As Sales Director of Wright Curtis Company, Post Office Box 12377, Tallahassee, Florida 32301, answer Truman Brown, contractor, 987 Fowler Avenue, Savannah, Georgia 31409, about the Handy-Power Convertor (5″ long, 3″ wide, and 3½″ deep), delivered price $29.95. It delivers 110 Volts AC electrical power from car or truck's alternator. Operates heavy duty impact wrenches, pipe threaders, drills, sanders, grinders, cement mixers, light bulbs plus many more uses. Easy to install. No belts or pulleys. No moving parts. Does not shorten life of alternator. Handy-Power will operate any 110 Volt brush-type motor. Nearly all power tools have brushes, and the performance is perfect. Handy-Power quickly starts cars with dead batteries thereby eliminating need for jumper cables. Provides fast, ten-minute or less battery charging (any voltage 6, 12, 24, 32). Good for arc welding of steel up to ¼ inch thick. Handy-Power convertor can be removed and installed into a new car or truck in 20 minutes. All convertors sold with warranty against parts and workmanship defects. The units will be repaired or replaced for five years for any unit that fails to perform properly (except unauthorized alterations or repairs damage) for a maximum charge of $5, regardless of condition of unit. Order will be processed and Handy-Power sent within 72 hours after receipt of enclosed order form.

Brown asked (1) time for battery charging, (2) warranty, (3) where repairs were done, and (4) installation procedure.

5. As Circulation Director for *National Osographic Magazine*, you have decided, in response to requests from several high schools and to build circulation, to send to all the Houston metropolitan high schools (one to each school) reprints of a recent *National Osographic* article entitled "The Influence of African Culture on American Society." This article is the first in a series of articles dealing with African, Asian, and Latin American influences on American society. Much has been said of American influences on Africa, Asia, and Latin America; but little about the influences these areas have had on American culture. Your articles will deal, among other things, with language, dress, foods, and even religion. You feel that the "African Influence" article will be particularly helpful in history, sociology, humanities, and political science classes.

Write a cover letter (form letter) to accompany the reprint, which, in addition to creating good will and underscoring the value of *National Osographic* as a teaching aid, asks for subscriptions.

6. As Gloria Benefield, owner, Bugg-Out Pest Control, Inc., 987 Shawnee, Topeka, Kansas 66601, answer the inquiry from Farley Moody, 809 Caldwell Street, Louisville, Kentucky 40208 (Case 6, p. 150). Send a brochure along but answer the questions with this information. For the best results from using Hurry-X, all cans of food should be removed from kitchen closets. Although the bombs are not harmful to people or pets, the odor is strong and can bother some people's eyes (watering) and make some feel slightly ill. The bugs will stay away generally for several months if sanitary conditions are maintained (leave no dirty dishes around at night, empty trash, remove old newspapers, etc.). The bombs leave no residue that is harmful. The nearest dealer is Carey Williams, Williams Feed Store, 2 Cameron Road, Louisville.

7. Reply to the direct inquiry (Case 5, p. 150) of DuMont Associates, DuMont Plaza, Providence, Rhode Island 02909, answering the most important questions first and sending along a brochure showing your golf course, swimming pool, and hotel. You cannot give anyone preference in seating in the dining room, but will of course honor reservations. Also, golf course cannot be closed for a private tournament, but your golf pro will try to schedule starting times to accommodate guests' wishes. You can and should answer all questions, subordinating weak or unpleasant items.

8. As Hilary Milton, Manager, Vulcan Supplies, 986 Lansing Road, Flint, Michigan 48505 (Case 7, p. 151), answer Bobbie Moore, 987 University Avenue, Ann Arbor, Michigan 48106. The ABM typewriters are ten years old, are not guaranteed for workmanship or parts. Originally they cost around $700. The all-steel typewriter tables roll smoothly on casters (no locks). Originally they were $9.00, are avocado color, measure 14 × 34 inches when open, 28 inches high. Swivel chairs have padded backs and seats in avocado, roll on casters. Chairs must be sold with typewriter tables. Chairs cost around $100 when new. Use an action ending to get Bobbie Moore's business.

9. Answer the inquiry of William and Alice Simpson, 14 Glendale Gardens, Pensacola, Florida 32560 (Case 17, p. 154), under the signature of Sales Director, Zodiac Simplex, 315 West Allegon, Lansing, Michigan 48910. For a 25-hp motor a Dinghie would not work, but Zodiac Master Runabout for $875 can take up to a 40-hp motor. Has rigid hull, handles and maintains course well, has two self-bailing transom plugs, handles on outer sides, comes with inflation gauge. Pump can also deflate. Internal one-way valves allow inflation from a single point (separate valves provide for deflation). Length is 12 feet, weighs 146 pounds. Comes with floorboards and foot pump, inflatable keelson, lifelines on outer sides, oarlocks, two oars, generous repair kit, dull gray finish. Can set up in 20–25 minutes. Can accommodate four passengers, but three more comfortably.

10. As Director of Sales, answer Ms. Mollie Pratt (Case 27, p. 157) with these facts: Tiny, lightweight behind-the-ear model; trim, distinguished eyeglass model; ultra-tiny in-the-ear model; or fine line of body-worn models. Closest Hearing Aid Center, 103 Overbrook Road, Wilkes Barre, Pennsylvania, operated by Henry Highsmith, who demonstrates any model without obligation. If not satisfied, return the aid (except for custom-made earmold) to Renith Dealer within ten days of purchase and money will be refunded under Renith's Ten-Day Money-Back Guarantee. During this month Renith has the following HOUSE SPECIALS: a trade-in allowance on all Renith hearing aids, free Renith custom earmold, free three-month supply of Renith batteries, free hearing test. Prices vary according to the model of aid. *Action:* phone or come by the Aid Center soon.

11. As a member of the customer service team of Auto-Train Corporation in Washington, D.C. (826 NW K St. 20009), reply to Shroud, Weeds & Cerement, Inc. (White and Sepulchre Streets, Golgotha, Virginia 12713 (Case 10, p. 152), about service between Deland, Florida, and Lorton, Virginia. One-way fare for two people and a car $195.46—5 percent discount for groups with noncancellable reservations and full payment in advance. Include brochures and a schedule, but also show what they get for $195.46. Emphasize the services and conveniences such as two meals (but no group dining), use of the game and club car, etc. Groups will be given seats together; sleeping accommodations for two cost $30 extra, subject also to the 5 percent discount. Make your train service attractive enough to get back (along with a check) the ticket order form you include.

12. As Harry (Harriet) Sweat, resident manager of Indian River Apartments, 2800 Archer Road, Norman, Oklahoma 73099, reply to Myron Bliss (118 West 49th St., Bayonne, N.J. 20031) about renting. Myron coming to Norman to work on Ph.D. in engineering. Writing to several apartment complexes about apartment availability and costs. Married, no children; a dog and a cat. Wants a two-bedroom, furnished apartment—second bedroom as a study. Move in after first of the year and begin course work in the spring.

Housing in Norman is a buyer's market. Want to get as many prospective tenants as possible to sign up as soon as you can. Myron can have a two-bedroom, furnished apartment on or after January 1. Make Indian River so attractive that he will come to you. Convince him that what he gets for $235 per month plus utilities (average $30–$35 monthly) is a better deal than competitor's offer. Include your brochure that shows floor plans and facilities.

13. You have been asked by Sylvia Carter, owner of the Portrait Studio, 109 Bernardino Road, Albuquerque, New Mexico 87104, to answer Decker and Decker about the oil portrait of the retiring comptroller (direct inquiry 22, p. 156). A fine oil 24 × 30 inches would cost about $500 and the frame another $100–$200, depending on the style selected. For $25 a simple light can be installed, but many times a light is not needed if there is desirable lighting around the area where the picture is hung. The strand of hair can be shaded away, and the eyes can be made to look clearer. Before Sylvia Carter could start on it, however, she would need samples of the hair, of the clothing, and a specific description as to skin tones. Generally she prefers to see the person, but her artists can do almost as good a job from several photographs as from a real-life sitting.

14. As manager of the Cleanamatic Company, 908 Main Street, Des Moines, Iowa 50309, answer direct inquiry 23, p. 156.

Facts on case: The cost for cleaning the wall-to-wall carpeting (15 × 30 feet) would be $72.90. A 100-percent wool rug cleans better than a rug that is part acrylic and part wool. The piano will not have to be moved because you have a tool that cleans right up to each leg of the piano. The steam jets will not bother the piano, for you can hardly see the steam when it comes out. Generally stains from soft drinks can be removed unless a chlorine bleach was used on the stain. It is impossible to remove urine stains from carpeting.

Inclose a reply card setting up an appointment for the cleaning of the rug.

15. *Your company:* Tools Unlimited, Meriden Avenue, Meriden, Connecticut 06450. *Your product:* Transpare, a material that can be written on with ball-point pen or other markers, or typed on, or run through a Fermo copying machine for a transparency. Transpare sheets are designed for use with any type of overviewer or overhead projector. They can be used on just one side. They always stay flexible and will not curl when left on an overhead projector. Transparencies are easy to make (just set the Fermo copying machine at about 2½, and place a sheet of Transpare on the face of the material to be copied). Transpare is available in boxes of 202 sheets (two sheets free to cover experimenting) at $15.50 per box (about 7 cents per 8½ by 11-inch sheet). *Your Potential Customer:* Morris Carlisle, purchasing agent, University of Colorado, 1105 N. Nevada Avenue, Boulder, Colorado 80903. He asked about typing on, making transparencies, cost, local dealer. Many of the teachers at the University will enjoy making their own detailed tests on Transpare, which would save Mimeographing costs. Graphs, maps, charts, tables, pictures, and in fact any copy can be transmitted to Transpare. Urge Carlisle to get in touch with the local dealer, Ward Supply Company, 1109 Colorado Street, Denver 80211, phone, 456–8765.

ORDER CASES

1. As directed by your teacher, assume the conditions of one of the acknowledgments (next section of the book). Write the order letter in the situation. (Federal law prohibits collection of sales tax on mail sales unless delivery is in the same state as the seller.)

2. One of your duties as head clerk for the Needle and Thread Sewing Center (379 West William, Ann Arbor, Michigan 48190) is to order bolts of cloth when the stock gets low. Your recent inventory shows that you will need the following materials: one bolt of red felt D–215 ($20), two bolts of light blue satin D–514 ($40 each), four bolts of cotton, assorted flower prints D–765 ($15 each), and two bolts of white-on-white dacron polyester D–981 ($18 each). Send your request to Kizer Kloth, 897 Ogontz Avenue, Reading, Pa. 28415. Your store has a credit account with Kizer Kloth (2/10, n/30). You'll want the cloth shipped airmail within five days since Dr. Marian Gallaway, director of the University Theatre Group, needs the printed cotton and satin for the production of a famous Greek play which opens in two weeks.

3. Move the clock up many years and assume that you are now 65 and are a member of AARP (American Association of Retired Persons). As a member you can order your drugs (and those of your spouse) at greatly reduced rates. Make up a typical drug order and send it to this organization, Pharmacy Department, P.O. Box 2400, Long Beach, California 90801.

4. Using your charge account at Neiman Marcus, Dallas, Texas 75227, write to the personal shopping department and order two items of clothing for yourself, one wedding present for close friends of yours, and one gift item for a five-year-old child in another city. Assume you have the current shopper's catalog, so you have catalog numbers and specific prices. A flat fee of $1.00 is charged for handling and gift wrapping of one article. You want the wedding present and gift to the child specially wrapped.

5. As historian for Gamma Omicron chapter of Sigma Omega Beta fraternity (sorority), 809 Colonial Drive, Morgantown, West Virginia 26506, you decide to brighten up the chapter house with photographs and drawings of the chapter's activities. You have a large file of materials for framing, but the cost of having the photographs and drawings matted and framed is considerably more than the $50 budget the treasurer allotted you. While thumbing through *House Lovely* magazine, you found an ad for the Redi-Frame Company (P.O. Box #998, Cucumber, West Virginia 24826) which listed frame sizes and costs. Your pledges can assemble and paint these unfinished frames and mat the pictures and drawings at a considerable saving. Order the following number of frames from Redi-Frame: 12–8″ × 10″ (A–108) @ $.75; 12–12″ × 15″ (A–109) @ $1.00; 8–18″ × 24″ (B–106) @ $1.50; and 6–20″ × 30″ (A–110) @ $2.00 each. Include a check to cover the cost and the $5.00 shipping charges by UPS.

6. From Habernickel Company, 265 North 9 Street, Paterson, New Jersey 07530, order two pairs alpine blue and surf green summer slacks, waist 40, inseam 30, $14.95; three large (16–16½) sport shirts in gold, light blue, and white for $6.95; and one zipper parka in gold, large size (42–44), $6.95. Send a check to cover the cost of the clothing plus $2.45 mailing charges. Use your school address.

7. From The Orange Shop, U.S. Highway 301, Citra, Florida 32627, order No. 11, one bushel of Valencia oranges, $16.95, and petite pack of Ruby Red grapefruit, $9.75 (prices include mailing costs), for yourself. For Mr. and Mrs. Levert Killough, 908 Hickory Hill, Scrant, Kentucky 40373, order No. 22, half-bushel of oranges, $11.25. Send a check to cover the costs.

8. Assume that you are Mrs. George Doster, Tower Lake Estates, Lincoln Road, Beloit, Wisconsin 53511, and you order the following merchandise from Field and Marshall, Chicago, Illinois 60678: two bath towels, 25″ × 46″, tigerlily orange @ $3.99 each; four wash cloths, 12″ × 12″ in tigerlily orange @ 89¢ each; one fitted Queen sheet and one flat Queen sheet, Wamsutta, in Colonial Stencil Design, $10.00 each; two standard cases in same design for $4.50; two twin-size bedspreads in girlfriend ensemble print @ $13.00; two pillow shams, ruffled edges, @ $6.00; four fingertip towels, 11″ × 15″, with initial *W* @ $1.39 in white; one box of two

Katherine Gray soaps with initial *W* @ $2.00. Charge these items to your account and ask Field and Marshall to mail them to you.

9. Since you started working for the Lively Music Company, Lincoln Square Mall, Ann Arbor, Michigan 48103, you've impressed Mallory Menninger, the manager, so much with your knowledge of country music that she has decided to let you try your hand at ordering some stock for the Country/Folk music section of the store. Mallory wants you to order ten each of what you feel will be the ten best selling albums for a floor display. At $2 each, that's an order of $200. Use the format suggested by your text, and ask for promotional material and a display rack. Ask for them to be sent C.O.D. You supply the album titles. Order from Discos Record Distributors, 4950 N. Ravenswood Ave., Chicago, IL 60640.

10. For Mrs. Roy Patterson, 906 High Forest, Boulder Junction, Wisconsin 54512, order from a mail order house called The Stitchery, Box 90-J, Durham, North Carolina 27705, three sets of crewel, Nos. Py–905, Py–906, and Py–907 at $4.00 each; one table cloth No. PB–909 for cross stitching $10.50; two canvases for needlepoint Py–547 and PBy–555 at $3.00 each. Send the goods parcel post and bill her accordingly.

11. You are to represent an organization to which you belong (assume a social or professional fraternity, a religious group, or a civic organization) at its national convention in Mexico City, Mexico, DF, at the Maria Christinia, Rhin 64. You want to stay at the Maria Christinia for two nights and three days of the convention. You prefer a single room at the minimum rate. Ask for such a reservation, and ask the Maria Christinia to confirm it.

12. As a thoroughly satisfied old customer, you are going to take the form-letter suggestion of the Maytag Cheese Company, Old Line Lexington, Bucks County, Pennsylvania 18103, and order now (November 1) gift boxes of assorted cheeses—one for yourself (six cheeses, $10.50 including postage) and two for friends in different cities (eight cheeses, $14.00; ten cheeses, $17.50). As suggested, be sure to give full names and addresses (including ZIP codes), to enclose the exact amount of money as a check or money order, and to indicate desired arrival date (otherwise shipment is immediate).

13. To help Mark Cook learn the metric system and also pass the time while recovering from a crushed pelvis, you order from Walker Educational Supply Company, 2218 University Blvd., Athens, Georgia 30601, the following items: one Metric Measurement with duplicating Masters by Hayes, Book 1, $2.50; one Duplicating Metric Workbook by Weber-Costello, $3.95; one Metric Activity Cards by Weber-Costello, $3.95; and a

Meter Measuring tape, $.50. Mark's address is Rural Route 9, Hickory, North Carolina 28601. Send a check to cover the supplies and the parcel post charges of $.72.

14. Odessa Hudson, Flatbush Elementary School, Flatbush, Mississippi 39146, orders school supplies from Walker Educational Supply Company, 2218 University Blvd., Athens, Georgia 30601. Assume that you help Odessa order the following to be sent c.o.d.: two yards clear contact paper at 59¢ a yard; one dozen liquid tempera paints in eight-ounce size, $18.00; one dozen eight-ounce finger paints, $11.00; one ream of plain newsprint 9″ × 12″, $2.15; one box letter size file folders, $4.25.

15. For your machine shop, which you own, Swarf Machining, 828 N. Clybourn Ave., Chicago, Illinois 60632, order from Turner & Miller, 1414 W. Lake St., Racine, Wisc. 53342, sixteen ¼″ × 1″ × 6′ bars of 24S13 aluminum, two 1″ × 3″ × 6′ bars of 3303T6 aluminum, twenty-four ½″ diameter × 6′ rods of free machining brass, and twenty-four 18″ × 18″ sheets of ¼″ thick mild steel, mill edge cut. You assume that the prices in Turner & Miller's catalog dated two months ago still hold. If not, T&M should contact you before making shipment. If T&M cannot ship all the aluminum in one shipment, hold the aluminum until all can come at once. The brass you need yesterday; the steel you won't need until today.

16. As the manager of La Señorita (a beauty shop in Guadalajara, Mexico), you order from Uniforms, Incorporated, 3618 Broadway, San Antonio, Texas 78241, six matching pant-set uniforms No. MP–765 in blue (five medium, one small) @ $10.95. Send a check to cover the cost and $2.40 shipping charges. Your address is Circunvalacion Norte 136, Las Fuentes, Guadalajara, Jalisco, Mexico.

17. Obscura (Case 8, p. 151) has sent you the information you wanted. Now send a letter order for 150 "Fold-A-Viewers," 250 filmstrips per the enclosed storyboard and color negatives, and 250 specially-imprinted folders per the layout on the form Obscura supplied. The prices of $1.50 per viewer, $.75 per filmstrip, $225.00 one-time charge for a master negative for the filmstrips, and $42.00 one-time charge for typesetting and keylining the folder are acceptable. You must have the entire package in four weeks—no later! Your company is well-rated—can bill you with shipment (which will be at Obscura's expense).

STANDARD ACKNOWLEDGMENT CASES

1. *To:* Mr. Frank J. DeRiggi, 1504 Almetta Avenue N.E., Atlanta, Georgia, 30307. *Your company:* International Publications, Inc., and you are Leslie I. Combs, Jr., Executive Vice President, 20 West Broadway, New

York, N.Y. 10021. Resale on the order you acknowledge (six-volume series *Executive Decision Making*) might include that these books observe the unique and clever way in which the authors blend sound management theory, profound behavioral understanding, and successful business experience. Many realistic case studies are included. Promote your sequential series entitled *The Junior Executive's Role*. Thank Mr. DeRiggi for his check for $22.95, which covered the mailing charges of parcel post.

2. As Pharmacist Roberta Dodson, The Pharmacy Department, American Association of Retired Persons, P.O. Box 2400, Long Beach, California 90801, acknowledge the drug order from retired Professor C. R. Matthews, 909 Del Rosa Drive, San Bernardino, California 92410, for the following: 100 tablets ℞ No. 470980, Dr. Daly $4.50; 100 tablets ℞ No. 514212, Dr. Patrick $10.75; 30 tablets ℞ No. 513746, Dr. Thomas $3.00; 6-ounce bottle medium strength Scope, $1.00; 1 box Johnson's unwaxed dental floss, $1.89; 3 bars Neutrogena soap, $3.00. Drugs are to be sent by UPS and charged to Matthews' new account. Since this is the first time Matthews has ordered, welcome him by telling him about your low prices and fast service. Enclose a card for other new member recommendations.

3. As a correspondent in the sales office of Elizabeth Barden, Inc., a cosmetic company, 8654 Upland Road, New Rochelle, New York 10803, you have to acknowledge an order from Louis Stegall, Stegall's Drug Store, 639 9th Street, Huntington, West Virginia 25706:

2 doz. Elizabeth Barden lipsticks (assorted shades)	$1.40 each	$ 33.60
1 doz. 2–oz. jars moisturizing cream	8.50 each	102.00
1 doz. 10–oz. jars cleansing cream	2.00 each	24.00
1 doz. 13–oz. cans of Volvo-5 hair spray	1.10 each	13.20
		$172.80

You are sending these cosmetics air express, charges collect to Stegall, a long-established credit customer. Tell Stegall about Elizabeth Barden national advertisements in *Seventeen* and *Glamour* and about the spot commercials on NBC-TV by the well-known Maurine Frances. Spot TV commercials are in the late afternoon and evening, Monday through Saturday. Suggest that if Stegall would like to increase his sales by tying in his local advertising with this national campaign, you can send him mats. Also tell Stegall about an allied product such as bath oil, eye shadow, or night cream.

4. After you read Case 6, p. 168, acknowledge the order for the Habernickel Company. Assume you are writing Douglas Cash, 879 Auburn Avenue, Pontiac, Michigan 48054. Assume too that you are having a closeout sale on cardigan sweaters made of 100 percent washable Creslan Acrylic with fleece backing on the inside in brown, navy blue, green, burgundy;

size L (40–42) should fit Cash. They were $8.95 and now just $6.95. These all-purpose sweaters are nice to take on weekend trips, can be worn with sport shirt or under best business jacket. Make ordering easy.

5. As William P. Powell, owner, The Orange Shop (Case 7, p. 168), write an acknowledgment to Mr. Charles Perry, 10 Mansfield Place, Lynn, Massachusetts 01904. You have the fresh, juicy fruit and are shipping it; but the prices have gone up $1.00 on the bushel of Valencia oranges and 50 cents on the half bushel and 75 cents on the petite pack. Ask Perry to send you the additional money; resell the fruit and the service of The Orange Shop. Perry is a new customer.

6. *Letterhead:* Warner-Borg, 900 High Street, Hartford, Connecticut 06105. *Inside address:* Mrs. JoAnn Bowers, JoAnn's Beauty Spot, Phipps Plaza, Springfield, Ohio 45501. *Signature block:* Sincerely yours, Creighton Smallwood, Sales Department. Use today's date. *Information:* Acknowledge the order of this new customer for the following merchandise to be sent C.O.D. as requested.

2 No. PGF–65 roller massagers @ $80	$160.00
2 No. PMR–76 electric progress-a-cyzers @ $60	120.00
2 No. PJT–98 portable plug-in steam baths @ $150	300.00
	$580.00

JoAnn's Beauty Spot is a combination of health and exercise salon and beauty shop. The beauty shop has been run successfully for 20 years. Choose one of the items to have resale talk and try to sell JoAnn on a deluxe dual-post belt massager for $70. This massager has one four-inch wide belt and one three-inch wide belt that massages two areas of the customer's body at the same time. Variable intensity and variable speed controls make for gentle or vigorous vibrations.

Enclose a descriptive folder of your other exercise equipment and a credit application.

7. *To:* The Green Thumb, 609 17th Street, Beaumont, Texas 77709. *From:* National Garden Suppliers, 6499 Casper, Baton Rouge, Louisiana 70802. *Send by UPS:*

1 doz. PYT ceramic hanging planters @ $4.00	$ 48.00
1 doz. PRE plastic terrariums @ $6.00	72.00
	$120.00
Shipping charges	2.28
	$122.28

Terms: 2/10, n/30. *Sales promotion material:* Revelation fruit-bearing fig tree generally bears fruit within 18 months. Average yield is about two crops a year. Reaches height of four to five feet indoors, nine to ten feet outdoors. Can ship this 15 × 22 inch tree by UPS for $6.00. How many does the Green Thumb want? Suggested retail price $11.00 (which includes one-gallon plastic container).

8. Reply to an order from Hampton Bush, owner of Radio Shack, 1659 North High Street, Columbus, Ohio 43244, for six Merrant's stereo sets (amplifiers, turntables, speakers). Each four-unit set (one amplifier, one turntable, two speakers) costs $200 wholesale. They retail for $300 (suggested price). Hampton included his check for $1,500 to cover the cost of the six sets and shipping. Shipping costs from your Chicago plant to Columbus are $30 for the six sets by Air Express, the way he asked you to ship them. Since this is the first order you've received from Bush, and it's a sizable one, you'll want to follow his directions carefully and add resale on your product and firm. Also include your brochure featuring Merrant's line of high quality stereo equipment. You'll also want to suggest future orders to this dealer and hold out to him the possibility of ordering on credit at your usual terms, 2/10, n/30. Enclose a credit application form. Tell him, too, how your company can help him sell Merrant's products. *Letterhead:* Chicago Instruments, Wacker Drive, Chicago 60609.

9. Reply to a direct order from Herman Howell, owner of Howell's Hardware, 987 Kirkham Avenue, Greensboro, North Carolina 27406. Herman ordered from your firm (Union Products, 444 Normandy Street, Akron, Ohio 48478) one dozen 20-gallon heavy-duty aluminum garbage cans with lids at $7.85 each, two dozen 20-gallon deluxe galvanized steel cans with lids at $5.50 each, and four dozen Wringo mop buckets with wringer attachments at $6.00 each. These mop buckets are also made of galvanized steel. Tell Herman that you've already shipped the cans and buckets. Give him some resale on the cans (lids fit easily and snugly, even on over-filled cans; domed design sheds rain and snow). Herman is a *new* customer who asked for credit. Ask him to fill out and return the enclosed credit-application form, pronto. Make him welcome and show your service attitude by telling him how he benefits by doing business with you.

10. M. J. Manning orders from Japan Food Corporation, San Francisco, California 94110, the following:

4 pounds Mung Beans @ 1.20	$ 4.80
6 boxes Japanese Noodles @ 40¢	2.40
3 woks @ 14.20	42.60
4 ginger roots @ 10¢	.40
Shipping charges	3.14
	$53.34

This is a first order and Manning says that there will be more. Check will follow when goods have been delivered. Send promotional material pushing the famous Dynasty oyster sauce and the special Kikoomun Soy Sauce. Manning just finished an Oriental cooking class and has a list of names of other classmates who might like to order direct rather than pay the high costs at Port I. Extend or invite Manning to charge his next order.

11. Reply to an order you received from M. S. Wilkens, owner of the Health Juice Bar, a health food store, 5200 Rush Avenue, Columbus, Ohio 43212, for the following organically grown canned foods:

6 cases turnips @ $3.00	$18.00
10 cases tomatoes @ $2.50	25.00
10 cases cut beans @ $4.00	40.00
	$83.00
Shipping costs	10.00
	$93.00

Wilkens sent his check for $100 but also included three credit references who rated him a good customer when you called them because he asked for credit later. Ship him the canned goods and ask him to fill out and return the enclosed credit application. (He is in a high-mortality type of business.) Your firm is Vita-Vegall of Fort Myers, Florida 32714. Your best ending will probably be resale on the firm.

12. As your instructor directs, write the appropriate acknowledgment for any of the order cases detailed in the preceding section.

CREDIT APPROVAL CASES

1. Mary L. Cannon, who owns and manages a large jewelry store in Chicopee, Massachusetts (1109 Dallaire Avenue) 01022, has sent a first order to the Pueblo Jewelry Company, 699 Abriendo Avenue East, Pueblo, Colorado 81097. Stephen Fox, your salesman who visited Cannon's store, reports that she seems to have a good turnover, an orderly store, and a good rating in Dan & Broadstreet (which you verify). There are only four jewelry stores in Chicopee, and hers is the largest and one of the oldest (in business 30 years). Grant terms of 2/10, n/30, and send the ordered turquoise and silver Indian-made rings, bracelets, squash necklaces, and earrings, $300. Tell her about your half-page ads in *Vogue*. Encourage other orders—say a new pinkie in the line which is going well.

2. Harry Gregory, proprietor of the Central Shoe Store, 987 Linden Avenue, Alexandria, Virginia 22310, sends in to the GENSCO (General Shoe Company), Nashville, Tennessee 37209, a first order amounting to $1,890. Gregory submits the following information to show his financial condition: annual sales, $400,000; total assets, $142,000; accounts payable, $500; accounts receivable, $7,000; no liability as bondsman or endorser. His references report him in good standing with all creditors. Write a letter to Gregory granting the credit and shipping the goods (on enclosed shipping list—assumed), sending a new catalog and envelope stuffers. Offer him merchandising, advertising, and point-of-purchase materials, which you supply at low cost.

3. You are credit director, Royal Office Supply Company, 800 Muhlenberg Road, Reading, Pennsylvania 19602. *Send to:* Kyle Office Supply Company, 1201 Elmwood Avenue, Charleston, West Virginia 25301, the following: Executive swivel chair, PYTR–89 at $50; Desk, PYTT–90 at $80; File cabinet, PYTM–91 at $50. *Terms:* 2/10, n/30. Shipment will go by freight collect. *Allied sales:* Secretarial swivel chairs with naugahyde vinyl upholstery with seat measuring 18 × 17 inches for $40. Send catalog that gives valuable information on other office furniture.

4. As the credit manager of Imperial Imports, 39th Avenue, Long Island City, New York 11101, acknowledge the first order and credit application of Mary Farley Craddock, owner of The Collector's Shop, The Ravensdood Mall, Lynchburg, Virginia 24504. She operates a new, exclusive, expensive gift shop. According to reports from the Lynchburg First National Bank her store is making progress and meets obligations in satisfactory fashion despite questionably high accounts receivable. On terms of 2/10, n/30 send the dozen Italian ceramic hand-painted pots for plants (No. Pm–932 at $15 each) and enclose a folder showing other Italian import ceramics. The usual markup is 50 percent.

5. J. P. Thayer, owner of Thayer's Unusual Foods, 464 Pleasant Street, Milton, Mass. 02186, orders from the National Food Industries, 4404 Reservore Drive, Washington, D.C. 20087, the following items for shipment on your usual credit terms (2/10, n/60):

1 case French artichoke bottoms	$12.00
1 case hearts of palm	12.00
1 case water chestnuts	6.00
	$30.00
Shipping charges by UPS	2.33
	$32.33

According to reports from the Milton City Bank, Thayer's is doing all right. The Bentwood Wholesale Grocery Company, however, reported some delays in payment and unusually numerous spoilage claims on slow-moving perishables. Send him some newspaper mats from which he can have some ads made promoting artichoke bottoms recipes for eggs Sardu, Arneau, Benedict. Caution Thayer subtly while approving limited credit.

6. As credit manager of the Midwestern Electric Company, 998 Wacker Drive, Chicago, Illinois 60698, credit a first order from Black's Appliance Store, 987 Sixth Street, Dubuque, Iowa 52001, for one dozen self-cleaning steam-spray-dry irons, No. WN–809 at $13.00 each; six oven broilers, No. WN–908 at $20.00 each; six push-button 16-speed blenders, No. WN–786 at $18.50 each; shipping charges $30.35. The company has a well-established credit rating. Resale (on the iron): At touch of button, lint and loose mineral dirt are flushed out through the steam valve tank and steam vents . . . keeps iron cleaner, helps prevent clogging and brown spotting. Can be used with tap water, lightweight and balanced design, up-front heat controls, eight-foot cord that reverses for right or left-hand use. National ads run in *House Lovely* (always half-page).

7. Ron Newsome, one of your salesmen, has just written you, the credit manager of the Wisconsin Dairyland Company, Stevens Point, Wisconsin 54481, about Edward McKnight, formerly a general manager for a large grocery store, who has opened a business of his own, The Cheese Corner, in Warsaw, Indiana 46580 (908 Water Street). As general manager, he bought about $4,000 worth of your merchandise a year, and now he would like to stock the same lines of cheeses. According to Newsome, McKnight will place a first order of $500, but he needs 90-day terms while he is getting started. You also learn from Newsome that McKnight has borrowed on his life insurance and home and has used all his savings. He is a good businessman and knows the cheese business; so you write him allowing him the 90-day terms he wants, but with a top limit of $500 and a subtle caution about cutting his capital cheese too close to the rind.

8. *Letterhead:* KoPlay Camera Company, 900 Expressway East, Rochester, New York 14612. *Inside address:* Graydon Turner Camera Corner, 1699 Rosewood, Spartanburg, South Carolina 29310. *Signature block:* Sincerely, Mike Howard, credit sales manager. Use today's date. *Information:* Acknowledge the first order of Graydon Turner for one dozen 410 pocket camera with electric eye at $35 each; one dozen 319 pocket camera with built-in electronic flash at $30 each; one dozen 126 easi-load cameras at $7.00 each. Shipping charges by UPS add $5.69. According to your sales representative, Alfred Tooson, Graydon Turner has built up a good camera business during the last three years, and he wants to do more business. He has no credit established with any jobbers because he always paid cash for the few accessories he bought. His bank reports that he built his business with some savings and some borrowing and repaying of small amounts under $200. Because the good camera season is near (holidays, weddings, vacations), you grant credit, but you carefully and specifically remind him of due dates and the advantages of the cash discount of 3 percent if paid within 10 days and the net due in 60. Check must be mailed by the tenth day from date of the invoice to take advantage of the discount. Neatly tuck in a cautioning comment about lump buying (by the dozen) on limited capital as if all groups of cameras sell equally well.

9. As Alvin P. Sellers, Credit Manager, Charles Scooners Publishers, 597 Fifth Avenue, New York, N.Y. 10017, write a credit-granting letter to Mrs. Esther Loomis, The Book Stall, 42 Green Bay Road, Wichita, Kansas 67216, and send the books she ordered totaling $375.56. Your terms are 2/10, n/30. Even though Mrs. Loomis has not had retail experience, she chose an excellent location for her store, has inherited money, has a husband who has a well-paying job, and is bright. Your salesman, John McCann, reports that she graduated with honors from Smith College 30 years ago. She got into the book business because she was bored with country-club life and because she had always wanted a book store. In checking Mrs. Loomis's accounts, you found she lived in a paid-for $80,000 home, had an excellent credit rating, was well thought of as a leader in the community as was her husband. By complimentary comment on the high intellectual level of her book selections, related to her personal background (including lack of business training or experience), try to hint that some Babbittry might be good business. In other words, as an analogy, a wise fisherman (though *he* loves steak) will use worms (not steak) for bait—because fish prefer worms.

10. For Richard Sullivan, Credit Manager, Chemical Division, Du Pont, Wilmington, Delaware 19805, grant credit and send $500 of X-ray films to Mercy Hospital, 232 West 25th Street, Erie, Pennsylvania 16507. Your sales representative reports that up to now Mercy has been using films from your big competitor Kodak. Explain briefly your terms 3/10, n/60 and make this new customer feel welcome. Promise fast deliveries, up-to-date information sheets on new films and film equipment.

11. This morning you received a letter from George Sanders, who was your sales representative for the North-Florida territory of Borg Electric, 986 Main Street, Orlando, Florida 32709, your small-appliance distributorship. George, now the Jacksonville director for the federal government's aid-to-small-businesses program, has written on behalf of Mr. Gary Richards, who has recently opened the Appliance Mart at 421 Center Street, Jacksonville, Florida 32814. Mr. Richards' location, you realize, is in the part of the city that was burned and looted during the riots three years ago. The neighborhood, which is on the edge of the ghetto, is predominantly black and has a high insurance risk. Mr. Richards, himself a black, has had some difficulty getting financial backing and credit from Jacksonville banks and businesses; and although there is a strong movement in the city to establish a black financial basis from which to finance black-owned businesses, Mr. Richards cannot afford to wait for black financial backing.

That same afternoon you received Mr. Richards' order for 6 table-model

TV sets @ $100 each and 12 portable radios @ $10 each. Mr. Richards sent a $200 check and asked you to extend credit for 90 days for the $520 balance. He also included several credit references which you checked out and found satisfactory. Write Mr. Richards a letter in which you ship his merchandise UPS and extend credit (explain your terms).

12. Two days ago you received an order from Pharquar Fumé, owner of the Potweed Factor, a pipe and tobacco store, 199 Bushnell Avenue, Alhambra, California 91877, for two dozen one-lb. cans of Seekmore aromatic tobacco @ $2.00 a can; six boxes of Hawser Deluxe cigars @ $10.00 a box; one dozen Al-Fatah genuine Algerian briar pipes @ $6.00 each; and two dozen Zuppo pipe tools @ $.75 each. Mr. Fumé asked you to extend credit for the cost of the merchandise and the $12 shipping charges (UPS). He included several credit references, which you checked out and found in order. Fumé has a preferred credit rating with the three companies he listed. Extend him credit for the merchandise and shipping costs and ship the goods ordered. He's a new customer; you'll have to state and explain your terms. Include some sales promotion on Grasse cigaret-making machines and Dottle pipe cleaners.

CLAIM CASES

1. Because you are moving out of the state, you scheduled two ads to run a week beginning Sunday, June 8, and you paid $32.76 the Friday before, June 6. Sunday, one ad for the house ran under 68A, p. 11C, column 3, under the Garage Sales, and the ad about your garage sale ran under 35, p. 6C, column 3, under House Sales. You were not able to call the paper Sunday (only the recorder answering service); so the ads ran the same way Monday (and more sales were lost). When you called early Monday, you were told that you would not be charged for ads run incorrectly. Later in the week you called to cancel the garage sale ad. Since you paid in advance for two ads for a week (and the check for $32.76 has cleared), you ask the classified department to figure and send the refund due. You will address Classified Department, Kansas City Star, Kansas City, Missouri 64132, from your present address.

2. When you checked in your most recent order from Dell Fabrics (Charwood Road, Wilmington, Delaware 19805), you noticed some discrepancies between the manifest and what you received. You've had troubles like this before, but Dell Fabrics usually straightens things out quickly. This time you got only 5 of the 6 pairs of size 6 Stepright slippers you ordered and were billed for, and instead of 18 T-shirts (assorted colors, size medium) you got 6 large T-shirts along with 12 medium. The six pairs of Larah bell-bottomed slacks (size 14, light blue) were exactly right. What you have to do is write D. D. Dell, manager, and explain what you got and ask for corrections. Since the bill is already paid, you'll ship back the six large T-shirts. Your store is Peppermint Poppy Boutique, Honey Creek Mall, Terre Haute, Indiana 47801.

3. When you opened your last package of Comet Coffee Filters, you noticed that you had only 18 in the package. According to the label you were supposed to get 30. You paid the full price (39¢ plus 2¢ tax) for a package that was 12 filters short. The other items in your order came out all right.

The fact that you got a sealed package with 12 filters missing bothers you (not the money—16¢). Write a friendly letter to Comet Filter Company (426 Apple-tree Road, Livonia, Michigan 30321) in which you present your situation and ask adjustment. Use a fairness approach; humor might work in this case.

4. As you stepped out the door of your apartment about three months ago, you collided with a half dozen protest marchers who hit the door just as you opened it. From this contact you discovered that you couldn't move your left leg. Some of the demonstrators called an ambulance, but you ended up in a cast and had to be on crutches for two months, to the cost of $200, paid out of your savings. In realizing that probably your student health policy ($100 deductible) might pay some of the money, you stopped by the infirmary, got the forms, and sent them to White Cross, and wrote a covering letter to the Claims Department, White Cross, White Shield, Inc., 404 Cook Avenue, Chicago, Illinois 60609. You have heard that the claims are long in processing; therefore you'll write a cover letter to go with the claim form to make sure that you have the $100 by August 1 to help cover your tuition for fall.

5. Current date: Write Chemical Control Corporation, Tarzana, California 91356, from Jeanne Lewis, 655 Orchard Avenue, Los Angeles, California 90064. After a household ant invasion, Jeanne Lewis purchased this company's all-purpose bug spray. The television commercials convinced her of its effectiveness. The house has continued to have ants—red and black, and fat as well as little ants that sting. She is writing to ask what might she have done wrong and also ask for another can.

6. While in Los Angeles, Mary P. Blake, 134 Bay Drive, Sacramento, California 95837, purchased a $32 nationally-advertised Barkay swimming suit from your speciality shop, Corliss, 98 Converse Drive, L.A., Zip 90063. The suit faded after the first wearing, ruining it. Mary is returning the suit with this letter (which you'll write). She has bought many clothes from Corliss and has always been satisfied.

7. M. S. Westover, 3196 Beverly Road, Columbus, Ohio 43204, bought an electric lawn mower, Lawn-Power, from Donlevy's Department store in Columbus last July. When the mower refused to work in May, Westover took it to Donlevy's. When Westover picked up his repaired machine a month and four-inches-more-grass later, he had to pay a bill of $20.45. Donlevy's had a work order that showed installation of motor and armature at the factory in Chicago. Westover was furious over having to pay the repair bill. He had just used this 18-inch mower (that cost $88.50) one summer. Sit in for Westover and write Lawn-Power Inc., 2000 Schiller, Chicago, Illinois 60610, asking for a refund.

8. As Fred Mack, 137 Windamere Drive, Hot Springs, Arkansas 71901, you purchased on your way to Canada four new nylon cord glass-belted tires called Co-op SPD, made by Triroyal, from Missouri Tire Company, 2901 Frederick, Saint Joseph, Missouri 64507. Two thousand miles later two of the tires developed tread separation. As you were driving in fog one night, a piece of rubber hurled from a defective Triroyal tire and ruptured a brake line. Fortunately, you were able to come to a safe stop. Careful driving and your mechanical emergency brakes got you safely to a town. You had to replace these worn-out tires with Canadian-made tires which cost $110.95—$4.49 more than you paid Missouri Tire Company—and pay $17.80 for repair of your brakes. Ask for your money back and see if you can get the $4.49 also.

9. As J. R. Moman, manager of Missouri Tire Company, 2901 Frederick, Saint Joseph, Missouri 64507, write a letter to Triroyal, Mount Vernon, N.Y. 10550, enclosing a copy of Fred Mack's letter (see preceding case), and his guarantee card. You have about 300 more of these tires to sell. You've been selling tires 40 years and have been selling Triroyal for 20. You take pride in your products and your customers. Ask for 300 new tires to replace the tires you have in stock, and where to send the tires you have—at no additional cost to you.

10. Write to Mr. Bob Neal, Bob Neal Pontiac, Inc., 897 North Marshall Street, Winston-Salem, North Carolina 27105, complaining about the charge for new blades on your windshield wipers. You complained to the Service Manager, but he just shrugged and charged you. You have had no complaint other than the squeaking windshield wipers in the nine months and 15,000 miles with your Pontiac. They squeaked from the beginning, as you have reported several times to the Service Manager. You've had eight new cars, traded all at 25,000 miles or less, and have never had any trouble with nor replaced a wiper blade. The original blades were never right and should have been replaced at Pontiac expense. Also, you have never been charged for labor for installation of regular maintenance items sold at a standard mark-up. Yet, this bill included $5.60 labor for washer fluid, air filter, and wiper blade installation. You are writing Neal because you felt that he might not be aware of the charges of this type and he might want to review the situation—and refund your $12.85.

11. Six weeks ago Mrs. Paul Palmer, 1085 N.W. 60 Terrace, Gainesville, Florida 32601, was given an Eastern Electric DMC 1 coffee maker (hot plate on which the decanter or carafe sits) by Mrs. Harold Switzer, New Haven, Connecticut. After a week, when the Palmers used the coffee maker they would get shocks from the hot plate unit and carafe. After a trip to downtown Gainesville, the Palmers were told by the store manager that they should write a claim letter to Eastern Electric, 9000 Fairway Avenue, New Haven, Connecticut 06522. He said that the Consumer Product Safety Commission (CPSC) had recalled several brands of electric drip coffee makers because of potential shock hazards. As Mrs. Palmer, write the letter to Eastern Electric.

12. When you painted your family room last Christmas with Gladden Aqua-Green paint, you were careful to select an indoor enamel that stipulated "no lead," since you have three small children and a pair of matched miniature poodles. Realizing that children and dogs would somehow get some of the paint into their mouths, you wanted a nontoxic, nonlead paint. Three months after you painted your family room, two of your children (ages one and three) became violently ill. So did your prize poodles; in fact the female died, aborting the litter of six puppies she was carrying. Both the hospital that treated your children and your veterinarian pointed to arsenic poisoning. On the advice of a chemist friend, you had chips of the paint analyzed. You discovered that the green pigment in the paint had an arsenic base. Surely the paint caused your children's illness, which cost $1,000 to diagnose and cure (Blue Cross paid $800 of it), and the sickness of one of your poodles and the demise of the other along with her six unborn pups. The cost of the vet was $200, not to mention the $500 cost of your champion female and the $300 each you would have got for her puppies had they lived (total $1,800). The chemical analysis of the paint cost $50. Your total costs, clearly the result of erroneous labeling on the part of Gladden Paints, was nearly $3,000.

Before you turn the case over to Williams and Pearson, your lawyers, which could cost another $3,000 in litigation fees, write a Direct Claims letter to Gladden Paints, 841 Levine Road, Binghamton, New York 13908.

13. Assume that you are Walter Reasoner, a small stockholder and a regular customer of Peril Oil Company. On your way from Washington, D.C., to Columbus, Ohio, you noticed undue vibrations in your car, so you stopped at a large service station outside Wheeling, West Virginia (one of the Peril Oil Company's stations with a slogan stressing that you can depend on the service at all such stations for all your car's needs). The man at the station sold you two new tires, balanced all tires, and put in new front shock absorbers for $151.18 for tires (including $8.68 federal tax and balancing of all five tires), $27.90 for shocks installed, and $5.70 state tax (4 percent). You questioned the prices but paid the bill.

Once home you checked the prices and found that your local dealer would sell you the identical tires for $85 (including tax), balance all five tires for $7.50, and install the same shocks for $15.90 ($12 cheaper). Federal tax on tires is the same and of course the 4 percent state sales tax, versus the local 3 percent, is not in question.

Though you have a carbon of the bill, it does not give the name or address of the station—it's a standard form used by all the big oil company stations, giving the New York address of that company. Write the Public Relations Department of the oil company and make claim for at least $35 overcharge. Send a photocopy of the itemized bill. Your main appeal should be based on the facts in relation to the company slogan. You admit that the workman did a good job in correcting your troubles.

14. Last November you ordered a van from H. T. Boyle, dealer in Birmingham. The sales representative said the van would be delivered within six weeks (by December 14) but has been ill and the truck sales manager has been transferred. The new sales manager says the manufacturer has acknowledged receipt of your order but has provided no additional information, even a possible production date of the van. In the time since November to now, February 1, you have spent more than $200 in maintaining an old van. Write the van company (P. D. Podge, Detroit, Michigan 48228) and ask about your missing van. Assume that you are Homer Hocutt, 897 Berry Street, Bessemer, Alabama 35020.

15. From The Collector's Shop, 908 Broadview Street, Petosky, Michigan 49770, you found a most unusual gift for the man who has everything —a "plantern" (a planter about ten inches square containing five different live plants and a two-foot high lamp). You turn the lamp on and off by simply clamping forefinger and thumb together on any leaf. The electronic planter has a foam rubber padding in the bottom that must be kept moist. You bought jade, aluminum, tiger and sword plants for the plantern and left them in their original pots. Two weeks after buying the gift in Petosky, you got ready to wrap it at home (1008 West Healy, Champaign, Illinois 61820) and you discovered that the plants when squeezed will not turn the light on. Before writing the gift shop, however, you took the "plantern" to several electric repair shops in Champaign-Urbana and found no one who knew how to fix it. Write the Collector's Shop and explain your problem and ask for help.

16. As Mrs. K. T. Litter, 14–11 Clauss Drive, Purr, N.C. 17120, you have a problem. Yesterday morning, when you opened a can of "Gourmet Beef Feast," both you and your cat received an unpleasant surprise. The horrible odor sent you out of the house to put the can in your garbage can, and your cat into the basement (from which she warily emerged some seven hours later). Your local supermarket's manager disclaimed any responsibility and suggested you write the manufacturer, Shaker Oats, Merchandise Mart, Chicago, Illinois 60654. Do so, pointing out that you are concerned about possible future threats to your beloved cat's health, and asking what Shaker Oats is going to do.

17. Thinking you were going to save money on Christmas cards this year, you ordered 100 cards and envelopes (and sent a colored negative along so that the cards would have a family picture printed on them) from The House of Gifts, 900 Hewitt Avenue, Minneapolis, Minnesota 55420. Today the cards and bill arrive and you are charged $24.00 for the cards plus 6 percent sales tax and $1.05 handling charge. The ad said nothing about the handling charge or 6 percent sales tax. In checking further you realize that you never have to pay sales tax on goods purchased from another state. To complicate matters more, your name was spelled incorrectly. Write a letter refusing to pay the sales tax and refusing to accept the cards. Ask if you may send the cards back for correct printing and the bill back for correct billing.

ADJUSTMENT-APPROVAL CASES

1. You are the adjustment manager for Powers Jewelry Company, 980 Conifer Street, Grand Junction, Colorado 81501. Eight days ago Lillian Steinway, Bar Eleven Ranch, Bonanza, Utah 84008, ordered and charged to her account one glass jewelry box to display her antique gold railroad watch. The 35-dollar case was trimmed in gold. She reports the arrival of the jewelry case with three of the four legs bent and the glass smashed. She wants another case just like the one that was broken and wants to know what to do with the one she has. You are having packed and sent another Stockman case in a larger carton with more packing, such as you'll use for such merchandise hereafter. Ask her to return the damaged one to you, shipping charges collect.

2. Piano tuning time came around to the home of Mr. and Mrs. Horace Humble, Cross Creek Acres, Salem, Massachusetts 01970. The faithful tuner of 20 years died, so the Humbles relied on the good reports they heard about a new, fashionably-modern tuner, Mike Melody, Melody House, 625 Huntington Avenue, Boston, Mass. 02109. In Mike's smooth way he talked the Humbles into having their piano stripped (black ebony removed so that the natural wood would show through), for which they paid him $200. When he brought the piano back, he said, he would tune it. Two weeks later the piano returned and looked handsome, but the decal saying Steinway was gone and Mike had not been at work for five days, the delivery men said. Every day the Humbles called but got just an answering service. The piano had never been tuned, but the tuning had been paid for. The truth was that Mike went bankrupt. You bought the business, and you are going to tune the piano at your own expense for the Humbles and replace the decal. You have tried to call the Humbles several times but, being unable to reach them, are writing a letter hoping to regain their good will, set a date for the tuning, and help business.

3. Read Case 5, p. 179 before you begin the following case: As Public Relations Director, Chemical Control Corporation, 925 Industrial Park Blvd., South San Francisco, send Jeanne Lewis another can of your potent ant spray and tell her that if she will read the label again on her old can, in the lower right corner, the directions say to buy this type of spray rather than the all-purpose. On the newly designed labels, you have made this fact much more eye-catching in order to help customers make the right selection.

4. *Letterhead:* The House of MoKo, 3101 Collins Avenue, Miami, Florida 33128. *Inside address:* Phillips Burger Department Store, 250 Rockton Avenue, Rockford, Illinois 61111. Use today's date. *Signature block:* Sincerely yours, Mildred Selko, vice president. *Information:* A good customer for 26 years, Janie Gibbons, returned to Phillips Burger a $36.50 purse she purchased two weeks before. The purse was genuine red leather with her initials in blue. During the two weeks she had used the purse about six times, and while using it she noticed that the leather was cracking and pieces actually peeled off from the bottom, she told the store. As Mildred Selko, write a letter asking Phillips Burger to have Janie bring the purse in and then mail it on to you. You will replace the purse exactly even though you question the type of use Janie gave this purse. Phillips Burger has been a good customer of yours, and you back up your quality merchandise. Include sales promotional material on Moko handmade jewelry done by some of the finest artisans of Mexico.

5. As Mary Farley Powers, owner of The Collector's Shop, 908 Broadview Street, Petosky, Michigan 49770, answer the claim from Mrs. Francis Andrews, 1008 West Healy, Champaign, Illinois 61820, about the plantern (Case 15, p. 182). Suggest that she try several different approaches to the plantern: (1) be sure that the metal disc in the center touches all of the pots; (2) the disc should not be sitting in water; and (3) the pots should be of about equal weight.

Resale on this product could be that Peggy Cederberg just bought one of these unusual planterns for the president of the United States for his birthday. Sales promotional material can be on the new Canadian handmade sweaters from Qiana yarn (the new lightweight yarn that washes, dry cleans beautifully). Enclose a folder on these sweaters and suggest she order.

6. Mrs. Andrews (preceding case) tried all the suggestions the Collector's Shop made and still the plantern doesn't work. Now she wants to know what Collector's is going to do about it. Tell her to return for replacement or refund.

7. As J. R. Moman, you have the job of telling Mack (Case 8, p. 180) that you will replace the two tires that went bad or you'll refund his money, $106.46. He must send you his guarantee card so that you can settle up with Triroyal. To your knowledge these tires were checked for conformity to federal safety standards. For sales promotional material tell Mack about your round fog light with a quartz-iodine bulb, swivel base, chrome-plated body $19.99, shipping weight two pounds.

Even though you cannot refund the $4.49 difference that Mack had to pay for the Canadian tires, you can reduce the price of this fog light from $19.99 to $15.00. Since Mack had trouble driving in fog, suggest that he use an enclosed card to order from you.

8. As Fred Turner, Director of Sales, Triroyal Tire Company, Mount Vernon, N.Y. 10550, answer J. R. Moman (Case 9, p. 180). You recall all his tires. You have had about 50 percent of these Co-op SPD tires develop tread separation within the first 4,000 miles. National Highway Traffic Safety Administration (NHTSA) is in the process of testing this model. Meanwhile you will immediately ship a supply of comparable tires to replace the Co-op SPD's. Keep Moman's good will by resale talk on other Triroyal tires. The AT–200, tubeless, "Splayfoot" has two tough fiberglass belts that work with plies to keep wide tread flat and is guaranteed 30,000 miles. Cost $25 but sell retail $35.

9. As Service Manager for Muller-Braun, 5960 Southwest 45th St., Miami 33155, you have received a letter from Roland Snipes, 907 Bellvue Drive, Hollywood, Florida 33020; in fact it is the third letter you have received from Snipes, not to mention his half-dozen or so personal appearances to complain about his new WW's stalling in the morning. Your mechanics have taken apart the carburetor, replaced some of the parts, and adjusted to the factory specifications for the automatic choke; but Snipes, who has written to the Better Business Bureau and even to Ralph Nader, claims that the car still stalls in the morning. A recent directive from the WW research center at Dieben, Germany, however, proves that Mr. Snipes has a point. It seems that the 19— WW automatic choke was designed for a cooler, drier climate than the Hollywood summer climate and will not function properly unless the overnight temperature drops below 70 degrees. Write a letter explaining the situation to Mr. Snipes and inviting him to make an appointment to have a new, improved choke installed.

10. As sales director for Sarah Jane's (bakers of fine white and dark fruitcakes, thousands of which are sold by mail), 4446 Pine Ridge Avenue,

Evansville, Indiana 47714, answer the letter from one of your unhappy customers, Louis M. Simpson, Apartment 202, The Williamsburg East, Urbana, Illinois 61801. He reports in sharp language that over a month ago he sent his order and check for one five-lb. Sarah Jane's White Fruitcake along with his card to be sent to his hostess of several days in Des Plaines, Illinois 60018, Mrs. Hamilton Fish, 399 Thacker Drive. In Des Plaines again last weekend, he called the Fishes and discreetly found out that the gift had never been received. "Unless you have gone out of business—in which case you'd surely return my check for $7.95—will you please trace this *or* send at once *and* write a note to Mrs. Fish confirming that I *did* order this gift very shortly after I was a guest in her home?" he ended. The facts are (*a*) you were caught short on the special raisins from Turkey and currants from California, without which Sarah Jane's White Fruitcakes would not be the distinctive culinary treats they are and (*b*) someone slipped in not notifying the buyer or the recipient of the atypical delay in shipment. You've resumed baking and shipping, filling orders in the order received; the cake in question is en route and may already have arrived. Write the necessary letters (to one or both Simpson and Mrs. Fish, as your teacher directs). (You should send Simpson a carbon of your letter to the lady.) Certainly you'll want to try to convince both that a Sarah Jane's White Fruitcake is an appropriate gift any time and is well worth waiting for.

11. Shirley Shaver, Apartment 202, 2153 California Street N.W., Washington, D.C. 20008, gave her three-year-old grandchild, Billy Weaver, a slot-racing set ($55.50). This complicated all-electric toy (transformer, controls, cars and track) came from your store, F. O. Sweeno, Lennox Shopping Center, Atlanta, Georgia 30388. Grandmother realizes that Billy is too young and too destructive for such a delicate toy; so it is sent back the day after it was given to Billy. Examination shows that the toy is in good shape and can be sold as new.

Refund Mrs. Shaver's money and suggest she order the "Checker-Flag Racer" set, a heavy-steel, wind-up race car toy. The cost is $20.50. Name other educational toys that Billy might enjoy . . . (Sesame Street, mock-up towns).

12. Answer Mrs. Paul Palmer's claim letter (Case 11, p. 181), as adjustment manager of Eastern Electric. If mailed back to you, you will replace the DMC 1 coffee maker with an improved CMD 1 coffee maker. You had to recall all your DMC 1 because if the cleaning instructions for periodic flushing of the main heating element with straight vinegar were not followed regularly, some minerals found in hard water could attack the main element's outer sheath. That could create an electrical path from the main element to the warming element. In that situation, someone in direct contact with an electric ground (a water pipe, for example) might get an electric shock on touching the warming element while the appliance was turned on. On the CMD I model insulation has been added to isolate the warming element from the main element. New instructions emphasize the need for proper cleaning, especially in areas (like Gainesville) where the water is hard. Stress the idea that drip-type coffee is brewed at just the correct temperature, not boiled, so the coffee oils remain pure and flavorful . . . making a clear cup of coffee with full-bodied taste. As an extra bonus, you have sent along 50 extra paper filters.

13. Read Case 13, p. 181. As Chairman of the Board of Peril Oil Company, N.Y. 00187, you decide to start an immediate investigation of the Wheeling station's prices, and you promise that the unhappy stockholder-customer will receive a report shortly. Your main purpose, of course, is to regain lost confidence and goodwill by making deserved adjustments or necessary explanations where no adjustment is warranted. Certainly you can't now promise anything except the investigation, a fair handling, any needed corrective measures, and your interest in seeing that customers are treated right.

14. As Retail Service Director (preceding case), you have your report from Wheeling and are to write the letter the Chairman of the Board promised to the unhappy customer-stockholder. People who operate service stations and carry your name and products are independent operators leasing the stations and hence can set their own prices and procedures—within broad contract limits. You select them carefully, however, and exercise some supervision and loose control. The leases are for short terms, renewable on mutual agreement. Your main methods of control are by suggestion, persuasion, and advice—decisions to renew or discontinue leases are usually handled by regional representatives.

The Wheeling representative found considerable variation in prices on tires and shocks in his marketing areas and has figured the averages. He informed all leaseholders in the area of what the averages are and of the dangers in being too far from the averages. He talked specifically with the manager, got him to agree to reduce his prices to the averages, and got him to write a check to you for $19.20 (the resultant reduction on the questioned bill). Send the check with this good adjustment letter.

15. As F. E. Line, Customer Relations Director of Shaker Oats Company, answer the claim (Case 16, p. 182) about the spoiled can of "Gourmet Beef Feast." You use only fresh, carefully prepared ingredients, precise cooking procedures, and modern, up-to-date canning apparatus. In fact, your pet foods are given all the care and attention in processing that you give your famous line of canned foods designed to please the most discriminating human palate. But occasionally microscopic pinholes occur in cans, and these can lead to spoilage. Enclose a coupon good for four free cans of Shaker Oats cat food, and thank Mrs. Litter for telling her troubles. You are as concerned about her cat's, and all cats', health as she is. Add some resale on your company by briefly describing your famous research facility where new foods are tested on well-cared-for cats for acceptance before they are marketed.

chapter 6 Special goodwill letters

Letters of deserved praise
Letters of sympathy
Letters of appreciation
Letters of seasonal greeting
Letters of welcome and invitation
Letters accompanying premiums
Letters offering helpful information
Letters anticipating resistance

FROM THE PRECEDING discussions and illustrations of various kinds of letters, you certainly realize that all letters should retain and even try to increase the reader's favorable attitude toward the writer while working primarily on something else.

Certain letters, however, have no other immediate purpose than the cementing of friendly relations between writer and reader. Although they may not ask for any immediate action, indirectly these special goodwill letters pave the way for continued business from old customers and new business from prospects.

Because your readers know you do not *have* to write special goodwill letters, these unexpected letters are especially effective in overcoming the impression of indifference—indifference to business given and to serving new customers.

All too often the only times a customer receives word from a firm are when it wants to make a sale or to collect for something or when it has to handle a claim. This apparent lack of interest is borne out in practically all reliable surveys of why firms lose customers. About seven out of ten lost customers just drift away. Yet eight out of ten are reclaimable if given some attention. Only 1 percent of lost customers have real grievances that need adjusting. And a large part of the 70 percent who do drift away would undoubtedly not do so if they were reminded that the business firm appreciates their patronage and has a continuing interest in their welfare.

Where people take their trade depends not just on quality, price, and convenience; these are usually comparable in several different outlets. We trade where we do partly because (1) we like the people and (2) we appreciate extra-service considerations—the personal and friendly aspects.

In theory, goodwill letters sell only friendship. Some do no more than that—ostensibly. But we should admit to ourselves that a letter on a firm's letterhead, signed by a representative of the firm, is promotional, regardless of its personal nature. The cultivation of business is inherent in the circumstance itself. No business writer need be reluctant to establish the virtues of a firm's services and goods and to place them at the disposal of the reader. The main thing to guard against is appearing to be offering only friendship in the first part of the letter and then shifting to an obvious, immediate sales pitch.

Some of these "unnecessary" special goodwill letters are of such highly personal nature that to use an obvious form would be insulting, to include sales or resale talk on either firm or merchandise would be ludicrous, and to write very much would likely result in gushiness. Letters of deserved praise and of sympathy certainly fall into this category. Letters expressing appreciation, extending seasonal greetings, issuing invitations, accompanying favors (or services), or offering helpful information also do if they are strictly goodwill letters; but most of these are form letters including sales-building talk and thus are promotional.

Letters of deserved praise

Although letters praising people do not have to contain the word *congratulations,* in them you are recognizing a significant event or accomplishment in the life of your reader: a job promotion, election to an office, receiving an honor, winning a contest, graduation, marriage, birth of a child, or completion of a new plant, office, project, or report. All these and many more are instances when you can show not only customers but also friends and acquaintances that you are interested in what happens to them. Some of the better ones are just a few lines:

When I saw that you've been named plant manager of Tri-States, I was delighted!

It's a well-earned recognition.

And it couldn't happen to a more deserving fellow!

(Any salutary effects of the foregoing passages would be lost if the writer followed with such an idea as "Now that you're earning more, surely you'd like to consider more insurance" or ". . . buy more clothes.")

I have just completed your article about credit control in the recent issue of Credit World.

Heartiest congratulations on a job well done!

--

I can appreciate your deep satisfaction and pride in John's graduation cum laude from Haverford last week.

Congratulations to him—and also to his parents.

--

We share your pride and happiness in the completion of the new Henderson plant.

It is a criterion of business, as well as civic, accomplishment.

Good wishes from all of us. (Or Sincere wishes for your continued success.)

If these examples strike you as being more like telegrams than letters, remember that timeliness is important in letters like these, probably of equal importance with what you actually say. The friendly thought behind the message counts most.

A note like the following would certainly engender good feeling (and probably stimulate the reader to do even better work.):

Your analysis of production difficulties at the Saginaw plant was one of the clearest, most easily read reports I've ever been privileged to study.

We're carrying out some of your recommendations immediately.

Several of us look forward to discussing the report with you when you return to the home office.

In the meantime, thanks for a job well done.

Many people in both their business and their private lives have discovered the gratifying responses of associates, customers, and personal friends to the receipt of a newspaper or magazine clipping of interest to the reader. A simple greeting (it may be no more than "Good morning") and a line or two like "This clipping made me think of you" or "I thought you might be interested in this clipping" are enough, followed by a handwritten or typewritten note like

Let me add my commendation to those you've undoubtedly already received as a result of the enclosed clipping.

It's a pleasure to know a man like you.

Still another variation of a letter deservedly praising someone is one you write to a third person about a second person who in your opinion merits recognition or appreciation or both. The man who wrote the following letter to an airline official made at least two friends for himself:

On your Flight 127 from Chicago to San Francisco last Tuesday, I was pleased with every phase of the service. But I was especially pleased with the conduct of Captain A. L. Lutz.

While at the controls he kept us well informed on flight conditions and frequently pointed out places of interest en route. When he walked through the cabin, he was the soul of hospitality and courtesy to every passenger—particularly to a six-year-old boy who was making his first flight!

As we came in over San Francisco in bright moonlight and

```
crossed the Bay, Captain Lutz pointed out sights of interest.
It was a thoughtful gesture that all of us appreciated.

The smooth, pleasant ride was made memorable through the
"little extras" of Captain Lutz.

My thanks and commendations to the line and to him.
```

Any time someone renders outstanding service is an appropriate occasion to relay, via letter, your understanding and appreciation of its significance. Such a gesture not only impresses the reader with the writer's "humanness"; but it also can and often does earn preferential treatment on subsequent occasions.

```
Last Friday your representative, Mr. John Wade, answered our
call for help when one of our motors failed at a crucial time.

We appreciated the promptness with which he came, of course.
But we appreciated even more the efficiency he displayed in
getting it running again.  He was considerate of all around
him and thoughtful enough not to leave a mess for us to clean
up.

Our thanks to you and to Mr. Wade; we shall remember on other
occasions.
```

Obviously, under such circumstances you could also write directly to the person whose performance you praise, as in the following instance:

```
If such an award were given by the U.S. Chamber Workshop,
you'd certainly get the "E" for excellence, John.

Your Thursday afternoon clinic met with more enthusiastic
reactions than I've observed in a long time.

It is a rewarding experience to work with people like you.
```

With a second letter to the speaker's dean, the writer could spread goodwill all around:

```
Everyone at MSU working with us on the U.S. Chamber Workshop
contributed and cooperated in exemplary fashion, Dean White.

We are most grateful to all of you.

John Fohr's Thursday afternoon clinic met with such
enthusiastic response that I feel I should report the group
reaction to you.  He had men like Ed Sherrer, the Memphis
division manager, eating out of his hand!

Deservedly so, in my opinion.
```

Congratulatory letters, including birthday and anniversary greetings, are practically always individualized. Sympathy letters—the most personal of any special goodwill letters—must be.

Letters of sympathy

Most of us are accustomed to lending a helping hand and extending expressions of encouragement when friends and family suffer some adversity. The same sympathetic attitude should prevail when a business friend experiences misfortune. Admittedly, letters of condolence are some of the most difficult special goodwill letters to write because of the melancholy circumstances (which can be reduced by avoiding specifics). But certainly everyone appreciates them. When a report of a retailer's illness reaches a wholesaler (or a manufacturer), a short, human, and essentially positive note like the following can gain goodwill:

> Sorry, Sam—
>
> —to hear that you're in the hospital again.
>
> But with rest and good care you'll be back at the store sooner than you think.
>
> I've always enjoyed you as a friend and valued you as a business associate; so for two reasons I hope all goes well with you again soon.

--

> We were distressed to learn of the automobile accident that hospitalized you and Mrs. Sigler recently.
>
> It's good to know, however, that you are now up and about. We certainly hope that Mrs. Sigler's condition will improve rapidly and without further complications.

As a result of accident, illness, and advancing age, most of us find ourselves having to write letters concerning the death of someone we've known. To the surviving partner of a business, for example, the following letter would be a comfort and goodwill builder by showing the writer's friendly interest and concern:

> We were genuinely distressed to learn of the death of Mr. Guin, your partner and our good friend for many years.
>
> Although the firm of Guin and Beatty will feel the effects of his absence, the greater loss is to the community and the Guin family. The good judgment, vision, and integrity Mr.Guin displayed as a business leader in your city undoubtedly carried over into his private life.
>
> In extending these words of sympathy, we should also like to add a few of encouragement and confidence in the future; we feel sure that would have been Mr. Guin's attitude.

Even though the writer of the preceding letter might not have met the widow (and/or the surviving offspring), certainly none of them would take offense at a message such as the following:

> For many years we enjoyed a business friendship with Mr. Guin.
>
> We respected him as a good businessman who insisted on high standards in serving the public and was always just, fair, and cooperative in his relations with us. We admired the good judgment, vision, and integrity he showed as a business leader in your community.
>
> To you who saw these and other fine qualities in greater detail and frequency than we were privileged to, we offer our sympathy.

May his contributions to your life in former days make the days to come easier.

Such a letter will necessarily have an emotional impact. But that effect can be less if writers will refrain from quoting Scripture or poetry. And sepulchral overtones will not be so powerful if death is accepted as the inevitability it is and the word itself used rather than euphemisms like "passed away," "passed to his reward," and "departed." Such a letter is going to be a greater comfort when it emphasizes the good characteristics and the outstanding contributions of the dead individual rather than the sorrow and anguish of the survivor. Possibly you will find writing such letters a little less difficult and will write more truly comforting messages if you accept the thought that good, worthwhile people continue to exert their influence in the hearts and minds of those who knew them.

Adversity also strikes in other forms—fires, floods, accidents and lawsuits, labor unrest, and work stoppage. When it does, the victim(s) will appreciate a message that says, "We're your friends; we understand the significance of this to you; we hope everything will work out successfully." If you really mean the offer and are in a position to extend it, you can add the equivalent of "Call on us if we can help." The following are examples:

All of us were sorry to hear of the fire that destroyed your warehouse night before last.

It's a tough break.

We're sure, however, that the same determination and ingenuity that helped you to build your business so successfully will also see you through this temporary setback.

Now, if this writer had some unused storage space and wanted to offer it, he might very well close with

We have a 30 x 40 room that we won't need for another 90 days; if that will help tide you over in any way, give me a ring.

But to propose to rent the space would change the complexion of the letter and destroy any goodwill built up in the opening passages.

Letters of appreciation

You have no doubt observed that most congratulatory messages also involve an element of thanks; likewise, most thank-you letters contain some commendatory passages. It's really just a question of where you want your emphasis to go.

Strictly goodwill thank-you letters—in response to a favor extended, for work on a project (member of a fund-raising team, for example), or for a contribution—have their origins in civic, educational, and religious surroundings rather than in business.

Many thanks for the untiring, cheerful way you worked on the recent United Fund Drive.

Through effort like yours we exceeded our goal.

Possibly the knowledge that you have helped materially to provide clothing, food, and medical care during the coming year for underprivileged children will be more gratifying with this expression of appreciation.

--

For the 32,000 youths of Athens . . .

Thanks a million!

Your generous gift to the new "Y" building is another evidence of your concern for the boys and girls of our city and county.

We want you to know how much we appreciate your cooperation in this project. As citizens and parents, we'll all be happy about our share in it for years to come.

As a matter of fact, you can't call the preceding letters pure goodwill letters, for obviously the resale phrases are designed to convince the reader of the worth of the projects and thus encourage a repeat performance the next time a request comes along.

Letters written by business firms are even more definitely promotional. *Any* time is a good time to express appreciation to good customers for their patronage or for handling accounts satisfactorily. Even the rubber-stamped notation on a current bill, "One of the pleasures of being in business is serving a good customer like you," has a heartening effect. But many stores wisely do more. Upon the first use of the account—or later in the first year—some stores send a thank-you note like the following:

Thank you for using your newly opened account. Surely you found it a quick, convenient way to shop at Tilford's.

To make sure our merchandise and service are just the way you want them, we'll always welcome any comments you may have about improvements you would like us to make.

We want you to continue to shop at Tilford's and we pledge our efforts to keep your trust.

Because of the rush of business, such letters too often go out only around holiday and special-event times. In too many such cases they don't do the effective job they might because too many other people and stores are sending greetings and goodwill letters on those special occasions. Arriving unexpectedly and without apparent reason at some other time, the following note is probably a more effective pleasant reminder of the firm's appreciation:

Believe us—

—we appreciate your continued patronage and friendship.

And to hold your friendship and patronage, we certainly intend to continue giving you the sort of service and honest values you deserve.

Come see us often.

When an account has not been used for some time and then a purchase is made, many credit managers wisely send a thank-you note:

```
Thank you for the purchase you made recently.

It's good to hear you say "Charge it" again, for we've really
missed you.

To serve you so well you'll want to come in more often is our
constant aim.
```

Letters thanking customers for paying promptly are simply a more specialized version of the ones we've been examining. They are also effective means of discouraging or reducing collection problems. Such a simple note as the following not only pleases the customer; it reinforces determination to maintain the good habit:

```
Your check this morning in prompt payment of last month's
purchases made me think, "I wish all our accounts were handled
so efficiently."

It's a real pleasure to service an account like yours, and we
thank you sincerely for your cooperation.
```

You can also easily tie in the expression of appreciation with a concrete reminder of the benefits the customer gains from taking care of obligations as promised:

```
Thank you for the splendid manner in which you paid up your
recent account.

Your record of prompt payments firmly establishes your credit
at Black's.  You will find it handy in adding fresh, new things
to keep your home alive and interesting.  Enjoying these things
while you save for them on small payments is thrifty and wise.

Come in often and make full use of the many services this
large, complete home store can render you, whether it's just a
window shade or a complete houseful of furniture.
```

If you keep your eyes and ears open, you'll find many other occasions for saying thank you to your customers and clientele. When a customer recommends you or your firm to another person, you'll certainly benefit in the long run by sending a cheerful, personalized note like the following:

```
Thank you for bringing Mrs. Stallings into the shop recently.
We enjoyed meeting her and seeing you again.

We appreciate this expression of confidence in us.  We shall
do all we can to serve her well and to continue to merit your
patronage and recommendation to your friends.

                          --

We appreciate your suggesting to Mr. Lee that he come to us
for quality men's wear.

He came in yesterday and seemed pleased with what we were able
to show him.

Thank you.  We're looking forward to his next visit.
```

When a firm writes such a letter of appreciation to an individual, no reply is expected. And when an individual takes the time to pay a business firm a compliment or express appreciation for good service, no answer is *required.* But you establish yourself as courteous and polite if you do reply. Furthermore, appropriate resale talk helps to strengthen the friendly feeling as well as build future business. The following letter emphasizes gratitude for kind words but adroitly stresses service:

The personnel of our Birmingham station quite proudly sent us your letter complimenting Delta personnel for their assistance in transporting Otto to his new home.

It was a real pleasure to receive such an excellent commendation, and we're happy to pass this along to all those who assisted.

In these days of rapidly growing transportation problems, and with the volume of traffic mounting so fast, we sometimes feel that Delta's past record of outstanding personalized service may not be attainable today in spite of our best efforts.

Then, at just the right time, along comes a letter like yours to show that our station personnel are still doing a good job of public relations. It is a genuine pleasure to hear of the excellent way they handled the many details, and we do appreciate your taking time to tell us.[1]

When you receive suggestions for improved service (some of which will be outright complaints requiring adjustment letters), an acknowledgment *is* required, particularly if you have invited the suggestion.

Thank you for pointing out how we can improve our system for providing free parking to shoppers at Wiesel's.

Starting next Monday, we shall have all customers pick up their tokens at the cashier's booth on the ground floor. And we shall have the parking lot entrance to the store completely cleared for easier flow of customer traffic.

Your suggestions for better service are most welcome, and we're sure that this change will make shopping at Wiesel's a greater pleasure than it was before.

Letters of seasonal greeting

A modified form of the thank-you letter is the one of seasonal greeting. By far the most common time is around Christmas and New Year, although some stores send such letters shortly before Easter, Valentine's Day, or Thanksgiving, when they have less competition from other mailings. Since they must be mass mailings in most firms (to keep down costs), they are rarely personalized.

---

[1] Reprinted with the permission of the author, W. D. Huff, manager of customer relations, Delta Air Lines, Inc., Atlanta.

The United Fund letter and the "Y" letter (pp. 194–95) were printed forms, thus conserving the funds of the organizations for more worthy causes. Business organizations, too, must conserve employee effort and time (as well as funds) by using some modifications of form treatment in many of the thank-you and seasonal greeting letters they mail. Ideally, these letters would be individualized; as a practical matter, they often are not. The undisguised form can be successful, however:

> Business firms, too, pause at this season to count their blessings.
>
> Good friends and customers like you are one of our greatest.
>
> So we want to tell you how much we appreciate your patronage at the same time we send heartiest wishes for
>
> A VERY MERRY CHRISTMAS AND A HAPPY, SUCCESSFUL NEW YEAR!

With the references to customers and patronage, the letter is promotional in effect. Most emphatically, you would not want sales material in a letter with such an opening theme. The following holiday greeting letter, however, is an overt attempt to cultivate business, and perhaps wisely so in the light of how a savings and loan association functions and the kinds of service it provides members:

> GREETINGS AT THE NEW YEAR!
>
> Hearts are never as full of peace and happiness as when friends and loved ones gather in the home at this season of good cheer and fellowship.
>
> Through the years your Association has played a part in providing homes for its members through sound home-financing plans that lead to real debt-free home ownership. Won't you please tell your friends about your Association and recommend its services to them? They will appreciate knowing of the easy, convenient terms upon which a loan may be repaid.
>
> Our officers and directors join in thanking you for your help in the past year and in wishing you happiness and health in 19— and for years to come.

Most of the time, however, you will be on safer ground if you exclude such promotional passages and concentrate on a simple wish for the customer's well-being, along with an expression of gratitude.

Letters of welcome and invitation

One of the most popular forms of goodwill letter is that greeting newcomers to a community and offering to be of assistance, particularly during the orientation period. Almost always it is an invitation to come in and get acquainted; it also emphasizes the services of the inviting firm. One unusual and unexpected example is the following from a public library:

Welcome to Evansville!

We're glad to have you as new members of our progressive city.

Your library card is ready for your use. We hope you'll be down soon to pick it up and to become acquainted with the staff and the services. For your reading pleasure and research over 100,000 volumes are available. Staff members will gladly assist you in finding what you seek. All of the leading magazines and newspapers are available in the lounge.

The children's room is also well supplied with both fiction and nonfiction books on a wide variety of topics of interest to youngsters 6 to 15.

If you enjoy musical recordings, you may want to check out some of the thousand-odd albums ranging from the most recent popular music to the classics.

We shall be glad to give you maps of the city, to supply directions—in short, to help you in any way we can to know Evansville better.

The library is open from 9 a.m. until 10 p.m. every weekday. We are glad to answer telephone inquiries during that time.

Please come in soon.

Such a letter—with no sales ax to grind—is the essence of goodwill in its spirit. It is more likely to be accepted at its face value than the usual letter from a firm with commercial/profit aspirations, such as the following:

As a new resident of our friendly city, you are cordially invited to visit the Federal Bank. We should like to get to know you. Even though you may already have selected a bank, it would be a pleasure to welcome you to Blankville personally and to explain the many services the Federal offers its customers.

The Federal has given prompt, courteous, and efficient banking services to the people of Blankville for over 75 years, and we would appreciate the opportunity of serving you.

Among the conveniences in Federal's modern banking quarters are the four drive-in teller windows that enable you to bank without alighting from your car. And in the parking garage right in our own building you may have 30 minutes of free parking while taking care of your banking business.

You may also bank around the clock at the Federal; a complete mail deposit service and a 24-hour depository are located in our parking garage.

Won't you come in for a friendly visit soon?

Most readers would probably recognize this letter for the wolf-in-sheep's-clothing it is. It is an obvious attempt to get a new account, and the attempts to establish friendly feeling are thin and transparent. Better to discard the talk of "get to know you" and "friendly visit" and get right down to brass tacks with an opening like "Since you are a newcomer to Blankville and will need a conveniently located bank with complete facilities, may we tell you what we can offer you at the Federal?"

On the other hand, the invitation to a special event extended in the following letter would probably be read with interest; it builds goodwill because it expresses a desire to render service; no resale (except that inherent in the action itself) or sales talk distracts:

Will you be our guest?

Beginning next Thursday, May 31, and every Thursday after that for the rest of the summer, Brentling's will present prominent lecturers and editors reviewing the most talked-about recent books.

All the reviews will be held in the auditorium on the sixth floor (air-conditioned, of course, like the rest of Brentling's) and will begin promptly at 2 p.m.

This Thursday Mr. I. George Levitt, popular literary editor of the Times, will review Robert Kukli's Cuddlesome Foursome—a powerful, gripping story.

We hope you will be with us to enjoy this initial literary treat and as many of the others as you possibly can.

Someone connected with credit control can easily maintain a list of newcomers to the community and mail a form letter (easily individualized, which does not promise credit, please note, but only invites the application):

Welcoming you to this community gives us a great deal of pleasure. We hope soon to count you as one of our good friends. Our Credit Department will be glad to handle your credit application at your request.

We invite you to use our lounging and rest rooms on the mezzanine, or the fountain luncheonette where you can get a deliciously prepared, well-balanced luncheon at a reasonable price. Rollins' spacious parking lot, located only 15 feet from the rear entrance to the store, is absolutely free to you when you shop here, no matter if your purchase is only a spool of thread. On Rollins' remodeled third floor you'll find home furnishings. The advice of our interior decorators is available to you with no obligation. And in the remodeled downstairs section you'll find an entirely new and complete food mart and new housewares department.

We are here to serve you. And we hope that you too will soon feel as one of our customers recently was kind enough to say to us, "The longer people live in this community, the more they trade at Rollins'."

--

This is just a note to express our appreciation for the new account you recently opened with us. We are happy to welcome you as customers and thank you for your confidence in us.

Please call on me or any of our officers whenever we can help you.

The following letter to a new shareholder is typical of what many corporations do to cement goodwill (and possibly forestall some gripes when things don't go too well for the corporation):

On behalf of the Board of Directors and employees of Pushman, I welcome you as a Pushman stockholder.

Through your shares in Pushman, you participate in ownership of one of America's leading corporations . . . and one with a bright and promising future.

Your company has operations in virtually every part of the world, activities that reach into a broad range of products and services that help to make human life better.

As your company progresses, you will receive regular reports. These will be primarily our annual and quarterly reports. In addition, we will send you special reports when circumstances warrant them.

Your company's latest annual report is enclosed, and it will give you an in-depth report on our achievements and status last year. If you would like more information on some aspect of our activities, please write me.

Again, welcome to Pushman. We look forward to sharing with you in the future.

When you can verify credit reliability (usually an easy thing to do), you may elect to set up the account and so inform the reader:

We know that stores, too, make a difference to a person establishing a home in a new community.

To serve you in as friendly manner as possible is one of our aims. As an earnest assurance of our desire to show you every possible courtesy that will make for a permanent and happy business friendship, we have opened a convenient charge account in your name.

The next time you are in the store, simply say "Charge it" to the person waiting on you.

We hope to see you soon—and often.

The following special invitation letter is frankly a low-pressure sales letter. It does offer a service in making shopping easier, but the primary emphasis is on sales.

For our best customers we're having an Open House the evenings of Wednesday, December 7, through Saturday, December 10. The store will be open until 9 these evenings, and you are invited to come and "just look" to your heart's content.

Refreshments will be served from 6 to 8, and our sales personnel will simply act as hosts. No public announcement will be made of this event.

With an eye to Christmas giving, you may want to examine some of the popular pocket-size transistor radios or portable TV's. Many GE and RCA models will be available for your inspection. The Whirlpool portable dishwasher is an especially welcome gift for a busy wife and mother. And of course, the 19— models of

GE refrigerators, washers, dryers, and other appliances will be on display. Any attendant will gladly demonstrate one of these for you.

This Open House is intended as a departure from business routine—one that will give you the opportunity of working out your Christmas gift problems at leisure. Won't you come in one or more of these evenings?

Letters seeking the revival of an account are but modified versions of invitation letters. When an account remains unused for any length of time—say three months or six months, depending on management's choice—it may be a signal that the customer is drifting away because of store indifference, or it may be the result of a real grievance. Letters inviting the customer back, reselling your merchandise or services, stressing "How can we serve you better?" and finally asking forthrightly, "May we continue to serve you?" can be mailed individually or in a series. One of the finest we've ever seen is this one:

Spring fever?

Here's a SURE cure—a Beachstone suit, coat, or dress, spiced with the right accessories.

Easy to choose, easy to buy too. Simply use your charge account at Wilson's. It's as good as new and just waiting for your "charge it" to be as useful as ever.

So come in soon! See and try on the beautiful new spring apparel, hats, shoes, and other accessories we have assembled for your Easter pleasure.

You can easily pattern any such letter after this one, which is built on sales promotion material and an action ending suggesting a visit to the store. Letters built around special events, such as Christmas, readily supply a theme (although they may lose some effect by competition with many others):

A welcome warm as Santa's smile awaits you at Bowen's!

We're all decked out with our Christmas best; so you can easily find the right gift for everyone on your Christmas list.

Practical gifts, starry-eyed gifts . . . and all conveniently in one store . . . Bowen's . . . where you can just say "Charge it" for ALL your Christmas giving.

Warmest holiday greetings!

Accompanying a new credit card, one letter solicited the renewal of the customer's business with:

Ordinarily we'd send you this enclosure with our monthly statement. Since your account hasn't been used recently, we're sending it along with some back-to-school suggestions.

Whether you're thinking of complete outfits for your child or a back-to-school gift for a favorite niece, nephew, or friend, you'll find complete selections of dependable quality Bowen merchandise in every department.

Your charge account is just as good as ever—whether you come to the store, phone, or shop by mail.

Some writers studiously avoid asking whether anything is wrong (see p. 419). Some stores send a dozen or so mailings before asking. A favorite form is the letter written on only one half of the page (usually the left side) with the caption "Here's Our Side of the Story." At the top of the right-side blank space appears another caption, "Won't You Tell Us Your Side of the Story?" Regardless of the format, most of these letters make a request much like this one:

One of my duties as credit manager of Bowen's is to check up on our service to keep it up to par.

Since your account has not been used for quite some time, the only way we can be sure we have pleased you with our merchandise and service is to hear directly from you.

Just use the handy form and the convenient stamped envelope enclosed to tell us whether you want us to keep your charge account open.

We will certainly do our best to please you.

Will you write us . . . now?

We'll surely appreciate it!

Letters accompanying premiums

Often as a goodwill reminder an alert executive finds some item to mail inexpensively along with a note reiterating the desire to be of service, such as the following from a jewelry and optical shop:

The special pocket-size Rausch & Lomb Star Ban spray accompanying this letter is for your use in keeping your handsome Everett glasses spotless.

Accept it with our compliments and the hope that you will be completely happy with your recent selection from Everett's collection of fine frames for the discriminating woman.

In a somewhat humorous vein one company recently mailed a pocketsize calorie counter to customers and prospects with this short note:

"Everything's expanding—especially my waistline," grumbled a friend recently.

Just in case you (or someone you know) may need to fight this perennial battle, we're sending you this handy calorie counter that you can use at home or at a banquet or at a lunch counter.

Accept it with our compliments—and the hope that we'll be seeing you soon.

Small gadgets galore are used in this manner. Like tricks in sales letters, however, they are better if related to the product or service of the firm. A real estate agency might appropriately send a pocket- or purse-size map of the city to which a person has just moved, along with the following:

Welcome to Jacksonville.

To help you get places faster and to know your new city better, this map shows the principal thoroughfares and locations of the principal landmarks and facilities.

Note that the Coleman Agency is located in an accessible area with adequate parking facilities nearby.

We would welcome the opportunity to help you in any way we can.

Letters offering helpful information

Large companies sponsoring radio and TV programs, as well as research projects and publications, rapidly accumulate names and addresses of people who are interested in being kept informed. As part of the public relations or goodwill program, many of these companies periodically send letters like the following (usually to selected lists of people supposedly interested):

Perhaps you will be interested in a program, "Life under the Sea," scheduled for Sunday, January 22, at 8 p.m. over NBS-TV.

"Life under the Sea" was directed by Emile Ravage, with the assistance of the marine biologist Albert Gaudin. It is the third in a series of such productions sponsored by the Rawlston System.

We hope these programs will help to broaden public understanding of science and to encourage some young people at least to consider scientific careers.

We shall welcome your comments after you have seen the program.

--

As a teacher of advertising, perhaps you will be able to use the accompanying brochure, "The Evolution of a *Woman's Home Journal* Ad."

You are welcome to quote liberally in your classes and to reproduce anything in it.

--

The exciting events in Detroit leading up to the introduction of the new models last month made a story too detailed to print completely in *Tempo*.

If you read the condensed version in the issue of two weeks ago, you'll agree that the accompanying report-analysis we're sending to selected educators and businessmen is a worthwhile expansion and supplementation. If you didn't . . . well, we think you'll want to now.

Letters anticipating resistance

In the interest of forestalling complaints and minimizing dissatisfaction, many business executives give advance notice when something like an interruption of service, a curtailment of service, or a price increase is scheduled to take place. (The same kind of advance mailing can also pave the way for the call of a solicitor for charitable contributions.) In almost all instances these letters (often only postcards) must be obvious forms. They need to stress service—improved service, if possible; at least, maintaining superior service or quality of goods—as an antidote for the inherently negative material the message has to establish. This message of a power company is typical (dates and times varied according to areas and so were stamped in):

> To provide better service for you and our other customers in your area, we have installed new equipment, which we plan to place in service
>
> April 15, 19—
> between 1 and 2 p.m.
>
> To safeguard the men who do this work, we shall have to shut off power during this time. Service will be restored as promptly as possible. We appreciate your cooperation in making this improved service possible.

A notification of a coming price increase is an even more unwelcome letter. Admittedly, it is never an easy letter to write. But with specific details supporting the increase, it may be successful in retaining the goodwill of some customers who would otherwise be lost or would become complainers or rumor-mongers. The following notice went to all customers of a diaper service:

> Dear Crib Customer:
>
> In the early 1940s when we first started lending mothers a hand with laundry for infants and babies, diapers cost 90 cents a dozen. Now they cost $5.97.
>
> Paper during the same period has increased from six to 37 cents a pound and soap from eight to 42 cents.
>
> To continue giving our customers satisfactory service, we had to increase our prices in the late '50s and again in the '60s. In the meantime all these items have continued to increase in price and now are from one fifth to one half more than they were then.
>
> Wages for our help, taxes, and other costs we cannot control have also risen appreciably.
>
> To continue the same twice-a-week pickup and delivery, and the same high standards of cleanliness and sanitation that we know you as a parent want for your child, we shall have to receive payment for services as listed on the enclosed card. These prices will go into effect at the beginning of next month.
>
> Please note that these increases average approximately three cents a day. You still are paying only 65 cents a day for service that makes life much easier for you, conserves your strength, and provides your child clothing that is sterilized to a degree impossible in most homes.

```
We appreciate the opportunity to serve you and shall continue
to do all we can to merit your confidence and your patronage.
```

* * *

We could classify and illustrate hundreds of situations in which a special goodwill letter would be appropriate and would cement a friendship for you and your firm. If you are alert to conditions, if you keep informed about what is happening to your clientele, if you honestly like people and enjoy pleasing them, however, you'll see plenty of opportunities to write such letters. In this short treatment, therefore, we have tried to concentrate on the most common instances; it is intended as a springboard for your thinking and practice rather than an extensive catalog.

We encourage you to

1. Write all you can of these "letters you don't have to write but should."
2. Make them specific enough to fit and be meaningful even when forms (NOT as one big company began, "If you are one of the many motorists enjoying the benefits of an XX credit card . . .").
3. In these most personal of business letters, be especially careful to get names, addresses, and facts right (if you write Mr. Wilkinson, he does NOT like to be addressed as Mr. Wilkerson; nor does Clarke like to be called Clark).
4. Avoid gushing in tone or length.

Special goodwill letters can do a big *extra* job for you, but remember that *all* your letters should build goodwill through courteous, sincere tone, and the service attitude. That is sometimes hard to do in the basically bad-news letters discussed in the next chapter.

GOODWILL CASES

1. For the president, Samuel P. Morey, First Alabama Bank, Post Office Box 2409, Tuscaloosa, Alabama 35401, write a thank-you for the new checking account to Mr. and Mrs. Simon Malchamps, 104 The Highlands, Tuscaloosa. Enclose a folder showing pictures of your four branch banks and give the banking hours. Invite the Malchamps to use your other services (savings accounts, safety deposit boxes, loans). Invite these new customers to ask questions regarding any of your services.

2. Draft a form letter for The Southland Corporation, 2828 North Haskell Avenue, Box 719, Dallas, Texas 75221, to go to stockholders who return their proxies for the next-month Annual Shareholders Meeting. Refer naturally to your recent Annual Report, which reflected the greatest year in Southland's 47-year history. You expect the next to be another successful year as new merchandising and marketing programs are being initiated and efforts toward reduction and control of expenses are being intensified.

3. Public libraries in Gross Pointe, Michigan, Canal Fulton, Ohio, and Cohoes, N.Y., lend power tools to community residents. The Minneapolis Public Library lends toys to children. But the Erie, Pa., Metropolitan Library, 212 Locust, Zip 16505, promotes lending of guinea pigs, rats, and mice for one week at a time. Not only is a child lent an animal, but also a cage, bedding, food, and a care-and-feeding instruction list. Also the young borrower must meet with the children's librarian for a preliminary discussion on handling and caring for the animal. Animal borrowing is not renewable. Write a form letter for the head librarian, Miss Lucille Stevens, to be sent to principals of all the elementary and junior high schools in Erie, telling the principals about your animal lending service and inviting the principals to encourage students to participate.

4. The Regional Library for the Blind and Physically Handicapped, 525 North Court Street, Talladega, Alabama 35160, uses a form letter to welcome people to the program of library services for the blind and physically handicapped. Regional is the lending agency for talking book machines and cassette machines for Alabama. These machines are lent to the agency from the federal government for as long as a person wishes to use them. Also for loan are books in braille, on recorded disc, cassette tape, and open reel tape. The recorded books and periodicals are lent for stated periods of time through this agency. All services are completely free, including free mailing of all materials to and from the library. Participants in the program are furnished without charge custom-built players for the phonograph discs and tape cassettes as well as attachments of earphones and speed-control units for cassette machines; headphones, pillow speakers, remote controls, speed control units, and plastic tone arm clips for the phonographs. Write this friendly form letter in which you offer your assistance. Sign the letter just as librarian after your name.

5. First Federal Savings and Loan, 1700 West 13th, Little Rock, Arkansas 72201, established since 1932, plans to open a branch office in a newly developed residential area. Prior to the formal opening of the branch, help Charles Thomas, head of the branch, write a letter to customers who had been doing business with the company in its main (and only) office and suggest to these customers that they transfer their accounts to the branch office for their own convenience (free, easy parking; five full-time experienced employees; convenient location). The branch at 10500 Dreher Road at intersection of Doyle Springs Road and Drew Road opens a week from today.

6. Using the information in the preceding case, assist Charles Thomas in drafting another letter to newcomers to the community telling them of the services of your branch office. (Thomas gets names at a nickel each from registration employees at the school, realty, telephone, and other utilities offices. Banks would not cooperate.)

7. Also (using preceding cases) write letters to be sent to others living in the area, urging them to open accounts. (You've given a clerk the job of making the mailing list by checking present customers' names against the City Directory.)

8. After 37 years of selling Fuilgas, you have sold out to Ugite Gas Incorporated, a company you felt would give your customers the same type treatment you have always given. You are sad to leave a business, people you love, and employees who have been part of the family, but you are glad to find a company with a hundred years of service. In a form letter thank your customers for their past loyalty and tell them about the new company (same phone number 376–5392). Ugite serves hundreds of thousands of residential, commercial, and industrial customers in ten states. The showroom at 12 S.W. First Avenue, Oklahoma City, Oklahoma 73120, remains open eight hours a day. Don Hunsberger is the District Manager.

9. As Phyllis Hutton, Treasurer/Manager, on the letterhead of the local Federal Credit Union, write a letter (or set up in memo form at your teacher's request) to members 60 years old or older of the Credit Union on the subject of Social Security Direct Deposit Program. Use the present date. The Credit Union has the necessary form to request that Social Security checks be mailed directly to the Union. No restrictions are on withdrawals. Money will earn dividends from the earliest possible date when member is away, ill, or too busy to make deposits. If not receiving Social Security benefits now, at least the member is aware of this option when eligible.

10. Use the current date and write Miss Roberta C. McMillian, Institute of Applied Science, 678 Boone Street, Denver, Colorado 80229, from International Publications, Inc., 171 Newberry Road, Boston, Massachusetts 02139, Leslie I. Combs, Jr., Executive Vice President, that you are delighted to have her new manuscript and welcome her to your publication family. Compliment her on a good job in making the changes reviewers of the first draft suggested. Send a publication schedule which will give her some idea of the time required for processing the manuscript and time needed for publication. As a little bug for her in this ice cream—and a little paving your road for a smooth-running publication schedule—tell this first-book author about a few weeks of hard work reading galley proof about six weeks hence and again reading page proof about four months hence.

11. As Cecil B. Morrow, Morrow Real Estate Company, your city, write a letter to Robert Shade, Bennet and Shade Insurance Company, also of your city, congratulating him on his two years of service to the YMCA. During Robert's term of office the YMCA opened a new cafeteria, new swimming pool lighting was installed, a new large gymnasium ceiling and improved lighting became a reality, dues were not raised despite increasing costs, and membership was the highest it has ever been since the Y was founded in 1915.

12. Millikin University is a private school in Decatur, Illinois. One of the main supports for this school is through gifts from individuals. Today, you (assume you are William R. Barnes, president of the Citizens National Bank, Landmark Mall, Decatur, Ill. 62523) write a note of congratulations to Karl N. Murphy (Murphy, Pierce, and Smith Accountants, 908 South Water Street, Decatur 62522). Murphy has been named chairman of Millikin University's Decatur community campaign this year. Murphy will head an effort by approximately 100 business people who will call on friends of the University to seek their continued support. Murphy is past chairman of the Millikin Associates and was special gifts chairman in Millikin University's building campaign. He happens to be a graduate of the Wharton School at the University of Pennsylvania with a master's in accounting and a CPA.

13. Over the signature of T. M. Elliott, Jr., Vice President, The First National Bank of Decatur, P.O. Box 2028, Decatur, Illinois 62529, write the Macon Woods Home, Incorporated (Phyllis Haring, manager), 46 Macon Woods, thanking the corporation for opening a new account with your bank. You have officers and employees who are helpful, friendly, and ready at all times to give their best attention. Name some other services available to businesses.

14. Write your alums giving a progress report on your fraternity/sorority, Alpha Mu Omega, your campus. At the National Convention in Atlanta a month ago your chapter received the National Trophy for outstanding achievement and the scholarship trophy. First semester the chapter took 35 new members. You have three of the eight officers of Student Government Association. The new president of the Accounting Society is an Alpha Mu. Two were taken into Mortar Board and one for Collegiate Who's Who. Two were invited to Alpha Lambda Delta, freshman honorary. One senior made Phi Beta Kappa. Call attention to the names and honors on an enclosed sheet. You may add any other appropriate details.

15. As publicity director of *National Osographic Magazine* you decide in order to build good will, to send to the Houston metropolitan high schools reprints of a recent *National Osographic* article entitled "The Influence of African Culture on American Society." The article is the first of a series of articles dealing with African, Asian, and Latin American influences on American society. Much has been said of American influences on Africa, Asia, and Latin America but little about the influences these areas have had on American culture. Your articles will deal, among other things, with language, literature, music, dress, foods, and even religion. You feel that the "African Influences" article will be particularly helpful in history, sociology, and political science classes.

Write a cover letter to accompany the reprint which, in addition to creating good will, underscores the value of *National Osographic* as a teaching aid. Be SUBTLE. DO NOT openly sell the magazine or ask for subscriptions. Remember: The primary purpose of your letter is to create good will.

16. After you review Case 10, p. 400, compose a brief thank-you letter to a firm in your city which has agreed to participate in the Youth Work Experience Program. Add appropriate details.

17. Recently you had the pleasure of staying at the Phoenix Inn, 379 Wagon Wheel Drive, Phoenix, Arizona 85021. Because you were so impressed by the friendly atmosphere, cleanliness, and good food, you write a deserved complimentary letter from your home address.

18. To vary the preceding case (and incidentally in the letter), assume that you left a personally autographed copy of *Communicating through Letters and Reports* in your room (214) (give specific date) and you would like for the manager to find the book and send it to you.

19. *Letterhead:* Alabama Power Company, Tuscaloosa, Alabama 35401. *Signature block:* Sincerely yours, A. Clayton Redman, Jr., Division Vice President. Use faked inside address and date this form letter to customers July, 19—. Since 1954 the cost of living has gone up about 183.5 percent. This increase has been caused by higher prices for clothing, food, housing, medical care, transportation, and electricity. The cost of building one mile of a typical electric distribution line in a residential neighborhood has increased some 140 percent since 1957. Explain how electricity is still a bargain. You are having to ask the Public Service Commission for a modest increase in some of your rates. On the average, the increase will add about three cents a day to the electric bills of residential customers. Even with this raise, rates will remain among the lowest in the nation. Last year the average cost of residential electric service from Alabama Power was below the national average. Promise to continue to provide the customer with electricity at the lowest possible cost and dependable service.

The point of the letter is to keep satisfied customers, to alert them to the increase in electricity costs, and to spread the good will of the power company. Specifically (but don't mention them) you want to take some steam out of the numerous—and largely uninformed and unfair—complaints about rapidly increasing rates.

20. For Roger Hemphill, Division Vice President, Regional Power Company, Winston-Salem, North Carolina 27103, set up a form letter to go along with a refund which is due the customer because on testing the meter was shown to be running fast. You have a regular program of testing meters. Stress the idea that your meters are the best you can buy, but they occasionally get out of adjustment. What you're doing is approved by the Public Service Commission. Any questions? They're welcome.

21. As Ralph B. Mason, Trust Department, First National Bank, 625 West Broadway, San Diego, California 92123, set up a form letter to be sent to widows acquainting them with your monthly bulletin, *Taxes and Estates.* This bulletin briefly presents facts and ideas which deal with the conservation of property and the protection for beneficiaries through modern estate planning. You hope that your bulletin will raise questions and generate comments so that your staff can assist in reviewing the overall estate plan.

22. From Mutual Savings, 1005 Congress, Austin, Texas 78767, send a form letter to your customers from the president, James O. Gant, telling them how much you appreciate their business. The enclosure of the 1099 form shows the earnings on the customer's savings last year (which is more money than customers could have earned at a bank in a similar type of account). The savings with Mutual are now FDIC covered to $40,000. Enclose a booklet that compares income rates from various types of investments (stock market, Treasury Notes or Bills, Money Market Mutual Funds, Floating Rate Notes, etc.). If, after reading the booklet, the customer feels that funds now invested in maturing instruments elsewhere, or funds from other sources, will best serve invested in one of Mutual's high-return, no-risk savings accounts, he/she can call or send the enclosed application form to Mutual.

23. To increase viewers, the television station you are Promotion Manager for, WHUH–TV, has been running a contest involving two game shows. Viewers are invited each day to send you the names of the winning contestants (in the viewer's opinion) on each show (one postcard per person per day). Cards are counted once a week to determine viewer-judged winners. Write a form letter to go to each week's winners, announcing that they have won, saying that they will receive their prize (an Oopster home appliance) shortly, thanking them for entering your contest. Without suggesting your inefficiency, suggest that they call you if they haven't received their prize in a few weeks.

24. As Executive Director of the Association for Scientific Communication, an organization for people teaching or practicing writing for scientific organizations or otherwise engaged in writing that is scientifically oriented, one of your pleasant duties is to acknowledge members' advancement to the rank of Senior Member. Draft a form letter that will be individually typed (and personalized) and sent to each new Senior Member. Be congratulatory, say something about what this professional recognition means to the member in terms of advancement both in career and the Association. The Senior Member certificate accompanies the letter; the Senior Member tie-tac or pin, as appropriate, is sent separately.

THE AL YOUMIN SERIES (SY, FOR SERIES YOUMIN)

Here in a compact package you find an interesting story and a varied series of 18 possible writing assignments involving the same few people and only two companies. We put it here, rather than somewhere else, merely because a goodwill letter started the whole thing.

Before writing any one of the assignments, you almost have to read all of the preceding and the appropriate text chapter (as indicated along with the kind of letter right after the case number).

On first looking at the series, you might be inclined to draw some moral —like "Don't write goodwill letters; they get you into trouble." But that misinterpretation of the facts is comparable to Mark Twain's intentionally humorous conclusion that being in bed is the most dangerous thing you can do because more people die in bed than anywhere else.

If you analyze the facts thoroughly, you should conclude, instead, that you should write all the goodwill letters you can find time for. The series shows how a simple goodwill letter led to one minor inconvenience for Al Youmin (writing seven letters) but brought him two big benefits—lots of favorable publicity and a good advertising manager for his business.

The series involves two goodwill letter situations (related to Chapter 6), five requests and one persuasive complaint (Chapter 11), three refusals (Chapter 7), three favorable replies (Chapter 5), one sales (Chapter 8), and (for Chapter 10) one personnel selector letter (inquiry), one letter "fielding" a loose job offer, and one job-resignation letter. That's six out of the eight chapters on specific kinds of letters treated in this book (skipping only Chapter 9 on self- and job-analysis, preparatory to writing applications, and Chapter 12 on collections).

SY 1 (Goodwill–6). You, Al Youmin, are owner of a machine shop specializing in high-precision metal working, Youmin Company, 3838 West Douglas Ave., Peoria, Ill. 60445. With your high investment in machines, tool life and downtime for resetting and retooling are primary concerns. Recently a customer sent you a job involving close-tolerance machining of some aluminum, one step of which involved difficult threading. Problems arose: Part was to specifications, but appearance was unacceptable, and micro-particle buildup on the cutting edge of the tool required resetting or retooling after every 40 parts were done. Tried kerosene as a coolant: Got better finish, but vaporizing created hazardous condition. Switched to "Slick-Flo 1000," mixed 15 to 1 with water. Great results: Beautiful satin finish on the part, and eliminated micro-particle buildup on the tool. Completed 600-part job with one tool, no resetting or retooling necessary, and tool was still capable of close-tolerance work. Saved $150.00 in tool costs, eliminated expensive downtime, did away with hazardous vaporizing. Customer so pleased he has given you additional work. Write your experience to the manufacturer of "Slick-Flo 1000," Levi Gate Specialties, Industrial Park, Ind. 68556.

SY 2 (Request–11). As the advertising manager of Levi Gate Specialties, reply to the unexpected but welcome letter from Al Youmin. You are so impressed with how well "Slick-Flo 1000" worked for him, you would like to feature him and his letter in your advertising and direct mail efforts. Ask his permission.

SY 3 (Refusal–7). When you wrote your letter to Levi Gate Specialties about "Slick-Flo 1000," you had no intention of publicly endorsing the product, and you do not want your company to be publicly "tied up with" any single coolant/lubricant maker. You want to stay good friends with all your suppliers. Nicely refuse the request for Al Youmin, making sure you stay on good terms with Levi Gate, too.

SY 4 (Request–11). That testimonial from Al Youmin is too valuable to allow him to withhold permission to use it. You won't necessarily want to print his letter *in toto* in your ads and direct mail, but want only to paraphrase parts of it and to use his name. Actually, by letting you do this, Youmin will gain invaluable publicity for himself and his company, build his reputation as a leader in the field, and do other people a professional favor by telling them (through your advertising and direct mail) about a product (yours, admittedly) that will help them. Add any other arguments you think that you, as Advertising Manager of Levi Gate Specialities, might use.

SY 5 (Favorable reply–5). That persuasive request from the Advertising Manager of Levi Gate Specialties is too good for you to turn it down. As Al Youmin, reply to him giving him permission to use your letter and your name in advertising and direct mail. Make sure he knows you want to see anything he does before it goes into print, if it has your name in it.

SY 6 (Request–11). Now that you have Al Youmin's permission to use his name and letter in your advertising and direct mail, thank him. You will send him photocopies of the material before you print or publish it. After all the trouble you had getting him to go along with you, you hate to ask for more, but you need a good black-and-white photograph of him and one of his company's buildings. Since he should already have these available, he ought to be able to send you copies. You will, of course, return them after use.

SY 7 (Favorable reply–5). That advertising manager at Levi Gate Specialities is pretty persistent. Now that you've gone this far, as Al Youmin send him a copy of your stock photograph of your building. For a picture of yourself, you have a snapshot taken a few years ago which may do. When does he expect to have the advertisement with you in it appear?

SY 8 (Request–11). The photographs Al Youmin sent you were not too helpful. The photo of his building wasn't bad, but the snapshot of him was barely usable. Taking a deep breath, you had it extensively retouched—it doesn't look much like him now, but it does look like a picture of a human being. By the time your advertising agency and your president, old Levi Gate, got finished, there wasn't much room left in the advertisement for his letter anyway, so all you could quote were a few generalized, congratulatory words. From what you sense about Al Youmin through your correspondence, he may not like all this, and he does have the right to pass on it before you print it. As Advertising Manager of Levi Gate Specialties, write Al, enclosing a photocopy of the advertisement, and sell him beforehand on approving it as it stands. You'll need lots of resale and success-consciousness, as well as the rest of the letter-writing techniques you've learned.

SY 9 (Refusal–7). As Al Youmin, you're sorry now that you ever let this thing get this far. The advertisement from Levi Gate is not the kind of thing you'd run. The headline ("Smooth Your Metalworking Path with Slick-Flo 1000") is unimaginative, the copy is dull, the picture of your building is so small the sign ("Youmin Company—Close-Tolerance Machining") can't be made out, and that picture of you doesn't look like you. You know this will create difficulties for the Advertising Manager at Levi Gate, but you must disapprove the advertisement. But do it nicely.

SY 10 (Request–11). The refusal from Al Youmin was a shocker. You know the advertisement featuring him is not a classic. But you have too much time and money invested to just drop the advertisement; so you elect for some quick revisions in the artwork: Make the sign on his building bigger so the "Youmin Company" at least pops out; retouch the photo of Al again. As the Advertising Manager of Levi Gate Specialties, write another letter to Al Youmin. Subtly point out the changes in the art, explain that the headline and copy lead directly into his testimonial (economy of using "Slick-Flo 1000"), and finally, using all your talent and experience to keep his goodwill, point out that he has approval rights over only the two photographs and those words in the copy directly quoted from his letter. Get him to approve the advertisement.

SY 11 (Favorable reply–5). When you (Al Youmin) receive the revised advertisement from the Advertising Manager of Levi Gate Specialties, his excellently persuasive letter and the changes in the pictures sway you. The picture of you, especially, is improved; it now looks like you; so you approve its appearance.

SY 12 (Sales–8). You are the advertising manager for the Levi Gate Specialities company. To merchandise your advertisement featuring Al Youmin's testimonial for "Slick-Flo 1000," write a sales letter to go to all your customers and prospects. It will accompany a copy of the ad and a copy of Youmin's testimonial letter. Since you have the ad and the letter to carry the burden of detail, you can use your cover letter to sell "Slick-Flo 1000's" main advantages: won't break down or vaporize at machining temperatures; compatible with all metals, ferrous and non-ferrous; easily cleaned and virtually infinitely reusable; economical. Point up the technical advice your company can give, your long reputation for quality products, and your quick delivery. Offer technical literature and a sample of "Slick-Flo 1000" on request.

SY 13 (Goodwill–6). Since you got Al Youmin's approval to run the "Slick-Flo 1000" ad featuring his testimonial, things have gone nicely. The plates have been made and sent to the trade magazines which will run the ad. Old Levi Gate (your president) is happy, and you're happy. Since you're the Advertising Manager of Levi Gate Specialties, to you falls the pleasant task of sending Al Youmin 5 copies of the advertisement, two of them mounted on easel boards. He will probably want to place them around his plant, and keep some to show to his customers. If he would like more, you have a limited supply from which you can send him some.

SY 14 (Complaint memo–11). You are Sam Lippery, West Coast sales representative for Levi Gate Specialties, and you're unhappy. Yesterday you called on one of your best accounts, Chip Braker Machining, and Chip threw a copy of *Technical Machining Magazine* in front of you, pointing to the latest Levi Gate advertisement, one for "Slick-Flo 1000" that features another customer, Al Youmin. Chip, in his inimitable way, wanted to know first of all how Youmin got to have all the publicity, and second, if "Slick-Flo 1000" is so good, how come you never told him about it. You couldn't very well remind Chip that you have been trying to sell him on "Slick-Flo 1000" for the last two years, but you smoothed his feathers, promised him a generous sample, and got out. Write a memo to the Advertising Manager back at Levi Gate's home office and suggest strongly that an advertisement featuring the testimonial of a West Coast machine shop would be a good idea, you could use the help in your territory, since Youmin in Illinois was featured it would be only fair, and you have a real good candidate.

SY 15 (Refusal memo–7). Being the Advertising Manager of Levi Gate Specialties is not all martini lunches and the glamorous ad biz. Take the memo you just got from Sam Lippery. After all the trouble you had with Al Youmin, you're not about to do another testimonial advertisement. They aren't all that great as a basis for advertising anyway. But you want to keep Sam happy, if possible; so point out to him that the Youmin testimonial was a one-shot, inspired by the purely unsolicited testimonial you got from him (attach a photocopy of Youmin's letter to your memo to Lippery). No plans have been approved to do more testimonial ads. If you do one for Lippery, you'll have to do one for each of the other representatives (all 32 of them!) to be fair. You can't be sure that everybody can come up with a customer who will write a strong testimonial. Tell him to explain all this to his customer, and also explain that to do an advertisement about that company would be unfair to all the other companies in the West Coast area. Be positive and success-conscious.

SY 16 (Personnel selector–10). Put yourself in the shoes of Al Youmin. Your advertising manager just quit after a row with Engineering, and left on short notice. You immediately thought of the advertising manager at Levi Gate Specialties, who ran that advertisement recently with that striking picture of you in it. He seemed imaginative, hard-working, persistent, pleasant, gentlemanly, and persuasive. On a hunch, write him to see if he would be interested in coming with Youmin Company. Be realistic when you describe the benefits, challenges, and opportunities—and be vague about the salary; no use chancing a too-high quote at the beginning.

SY 17 (Invited application–10). When Al Youmin wrote to you about the possibility of being his advertising manager, you were intrigued. Things haven't been going well for you at Levi Gate Specialties lately, and a change might be a good thing. Putting yourself in the place of Levi Gate's advertising manager, write a very careful letter to Al Youmin expressing your guarded interest, indicating that the salary area he talked about is too low, and asking whether he will pay your relocation expenses.

SY 18 (Job resignation–10). Al Youmin upped his salary offer and agreed to split your relocation expenses. Along with everything else, it looks like a good opportunity. Now write your resignation letter to old Levi Gate, the president of Levi Gate Specialties, where (you reflect) you've worked for six years, had your ups and downs, learned a lot (and, you feel, contributed something too), made some hits and some errors (and a lot of friends—including old Levi, the devil, who at least always treated you right). Of course you won't *say* all of that, and you *will* remember one of Levi's first pieces of advice: "Always be kind to others on your way up the ladder of success; you may meet them on your way down."

chapter 7 Disappointing messages

[Character requires the courage to say no firmly but pleasantly when saying yes or saying no unpleasantly would be easier.]

UNLESS YOU recall clearly the suggestions about handling disappointing messages in Chapter 2 (pp. 37–39), turn back and quickly review them. What we said there is especially important as a basis for this whole chapter.

REFUSING REQUESTS

Most people are disappointed, irritated, or downright angry when told they can't have something or can't do something unless given at least one good reason. And in any of these emotional states they will not give full attention to your explanation.

Back of most refusals is some good reason dictated by sound business judgment. And usually it can be told. That is why we say that most refusals have an educating job to do: They usually have to explain some facts or circumstances of which the reader is apparently unaware. Hence the emphasis on *explanation before refusing*.

Furthermore, one of the first lessons in good human relations any sensitive person learns is that when you take something away from or deny someone something, you give a reason, you give something else to compensate for the loss when you can, and you try to extend some gesture of friendliness.

Simply stated, the desirable pattern for most refusals is therefore

- A buffer beginning (establishing compatibility; defined and illustrated below)
- A review of facts (reasons)
- The refusal itself, subordinated } *or* a counterproposal which implies the refusal
- An off-the-subject ending }

Before studying an analysis of this suggested structure, however, read the following refusal of the request for toothpaste samples (p. 386):

> Sales-minded businessmen are keenly aware of the advertising possibilities which usually accompany such an occasion as "A" Day at your university.
>
> Where they have found such advertising to be sufficiently productive to warrant the cost, they are glad to participate.
>
> We here at Rigate have experimented with many different forms of advertising. We have found that we obtain best results at the least expense by advertising in nationally circulated magazines and by sponsoring the Picote Theatre, which millions of Americans enjoy every Sunday night.
>
> The results of advertising by distributing sample tubes of Picote did not warrant the relatively high cost of manufacturing, handling, and mailing the samples; so we now concentrate on magazine and radio-TV promotion. As a result, we have been able to make a substantial saving, which we have passed on to users of Picote by lowering the price of the product.
>
> In addition to this price reduction, in January and February Rigate will offer an economy-size tube of Picote for just one additional penny with the purchase of a bottle of Rigatine. The first time you drop by your drugstore in January, take advantage of the savings Rigate passes on to its users.

The buffer beginning

Since people don't normally ask for what they don't expect to get, on opening your reply to a request the reader almost certainly expects pleasant news. Usually the request involved some strong feelings and carefully figuring out seemingly good reasons why you should do as asked. If you present a refusal immediately, you appear to ignore those feelings and reasons—and are likely to arouse a negative reaction, causing a mind closed to anything else you say.

If you pitch right in with a presentation of your reasons, you appear to be arguing—and dander, or at least suspicion, rises.

To prevent mental impasses and emotional deadlocks, show your reader that you are a reasonable, calm person by indicating some form of agreement or approval of the reader or the project. Frequently you can agree completely with some statement made in the request. At least you can say something which will establish compatibility, even if it's nothing more than that you have given the proposal serious thought. This is your buffer.

The turndown of the request for the correspnodence manual (p. 39) could easily begin with

```
You are certainly right about the pressing need facing most
business firms for more effectively trained business writers.
```

Or it could start this way:

```
Students attending Harwood College are fortunate to have a
faculty who try so conscientiously to correlate college
training and business practice.
```

Both beginnings acknowledge the receipt of the request, clearly imply careful consideration, establish compatibility, and set the stage for a review of the facts in the refusal later.

Six warnings should be sounded here, however, about writing buffers for this and other kinds of disappointing messages. The *first* is that if you appear to be granting the request, you are building your reader up to an awful letdown! Such beginnings as these would mislead most readers:

```
I certainly would like to see each Harwood letter-writing
student have access to a copy of the Southern Atlantic manual.

--

"A" Day surely would be a good opportunity to acquaint
potential customers with Picote toothpaste, Mr. Willet!

--

Our policy of making fair adjustments. . . .
```

The *second* warning is against beginning irrelevantly or so far away from the subject that the reader isn't even sure the letter is a reply. The buffer beginning must clearly identify the general subject. Otherwise, incoherence and rambling are inevitable results. Even such a beginning as the following is irrelevant:

```
Your interesting letter describing "A" Day brought back to
mind many pleasant memories of my own college days.
```

The job of getting to the facts would be harder with such a start.

The *third* warning is against recalling the disappointment too vividly and negatively ("We regret your dissatisfaction . . .").

Also, as the *fourth* warning, you need to be careful about buffer length. You can easily go wrong either way—making the buffer too short to get in step with the reader and hence not really get off to a pleasant start, or too long to suit an impatient reader.

As the *fifth* warning, you need to phrase the buffer well so that it makes a smooth and natural transition to the next part (your explanation).

Despite the fact that many writers advocate beginning refusals with

```
I really wish we could. . . .
```

we do not believe it can do as good a job for you as some other opening. It is stereotyped, it sounds insincere to many readers, and it invites the belligerent response, "Then why don't you?" But the greatest disadvantage (and the *sixth* warning) is that it defeats the whole psychology and strategy of B–plan letters—it establishes the refusal unmistakably in the opening before showing any reason why.

Reasons rather than apologies

If you will apply the positive thinking and positive phrasing we talked about under "Positive Statement" (p. 46) and "Success Consciousness" (p. 48), you will resist the common impulse to apologize anywhere in a refusal *and especially in the beginning.* Apologies are no substitute for action or explanation. And they inevitably force you to phrase in distinctively negative terminology the very idea you should avoid, that you *will not, cannot, are unable to, do not have,* and similar negative expressions.

You will of course run into some situations where you have no reasons (nonexistence of certain information or plain and simple unavailability) and some where the reason is so obvious that it need not be put into words.

But in most cases when you have to refuse, that refusal is based on good reasons. *Those reasons—not some apology or policy—form the bedrock of your explanation.*

As much as possible you will want to search out and emphasize those reasons which reflect benefit to the reader—if not directly, then indirectly by identification with a group with which the reader might be sympathetic. The writer of the Picote-sample refusal letter did a good job of relating reader benefit to the refusal.

The following letter from a manufacturer refusing a dealer's request for samples also stresses reader benefits:

```
Congratulations on the 25 years of service you have given to
your community!

Through continued association with retailers, we know that
only those whose businesses are based on sound managerial
policies and services succeed over so long a time.

We have tried to help in these successes by cutting costs
whenever possible and passing these savings on to retailers in
the form of lower prices.  This aim led us to eliminate the
high (and often unpredictable) manufacturing and shipping costs
of special samples.  You and hundreds of other druggists have
benefited from these cost reductions for the past five years.

If you'll fill in and mail the enclosed card, Mr. Robert
Abbott, your Walwhite representative, will be glad to arrange
a special Walwhite exhibit for your anniversary sale.  This
attractive display will attract many customers.
```

You cannot, however, apply such reader-benefit interpretation in every case. To attempt to would result in artificial, insincere talk. The following letter refusing a request for permission to reprint some sales letters of a mail-order house would not be likely to offend when stripped down to its fundamentally selfish message:

> You can count on a large, interested readership for the article you are writing about the importance of sales letters in business.
>
> In our company, as you know, we depend upon letters exclusively for sales. Of necessity, then, we have tested extensively to find out the most effective procedures. Our highly paid writers are continually revising, sending expensive test mailings, and comparing the returns. The best letters represent a considerable investment.
>
> In the past we have had some of our standard letters used without consent by rival companies; so we now copyright all our sales forms and confine them to company use. Should we release them for publication, we would have to incur the same expense once again, for their effectiveness for us would be materially decreased.
>
> I'm sending you some bulletins and a bibliography which may help you with your article. Will you let me know the issue of the magazine your article appears in?

Even though the reasoning is frankly selfish, it is reasonable, and the writing is friendly and positive.

If you establish good reasons, you have no cause to apologize.

The derived, positive refusal

Ideally, your explanation and reasons so thoroughly justify you in refusing that anyone would infer the turndown. Thus prepared, your reader is far more likely to accept your decisions without ill feeling.

But you cannot always afford to depend exclusively on implication to establish the turndown unmistakably. The refusal must be clear; but even when you have to state it, it need not be brutally negative. In fact, it need not be negative at all.

If you will look back at the sample refusals in this section, you will see that the writers established the idea of what they were not doing by a statement of what they were doing. To establish the idea of "We don't distribute samples," one writer said, "So we now concentrate on magazine and radio-TV promotion." That letter might have expressed the idea more definitely with "We advertise exclusively through magazines and radio-television." Instead of saying, "We cannot let you have samples of our sales letters," another phrased it, "We copyright all our sales forms and confine them to company use." When you incorporate the limiting words *only, solely, exclusively* (even phrases like *confine to* and *concentrate on*), there's no room for doubt.

Saving some of your reasons until after establishing the refusal enables you to embed the disappointing news and thus, you hope, to reduce the impact of the refusal. In any event, you certainly want to take leave of your reader on a more pleasant note than the refusal.

The pleasant, hopeful ending

In some cases when you must refuse you can do little but reassure the reader through a few additional words that you are not utterly callous—or even merely indifferent. Good wishes for the success of the project, the suggestion of other sources, possibly the suggestion of being helpful in other ways, sending something other than what the reader has requested—all these are possibilities for ending your letter with a friendly gesture.

Sometimes you cannot comply with your reader's request but can suggest an alternative action, a "counterproposal" or "compromise proposal," which will be of some help. In many instances it can successfully absorb the statement of the refusal and furnish you with the positive ending you seek. The following letter is an example of this technique:

> Prudential's employees and clients will no doubt benefit materially from the reports manual you are planning, Mr. Lee—especially if it is the same caliber as the letters manual your staff prepared recently.
>
> I'm sure many college teachers would be glad to furnish you illustrative material. And I am no exception. In the past fifteen years of working with business and college people trying to improve the quality of their reports, I've collected much HOW NOT TO and HOW TO teaching material.
>
> For most of this I have only my single file copy, which I use in teaching a report-writing course three times a year and which I carefully keep in my office.
>
> I'm sure my student assistant would be glad to photocopy it for you during off-duty hours at the regular rate of $2.60 an hour. Since the job involves no more than 50 or 60 pages, I feel reasonably sure that securing the material this way would cost you only about $10–15 (including cost of materials, copier fees, and time).
>
> I shall be glad to make the necessary arrangements if you would like me to. I'm sure I can have the material to you within four or five days after hearing from you.

Please note again that this writer does not resort to negative phrasing or apologies. You too should resist the common tendency to resort to such expressions as "I regret, I assure you, my inability to do as you asked," "I'm sorry to have to refuse your request," or—much worse—"I hope you will understand our position," especially at the end. For these weaklings, substitute appropriate positive ideas such as those used in the examples in this section.

For writing goodwill-building refusals, keep in mind the reminder list of points on page 223.

Checklist for Refusing Requests

1. Your buffer opening must pleasantly establish compatibility.
   a) One of the poorest starts is talk about how pleased or flattered you are. It's vain and selfish.
   b) Shift the emphasis to your reader.
   c) Don't appear to be on the verge of granting the request.
   d) Nor do you want to intimate the refusal at this point.
   e) Beginning too far away from the subject results in incoherence.
2. Your transition must follow coherently and logically from your buffer.
   a) To avoid selfish-sounding turns, keep the emphasis on the reader.
   b) *Although, however, but* and *yet* signal a turn for the worse. Avoid them as sentence beginnings.
   c) Avoid also the insincere "Although I should like to. . . ."
   d) Supply the bridging sentence showing why you are explaining.
3. Give at least one good reason before implying or stating the refusal.
   a) Emphasize reasons which are for the benefit of someone other than yourself if you can.
   b) Don't hide behind "our policy." Policies merit little respect; the reasons behind them merit a lot.
   c) For believability, you need specificness.
   d) Stick to plausibilities.
4. The refusal itself should be
   a) A logical outcome of the reasons given. Ideally, the reader should deduce the refusal before your definite indication of it.
   b) Presented positively—in terms of what you can do and do do.
   c) Preceded (and preferably followed) by justifying reasons.
   d) Unmistakable but implied or subordinated (maybe counter-proposal).
   e) Written without negative words like *impossible, must refuse,* or *very sorry to tell you that we cannot.*
   f) Without apologies, which just weaken your case. Concentrate, instead, on what is hopeful.
5. Continue to convince your reader of your real interest and helpful attitude, without recalling the refusal.
   a) Your ending must be positive and about something within the sphere of the reader's interest.
   b) Watch for bromides and rubber stamps in the end.
   c) Be wary of the expression "If there is any other help I can give you, please let me know." It can produce some sarcastic reactions.
   d) Follow through specifically with any wanted action.

REFUSING ADJUSTMENTS

The letter refusing an adjustment is obviously a bad-news (B–plan) letter. Your psychology of saying no is therefore important. So unless you thoroughly understand it, read the explanation beginning on pages 37 and 217.

For your buffer-paragraph beginning, you look for something in the situation which you and the reader agree on and which is pleasant. Appreciation for the information could serve in most cases.

Although you may introduce a sentence that serves as a transition and resale on the house, you need to get to your explanation or review of facts and reasons fairly early. And you need to give the facts and reasons fully in a clear system of organization.

Several special techniques are important if the explanation is to rebuild goodwill while refusing to do what the reader asked. You already know better than to hide behind the word *policy* or to give no reason at all. A flat-footed announcement of what the guarantee states is just as bad as unsupported talk about policy.

Since you are refusing, obviously you are not charging responsibility for the dissatisfaction to either the firm or the product. You must clear that point up with adequate explanation as a basis for refusing. Resale at this stage (before the explanation) in the area of the trouble is *not* the way, but only a head-on collision with what the reader thinks. You *have to* give the basic fact(s) on which your refusal depends. This of course, makes the reader guilty; but you don't want to accuse directly. Preaching or belittling will only make matters worse.

Your best technique is to fall back on the impersonal presentation (something "was not done" instead of "you didn't"), rather than accuse. The reader will be able to see who is responsible if you explain well that your goods and your firm aren't.

In fact, if you arrange your reasons and explanations carefully, they will probably make the negative answer clear by implication without the necessity of stating it. Thus you may subordinate the negative refusal. If not this way, at least you subordinate it by burying it (that is, putting it in the middle of a paragraph where it doesn't stand out unduly).

After the refusal, which must be clearly there whether by implication or by direct statement, you may do well to add some more reasoning and explanation in support. Be sure you say enough to make your refusal convincing and justified.

Your ending then becomes an attempt to get agreement or the reader's acceptance of your refusal as justified. That is, you write with as much success consciousness as seems reasonable about the future outlook. This does *not* mean that you write and ask for an answer as to whether your action is all right. If it isn't, you will know without asking.

Often the best ending assumes that the preceding explanation and decision are satisfactory and talks about something else. Rather than looking backward, it may better look forward to the next likely relationship between writer and reader. The following letter illustrates most of the points, especially the clear reasoning that makes direct refusal unnecessary:

> We certainly agree with you that your company has always ordered high-quality products to sell to your customers. We, too, try to keep our products up to a high standard.
>
> That is why we appreciate your fairness in giving us a chance to analyze the sample of screws you sent.
>
> Our chemical analysis shows that the screws are brittle because they are high in phosphorus and low in carbon and sulphur steel, whereas our screws are of a very different analysis. Physical analysis shows that the sample screws have been severely cold-worked without stress relief, whereas our screws are never made that way.
>
> To check our laboratory report, which practically proved that we could not have made those screws, I have checked your former orders and found that the screws we have sent you were always blue steel finish, instead of the cadmium finish of the sample.
>
> We should be glad to supply you again with our hard but tough screws that will give your customers the quality they have come to expect from you. Our descriptive price list is enclosed. May we look forward to your order?

The checklist on page 226 reviews the highlights of refusing adjustments.

COMPROMISING ON ADJUSTMENTS

When you decide to try to compromise—usually because of divided responsibility, or uncertainty about responsibility or correction for the trouble—you may use either of *two* plans.

In the *first* you follow the refused-adjustment plan exactly down *to* the refusal. There you make your proposed compromise instead, explicitly. In effect, you are refusing the adjustment requested and are making a counterproposal—a compromise. When you ask acceptance of it, your success in getting a favorable reply will depend not only on how well you have presented facts and reasons to justify the compromise but on your success consciousness in presenting it and on your phrasing it to encourage rather than discourage acceptance.

The following letter in answer to a strong request for removal of the heater, cancellation of remaining payments, and refund of the shipping and installation charges illustrates the points. You will notice that it offers to compromise to the extent of canceling the remaining payments, but it proposes another action instead.

Refused-Adjustment Checklist

1. Make your buffer positive, related, adequate, and progressive.
   a) Reflect pleasant cooperation (try to agree on something).
   b) But begin closely enough to the situation to acknowledge.
   c) Don't imply that you're granting the request.
   d) Avoid recalling the dissatisfaction more than necessary.
   e) Watch buffer length: neither too breezy nor too long.
   f) Early resale in the trouble area bluntly contradicts.
   g) Should you show appreciation for the report?
2. Make your facts and reasons courteous, thorough, and convincing.
   a) An immediate plunge (beginning of the second paragraph) into "our guarantee" or "our policy" is abrupt.
   b) Don't accuse the reader or preach. Phrase your explanation impersonally—and let the reader decide who's guilty.
   c) Establish the explicit, adequate facts—the basis for refusal.
   d) Even intimating refusal before reasons is bad psychology.
   e) When possible, interpret reasons to show reader benefits.
3. Make the refusal logical, subordinate, and impersonal but clear.
   a) Preferably the reader sees the refusal coming.
   b) Give it little emphasis. Consider implying it.
   c) Keep it impersonal and positive—in terms of what you do.
   d) Be sure it is there, however; unclear is as bad as too strong.
   e) Follow the refusal with reasons, showing any reader benefits.
   f) Customer education or counterproposal may imply the refusal.
   g) What about the returned product (if applicable)? Resell it?
4. Make your ending pleasant, positive, and success-conscious.
   a) When you need reader action, ask for it positively.
   b) Otherwise an off-the-subject ending about services, seasonal goods, or some other topic of interest is appropriate.
   c) Don't suggest uncertainty of your ground. Watch *hope/trust.*
   d) Apologies are unnecessary reminders of trouble; your explanation has already made the best apology.

For the COMPROMISE ADJUSTMENT, use these for Items 3 and 4:

3. Make your counterproposal as logical, helpful relief.
   a) Be careful to make a smooth transition from the explanation (which implies refusal) to the counterproposal.
   b) Offer it ungrudgingly, without parading your generosity, but let the service element prevail.
   c) Don't belittle it ("the best we can do") or make it sound like a penalty ("a service charge will have to be made").
4. Use a modified action ending.
   a) Ask permission; you wouldn't go ahead without agreement.
   b) Tell what the customer is to do, but don't urge acceptance.
   c) For service attitude, talk prompt satisfaction.

> You are right in expecting your Warmall heater to heat a large room such as your entire store, for that was what it was designed to do.
>
> To do so, the Warmall requires careful installation. It must be located so that the air currents can carry its heat to all parts of the room. Our engineer reports that the stove was installed in the proper position but that later remodeling of your store has blocked circulation of air with a half partition.
>
> Your stove can be all you want it to be when properly located; so removing it would be useless. That would mean losing your down payment and what you have paid for shipping and installation, although we would of course cancel the remaining payments. Moreover, you must have heat, and the Warmall will do the job.
>
> We have absolute faith in our engineer's judgment, but your satisfaction is more important. So we want to do what is fair to us both.
>
> At your convenience we can move the stove to the position suggested by our engineer; and, if it does not heat to your satisfaction, we will not charge you a cent.
>
> Will you suggest the most convenient time for the change that will make your store warm and comfortable? We can do the job so quickly and efficiently that your business can continue as usual.

(For a checklist following this plan of compromise adjustment letter, see p. 226.)

A *second* method of compromising—usually called the full-reparation beginning compromise—sometimes works better. You follow the plan of the letter *granting an adjustment* at the beginning, through the explanation. The facts, of course, will indicate divided responsibility or uncertain responsibility. Your resale talk will indicate that the repaired product (or a replacement up to par, in case the original was beyond repair) will give the service the customer wanted.

Since presumably the original desire for that service still exists, you ask the customer to make a choice—the refunded money or the product. And of course you word it to encourage choice of the product, because that way you have a customer satisfied with your products as well as your fair-minded practices.

Your main purpose is to restore goodwill and confidence. Your success depends on a start which offers everything requested and thereby pleases the customer, your explanation which shows the justice of a compromise, and your fair-mindedness in allowing the choice. The danger—not a very serious one—is that some people might try to keep both the money and the product.

> Attached to this letter is a credit memorandum for $43.75, which we cheerfully send you for the five Bear Mountain hunting jackets you returned, as an indication that you'll always be treated fairly at Bowen's.

Under the assumption that these jackets would find a ready sale at a reduced retail price despite slight imperfections (a button mis-matched, a crooked seam, or maybe a little nick in the fabric), we offered them "as is" and priced them at $8.75 instead of the regular $12.75. We felt that marking them "as is" indicated special circumstances.

Generally we follow the accepted business custom of making all such sales final for an entire lot. But as we evidently did not make the situation perfectly clear, we are leaving the decision up to you; if you feel that you're entitled to the adjustment, it's yours.

Many of your customers, however, would probably be glad to get nationally advertised Bear Mountains at perhaps $21 instead of the standard $25. And even if you sell these five at, say, only $16, your percentage of profit will be about the same as if you sold perfect jackets at full price. So if you'd like to reconsider and want to offer these jackets at a saving, just initial the face of this letter and send it to us with the credit memo. We'll absorb the freight charges.

Even though slightly imperfect, these jackets are still ready to stand a lot of hard wear. They are made to suit hunters' needs, with ample pockets for shells and with comfortable tailoring. Selling them should be easy, especially at a discount. We'll look for your decision, but we think you can make a good profit on them at the special price.

Application of the checklist for compromises with full-reperation beginning (p. 229) to this letter will show that it is pretty good and will review the principles for you.

REQUESTS FOR CREDIT INFORMATION FROM CUSTOMERS

Many applications for credit do not give all the data you must have. You therefore write, asking for the needed information. The major problem is to avoid arousing the customer's suspicion or indignation.

To soften the effect of the delay in approving credit and to quell suspicion, you begin with buffer material, stress the benefits of complying with the request, show that you treat all customers alike, make action easy, and promise quick action. If character is not in question, be sure to say so. And to encourage response, use resale or sales promotion as the matrix for your explanation.

The following letter to a housewife is typical in stressing "All our customers fill out this application . . ."; it is an appropriate covering letter for the form request discussed on pages 98–99.

Your interest in the conveniences of an Allen Tilby charge account is most welcome, Mrs. Lee.

So that we may assist you as quickly and as easily as possible, will you please fill out the routine credit application which is enclosed? All our customers fill out this form as a help to both them and us. The information is strictly for our

Checklist for Compromise with Full-Reparation Beginning

1. The beginning giving everything asked for is basic—to dissolve reader emotions and get you a reasonable hearing.
   a) Make it immediately, specifically, and completely.
   b) Build up the wholesome effect by a friendly, adapted expression to emphasize your reliability and prevent a curt tone.
   c) Don't apologize more; Item 1(a) does lots more.
   d) Carefully avoid unnecessary negative reminders.
   e) Beginning with the compromise would infuriate readers. Since they think they're entitled to what they asked, you have to show otherwise before compromising.
2. The explanation (facts and reasons) must show that the claimant is expecting too much.
   a) Don't be too slow about getting to at least some of the explanation.
   b) Interpret it with a reader viewpoint and positive statement.
   c) Do not directly accuse; show blame impersonally (perhaps by customer education on the use and care of the article).
   d) Establish the facts to show that the claimant is at least partly responsible or is overestimating the loss.
3. Show the service attitude and your fair-mindedness in your proposal.
   a) As the foundation of your proposal, stress serving your reader.
   b) Recall the original desire for the service the reader wanted.
   c) Continuing the reader-benefit interpretation, state your proposal.
   d) Follow your suggestion with any other plausible sales points.
   e) Don't parade your generosity in the loss you take.
   f) Suggest—don't command or preach or high-pressure the claimant.
4. The modified action ending should give a choice but encourage the one you prefer.
   a) Tell what you want done: reject (return) the full reparation and accept your proposal.
   b) As in any action ending, make action easy.
   c) Do not bog down with apologies or emphasis on the full reparation.
   d) End with a short suggestion of reader satisfaction resulting from the proposal.

confidential files, to be used in setting up the best credit arrangements we can make for you.

You can be sure that we will give your request our immediate attention. Just use the stamped, addressed envelope enclosed for your convenience in returning the application.

A letter to a dealer employs the same strategy:

Corone fishing gear is a good line to handle. Dealers throughout the country report favorable reaction of fishermen. And our advertising in Field and Stream, Sports Afield, and True continues to create demand for Corone dealers.

We're just as eager as you are to have your Corone sales start; so will you supply the usual financial information that all our dealers furnish us, along with the names of other firms from which you buy on credit? Most of our dealers use the enclosed form, but if you prefer to use your own, please do. This confidential information will enable us to serve you efficiently—now and in the future.

Occasionally such a request backfires, with a protest from the customer (sometimes quite vigorous!). In such cases all you can do is write again, using a pacifying buffer, and then pointing out the value of credit and the importance (to you and your reader) of careful selection of credit customers. The letter reiterates the normalcy of the request and closes with a request for action. It is also a modification of the B–plan letter, as in this example:

We're glad you let us know unmistakably how you feel about sending financial information. And we're sure that as an open-minded business manager you'll want to look at your supplier's side of the story. Only through complete frankness can we work together successfully in a credit relationship.

We have some pretty definite ideas too—learned from selling about 2,000 successful dealers like you several million dollars' worth of Corone fishing equipment in the last 20 years . . . about 90 percent of it on credit.

Because of our credit arrangements, Corone dealers can do a large amount of business on a small investment. In effect, we take the place of your banker, for the goods we send you on credit are the same as cash. Like your banker, we can make loans only when we have evidence of ability and willingness to pay later. The only way we can protect all our dealers against price rises due to losses from bad debts is to check every credit applicant and select carefully.

If you applied for a loan at your bank, you'd expect to show your financial statements to your banker. We are in the same position—except that we have no mortgage to protect us, and we are not so well informed as your banker about you and your local market.

The confidential information we've asked for is strictly for business purposes. It helps both of us. Since the peak sales months are close at hand, I'm enclosing another form and an addressed envelope so that you can get this information

```
back to us in time for us to get your fast-selling Corone
fishing gear started to you by the first of next week.
```

(Because most requests for credit information from customers are simply modifications of direct requests and refusals, we run no checklists or cases.)

CREDIT REFUSALS

In the light of poor standing on any or all of the four C tests for credit (p. 131) you will have to refuse some credit applicants. The most likely bases are unfavorable reports from references or an unfavorable financial position. Your job will sometimes merely require suggesting some modification of the arrangement the customer has requested. In the case of an old customer it may be a refusal of a credit-limit revision or a suggestion of curtailed buying. All these situations are inherently disappointing; they are a reflection on the ability of the customer; they *may be* interpreted as a reflection on honesty; and so they are fraught with negative possibilities.

As in any disappointing-news letter, you need to analyze the situation, search out any hopeful elements (especially character), line up your reasons, and write a B–plan letter.

The applicant may have receivables or payables out of line, or be too slow in meeting obligations, or be undercapitalized. *Whatever the reason, you have to establish it,* and in this function you have some educational work to do—without offense if at all possible.

You certainly do not want to close the door irrevocably on any debtor (except possibly deadbeats). A poor account at the time of writing may be a good one a year from then (and if your wise counseling has helped in the improvement, you have established yourself as a helpful friend and are thus more likely to receive the customer's business).

For that reason, most good credit refusals establish good feeling in a short buffer, show the reasons in an analysis of the circumstances, identify the deficiency, refuse in positive fashion, suggest how the customer can remedy the deficiency, and invite a later application. If possible, the letter may make a counterproposal and point out its advantages and then ask for action on that basis. The best ending is an attempt to sell for cash. After all, the reader wants your goods and possibly can't get them on credit elsewhere either.

In the following instance, involving an order for $176 worth of work overalls, the dealer quickly responded with a financial statement and references in response to the request for them. Accounts receivable and payable were both too large; the trade association reported that strikes in the mines of the dealer's community affected all local trade. Since the references reported that the customer's payments were good enough during normal times, the credit writer sought to cultivate potential business while declining the account at present:

Your large order for Stalwart overalls suggests the prospect of an early strike settlement in your area. We're glad to hear that.

When the miners go back to work, the steady revival of business in and around Canyon City will no doubt help your collections so that both your accounts receivable and accounts payable can be reduced. In that way you can probably quickly restore your current ratio to the healthy 2:1 we require because we've found over the years that such a ratio places no burden on our customers. Such an improvement will enable us to consider your credit application favorably. Will you please send us subsequent statements?

You'll probably need your Stalwart overalls sooner than that, however; they're a popular brand because they wear well. Workers like the reinforced pockets and knees. They'll easily outsell other lines you might carry.

You can stock this popular brand and thus satisfy present demand by paying cash and taking advantage of the liberal discount we can give you. On this order, for instance, the discount at our regular terms of 2/10, n/90 would amount to $3.52—more than enough to pay interest for three months on a $100 bank loan.

Or you might cut your order in about half and order more frequently. But with a $100 bank loan at 8 percent and a stock turn of 12—which is a conservative estimate, Mr. Wolens—you'd make an annual saving of $16 after paying your interest charges. I don't need to tell you that that's 3 pairs of dependable Stalwart overalls absolutely free—overalls that you still sell for $7.80 a pair.

To handle the order in this profitable way, attach your check to the memo I've enclosed and mail both of them back to me in the enclosed envelope. We can have your Stalwart overalls to you in about five days.

Usually you can specifically isolate the sore spot in a dealer's situation (as in the preceding letter) and by impersonal, positive phrasing save the customer's pride, suggest the remedy, and leave the way open for future negotiations.

In consumer letters involving a retail customer, however, nine times out of ten the reason for the refusal is the customer's failure to take care of obligations. This is a highly personal reflection, one which many retail credit people shy away from by feigning incomplete information and inviting the customer to come in and talk the matter over.

We do not agree with that dodging procedure. We think that a better method is the forthright credit refusal in the usual pattern of buffer, reasons, positive refusal, forward look, and counterproposal in the form of a bid for cash business.

Your request for a credit account at Aiken's has received our interested consideration, and we take it as a compliment to our way of doing business.

For 50 years Aiken's has been bringing its customers quality merchandise at fair prices. This, as you realize, requires careful merchandising policies on our part. Not the least of these savings—the policy of paying cash for merchandise, thereby receiving discounts and eliminating interest charges, which we are able to pass on to Aiken customers in the form of lower prices—necessitates that we receive prompt payment from our credit customers.

As you were an applicant for a credit account, we followed our usual practice and asked for information from retail credit sources.

We realize that meeting all obligations promptly is often temporarily difficult and that very likely in a short time you will have qualified for a charge account at Aiken's by taking care of your other obligations.

Meanwhile you will continue to receive the same courteous treatment that made you favor Aiken's in the first place. We certainly want to have you as a customer. With our will-call, budget, or layaway plans at your disposal, you may own anything in Aiken's within a short time by making convenient payments of your own choice. Come in soon and let us serve you in this way.

The following letter refusing credit to a young man just out of college and with unsteady, low-income employment talks concretely and sensibly; it's a good credit-education letter. Note how the writer stresses the idea that character is not the basis for refusal.

When you wrote last week asking for credit, as a member of the Illinois Credit Union we automatically asked the Union for your record. You can well be proud of the report we received, showing absolutely no black mark against you.

Such a complimentary report on your excellent character indicates a promising future. The fact that you have never defaulted or delayed in paying an account means that you will be able to get credit easily when your income becomes steady.

We could extend credit to you on the basis of your personal record alone, for we know that you fully intend to meet any obligations you undertake. But if some unforeseen expense should come up, with your present fluctuating income you probably could not pay your account. As a cooperating member of the Credit Union, we would then be compelled to submit your name as a poor credit risk. Such a report would limit your chances of obtaining credit in the future—perhaps at a time when you need it more than now. For your own benefit you'll be better off to stick to cash purchases now.

Thank you for thinking of us. We shall look forward to the time when you can comfortably and safely contract for credit purchases with us.

Meanwhile you can make your dollars reach further by buying from Bowen's for cash, for we can buy in quantity, save on shipping costs, and take advantage of discounts. We pass these savings on to you in the form of lower prices. When you buy at Bowen's, your income is inflated because you get quality merchandise at low prices.

Letters limiting the credit of an old established customer are no different from refusals to new customers; they just adapt the talking points.

> The $635 order for September delivery you gave Mr. Ray indicates a bright outlook for fall sales. Apparently you are selling lots of Carlton heaters. I'm glad to see that.
>
> We want to work right along with you. In trying to be of service to you as always, we want to make a constructive suggestion. The large order you placed in March, together with this current one, leads us to believe that you may be overstocking Carltons.
>
> With this shipment your account would stand about $500 beyond the limit we agreed on when you first started to deal with us five years ago. Since we believe that the proposed balance would be too great a burden upon you because it would throw your payables out of line, we suggest two alternative courses of action.
>
> If your ordering such a stock of Carlton heaters indicates an extensive home-building program going on in Fairview, your comments on local conditions and the information requested on the enclosed form may serve as a basis for extending your credit limit to the point where it will take care of your needs.
>
> Or we will extend to July 10 the 5 percent discount on your $940 March order. By sending us your check for $893, you will not only put your account in shape for the present order; you will also mark up greater profits on the sale of your Carltons.
>
> We're just as anxious as you are, Mr. Skinner, to send you this latest shipment. Please take one of these courses so that we may ship your new stock of Carltons in time for the fall season.

As in any good refusal, none of these letters apologize or hark back to the refusal in the end. To do so indicates that you are not confident in your decision. The checklist on page 235 incorporates the major suggestions for handling credit refusals or limitations.

ACKNOWLEDGMENTS OF INCOMPLETE OR INDEFINITE ORDERS

[*Any firm which sells by mail will receive some orders which can't be handled as the Standard ("all's well") Acknowledgments discussed on pp. 126–31. Some orders will be incomplete or vague, or for goods temporarily out of stock, or from people to whom you cannot sell, or for something a little different from what you have, or for several items involving a combination of these difficulties.*

Keeping most of these problem orders on the books (and hence the profits from them in your income statements) is often the difference between success and failure. While a firm may occasionally get into a situation where it can succeed in business without trying, smart competitors soon

Credit Refusal Checklist

1. Your opening:
   a) Your best beginning talks about something pleasant: the market; timeliness; the reader. . . .
   b) Beware the selfish note of "We are glad to receive. . . ."
   c) To keep your reader from considering buying elsewhere, get resale (product and/or house) early in the letter: consumer pleasure in use or dealer profit possibilities.
   d) References to the order, if there was one, should be worked in incidentally while you say something of more significance.
   e) Be careful not to mislead the reader.
2. Your explanation and refusal:
   a) Stick to the theme of a strong, healthy financial condition.
   b) Do not begin your explanation with writer-interest reasons.
   c) Give some justifying reasons before the refusal.
   d) Meet the issue squarely, making clear whether character is or is not the reason. Advantages in cash buying are not reasons for refusing credit.
   e) Avoid the negative, critical, nosey, or patronizing tone; state your reasons as helpfulness to the reader. Give just enough facts to show that you know without implication of FBI investigations.
   f) Be sure you've made clear that you will not now approve credit.
   g) Hiding behind "policy" evades the issue (and appears selfish).
   h) Phrase your reason in terms of your experience with others.
   i) Always leave the way open for credit extension later.
   j) But you can't make promises, except to reconsider.
3. Your counterproposal:
   a) Introduce a cash, reduced-shipment, or other plan as the solution.
   b) But first show why (help to the reader).
   c) If you propose cash with a discount, figure the savings.
   d) Possibly project the savings over a year's business.
   e) Can you suggest smaller orders? Local financing?
   f) Use the conditional mood in your explanation and proposal.
4. Your ending:
   a) Leave no details uncovered in your present proposal.
   b) In regular action-ending style, drive for acceptance.
   c) Success consciousness precludes the use of "Why not. . . ."
   d) You have to get approval before taking unasked action.
   e) Your last picture should show the reader's benefits.
5. Your tone:
   a) Throughout your letter retain an attitude of helpfulness.
   b) Sales promotion material on other goods is inappropriate.

learn about such a gravy train and jump aboard. The former lone rider who doesn't know how to compete for the problem-order business will lose it—and the profits that go with it.

For that reason, we devote the remainder of this chapter to Disappointing (B–plan) Acknowledgments of Orders. And we do it in terms of letter writing—for good reasons.

In nearly all cases a well-done acknowledgment letter is the best way to keep the order on the books and the customer well served and satisfied. You could hardly expect to succeed with form letters because they cannot adapt adequately to highly varied circumstances and because their impersonality does not work well in handling negative situations. Telephone calls, while having the advantage of speed, lack two important advantages of a good letter:

1. *They do not give the firm the chance to phrase the message so precisely, concisely, and persuasively as in a carefully done letter.*
2. *They do not provide the written agreement on the many details often important in the buyer-seller contract.*

In messages acknowledging various problem orders, you need a high level of know-how with various letter-writing principles and techniques. Since all are inherently negative (always delay and inconvenience, for example), you need to know how to keep the picture as bright as possible. You need resale to keep reader interest. Adaptation becomes important because of the varied and special circumstances. And since you often must ask the reader for a change of mind or for further action, you need all the principles of persuasion, including skill with action endings. None of these are likely to come out as well in form letters or telephone conversations.]

When you get an order that is incomplete (and therefore vague), you can either try to guess what the customer wants and thereby risk extra costs and customer dissatisfaction, or you can write for the needed information. Usually you write.

Since it is a *bad-news* letter (because of the additional trouble and delay), you will wisely use a buffer. Resale, thanks, and (if a new customer) a hearty welcome are all good buffer material and need to come early in the letter. A problem here is to avoid misleading the customer into believing that you are filling the order.

Very early—perhaps by starting to interweave some of it into the first part of the letter—you should stress the resale element. The more specific it is, the more emphatic it is. If you say the customer will like the product, make clear specifically why you think so. Reassuring the customer that the product is good is resale that will help to overcome the drawbacks. In this case it has a much more important role than in the standard acknowledgment. Although small bits of it may be scattered throughout the letter, at least some of it comes before the reader learns the bad news—to bolster the original desire in the moment of disappointment. It can be very short:

```
Fashion-conscious women everywhere are wearing Ban-lon
sweaters like the one you ordered, not only for their wide
color choice and style but because of their ability to be
tossed around and still keep looking nice.
```

When you have thus prepared the reader psychologically, asking for the needed information will reveal the bad news. Thus you save words, weaken the bad news by putting the reader's main attention on complying with your request, and avoid any goodwill-killing accusations. More specifically, your technique at this important crux of the letter is: In one key sentence beginning with a reader-benefit reason for your request, ask for the information. For example:

```
So that we may be sure to send you just the sweater that will
suit you best, will you please specify your color choice?
```

Now, if you add a touch of satisfaction-resale to motivate the requested action, do what you can to help the reader decide and answer (to overcome the extra trouble), and promise speed (to overcome as much as possible of the delay), you'll probably get the information you want, without ruffling your reader's feathers:

```
Coming in four subtle shades of harvest brown, lettuce green,
tile red, and sky blue, Ban-lon sweaters provide you a pleasant
color to match any complexion or ensemble.

Just use the handy return card, and you'll be enjoying the
sweater of your choice within two days after we receive the
information.
```

When circumstances permit, even a better idea is to get the customer to return your letter with the necessary information marked on it. Beyond making customer response easy, you get the desirable effect of removing your reminder of shortcomings from the customer's sight. The letter above could also have ended this way:

```
Just check the box at the bottom of this letter to tell us
what color you want, and return it in the stamped, addressed
envelope.  You'll be enjoying the sweater of your choice
within two days after we receive the information.
```

Notice that although they treat an inherently bad-news situation, nowhere in the four paragraphs of this letter is there any negative expression ("delay," "inconvenience," "incomplete," "regret," "sorry"). Most of all, the acknowledgment does not irritate by accusing with such expressions as "you neglected," "you forgot," or "you failed."

The following letter illustrates good technique for an acknowledgment when you can fill part of the order but have to get omitted information about another part. If you want to consider it as a simple acknowledgment of an incomplete order, however, you can read it without the first paragraph and the phrase "the file and" in the next-to-last paragraph.

```
Soon after you get this letter you should receive the very
protective locking and fire-resistant Chaw-Walker file you
```

ordered October 2. It is to go out on our Meridian delivery tomorrow.

The sturdy but light Model 94 Royal Standard typewriter you specified is our most popular one this year, perhaps because of its wide adaptability. Readily available in two type sizes and six type styles, it is suitable to all kinds of work and to various typists' tastes.

To be sure of getting the size and style you like best, please check your choices on the enclosed card of illustrations and return it.

Although your letter was written in Executive style elite (12 letters to the inch), you may prefer the more legible Professional style pica (10 letters to the inch) if you are buying for your reporters. It is the most widely used in newspaper work.

All prices are the same—except $10 extra for the modish Script style, which you probably will not want—and your check exactly covers the file and the three typewriters you ordered in any other choice.

By returning the card with your choices of type size and style right away, you can have your three new Royals Friday, ready for years of carefree typing. We'll send them out on the next delivery after we hear from you.

For requesting additional information in business-building fashion, apply the suggestions in the checklist for incomplete orders (p. 239).

DELAYS AND BACK-ORDERING

Sometimes the problem in an acknowledgment is that you can't send the goods right away. In the absence of a specified time limit, sellers-by-mail usually try to keep the order on the books if they feel they can fill it within a time that is really a service to the customer—that is, if they feel the customer would prefer to wait rather than cancel the order. After a buffer, they tell when they expect to fill the order and usually assume (without asking) that such an arrangement is acceptable. If the date is so far off that doubt arises, they may ask instead of assuming. In either case the wise business writer will acknowledge the order promptly.

Again your main problem is keeping the order. This time, though, the only drawback to overcome is delay. Your main element is resale—to convince the reader that the product is worth the wait. It may include both resale on the house and resale on the goods. If the order is the customer's first, resale is even more important and more extensive.

The plan and technique are the same as for the acknowledgment of an incomplete order, at least through the first paragraph and some resale talk.

Your order 5B631 of April 7 for Tropical brand playsuits in the new Wancrest Glachine material is another reflection of your

Checklist for Acknowledging Incomplete Orders

1. If you are sending any goods, say so immediately and give necessary details.
   a) If not, begin with a short buffer which is basically resale.
   b) Quickly but subordinately identify the order by date, number, and/or description.
   c) Slow: "We have received . . . ," "Thank you for your. . . ."
   d) Selfish: "We're glad to have. . . ."
   e) Provide some resale on the problem article before the bad news, but don't imply that you are sending the article now.
   f) Make the resale specific, not "We're sure you'll like these shoes." Say why.
   g) Use only brief phrases for resale on goods sent, or for any new-customer aspects, until you've asked for the missing information.
2. Ask for the information naturally, positively, and specifically.
   a) The natural transition to the request follows from preceding resale talk.
   b) Preface the request with a reader-benefit phrase—something like "So that you'll be sure to get just the X you want, please. . . ."
   c) To avoid puzzling, make the request fairly early—but not too quickly or abruptly.
   d) Avoid the accusation and wasted words of such phrasing as "You did not include" or "We need some additional information."
   e) Name the customer's options; color choices or different models, for example.
   f) Add explanations to help in the choice (or decision), to resell and to show your interest in satisfying.
   g) Keep the you-viewpoint: "You may choose from . . . ," not "We have three shades."
3. Close with a drive for the specific action you want.
   a) If many words follow the first indication of what you want done, repeat specifically.
   b) Make replying easy (maybe a return card to check).
   c) If appropriate, have the reader mark your letter and return it.
   d) Refer to the enclosure subordinately; action deserves the emphasis.
   e) Stress your promptness—preferably a date of arrival if you get prompt response.
   f) But keep it logical; post-office speed is not that of an automat.
   g) Try to work in a last short reference to reader satisfaction.

If resale on the house and/or sales promotion material would be appropriate—as the first surely would be in a new-customer situation—use Items 3 and 4 of the checklist for standard acknowledgments (p. 130) as additional Items 4 and 5 here.

> astute buying. From all indications they will be the prevailing style this season.

The parting of the ways comes where the incomplete asks for information and the back order explains the situation. The explanation should picture the goods on their way (and imply receipt of them) in the first part of a sentence which ends with a clear indication that that does not mean now (usually by giving the shipping date):

> By making every effort to get your supply to you before spring, when your customers will start calling for these popular playsuits, we are able to promise you a shipment by April 27.

As always in letter writing, explaining in positive terms what you can do, have done, and will do is better than telling in negative terms what you can't do, haven't done, or won't do. As the writer of the preceding paragraph did, a good letter writer will avoid such unnecessary negatives as "out of stock,""cannot send," "temporarily depleted," "will be unable to," "do not have," and "can't send until."

Only a poor business manager is caught short without a justifying reason. A good one will have a reason—and will explain it to customers to avoid the impression of inefficiency. Often it is basically strong resale material if properly interpreted. For example:

> The Wancrest people have assured us that although we're insisting on the top-quality material which has made these playsuits so attractive to store buyers, they can catch up to our recent order and have a new shipment to us by the 21st. Thus we can promise yours by the 27th.

More resale may follow the explanation to make the reader want the product badly enough to wait. Because it has such an important job to do, it is probably more important in the back-order acknowledgment than in any other. It should be short, specific, and adapted to carry its full effect. It may include both resale on the house and resale on the goods. Since so much of both kinds has already appeared in the letter we're developing here, however, more hardly seems appropriate.

The ending of the back-order acknowledgment may go either of two ways:

1. You may ask outright whether you may fill the order when you have said you can. This plan is preferable if you seriously doubt that the customer will approve.
2. You may phrase it so that this letter will complete the contract unless the reader takes the initiative and writes back a cancellation. That is, you look forward with success consciousness to filling the order when you have said you can. Your assumption (that your plan is acceptable) will hold more frequently if you never suggest the thing you don't want your reader to do —cancel.

The following letter illustrates the handling of a back-order problem:

You will be glad to know that the women's white tennis dresses you ordered April 7—

4 dozen—style No. 16J7 women's tennis dresses, 1 dozen each in sizes 8, 10, 12, and 14 @ $180.00 a dozen; terms 2/10, N/30

—are leading the summer sportswear sales of more than 400 of our customers from Maine to California.

We are increasing production on this model and have booked your tennis dresses for rush shipment April 27 by air express.

The unusual preseason popularity of this trimly cut tennis dress owes much to the shimmering polyester and cotton fabric of which it is made. We used up our stock of the genuine combed cotton material; and rather than use a substitute, we shut down production on this model. A large stock of Glachine cotton fabric is already en route here from Wancrest's famous North Carolina mills; thus we are able to promise your shipment by April 27.

For this chance to prove once again Tropical's continuing fashion superiority, we thank you sincerely.

Much of the back-order acknowledgment technique is the same as that used in standard and incomplete-order acknowledgments. The checklist for back-order acknowledgments points out the similarities and additional considerations (p. 242).

ACKNOWLEDGMENTS DECLINING ORDERS

Only three likely reasons might make you decline an order:

1. The customer has asked for credit, and you are not willing to sell that way. In that case the problem is a credit problem (discussed on pp. 231–34).
2. You don't have the goods (or a suitable substitute), and you don't expect to get them in time to serve the customer. You then explain the situation, tell where to get the goods (if you know), maybe present resale on the house and sales promotion material on any other goods which seem likely to be of interest, and end appropriately.
3. You don't market your products in the way proposed. Most of these problems arise because of one of the following two situations: (*a*) the orderer is an unacceptable dealer; or (*b*) you sell only through regular merchandising channels and the orderer (usually a consumer) does not propose to go through those channels.

Declining because you don't have the goods is well illustrated by the following letter from a Florida orange grower to a former customer:

Your recent and additional order for one bushel of navel oranges is evidence that you find our fruit to be of high quality. That's a reputation of which we are very proud.

Although this valley is known as the land "where sunshine spends the winter," a snowstorm and freeze in early January caused extensive damage to our current fruit crop. Some of the fruit looks and tastes good, but we do not trust it to keep more than a week after it has been picked.

Back-Order Checklist

1. If you are sending any goods, say so immediately and give necessary details.
    a) If not, begin with a short buffer which is basically resale.
    b) Quickly but subordinately identify the order.
    c) Slow: "We have received . . . ," "Thank you for your. . . ."
    d) Selfish: "We're glad to have. . . ."
    e) Provide some resale on the problem article before bad news.
    f) Make the resale specific, not "We're sure you'll like. . . ." Why?
    g) Use only brief phrases for resale on goods sent, or for any new-customer aspects, until you've handled the key point.
2. Handle the bad news as positively as you can.
    a) Picture the goods moving toward or being used by the customer *before* indicating that you do not now have them.
    b) Avoid negatives: "out of stock," "can't send until. . . ."
    c) Adapt to the one situation rather than a universal, like "In order to give you the very best service we can. . . ."
    d) Explain the reason for being caught short (if any)—preferably resale in effect.
    e) Do make clear when you can ship.
    f) To avoid cancellation of the order, some resale is important.
3. Resale on the house helps too, especially with new customers.
    a) For consumers: personal shopping, delivery schedules, credit. . . .
    b) For dealers: sales representatives, manuals, displays, advertising aids.
    c) If you talk advertising, give publications or stations, amount of space or time, and schedules; show how it promotes sales.
    d) If you talk credit, invite application rather than promise.
4. Sales promotion material shows service attitude and builds sales.
    a) Keep it appropriate—usually on allied or seasonal goods.
    b) You-attitude and specificness are necessary to effectiveness.
    c) Emphasize service to the customer, not desire to sell more.
    d) In referring to enclosures, put the emphasis on reader action.
5. Look forward to future orders.
    a) If sales promotion is the basis, suggest specific action.
    b) If resale is the basis, talk of reader satisfaction.
    c) Guard against bromides and Greedy Gus wording as you close.
6. Word the back-order action phrase to stress the action you want.
    a) Ask only if you doubt that your plan is satisfactory.
    b) Suggest acceptance; avoid the idea of cancellation.
    c) Also avoid reminders of the delay.

Since one of the qualities you have a right to expect in fresh fruit is its ability to keep, and since we are unwilling to risk the chance that you might be disappointed, we are returning your check for the one bushel of oranges.

The groves around Citra (30 miles south of here and surrounded by lots of lakes) were not damaged. Mr. Charles Perry, manager of The Orange Shop there, told me yesterday that he still has excellent fruit (Zip 32627).

The damage to our trees is only temporary. We are looking forward to another crop of high-quality fruits next year. May we serve you again next season with some of our choice fruits?

Unacceptable dealer

A dealer may be unacceptable because (1) you sell only through exclusive dealerships and you already have a dealer in the territory or (2) because the orderer does not meet your requirements for a dealership. For example, the dealer may insist on consignment sales.

The first part of the declining letter would be the same in each case and (except for the omission of resale) the same as the beginning of other bad-news acknowledgments we have discussed. In the first case your explanation (usually beginning in the second paragraph) would be how you operate and why you operate that way plus the simple fact of the existing dealership. In the second case it would be a simple explanation of your requirements, with justifying reasons. The ending for the one would be a purely goodwill ending of "keeping in mind" in case you should later want another dealer. The other would end with an offer to reconsider if a change or additional information shows the requirements are met.

Improper channels

Some buyers think that all manufacturers or producers should sell to anybody who has the money and omit jobbers, wholesalers, and retailers (who add so much to the cost of goods). Those who howl the loudest on this point also howl loudly when a producer from afar does not make the goods available in local stores. Both methods of merchandising have advantages and disadvantages. Which is the more desirable is a question we need not answer. We must grant, however, that a producer has the right to sell goods any legal way. And whatever plan you encounter has no doubt been chosen for certain reasons. At least some of them should be in terms of how best to serve customers.

Assuming that the firm has taken the customer-service attitude, you are in a good position to acknowledge the order of a person who does not (through ignorance or intent) choose to follow your plan—usually a consumer asking for goods from a wholesaler or producer instead of through the regular retail channel.

Some of the customer-service reasons you can point out for selling only through local retail stores are the advantage of being able to get goods quickly from local stores; of being able to see, feel, and try them; of being able to get adjustments and service easier—indeed, all the disadvantages a seller-by-mail usually has to overcome are now in your favor.

Your bad-news letter begins in the same way as those acknowledging incomplete orders and orders you cannot fill immediately: with a buffer, including resale to help keep the customer interested in the goods (on which you *do* make a profit, of course). As before, you are careful not to mislead.

After this beginning, you explain how you merchandise your goods (not how you don't, except by implication) and why you operate this way. As far as possible, you explain the why in terms of benefit to the customer (you-viewpoint)—not the benefits to you. At least a part of the reader-benefit *why* should come before the part of the explanation which conveys the bad news (by implication) that the order is not being filled.

If your explanation is good, the reader will decide yours is the best way. If your resale talk has been good, the desire for the product will still be there although the purchase has to be elsewhere. You tell exactly how and where to get it, and you give a last touch of resale to encourage ordering the way you suggest.

If you have several equally convenient outlets, you name them all to give a choice and to be fair to all. This letter follows the directions:

> Karsol shower curtains like the ones you saw advertised will give you the wear you want for rental units.
>
> So that you will be able to select personally the exact patterns you prefer (from eight different designs offered), we have set up a marketing plan of bringing Karsol shower curtains to you through local dealers only. This way you will save handling, shipping, and c.o.d. charges. You will be able to get your curtains at the White House, located at 300 Main Street in Montgomery, thus speeding your purchases and avoiding unnecessary delays ever present when ordering by mail.
>
> We have recently sent a large shipment of Karsol shower curtains to the White House, and you will be able to see for yourself that although these waterproof curtains are of exceptional strength and durability, they are soft and pliable.
>
> Stop by the White House next time you are in town and select your favorite pattern of Karsol shower curtains that will satisfy your tenants.

If you are really a good business manager, you will notify the retailers, so that they can write or call the interested prospect who doesn't come in (especially if the order is for a big-ticket item).

The reminder checklist on page 245 summarizes most of the guide points.

Checklist for Rechanneling Orders

1. Your buffer beginning is a good place to work in resale.
   a) An exact reference to the merchandise ordered is a form of resale in that it attempts to etch the choice in the reader's mind. Other identifications (quantity, date of order, and the like) aren't so important here, since this is an outright refusal.
   b) But don't even intimate the refusal at this point.
   c) Nor do you want to imply that you are shipping the goods.
2. To avoid abruptness, continue the idea of reader benefit as you turn from the resale to your explanation.
3. Think—and write—positively in your explanation.
   a) As appropriate to your reader (a consumer or a dealer), focus on benefits (fresh stock, less inventory, savings on shipping costs, examination of all choices before purchasing, credit and adjustment services).
   b) Establish at least one good reason for your merchandising plan before stating it (the statement of the plan is the refusal).
   c) State the plan in terms of what you do, not what you don't.
   d) Make it clear; otherwise, you may get a second, more insistent order.
   e) Follow the statement of the refusal with additional customer advantages.
   f) Is there any advantage in pointing out benefits other than those for the customer?
   g) When a price difference exists (as is usual), admit it but minimize it.
4. Your action ending should urge the reader to place the order with the appropriate outlet.
   a) Be as specific as you can (name and address if only one place and hence no playing favorites), and build up the image of service.
   b) Work in specific resale material as a safeguard against the possibility of brand switching when the reader places the order again.

SELLING A SUBSTITUTE

Many times you will receive orders you can't fill exactly because you do not have the special brand, but you have a competing brand or something else that will render the service the customer obviously wanted. You know that in most cases people buy a product not for the name on it but for the service they expect from it. If you think your brand will serve (and ordinarily you do, or you wouldn't be selling it), you remember your service attitude and try to satisfy the orderer's wants. As a point of business ethics, you should not try to sell a substitute unless you sincerely believe you can truly serve by saving the customer time, trouble, or money in getting wanted products or by giving service at least comparable to what is available elsewhere in terms of cost.

Once you decide that you are ethically justified in selling the substitute, you need to remember several working principles:

1. Don't call it a substitute. Although many substitutes are superior to the things they replace, the word has undesirable connotations that work against you. Burma Shave once used the connotation effectively in a roadside advertisement reading "Substitutes and imitations—give them to your wife's relations. Burma Shave."
2. Don't belittle the competitor's product. Not only is this questionable ethics, but it criticizes the judgment of the orderer who wanted to buy that product.
3. Don't refer to the ordered product specifically by name any more than you have to—perhaps not at all. Once should be enough. You want the would-be buyer to forget it and think about yours. When you use its name, you remind your reader of it—in effect, you advertise it. Conversely, stress your product, perhaps repeating the exact name several times.

Except for the fact *that the identification and resale are in general terms broad enough to encompass both the product ordered and the substitute,* and show their basic similarity, your beginning of the substitute-selling acknowledgment is the same as other buffers for bad-news acknowledgments. If you phrase the beginning well, you'll have no trouble making a smooth transition to further talk about the substitute.

```
Your repeat order of September 10 for 60 regular-duty
batteries suggests that you have found your battery business
quite profitable.  We're glad to hear it, but we think we can
show you how you can do even better in the coming season.
```

You arrange to introduce at least one sales point favorable to the substitute *before* revealing that you can't send what was ordered. You need to convey the negative message fairly early, however, to keep the reader from wondering why all the talk about the substitute. Your best technique is the standard one for subordinating negative messages: Tell what you *can* do in a way that clearly implies what you can't.

In our continuous effort to find the best automobile accessories and equipment at reasonable prices, we have found that the new Acme battery excels others of its price class in power, endurance at full load, and resistance to cracking. Because of those desirable qualities, we decided two months ago to stock the Acme line exclusively. Although Powell of Dayton still has the Motor King, we think your customers will be ahead in service and you'll make more profits with the Acme.

Once you are over that rough spot, clear sailing lies ahead. You continue your sales talk, concentrating on why you carry the substitute and what it will do for your reader, not on why you do not carry the ordered product. You give a complete, specific description of the substitute's good points in terms of consumer or dealer benefits (as the case may be).

A good test of the adequacy of your sales talk is whether it is all *you* would want to know if you were being asked to change your mind about the two products.

Because of its 115-ampere power and its endurance of 5.9 minutes at full load, your customers will like the fact that the Acme keeps a hard-to-start engine spinning vigorously and increases the chance of starting. They'll also like the tough new plastic case that avoids the cracking and loss of acid sometimes experienced with hard-rubber cases.

Sometimes your price will be higher than that of the product ordered. If so, presumably you think your product is better. Your method of meeting the price competition, then, is to sell the advantages and then point to them as justifying the price.

When you explain the advantages the Acme has over its competitors, you justify at least a $2 higher price in the customer's mind—and you produce a prompt purchase. The Acme battery will back you up, too, in the customer's long experience with it. It carries the usual 36-month pro rata replacement guarantee. And the fact that it wholesales to you at only $1 more means an extra $1 profit to you on each sale.

Sometimes you will have to admit (tacitly) that your product is inferior but adequate. Your technique then is to sell its adequacy and the fact that it is a good buy because of the price. If the customer had ordered a higher priced battery than you now sell, for example, you could replace the three preceding paragraphs with these:

In our continuous effort to find the best automobile accessories and equipment at reasonable prices, we have found that the Motor King is a leading seller. Because of its low price, strong customer appeal, and complete range of sizes, we now offer only the Motor King for all cars. The fact that you could fit <u>any</u> car would give you a big advantage over competitors selling brands that come in only a few sizes.

The $2 saving you can offer on the Motor King will have a strong appeal to many of your customers who are unwilling to pay higher prices for more than standard specifications for

> regular-duty batteries: 105 amperes, 48 plates, 5.3 minutes' endurance at full load. The Motor King meets these specifications, and it carries the standard 36-month pro rata replacement guarantee.
>
> And while your customers would be saving, we estimate that you would be making more profits because of increased volume that would almost certainly come from a complete line at favorable prices.

Usually, however, quality and price are about the same; and you simply sell the product on its merits and as a service or convenience because it is available.

When your selling job is done, you are ready to try to get action. You can do either of two things:

1. You can ask the orderer whether you may fill the order with the substitute, or ask for a new order specifying it; or
2. You can send the goods and give the orderer the option of returning them entirely at your expense—that is, you pay transportation both ways. Thus no question of ethics arises.

The second way will sell more goods if you word the offer carefully to avoid a sound of high pressuring. You should use it, however, only in an attempt to give the best service you can—for example when the customer indicated pressing need, and transportation costs are small, and you are reasonably sure of acceptance. Indeed a recent Supreme Court decision seems to relieve the receiver of any responsibility for returning or paying for unordered goods.

If you do send the goods on option, you can greatly affect your chance of having them accepted by the wording of your offer. Note the difference between these two ways:

> 1. We believe you will find the Acmes satisfactory. Therefore we are filling your order with them. If you don't like them, just return them to us collect.
>
> 2. Because we are so thoroughly convinced that you will like the Acmes, we are filling your order with them on trial. When you see how they sell and satisfy your customers, we believe you will want to keep the whole shipment and order more.

The second puts the emphasis on the customer's accepting the merchandise, where it should be; the first, on returning the goods. The second way will sell more.

Whether your acknowledgment letter selling a substitute asks approval or explains that you are sending the goods on trial, you should merely ask or suggest the action and make it convenient. A last touch of resale may help, but you should not urge action—certainly not command it. This type of letter has the onus of suspicion on it from the outset. High pressure is out of place anywhere in it, especially in the end. Here's a good substitute letter:

Your request for another Simpson product shows that you have been well satisfied with these high-quality electrical supplies. One of the reasons we've been able to please you is the practice of introducing new and improved products first.

Our latest electric fan featuring the newest improvements is the Matthews. Because of the new-style oscillating gear, this new fan delivers 12 percent more cubic feet of air per minute than any other fan of similar size. The crackle finish looks new longer because it resists scuffs and scratches.

Since the demand is rapidly growing for the improved Matthews, we now stock it exclusively. You may still be able to buy the Seabreeze from Gardner, Perkins, and Simons in Cleveland. We believe, however, you'll prefer the Matthews.

In addition to the standard 10-inch Matthews priced at $12.83 and the large 12-inch at $18.16, with the Matthews line you can also offer a new model, the Matthews Midget. This is an 8-inch fan priced at only $9.08. The Midget has all the new improvements found on the larger fans. Like all Matthews fans, the Midget also carries a one-year guarantee.

To order, simply fill out the enclosed card and mail it. We will ship your Matthews fans by freight collect. When you see how well Matthews fans sell, you will fully realize that you made a sound buy.

The checklist for selling substitutes (p. 250) summarizes the points you'll want to observe in writing successful letters of this type.

COMBINATIONS

In acknowledging orders, you will often find one for several items, some of which you have and others of which you don't. To answer such an order, you have to combine the principles discussed for different types of acknowledgments. The writer of the following letter to a new customer had to combine several types because the firm could send one item immediately, had to delay another shipment, couldn't provide another item, and had to substitute for still another:

Your two dozen F78 x 14BW Firestone tires are already on their way to you. They should arrive by Motor-Van truck Thursday, ready for your weekend customers.

Welcoming a new customer to our long list of dealers who look to us for automobile suppliers is always a pleasure. We shall always try to serve your needs as best we can, by keeping up with the market and providing you with the best goods available.

The GR78 x 15WS tires are a case in point. In another effort to assure our customers of the advertised quality of all products we handle, we returned to the manufacturer the last shipment of GR78 x 15WS Firestone tires because they had been slightly bruised in a shipping accident. Since we are assured of a new shipment in two weeks, may we fill this part of your order then?

Checklist for Suggesting a Substitute

1. Your opening:
   a) For acknowledgment, rely mainly on implication: maybe the date of the order and a general reference to the class of goods.
   b) Make the reference broad enough to encompass A (product ordered) and B (substitute).
   c) But don't call either by specific name, model, or number yet.
   d) Let the buffer be resale in effect, but not specifically on A.
   e) Intimating at this point that you're going to ship anything could mean only A to the reader.
   f) Establish early the kinship—the similar nature—of A and B, with emphasis on points in B's favor.
   g) Show gratitude for the customer's coming to you with business.
   h) The routine "Thank you" or the selfish "We're glad to have" is usually not the best way.
2. Your transition:
   a) Introduction of B should follow naturally from what precedes.
   b) Before revealing that you can't send A, introduce B and at least one of its strong points.
   c) Calling B a substitute or "just as good" defeats your strategy.
3. Your statement of unavailability:
   a) Stress what you can do, not what you can't; saying that you can send only B makes adequately clear that you can't send A.
   b) Identify A by name no more than once—when you clear it out of stock.
   c) Present the bad news early enough to avoid puzzling.
   d) Make perfectly clear that you can't send A.
   e) Stress why you carry B rather than why you don't stock A.
4. Your sales message on B:
   a) Sell B on its own merits; it's a good product; no apologies needed, and no belittling of A.
   b) Seek out the sales points, and apply them specifically.
   c) Interpret these points in terms of reader benefits.
5. Overcoming price resistance (See p. 112):
6. Your action ending to keep the order and goodwill.
   a) Make responding easy, as always.
   b) Work in a last plug about satisfaction with the product.
   c) High pressure is out of place in this letter, especially in the end.
   d) If you send the substitute, make returning it a free option.
   e) But emphasize keeping, rather than returning.

In trying to keep our operating costs and consequently our prices at a minimum, we have discontinued handling A78 x 13WS tires because of the small demand for them. Probably your best source for them is the Kimble Supply Company, 401 South State Street, Chicago 61382, which carries a large stock of obsolete auto parts and supplies.

When our buyer was in the market last year, he found a new automobile paint that seemed superior to other paints he knew. It is a General Motors product in all colors, with the standard General Motors guarantee. Our other customers have been so well satisfied with its quality and price (only $2.85 a quart and $9.85 a gallon) that we now stock it exclusively. As I feel sure that you, too, will be satisfied with this new product, I am filling your order with the understanding that you can return the paint at our expense unless it completely satisfies. I think you will like it.

Since I am awaiting the return of the enclosed card with your decision on the paint (sent with your F78 x 14BW tires) and the GR78 x 15WS tires to be sent in two weeks, I am holding your check to see how much the refund is to be.

For your convenience and information, I am sending a separate parcel of our latest catalog and a supply of order blanks. We shall be glad to handle your future orders for high-quality automobile supplies.

Note how the letter would have read if the order had been for only the paint. Read only the second, fifth, and seventh paragraphs.

The checklists on preceding pages for standard (p. 130), incomplete (p. 239), back-order (p. 242), rechanneling (p. 245), and substituting (p. 250) acknowledgments apply to the combination cases which follow.

CASES FOR REFUSING REQUESTS

1. As Chairman of the Treasurer Search Committee of your company, draw up a form letter that can be used to turn down job applicants for the position of treasurer which you had open. You have had an incredible number of applications and have tried to give the most careful consideration to each one. Naturally, you appreciate the applicant's interest in your company, but you have filled the position with one whose qualifications seem specifically suited to your needs.

2. With the high cost of printing and publishing, many book companies have to turn down requests for free copies to teachers. For your publisher, Richard D. Irwin, Inc., 1818 Ridge Road, Homewood, Illinois 60430, write a letter that turns down a request for a free copy of *Communicating through Letters and Reports* to Florence Dana Moorhead, a teacher, San Jose Junior College, 1000 Brady, Davenport, Iowa 52808. Make the ordering of the book easy by enclosing a card. Teacher's desk copy of book and manual free when book is adopted as text and at least ten books are ordered. Can order and (if adopted) get charge canceled. Resale might stress that this text is used by over 200 universities and that it has been a leader in the field for 20 years.

3. As booking agent for the Open-World, an open-air concert facility in your town, one of your jobs is to regulate performance schedules for the bands you hire. Shortly after the last wage-price freeze went into effect, you booked Merry Chrishna and the Transcendentalists for an October 31 Halloween show. You sent out the contract late in September, and it was returned October 1, signed and accompanied by a letter asking $500 for the performance rather than the $400 stipulated in the contract. You checked with government agency and found that band costs are covered by the freeze. Besides, the band has signed a contract to play for $400. Write to Charles Dodson, the band's manager, World Enterprises, 21 Madison Avenue, N.Y., N.Y. 12321, refusing to pay the extra $100 and cancel the contract, since the band seemed less than eager to play the Halloween date. Besides, you have already got the San Franciscans to play in place of Merry and his group. You might offer Dodson a date later in the year.

4. Recently you received a direct inquiry from a student at the University of Illinois for a ruling on the tax status of the ⅓-time assistantship. He included all the information necessary for you to make a ruling. After looking over the documents he sent you, you have to rule that his assistantship is taxable income since the teaching he does is not a requirement for all candidates for the Ph.D. degree. Write him a B–plan letter in which you tactfully let him know your decision. Your job is Associate Referee for the IRS Midwest Division, 400 West Van Buren Street, Chicago, Illinois 60655. You can assume that the student's name is Bud Creighton, 904 South Lincoln Street, Urbana, Illinois 61801.

5. As the secretary of the English Department in X University, you receive a memo from Professor A in another department saying he will be taking a group of students (14 names listed) on a three-day field trip ten days hence. He asks that you inform English teachers and request that they excuse the student absences, though students will be expected to make up missed work.

Your department has 59 teachers and 5,800 student enrollments in 89 courses (many of which have several sections). You aren't about to look through all the rolls to see what teachers have the listed students—or to pester all 59 teachers with a memo about the absences of the 14 students. Of course you won't tell all of this to Professor A. You do want to be helpful, but he's expecting too much. You wonder if he's unthinking, inconsiderate, or just trying to pass the buck of a lot of work to you. If he wants you to notify the professors involved, Professor X will have to tell you the

English course (or courses) and section(s) each of the 14 students is taking.

Send his list back to him and explain.

6. Assume that you are Governor Arthur Leon Polhill of Virginia. You are asked by Lucy Armstrong, University of Virginia Young Autocrats Club, 909 Monument Avenue, Richmond, 23240, to debate campaign issues with two of your opponents for the nomination to run for the Office of Governor. As the incumbent Governor you have too many official pressures that you have to face/do not have the time to campaign around the clock every day/daily receive challenges to debate Mr. Kelly and Mr. High (the opponents)/feel that if these two men want to debate between themselves that is their business/dignity of Governor's office should not permit incumbent to participate. More than 30 years have been supporter of University of Virginia and all activities and efforts of faculty and student body/been proud to be named Honorary alumnus of University by University's Alumni Association/were made an honorary member of Sigma Phi Epsilon. Your support of higher education is matter of record/would be happy to receive, as Governor, invitation from proper authorities to address student body.

7. Richard Rhone, librarian at Houston High School, 3320 Wheeler Avenue, Houston, Texas 77001, replied to your letter (Case 5, p. 164) containing the reprint of "Africa's Influences on America" by filling out your subscription blank for a year's subscription to *National Osographic* and requesting 60 more copies of the "Africa's Influences" reprint, which you cannot send. One alternative you might suggest is Rhone's photocopying parts of the second copy of the reprint included with this letter. Give solid and believable reasons why you can't send 60 additional reprints (cost, paper shortage, etc.)

8. The program chairperson for the next national convention of your professional association has asked you to take an important part on the program, not as a speaker but as head of a session.

Your employer encourages employees to attend and participate in meetings of their professional groups by paying all or part of the expenses of attending when they are on the program. But employees never know just how much the employer will pay until they get the answer in view of the specific situation. You have asked your employer how much expense money you may have this time but have been told that the answer can come only when your request and numerous others are considered together and compared with available funds.

Furthermore, the convention dates are December 28–30, and you have been unable to get your spouse to say whether your attending will conflict with Christmas plans.

You'd be glad to take the assignment if favorable answers could be had from your two bosses, both of whom are delaying. You realize that the program chairperson must proceed with plans; so you must write a negative reply, at least for now. You still hope to attend the convention, and you will let the chairperson know your decision as soon as it can be firm. Suggest getting somebody else.

9. As curator of the computerized census information at the University of Florida Libraries (Library West, University of Florida, Gainesville 32612) reply to C. H. Holmes, the merchandising coordinator for Marcus Brothers, a large department store chain whose headquarters are in Orlando (45 East Main Street, 32802). Mr. Holmes wanted a computer printout of the names and addresses of Florida residents who owned homes appraised at $30,000 or more. He told you that he was making up a storewide mailing list for all Marcus Brothers stores. Although it's legal to send him the list, you can't do it for free as he requested, even though he was right to point out to you that the University is a public-funded institution. The standard charge for census printouts is $10 per city and $15 an hour for computer time. You estimate that it will cost Holmes a total of $15 for every city with a population between 30,000 and 200,000. Write a letter in which you explain the charges clearly and ask him to submit, along with his check, a list of the cities he wants printouts for.

10. *From:* John P. Gray, Director, Institute of Food and Agricultural Science, University of Florida, Gainesville, 32600. *To:* Robert A. Piotte, Regional Information Officer, Canadian Forestry Service, Box 650, Sault Ste. Marie, Ontario, (Case 3, p. 158). *Facts:* School of Forest Resources and Conservation has held two short courses in communications for wildlife information and education personnel of the Southeastern States Game and Fish Commissions. Enclose a photocopy of program. Main people teaching in program were from Florida's Division of Business and Technical Writing (mostly retired or gone now) and College of Journalism and Communications. Three who weren't and who are excellent are Dr. Lewis Davis, Professor and Chairman, Department of Wildlife Biology, Colorado State University, Fort Collins, Colorado (keynote speaker and taught two sessions); Luther Richardson, Office of Conservation Education, Bureau of Sport Fisheries and Wildlife, U.S. Department of the Interior, Washington, D.C.; Jerome T. Goldman, Audio-Visual Service Department, Eastman Kodak, Rochester, New York. Mary Cook of the Forest Service, U.S. Department of Agriculture, Information and Education Division, Washington, D.C. was effective also. You will not be rescheduling any short courses this year.

11. Draft a form letter to be used by your law firm, Monroe and Williams, 946 Broadway, New York, New York 10005, to turn down applicants to your law firm. Because of the limited number of places available in your hiring program, you can not grant an interview, but you can keep the applicant's résumé and wish success in legal career.

12. Since you will graduate in June of this year, you have already scheduled some interviews with prospecting employers through the University Placement Center. One of your interviews for work (pick something out of your major or minor) was with American Intergalactic of a nearby city (you name the city near you). Mr. MacDonald, the American Intergalactic representative who interviewed you on campus, invited you to come see him for a follow-up interview. Two weeks later you got a letter from MacDonald offering you a job as a (pick one out) at $12,000 a year. In the meantime you had applied to graduate school, and surprisingly enough, you were accepted and awarded a half-time assistantship that pays nearly $5,000 for nine months. Your wife makes $8,000 a year as a high school teacher. To go with A-I, you would have to take a cut of more than $1,000 a year, if you assume that your wife will remain at home. Besides, you want to go to graduate school. With a Master's degree you will be better qualified and could possibly get a higher starting salary. Write a letter to MacDonald in which you gracefully refuse the job offer, but keep the door open for a year or two from now when you will have a Master's degree and will be ready to move.

13. Recently your magazine, *Music Trends*, received a request from Ms. Regina Stafford, librarian, Des Plaines High School, Des Plaines, Illinois 60018, for 100 reprints of a recent article, "Swing to Jazz," a historical survey of music from the twenties to the seventies. The cost of reprinting this 20-page article, not to mention the color reproductions and paying the postage, are prohibitive (about $.85 a reprint; and Ms. Stafford clearly implied that she wanted the reprints free). Write a letter refusing to send her the reprints. As a counterproposal send her one reprint and give her permission to copy it.

14. Sit in for Lois Webber, wife of Professor Melvin Webber of Millikin University, Decatur, Illinois (524 South Siegel Street) 62522. Two weeks ago you finished serving on a jury for an armed robbery case. Today you get another request to serve from the Circuit Court, Springfield, Illinois 62706, the court session beginning in two weeks. You and your husband have planned a trip to South America and are scheduled (plane and boat reservations) to leave Decatur two days after court convenes and you are expecting your daughter to come home and visit before you leave. According to Chief Judge John J. Crew's letter, reasons for not serving are: hospital, work hardship, or out-of-town (if plans were made ahead of the time you received the jury notice).

15. *Letterhead: Modern Living* Magazine, 908 35th Street, Norwich, New York 13517. *Inside address:* Mr. Arthur Wilkes, 87 Luna Road, Gallup, New Mexico 87301. Use today's date. *Signature block:* Sincerely, Fred T. Brayton, Editor. *Information:* Wilkes has sent you an article he wrote on "College and Movements for Christ" which he would like published in your magazine and which you are returning. In next month's *Modern Living* you are running a similar article by Dr. Spencer Shellabarger, prestigious authority on religion. Tell Arthur that *Modern Living* is expanding and will soon be published bimonthly. With the new format you will need many more articles; ask him to send more work to you.

16. Your school, like most good universities, encourages selected faculty members to improve themselves by giving them time off for research and development at full pay. Instead of regular sabbatical leaves (available after seven years of duty), during which most universities allow the faculty member to choose how the time is spent, your program requires applications with definite proposals of worthy projects the applicants want to pursue. You have a campus-wide committee of seven members to consider all applications and award study grants (equaling a selected faculty member's full salary for one to three terms) from a special fund. As head of the committee, you now have the unpleasant duty of writing two refusal letters.

a) A form letter to 27 applicants who were not selected because, according to your criteria attached to the setting up of the special fund (see the criteria in b), they did not make it.

b) An individualized letter to Professor Melvin Altew. The reasoning:

1. The competition is primarily on the basis of the merit of the proposals, which are scored and ranked according to Merit Points (MPs). (DO NOT COPY any of the phrasing below; where you need to use the information, rephrase it your own way.)
2. After ranking by MPs, the committee uses a complex of plus and minus points to arrive at the final winners.
3. The sum for all salaries of Study-Grant (S-G) winners must stay within the $250,000 a year the special fund provides.
4. By the time the committee totted up final scores and ranked them, that for Professor Altew put him down the list below where the fund could pay.

The fact that Professor Altew lost MPs because his research plan was not thoroughly worked out and he had not really made a start on his own suggests that he might well gain MPs by doing further planning and move forward a bit before resubmitting the proposal—maybe next year.

Though Professor Altew will lose more DPs (Development Points) with increasing age (because the fund requires giving points to young faculty members likely to serve longer), he would likely gain FPs (Financial Points) by having the project under way so that he could complete it in two thirds of a year instead of a whole year and thus not take such a big bite, with his high salary, out of the fund (and thus not reduce the number of S-Gs so much).

17. Assume that you (Case 25, p. 405) have received a stern second notice from National Bank Credit Card telling you that you owe on your account (43389–81–09–64320) $250 for purchase No. 9876 of CRA stereo system from Newsome Music House, 987 Langdon Street, your city, three months ago. You refuse to pay this amount because the stereo would not work right after three weeks. Explain that since then you have called Newsome twice and written once to come and get it or fix it but only got brushed off. You also wrote NBCC about a month ago—when you got the first bill. Write National Bank Credit Card (52000 Olive Road, South Bend, Indiana 46628) again, making clear that you don't intend to pay. (A federal law effective October 28, 1975, holds a credit card issuer responsible for resolving disputes over which the credit card holder and a merchant honoring the card cannot agree—or stopping attempts to collect.)

CASES FOR REFUSING ADJUSTMENTS

1. As Sales Manager for Lawn-Power Inc., 2000 Schiller, Chicago, Illinois 60610 (Case 7, p. 179), refuse the request of M. S. Westover, 3196 Beverly Road, Columbus, Ohio 43204. Your repair shop tells you that it was necessary to install a new motor and armature in his electric lawn mower. In most cases, failure of the motor and armature is caused by using a dull blade, which creates an extra drag on the motor. It may also be caused by using an abnormally long extension cord, which creates a voltage drop from the electrical source and results in damage to the motor. Lawn-Power's guarantee warrants for the life of the mower any defective parts and material. Normal wear, misuse, or abuse, of course, do not fall under the warranty policy. In reviewing the paper work on this transaction, you find that the repair cost as quoted was correct for both material used and labor costs.

2. *To:* Miss Rae Allen, 1120 Viscose Drive, Decolletage, California 95021. *From:* (You), Adjustment Manager, A. C. Tate's, North Ilan, California 95303. *Case:* Last week Miss Allen charged at your store a white Dacron and cotton formal evening gown, priced at $75. This week she sent it back to you with a note saying that the gown did not fit. She wants you to take the gown back and remove the charge from her account. Upon examination, however, you find traces of face powder or make-up base around the neckline and there are smudges of dirt at the bottom of the dress. Your company policy is that clothes cannot be worn and then returned; this is for the protection of your customers and to insure that all the clothes you sell will be fresh and new. Write a tactful, polite letter explaining that you cannot accept the dress for credit and that it is being returned to her separately. Don't lose her as a future customer! A white evening gown of Dacron and cotton can be worn for years and all through the year.

3. *To:* Mr. L. P. Lumpkin, 416 Macon Street, Laydell, Arkansas 46515. *From:* (You), Adjustment Manager, Mason Company, Sideboard, Arkansas 46381. *Case:* 18 months ago Mr. Lumpkin bought from your store a top-loading automatic washing machine (Model No. 98–0864). It cost him $260.95 and carried a one-year guarantee against defects in workmanship or manufacture. Ever since he got the machine, it has persistently skipped the second wash-rinse cycle and consequently has failed to properly clean the clothes placed in it. In addition, skipping the cycle occasionally means that he gets four inches of suds on his basement floor. During the one-year guarantee period, your store has made four service calls on his washer, two to adjust the timer and two to replace the entire timing mechanism. The last time, about six weeks ago, you went with the repairman and all three of you agreed the washer worked properly. Now Mr. Lumpkin has sent you a letter that bitterly complains about the inferior machine and encloses a bill from the local repair shop for $20.00 labor and $8.95 for a new timer, total $28.95. He wants you to pay this bill. Refuse to do so. Return the repair shop's bill to him and try to keep his good will.

4. *To:* Miss Beatric Folrath, 14 Windsor Drive, El Paso, Texas 79922. *From:* You (Manager), Frank M. Bromberg, Bromberg's Jewelry Store, 1300 Daytona Street, Dallas, Texas 75216. *Case:* Miss Folrath has returned to you the ruins of a diamond-chip and pearl pin she bought from you six months ago for $55. The metal mounting of the pin is scaled and discolored, and the diamond chips and small seed pearls it was decorated with have fallen out. She's pretty unhappy; in her letter accompanying the remains of the pin, she suggests that it must have been made of cheap pot metal, and the diamonds and pearls probably aren't genuine. You examine it closely and discover the pin was not defective in any way. Apparently she has exposed it to one of several types of weak acids, some of which are found in cleaning solutions, photographic developing solutions, and in materials for home handicrafts like copper enameling. Except for watches, little jewelry carries any guarantee except that it is as represented. Her pin was iridium, and the diamond chips and pearls were real. Therefore you glue the chips and pearls back into the setting after cleaning it as best you can—it still looks like something out of the black lagoon—and return it to her. You make no charge for the "rebuilding" job, but you also will make no adjustment. Keep her goodwill toward Bromberg's.

5. *Letterhead:* White Crusaders Pest Control, 611 Milledge, Athens,

Georgia 30601. *Inside address:* Calvin Hall (Rural Route 91, Box 509, Whitehall, Georgia 30689). *Signature block:* Sincerely yours, Morris Neal, Manager. *Situation:* When Calvin bought three 100-lb. bags of tri-nitre micrate, your combined fetrilizer and bug killer (@ $50) for his two-acre truck farm, you were careful to tell him to make sure to plow the stuff in at least three inches. More important, you told him to keep his livestock out of the field for at least three weeks. (The micrate poison becomes benign after three weeks.) You remember that you sold Calvin the TNM yourself and were careful to explain how to use it as directed on the bag, and not to overdose. You even remarked that 200 lbs. would be enough for his two acres and that he should hold onto the other 100 lbs. until next spring.

About a week after you sold Calvin the TNM, you got a nasty letter threatening to haul you into court and demanding that you "fork over" $200 to pay for his 3 hogs and 50 chickens that got into the field and were poisoned. "It looked like Dunkirk," he wrote, "pigs and chickens dead all over the place." When your entymologists investigated, they found that Calvin had spread the entire 300 lbs. over the top of the plowed field and hadn't bothered to plow it under. Naturally the chickens and rooting pigs got poisoned and died. Refuse to pay for Calvin's livestock and reeducate him on the use of strong pesticides. Don't antagonize him; you want to keep his business. Besides, Calvin has a reputation for gossiping; and he knows everybody in the county.

6. *Letterhead:* Customer Service Department, East Bend Company, East Bend, Wisconsin 53095. *Inside address:* M. J. Curry, 91 Bainbridge Road, London, Ontario, Canada. *Signature block:* Sincerely yours, Milton Rose, Adjustment Manager. Use today's date. *Information:* M. J. Curry, a gourmet cook of oriental foods, returns an electric wok saying that the wok won't heat up and that the finish inside the wok looks worn and white-like. He had taken it to a local repair shop where the estimate of parts and labor was $15. The wok retails for $29.25. He requests that you fix the wok free. Write a refusal in the light of the following facts: The automatic heat control had been immersed in water and would have to be replaced. On the bag that held the thermoplug in big red letters East Bend had cautioned users against immersing the control in water. The same instructions were repeated in the *Chopstick Cookery* booklet that accompanied the wok. Also the instruction booklet makes it very clear that "The no-stick finish must be conditioned again after each time it is (1) cleaned in a dishwasher, (2) treated with a commercial cleaner for nonstick finishes, and (3) treated with lemon juice or vinegar to remove a mineral film." From the looks of the inside of the wok these directions had not been followed. Your one-year guarantee against defects in workmanship and materials does not cover damage caused by misuse of the appliance, accidents, or alterations to it. The wok will have to have a new thermoplug and the inside of the bowl will have to be treated with a special oil process, at a cost of $10.00 (actual cost). You'll need his authorization before you repair it. You'll return it c.o.d. or if he prefers to save c.o.d. charges he can send you a payment of $11.95 (including return shipping charges). You can have it to him in a week after you hear from him.

7. Last week, as claims agent for the All-Nation Insurance Company, you received an irate letter from Barney Coleman, 987 Blair House Apartments, Cedar Rapids, Iowa 52409. Barney demanded that you pay him $300 for the damage done to his car by one of your clients, Irving Webber. Barney threatened to sue your company if he didn't get his money. Your client was not charged with any traffic violation. Write Barney a letter in which you cordially, but firmly, tell him that under the new Iowa No-Fault insurance law, he should seek reparation from his own insurance company.

8. At the Neenah Paper Company, Neenah, Wisconsin 54956, you handle requests for adjustments on the printed monogrammed stationery and postcards you send to thousands of retail outlets handling stationery supplies. Ordinarily when a request comes in for correction (and such requests are rare), a company policy is to print and ship the corrected copies without question and without charge. But one customer, Jayne's Gift Shop, 1005 Fifth Street, Decatur, Alabama 35601, stands out in your mind because it has sent in so many requests in the last few months. Today you have another letter, asking for replacement of 100 personalized postcards which Stanley M. Washburn, 10 Freemont Drive, Northport, Alabama 35476, ordered through Jayne's and which were delivered with the street name "Fairmont Drive," and for a replacement of a box of 200 sheets and 100 envelopes for Miss Sarah Wentworth, Montevallo University, Montevallo, Alabama 35215, who received her stationery with the imprint "Alabama College." Checking back, you find that the order forms filled out by someone at Jayne's clearly printed in both cases what your printer faithfully followed in printing the items ordered. And so you are going to refuse to furnish the replacements gratis; they will be billed to Jayne's at the usual wholesale prices. You are enclosing with your refusal photocopies of the original orders.

9. You are General Manager of Folio, Inc., 784 No. Leaf St., Errata, PA 18665. Recently you supplied 700 three-ring binders, two-inch capacity, red vinyl, patent hinge, imprinted front and spine with company name and logo, with sheet protectors, to American Poultice, Nostrum Square, Anodyne, MO 64550. American Poultice supplies a complete line of syringes, scalpels, bandages, and allied items to clinics and hospitals. AP wanted the binders for salesmen to use to hold their constantly changing price and specification sheets. Now you have one of your binders back

from Abner Sorbent, American Poultice Sales Manager, with a complaint —the rings spring, allowing pages to drop out, the covers are all becoming torn and bent, and the hinges are tearing. A cursory examination shows what happened: someone tried to stuff 2½ or 3 inches of paper in it, attempted to shut the binder, the paper sprung the rings apart, bending the locking mechanism and preventing the rings from ever closing completely, and thus exerting enough pressure on the covers to cause even your patent hinge to give way. Also, the sheet protectors are missing. Tell Sorbent what went wrong (gently—he's a customer) and offer to provide 700 new binders at the same price as before, but without the one-time charge for the plate for the imprint, since you still have it on hand. Quote him prices for three-inch and four-inch binders, too. They appear to be what he really needs.

10. For a couple of years now, your company, Staple Products, 4445 Clasp Rd., Copula, IL 62498, has been selling blind rivets to Lorry Trailers, 17 Drawbar St., Pintle, TX 72113. Lorry makes the small rental trailers people hook onto their cars to move furniture, etc. Last week you received a rather sharp letter from Litel Waggen, Lorry's purchasing manager, saying that the last batch of blind rivets you shipped are defective. The pins that should pull up the rivet and then break off are instead ripping all the way out, tearing up the rivet, and consequently slowing down production and jeopardizing shipping schedules. Lorry is using up some old rivets found in the back of the plant and wants to know how you plan to rectify the situation. Waggen hinted that beyond taking back the defective rivets, some sort of indemnity might be in order. An emergency call to your sales representative in Texas sent him to Lorry, where he was able to get some of the rivets in question, some of the old rivets Lorry is using up, and a piece of aluminum panel with the rivets torn up from the pin ripping out. The salesman mentioned that Lorry was now using the new "Super-Puller" pneumatic tools to pull the pins instead of the hand-operated tools formerly used. A quick look at the material he sent revealed what happened: Obviously the new tools exert far too much clamping force and pull the pins from below the break line, thus yanking them through the rivet. The rivets are quite up to standard. The old rivets now in use are steel, not aluminum, and of course can take the punishment the new pneumatic tools hand out. Write Waggen, refusing to make any adjustment and pointing out where the trouble lies. But keep this good customer's goodwill while you point out the mistake.

11. As Chief Engineer for Standard Car Co., 205 S. Michigan Ave., Chicago, IL 60604, reply to Edward Ballast, Director of Operations, Gonad and East Turndown Railroad, Spur Building, Signal, PA 17156. Ballast reported recently that some open-top hopper cars you supplied last year (Lot 6225) are developing severe weld fractures in the body bolsters and at the bottoms of the side posts. The cars will have to be removed from service for repair, and he wants Standard to foot the bill. Your field engineers made an immediate investigation and discovered the cars were hauling coal to the big Bright Electric Power Company generating plant at Plugg, Ohio, where a shaker unit was being used to empty the cars faster. Write Ballast, enclosing (imaginary) a report from your field engineers. Point out that the hopper cars were not designed for shaker service; that would require shaker bars on the top plates, special corner caps, bigger side posts and thicker side sheets, and special center sill and body bolster fabrication. The order for the freight cars didn't specify such, nor did anybody ever indicate that the cars would see shaker service. Thus your standard guarantee for your cars would not apply. You won't, therefore, be able to contribute anything toward the cost of repairs and the loss from the cars' downtime, but you will have your design engineers work with the Gonad and East Turndown people on the best way to make the repairs, and on possible modifications to the cars. Remember that as a freight car manufacturer, your best and just about only customers are the Class I railroads. There are only 17 Class I railroads, and the Gonad and East Turndown is one of them.

12. As advertising manager of *The World's News* magazine, you are to handle the request of the Copus Supply Company for a discount because the correction Copus made in the proof for a recent ad did not appear in this month's issue. You'll have to refuse the request (even though Copus is a regular advertiser, usually buying at least half a page, frequently full page) in the light of the following facts: Your rate card (based on 400,000 circulation) clearly emphasizes that all copy and revisions must reach you by the 18th of the month preceding publication. On the 10th you sent proof of the ad. Copus made a couple of minor changes and returned the proof to you on the 20th, after you had already run off 15,000 copies. However, there was a mechanical breakdown, and the press had to be stopped. This gave you an opportunity to make the corrections the Copus people had made in the ad. Contractually, of course, you were not obligated to do it; but as a matter of customer service you were glad to do so. Then the press resumed and turned out 435,000 more copies with the changes as specified. In inductive order you'll review the facts and, of course, send the page proofs of the original and the corrected ads. The answer—as positively as you can make it—is no. Incidentally, the first-of-the-month Audit Bureau of Circulation figure will be 450,000—but with no change in rates.

COMPROMISE ADJUSTMENT CASES

1. As customer relations manager for Radio Shack, 67 Kingsberry Drive, Springfield, Illinois 62743, reply to a letter from Marilyn Moore, Randolph-

Macon College, Bristol Hall, Lynchburg, Virginia 24566. Marilyn reports that the AM–FM radio purchased from your store blew up with sparks and pops in a cloud of smoke the minute it was plugged in. The radio was sent back to you with a letter demanding $31.45 back. When your service person took off the back of the radio, the plug wire had been pulled off its connection and the bare ends had come together causing a short circuit. The radio was untouched, except that the back was a little singed. However, it cost only $1.00 to reattach the wire and put a new back on. The wire was probably pulled loose in packing after you took the radio off the shelf. Marilyn got the radio ($60 retail) at the $31.45 discount since it was a display model reduced for quick sale. You make no refunds on sale items; all sales are final. But you do honor warranties. Besides, you don't want Marilyn spreading the word around Springfield and among her prominent friends that the Radio Shack was not fair. Resell Marilyn that the radio is now good as new. It's still a bargain at $31.45. Use a full-reparation opening.

2. Harriet E. Richards, your boss at Texas Bug Control, 1190 Danbury Lane, Corpus Christi, Texas 78450, has just asked you to reply to one of your enraged customers, Mr. Ronald Roberts, 5678 Kingsville Road, Robstown, Texas 78466. Ron claimed that the roach powder your service man spreads around his house has had no effect on the bugs. They line up to eat the stuff when they see him coming with it. He claims that the bugs are driving him out of his own home. Write a letter in which you *subtly* stress the necessity of keeping the premises clean and promise him that your service man will be out by the end of the week to spread around a new nonchlorinated-hydrocarbon pesticide, Cyclone-Z, which kills roaches quickly by attacking their nervous systems.

3. To your desk as sales manager for the Eastern Office Equipment Company, 755 Brewster, Springfield, Massachusetts 01119, comes the following letter from Alton Burr, Burr Insurance Company, 943 Main Street, Bondsville, Massachusetts 01214 (good customer for ten years):

I'm returning the file cabinets you shipped me in response to my request of two weeks ago. I specified No. 3 PT 543 four-drawer steel files at $40, and you sent No. 3 PT 763 at $60. If there were only one file involved, I'd probably pay the difference; but, as you can see from the invoice I'm returning, there are four. Please refund the $10.87 shipping charges that I paid and send me a credit memo for $240. I'm returning the four, shipping charges collect. As far as I'm concerned you can forget the whole thing.

Several months ago you sent out a correction slip for your current catalog indicating that you no longer carry the No. 3 PT 543. Since you notified everyone to whom you had mailed a catalog, you assumed that Burr realized you'd fill his order with No. 3 PT 763 (as your correction slip indicated). Possibly it didn't reach him; maybe some of the office help threw it away. Whatever the reason, you certainly want to sell him this superior file with its improvements: heavier steel, baked-on enamel colors (instead of sprayed), satin-finish aluminum drawer pulls (instead of chrome-plated) plus automatic stops that prevent drawers from rebounding or being accidentally removed. You are convinced that they are well worth the additional cost. Before you can hope to convince Mr. Burr, however, you'll need to refund the $10.87 and assure him that you'll send him a credit memo for $240 as soon as you receive the file cabinets. You'll also want to explain why you did not follow his original instructions. But most of all you want to sell him No. 3 PT 763. You'll be willing to ship the four cabinets charges prepaid if he'll reconsider.

4. *Letterhead:* Du Bois Interiors, 908 San Rafael, Santa Barbara 92898. *Inside address:* Mrs. Jane B. McMillan, High River Ranch, Los Alamos, California 93440. *Signature block:* Sincerely yours, Jacques Du Bois. Today's date. *Information:* On a dark, cloudy night you, Jacques Du Bois, went to Mrs. McMillan's ranch and measured for a padded headboard and matching draperies for her master bedroom. Together you selected the right shade of blue (No. 765) costing $400. While she was visiting her family in Nevada, her house boy let you in to hang the new draperies and mount the headboard on the queen-size bed. Instead of being the soft powder blue she thought she ordered, she has bright aqua blue draperies and headboard that clash with the walls. Today you get a letter from her from Nevada, but asking you to answer her at home with a letter guaranteeing to change the draperies and headboard. Because you showed her the color number, and she agreed to number 765, you are going to compromise with her. You will furnish all the new material, but ask her to pay $150 for the labor.

5. As Service Manager for Lawn-Power, Inc. (Cases 7 and 1, pp. 179 and 257), write a compromise adjustment to M. S. Westover. Because your company failed to contact Donlevy's Department Store before the repairs were made and to quote an estimate for repairs, you are sending Donlevy's a credit memorandum for $15.50 to offset the original charge with the exception of the shipping costs involved. Westover should get in touch with the store for a refund. Remind Westover that his 18-inch mower has 5 cutting heights, adjustable handle that folds for storage, twin blades, and aluminum die-cast housing.

6. Today's mail brings a package with a faded Barkay swim suit and a letter of complaint from Mary P. Blake, 134 Bay Drive, Sacramento, California 95837 (Case 6, p. 179). The label points out that the suit is not guaranteed against fading. Offer to let Mary have another suit of her choice for 50 percent off the label price, and you'll keep this suit. To make

Mary want to come back to your store right away, tell her about the half-price sale you are having on summer dresses. Sign the letter Abraham Goldfarb, owner.

7. Last year your company, Standard Car Co., 205 S. Michigan Ave., Chicago, Il 60604, delivered 30 subway cars to Boston. The cars are pretty well debugged, but now a new problem has surfaced. Water is leaking into the air conditioning control boxes, causing short circuits and distressingly acrid smoke. Your field engineer found that the controls for the air conditioning were installed improperly at your plant because the manufacturer of the controls had failed to supply you with proper instructions. Boston service men had repositioned the controls in the cars but had not properly reinstalled the gaskets on the control boxes (manufactured by Standard Car). Although the air conditioning control supplier had accepted the responsibility (and the cost) of fixing the controls, the Boston subway people should have made sure the boxes were properly sealed after the job was done. However, since you are the supplier of the boxes, some responsibility may rest on you for seeing that the Boston people were properly instructed about the box gaskets. Offer to pay half the cost of the necessary repairs to the air conditioning controls and boxes as a fair way of resolving the matter. Write to Operations Manager, Boston Public Transportation, City Office Building, Boston, MA 08935.

8. Abner Sorbent didn't like your letter refusing responsibility for the unacceptable performance of your binders (Case 9, p. 260). He says that he specifically ordered three-inch binders and that since your company sent the binders direct to American Poultice's district offices, he didn't know until too late that they were two-inch capacity binders. Your sales representative claims Sorbent ordered two-inch binders, and that's the way the order was processed through your district office and your plant. But Sorbent gave your rep an oral order; so if there was a breakdown in communication, there's no way to place the blame. But you're not going to give Sorbent 700 new three-inch binders (imprinted) for free; any of his district managers should have said right away that the binders were too small to carry the load of paper. This whole situation is getting out of hand, but you don't want to anger American Poultice—a possible big customer. Write Sorbent, using all your most effective letter-writing tactics, offering to supply 700 new three-inch capacity imprinted binders at half price, since the blame appears to lie partly on each of your companies. Stress your fairness, not your generosity.

CASES FOR CREDIT REFUSALS AND MODIFICATIONS

1. Recently you received an order from James B. McLester (The Book and Machine Center, 512 Main Street, Madison, Wisconsin 54303), your

SCN dealer in Madison, for 25 SCN T–125 portable typewriters—popular with college students for $69.95 (cost to dealer $50). The $1,250 cost of this shipment would be $500 over the $750 credit limit you agreed to at terms 2/10, n/30. Besides McLester still owes you $500 (now 15 days past due) on his last order. Restate your credit terms, mention the $500 past due, refuse credit extension, and ask him to send in his check to cover the past-due account and at least $500 on his new order. Suggest, however, that he might reduce his order to 12 typewriters, since summer is coming and students will be leaving school, and carry the new order on credit if he sends the $500 due. Your firm is SCN Business Machines, 4500 Freemont Road, Saint Louis, Missouri 63110.

2. Ellen Powers, owner of the Stay-Slim Salon, 908 Fairview Avenue, Columbia, Missouri 65201, ordered from your company, Warner-Borg, 900 High Street, Hartford, Connecticut 06105, two roller massagers @ $80 each, No. PGF–65; two portable plug-in steam baths, No. PJT–98 at $150 each; two electric progress-a-cyzers, No. PMR–76 at $60 each. After reviewing what two reliable sources said about her credit and after viewing her application, you have to deny her credit (but maybe not decline her order). Two sources reported she paid bills 30 to 60 days slow and her financial statement showed that she is undercapitalized. With a conventional loan she can take advantage of your 2 percent cash discount, which will at least offset her interest costs. Drive for the order on a cash basis.

3. For some time now you have been doing business with Walt Morey, owner of Walt's Pit Stop (90 South Pine Street, Sumpter, Florida 33108), a high-performance center specializing in equipment for enhancing dragsters and custom cars. When you started doing business with Walt five years ago (your company is Palmer Auto Parts, 987 Branch Avenue, Detroit, Michigan 66344), you agreed to a $1,500 credit limit. Walt's most recent order, $450 worth of Treadwell tires, would put him over the limit you agreed upon. Walt hasn't paid his last two bills—$400 now 40 days past due and $700 now 10 days past due (terms 2/10, n/30). Write Walt a letter in which you tactfully refuse credit until he takes care of his outstanding bills. But try to get him to buy the tires on a cash basis. What you want to do is to keep his goodwill and his account, which averages about $600 a month.

4. As Roland M. Short of Autorite (333 5th Ave., New York, N.Y. 10022), you received an order from Harry James, the owner/manager of James's Auto Works (546 Jackson Avenue, Jersey City, New Jersey 10344), for three dozen 4-ply polycord tires @ $20 each and 12 sets of load leveler shock absorbers at $30 a set. Mr. James included his check for $1,080 and asked to be allowed to make future purchases on credit. Investigation revealed that Mr. James had a good credit rating in 1970 when his store, located at the edge of the ghetto, was looted and burned out by rioters. His insurance covered much of the damage, and he was able to remodel and reopen within six months. However, he now has an outstanding debt of $10,000, half of which is already past due; and his prospects for increased business are dimmer now with the recent increase in the prime interest controls. Ship James the items he ordered and paid for, but refuse him credit until he gets his Credit/Debit ratio down to the 2:1 you recommend.

5. Last week your company (Haines Moore Paints, 123 Sullivan Parkway, Rahway, New Jersey 07065) received an order from John King, Brush and Roller paint store, 567 College Road, Manchester, New Hampshire 03156, for 100 gallons of Show-Glo Supertone latex paints, assorted colors (50 antique white, 20 shell white, 10 blue, 10 red, and 10 green). Show-Glo Supertone, the top paint in your line, sells for $5 a gallon to the dealer and $8 a gallon retail. This is the third credit order that King has asked for in the last three months, and he has yet to pay for the first two; one for $200 is 30 days past due, the other for $250 comes due in 2 days. When King assumed your dealership a year ago, you agreed to a $500 credit limit. He usually pays at the end of the net period, and twice he was ten days late. Refuse to extend credit for his new order until he takes care of his outstanding bills. Try to get him to pay cash for the new order when he sends in his check for the two unpaid orders.

6. As credit sales manager of the Robinson Company, Kansas City, Missouri 64105, you have to acknowledge the order of Victor Van Law, who (according to the financial statements he sent with his application for credit and for his first order for work pants amounting to $300—he buys for $3 and sells for $6) is the sole owner of the Van Law Dry Goods Company, Eureka Springs, Arkansas 72632. You followed up the references he gave, and they spoke well of his personal integrity and indicated that he is a reasonably good payer. Two sources said he pays within the terms; three said he was 15–45 days slow; one said "slow but sure." You are reluctant to extend credit to a man in a predominantly agricultural area who, at a time when farm income is high, has allowed his current ratio (quick assets to liabilities) to fall closer to 1:1 than to the desirable 2:1. Furthermore, with the uncertainty of the government's action on farm supports, you think now is a poor time (from Van Law's point of view as well as your own) for him to be taking on new obligations without straightening out his present ones. You suspect maladjusted inventories and lackadaisical collections. As much as you'd like to fill this order, you have to refuse. It's wiser for him to cut his order in half and pay cash (he'll still get the customary 2 percent discount). Since rush orders can be handled within four days, he can keep adequate stocks on hand. Perhaps later on when he has reduced his current liabilities and strengthened his cash position, your regular credit privileges of 2/10, n/30 can be made available. After you give him the business reasons for refusing, offer a compromise solution as attractively as you can, and strive to convince him that Robinson pants are the best buy he can make.

7. Benjamin Smith Manufacturing Company, 900 Ackerman Road, Clifton, New Jersey 07013, receives an order from Tony's Paint Center, 197 Butler Avenue, Scrant, Pennsylvania 18519, for a variety of house paints totaling $528.75. You (the credit manager) look Tony's up in Dun & Bradstreet and discover that Tony Hobson has a small store with a very limited credit rating. Tony wants you to ship the paint on account, but you are reluctant to do so.

Send Tony a credit form to be filled out and returned along with a financial statement. You will ship the paint right now on c.o.d. or cash-in-advance basis if Tony is in a hurry. It will take a little time to complete your credit investigation. Or, if he will scale down his order, you will ship up to $175 on account. Since he will have to reply before you do anything, write a letter designed to get action. Make it easy for him to answer your questions and inform you of the course of action he prefers.

8. As credit sales manager of Martin Wire Products, 909 Cherokee Lane, Muskogee, Oklahoma 77401, you are not granting credit to Enrique Gonzalez, 96 Fernandez, Madrid, Spain, on his order for 4,000 50-foot rolls of 48-inch Sunscreen at 14 cents a roll. Although you aren't going to tell him this, you have from the Spanish Embassy in Washington the name of a possible dealer in Madrid—not Gonzalez. Before you can do business with Gonzalez, you'll have to have more credit information about him (history and nature of business, financial statements, and bank and credit references). This is a temporary refusal based on a lack of financial and credit information.

9. Floyd Taylor, traveling salesman for the Haines Hardware Company, Sixth Street at River Road, Sioux City, Iowa 51110, sent in an order for miscellaneous hardware supplies, amounting to $600, given him by Howard Gray, manager of the Jemison Hardware Store, 908 University Avenue, Iowa City, Iowa 52240, an old customer (six and a half years), whose rating is "fair," because he is slow in meeting his obligations. Assume that the order has been referred to you, the credit manager of the Haines Hardware Company, for attention. You believe the order is too large to be disposed of by your customer promptly and profitably. Write a letter to Mr. Gray, suggesting that the order be split up into three parts so that he may cancel unfilled portions of it should the goods not find a ready sale under the present business conditions. You can ship the first installment now.

CASES FOR INCOMPLETE- AND BACK-ORDER ACKNOWLEDGMENTS

1. *Letterhead:* Hotcenter Appliances, 2400 Fern Road, Wichita, Kansas 67211. *Inside address:* Richard Mallett, Mallett's Appliances, 910 Wabash Avenue, Terre Haute, Indiana 47807. *Signature block:* Sincerely, Alan Godwin, Director of Sales. *Information:* When you received this month's order from Richard Mallett, you were glad to see that sales were going well (50% increase in order). Richard must have been in a hurry; he forgot to check off the colors of the three Hotcenter dishwashers he wanted (they come in white, bronze, green, and yellow)—and whether the six clothes washers and six driers he ordered were the permanently mounted type or the smaller portable type (same price). Since Richard is a regular customer, he didn't send payment; you assume your 2/10, n/30 terms would be in effect. Write for the missing information.

2. As mail sales coordinator for Mallory, a prestigious mail-order house in Cedar Rapids, Iowa (1300 Elmhurst Drive, 52433), reply to Clarence Day, owner of the Green Door, an exclusive boutique and jewelry shop in Louisville, Kentucky 40216 (Phipps Plaza). Day ordered six Karl Couturier wigs @ $50 apiece and two dozen Montezuma imitation Aztec rings at $20 each. He included his check for $800 to cover the cost of the merchandise and shipping. You can ship him the rings; and though he indicated colors (two in each—brunette, blond, and red), he forgot to tell you the styles of the wigs he wanted. They come in shag, Afro, and standard (straight hair to the shoulders) styles. Get him to match up the colors and styles of wigs he wants.

3. *To:* Mr. Russel Larcom, Larcom's Hardware Company, 816 Dover Street, Abbyville, Kansas 67510. *From:* You (Sales Manager), Healy and Hagler Company, 109 Everett Avenue, Louisville, Kentucky 40206. *Case:* Larcom ordered from you: 42 No. 4–M Teflon-lined 4-quart waterless cooking saucepans, 14 each in aqua, orange, and coppertone @ $3.15, and 12 No. 9–M Teflon-lined Dutch ovens @ $5.15. Terms 2/10, n/30; freight charges collect. On his order there was no mention of colors for the Dutch ovens (aqua, orange, coppertone, black, yellow, and green). Some people like to mix the colors to brighten their kitchens. You can send the 4-quart saucepans immediately; but to save freight charges, you'll wait and send all of the saucepans and Dutch ovens in one shipment. Resale on the cooking-ware: Advertised in *Good Homemaking* and *House Lovely;* matching colored lids make a waterproof seal (can be used for waterless cooking); teflon linings mean no-stick, no-burn cooking, and very easy cleaning; pebbled texture of the outsides and handles makes them easy to handle without slipping; the colors, general design, and ovenproof quality suitable for serving dishes on the table.

4. Work out a simple form letter for Diebold, Inc., Canton, Ohio 44711, over your signature as Assistant Secretary. This form is to acknowledge proxy cards that have not been signed by the shareholder. Explain that in order for the proxy to be voted, the card must be signed. Ask the reader to sign, date, and send back the enclosed card in the addressed, stamped envelope.

5. As Lee O'Brien, Director of Customer Service for Me-Books Publishing Company, 11633 Victory Blvd., North Hollywood, California 91690, ask Mrs. Victor Bliss, Rolling Hill Road, Skillwau, New Jersey 08558, for some missing information on her order of the Me-Book she wanted sent to her grandchild in Bloomington, Illinois. Children enjoy these books because they can see their own names, street addresses, phone numbers, and names of pets, siblings, friends, grandparents, parents, and givers. Mrs. Bliss failed to indicate the names of pets, siblings, and one set of grandparents. (Could the omissions have been intentional?)

6. For variation, read over Case 8, p. 168, and change the situation around so that you assume Mrs. George Doster of Beloit did not tell you the initials she wanted on the fingertip towels or the soaps. You will be sending the other goods but will ask her to specify the initials she wants. Tell her also about the special you have on fringed oval contour bath rugs in solid colors of moss, topaz, blush-pink, Dresden blue, yellow, cornsilk, brown, or white colors—regularly $5.00 but this next two weeks 2 rugs for $7. They are made of DuPont nylon pile with a deep fringed edge. Machine washable.

7. As mail-order supervisor for the Redi-Frame company (P.O. Box 998, Cucumber, West Virginia 24826), acknowledge the order of Zelda Lincoln, historian of Gamma Omicron chapter of Sigma Epsilon Xi sorority (904 South Busey Street, Oxford, Mississippi 38655). Zelda forgot to tell you what sizes she wanted, or whether she wanted nailed corners or easy-clip corner assemblies on her 24 picture frames. Send her the ordered 12 sheets of off-white marbled mat-board (@ $.40 a sheet), ask her tactfully to tell you what kind of frames she wants, and acknowledge her check for $50.

8. Acknowledge the order from Mrs. George C. Doster of Tower Lake Estates (Case 8, p. 168). Before sending the goods, however, you need to clear up some confusion on her charge information. You do not have a Doster at Tower Lakes in Beloit, but you do have a George M. Doster at 305 Cook Street, Beloit, and a G. C. Doster at 35 Wimberly Drive, Beloit. How is her account listed? She might be interested in the special you have for the next ten days on Dacron polyester fiberfill pillows with cotton ticking at the low price of two for $8 standard size, two for $11 queen size, or two for $13 king. Suggest she order the pillows when she sends you the information on how her account is listed.

9. Yesterday you (James P. Younger) received an order from the Ebb and Flow Beach Boutique, 777 San Ladron Avenue, St. Augustine, Florida 32816, for two dozen High 'n Dry giant beach towels @ $2.00 apiece, six dozen pairs (size medium) of Sun-Yat-Sen zori @ $.50 a pair, and six Va-Va-Voom mini bikinis @ $12 apiece. Mr. Eugene Bridgers, the owner of the Ebb and Flow, included his check for $160.25 (cost of the merchandise and $4.25 shipping by UPS). Ship him the towels and zori, but back-order the swimsuits for two weeks. These new-this-year handcrafted cotton-Dacron swimsuits (made in Italy and imported by Cosa Nostra Novelties of New York for exclusive distribution through member stores of the Coastal Boutique Association) caught swimmers' fancy more widely than the manufacturer planned for; but Cosa Nostra has promised to ship you a fresh supply of swimsuits by next week. Your firm (Sand and Surf Supply of 43 Broadway, Bayonne, New Jersey 10106) can promise his swimsuits a week later.

10. Assume that you are in Mail-Sales for Uniforms, Incorporated, 3618 Broadway, San Antonio, Texas 78241. You must write Señor Juarez, manager of La Señorita (a beauty shop catering to Americans), Circunvalacion Norte 136, Las Fuentes, Guadalajara, Jalisco, Mexico, that you can send (for the operators) five matching pant-set uniforms, blue, size medium No. MP–765 in about three weeks, when you expect to catch up your production. You have mailed the two small-size today. Add resale about the garments (extra-strong seams, won't fade, handy two-patch pockets, double-knit of polyester). Try to sell more of your uniforms and make ordering easy.

11. You are sales manager for the Julian Rothchild Clothing Company, 6028 West 76th, Los Angeles, California 90045. Today you have an order from Jay Gray, buyer for L. O. Adrian and Company, 987 Shattuck Road, Saginaw, Michigan 48602, for 3 dozen blue denim shorts, Style #7464, one dozen each of sizes 8, 12, and 14 @ $9.00. Because of the unexpected popularity of the shorts, your stock is exhausted. You've ordered new material, and it is due within a week; so Mr. Fabian, the production superintendent, tells you that he'll have the shorts ready to ship within ten days. Include some resale talk on these easy-to-wash, no-iron shorts. Word your letter so that the order will remain on the books. The L. O. Adrian Company is a good credit customer of yours.

12. The Carter's Manufacturing Company, 50 Ellison Way, Independence, Missouri 64099, receives a first order (via your salesman, Albert Miller) from Roy P. Spiller, Spiller Feed and Flower Shop, 999 Bonner

Street, Abbyville, Kansas 67510, for a case (24) of Carter Anti-Pest Powder in 1-lb. sizes @ $9.60 a case. The Order Department passes it along to your (the sales manager's) desk because of the routine plan of having you write a letter to each new customer. On the bottom of the order is a note that says you cannot ship the powder for another two weeks because you have no 1-lb. plastic containers; your next shipment of containers is supposed to arrive from Chicago in about that time. The government banned all the X-Y-210 containers for health reasons. Write Spiller welcoming him as a new customer and handling the back-order element positively, with emphasis on when he will receive the shipment.

13. For the president of Obscura Co. (Case 17, p. 170), tell the advertising manager of Lambent Products that the filmstrips and folders are coming along nicely but there is a strike at Rezzin Plastics, which makes the plastic viewers for you. Since Rezzin has the molds, you have to wait until the strike is over before you can get viewers. You can make delivery date on the filmstrips and folders but can't even recommend an alternate source for viewers since the filmstrips are your own special size and cannot be used in any viewer but yours.

14. On behalf of American Metal Stampings, 14 Webster Drive, Crown Point, IN 46307, write to the Purchasing Agent, Lorry Trailers, 17 Drawbar St., Pintle, TX 72113. You will ship 4,000 of the ⅝″ galvanized steel washers by the end of this week. Your supplier has back-ordered the copper-bearing steel strips you ordered to fill Lorry's order for 1″ O.D. × 33/64″ I.D. × 1/32″ washers stamped out of that material. He promises you will have the steel within 14 days. You have completed the tooling for the back-ordered washers, and will go on them the day the steel arrives.

CASES FOR DECLINING ORDERS

1. *Letterhead:* Hogate Manufacturing Company, 900 Cresent Rim Drive, Boise, Idaho 83701. Use today's date. *Inside address:* Ms. Rose Hill, principal, Kirkwood Elementary School, 987 Hugo Street, Hibbing, Minnesota 55746. *Signature block:* Cordially, Irene Marshall, Sales Director. *Information:* Your company (Hogate), manufacturers of educational toys and equipment, had a serious fire last week which burned up your on-hand stock and your local manufacturing facility. Your nearest affiliate is in Baltimore, Md. What your staff is now doing is declining orders that you can't possibly fill or divert to your Baltimore branch. Write a letter to Rose in which you decline her order for your Giant Jungle Jim and Obstacle Course. This order of playground equipment (made out of safe, indestructible plastic) would have been $500. You can't divert her to Baltimore, since the shipping costs from there would be over $200. It simply wouldn't pay her to order from Baltimore. Decline her order for

the present, resell her the equipment, and hold out for another 6 months when your Boise operation will again be in full production.

2. As Head of Sales for Meadowcraft Outdoor Furniture, 923 Penn Avenue, Pittsburgh, Pennsylvania 15219, decline the order from Safer's Department Store, 4301 North Charles, Baltimore, Maryland 21202, for $2,456.89. You have given the exclusive furniture franchise to City Furniture, 905 15th Street, Baltimore, for 12 years. (Since that has only two years to go, try to *hint mildly* of Safer's chance. You have thought of the need for another dealer in the big City—different section, where Safer's is—especially since your Patio Set of wrought iron won two Outdoor Furniture Association National awards last year—for design and for weather resistance, attributable to your patented mix of just the right amount of lead in the iron.) Perhaps Safer's could work out an arrangement with City to be a subdistributor. You have a store in Urbana, Illinois, that is the subdistributor for an exclusive franchise held by a business in nearby Champaign.

3. On your desk in the office of the sales manager of the National Cereal Company, 99 Beachfield Drive, Battle Creek, Michigan 49014, appears an order for two cases of N&N (Natural and New, one of your popular new cereals), to be shipped direct to Jackie Simpson, Quick Food Shop, Five-Points, Hamburg, Minnesota 55339. His check for the correct amount at your jobbers' prices is pinned to one of your current Mimeographed jobbers' lists. You don't know how he got the list, and you don't propose to mention it in the letter. You cannot sell to him direct or at jobbers' prices, list or no list. Your exclusive distributor for his district is the Roberts Wholesale Grocery Company, St. Paul, Minn. 55143. Certainly you want Simpson to handle your popular new breakfast cereal; so you will return the check and ask him to place the order with Roberts. In the light of the ultimate advantages to retailers, make a presentation that emphasizes Simpson's advantages rather than your own or your jobber's.

4. You've just received an order from Dr. Gordon Shaver, the chief veterinarian for Macon County, Illinois, for six electric, continuous-flow vaccinating guns. There's been an outbreak of hog virus in Iowa and Missouri, and Dr. Shaver wants to help Macon County farmers innoculate their hogs before the disease spreads to Illinois. You'd really like to ship the guns to Shaver, but he can get them faster (although they will cost $2.00 more apiece) from Lincoln Feed and Grain, 1098 Gibbs Road, Kansas City, Missouri 64154, your local franchised dealer. Besides, you have an agreement with your franchised dealers that you will divert any orders you get from their territories to them. Write a letter to Dr. Shaver in which you divert his order to Lincoln in Kansas City. Give him the reasons first before you divert his order, e.g., quick delivery, service, a full line of veterinary equipment. (Your firm is Ortho-Vet, Inc., 504 Locust, Des Moines, Iowa 50320).

5. When John Wiggins graduated from junior college last spring and decided to open a variety store in his hometown (698 Main Street, Springtown, Texas 76082), he wrote to you for suggestions about what paper products he should carry in stock. As sales manager of the Celluton Products Company, Ft. Worth 76102, you drove out (30 miles) to see him. He appreciated your suggestions; but, because of limited finances and heavy expense of getting the business started, he cut your suggested order drastically.

Since it was late fall, the two of you settled on a good stock of toilet and cleansing papers and your colorful Christmas papers. When the order totaled only 18 cases, you told Wiggins about your policy of not accepting orders for less than 25 cases; but you agreed to accept this first order anyway, to get the new customer started handling your products. But you asked for, and got, Wiggins' promise of his financial statement at the end of the year.

Wiggins ordered 15 cases of school writing supplies and toilet and cleansing tissues in January, when you were in the hospital, and the order was filled by a clerk who saw that you had approved the previous order for only 18 cases. You wouldn't have filled it in view of the financial statement Wiggins sent January 4.

Now it is March, and you have an exact duplicate of the January order. Wiggins seems to expect to make these small orders about every two months. There is no use to let him get by with this plan, contrary to your policy, which was established as much for his benefit as for yours. Besides, he has not even tried some of your products.

In the spring and summer the need for school supplies will decrease; but the people of Springtown do lots of picnicking (at Lake Worth and Possum Kingdom) and use lots of paper cups, napkins, and plates.

For people in business, you have memo pads and blotters in various sizes and colors. Homemakers will be doing spring cleaning. Your decorative shelf papers might help. Your tough, chemically treated special paper for washing dishes and windows is catching on everywhere that housewives have tried it.

Wiggins, now financially able to order more heavily, could easily make up an order of 25 cases of quick-selling paper products if he would. Then he would not need to order so frequently; he would comply with your policy; and he would enable you to keep your prices to him down where they are by keeping your per-unit costs for handling, packaging, and transportation down to the minimum.

Instead of filling his order, hold it and write him a letter. He has your complete price list, unchanged since last fall.

CASES FOR SUBSTITUTE-SELLING ACKNOWLEDGMENTS

1. Waverly Department Store, 807 South Chalmers, Sioux City, Iowa 51109, orders one dozen DMC 1 coffee makers from you, Eastern Electric, Inc., 9000 Fairway Avenue, New Haven, Connecticut 06522. This particular model has been recalled from all your dealers because if it wasn't cleaned according to the instructions (clean main heating element with straight vinegar), customers frequently got shocks from the heating element. In its place you have the CMD 1 which has added insulation around the heating element. The same paper filters ($3\frac{1}{4} \times 3\frac{1}{4}$) fit both models. The CMD 1 comes handsomely styled in white with Indian brick color trim. The body of the carafe is molded polypropylene and it sits on phenolic base with stainless-steel warming plate. Drip-type coffee is brewed at just the correct temperature, not boiled, so the coffee remains pure and flavorful. Also tell Waverly's about your special on high-dome frying pans made of solid cast-aluminum for even heat distribution, non-stick interior for fast clean-up, snap-off handles for easy storage and cleaning (regularly sells to dealers for $20, now $16.50).

2. Keystone Electronics Corporation, 865 Main Street, Tempe, Arizona 85281. Attention Mr. S. J. White, White's Dickory, 5650 Congress Avenue, Austin, Texas 76743. You regret that the Model 605–1 Majestic Headsets are no longer in production. As a substitute, you can offer the new Model 610–2, an improved headset of high-impact plastic construction and nickel-plated metal parts with removable ear cushions and standard ¼″ molded phone plugs at $16.50. Ask for White's approval to ship six Majestic 610–2 Headsets. Also send (as ordered) 12 Omni-directional Microphones, $17.25 each, and 12 Universal Patchcord and Connector Kits for recording from components, radio, and other signal sources with tape deck or cassette recorder, $3.00 each. The goods will be charged to White's account.

3. At Nelson-Lamb hardware wholesalers, 1780 Hudson Road, St. Paul, Minnesota 55103, you have an order from Patton Brothers, 1699 Wallace Avenue, Duluth, Minnesota 55802, for two dozen Flame-Free fire extinguishers, auto size. About 13 months ago you shipped Patton Brothers four dozen Flame-Free extinguishers in the larger sizes. Four months ago you acquired the Minnesota distribution of the nationally advertised Stampire extinguishers and have sold out your entire supply of Flame-Frees in the size ordered. The Stampire is a more effective and dependable instrument than the Flame-Free—fights all fires (flammable liquid, cloth, wood, paper, and electrical equipment; the clean, odorless carbon dioxide gas smothers fires and won't conduct electricity; approved by the Underwriters' Laboratories, Inc., and the Coast Guard. The 1-quart size comes with clamps for installing it on the automobile steering post without drilling holes or inserting screws. This model is $6 a dozen higher than the Flame-Free, but sells better—vigorous national advertising. Ask permission before substituting the Stampire. If Patton's still prefers Flame-Free, try Hardy Hardware Company in Minneapolis, the nearest distributor you know of.

4. As mail sales coordinator for Sturdevant Stereo Components, 230 North Michigan, Chicago, Illinois 60644, reply to an order from John Bickley, Apt. 605, 2000 Milledge Avenue, Athens, Georgia 31906, for two of your Fissure A–800 stereo speakers. John must have looked at a 2-year-old catalog, since you stopped making the A–800 two years ago. You replaced the A–800 in your speaker line with the A–850. The A–850, unlike the A–800, comes in a solid mahogany cabinet. The A–800 was walnut. Of course you've improved the speakers too; the 10″ double woofers and 6″ triple tweeters produce a fidelity and clarity that the A–800 could not match (add some details). And John can have all this quality for only $20 more per speaker. John sent you a check for $200 to cover the $190 cost of the two speakers and shipping. He must have misread the catalog because the cost of the two A–800's would have been $160. Fill John's order with two Fissure 850's. His check for $200 will just cover the cost. You will absorb the $10 shipping charges. Remember to sell the 850's on their own merits before you fill John's order; and be sure to give the option of returning them if not satisfied. However, stress John's keeping the 850's.

5. As Oscar Hoover, Director of Sales, Pheeser Pharmaceuticals, Alameda Road, Abilene, Texas 79802, Cattle Care Division, reply to an order from Leland Smith, Smith-Lee Feed and Grain (800 South Main Street, Lawton, Oklahoma 73501). Leland ordered 50 one-gallon bottles of Terramycin X, an antibiotic used in calf feed to protect the young animals from viral and other infections. You don't sell Terramycin X any more, but you do sell Neo-Terramycin XX which replaced Terramycin X four months ago. Neo-Terramycin XX costs $15 a gallon; that's a dollar more per gallon than Terramycin X. And Neo-Terramycin XX is effective against more diseases than the old product, especially blackleg. Fill Harry's order with Neo-Terramycin XX. Sell the substitute on its own merits, and at its regular price.

6. *Letterhead:* Warner Inc., Townsend Way Southeast, Salem, Oregon 97303. *Inside address:* Beverly Huff, Huff Music Company, 980 Main Street, Aberdeen, Washington 98520. *Signature block:* Sincerely yours, J. B. McLester, Director, Western Sales Division. *Information:* Huff ordered 12 sets of Palmer tape heads for reel-type tape recorders @ $10 apiece (retail $15) and 6 Stanley A–622 sapphire needle cartridges for Girrard stereo turntables @ $6 (suggested retail price $8). You carry the

Stanley A–625, which replaced the A–622 in the Stanley line because it gives better pick-up and tone quality. These new antimagnetic, synthetic diamond needles last almost twice as long as the old sapphire needles and cost only $7.50 (suggested retail price $10). Since Huff wanted you to bill him at the usual 2/10, n/30 terms, sell him the A–625 on its own merits and ship them on trial along with the tape heads. Stress his keeping the substitute at the end rather than sending it back.

7. To Young Engineering Associates, 808 S.W. Broadway, Portland, Oregon 97205, from Crosswhite Wholesale Suppliers, 477 Alamo Avenue, S.E., Albuquerque, New Mexico 87100. Order number: GJ–5032. You can not send the ordered five Craft electric wrenches, but you can substitute a new and improved Wannamaker wrench that is double insulated, has polymer motor housing ($25 each instead of discontinued Craft's $21.88). Motor develops ⅕ HP at 1,700 rpm and delivers 40-foot-pounds of torque in five seconds. Ask Young for permission to send the improved electric impact wrench. Welcome this new customer with talk on quality of your service (been in business 50 years), your four research laboratories that are constantly finding new products.

8. Before you begin, read the order case to the Habernickel Company (Case 6, p. 168). Assume that you work for Habernickel and that this order came from Hugh Mate, 3299 Carlson Street, Apartment 204, Duluth, Minnesota 55815. You can send Mate every item of clothing ordered except the zipper parka in gold for $16.95. The imported chambline you used to make the parkas can no longer be imported; so you have postponed parka production for the time being. For the cold climate of Duluth, Mate might enjoy Habernickel's heavy-duty 100 percent cotton tight-ribbed corduroy jacket, fully lined with plush acrylic fleece. Jacket has double-snap cuffs, five-snap front, two big chest pockets and two deep, warm hand pockets with quilted lining in sleeves. It comes in navy, gold, or burgundy and sells for $24.75. Justify the price difference of this jacket in terms of warmth and quality.

9. *From:* Rosenburger Trunk Factory, 900 Danebo Avenue, Eugene, Oregon 97401. *To:* Mrs. James Weston, Cedar Hills Ranch, Route 12, Cave Junction, Oregon 97523. *Facts:* From your recent catalog (she said) Mrs. Weston ordered for her husband's birthday (exactly one week from today) an all-leather olive-green molded attaché case M–987 at $25.95. Since Mrs. Weston is on the list to receive your catalog, obviously she ordered from your catalog of two years ago—when you did have what she ordered. Since you dropped that line, you do not have an attaché case at that price nor do you have one listed at that number. Your all-leather brown or black attaché case M–798 with aluminum frame, recessed spring-action chrome-plated metal locks, and three-pocket lid file runs $35.95.

The all-leather cases have the approval of the National Luggage Dealers' Association. You'd gladly charge this case to Mrs. Weston's account, or send it c.o.d.—if you knew what case to send. You can't call—she added a postscript that she and her husband were going to Hawaii this week (wedding anniversary) but would be back for the birthday party. Whatchagonnado? Make up your mind and do something.

10. As sales coordinator of Universe Industries, a large American munitions conglomerate (No. 10 Beakon Road, South Amboy, New Jersey 08654), reply to an order from Ku-Fung Wong, leader of the military junta of Tiev, a small Southeast Asian country. Tiev is presently engaged in a war with its neighbor, Aidomac. Wong wants ten used F–92 Fox-Fire Jet Fighter Bombers. The Fox-Fire is a good plane, but you no longer handle it, since the F–3 Cobra came on the market. The Cobra is superior to the Fox-Fire in range, maneuverability, and firepower, and spare parts are more readily available. Wong sent along his Swiss Bank draft for $5 million as earnest money on the planes he ordered. Ask him for permission to send the Cobras. Sell the plane on its own merits. Assume that both planes cost about the same, depending on the electronics and armament specified.

CASES FOR COMBINATIONS

1. Last Friday you (Mary Spann, O'Neill's Odd Balls, 5090 Cermak Street, Chicago, Ill., 60698) received an order from George Kuhns, owner of The Dickory, a psychedelic shop, 907 Landrom Avenue, Madison, Wisconsin 53716, for six brass hand-hammered and handspun cymbals and six tablas (a small drum). George is one of your regular credit customers. He neglected to give you the stock number and sizes of the cymbals. They come in 14-inch, $10.00 each; 18-inch @ $17.00; 20-inch @ $24.00, and 22-inch @ $30.00. Ask him to indicate on an enclosed card the kind he wants.

You can't send him the six tablas he wanted; you're out of stock (so popular). Your supplier, however (Chater's, 4 Garden Row, Kent, England Br-1), has promised you a new supply of tablas in two weeks. Back-order the drums for two weeks plus your delivery time. Remember to use exact dates. George wants to know when he will get his merchandise.

2. *From* General Wholesalers, Inc., Baltimore, Maryland 21224. Consigned to and destination Hopewell Stores, Inc., 3600 West Broad Street, Richmond, Virginia 23230. *Customer order no.* 985432A, *Delivering carrier* Eastern Trucking Co. *Car initial and no.* YM87643.

No.	*Description*	*Cost*	*Total*
4	Camera cases, leather	$ 2.00	$ 8.00
6	Flight bags, leather, 22″ × 13″ × 9″	15.00	90.00
8	Attaché cases, 18″ × 12½″ × 5″	15.00	120.00

Because of their popularity, you'll have to back-order the ordered 12 men's 42″ travel bags. Delivery should be in two weeks. The sports bags (eight ordered in 12″ × 19″ × 11″) come only in vinyl (not leather as ordered). Gym suit, basketball, or football uniform or wet swim suit can be put in this vinyl bag that resists moisture in and out. The reinforced hard bottom retains its shape after rugged use. The end-to-end zipper is for easy access to every corner. Ask for permission to send the vinyl bags. Retail price runs $5.00 for each bag. Terms 2/10, n/30.

3. For your company, Crosswhite Wholesale Suppliers, 477 Alamo Avenue, S.E., Albuquerque, New Mexico 87100, handle this special letter involving a combination back order and substitute from Young Engineering Associates, 808 S.W. Broadway, Portland, Oregon 97205, Order No. GJ–5097. Because of the shortage of copper, you have to back-order the ten 60-foot coils of ⅜-inch copper tubing at $10 each for total of $100.00. Rally doesn't make the special cleaning powder for cars anymore. Your Super Satin Car Wax (only kind you sell) has a cleaner built into it. Most towns do not have places where cars can be waxed; so customers prefer the short-cut procedure of cleaner with wax for one operation. The 10 cases 30-wt. oil, 2 cases of plastic funnels, and 50 rolls of repair tape went out this morning by Blue Bell Express. Tell Young about your special on welders' goggles (NX 4215), usually $8.50 but now $6.00 this month.

4. *Letterhead:* The Orange Shop, U.S. Highway 301, Citra, Florida 32627. *Inside address:* Mr. and Mrs. Levert Killough, 908 Hickory Hill, Scrant, Kentucky 40373. July 20, 19—. *Signature block:* Sincerely yours, William P. Powell, owner. *Information:* You cannot send the ordered bushel and half-bushel boxes of navel oranges, but you can send the fruit that is in season, the round, juicy Valencia oranges (smaller, travel and keep better, especially in hot weather). You do not have any Ruby Red grapefruit at this time. In fact, you don't have any good grapefruit at this time of the year; but in about six weeks you will have good ones. Ask for permission to send the No. 11 (bushel) and No. 22 (half bushel) Valencia oranges at costs of $16.95 and $11.25 now and back-order the bushel of Ruby Reds.

5. Last Friday you received a rush order from Dr. Conrad Fulton, the County Veterinarian of Alachua County (office in Alachua, Florida 32616), for two gallons of equine encephalitis vaccine (V–211), six large syringes (B–201), and four continuous-flow vaccinating guns (V–316). Dr. Fulton neglected to tell you whether he wanted glass or plastic syringes or whether he wanted battery-powered or plug-in vaccinating guns (no differences in the prices of the syringes or vaccinating guns). Write Dr. Fulton to find out what kinds of syringes and vaccinating guns he wants and tell him you have only two plastic syringes until a promised new supply arrives ten days from now (a severe outbreak of equine encephalitis in the area has exhausted your supply). You are Oscar Hoover, Director of Sales, Pheeser Pharmaceuticals, Alameda Road, Abilene, Texas 79803.

6. To your desk in the sales division of Holgate Manufacturing Company, 1599 North Sedgwick, Chicago, Illinois 60610, comes a letter from Horace P. Love, buyer, Washburn's Department Store, 900 Sycamore Street, Sunny Slope, Missouri 64110, authorizing the shipment of six dozen skate boards (Bv–986) with Chicago clay wheels at $2.00 each plus shipping costs $3.89. Apparently Washburn's used an old catalog. When skateboards first came out, they were equipped with Chicago clay wheels which did not take turns well, thus injuring many young people. Skateboard technology has advanced and the boards are now being manufactured with safe urethane wheels, which take turns exceptionally well; but they do not sell at $2.00. Prices range from $8 (retail) to $60 (suggested price) but to this department store $4–$30. Enclose your price list, ask for his action, and tell him that because of their popularity (especially in Florida and California) your stock is depleted. You should be able to fill his order in two weeks.

7. Zelda Lincoln (Case 7, p. 270), really got the word out at Oxford, Mississippi, about your reasonably priced framing materials. You have had no less than 20 orders from campus organizations, which have seriously depleted your stock on hand.

Yesterday you received an order from Dick Mims, the historian of Nu Omega chapter of Sigma Omicron Beta fraternity (202 Vermont Street, Oxford, Mississippi 38655) for the following picture frames: 12 8″ × 10″ (A–107), @ $.75; 12 12″ × 15″ (A–108), @ $1.00; 8 18″ × 24″ (A–109), @ $1.50. Ship Dick the (A–107) and (A–109) frames he ordered. Back-order the (A–108) and explain that you have been having trouble getting the special birch lumber you make them out of. Dick also ordered 6 20″ × 30″ (A–110) sheets of plain white matboard @ $2.00 each, 12 18″ × 24″ matboard @ $.50 each, and 24 24″ × 36″ sheets of cream-colored matboard, @ $1.00 a sheet. Ship him off-white in place of the out-of-stock plain white matboard he ordered (sell it to him first), and ask him to specify whether he wants a marbled or smooth finish on the cream-colored matboard. They sell for the same price. Push the marbled finish; it looks better, and you have a lot on hand. Acknowledge his check covering the cost and shipping by UPS.

8. An old customer of yours, Hargrove Green, owner of Green Sporting Goods Store, 406 North Broadway, Baltimore, Maryland 21203, ordered from your wholesale catalog six 30-second sweep stopwatches at $11.95 each. He did not specify if he wanted No. B, which starts, stops, and returns from stem control with a 15-minute center recorder, or No. C, which has a side control and center dial recording up to 30 minutes. As sales manager for Blakeney Fine Sports and Gym Equipment Company, 735 Chestnut Street, Springfield, Massachusetts 01107, find out which type of stopwatch he wants, and back-order the dozen tetherball sets No. MTS ($10.95 a set) he ordered. The tetherball set (9-foot post of 2-inch galvanized steel tube with full-size tetherball) has become very popular in schools throughout the country. You have the manufacturer's assurance of a new shipment of No. MTS sets within 10 days and will ship them express collect to Green.

9. *Letterhead:* Imports Center, 109 Franklin Avenue South, Valley Stream, New York 11582. *Inside address:* Horton Fenimore, Bremer Arcade, Washington, D.C. 20004. *Signature block:* Sincerely, Claude Allen, Mail Order Department. *Information:* Horton asks you to ship to his psychedelic shop and organic delicatessen, the Polyethylene Pickle, ten cases of OM organically grown bean sprouts (Z–641), @ $4.00 a case; five cases of Frangipani incense (no code included), @ $2.00 a case; and two cases of water pipes (Z–682), at $15.00 a case. Since you don't have the water pipes on hand, back-order them for two weeks. They have to be made specially by Rising Sun, Inc., your Hong Kong subsidiary. Request more information about the incense. You have to know the form (block, stick, or candle); you can guess the size box he wants from the price. Ship him the bean sprouts. Assume that Harry sent in a check for $100 which covers the cost of the merchandise and shipping by Ryder truck line, balance to be refunded.

chapter 8 Persuasive messages: Sales

In these times of mass production, most products are made for sale to satisfy the needs and desires of other people—rarely for the maker's own use. If such potential users realize their needs and desires, marketing the product is a matter of making it available when and where wanted at an acceptable price, and filling the orders. Often, however, the ultimate users are not conscious of their needs or desires until somebody else points them out. In those cases, marketing also involves sales promotion—pointing out needs and desires, and how the product will satisfy them—by personal selling, advertising, and mail.

GENERAL SALES STRATEGY

Whether you sell by mail or in person, your procedures are essentially the same. You seek to gain attentive interest, convince your prospect that your proposal is worthwhile, and confidently ask for the action you want—usually an order.

In some cases you already have favorable attention, as when you answer an inquiry about your product or service. In those cases your job is to marshal your sales points and adapt them to your reader in a message that satisfactorily answers questions, convinces, and asks for action. You've already learned to do this in your study of invited sales (Chapter 5).

But in prospecting—or "cold turkey" selling, as many professionals call it—you have the preliminary job of getting your reader's attention and then arousing interest so that your reader will be eager to see what you have to say.

The surest way to get your reader to read, and ultimately to buy, is to stress some reader benefit coming from what you have to sell. To construct this benefit theme, you must know a good deal about your product or service, its uses, and the kind of people who will benefit from having it. From analyzing your product and your prospects comes the selection of the appeal to emphasize. And from a knowledge of marketing methods and people's buying habits comes the decision of what you want your prospect to do after reading your message.

Analyzing the product or service

Experienced, successful sales executives know that a thorough knowledge of the product or service is essential to successful selling. You will have a hard time convincing someone to purchase something if you are not an authority on what you are selling, or at least appear to know enough to be an authority. So you begin your sales effort by thoroughly analyzing what you want to sell.

Begin with the concept. Why was this product, say, created? Was it to satisfy a need which existed and was recognized? Or was the product perhaps created for a need which does not yet exist or which is unrecognized? In either case, you must ascertain how the product meets the need.

Get to the designers and engineers, if applicable. What did they do in designing the product? What was their reasoning behind the overall design? What problems did they meet, and how did they overcome them? What do they see as the outstanding features of the product? Get all the information you can. The more you have, the better (and more easily) you'll do your job.

Now you should have the tools you need to answer the most important question in marketing any product: *What will it do for people?* How will it make their lives better, their jobs easier, add to their security, increase their status, or otherwise satisfy a need or desire?

Although you need to know a great deal about the physical characteristics of the product (overall size, shape, color, length, breadth, height, composition, construction, operation, for example), physical description of the product will not sell it. *The psychological description—interpreta-*

tion of physical features in terms of reader benefits—is the effective part of selling.

Aluminum cooking ware, for example, may be just metal pots and pans to you. But to a chef, cast aluminum utensils (in psychological description):

—Will last for years, even in restaurant service.
—Keep their smooth surfaces because they do not nick, chip, crack, or peel.
—Provide even, uniform heat, thus decreasing chances that food will burn on the top, bottom, and sides, yet be raw in the middle.
—Allow the chef to do waterless cooking or cooking at reduced temperatures, preserving the flavor and nutrition that would go down the drain in the case of some foods.
—Make dishwashing easier and more effective, reducing costs and aiding in keeping sanitary conditions.

A dictation machine has buttons, wires, wheels, lights, and a motor. So what? It enables a business executive to record ideas, it is true. But it also allows the executive to:

—Release the high-priced dictation time of a secretary for other duties.
—Dictate when (and with a portable machine, where) desired—as time permits and as ideas occur.
—Arrange work for the office staff in the executive's absence.
—Have a record which does not get "cold," which anyone can transcribe with greater accuracy than is often possible with an individual's shorthand notes.
—Have a record to play back without needing an interpreter.

Insulation is not just pellets or batts of certain sizes and materials. To a true marketer, it keeps houses warmer in winter, cooler in summer. It thus reduces heating costs in cold months and cooling costs in warm months. It also deadens outside noises. Since it is fire-resistant, it reduces chances of fire and also decreases fire damage if and when fire breaks out. In view of all these reasons, insulation adds to the resale value of a house.

Even a child's tricycle (made of steel and chrome, with first-grade rubber tires) does more than provide pleasure for its youthful owner. It teaches muscular coordination, helps to develop visual perception and judgment, and develops leg muscles. It also releases parents from a certain amount of time spent in direct supervision.

Such analysis identifies the promises you can make your reader, the benefits you can hold out that will result from using your product or service. Such psychological description helps the reader see your offer in terms of benefits to be received. Selling is the creation of recognition of value. It is what turns a prospect into a customer.

Psychological description is interpretation, which deserves primary emphasis. Physical description is specific detail, evidence incorporated *subordinately* to bear out the promises established in psychological-description phrases and passages.

For convincing your reader that your product is the one to spend money for rather than miss the benefits it will give, you must have details concerning how, of what, by whom, and where it is made and how effectively it operates. The circumstances under which it is sold (warranties, guarantees, servicing) also affect your analysis and subsequent presentation. This physical description is necessary for conviction, but in the final sales presentation it is subservient to psychological description—the interpretation of the thing to be sold in terms of pleasure, increased efficiency, increased profit, or whatever benefit you can most specifically promise your prospect.

Finding the prospects

True prospects are people who need your product or service, can pay for it, and do not have it. In selling by mail, determining who these people are and their addresses is the job of making a mailing list. Of course you can easily get names and addresses; but are all these people *prospects?*

Some people who appear to be prospects will already be enjoying the benefits of your product or service or one like it. In that case they are suspects, not prospects. But unless you know for certain, you need to find out. And the cheapest way to find out is to solicit them.

If you are selling a product everybody needs, all you have to verify is your prospects' ability to pay. But few products are used by everybody (and when they are, direct mail is not the best way to sell them; direct mail is a specialized class medium rather than a mass medium).

In determining need, you have to start with logical analysis. For instance, you wouldn't try to sell bikinis to Eskimos or snowblowers to Puerto Ricans. Nor would you try to sell a central heating unit to apartment dwellers or baby carriages in a retirement community.

You would seek to sell a piece of office equipment to some business owner or manager, aluminum cooking ware to homemakers and restaurant owners, insulation to homeowners.

Sex, age (and a close corollary, physical condition), family and dwelling status, vocation, geographical location, and financial situation are some of the more significant considerations in assuming that someone is a logical prospect for your product. In some cases you will need to go further than a logical analysis and make a marketing survey.

Logical analysis, and a marketing survey if necessary, will give you a list of characteristics that describe the most likely prospects for your product or service. If enough people share these characteristics to make it practical to approach them by sales letter, you have a direct-mail market. If they are too numerous to send letters to, then you have a "mass market," and you should use a mass medium such as one of the forms of advertising. If they are so few that letters are not specialized enough—very rare—then individual phone calls or visits may be more practical.

Most sales letters have to go out in large numbers to secure the volume necessary for profit. But even when they go out by the thousands, you send them to a *selected* mailing list. As one direct-mail specialist put it, sales letters and direct mail are "not *mass* media but *class* media."

Assured of a direct-mail market, you next need a *good* mailing list. That means names and addresses that are accurate (no waste on incorrect or obsolete addresses), *pure* (all true prospects), and *homogeneous* (having the desired characteristics in common—the more the better for adapting your letter).

To get such a list, you can make your own, buy one, rent one, or—if you've already made one yourself—trade for one, but usually not with a competitor. Making your own list may be the best way *if* you know how and can afford the time and the money for necessary tools. At least your own list will be private—your competitors and others won't share it with you.

The obvious place to start compiling a list of prospects is your list of customers—people who have already bought from you. If your marketing plan includes advertisements, especially in trade magazines, inserting coupons in them offering free literature on the product or service will bring in names and inquiries of interested people.

Several directories (Dow's, Poor's, and others) classify names of companies by type of business and areas of operation. The Yellow Pages are a fertile source of prospects, especially if you are restricting your effort to a limited geographical area. Another alternative is to hire a clipping service to send you clippings of items (with names) printed in consumer and/or trade publications that deal with the type of people or companies you are seeking.

Like many other activities, however, *making* and *maintaining* a good mailing list requires not only more time and money but more KNOW-HOW and facilities than most people can and will devote to the job.[1] Therefore, unless you are going to study the subject to learn the procedures and techniques, and spend the money for the tools of the trade, you probably will do better to buy or rent your list from one of the many firms that specialize in them. Doing otherwise is likely to have results comparable to what usually happens (a mess of costly errors) when Tom, Dick, and Harry (without learning how) act as their own doctors, lawyers, conductors of surveys, architects, index makers—yes, and writers of letters and reports.

Hundreds of companies are in the business of making, selling, and renting lists. In fact these list houses are so numerous that the Department of Commerce publishes a directory of them. You can purchase virtually any list you want from list houses. Most of them have catalogs of the read-

---

[1] Yeck and Maguire, *Planning and Creating Better Direct Mail,* devote 28 pages to the subject.

ily available lists they offer, giving the size of each list and the cost. If they do not have the list you want, they will build it for you according to your specifications, if you are willing to pay the price.

As a rule, mailing lists are priced according to the difficulty in compiling them, usually varying from two to ten cents per name. A major factor is the number of characteristics you specify that the people on the list must have in common. That same factor, however, affects directly the desirability and purity of the list. This last is important; it refers to the percentage of names that may not belong on the list. That is, they are mis-classified according to at least one important characteristic (or you failed to specify classifying by that characteristic) and hence are not likely prospects. A certain percentage of these will creep into almost any list, but you will usually not be charged for those you identify.

An example will clarify the matter of varying list costs and purity. You can buy a big list of auto owners very cheaply (probably no more than two cents a name because of specifying only the one characteristic). But for promoting purchases of new Cadillacs, the list would have very low purity. Many of those people would have relatively new cars and others would have too low incomes. To purify your list considerably, you could add as specifications that the presently owned cars be at least four years old and that the annual incomes be at least $25,000. Your list would now be much smaller, and the cost might be just as much because of the much higher cost per name, but you would save lots of money you might have wasted on people who weren't prospects. Furthermore, you might sell more cars, especially if you made good use of the new information to *adapt* your letters by references to the financial status of the readers and the age of their cars. These facts point up an ever-present question in selling by mail: How far should you go in purifying the mailing list?

Another big problem—this one of maintaining rather than making—is the list's accuracy, the percentage of incorrect names and addresses. About 18 percent of the people in America change their addresses each year. People who use old lists—whether they make, buy, rent, or trade for them —and are not aware of this situation are unpleasantly surprised at the number of undeliverable letters. Over half a list can be obsolete after only three years!

Mailing-list houses usually do not charge for incorrect addresses if you report them. This is how lists are qualified (the inaccurate names and addresses deleted). As a rule of thumb, any list that has not been qualified within the past year is suspect, and you can expect a good part of it to be useless. First-class mailings, or third-class with return instructions to the Postal Service, are how you qualify a list.

Whether you buy, rent, trade for, or compile your list, however, for sales effectiveness it must contain the correct names and addresses of people or companies with enough desirable characteristics in common to make them a group of likely prospects; a market, for your product or service.

Only then can you adapt your talking points and your references in persuasive fashion, as discussed on pages 42–46.

Choosing the appeal

From the analysis of your product will come your sales points. You know your product or service, and you know things about it that might convince people to buy. Obviously you can't put all of them in detail into one letter, or you'll have a cluttered message with so much in it that nothing sticks with the reader. Your next step is to select for emphasis the *central selling point*—the one big theme around which to build your letter. It is the answer to this question: *What one feature of the product or service is most likely to induce the prospect(s) to buy?* Your other sales points you can interweave, relegate to an enclosure, or leave for a subsequent mailing. In selling completely by mail, one incidental point that you need to make clear (by explicit statement or implication) is *why* the reader should buy by mail instead of at a local store.

People buy for many reasons: to make or save money, to build or protect their reputation or status, to preserve health, to save time or effort, to protect themselves or their families or companies, for example. If you want to, you can find them listed in multitude in countless books on psychology, salesmanship, sociology, advertising, and marketing. Pride, love, beauty, acquisitiveness, self-indulgence, self-preservation, curiosity, and sometimes fear play their parts in inducing interest and stimulating the final action—making the purchase.

People are both rational and emotional. They need a rational reason to support an emotional desire for something. Arguing the relative importance of rational and emotional appeals in selling is comparable to a vigorous debate over which came first, the chicken or the egg. In writing good sales letters, if you remind your reader of a need your product will meet and supply evidence to back up your promise, if you stress what you think is the most important reason why the particular group of readers will buy, you won't need to worry about whether you are employing rational or emotional techniques. You'll be using both. And that's as it should be.

You may, however, need to vary the division of emphasis according to the kind of thing you're selling. Goods that are durable (long-lasting), tangible (touchable), expensive, and essential call for major emphasis on rational appeals. Conversely, selling things that are ephemeral (quickly used and gone), intangible (like entertainment), inexpensive, and nonessential (luxuries) calls for more emphasis on emotional appeals.

Certainly effective adaptation is necessary. Your choice of theme for your message will be affected by one or more of the significant considerations of the prospect's sex, vocation, location, age, source and amount of income, and social, professional, educational, or corporate status. One of the most obvious differences that affect your choice of theme is that between manufacturers and dealers on one side and consumers on the other. Manufacturers buy for the ultimate *profit* they will make by using your product or service to improve their manufacturing or other activities.

Dealers buy for the *profit* they will make on reselling. That depends on the *number* they can sell and the *markup*, less any expense and trouble necessary in backing up guarantees with replacements, repairs, and service calls. The logic of selling to dealers lends itself to formula statement as $P = VM - C$ (profit equals volume of sales times the markup, minus operating costs). Consumers buy for the various benefits the product or service will render. But even in dealer letters you wouldn't write the same things to a large metropolitan department store that you would to a small rural variety store.

You can't always be certain, either, of the wisdom of your choice of theme. Testing two or more different letters on a part of your list in a preliminary mailing (about which we'll say more later) may help you to arrive at a choice, but sometimes even testing does not resolve your dilemma.

For example, in selling steel desks and chairs to fraternity houses, two writers came up with two different themes. One played up comfort and subordinated the factor of appearance; the other stressed appearance to the subordination of durability and comfort:

How many hours of each day do you spend at your desk?

Three? Four? Maybe more?

From experience you know how important it is that your desk be roomy and your chair comfortable. You can be assured of the comfort and convenience you need with Carroll steel desks and chairs. Especially designed as a study unit for college men, they are also sturdy and good looking.

Since the desk is 31 inches high, you can cross your knees beneath the top. Or if you want to sit with your feet on the desk, propped back in your chair, you can do so without marring the surface or breaking the welded steel chair.

Whether you choose the steel top at $40.75 or the laminated plastic top at $35.75, you don't need to worry about

Wouldn't you be proud to show your rushees uniform desks and chairs?

Fine-looking study equipment will create an initial favorable impression. And they will realize, as you do, that following rush week comes work.

In Carroll steel desks and chairs you'll have study equipment that will stay good looking and provide years of comfortable use. The top has been chemically treated to avoid burns and scratches and to eliminate stains from liquids. Welded steel construction assures you that your Carroll desk and chair will retain their attractive straight lines. And a choice of battle gray, olive green, or mahogany enables you to select a color which will blend in well with your present furnishings.

Either the steel top at $40.75 or the laminated

```
nicks and scratches.  Either
top, 28 inches wide by 42
inches long, gives you ample
room for all the books and
papers you have in use.
Shelves at one end and a large
drawer keep your other books
and supplies at hand.

And you can have Carroll desks
and chairs in battle gray,
olive green, or mahogany.

After you've had a chance to
read over the enclosed leaflet
(which explains the attractive
quantity discounts available
to you), you'll see why
Carroll study equipment was
recently chosen for
dormitories at Michigan, Iowa,
and Princeton.
```

```
plastic top at $35.75 will
retain its attractive
appearance over the years.

The ample work space of the
desk—28 inches wide, 42
inches long, 31 inches high,
with shelves at one end and a
generous drawer—and the
swivel chair of body-comfort
design mean comfort for study
as well as for long bull
sessions.

After you've had a chance to
read over the enclosed leaflet
(which explains the attractive
quantity discounts available
to you), you'll see why
Carroll study equipment was
recently chosen for
dormitories at Michigan, Iowa,
and Princeton.
```

Both these letters are well-knit presentations of their selected themes. Each establishes the same information about the product. But we suspect that the first version would sell more chairs to house committees, because on most campuses comfortable study conditions are more important than appearance, and for a longer time than rushing conditions. You would have to test to be sure.

A letter addressed to the appropriate purchasing agent for the dormitories would wisely have stressed still a different possible theme—holding down maintenance and replacement costs.

Identifying the specific goal

You may know before you begin your prewriting analysis exactly what you want your reader to do. But you'll want to *be sure that the action you request your reader to take is logical* in the light of purchasing conditions, which are governed by the nature of the product, the circumstances of the customer, and authorized, organized marketing channels.

Many sales letters cannot and should not drive for completion of the sale. All they do is ask for a show of interest (and thus help to weed out the "suspects"). You may want your reader to request a booklet, come to your showroom, or give you some information; or you may want authorization for a sales representative to visit. In many instances, of course, you can logically ask for an order. Regardless of what the appropriate action is, decide on it and *identify it specifically before you begin to write*.

All possible versions of the letter about fraternity desks and chairs should have some type of action ending, identifying payment and shipping conditions if an order by letter is appropriate or—more likely in this case—inviting the readers to come to a display room or to authorize the visit of a representative.

WRITING THE PROSPECTING SALES LETTER

After thorough study of your product and prospect, selection of theme, and decision on your specific goal, you develop your theme in a C–plan letter patterned by some adaptation of the standard sales presentation: Attention, Interest, Conviction, and Action. If you want to substitute *Desire* for *Conviction* in letters appealing largely to emotion, go ahead; it won't alter your basic procedure. If you want to call it Promise, Picture, Prove, and Push, you won't go wrong because of your labels.

But don't think of a presentation in four or five or even three parts—like a play in three acts. In a good letter, smoothly written for coherence and unity of impression, you can't separate the parts cleanly. Although we analyze the writing of a sales letter in terms of getting attentive interest, establishing belief and trust, overcoming price resistance, and confidently asking for action, the final version of it should be a presentation that is smooth because of its coherence and persuasive because of its singleness of purpose (giving it unity) and progression of thought.

If there is a key to selling, we think it is this: Help your prospects imagine themselves *successfully* using your product or service. Note that word "successfully," for it is essential. The readers must clearly picture mentally how your product or service will contribute something wanted—status, well-being, self-satisfaction, and so forth.

You help your readers imagine themselves successfully using your product or service through psychological description. To help them justify themselves logically in acting to get the benefits you have made desirable, you interweave and follow up with physical description and other evidence that they can get the wanted benefits.

The letters in this chapter all exhibit this fundamental pattern of persuasion, and we will examine it in detail.

Getting attentive interest

If you believe in your product and what it can do for your reader, you'll have no big problem starting a sales letter effectively. All you need to do is *hold up the promise of the big benefit your product can contribute to the reader.* If it's a genuine benefit and your message is to a real prospect, your reader will finish your letter.

Yet because of the clamor for attention which many advertisers talk and write about, many advertisements and letters put on a show with the bizarre, the irrelevant, and the irritating to make the reader stop and listen. They seem to say: "We know you won't listen otherwise; so we're standing on our heads to attract your attention. Of course, standing on our heads won't tell you a thing about our product or what it can do for you, but it'll make you sit up and take notice."

To that, all we can say is: "Sure! The freak at the circus commands attention. And if sheer attention is all you want, walk naked down Madison Avenue or Michigan Avenue. You'll get attention. But is it appropriate? Is it in good taste? Will it really help to induce the reader to buy?"

Relevancy is important. Without it, your trick or gadget will likely be a distraction and a detriment rather than an assist to your sales effort. Tricks are legion, and they create talk, even notoriety, about you. But *unless they lead naturally, plausibly, and shortly to what your product can do for your reader, they're not worth the effort and expense.*

The American public is an educated and sophisticated public. It is quick to criticize or, worse yet, to laugh at advertising and its methods. It hasn't bought the Brooklyn Bridge for a couple of generations. It recognizes a gold brick for what it is worth. The farmer's daughter has been to town—even if it's only via TV. Smug patter about the 14-year-old mentality is beguiling—and dangerous. Even the 14-year-old mind recognizes the difference between showing off and real selling.

You'll read much and hear much about tricks, stunts, and gadgets. Good-luck pennies, four-leaf clovers, keys that open the door to everything from business success to a happy home life with your dog, rubber bands (which most of the time only stretch the reader's patience), cartoons, faked telegrams in yellow window envelopes, simulated handwritten messages, names of readers written at the top of the page in red, blue, gold ("the symbol of things precious, and your name means much to us!"), boldface numbers ("**2,400,001!** What's the 1 for? That's *your* copy!"), shorthand copy, Chinese writing, the early bird with the worm in its mouth, checkerboards, mirrors, alarm clocks—all these and many others may distract from your sales message rather than assist it unless they enable you to *cut through quickly to the benefit your product can render.*

Such tricks have been overused and misapplied in so many instances that one advertiser recently sent the following letter (which you'll recognize as a trick in itself):

> I have never tried to fool you.
>
> I have never sent you an order form that looks like an authentic bank check, with or without signatures and countersignatures!
>
> And I've never sent you a bondlike certificate apparently so valuable that it startles you briefly—before you throw it away.
>
> I have never used a brown envelope to make you think your tax refund has finally arrived.
>
> In fact, I've never even sent you a postage stamp!
>
> We here at Bowen's think you're too intelligent to fall for such nonsense!

> We're convinced that Bowen customers are an alert and critical, not a gullible, audience. New gimmicks and catchphrases are not going to influence you. . . .

You may dream up a trick or gadget occasionally that isn't old stuff to most of your audience and that naturally, plausibly, and quickly illustrates or introduces the benefit your product can render. If it can meet the tests of relevance, plausibility, good taste, and speed, you may want to use it. A fire-sale letter typed in red may have salutary appeal. A check form made out to the reader, immediately followed by the lead, "What would it mean to you to get a *real* check like this *every month*?" may plausibly preface sales talk about an annuity or health insurance.

The sales manager who sent a letter on cellophane with the lead, "Here's a value for you that is as clear-cut as the paper on which it is written," used a good (but very expensive) gadget to command attention.

So we do not mean to imply that all tricks, gadgets, and humorous letters are undesirable. Certainly you'll find occasional opportune times for the whimsical, the gracefully turned phrase, the chuckling at humanity's idiosyncrasies, and the outright humorous. But before you use what you think is a bright, clever, or punny approach, recall the story that seasoned advertisers tell of the woman who asked her husband if he had seen a certain clever ad. "What was it about?" her husband asked. "I don't remember," the lady replied, "but it was right next to that homely X, X and Y ad."

If you can phrase an opening which is deft, novel, and catchy, use it —provided it paves the way quickly and naturally to the introduction of what your product can do for your reader. If you can't, forget about it.

The benefit-contribution-product beginning is always applicable and always good. Associate the benefit with your reader, then bring in the product as the provider of the benefit, and you have a good opening.

A business-reporting service used the following successful opening in a letter to contractors:

> A lot of money spent
> on new construction
> in your area—
> —is going to wind up in somebody's pocket . . . and it might as well be yours instead of your competitor's!

Another reporting agency got good attention with this opening:

> WHAT SORT OF GOVERNMENT
> WILL DOMINATE YOUR BUSINESS
> IN THE DIFFICULT PERIOD AHEAD?

A laundry got the favorable attention of homemakers with

> Would you wash a shirt, iron it to please the most demanding man, and wrap it in cellophane—for 40 cents?

A savings and loan association led with

> Do your savings work hard enough for you?

And an insurance company seeking to sell education insurance to parents of small children paved the way with

> A small monthly saving now will buy your youngster a gift worth $220,000. There's no catch to it.
>
> The $220,000—an estate even a wealthy family could be proud to leave a son or daughter—is the difference between the average lifetime earnings of a college graduate and one without this special education, according to a recent national survey made by the Bureau of the Census.

Selling word processing equipment to office managers, the following opening (below a clipped-on photograph of a girl powdering her nose while surrounded by three of the machines referred to) pinpoints a real problem and its solution:

> What happens when a girl "powders her nose" in the offices of the Northeastern Mutual Life Insurance Company?
>
> When her typewriter stops, production ceases. And office costs go up.

A variation of theme for the same product went this way:

> "I've had five years' experience with the Mutual Life Insurance Company, can type 140 words a minute, am willing to work each day indefinitely, do not get tired, and demand no salary."
>
> Would you hire this typist? We did. And she typed this letter in two minutes.
>
> Of course, it isn't human. It's a machine—the Robo-Typist—which types any letter you want from a magnetic tape at 140 words a minute.

Note that in all these quoted openings *the lead is simply a reminder of a need for which the product comes in shortly as an agent for satisfying that need.* They do not command, preach, cajole, beg, or exhort. They do not challenge. They do not scream in superlatives (finest, amazing) with exclamation points! They do not begin with talk of the product itself ("Now you too can have XYZ dog biscuits!") or the company ("53 years of doing business . . ."). Here's an example of an opening that does just about everything wrong:

> Recently I was appointed Director of Sales—Midwest Region for the Hardly Used Tool Company and I will now have the pleasure of working with you in handling your used tool requirements with our company.

Good openings positively, specifically, and vividly, but believably, say or imply, "As help in handling this specific problem, I suggest. . . ." They get attentive interest through psychological description of the product in use benefiting the reader personally. Thus they cause the reader to want more information, especially on how the product can fulfill the promise.

Establishing belief and trust

Having made the promise, a letter must quickly supply evidence to back it up. If the opening is successful, it has established tentative favor or agreeableness rather than serious doubt. In effect, the reader has mentally nodded in agreement. The next part of your sales letter—which ordinarily consumes the greatest amount of space—tells how your product does meet the need and *gives specific information that will make your reader believe you.* You thus maintain and continue the agreement you establish in the start of the letter.

Explanations and descriptions of the product or service *in use* are how you handle this part. Word pictures of how it works and how it is made, performance tests, testimonials of users, statistics of users, facts and figures on sales, guarantees, free-trial offers, offers of demonstrations, and samples are some of your most common devices. Note how the following letter supplies evidence to support its opening claim.[2]

```
The Carriage Return Lever
On a Manual Typewriter
Is Costing You Money . . .

. . . and it's money you don't have to spend any more.

Human Efficiency, Inc., of New York City, has completed a
series of exacting tests and confirms that you can save as
much as one hour each day for each typist you employ when
you install Speedo Carriage Returns on your manual typewriters.

Watch one of your typists.  Every time she returns the
carriage to the next line, her left hand makes three
movements.  When the bell signals the end of a line, her hand
moves from the keys to the lever, throws the lever, and then
returns to the keys.  It looks fast and easy, doesn't it?  It
is—an expert typist can do it in just one second.

Just one second, but one second becomes one minute when your
typist types 60 lines.  And that one minute multiplies to one
hour every 3,600 lines.  From your experience as an office
manager, you know that 3,600 lines aren't very many for an
efficient stenographer to type, especially the short lines
required for orders and invoices.
```

---

[2] We have two comments before you read the letter: (1) Though the product sold is becoming obsolete because of electric typewriters, the letter is an excellent one to illustrate the point of convincing the reader by detailed logic and facts about the product *in use.* (2) Yes, this letter is long—as most effective sales letters are. If you're worried about length, remember that the firm which has tested more of its sales letters than any other, Time, Inc., never writes one-page sales letters any more—they always pulled less under test. Remember, too, the statement of one of the nation's most renowned consultants, Howard Dana Shaw, that in general a long letter will outpull a short one if it tells, in an interesting way, something of value to the reader. But don't confuse length with a lack of conciseness.

Using a Speedo, your typist performs one step—not three—to return the carriage to the next line. When the bell signals the end of the line, she presses a foot pedal; the carriage automatically spaces correctly and returns to the left margin. One tenth of a second—not one second—has elapsed.

And because her hands do not have to leave the keyboard, accuracy increases when you install Speedos. Human Efficiency tested 150 typists using Speedos for two weeks in 20 different large plants. They showed a 16 percent reduction in errors—and, naturally, a similar 16 percent reduction in time spent erasing errors.

Part of the explanation for the increase in output and decrease of errors is a reduction in fatigue. Throwing a carriage just once doesn't amount to much, but when your typist repeats hundreds of times she uses up as much energy as if scrubbing the floor. The Speedo not only reduces the strain by two thirds but shifts it to the leg and foot, which can bear it far better than the arm. Tests of 45 typists employed by the Kenoya Wholesale Grocery Company of Columbus, Ohio, showed that after two weeks they increased by 9 percent the amount of copy produced daily.

Clamped to the carriage-return lever, the Speedo connects to the foot pedal by a thin wire. The adjustment is simple; you can put one on any standard typewriter in less than five minutes.

Turn to pages 1 and 2 of the enclosed folder and read the complete report of the tests. On page 3 you'll find comments of typists who've used the Speedo and the comments of their office managers. Read how the typists all agree that they had no difficulty learning to use the Speedo efficiently.

Page 4 gives you data on prices and shipping. Note that the Speedo with all its advantages—plus an unconditional 90-day guarantee—is yours for only $4.50 because we sell Speedo only by mail to help keep the cost down. And by ordering a dozen for $46 you save 70 cents on each one.

Fill out the enclosed order blank and send it to us in the return envelope provided. We'll immediately ship your Speedos by whatever method you direct, either prepaid or c.o.d. Within 10 days at the most you'll be able to see the increased output and accuracy of your typists.

Surely you remember that sincerity is essential to the reader's belief and trust, that you-viewpoint description is vital, that psychological description in terms of the reader's use and benefits is far superior to mere physical description of the product, that specific words in positive language are necessary to effective sales techniques, and that enclosures (properly introduced) can often supplement letters effectively. If not, turn back and review the persuasion principles in Chapter 2 and the analysis of the invited sales letter in Chapter 5. All we're suggesting is that you apply the same principles.

Overcoming price resistance

You've already studied effective ways of handling dollar talk too (back in the discussion of the invited sales letter, pp. 112–13). The principles are the same in prospecting sales. Were we to repeat them here, we'd just take up space which would merely waste your time if you remember the former discussion.

Asking confidently and specifically for action

Likewise, if we discussed again what we've already told you and illustrated for you repeatedly about action endings (indicate confidently what you want your reader to do and how to do it, make it easy and make it sound easy, and supply a stimulus to prompt action in a quick reference to the contribution the product can make to the life of the reader), we'd be using your time unnecessarily and adding to production costs. Furthermore, the summary checklist (p. 298) itemizes the points specifically. It helps you to review and your instructor to evaluate your letter.

ADAPTING TO CLASSES

All good sales letters follow the basic procedures advocated in the preceding pages. Only in their talking points and in their interpretation and references do they differ as they go to farmers instead of bankers, to lawyers instead of engineers, to consumers as opposed to dealers or manufacturers.

Much fluff is written and said about letters to women. Such talk is misleading. Lots of evidence points to the fact that the American woman—and the homemaker in particular—is a sharp customer, as demanding and calculating in reading the pages of catalogs and magazines as a purchasing agent for a firm is. She's no different when she reads a letter.

If you are a person of feeling and imagination and are unselfish enough to forget yourself in analyzing another person's (or group of persons') circumstances, you won't have much trouble writing successfully adapted letter copy.

As an illustration of how tone and talking points differ, study the following two letters. The first is to a homeowner, the second to a dealer. In both cases the product is a special kind of lawn mower which eliminates hand clipping.

```
                                              Lawn-mowing Time
   Extra Time for
   Summer Rest and Fun!

   You can cut your lawn-mowing time in half with an easy-
   operating Multimower because you can eliminate the hand
   clipping and trimming.
```

Prospecting Sales Checklist

1. Get started effectively and economically.
   a) Suggest or hint at a specific reader benefit in the first sentence.
   b) Show a need before naming the product as serving it; but usually use positive selling, not predicament-to-remedy push-overs.
   c) Concentrate on a well-chosen central selling point at first.
   d) Quickly get to the distinctive thing about your product (not just anybody's). Avoid unnatural or delaying gimmicks.
   e) Don't begin with an obvious statement or foolish question.
   f) Suggest, remind, but don't preach: "You will want. . . ."
   g) Don't claim too much for your product. Be reasonable.
2. Back up your opening promise with a persuasive description.
   a) Interpret physical features in terms of the reader's benefit.
   b) You-viewpoint is not automatic from use of you ("you will find" and "you will note"); but as the subject or object of action verbs, *you* helps.
   c) Guard against stark product descriptions (beginnings like "Our goods . . . ," "We make . . . ," or "XYZ is made . . .").
   d) Specificness in description is necessary for conviction.
   e) Even in form letters, refer to some action or condition that applies and avoid references which brand them as forms.
   f) The history of the product or firm will bore most readers.
   g) Eliminate challenging superlatives.
   h) Guard against the trite "truly" and "really" and the indefinite "that" ("that important conference").
3. Be sure to cover all important points with proper emphasis.
   a) Develop the most appropriate central selling point adequately.
   b) Stress your central theme for singleness of impression.
   c) Give enough detail to sell your reader on reading an enclosure, when you have one, and even more when you do not.
   d) Provide adequate conviction through selected methods.
   e) Introduce any enclosure only after most of your sales points, stressing what the reader is to do with it or get from it.
4. Remember the price; it is an integral part of any sales message.
   a) Unless using a recognized-bargain appeal, minimize price.
   b) Keep price out of the ending, at least the last sentence.
   c) If you choose not to talk price now, offer to sometime and reassure the reader that it is not out of line.
5. Forthrightly ask for appropriate action (and tell why buy by mail).
   a) Name the specific action you want your reader to take.
   b) Be confident. Avoid "If you'd like . . . ," "Why not . . . ?"
   c) Avoid high-pressure bromides: "Why wait?" "Don't delay!"
   d) Refer *subordinately* to ordering aids (blanks or envelopes).
   e) End with a reminder of what the product will contribute.
6. Check for any unintentional promises of safety or warranty.

The Multimower gathers all the grass it cuts too.

So with just one run over the lawn with your Multimower, your lawn is in shape. And it's just a light workout. You can cut your grass flush against fences, trees, and flower beds. The interlocking rotary cutters enable you to mow tall grass and tough weeds with no more effort than it takes to cut short grass. And you're less tired when you get through because you handle only the minimum weight when you use this 58-pound mower. It's light enough for almost any member of the household to use.

Even though the Multimower is light, you have a precision mower of sturdy construction and strength-tested materials. The drive shift is mounted on free-rolling, factory-lubricated, sealed ball bearings which keep dirt and water from rusting these parts. And the cutters are self-sharpening. So your Multimower is always ready for you to use. All you need to do is put in the gas.

If the weather keeps you from mowing your lawn on schedule and grass gets a little too high, simply adjust the handle knob to the cutting height you want, and drive your Multimower easily across your lawn, cutting a clean, even 21-inch swath.

Many of the 8,000 enthusiastic Multimower owners have been using theirs for over two years. Some of their statements, along with illustrations and the details of our 90-day structural guarantee, you can read on the two inside pages. You'll see, too, that we pay shipping charges to your door. Multimower is available only by mail at the economical price of $139.95. The time you save on the first summer's Multimowing is probably worth more than that.

Use the handy order mailer to send us your check or money order. Within a week after you mail it, you'll be able to cut, trim, and gather up the grass on your lawn in only one easy, timesaving Multimowing.

The letter to a dealer stresses the same points, to show *why to expect high-volume sales to customers;* but it does so more rapidly and concisely, in order to concentrate on sales aids, price spreads, promptness and regularity of supply, and service as parts of the profit-making picture. Remember the formula $P = VM - C$. And since the V (volume of sales) is usually the main variable, give it the major attention it deserves by pointing out how the features of the product will appeal to buyers.

Certainly, of necessity, a dealer is habitually more money-conscious than the average consumer. And the reasons for buying are more complex. A dealer may be more rational in evaluation of a product than a consumer and probably is more critical. Still the approach is the same as in any sales letter: It seeks the answer to the ever-present question, "What will it do for me?"

To a dealer the answer is always "profits," but profits depend on salability (the features of the product that cause people to buy), on serviceability, and on markup. Since salability—features attracting buyers—is usually the main point, the psychological description becomes *interpretation of those features in terms of consumer appeal.* A dealer is also interested in your promptness and regularity in filling orders, in guarantee and service arrangements, and (if you provide any) advertising or other selling aids to help sell more—as in the following letter:

> When you show a customer a Multimower, a lawn mower completely new in design and principle, which cuts and trims a lawn in one operation, you have a quick sale, a satisfied customer, and a $46.65 profit.
>
> Your customers will like the Multimower because it gives them more time to spend in enjoyable summer recreation. It cuts right up to walls, fences, trees, and flower beds and thus eliminates the need for hand trimming in spots not reached by ordinary mowers. Its easily adjustable cutting-height regulator and self-sharpening cutters that slice down the toughest kinds of grass, dandelions, and weeds will assure them of having a trim, neat lawn in half the time they've formerly spent.
>
> Both men and women like the Multimower because its light weight—only 58 pounds—means easy handling. The quiet operation of the interlocking cutters has won approval of 8,000 Multimower users. They like it, too, because it is permanently lubricated and self-sharpening. With a minimum of care it's always ready for use. Just put in the gas, and it's ready to go.
>
> No doubt many of your customers have been reading about the Multimower in the full-page, four-color monthly ads that started running in *Homeowners* and *Vacation* magazines in March and will continue through July. A reprint, along with testimonials and conditions of our guarantee, appears on the next page. Note the favorable guarantee and servicing arrangements.
>
> In these days of high prices, the $139.95 retail cost of the Multimower will be popular with your customers. Our price to you is only $93.30.
>
> By filling out and returning the enclosed order blank along with your remittance today, you'll be sure to have Multimowers on hand when your customers begin asking for them.

The checklist on page 301 summarizes the significant points to keep in mind for selling to dealers.

LEGAL CONSIDERATIONS

One point that you as a sales writer must definitely keep in mind involves questions of legal responsibility. Recent court decisions have firmly placed the responsibility for product liability squarely on the manufacturers and designers of products. If a defect in design or manufacturing or material of a product causes injury or other harm to the user, the legal responsibility for the harm or injury rests on the product's creator. And this may be the case even if the user admits reading and understanding clear instructions for use supplied with the product. This matter of prod-

Dealer Sales Checklist

1. A dealer sales letter opening has to move fast.
   a) Devote at least the beginning to the reader and benefits to come—not yourself or even the product per se.
   b) Picture the act of selling and the product's consumer appeal.
   c) Stress a distinctive point; avoid obvious, slow, general copy.
   d) Avoid exaggeration and questionable superlatives.
2. Though you might mention profits, the first point to develop is salability (Volume). Without consumer appeal the product stays on the shelves and makes no profit regardless of price spread.
   a) To stress consumer demand, explain the product's points in terms of customers' reactions, demands, and approval—hence high-volume sales.
   b) Talk about the dealer's selling—not using—the product.
   c) Adaptation here means talking of sales demonstrations, wrapping up a purchase and handing it across the counter, ringing up a sale, answering customers' questions, and the like.
3. Show how the manufacturer helps to push the sale, if applicable.
   a) Refer to whatever dealer aids you have (advertising, displays, mats, cuts) with emphasis on how they build local demand.
   b) Give working ideas of size (quarter page, half page), extent (time it will run), and coverage (specific medium—magazine, newspaper, radio, and/or TV station—and type of audience).
   c) Interpret any advertising as promoting inquiries and sales.
4. Continue pointing to appeal and profitable selling in the price talk.
   a) Price is most appropriately handled late, most naturally as you ask for an order and talk payment details.
   b) Include a specific mention of price spread, percentage, or both.
   c) Terms and manner of payment have to be cleared up.
5. You will almost always have some enclosures to handle.
   a) Don't divert attention to the enclosure until near enough the end that the reader will complete the letter.
   b) Make the reference to an enclosure carry a sales point too.
   c) Don't depend too heavily on an enclosure to do the selling.
6. Make the action ending brief and businesslike too.
   a) Probably better avoid commands to the seasoned buyer.
   b) Exaggerated superlatives are out of place here too.
   c) Of course, you name the specific action you want.
   d) And you make that action easy.
   e) Use a whip-back suggesting prompt handling and profitable selling.
7. Check for any unintentional promises of safety or warranty.

uct liability is presently being more precisely defined through legal cases, but clearly the ancient doctrine of *caveat emptor*, "let the buyer beware," is changing to *caveat venditor*, "let the seller beware."

As an example, the Multimower letters above wisely avoid the question of safety. But the writer was tempted, we imagine, to say something like

```
The unique spring-loaded on-off switch, deflected cuttings
exhaust, and rugged blade shield make Multimower safe to use.
```

But if worded that way and the spring in the switch broke and hurt the user, or if the mower accidentally got on someone's feet, severely injuring them, that sentence would make Multimower's position in court indefensible. The letter would have made in writing an absolute claim for safety, and the company would be held legally responsible for making that claim good.

If the writer of the Multimower letter had to talk about safety, he would have been wise to qualify his statements with something like

```
. . . safe to use, provided normal safety precautions are
observed.
```

or

```
In normal use, and observing proper safety precautions. . . .
```

Product liability extends to manufacturers of industrial items as well as consumer goods, and to suppliers of advice and designs, such as architects, consulting engineers, and the like. In a recent case, for example, a large machine tool shifted when the bolts fastening it to the floor sheared off, resulting in severe injury to a worker. The worker sued the employer, who sued the manufacturer of the machine tool. The manufacturer in turn sued the manufacturer of the special bolts that had fastened the tool in place, and the maker of the bolts in turn sued the steel company that had supplied the steel for making the bolts. Responsibility for a product's safety may extend back a very long time, too, the statute of limitations for product liability being a foggy legal area. In the case of the machine tool above, it had been installed almost twenty years before the accident! We do not know how the case was resolved.

Warranties and guarantees are an area in which writers of sales letters are more likely to get into trouble unwittingly, usually by making one of two mistakes: the writer (1) implies a warranty where no warranty exists or (2) extends an existing warranty infinitely. As an example, the last two sentences of the fifth paragraph of the Multimower consumer sales letter read:

```
So your Multimower is always ready for you to use.  All you
need to do is put in the gas.
```

First, the writer has implied a warranty where surely none was intended, saying that *all* that is needed is gas, and the mower will be operable. Sec-

Avoid general guarantees.

ond, whatever warranty or guarantee the company does make is extended infinitely by that "always." Always means forever—the writer unintentionally made a firm promise that the Multimower would perform until time and the universe end, provided only that the user put in gas!

The first time an owner of a Multimower gases it up and it doesn't start, he can hold the manufacturer liable for any necessary repairs or maintenance, including possibly court costs and punitive damages. Here's how those sentences could have been rewritten to avoid the problem:

```
A minimum of easy maintenance will help keep your Multimower
ready for use.  Virtually all you need to do is put in the
gas and start it.
```

Observing the restrictions of legal responsibility and warranties is just about impossible if you are going to write an effective sales letter. We therefore suggest that you do what most good sales and advertising writers do. Go ahead and write a letter that *sells.* Get the reader's attention, create in the reader a desire for your product or service, give some logical reasons for fulfilling that desire, and then specify the action you want taken. Use all the tools at your command—emphasis, positive phrasing, you-attitude, success consciousness, specific words, and the rest—and marshal all the selling points about your product or service in the best order. Later, when you are revising your letter, is the time to make sure you haven't created some problems that will make your company lawyer hate you.

Words to watch out for are *always, whenever, all, perfectly, trouble-free, simply,* and others like them. They signal that you may need to reword what you said, or qualify it.

TESTS AND TESTING

Testing a mailing to pre-determine the returns (or the pull or the pulling power) of a letter is serious business among high-volume mailers. Testing means simply mailing the letter to a portion of the names on your list to see whether you can get a profitable percentage of people to take the action you want. You can see why a business executive would be wise to test a mailing before risking the money to send 10,000 letters, especially if the mailing pieces are expensive.

Suppose your mailing pieces cost 30 cents each (not unusual in a mass mailing) and you make $3 on each sale. Obviously, you have to make sales to 10 percent of the list to break even. Now suppose you have a 90 percent accuracy factor (that is, the percentage of correct addresses). Each 100 letters have to bring 10 orders from every 90 people who get them. Further suppose the purity (how many names on the list are likely prospects instead of deadwood) is 70 percent. This means that your 100 letters have to bring 10 orders from every 63 good prospects (70 percent of 90). This requires about 16 percent pulling power from your letter (10/63). Most sales letters don't do so well. But you could change the situation into one that would be more likely to be profitable by increasing any or all of the accuracy, the purity, or the pulling power—or by decreasing costs of the mailing or increasing the profit on the sale.

Faced with the prospect of a required 16 percent, you'd probably revise plans in order to lower it. And then, to be on the safe side, you'd mail your proposed mailing to a part of your list. On very large mailings the percentage may be small—5 percent or less. If the replies from the sample meet the necessary percentage figures for profitable operations, you'll go ahead. If they don't, you'll revise or drop the whole plan without losing as much money as you would have if you hadn't tested.

Another reason for testing is to find out which of two or more messages has the greater pull or which of two times (day or week or month the mailing piece arrives) is more profitable. *But you can test only one factor at a time!*

You can test one color against another; but if you also vary size, copy, or time, your test doesn't mean a thing. You can test position of coupon *or* order blank versus order card; but if you allow any variation of other factors, your findings are not reliable. You can test one lead against another; but if the rest of the copy, the color and size of the paper, the envelope and stamp, and the time of arrival are not the same, you still have no basis for saying that one lead is better than the other.

Many test results have been published concerning format and timing. If you talk with enough people in the field or read long enough, you'll be reassured—often vehemently!—that every color you've ever seen is the best color for a mailing. You'll find one person swearing by third-class mail and another at it. You'll find out, however, what all experienced persons with judgment discover: Because people and circumstances constantly change, so do the results of testing; what a test suggests this week may not be true next week and probably will not be next year; the only way to be safe is to test in each new situation and then follow through as fast as you can.

Even so, you usually expect only 5–10 percent pulling power. But especially effective copy, carefully selected mailing lists, or unusual offers often increase these percentages. And obviously the reverse of these conditions decreases the pulling power sharply.

Because some series depend on large volume and succeed on small margins, even such apparently insignificant things as the time of arrival are important. Experience has shown that such letters should not arrive in an office at the beginning or ending of a week or month or at the homes of laborers or farmers in the middle of the week. Around Christmas time and April 15 (income tax time) are especially bad times of the year. In general the fall and winter months are better than spring and summer. Of course, seasonal appropriateness of the goods and geographical locations can easily affect this. Even temporary local conditions may.

By keeping careful records on the tests and on the whole mailing, through the years users develop a considerable quantity of experience data that may help guide them in future work.

Before you accept conclusions, however, know the circumstances back of the quoted figures. The results may be worth no more than the paper they're written on, or they may be reliable.

WRITING SALES SERIES

The sales letters we have been discussing are lone efforts to produce or promote sales. Because single sales letters frequently cannot do all the work a series can, probably *just as many* or more sales letters are sent as part of a series as are sent singly. Usually they are obviously processed (form) letters, sent out in large numbers by third-class mail. For further economy they often use some simulated address block instead of an inside address and salutation (like some of the examples in this chapter). By careful phrasing, however, a skillful writer will make the one reader of each copy forget the form and feel that it is a well-adapted message that certainly fits personally.

Whether a letter is a single sales letter or one in a series makes little difference in the techniques or preliminary planning, but in one of the three types of series the letter's organization is more complicated.

The wear-out series

Probably the most widely used of sales series is the wear-out. In it each mailing is a complete sales presentation sent to a large group by almost any firm with a relatively inexpensive product to sell (usually not over $25). The product almost has to be inexpensive, because one letter cannot hope to succeed in persuading most people to buy expensive items by mail from a complete stranger.

After the market analysis, preparation or purchase of a mailing list, and preliminary planning comes the writing of the letter. Probably you and several other executives, and perhaps a letter consultant, will spend hours preparing the letter, or several versions of it. These first few copies may cost several hundred dollars in time and consultant's fees.

Then you test your list, and perhaps several versions of the letter. If one letter seems to have the best pulling power (and that is high enough to make it profitable), you run off hundreds or thousands of copies and mail them out at a carefully selected time. Now that the big investment has been divided among so many, the cost per letter is not so big (maybe only 25–50 cents).

After an interval, usually of one to three weeks, you remove the names of purchasers (unless the product has frequent recurring demand) and send another letter (or sometimes the same one) to the remaining names. Sometimes the second or even the third or fourth mailing brings better results than the first, even with the same letter, because of the buildup of impact. You continue to repeat the mailings until you reach a point at which the percentage of returns from each mailing no longer yields you sufficient profit to continue. Those left on the list are the "hard cases" that apparently won't buy no matter what. The list is worn out; hence the name.

The campaign series

What has been said about the cost of the first copy, the general preliminary planning, the testing, and the usual interval between mailings of the wear-out series also applies to the campaign series. But there the similarity stops.

Contrary to the wear-out series, the campaign series is preplanned not only for the construction of the letters and the intervals between them; you decide, before you start, how many mailings you will send and how long the whole series will run. It is also different in that it is better used to sell or to help sell rather expensive items.

This fact (cost of product) really determines its nature. The theory is that people buy some (usually inexpensive) items quickly, without much thought. These things can be sold by one good complete sales letter, as in the wear-out series. But before buying certain other types of items (usually more expensive but not absolutely essential), most people ponder for a month or more and talk over the situation with friends, financial advisers, and other members of the family. To send a letter which first introduced such an item and, after only two minutes of reading time, asked for the decision on an order card would be to pour money down the proverbial rathole. The reader would laugh at you. Instead of the wear-out, you would use the campaign series for such a situation. You usually do not talk price in the earlier mailings and sometimes not at all. Your action requests (at least in the first few mailings) are to get a show of interest: Write for more information, come to a showroom, authorize the visit of a sales representative.

Having done your preliminary planning as explained, you are ready to plan the series. You decide approximately how long most people on the mailing list would want to think over your offer before making up their minds. Then you decide how frequently they should be reminded to keep them thinking about your product or service. On that basis you decide how many mailings you want to send for the whole series.

The essence of planning the series of letters (whether two or a dozen) is to make the whole series cover the parts of a complete sales presentation and knit them together. In any case the first letter will try hard to get attention and start working at interesting the prospect. Further letters will develop the succeeding sales steps until the last makes a strong drive for action. As people respond, you remove their names from the list.

The last letter is not the only one, however, to which a reader can easily respond. Sellers by mail know that they will not usually get any action from more than half of their prospects. But they also know that in almost any large group some people will be sold on the first contact. Consequently, they usually provide order forms with almost every mailing.

If you have ever let your subscription to a magazine lapse, you have probably received campaign series letters. To help illustrate further the differences between a campaign series and the single-letter sales presentations discussed earlier, however, we have included a typical campaign at the end of this chapter.

The continuous series

The wear-out and campaign series are different in many ways, but they are much more like each other than like the continuous series. Both the wear-out and the campaign series are usually complete sales presentations which try to bring in orders. The continuous series rarely does. Instead of being used by almost any kind of firm, the continuous series is most frequently used by department stores as a goodwill or sales promotion medium, and by oil companies and credit card organizations as a direct-mail selling system. The mailing list for the continuous series is usually the list of the firm's charge customers, instead of one specially prepared in view of a market analysis for a particular item or service being sold. The continuous series usually costs little or no postage because it rides free with the monthly statements; so the usual interval between mailings is longest in the continuous series.

Still, perhaps the biggest distinction is the rigid planning of the campaign series as compared with the hit-or-miss, haphazard nature of the continuous series. It commonly includes special mailings at Easter and Christmas but also on almost any other special occasion the sales manager chooses. As such, it does not run for any set length of time or for any definite number of mailings; and it may *promote* a great *variety* of products while the campaign and wear-out series are *selling one.*

* * *

The following direct-mail campaign directed to accounting firms, tax services, and law firms emphasizes the economy of making dry photocopies instantly with an Adeco Auto-Copier (costing about $350) instead of having papers and carbons typed. Although planned for firms in Alabama, Georgia, and Florida, the letters could just as well be sent within one city or over the entire country. A sales representative within a city could readily assemble a mailing list from the Yellow Pages of the phone book. The Atlanta district manager (for the three states) could assemble a list also from the Yellow Pages of phone books for cities in the area (available in any large library, such as the Atlanta Public Library), or buy the list. Certainly a nationwide mailing list would be more inexpensively purchased than assembled.

The mailings are planned for intervals of about three weeks. For economy they use a simulated address block instead of an inside address and salutation, are printed, and go third class. Each mailing includes a reply card which reads something like this:

Adeco Auto-Copier

Yes, I would like to know more about how the Adeco Auto-Copier will help me. Please call me and arrange an appointment.

The card provides blanks for indicating name of individual, position, company, and address.

The first mailing includes a 12-page, two-color booklet containing illustrations, savings estimates and comparisons, and information about the company and its organization.

You can save
Up to 80 percent on
Copying jobs . . .

. . . by letting your typists make black-and-white photocopies with the Adeco Auto-Copier.

In less than 45 seconds an unskilled operator can turn out a legally acceptable, error-proof copy of an original—one that would take your typist at least 10 minutes to copy. If your office produces only 15 copies a day, the Auto-Copier can save you about $3 each working day. When you need to turn out large numbers of copies, the Auto-Copier makes them for you as fast as 75 an hour, at proportionate savings.

Your Auto-Copier takes a picture without using a camera. So in turning out copies of complicated tax forms, accounting forms, government records, and deeds, it assures you of error-proof, smudge-proof copies. One compact photocopy unit does it all; the Auto-Copier is a fully automatic, continuous copier and processing unit combined. Since it dries its prints automatically, they're ready for your instant use.

And you don't need a separate timer or printer either. In just two simple steps you can turn out prints made from any original up to 11 by 17 inches whether printed on one or two sides.

Just put the Auto-Copier on any convenient desk or table, plug it in, and you're ready to start. You can copy any confidential material right in the privacy of your own office in just a few seconds. Read the description in the enclosed folder of the Auto-Copier's easy, simple operation.

The Auto-Copier will actually enable you to have one unskilled clerk do the copying work of six expert typists. Just sign and return the enclosed card so that your Adeco representative can stop by and show you how to let the Auto-Copier cut the high cost of duplicating records.

(Signature)

Auto-Copies of tax forms are fully acceptable and approved by the Internal Revenue Service.

The second letter accompanies a four-page, two-color folder headlined "Make dry photocopies of tax returns instantly!" In the upper left corner of the letter appears the picture of an office worker operating an Auto-Copier. To the right of the illustration is the headline

MAKE
TAX RETURN COPIES
INSTANTLY
with the Adeco Auto-Copier.

Now your typists can
Turn out tax return
Copies in just a few seconds!

Tax copying work which used to take hours you can now do in seconds with the Adeco Auto-Copier. And these copies are fully accepted and approved by the Internal Revenue Service.

You can actually reduce by one third to one half the number of statistical typists you employ. Since the average statistical typist in this area makes about $100 a week, you'll be able to save at least $30 each week for each one you now employ. Or your typists can use the time saved to get out your other important papers and reports.

You know how difficult it is to type tax copies speedily, align them accurately, and avoid carbon smudges. With the Auto-Copier you need to type and proofread only the original, then turn out error-proof, clean, legible copies at a rate as high as 75 an hour—copies your typists never have to align, erase, or proofread.

And on involved legal reports or contracts you'll find your Auto-Copier especially helpful. Whether your paper is opaque or translucent, you are assured of clear copies, and you can reproduce copies on both sides of a single sheet too.

Eliminate the expensive, time-consuming job of typing extra copies of tax returns in your office. Whether you're working on state or federal tax forms, corporation or individual, you can get the copies out three times as fast with the Auto-Copier. Just sign and return the enclosed card so that your Adeco representative can come by and show you all the ways you can use an Auto-Copier.

(Signature)

Turn to page 4 of the enclosed folder and note the three simple steps in making tax return copies.

Letter No. 3, accompanied by a one-page folder, drives for a demonstration (with the postcard altered in wording accordingly):

When you need copies . . .

. . . of tax forms, accounting records, government forms, or letters, you can be confident that any made on the Auto-Copier will be as clear, unsmudged, and error-proof as the original. No more faulty copies because of poor alignment or carbons that are too light to use. And your copies are turned out from 3 to 10 times as fast as carbons ever can be.

The average typist, even the good typist, is hard pressed to turn out in one hour even six perfect copies of a tax return or many other government forms the average business has to produce. The Auto-Copier can turn out 75 perfect copies. And no proofreading or corrections are necessary.

Your Auto-Copier takes up no more space than a standard typewriter. Just plug it in, and your typist is ready to copy. Because the Auto-Copier is completely electric, you can do all your copying work automatically from start to finish.

Try the Auto-Copier for a week. We'll be glad to bring one around for you to see how easily it will fit many of your copying needs. Fill in and return the enclosed card so that your Adeco representative can demonstrate in your office its value to you and your company.

(Signature)

Notice Auto-Copier's other exclusive advantages described in the enclosure.

The fourth letter shows an office worker turning out copies on the Auto-Copier while looking directly at the reader and saying:

I've typed thousands
of tax returns.

And I know the Adeco Auto-Copier can save you money because it can reduce your tax copying work up to 80 percent.

For two years I have typed tax forms in the offices of C. C. Putnam, CPA, 166 Stallings Building, Atlanta 30218.

Turning out an original copy of a complicated tax form is a job in itself, but typing 10 or 12 clear, unsmudged carbon copies is next to impossible.

Now just a minute! I'm not a poor typist. I can type 60 words a minute with no errors on a 10-minute test. That is certainly as good as the average typist, and, I confidently believe, a lot better. But I still have trouble aligning carbons, making corrections, and typing sufficiently clear and legible copies.

With the Auto-Copier I simply type the original and run off as many copies as I need. I can now turn out in one day reports that used to take at least two days. Each detail of the original is accurately and legibly reproduced—and the only copy I have to proofread is the form itself!

Our clients like Auto-Copied forms. And they're fully accepted by the government.

In addition to tax form copies, I use the Auto-Copier for letters, bank records, claims, graphs, or invoices. No more costly retyping or hand copying! And no more messy, time-consuming carbons!

My employer and I agree that the Auto-Copier is the answer to our copying needs. Your Adeco representative would like to show you how the Auto-Copier can solve your copying problems too. Check the enclosed card today for a demonstration in your office.

The letter carries the signature of the speaker and the title as secretary to Mr. Putnam.

The fifth mailing reestablishes the main talking points and stresses much harder the advantages of having the sales representative come in and demonstrate:

> Can your typists turn out
> 75 perfect copies an hour?
> With the Auto-Copier they can!
>
> The Auto-Copier will enable you to have one unskilled clerk do the copying work of six expert typists.
>
> In addition, you are assured of perfect accuracy—each detail of the original is accurately reproduced without any possibility of error. And there's no need for tedious, time-consuming proofreading and checking either.
>
> In turning out copies of complicated tax forms, legal reports and records, and accounting data on the Auto-Copier, your typist can run off up to 20 clear, unsmudged copies in no more than five minutes. Since no errors appear, Auto-Copier eliminates erasing time and messiness.
>
> You can put your Auto-Copier on any convenient desk or table, since it measures 20 by 11 inches. You simply plug it in, and you're ready to start using it. No special installation is necessary. Anyone can run it.
>
> Since Auto-Copies are processed and dried automatically, they're ready for your instant use. You need no developing, washing, drying, or printing space because the Auto-Copier does everything in one simple operation.
>
> Your Auto-Copier representative would like to talk with you about your particular copying needs and show you how other companies are using Auto-Copier to help cut copying costs. Just sign and mail the enclosed card for a demonstration in your office.

The sixth mailing is a copy of the first letter, with a reminder memo attached.

Mailing No. 7 is the booklet sent with the first letter. Attached to the booklet is a memo in simulated handwriting:

> If you didn't get a chance to read the first copy of the booklet I sent you recently, here's another.
>
> It will show you how the Auto-Copier can help you cut the high cost of duplicating records.

Of course, the reply card is also enclosed.

The eighth and final mailing is another memo, this time attached to the same folder that accompanied the second letter:

> You can make photocopies of tax forms instantly with the Auto-Copier. Notice in the enclosed folder the three easy steps necessary to turn out tax copies fully acceptable to the Internal Revenue Service.
>
> To find out how the Auto-Copier can lighten your tax copying problems, return the enclosed card.

CASES FOR SALES

1. *Company:* McMillan's Boat Charter Service, 659 River Road, Manistee, Michigan 49660, Phone: 616-765-9876. *Mailing list:* Former customers who like to fish. *Facts:* Light-tackle fishing; Lake trout and Salmon Charters; two five-hour trips daily, 7 and 2:00; all tackle and bait furnished; minimum of four people; maximum, six people; Captain: Marion Spence; $4.00 per hour per person; fishing was best 1974–75; lakes well stocked. *Enclosure:* Folder with picture of a Dagati, of three people with ten fish.

2. Although the high-water mark of the trading stamp industry was reached several years ago, your firm, Pibald Stamps, 432 Michigan Avenue, Chicago, Illinois 60698, has been leading the industry growth charts for two years. Your secret is well-staffed and -stocked regional redemption centers and one-week mail-order service out of your local centers. A survey you took when you worked for S & S Green Stamps showed that many people were told at the redemption center that the item they wanted was out of stock or on the next weekly truck. And if they ordered by mail, they rarely received their premium within the four-week period suggested on the order forms. By significantly reducing the time the customer had to wait to get premiums, and by maintaining a 97 percent on-hand-when-asked-for ratio, your company has continued to grow in spite of the current trend away from trading stamps among some sectors of American business.

Write a form letter that could be sent to gas station owners in California in which you present and sell your Pibald program. Your six regional centers—Los Angeles, San Diego, Fresno, San Francisco, Sacramento, and Bakersfield—are store and warehouse operations that handle both in-person and mail-order redemptions. The cost to the dealer is $150 for $15,000 worth of stamps; that's $100 in stamps for each dollar invested. Stamps come in three denominations: $.10, $1.00, and $5.00. Your action ending will be to get the reader to initial and return a card that authorizes a visit from your sales team.

3. *Company:* Zodiac Simplex, 315 West Allegon, Lansing, Michigan 48910. *Mailing list:* Subscribers to *Field and Stream. Product:* Inflatable boat you can stow in a closet, transport in a car's trunk, set up and launch at beach, riverbank, or dock. Unparalleled stability and load-carrying capability. Safe and seaworthy (avoid possible legal problems). The dinghie looks like an oblong doughnut, is called Zodiac Simplex. Floorboards stiffen the fabric bottoms and make them feel more stable. Rowing is easy because this model has a keelson (a separate, inflatable chamber running fore-and-aft the floorboards). It comes with oarlocks, outboard-motor bracket (or transom assembly), and floorboards. Can be set up in ten

minutes by one person. Holds three people comfortably. Maximum motor, 4 hp. Price $531 (including floorboards and outboard bracket). *Action:* Ask reader to fill out a card for more information.

4. *Company:* Glory, 3200 West Peterson Avenue, Chicago, Illinois 60659. *Mailing list:* Office managers of industrial plants. *Product:* Glory Coffee Service Plan. If the office manager buys just the Glory coffee, you furnish the Glory brewer, creme, sugar, and filters free. The coffee is Glory's finest—a gourmet blend found in elegant hotel dining rooms or exclusive restaurants. The free service is that you see to it that the office is fully supplied at all times and you personally phone each month to make sure everything is running smoothly. The coffee costs just a few cents a cup. Ask the reader to fill out a card you'll enclose. The card brings 100 free cups of Glory's Finest Coffee and will introduce the reader to the finest, fastest, most attentive Coffee Service Plan in the business. The employees will have more energy, production time, and appreciation than before Glory.

5. With a mailing list of members of the Nationwide Spa in the Midwest, set up a form letter with a faked inside address. Your company, Greenwood Associates, Inc., Glenview, Illinois 60005, has a new product called the French Twist Automatic Calorie Counter which it hopes to sell by mail for $14.95. This watch-like device, which is clipped to a belt as you would a pedometer, automatically computes the calorie burn-off with each step the wearer takes. Walking, jogging, jumping, and similar activities cause a hand on the dial to revolve, and the measurements accumulate as calories expended. A doughnut contains about 151 calories, equivalent to the energy expended by an average person jogging for about 14 minutes or walking for about 49 minutes. Enclose a folder with pictures of the French Twist Automatic Calorie Counter and an order card.

6. As Oliver Davidson, Director of Sales for Collector's House (P.O. Box 567, Boston, Massachusetts 02118), you want to try selling by mail your decorator-designed, precision-crafted (by Thomalison Instrument Company, a respected leader in its field) Clock Weather Stations to a specially purchased national mailing list of homeowners (homes tax-assessed at $30,000 and up), at $34.95 plus $2.01 for postage and handling, billed after a 15-day free trial period (or $6.71 a month for six months, including postage, handling, and interest of 1½ percent a month, 18 percent annual rate). An enclosed franked and addressed order card states the 15-day, no-obligation, free-trial offer and has blanks for the number of Clock Weather Stations ordered (make wonderful gifts), the choice of payment plan, and the signature.

You will also include, with the letter, a full-size, full-color illustration (on heavy paper) for the reader to hang on a wall to see how it looks (gold faces with black hands in sculptured dark oak frame, blends with any decor). On the back will be directions for mounting, restatement of the basic offer, a reduced-size picture of the three-dial instrument (one right under the other), and a picture of the bonus for ordering this month —a round outdoor thermometer. By the three dials will be the wording:

Barometer—a fine instrument for weather forecasting; indicates atmospheric pressure changes preceding likely weather changes; adjustable to your altitude; enables you to check on the U.S. Weather Bureau just like a professional.

Clock—a truly fine U.S.-made clock with no wires (operates on size "C" flashlight batteries).

Temperature and Humidity—Accurate indoor thermometer and measure of the wetness or dryness of the air.

As usual, however, the main sales piece will be your letter—a strict form with facsimile inside address and salutation—which you now have to write.

7. Commonwealth Manufacturing Company/165 North Broad Street/ Philadelphia, Pa. 19121/Attention Mr. John Still/from Capital Travel Service, Inc./Edward E. Rankin, Manager/International Tours Division/ 919 Linden Avenue/Minneapolis, MN 55403/Subject: Executive "Sea-School." Beginning next February 14, Capital will launch another of its famous "Sea-Schools" for top-echelon executives. Leaving San Francisco Harbor, Capital sails on one of the most luxurious ocean-going vessels afloat. This 20-day cruise includes stops at Hilo, Kahului, and Honolulu, Hawaii. En route, seminar sessions, held in beautifully appointed meeting rooms, will be led by leaders of international reputation. Growing professionally while enjoying soft Pacific breezes is the deal of a lifetime! Complete details enclosed give dates, prices, seminar leaders, and social events —all planned with executive interests in mind. Action ending. Make it easy for John Still to reply with an addressed, stamped card.

8. With the love-bug season approaching, you feel it will be a good time to introduce your new Bug-Off insect deflector screen. The Bug-Off screen fits across the front of any automobile and catches bugs before they spatter on the paint and windshield. Love-bugs take the paint off with them when you try to wash them off. The Bug-Off protective screen has a thin linen backing that catches the smashed bugs that pass through the $\frac{1}{16}$ inch squares of the nylon screen, but the cloth is not thick enough to block the flow of air to the car's cooling system. And the adjustable Bug-Off screen fits all cars, from Cadillacs to VW's. The screen can be cleaned simply by spraying with a garden hose and scrubbing the bugs off with a broom or a stiff bristle brush. Write a form letter that could be sent to car owners in the Gainesville/Orlando, Florida, area. In your letter, present and sell the Bug-Off screen to the prospects on the mailing list

you purchased from the Florida Department of Motor Vehicles. The screen costs $5.00 and $.50 for mailing costs. All the customer has to do is take it out of the mailing tube and tie it on to the car. Your company is Bugs-Away, 811 St. Johns Ave., Jacksonville, Florida 32666.

9. Using the information in the previous case, write a form letter that you can send to auto accessories and hardware store owners in the Gaines-ville/Orlando area. Point out to the dealer the advantages of stocking and selling the Bug-Off screen now that the love-bug season is approaching. The cost to the dealer is $3.00; the suggested retail price is $5.00.

10. As mail sales executive for the Redi-Frame picture frame company, 987 Springside Avenue, New Haven, Connecticut 06517, write a form letter to accompany your brochure (featuring your complete line of hard-wood and metal frames and colored matboards). You want to send this letter (and brochure) to the treasurers of all the sorority and fraternity houses in Connecticut. Your own fraternity/sorority experience as an undergraduate at Central College has convinced you that you have a market here; your chapter spent over $200 a year for framing materials to preserve the annual chapter composite and important social events. You add the details. This is a C–plan letter. You may want to talk prices.

11. Write the same letter as described in preceding case, but to a dealer, the Frame Frontier, 862 Hoyt Avenue, Hartford, Connecticut 06876. Show Mr. Ford Sutton how he can make money in a university town by providing a framing service for faculty and students, featuring, of course, your complete line of custom-cut frames and colored matboards. You will want to include your brochure and, perhaps, some sales-promotion materials.

12. As Richard Burgtorf, Corporate Card Sales Manager, United Express Company, 100 Colony Square, Suite 522, Atlanta, Georgia 30309, telephone (404) 892–7458, promote United Express Corporate Card to a mailing list of members of American Automobile Association. Ninety percent of all travel expenses can be paid with the United Express Corporate Card. The holder of the card reduces bookkeeping expenses; the uniform expense reporting gives a monthly descriptive bill broken down by region, district, department, and provides substantiation for every expense incurred; increases profits by not having to use cash. Ask the reader to return the enclosed card so that a sales representative can show the receiver how the Corporate Card is different from the personal card or any other company card arrangement.

13. *Company:* Middleton Design and Equipment Company, 409 Linton Avenue, Providence, Rhode Island 02908. *Mailing list:* Hospitals in the Southeast. *Product:* Fly-Grid, a unique, all-electric flying insect electrocutor. Each Fly-Grid unit consists of three basic parts: (1) a certified radiant energy black light fluorescent lamp that attracts flying insects, (2) a grid charged with high voltage that electrocutes insects on contact, and (3) a removable insect catch tray to trap and contain all insect remains. Five models are available but the most popular is the five-foot tall "Big Boy" which is used around food processing plants, zoos, catering places, etc. Another popular model is a small, light-weight portable unit which can be used for patios, small office areas, and dining rooms. The Fly-Grid is the only system which health departments will allow to operate 24 hours a day. The Fly Grid is guaranteed for three years except the bulb, which must be replaced once a year.

Action: Enclose a card so that a sales representative can call on the hospital. Price will depend on the model. *Testimony:* Virginia Fried Chicken processing plants use Fly-Grid exclusively.

14. *Company:* Advent Corporation, 3600 Riley Avenue, Camden, New Jersey 08109. *Mailing list:* 500 stereo-component stores. *Product:* $2,495 television set with a 4 × 6 foot screen. Carlin Audio, small hi-fi shop in Dayton, Ohio, test marketed it and sold 12 sets and turned down orders for 30 more. Five of the sets were purchased by individual consumers and the remainder by businesses like bars and banks. One early customer, Richard Gibbs, an executive of an oil-distributing company, says that he "couldn't be any more thrilled even though the first few weeks it has you mesmerized." He figures he now watches up to twice as much television as before he bought the set. Lang's Bowlerama, a Crenston, R.I., bowling alley that has an Advent set in its 125-seat cocktail lounge, turned away "dozens of people" who wanted to watch the Super Bowl. Its profits are up 20 percent since it bought the set.

The set isn't designed for your average living room or recreation room. It comes in two pieces. A 33-inch-high white plastic console with conventional TV controls projects separate red, green, and blue images 8 feet onto a curved, 4 × 6 foot aluminum-foil screen, where the images merge into a bright, sharp picture. Sets are easily serviced by knowledgeable TV servicemen, who can be quickly familiarized with the set's operations. It's best viewed in a darkened room and is difficult to move. Because the screen is curved, it can't be seen by anyone sitting too far to one side. The screen is so fragile it can be damaged simply from the touch of a finger.

Enclosures: Folder with picture of the television screen and card for representative to come by the stereo-component store.

15. The bicycle thief is probably the busiest person on most campuses these days. Despite proliferation of chain locks, yokes, and burglar alarms, the demand for high-cost, ten-speed bikes makes the thefts a lucrative business. "Thieves were stealing an average of two bikes a day from the racks," says Ken Smith, student body president of American River College in Sacramento, California. Last fall the student body association installed 34 bike lockers—a kind of mini-garage for bicycles. Nearly impregnable, the polyester-laminated fiberboard boxes have aluminum frames and pick-proof, seven-pin tumbler locks. They sell for $146 each and rent for about 25 cents a day. As Director of Sales for Rodney Corporation, 609 St. Charles Avenue, Los Angeles, California 90041, write a sales letter to the purchasing agents of all major universities telling them about your Bike Lokr, suggesting they purchase directly from you, and then rent (coin-operate) the lockers to students. Within the past year Rodney Corporation has placed coin-operated units at bus and rapid transit stations, shopping malls and at the University of Miami.

16. *Company:* Wright Curtis, Post Office Box 12377, Omaha, Nebraska 68102. *Mailing list:* People who own campers. *Product:* Handy-Power Convertor (5″ long, 3″ wide by 3½″ deep). Delivers 110 Volts AC electrical power from car. Operates lawnmowers, coffee makers, heaters, hot plates, light bulbs, iron, plus many more uses. Easily installed in just minutes by anyone. No belts or pulleys. No moving parts. Does not shorten life of alternator. Handy-Power unit quickly starts cars with dead batteries eliminating need for jumper cables. Helps overcome inadequate camping facility difficulties for the camper, sportsman, and other outdoorsmen.

Cost: $29.95.

Warranty: All Handy-Power Convertors sold with warranty against parts and workmanship defects. The units will be repaired or replaced for a period of five years for any unit that fails to perform properly (except unauthorized alterations or repairs damage) for a maximum charge of $5.00, regardless of condition of unit. Orders processed and Converter shipped within 72 hours.

17. As Wright Curtis (preceding case) you find that you do not have time to handle all of your sales individually—business is too much for you and your wife. So you decide to sell partly through dealers—and have acquired a good list of mobile home dealers in the Midwest. Write a form letter selling the Handy-Power Convertor to them at $20 delivered (in cartons of 5, 10, and 20), with return privileges on any not sold in six months.

18. After seven years of preparation, The Book-of-the-Month Club, Camp Hill, Pennsylvania, developed a comprehensive home-study program for reading improvement. Reading speed can be increased as much as 50 percent in just two weeks' time without cost or obligation. For the first two weeks, the subscriber will use a portfolio ($5.75) and a Reading Pacer ($70.50) which will be used with other portfolios. If, after studying and using the first portfolio, the reader wants the others, they will be sent at the rate of one every three weeks. If the reader is not sure of improvement, then all the materials may be sent back within two weeks and pay nothing.

The First Portfolio contains: Basic Instruction Guide, Training Manual, Eye-and-Mind Practice Section, Speed-and-Comprehension Practice Material, Practice Material for the Reading-Pacer, Speed-and-Comprehension Tests, Reading Improvement Chart. Each of the portfolios takes up a different reading problem, and in each case the problem being covered is first explained, and then the particular weakness causing it is dealt with by means of specially prepared practice materials. The serious student need spend no more than an average of 15 minutes a day to keep up with the instruction. Psychologists have found that the ability to read swiftly and with complete comprehension is an acquired and not an inborn skill. Slow readers are almost invariably the product of poor training at an early age.

Write a special sales letter to your large membership list. Include (assumed) a picture of the Reading Pacer and the Portfolios along with an order form and envelope.

19. Already 80,000 users enjoy Hydro-Fin (by Hydro-Fin, Inc., 175 Ichthus Street, Detroit, Michigan 48224). Attaches somewhat like a small outboard. Operates with one hand. Leaves one hand free to troll or cast. Propels boat silently, easily, up to three miles per hour. For fishermen, duck hunters, sail boaters. $17.95, fully guaranteed. Try to get an order on the enclosed blank. Enclosed booklet shows pictures, details, and testimonials. How would you get a mailing list?

20. For the Infant's Diaper Service, your city, set up a letter to go to parents of new-born children informing them of your once-a-week diaper service. The soiled diapers are picked up, sterilized, and laboratory tested for cleanliness, and returned to the parents. Enclose a price list. Average new baby uses 100 diapers a week, a cost of $4.10 or about 4 cents a diaper. With the service comes a plastic hamper for $3.25. The customer may keep the hamper after using the service one month. Disposable diapers for daytime and nightime for new-born would run about 5–6 cents depending on quality.

21. Your company, Stanley and Stroughton, Inc., 497 Newburg, Neenah, Wisconsin 54946, manufactures Firmaides, dinner napkins 17 inches square made of triple-ply, fine-quality cellulose. Market research shows that some commercial restaurateurs pay more for rented table linens than the cost of these napkins (one case of 2,000 napkins sells for $30). When they use their own linens, pilferage losses and replacements due to fraying and cigaret burns amount to a significant cost. Operators who are using paper service are dissatisfied with the small size and poor quality of the napkins, but operators of fine establishments are interested in a luxury type of paper napkin for cocktail lounge or luncheon service. With economy and quality appeals, write a letter to hotel managers in the East. For our sample you write Mary Hunter, Hunter's Lodge, Portland, Maine 04155. See whether you can convince your prospect that this snowy-white napkin is far superior to ordinary paper napkins. It is intended for use instead of linen in the finest inns, hotels, and clubs, where patrons expect the best.

With these large paper napkins that won't slide off laps, the hotel or lodge avoids laborious ironing, sorting, counting, bundling, and handling. Also Firmaides have no holes, no frayed edges, no rust spots, or stains. Besides calling Hunter's attention to the enclosed sample napkin, suggest ordering by filling out the reply card.

22. *Company:* Champion Travel Bureau, Inc., Champion Building, P.O. Box 4327, Birmingham, Alabama 35206. *Mailing list:* Heads of Science departments, High Schools in Alabama.

Message: Low-cost trip to Australia June 1–23 with the Alabama Astronomical and Biological Expedition, led by Conrad Klein, director of the Birmingham Zoo. Travel to Sydney, Cairns, Green Island, Alice Springs, Ayers Rock, Melbourne, Perth, Brusselton and see fauna, coral reefs, aborigines, eclipse of the sun around 1:15 P.M., June 20. Stop for visit in the Fiji Islands on return. Cost from Birmingham back to Birmingham is $2,595 per person, share basis at hotels, $198 extra for single room if desired and available. Deposit of $50 per person required at time of booking. *Enclosures:* Tour Reservation Form and descriptive picture folder.

23. With a mailing list of 50,000 owners of homes valued from $40,000 to $65,000 in the Northwest, your company, Alliance Swift Door, 9008 Prospect, Tulsa, Oklahoma 74112, sends a letter and pamphlet on the integrated-circuit door opener for garage doors. Previously you have handled automatic door openers that operated by radio control. Some customers complained that they were highly temperamental. Now your company has perfected a garage door opener that is operated by small integrated circuits, or IC's. The garage door is automatically opened, and the light goes on automatically when the driver pushes a small panel (2 by 4 inches). The receiving panel in the garage and the pushbutton transmitter are the size of a 3- by 6-inch box. Although these operate the same way as the radio control, the units are smaller and cost more ($180 instead of $160), but they last longer. These have a five-year guarantee instead of two. They have been tested on 60,000 single and double garage doors in six major areas of the United States (East, Southeast, West, Midwest, North, and Northwest). The company will repair or replace without charge any defective Alliance Swift door opener within five years of date of purchase. If the homeowner has several cars, there is no problem of mounting a control set in each car.

Only the driver can open the garage from the car. Safety is a big selling point for this item. The family or just one member of the family can feel secure in driving up to a dark house, pushing the IC panel, and having the garage light come on and the door open. Before leaving the car, the driver can close the door from the car panel, or from the garage reset panel.

24. Since 1961 the rate for all serious crimes has more than doubled. From 1973 to 1974 it jumped 17 percent. In the past 14 years, the rate of robberies has increased 255 percent, forcible rape 143 percent, aggravated assault 153 percent and murder 106 percent (*Time*, June 30, 1975, p. 10).

Whether it's a drug addict in desperate need of a fix, a vandal out for kicks, a burglar looking for available cash, or a maniac looking for rape, the homeowner has become a leading target for criminal attack.

More homes are unattended during the daytime than ever before because in many cases both husband and wife work, because more families own two homes, and because we enjoy longer vacations. Another reason, reports FBI, is that prevention and detection are most difficult for law enforcement agencies due to the tremendous volume of offenses and lack of adequate police patrols. Also, law enforcement agencies are successful in solving fewer than one out of every five cases of burglary. This low clearance rate indicates the lack of deterrent and the slight risk of detection.

No lock—regardless of size or cost—will keep a determined criminal out. At best, it will only slow him down.

As an authorized dealer for American Protective Services, Inc., of your city, write a letter to homeowners ($30,000 and up) pointing out their need for a Safograph Security System. With this system, the homeowner has a system designed for individual needs. If desired, the system can even notify the police.

Urge the homeowner to mail the enclosed business reply card for more information. There is no cost or obligation for the security survey and equipment demonstration. You will not talk price. These installations can run anywhere from $600 to several thousands depending on degree of protection the homeowner wants (mere alarm, hookup with police or fire department and the like). These points have to be discussed with the prospect face to face.

25. Your company—Samuels, Speery, and Sand, 5340 Delmar Boulevard, Saint Louis, Missouri 63196—perfected a formula for protecting tools from rot, rust, heat, and cold. Tool-Guard stops splitting of wooden handles, waterproofs joints, penetrates wooden surfaces, sets up a weather-resistant, glovelike coating, leaving no sticky surfaces, making tools grip easier, safeguards metals. As a test 5,000 tools were tested two years ago in Saint Louis. During the two years the tools were exposed to rain, snow, sun, and sleet, but they didn't rust, nor did the handles deteriorate in any way. In a short time this product pays for itself. A 1-gallon metal drum,

$19.50 retail, is enough to paint 600 tools. Also available in a 4-ounce plastic bottle with applicator top (20 tools, $1) and 16-ounce bottle ($2.95). You're going to send a one-page letter to all contractors in the New York-New Jersey-Pennsylvania area. Your mailing will be a four-page folder: the letter on the first page; two-color illustrations, copy, and endorsements on the rest. (For class purposes just write the letter and assume the rest.) On the fourth and final page will be an order blank. To cut down on the expense of mailing, use a faked inside address imitative of the three-line inside address. Even your signature as sales manager can be processed.

26. Try a mailing promoting Tool-Guard to hardware dealers in the New York-New Jersey-Pennsylvania area (see preceding case). A 4-ounce plastic bottle with applicator top wholesales for 50 cents, 16-ounce bottle, $1.75. To make ordering easier, you've enclosed an order blank along with pictures of the product. You can afford to send card displays and envelope stuffers to help promote Tool-Guard. You are running full-page ads in the monthly *Hardware Review.*

27. One of your direct-mail jobs is to write a two-letter campaign for Mark Baldwin Company, 6719 Hanover Street, Madison, Illinois 60053, to promote a brown simulated leather desk diary called the Executive Organizer which sells for $4.95. Your mailing list: executives, supervisory personnel, dealers, and distributors. Main theme of first letter: "Give a gift your friends will truly appreciate this Christmas." Theme of second letter: "You are in good company when you use the Executive Organizer as a Christmas gift." First mailing: August; second in September. Each mailing includes an order blank and a picture of product.

Features: page size—6¾″ × 8¾″ with ruled lines spaced just right; all entries written on flat surface from first page to last so executive can see a "week at a glance" with room for notes, dates, appointments; gold embossed tab indexing for every month of year, plus removable A to Z name, address, and telephone index helps user organize and plan; separate expense section for tax records; telephone area code numbers for every section of country; auto mileage distances between 192 principal cities; guide to fine dining; basic weights and measures; buying power by sections and states; dates to remember; vital facts, decimal equivalents. Every Executive Organizer comes in attractive gift box at no extra charge. A custom-made mailing carton comes for each at no extra charge. Name of each gift recipient can be embossed on front cover for 40 cents per unit. In this two-letter campaign ask your reader to order the Executive Organizer for Christmas gifts to business friends.

28. A recent survey shows that 80% of the families living in homes assessed at $30,000 or more have outdoor cooking facilities. You know from your own experience and that of your friends that the most common (and much preferred—for food flavor) fuel is charcoal and that an almost universal problem is getting it started and the fire spread throughout, ready for use. Whether you (or anybody you know) uses kindling, a liquid starter fluid, or an electric starter, it takes at least 40 minutes before you're ready to cook. Your company, Holiday House, Inc., P.O. Box 62, Kansas City, Missouri 64133, has therefore put on the market a handy gadget called FireFly (a small blower). Eleven ounces, starts fires in minutes, revives fires in seconds. Hand-operated, directing a flow of air where you want it, Firefly has even a charcoal fire ready in ten minutes. Ideal gift, beautiful charcoal color, textured finish, hand-fitting handle. Fully guaranteed. $5.25 plus 50 cents for postage and handling. Write a letter to sell this needed, popular-where-used product to a large mailing list and attach an explanation of how you would get your mailing list. Assume an enclosure sheet with details and picture.

29. Sell the Firefly (preceding case) to hardware dealers in quantity at $4—as the manufacturer (Outdoors Specialties, 6340 South Jefferson, St. Louis, Missouri 63166) which also supplies Holiday House. Assume the enclosure.

30. As your teacher directs, writing from Holiday House or the manufacturer, sell the electric charcoal starter mentioned (preceding two cases) to appropriate mailing lists, assuming appropriate enclosures. It's a looplike heating rod on cool wooden handle; six-foot cord; uses 110 volt current; runs ten minutes. Then fire spreads in 30 (or with blower in 10). No kindling or messy liquid starter required; hence no danger, objectionable odor, or chemical tastes in food.

31. Six months ago a major manufacturer of auto batteries decided to put out a really superior battery and sell it at a low-profit price, thinking that the public would recognize its quality (from description) and appreciate the quality enough to buy in high volume, though paying a little more than for ordinary competitors' batteries. Sales were slow. So a marketing consultant suggested trying to use members' confidence in the AAA to overcome buyer doubts. The manufacturer convinced the Peninsula Motor Club (Florida branch of AAA) to promote and back the battery, and get AAA-authorized service stations as sales outlets (sales to AAA members only).

As advertising manager in the offices of the PMC (1515 N.W. Shore Boulevard, Tampa, 33602), you have induced the service stations to handle the batteries in all sizes and have been running quarter-page ads in monthly issues of the much read and respected newspaper for members, *The PMC Explorer*. Above a picture, the heading reads, "Introducing the battery so good it's guaranteed by your AAA club." Underneath, the copy says new case more durable, 12 percent more lead and electrolyte inside, will crank your car twice as long and 29 percent faster than original equipment, more reserve power, more dependable; sellers will replace free if battery fails within 18 months or replace at pro-rata charges between 18 and 48 months. A table gives the price list (no-discount prices of $30.95 to $34.95) by sizes and kinds of cars they fit.

Now you have decided to try a sales letter to go to your membership list, as a means of selling even more of the now fast-selling battery.

32. As the sales manager of the manufacturer referred to in the preceding case (ECCO Batteries, Joplin, Missouri 64801), write the letter (with assumed appropriate enclosures) to convince the Peninsula Motor Club to handle the batteries as it is doing.

33. Because of the recent rash of burglaries in the Wilkinsburg, Pennsylvania, area, your company, Sutton Protective Systems Corporation, 625 Stanwix, Pittsburg, Pa. 15230, decides to offer your line of home-protection devices for sale to Wilkinsburg home owners. You sell items such as taped human voices and taped dogs barking that are set off when someone enters the house, silent alarms that call the police but don't alert the burglar, special locks, some that work on radio frequencies or voice commands, etc., not to mention your complete line of non-pickable key and combination locks and door chains. Most of the items are quite expensive.

To introduce your line of merchandise you will use a mailing campaign in the Wilkinsburg area. You will interest your potential customers by offering to sell them Light-On automatic relay switches that periodically turn the lights off and on in a house, making it appear that someone is at home. You can sell half a dozen of the relay switches for the low price of $4.98 plus $.50 handling charge (that's $2.00 below the normal retail price). What you really want to do, however, besides selling Light-On switches, is to get the customer to authorize a visit from one of your home-protection consultants who can sell a complete protection system tailored to the needs of a particular dwelling. Selling the Light-On switches at a small profit gives you a foot in the door, the chance to sell a more expensive (and profitable) protection system. Make it easy for the customer to reply. Tell him exactly what you want him to do. You may want to use several enclosures.

34. Two weeks later follow up the mailing described in the preceding case. This mailing centers around a success story of how Dr. William Simpson's home (87 Woodridge Road, Philadelphia, 19119) was protected by tapes and Light-On automatic relay switches. Robbers attempted to break in but heard the taped recorded dog barks and people talking. They became scared, so broke in next door and took a new colored television and some jewelry. Enclose a card for easy replying.

35. Write a letter offering the products mentioned in the two previous cases to hardware dealers and building-supply stores in Pennsylvania's major cities. Read the check list carefully; make sure you understand the "whip-back" technique.

36. *Letterhead:* Schwanz Hillmaster Bicycles, 900 Acorn Road, Rahway, New Jersey 07066. *Inside address:* Martin Straight, owner of Straight's Cycle Shop, 804 West University Avenue, Urbana, Illinois 61801. *Signature block:* Sincerely, Melba Garrett, Sales Director. *Information:* Convince this local dealer that the Schwanz Hillmaster will sell well and earn a reasonable profit. The Hillmaster wholesales for $60 and retails for $100 (suggested retail price). That's a 67 percent markup over the cost price. Aim details to the dealer and show him how you will help him sell these new Schwanz bicycles. Facts that you can interpret: wide ratio ten-speed derailleur for fast acceleration, easy hill climbing, practically effortless touring; lightweight racing saddle spring-mounted for comfort; toe clips make pedaling more effective; dual-position brakes allow braking from touring or racing position; designed in bicycles for men and women.

37. Because of the oil shortage, your market analysts tell you that now is a good time to introduce your new Schwanz 12-speed, lightweight, Hillmaster bicycle to the public, especially to college students. Your Schwanz representative (preceding case) has gathered a fairly pure mailing list of University of Illinois students who do not own bikes by checking police department registration records against the new student directory. You need a letter introducing this latest design, racing-type bicycle to the students. Hillmasters come in a variety of colors and with a complete line of bicycle accessories (for all Schwanz bikes). The Schwanz Hillmaster costs $100 retail and can be purchased at Straight's Cycle Shop (804 West University Avenue). Although $100 is a good price for a 12-speed bike, most college students can't write a check for $100 immediately. Therefore, your action ending will ask them to show their interest by sending back the enclosed postcard that already has their names, addresses, and phone numbers. You will, in turn, forward the cards to your Schwanz dealer in Urbana (Straights). You supply the details about the bike.

38. With a critical fuel shortage looming ahead, you feel that now will be a good time to sell home insulation in Jonesboro, Arkansas, before the cold months get here. You used the census information in the University library to prepare a list of 3,000 names of homeowners whose homes have central heat and air and are valued at or above the $30,000 price bracket.

Your firm, Imperial Industries, Markham and Broadway, Little Rock, Arkansas 72201, has developed a technique of pumping insulating materials into attics and walls by hoses and air pressure. Since most of the homes in Jonesboro are block construction, you decide to concentrate on insulating the attics. Eighty percent of the heat loss in a home occurs through the attic and roof. By applying a 7-inch layer of your special asbesto-polyfiber insulator, you can cut the heat loss by two thirds and save the customer about 15 percent of the cost of heating (or cooling) his home. That's about $90 a year for a home with a monthly electric and gas bill of $50.

It takes only two hours to fully insulate the attic of a three-bedroom house. Your three Jonesboro dealers will subcontract any jobs you get. You will ask your customers to authorize a visit from your salesman rather than send the $300 cost of doing the job. Write a prospecting sales letter (form letter) that can be sent to the 3,000 names on your list. Sign the letter with your name as Director of Sales and date it simply—Fall, this year.

39. For more sales-to-dealers situations, make appropriate modifications and sell the product listed in Cases 19, 23, 24, or 30.

chapter 9 Evaluating yourself and potential employers

UNLESS YOU ARE an extremely fortunate (or unambitious) person, sometime in your life you will write letters to help you get work: summer jobs; jobs launching a career when you graduate from some institution of learning; a change of jobs for more money, for a better location, for work that has greater appeal to you—and even jobs for retirement or widowhood days.

And even if you never write such a letter, the assurance and confidence from realizing what you could do if you have to are good equipment for successful living. Too, from a practical standpoint the experience of job analyzing is desirable preparation for interviewing—an inevitable part of the procedure in job seeking.

As in sales, when you seek work, you are simply marketing a product: your service. You market that product to some prospect: business firms or other organizations which can use your services. In some cases those firms make their needs known—through advertisements, word of mouth, placement agencies, or recruiting personnel. In these circumstances the application is *invited*. In other cases firms do not make their needs known; so it's a case of *prospecting*. You'll find, then, that job-getting letters will be directly comparable to either the invited sales letter or the prospecting sales letter. Both must convince someone of your ability to do something; the big difference between the two is in the approach.

If you are content to accept what life doles out to you, you will probably never write anything but an invited application letter. But we assume that you would not be reading this chapter if you were not trying to improve yourself. For that reason and others listed below, we believe we can help you more by *beginning this analysis with the prospecting letter.*

The *prospecting application* is the logical first choice for learning to write applications because you will write better applications of any type as a result of thorough analysis and writing of this kind. Moreover, in real-life applications the prospecting letter has these advantages over the invited:

—You have a greater choice of jobs and locations, including jobs not advertised.
—You don't have as much competition as for an advertised job, sometimes no competition, as when you create a job for yourself where none existed before.
—Often it is the only way for you to get the exact kind of work you want.
—You can pave the way for a better job a few years later after having gained some experience.

Of course you need to know what kind of work you want to do before you ask someone to let you do it. You may now know exactly what you want to do—that's fine! You may even know exactly the organization where you will seek employment and be thoroughly familiar with its products, operations, and policies. But if you don't know for sure, the following few pages will help you in arriving at those important decisions.

And even if you think you know, you will profit from reading—and maybe revising your present plans. Life holds many changes, occupational as well as personal. Many a job plum turns out to be a lemon. One's goals at 30 often contrast sharply with those one had at 20. Sometimes changes come through economic necessity, for health reasons, because of changes in personal situations (one's marital and family status), because of shifts in demand for a product or service (the prosperous livery-stable owner in 1900 was no longer prosperous by 1910 and was no longer in business by 1920). For you, probably the most significant reason will be your ambition to get ahead: to assume more responsibility in work that is challenging and interesting and thus merit respect and prestige in the eyes of other people, with consequent increased financial returns.

The starting point in your thinking and planning, in any case, is yourself.

ANALYZING YOURSELF

If you are going to sell your services, you will do so on the basis of *what you can do* and *the kind of person you are.* That is your marketable product and it deserves careful analysis, as launching any product does. The *education* you have, the *experience* you've had (which is not so important in many instances as college students assume it to be), and your *personal attitudes and attributes* are your qualifications which enable you to do something for someone.

Early in your career, especially, attitudes and attributes may be the most important of the three: If you don't like a particular kind of work, you probably won't be successful in it. Of all the surveys of why people lose jobs, none has ever cited less than 80 percent attributable to personal maladjustments rather than professional deficiency.

No one but you can decide whether you will like a particular kind of job or not. Your like or dislike will be the result of such general considerations as whether you like to lead or to follow, whether you are an extrovert or an introvert, whether you prefer to work with products and things or with people, whether you are content to be indoors all your working hours or must get out and move around, whether you are responsible enough to schedule your own time or need regular hours guided by punching a time clock, whether you want to work primarily for money or for prestige (social and professional respect and greater security can partially compensate for less money). Certain kinds of work call for much traveling, entertaining after work hours, frequent contact with strangers, staying "dressed up" and "on call" physically and mentally; other kinds are just the opposite.

For most readers of this book, education is already a matter of record or soon will be. In some college or university you are laying a foundation of courses pointing to job performance in some selected field. While graduation is a certification of meeting certain time and proficiency standards, the individual courses and projects have taught you to do something and have shown you how to reason with judgment so that you can develop on the job. Unless you intend to forfeit much of the value of your training (which for most people who go through college represents an investment of $10,000 to $30,000), you will want to find work in the field of your major preparation.

Experience, likewise, is already partially a matter of record; you've held certain jobs or you haven't. Most employers look with greater favor on the person who has already demonstrated some good work habits and exhibited enough drive to work and earn than they do on the person who has held no jobs. But if you've never earned a dime, don't think your position is bleak or unique. Many employers prefer a less experienced person with vision, judgment, and a sense of responsibility to some experienced plodder with none. And as you know, many employers prefer to give employees their own brand of experience in training programs.

Regardless of your status, when you show that you understand and meet the requirements for the job, you have an effective substitute for experience. Furthermore, if you discard the kind of thinking that brands your education as "theoretical" or "academic," you will begin to realize that it is as down to earth as it can be. And that is true whether you have stressed cost accounting or a study of people and their environment.

But since you may still need to come to a vocational decision, because your learning may be applied equally well in many different lines of business or industry and because you probably don't know as much about job possibilities as you could (most folks don't), you'll do well to do some research.

To get some idea you may want to read a description of job requisites and rewards concerning the kind of work you are considering. Publications like *Occupational Briefs* and other job-outlook pamphlets published by Science Research Associates (259 East Erie Street, Chicago, Illinois 60611), and the publication *Occupational Outlook Handbook,* put out by the Bureau of Labor Statistics assisted by the Veterans' Administration, will help you. If you check in *Readers' Guide, Applied Science & Technology Index* and *Business Periodicals Index,* or *Public Affairs Information Service* under the subject heading of the vocation you have chosen or are contemplating, you may find leads to more recent publications.

You may want to consult some guidance agency for tests and counseling. Most institutions of higher learning have facilities for testing aptitudes and vocational interests, as well as intelligence. So do U.S. Employment Service offices and Veterans' Administration offices. And in practically any major city you can find a private agency which, for a fee, will help you in this way. Reading and talking with other people can help you, but only you can make the choice.

Having chosen the particular kind of work you want to do, you should make an organized search for those who can use your services.

SURVEYING WORK OPPORTUNITIES

If you are dead sure that you have chosen the right kind of work and the right organization, that the firm of your choice will hire you, and that both of you will be happy ever after, this discussion is not for you.

Most job seekers, however, are better off to keep abreast of current developments as signs of potential trends in lines of employment and specific companies.

The publications of Science Research Associates (already referred to) give you business and employment trends that help you decide whether you are going to have much or little competition in a given line of work (as well as what is expected of you and approximately how far you can expect to go). The annual Market Data and Directory issue of *Industrial Marketing* and Standard and Poor's Industry Surveys analyze major industries, with comments on their current position in the economy (the latter also identifies outstanding firms in each field). The *Dictionary of Occupational Titles* (U.S. Employment Service) and the *Occupational Outlook Handbook* help you to keep informed on vocational needs. The special reports on individual fields which *Fortune* and *The Wall Street Journal* run from time to time are helpful also. And study of trade journals devoted to the field(s) in which you are interested can help you decide on a given kind of work.

Once you make that decision, you seek names of specific organizations which could use your services. You can find names of companies in *Career, The Annual Guide to Business Opportunities* (published by Career Publications, Incorporated, Cincinnati and New York), *The College Placement Annual,* Standard and Poor's *Manuals,* Moody's *Manuals,* and the Dow directories. Trade directories are useful. If you are concerned with staying in a given location, the city directory—or even the classified section of the phone book—will be helpful. Even if there is no city directory, the local chamber of commerce and local banks can help you.

If willing to spend a little time, you can assemble a good list of prospects from reading business newspapers and magazines. When significant changes occur within a company—for example, a new plant, an addition to an already existing structure, a new product launched, a new research program instituted, a new or different advertising or distribution plan announced—some newspaper or magazine reports that information. Widely known and readily available sources of such information are *The Wall Street Journal* and the business section of an outstanding newspaper in the region of your interest. *U.S. News & World Report* and *Business Week* (in their blue and yellow pages) give you outstanding developments; *Marketing Communications* summarizes what is happening in marketing.

Of special value are the thousands of trade magazines. No matter what field you are interested in, you can find a magazine directed to people in that field, from tropical fish breeding to archery equipment manufacturers, wholesalers, and dealers. The monthly "Business Publications" edition of *Standard Rate & Data Service* (*SRDS*) lists trade magazines by the fields they serve. If your library does not subscribe to *SRDS,* advertising agencies do, and a local one will probably be willing to give you an old copy or let you look at a current issue. Most trade magazines have student subscription rates (often free), and will also usually send a copy or two at no charge, or supply copies of specific articles. From such reading you can assemble a list of companies, the nature of each business, the location, and sometimes the names of key personnel.

Many large companies distribute pamphlets dealing with employment opportunities with the company and qualifications for them; all you have to do is write for one.

If you're interested in a corporation, frequently you can get a copy of its annual report from a business library in your locality. If not, you can get one by writing for it. The report will also often identify key personnel, one of whom may be the person you should direct your letter to.

Certainly other people can also help you. Teachers in the field of your interest and business people doing the same thing you want to do can make many good suggestions about qualifications, working conditions, opportunities, and business firms. Before taking their time, however, you should do some investigating on your own.

ANALYZING COMPANIES

The more you can find out about an organization, the better you can write specifically about how your preparation fits its needs. And remember, that's what you have to do in a successful application—*show that you can render service which fits somebody's need*. For that matter, even if you are fortunate enough to have interviews arranged for you, you'll want to find out all you can about the company: its history, operations, policies, financial structure, and position in the industry—even its main competitors.

Probably the best source of such information—and the easiest for you to obtain—is the annual report. And most annual reports contain much more than financial information; their intended readership includes stockholders, employees, customers, sources of supply—almost anyone, in fact. So they summarize the year's overall activities in terms of products, employment, sales, stockholders, management conditions affecting the industry and the company (including governmental activities), and a wide range of other topics. Careful reading of the last five years' annual reports makes you well informed on the company.

Standard and Poor's *Manuals* and Moody's *Manuals* summarize the history, operations (including products or services, number of employees, and number of plants), and financial structure. These are usually available at stockbrokers' offices as well as libraries.

If you can't find the needed information in sources like these, you may be lucky enough to find it in some magazine. *The Wall Street Journal* is a basic source; and *Fortune*, for example, has published many extensive résumés about specific companies. *Time* does regularly. Indexes—*Readers' Guide, Applied Science and Technology, Business Periodicals, Public Affairs Information Service*—may show you where you can find such an article.

We have mentioned trade magazines as a basic way of learning about the field you are interested in. Another source you should investigate is the association of people in that field. Such trade associations abound, and they are the medium for exchanging information about new developments, who's who and where, and who has job openings or is looking for a new position. If you have pretty definitely settled on the field you want to work in, you can do some invaluable spade work by joining the appropriate trade association, especially if you are still in school. Most associations welcome student members (and at reduced dues).

If you want to get a head start on your competition, tell the officers of the association you want to get involved actively, perhaps by working on some committee. Associations need *active* members, and you are pretty sure to be welcomed with open arms. Such association work is generally not too demanding, and will have the immediate benefit of giving you information useful in pursuing your major. But most important, people working with companies will get to know you, and they can provide entrée to job opportunities you might otherwise not learn about—and may serve as references.

From whatever source you can find, learn as much as you can about what the company does, how it markets its products or services, the trends at work for and against it, its financial position, its employment record, what kind of employees it needs and what it requires of them—plus anything else you can.

FITTING YOUR QUALIFICATIONS TO JOB REQUIREMENTS

Actually what you are doing when you analyze yourself in terms of a job is running two columns of answers: What do they want? What do I have?

The answers to both questions lie in three categories: personal attitudes and attributes, education, and experience—but not necessarily in that order of presentation! In fact, as explained in greater detail in the section "Compiling the Data Sheet" (pp. 337–49), you will usually put yourself in a *more favorable light if you follow an order emphasizing your most favorable qualification in the light of job requirements. This rarely means little personal details like age, weight, and height. But desirable attitudes and personal traits and habits are basic equipment in* any *employee (and for writing a good application). Without them, no amount of education and/or experience will enable you to hold a job, even if you are lucky enough to get it.*

The right work attitude

A company, other organization, or individual puts you on a payroll because you give evidence of being able and willing to perform some useful *service*. That means work. The simplest, easiest, and most effective way to think, talk, and write about work is in terms of doing something for someone. The only way you'll convince someone that you can do something—better than someone else can—is first to realize that you're going to have to be able and willing to produce; that hard work is honorable; that recognition in the form of more pay, more benefits, and flexible hours comes only after demonstrated ability; that you have to be as concerned with *giving* as you are with *getting*, and that you have to give more than you get, especially at first; that you know you can learn more than you already know, and are willing to in order to grow on the job; and that glibness does not cover incompetence or poor work habits—not for very long, at any rate.

The only way you can earn the right to stay on a payroll is to give an honest day's work and to give it ungrudgingly. That means punctuality, reliability, honesty, willingness, cheerfulness, and cooperativeness.

Without a desirable outlook toward work and the conditions under which it must be carried on, competence can be a secondary consideration. Before you can ever demonstrate competence, you have to gain the approval of other people. You can be good, but if you don't get along well with people, your superior abilities won't be recognized. Even if recognized, they won't be rewarded.

You can be very good, but if you indicate that you think you are, you're going to be marked down as vain and pompous. One of the most frequent criticisms of college graduates is that they have overinflated ideas of their abilities and worth. Of course, if you don't respect your own abilities, someone else is not likely to either. The key is to recognize that you can do something because you've prepared yourself to do it, that you have the right mental attitude for doing it under normal business conditions, that you believe you can do it, and that you want to.

Confidence in yourself is essential, but so are humility and modesty. You can achieve a successful blend if you imply both in a specific interpretation of how your education, experience, *and disposition* equip you to perform job duties.

Specific adaptation of personal qualities

The work-for-you attitude in an adaptation implying confidence is basic in any application. Other attitudes or personal qualities need to be evaluated in the light of the particular circumstance. Affability, for instance, is highly desirable for work in which a person deals primarily with people (saleswork, for example); it is not so significant in the makeup of a statistician or a corporation accountant. Accuracy is more to the point for them, as it is for architects and engineers. Punctuality, while desirable in all things and people, is more necessary for public accountants than for personnel workers; for them, patience is more to be desired. While a salesperson needs to be cheerful, a sales analyst must be endowed with perseverance (although each needs a measure of both). A young person asking to be a medical secretary would stress accuracy in technique but, equally, poise and naturalness in putting people at ease; but in applying as a technician, accuracy would be the primary consideration, probably to the exclusion of the other two. Certainly in any position involving responsibility, the candidate for the job would want to select details from personal experience which would bear out the necessary virtues of honesty as well as accuracy.

While all virtues are desirable—and truth, honor, trustworthiness, and cheerfulness are expected in most employees—a virtue in one circumstance may be an undesirable characteristic in another. Talkativeness, for example, is desirable for an interviewer seeking consumer reactions; the same talkativeness would be most undesirable in a credit investigator (who also does a considerable amount of interviewing). Both would need to inspire confidence.

Indeed, finding the right degree of confidence and aggressiveness to sit well with the reader and the job (and reflecting it in style and content) is one of the hardest things about writing good applications. Most employers want neither a conceited, cocksure, overbold and uninhibited, pushy extrovert nor the opposite extreme. They do not want new employees to take over their own jobs in a few weeks, but they know that the meek do not inherit the leadership needed in future managers either.

In any application analysis, estimate what you think are the two or three most important personal characteristics and plan to incorporate evidence which will imply your possession of them. The others are then likely to be assumed. You can't successfully establish all the desirable ones. Besides, you have to show that your education and experience are adequate in selling yourself to a potential employer.

Enhancing your college preparation

With the desirable work-for-you attitude, you'll think in terms of job performance. If your reading has not given you a good idea of the duties you would be expected to perform on a particular job, you'll profitably spend some time talking with someone who has done the work and can tell you. You cannot hope to anticipate everything you might be called upon to do on a given job (nor would you want to talk about everything in your application); but if you anticipate some of the major job requirements and write about your studies in a way that shows you meet these requirements, you'll have enough material for conviction.

Although recruiting ads often stipulate a level of academic attainment, your academic status (units of credit) or a diploma is not what enables you to perform a useful service. *What you learned in earning them does.* To satisfy the arbitrary requirement when you apply to some firms, you'll need to establish your graduation (or the completion of as much work as you have done). But the *primary emphasis in your presentation needs to go on those phases of your education which most directly and specifically equip you for the work under consideration.* In planning your application (but not in writing it), you should list, as specifically as you can, job duties you can be reasonably sure you'll have to perform and, in a parallel column, the background that gives evidence of your ability to do them.

An applicant for work in a public accounting firm knows that the job requires analyzing financial data, preparing working papers, assembling financial statements, and presenting a report with interpretive comments. The direct evidence of having learned to do these things is experience in having done those same things in advanced accounting courses and/or work experience. The applicant must also communicate findings intelligibly and easily to clients, and (as evidence of ability to do so) should cite training in report writing (and letter writing) as well as in speech. If the applicant assumes that pleasant relations with clients are a desirable point to stress, citing study of psychology and sociology might be useful.

Helping clients to evaluate the significance of what the accountant discovers may draw on a knowledge of law and statistics.

A secretarial applicant writes about dictation performance as evidence of ability to record an employer's ideas; as evidence of ability to reproduce them rapidly in attractive letters, memos, or reports, the applicant writes in terms of transcription performance. The job-seeker appears more valuable by talking in terms of relieving a busy employer of much routine correspondence as a result of having studied business writing. Since the job would involve handling callers both face to face and on the telephone, the applicant cites courses in speech and in office procedures.

If you are interested in sales as a career, your specific work in direct selling (both oral and written), market analysis and research, advertising principles and practice, and report writing needs emphasis (along with any other specifically desirable preparation that you know about).

Likewise, the management major stresses study of principles, industrial management, and personnel selection and placement—and if particularly interested in industrial relations, will focus on work in industrial management, motion and time study, and labor economics, law, and legislation.

In all instances, applicants need to be selective, concentrating on that study which most nearly reflects the most advanced stage of preparation. For example, the successful completion of an auditing course implies a background of beginning and intermediate principles of accounting. Similarly, a person who cites evidence of training in market analysis and research will certainly have studied marketing principles. The careful selection of the most applicable courses precludes the necessity for listing qualifying courses and thus enables you to place desirable emphasis on the most significant.

Making the most of experience

Any job you've ever held that required you to perform some task, be responsible for successful completion of a project, oversee and account for activities of other people, or handle money is an activity you can cite with pride to a prospective employer. You may not have been paid for it; that doesn't matter a lot. The college student who directs a campus unit of the United Fund drive gets a workout in organization, delegation of authority, persuasion, systemization, persistence, punctuality, responsibility, honesty, and accuracy that is good work experience. It is experience which is more valuable than that of the student who operates a supermarket cash register four hours a day—and nothing else. Especially if both are aiming at managerial work or some kind of contact work, the one who has earned no pay but has had more experience working with people and assuming authority and responsibility is more desirable.

You may not have held the job for any length of time—maybe for only a summer or over the holidays or briefly part time while in school. But didn't you learn something that increased your ability to render service?

You may have held a job that does not appear to be related to the work you hope to do. The checker at the supermarket, for example, has punched a way through college because that is the only way to pay to prepare for a career in marketing. But hasn't that person demonstrated vision, perseverance, accuracy, the ability to work under pressure, the willingness to be cheerful and polite to customers, and—if observant—had a good workout in interpreting consumer demand?

Even the person of limited experience can interpret it in relation to job requirements, giving the most significant part the emphasis of position. The most directly related phase of experience is the one most nearly preparing you to do something. For example, if the supermarket checker had also been a fraternity or sorority house treasurer (involving handling and accounting for money), an application for accounting work would want to emphasize the treasurer's duties over the checker's job; but, an application to do selling would make the checker's job more significant.

If you are fortunate enough to have a wide range of experience, your problem is simply one of picking and choosing and presenting in an order of descending applicability to the job sought. Chronology (a time sequence) rarely should be your governing choice at graduation or even for a few years after. Later as an experienced employee changing companies, however, you might wisely elect to present job experience in chronological order (or the reverse), emphasizing progress to your present state of preparation. Such order-of-time presentation suggests a well-defined goal and success in attaining it.

Whatever experience you elect to present, you want to show as directly and specifically as possible that as a result of this experience you come equipped to do the job or at least to learn how quickly. The surest way to present this information about yourself in the *most favorable light is to describe past-experience job duties related to the job you're seeking.* You will strengthen your application if you interpret the experience to show what it taught you about important principles, techniques, and attitudes applicable to the hoped-for job. Evaluating work experience is the same as evaluating education; it's matching-up as far as possible the answers to "What do I have?" with the requirements under "What do they want?"

You will rarely, if ever, meet all job requirements; and you will always have some points that are stronger than others. Outright lack of a specific point of preparation or below-average standard are negative points to be handled in the same manner that any good writer handles them: embedded position and corollary positive language.

Determining a favorable order of presentation

After you have listed the necessary and desirable qualifications of the person who will be hired and your own specific preparation as defined by personal qualities, education, and experience, you will then need to decide on an order of presentation that is most favorable to you.

Most jobs are secured in the first place because of competence, not personal charm or good looks. While undesirable personal attributes and attitudes can keep you from getting the job of your choice (sometimes from getting *a* job!) and may result in your losing the job even if you fool someone and are selected, good personality will not ordinarily get you the job unless you first show ability to do the work. Competence stems from good education or worthwhile experience, or a combination of the two.

If your strongest point is thorough preparation, that is what you want to start with; if it is experience, begin that way. And within each of these categories, arrange your qualifications so that the best comes first (as any good seller does).

Without telling your reader what they are (surely your reader knows them!), be sure to give evidence that you meet all important job requirements. And write your evidence *not* in the order it occurs to you, or even in an order of what you estimate is of greatest significance in the evaluation, but in an order that stresses your strong points.

For this comprehensive presentation, a data sheet (often called résumé or personal record sheet) is the preferred form.

COMPILING THE DATA SHEET

We emphatically recommend that you prepare your data sheet *before* you write your letter. Making the necessary self- and job-analyses helps you recognize your assets and truly see yourself realistically in relation to the job you want. Thus it can bring you back into alignment if you have swung too far up (overconfident) or too far down (in the dumps). Perhaps more important, organizing your data sheet usually shows you what to stress in your letter, the problems of which we will discuss more fully in the next chapter.

The purpose of a data sheet is *to help sell you to a prospective employer*. It can accompany either a prospecting or an invited application letter—and often serves to start off an interview under favorable conditions. It tells your complete story—the little details as well as the big points—thus *enabling your letter to be shorter and to concentrate on showing how the high spots of your preparation equip you to do good work.*

As one authority said, a data sheet gives your life's history in two minutes, indicates your organizing and language ability, and leaves your letter free to sell. It is a tabulation of your qualifications, giving pertinent, specific details concerning your education, experience, and personal data and —except in atypical circumstances—supplying the names of references who can verify what you say about yourself.

Though we will treat the main contents and forms later, here we want to clear up two minor problems. First, almost traditionally company application forms have asked *first* for name, address, and lots of personal information that relatively recent Civil Rights legislation now prohibits prospective employers from considering (race, religion, age, marital and family status, and photographs). Of course no law prohibits you from volunteering such information in a personally planned data sheet; but since personnel people cannot consider it in their decisions, it at least becomes useless. Even worse, because many of them are scared by some of the not-yet-court-tested-and-defined new legislation, some of them say they *prefer not to have* the personal information (lest they be accused of using it).

The second minor problem is where and how to put in the chosen personal information, including your address (and, if likely to be wanted, telephone number). Certainly the person answering will want your address; and you cannot depend on just putting it on letters (which sometimes get separated from data sheets). Though necessary, such information *is not influential* in whether you get the job and hence *does not deserve the emphatic first position.* It is *not* what gets you a job. Your problem is to find the best way to *present it so that it can be found readily but is not overemphasized.*

When you are preparing your own data sheet, *you want to sell yourself.* Remember that the company isn't trying to sell you, but you are! *You will sell yourself more by emphasizing initially your best point of preparation*—either education or experience details, followed by the other. In most cases you have a stronger presentation by establishing these significant points before you take up the necessary personal details. Notice that the four data sheets which follow (pp. 346–47) desirably emphasize each candidate's strongest selling point first.

Since the data sheet must carry a wealth of detail and condense the material into a small amount of space, it follows good outlining principles and form. You need to use the space-saving devices of tabulation and noun phrases (rather than sentences and conventional paragraphs). To facilitate rapid reading, you should use headings, differentiate in type for the various classes of information, and observe uniform indentions for rows and columns of information. Parallel construction in phrasing requires special care. (If you stick to noun phrases, you'll eliminate your problems in this respect.)

Impersonal style, without opinions and comments, is usually best for this concise, basically factual presentation (but be careful not to fall into unnatural, stuffy, pompous phrasing).

The best form is that one which enables you to make the most favorable presentation of your qualifications, attractively displayed and concisely stated. Study thoughtfully the examples following. Note the variation in the use of rows and columns of information, in the type and placement of information, in the classification of the information, and in the points the writers stressed.

Your data sheet definitely should be typed. When you type each one, you can desirably fill in the name of the organization addressed and make other minor changes for better adaptation.

As a practical matter, however, you may have to run off multiple copies. If so, get the best quality printing job you can afford. Never send a prospective employer a carbon copy or a photocopied, Mimeographed, or Dittoed data sheet. Until you get an interview, your data sheet is your representative. Make sure it has a quality appearance—like you.

You may choose to omit references if you are prospecting or if you are answering a "blind" (anonymous) advertisement and fear the effects of an inquiry at the firm where you are working. Or you may not want to ask references to take time to answer inquiries until you know for sure that you are interested in the job. In either case you would need to indicate willingness to supply the names of references upon request or after an interview; the evaluation by those who have supervised you in classrooms and on jobs is of real use to the people who consider employing you.

In most cases—especially for college students seeking a career—the names of references to whom the potential employer can write are a necessary part of data sheet information. Logically, they conclude the presentation.

With careful planning and only minor changes, if any, you will be able to use the same data sheet information over and over as you mail out applications for the same kind of job. Often a simple substitution of company name in the heading is all you'll need. When the kind of work you're applying for changes, however, reevaluate your qualifications in the light of the circumstances. Some of the data sheets shown on page 340–47 would have stressed different aspects of education had the applicants been applying for work in their majors.

We have purposely given you illustrations varying considerably in content and form. The first (p. 340) is perhaps the most typical for college undergraduates. Since Mr. Smith had no particularly pertinent course work outside the standard major, chose not to include a picture or reference to religion, and relegated the address to the end, he was able to give the significant data on one page and lead with his ace (education). Miss Crane also chose to begin with education and detail it and activities specially pertinent to a particular job. You might notice also how she subordinated the address and incidentally revealed religion in making the important point of activities that amount to experience. Though we question the emphasis Mr. Adams put on the address and his including a picture (even for a job before the public), by careful phrasing and conciseness (especially in "Personal Factors"), he still presented a Master's degree, special courses, and experience on one page.

The fourth data sheet is a special situation. The applicant was a little older, more educated, and more experienced than most of the readers of this book are likely to be. Moreover, he was shooting for (and got) bigger game. The presentation was a commercially printed fold-out on heavy paper. With the photograph, the art work, and the extra postage, the cost was far higher than many students just graduating from college can afford or need to spend. But this applicant had more qualifications to present, and he gave a more complete picture. He also included two additional pieces of information many readers want—the date of availability and a full statement of objectives or goals. It is a good example of what a person might want to do after a few years of experience, however, or an advanced degree or two.

After studying the four examples, review the checklisted items (pp. 348–49) as a basis for preparing your own data sheet.

EUGENE N. SMITH'S QUALIFICATIONS

FOR ACCOUNTING WORK FOR SPERRY-RAND, INC.

EDUCATION:

Bachelor of Science in Business Administration,
University of Florida, with a major in accounting
Expected date of graduation, August, 1976

WORK EXPERIENCE:

Summer employment:

1975: Supervised 8 adults and 50 carriers in circulation department of Miami News
Worked as sales clerk for Masters Department Store, Miami
1974: Worked as laborer for Fleming Construction Company, Miami
1973: Worked as office clerk and key clerk for seven months for Southern Bell Telephone Company in Miami

Other work:

Worked as bag boy, telephone clerk, service station attendant, and bus boy

SCHOOL ACTIVITIES:

Head parade marshal, 1973 Homecoming Parade, University of Florida
Special Projects Chairman for Student Union, 1974
Academic Chairman, Interfraternity Council, 1974
Rush Chairman, pledge master, house manager, and secretary for Kappa Kappa Rho fraternity

PERSONAL DATA:

Appearance: 6' tall, 175 pounds, excellent physical condition
Hobbies: Reading, sports, and dancing
Birth: Born July 2, 1954, in Miami
Marital Status: Single, but engaged to be married
Memberships: Kappa Kappa Rho social fraternity

REFERENCES BY PERMISSION:

Mr. Joseph Williams
Accounting Department
Southern Bell Telephone Company
Jacksonville, Florida 32102

Brother Henry Armstrong
Columbus High School
3000 SW 87th Street
Miami, Florida 32211

Mr. Brit Benedict, Business Manager
The Miami News
417 Eucalyptus Drive
Miami, Florida 32211

Dr. Emmet E. Wilson
Accounting Department
Matherly Hall, U of F
Gainesville, Florida 32611

ADDRESS: 1027 SW 7th Avenue, Gainesville, Florida 32601, Tel. (904) 378-3732

MARIAN CRANE'S QUALIFICATIONS FOR

EFFICIENT PUBLIC RELATIONS WORK

WITH SOUTHEASTERN HIGHWAY TRANSPORT, INC.

Thorough University Training

Three and one-half years of work in the School of Commerce, University of Alabama, with only five hours of advanced electives left (for completion by correspondence) after June 2, 1976, for a B.S. degree.

"B" average in the following courses related to public-relations work with Southeastern Highway Transport:

Transportation
Traffic Management
Employee Supervision
Business Statistics
Business Correspondence
Business Report Writing
Personnel Management

Experience Working with People

Active participation in these campus organizations:

Beta Beta Alpha--organization for women Business Administration majors.

Newman Club--organization for the promotion of religious social activities of Catholic students.

Wica--independent women's social organization.

Campus League of Women Voters--meetings used for the discussion of current events, trends, interests.

Three and one-half years of life in a cooperative house--an organization of 16 University girls who cooperate to do all the planning, managing, and work of this living unit.

Coordinator of this organization during senior year. Managerial responsibility.

Member of the advisory committee, with special duties of talking to any member of this co-op who caused any friction within the house.

Active member of the Interco-op Council, the board representing all co-op houses on the campus. Working on problems of all the houses as a whole and planning a definite expansion program.

MARIAN CRANE'S QUALIFICATIONS--page 2

General office work with Ford Motor Company of Evergreen, Alabama. Typing, dictation, bookkeeping. Summers, 1973, 1974, 1975.

Secretary to Representative Stark in the Legislature during the last session. Spring, 1974

Office assistant at Radio House, University of Alabama. General office work of typing, dictation, mimeographing. Part time while in school.

<u>Personal Details</u>

Nativity: Born in 1956 in Alabama
Family status: Unmarried.
Physical characteristics: 5 feet, 4 inches; 120 pounds; blond hair; hazel eyes.

Health: Good. Perfect hearing and eyesight.
Hobbies: Participation in sports; listening to classical music; designing and sewing wardrobe.

Address: (until June 1, 1976) Box 1773
University, Alabama 35486
(after June 1, 1976) Box 47
Evergreen, Alabama 36401

<u>Persons Who Will Testify</u>

Dr. M. W. Whitman
Professor of Transportation
University of Alabama
University, Alabama 35486

Dr. John Robert Blocton
Professor of Business Statistics
University of Alabama
University, Alabama 35486

Mr. Layden D. Osmus
Director of Radio House
University of Alabama
University, Alabama 35486

Mr. D. R. Lanning
Professor of Marketing
University of Alabama
Tuscaloosa, Alabama 35401

Mr. L. A. Jarosek, Manager
Ford Motor Company
1813 N. Main Street
Evergreen, Alabama 36401

Qualifications of Harry E. Adams

for Representing Bedford, Mace, and Company in the Field

Until June 1, 1976

Box 3652
University, Alabama 35486

Conservative picture in a business suit. Front view.

(Detachable)

After June 1, 1976

Rainbow Drive
Gadsden, Alabama 35901

Education and Teaching Experience

Master of Science degree, June, 1976, University of Alabama, with major concentration on economics and labor.

Courses of value in representing a publisher to the college trade (in addition to specialization):

Public Speaking	Business Correspondence	Business Research
Psychology	Business Report Writing	Advertising
Marketing	English Composition	Business Law

One year (1975-76) of teaching Economic Principles, University of Alabama. Responsibility for planning and delivering lectures and for all testing and grading.

Personal Factors

6 feet tall, 170 pounds, brown hair and eyes, dark skin, conservative dress.
Born January 24, 1951, Gadsden, Alabama.
Honorable discharge from U.S. Navy after 24 months of service

Delta Chi social fraternity.
Single (free to travel).
Active participation in tennis, golf, swimming. Frequent bridge and dancing. Wide reading of fiction and business publications.

University of Alabama References

Dr. Ralph M. Hill
Professor of Economics
University, Alabama 35486

Dr. R. E. Lampkin
Professor of Management
Chairman, Commerce Graduate Division
University, Alabama 35486

Mr. D. H. Brennan
Professor of Marketing
University, Alabama 35486

Dr. Paul W. Paulings
Professor of Economics
University, Alabama 35486

Training

and

Experience

REPORT

on

CHARLES E. COMPTON

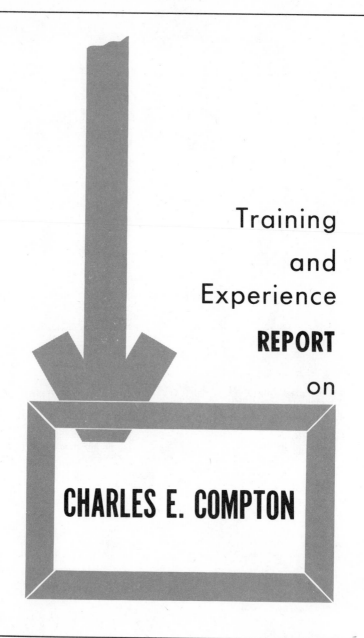

To: Busy Executives, Personnel Managers, and other Company Leaders

– A one minute check list to save you time –

Do you need a career minded young man who–

IN MARKETING

1. Can adapt ☐
2. Can help develop marketing mixes for nontechnical products ☐
3. Knows basic consumer behavior ☐
4. Can help identify new markets ☐
5. Can structure surveys – interpret findings ☐
6. Can write reports – present results ☐
7. Has ideas – some good – some bad ☐

IN ACCOUNTING AND FINANCE

1. Can analyze financial reports and data ☐
2. Can make cost and price analyses ☐
3. Can evaluate operating results ☐
4. Knows something about stubborn overhead cost growth ☐

IN BUSINESS

1. Can communicate with people at all levels ☐
2. Can think in detailed or broad terms ☐
3. Seeks continued challenge and growth ☐
4. Works without close supervision ☐
5. Accepts responsibility ☐
6. Will work hard – Will study hard – to learn the business he serves ☐

CHARLES E. COMPTON'S QUALIFICATIONS
for
MARKETING LINE or STAFF WORK

334 Bruce Street Apartment E
Warner Robins, Georgia 31093
Home Phone: 912- 923-7442
Office Phone: 912- 926-2151

PHOTO

Age: 27
Health: Good
Married 1971, no children
Wife (Roberta) Pharmacist

Height: 6′ 2″
Weight: 195

Current Status: Captain, USAF
Central Procurement Officer

Will separate in July 1976
Available upon separation

OBJECTIVE

To work in a marketing line or staff job. To handle projects and assignments concerned with the various aspects of marketing and offering cross training into other major functional areas. To gain additional business knowledge, experience, and judgment necessary for advancement.

THOROUGH COLLEGE TRAINING

M.B.A. Degree top third

Master of Business Administration degree, 1972, University of Alabama, with major in General Management. Ranked in top third of class. Completed advanced courses in management, finance, accounting, statistics, marketing, business law, and economics. Earned Graduate Research Assistantship. Secretary of Commerce Graduate Association. Passed all seven fields on written comprehensive M.B.A. Field Exam. M.B.A. paper on Product Management. Other research papers on Brand Imagery, Corporate Organizational Structure, and Product Deletion.

B.S. Degree top 10%

Bachelor of Science in Commerce and Business Administration, 1971, University of Alabama. Graduated in top ten percent in class of 175. Marketing major with emphasis in Sales Management and Professional Selling. Earned A's in Marketing Research, Report Writing, International Marketing, Marketing Analysis and Control, Marketing Seminar, and Industrial Marketing and Wholesaling. Earned B's in Promotion, Salesmanship, and Retailing. No C's. Elected liberal arts courses in mathematics, speech, and behavioral sciences with B average. On Dean's List junior and senior years with QPA of 2.8 on 3.0 system each year.

College Activities

Alpha Kappa Psi, Professional Business Fraternity, Vice President junior and senior years. Theta Chi Fraternity, social, elected officer two years. Active member in Marketing Club. Member of academic honor society. Active in intramural sports. Earned seventy-five percent of college and living expenses.

BUSINESS EXPERIENCE REQUIRING ACCURACY AND JUDGMENT

Four full years of responsible Procurement work for the Air Force while stationed at Warner Robins Air Materiel Area (WRAMA), Robins Air Force Base, Georgia. Two concurrent years teaching college business courses at night.

AIR FORCE BUSINESS EXPERIENCE

March 1974 to present **Principal Negotiator**	Contract Price Analyst and Negotiator – Work as a Price Analyst and Principal Negotiator on fixed price and cost type contracts in excess of $100,000. Negotiate with major defense contractors. Analyze all cost and profit elements to develop formal Government price objectives. Responsible for total negotiation and price justification. As negotiation team leader, maintain close contact work with engineers, auditors, production personnel, contracting officers, and top management.
Price Analyst	Experienced in analyzing proposals, and evaluating audit reports and technical reports. Evaluations include analysis of labor hours and rates, overhead cost and base, material costs, and profit factors. Analytical tools include variable and fixed cost analyses, weighted averages, learning curve applications, and regression analysis.
Central Staff	Negotiated twenty-four contracts across-the-table or by telephone with twenty contractors obligating about $15,000,000 during the past year. Currently work in a central staff office with fourteen analysts supporting 530 Directorate of Procurement and Production employees.
1972–1974 **Buyer**	Government Buyer – Experienced in Government procurement system, methods, and regulations. Wrote solicitations, evaluated proposals, made awards, and wrote final contracts up to $100,000 in value.

TEACHING AND SELF EMPLOYMENT

College Teaching	Taught seventeen quarter courses at night in Georgia colleges since April 1974 in four business fields. Course Titles: Accounting – Business Finance – Business Organization and Principles – Basic Marketing – and Wholesaling, Retailing, and Logistics Management. Held complete responsibility for developing course content and presentation.
	Small Business – Advised two local retailers on product lines, product display, and accounting controls.
1972–1975	Real Estate – Worked with Georgia realtor in conducting feasibility analysis for a city trade area shopping center.
	Amway Cleaning Products – Sold to institutions. Developed a small distributorship of home retail salesmen.

OTHER WORK – INTERESTS – MEMBERSHIPS

Other Work	Graduate Research Assistant, University of Alabama (1971–1972). Timber Management of personal property (1971–1976). General Reserve in paper mill during summer (1967–1969). Cattle Farm work and management (1966–1967). Retail Clerk in shoe store – Tupperware Salesman (1964–1965).
Interests	Conversation with business leaders – Travel and meeting people – Income tax accounting – Remaining current on business conditions – Stock market activities – Real estate investments – Church – Physical fitness – Hunting – Golf.
Memberships	American Marketing Association.

REFERENCES

References	References gladly furnished upon request.

Résumé (or Data Sheet) Checklist

1. Give your data sheet an informative heading worded for the appropriate degree of "selling."
   a) Identify your name, the type of work desired, and (preferably) the company to which addressed.
   b) Be sure you apply for work, not a job title.
   c) Write concisely; avoid "data sheet of" and "position as."
2. Emphasis, ease of reading, and space saving are the main factors affecting the physical arrangement.
   a) Balance the material across the page in tabulated form.
   b) Use difference in type and placement to affect emphasis and show awareness of organization principles.
   c) Centered heads carry emphasis and help balance the page.
   d) Capitalize the main words in centered heads and underline the heads. Unnecessary to underline one in solid caps.
   e) If you have to carry over an item, indent the second line.
   f) Remember to identify and number pages after the first.
3. Lead with whatever best prepares you for the particular job.
4. Education details should point up specific preparation.
   a) Show the status of your education early: degree, field, school, date.
   b) Highlight courses which distinctively qualify you for the job. Listing everything takes away emphasis from the significant and suggests inability to discriminate.
   c) In listing your courses, give them titles or descriptions which show their real content.
   d) You may briefly give specific details of what you did in courses.
   e) Give grade averages in a form which any reader will interpret accurately: letter, or standing in quartiles, or percentages (GPA systems vary too much).
   f) Expressions like "theoretical education" deprecate your work.
   g) Arrange listed courses in order of significance or applicability, best first.
5. Experience: All is good but some better than other.
   a) About the experience you list, give at least job title, duties, the firm or organization, the place, the specific dates, and *responsibilities.*
   b) If experience is part time, identify it as such.
   c) Account for the chronology of your life since high school; gaps of more than three months may arouse suspicion.

Résumé (or Data Sheet) Checklist

(continued)

6. The personal-details section should present a clear, true picture.
   a) It ordinarily includes physical indications (age, height, weight, general condition of health). (Though law prevents employers from asking, no law prohibits you from volunteering information about race, religion, and marital status.)
   b) Tabulate, but try combining ideas to reduce overlisting, saving space and words:

      Born in Birmingham, Alabama, 1955
      5′11″, 185 lbs.
      Good health, glasses for close work
      Married, no children
      Member of (list appropriate organizations)
      Like fishing and reading

   c) Give your address(es)—and phone(s) if likely to be used—in minimum space where easily found but not emphasized.
   d) Some employers want (but cannot legally require) a small photograph. If used, attach with a paper clip, not staple, glue, or tape.
7. References ordinarily conclude data sheets (unless you have some reason for a "blind" situation).
   a) Give the names, titles, addresses, and telephone numbers of references for all important jobs and fields of study listed.
   b) Always give proper titles of respect: Mr., Professor, Dr., Honorable—whatever is appropriate.
   c) Unless character references are requested, omit them.
   d) Unless obvious, make clear why each reference is listed.
8. Remember these points about style:
   a) Data sheets are usually impersonal presentations; avoid first- and second-person pronouns.
   b) Noun phrases are the best choice of grammatical pattern.
   c) A data sheet is ordinarily a tabulation; avoid paragraphs and complete sentences.
   d) Items in any list should be in parallel form. See Para. in Appendix C.
   e) Keep opinions off data sheets; just give the specific facts.
   f) Avoid superlatives or other "advertising." Leave the selling to your cover letter.

chapter 10

Letters about employment

WRITING THE PROSPECTING APPLICATION

A SALESMAN, like a fisherman, almost has to have a feeling of success consciousness and optimism so that he can think positively. You can hardly force yourself to really try to catch fish or make sales unless you feel that you have an attractive bait or an appealing product or service. Other people (and seemingly even fish) sense quickly how you feel about yourself, and respond accordingly. And since application letters are sales letters in every way—sales letters selling your services—you have to have self-confidence and positive thinking.

That, you remember, was one of the reasons we urged you in the preceding chapter to prepare a good data sheet *before* writing your application letter to go with it. Especially if you're down because you are earning less than *A*'s in courses or encountering questions about whether you'll graduate—or your present job is going sour (or worse, you've been fired) *—realistically assessing your strong points through preparing a good data sheet can be a big step toward retaining and increasing your own self-confidence and optimism.*

With a well-prepared data sheet you will have done a good job of lining up your qualifications, of realizing what you can do, and of deciding on those qualifications which most nearly equip you for efficient performance. You are then in much better shape to write an application letter—a sales letter selling your services.

At times you may want to send a prospecting letter without a data sheet. That's your decision. We don't think it's the better decision; most personnel people prefer to receive a data sheet. Even if you elect not to use one, you'll write a better letter for having prepared one. Having prepared it, you're throwing good money away if you don't let it work for you.

You're also being very foolish if you fail to capitalize on your investment of time and effort (and maybe even cash) by slavishly following the points and aping the style of another person's application letter. The good "model" application letter doesn't exist—and never will for applicants of average intelligence and above. They realize that *the application letter must be an accurate reflection of the writer's personality as well as aptitudes.* And so they will write their own.

Securing favorable attention

As in sales letters, the infallible way to secure interest in your application letter is to stress your central selling point in writing about serving the reader. Your central selling point may be an ability based on education, experience, or personal qualities or a combination of them. The young man who compiled the third of the data sheets you studied (see p. 343) successfully combined all three:

> With my college background of undergraduate and graduate work, my teaching experience, and a temperament which helps me to adapt easily to college people and circumstances, I believe I could do a good job as a field representative for your firm.
>
> And after talking with several field representatives about the nature of the work, I know I'd have the added factor in my favor of being very enthusiastic about it.
>
> While I certainly don't know all the reasons why college teachers choose certain textbooks, I have taught enough while completing a master's degree at Alabama to realize that format and price are only minor factors affecting a teacher's decision.
>
> Possibly the most significant realization from my year as a graduate student and instructor is that there is no true "academic" personality—that a successful representative has to be prepared to meet and talk freely and convincingly with a wide range of personalities.
>
> Teaching classes in Economic Problems and Policies, discussing my thesis with committee members both collectively and individually, and talking with staff members about teaching problems (in staff meetings and in bull sessions) have helped me to think on my feet, to have self-assurance when speaking

to groups and to individuals, and to adapt myself to varying situations. I've learned to feel at home with all types of college teachers.

The fact that I have studied business at Alabama rather than liberal arts at an Ivy League school may actually make me a better representative, Mr. Dayton—especially if I'm assigned to the South, where I already know the territory. I could serve happily as your representative in any district, however; I've traveled over most of the U.S. (and to Europe and the Far East while in the Navy) and can adapt readily to the fine people and country one finds everywhere.

I believe you'd find me quick to learn; the men I've listed as references on the enclosed data sheet will probably tell you so if you'll write them.

After you've had a chance to verify some of the things I've said about myself in this letter and on the data sheet, will you write me frankly about the possibilities of my working for you?

Possibly I could talk with one of your regional representatives in this area as a preliminary step. And I can plan to go to New York sometime this summer to talk with you further about my successfully representing your firm.

(You may be interested to know that the 22 copies of this letter brought 22 replies within a couple of weeks. Half a dozen of the firms wanted to interview the applicant right away, another half dozen, within a month afterward. The writer had four job offers.)

To get started rapidly and pertinently, one applicant began her letter to the American Red Cross this way:

I can be the versatile type of club director the American Red Cross seeks.

As a result of five years' specialized training in dietetics and institutional management and 10 years' practical experience in meeting and serving people as a volunteer worker in service clubs from New York to Trinidad, from France through Germany, I know the kind of program which will best meet the needs and interests of service men and their families everywhere.

A young man just graduating from college got favorable attention with this:

Because I have had an unusual five-year educational opportunity combining the study of engineering and management, I feel sure of my ability to do efficient work in your industrial engineering department and to steadily increase in usefulness.

I could conduct a time study with a technical knowledge of the machines concerned or work on the problems of piece wage rates without losing sight of the highly explosive personnel situation involved.

A 19-year-old-girl with two years of college summarized her outstanding qualifications in the following well-chosen lead:

```
As a secretary in your export division I could take your
dictation at a rapid 120 words per minute and transcribe it
accurately in attractive letters and memos at 40 words per
minute—whether it is in English or Spanish.
```

There's nothing tricky about these openings. They just talk work.

You may be able to capitalize on a trick in some situations—provided it shows knowledge of job requirements. The young advertising candidate who mailed a walnut to agencies with the lead "They say advertising is a hard nut to crack" got results from the message he had enclosed in the walnut. The young man who, in seeking radio work, wrote his message in the form of a radio script marked "Approved for Broadcast" and stamped with a facsimile of the usual log certification indicated above-average knowledge of working conditions. The secretary who started her letter with a line of shorthand characters indicated qualifications from the start. The statistical worker who drew at the top of his letter a line graph showing the Federal Reserve Board Index of Industrial Production and in the opening lines of his letter commented on the significance of its recent movements certainly had a head start on other candidates for the job. If you can think of one which is pertinent, in good taste, and not stereotyped (such as the balance sheet from an accounting candidate), it may help you. But it is by no means a must and can do you more harm than good unless you handle it carefully and thoughtfully.

You do need to concentrate on rapidly and naturally establishing your qualifications with the attitude that you want to put them to work for the reader in some specific job. Having held out such a promise, you need to back it up.

Supplying evidence of performance ability

Your evidence in an application is simply an interpretation of the highlights of your data sheet. For persuasiveness, you phrase it in terms of "doing something for you." If you didn't notice how each of the paragraphs two through seven in the letter beginning on p. 351 gives evidence in support of the opening promise, go back and read the letter again.

The applicant to the Red Cross whose opening you read in a preceding passage continued her letter this way:

```
With the full realization that the Red Cross necessarily
operates on an economical basis, I can use my thorough college
training in institutional organization as a sound basis for
financial management, cost control, personnel management,
employee training, and job specification, all of which I know
are vital in a well-run Red Cross club.

When it comes to food service, I feel at home in the planning,
selection, buying, preparation, and serving of party food for
a group of 500 or 1,000 or behind the snack bar of a canteen
or in planning the well-balanced meals for the hardworking Red
Cross girls who live in the barracks.  During my year as
```

assistant dietician at Ward Memorial Hospital in Nashville, I successfully supervised the preparation and serving of from 3,000 to 20,000 meals a day.

Having been an Army wife and lived in many places under varying circumstances, I have learned to use my own initiative in developing the facilities at hand. I've learned to be adaptable, patient, resourceful, and—through grim necessity as a widow—cheerful! I believe in punctuality but am not a clock watcher. And I know from experience that I can direct people without incurring resentment.

I've always enjoyed and participated in the many sports and social activities that are listed on the enclosed data sheet. As a Red Cross director I could help others to share their pleasures too.

The industrial-management applicant followed up his opening like this:

The program I followed at Northwestern University required five years of study because I felt that qualification for work in industrial management should include basic engineering information. The scope of such courses as Business Organization and Cost Accounting were therefore enhanced and expanded by related work in Machine Design and Properties of Engineering Materials.

Three years in the Corps of Engineers of the U.S. Army form the main basis of my experience. A large part of this time I spent as a section officer in a large engineer depot. The knowledge, skills, and experience I gained concerning layout, storage, freight handling, and heavy packaging relate very closely to the problems of factory management in the production of heavy machinery. While working with the problems of shipping bulldozer blades, I was gaining experience that will aid me in understanding the special techniques required in handling cotton pickers and tractors.

I've learned how to get my ideas across in business-writing courses here at Northwestern as well as through being a reporter for the Daily Northwestern. As a member of the student governing board and the senior council, I've had good lessons in cooperation and patience. And despite a pretty rugged schedule of classes and extracurricular activities, I've kept myself in good physical condition by participating on my fraternity's intramural basketball and football teams.

The enclosed data sheet and inquiries to the men I've listed will probably give you all the information you want about me before seeing me, but I shall be glad to furnish any further particulars you may wish.

And the secretarial applicant to the exporting firm continued (after her opening) in the following vein, drawing exclusively on her schooling:

In secretarial courses during my two years of study at Temple College, I've consistently demonstrated my ability to handle material at these speeds. And as a matter of practice in my course in conversational Spanish I take down what my teacher and my classmates say. I have no difficulty transcribing these notes later.

```
I learned a good deal about your markets and your clientele
while doing research for a report I submitted this semester in
marketing, "Some Recent Developments in Latin-American
Markets."  In the process I became familiar with such
publications as The American Importer, Exporting, and The
Foreign Commerce Yearbook.

I'm neat and conservative in appearance.  Early in my life
mother impressed upon me the desirability of a low-pitched
voice and distinct enunciation; probably for that reason my
college speech teacher has been especally interested in
helping me to achieve poise and dignity before a group of
people.  On the telephone or in person I could greet your
clients pleasantly and put them at ease.

After I start working, I hope to further my knowledge of the
people and language of Latin America by using my vacation
time for trips to Mexico, Central America, and South America.
```

Overcoming deficiencies is a function of the letter, not the data sheet. In almost any application situation you'll have one or more. In many cases the wiser course of action is simply not to talk about it! In other cases, if you feel that it is such an important consideration as to merit identification and possibly discussion, embed it in your letter, and endow it with as much positiveness as possible.

The young man wanting to be a publisher's representative had two strikes against him and knew it: he had gone through a commerce school and he was a product of a state university in the South rather than an Ivy League school. Turn back and note how in the fifth paragraph of his letter he met the issue head on and capitalized on it.

The industrial-management applicant had no experience. But did he apologize for it? Not at all! He held out his service experience confidently and showed its relation to the job sought. "Three years in the . . . U.S. Army form the basis of my experience," he wrote—instead of the weak-kneed statement, "The only experience I've had was in the Army," or even worse, "I've had no experience. But I did serve with the Corps of Engineers in the Army."

Probably one of the finest examples we've ever seen of turning an apparent handicap into a virtue is that of a young woman who at first didn't know where to turn when confronted with the necessity for getting a job. After thoughtful analysis of what she had done in college and how it could be used in business, she sent the following letter to a large Chicago mail-order firm. The third paragraph is the epitome of positive thinking.

```
Isn't one of the significant qualifications of a correspondent
in your company the ability to interpret a letter situation
in terms of the reader?

Because I believe that I could express an understanding of a
situation clearly and imaginatively to your customers (a degree
in English from the University of Illinois, an A in Business
Communication, and the editorship of my sorority paper suggest
that I can), will you allow me to become a trial employee in
your correspondence division?
```

> Learning your particular business policies and procedures in writing letters would come quickly, I believe; I am used to following assignments exactly, and I have no previous working experience to unlearn.
>
> I have a good background in writing. I can type 60 words a minute. And the varied extracurricular activities listed on the enclosed data sheet are my best evidence for telling you that I've successfully passed a four-year test of getting along with people.
>
> Will you call me at 876-2401 and name a time when I may come in and talk with you?

It worked! And the same kind of positive approach to any handicap you may have—physical or otherwise—is probably your best way to treat it.

Talking the special language of your reader's business also convinces your reader of your performance ability and helps to overcome any deficiency. In all the examples you've been reading in this analysis, you've probably noticed that each incorporated specific and special references to conditions or products or activities peculiar to the given job. Such references certainly further the impression that you are aware of job requirements and conditions. The would-be publisher's representative referred to books, teachers, college circumstances, and adoptions (the end and aim of that particular job). The industrial management applicant referred easily and sensibly to two products of the company, tractors and cotton pickers. The applicant to the Red Cross referred to service clubs, canteens, and the hardworking Red Cross girls who live in the barracks.

From your research you can readily establish such references. If significant enough information, they may be good choices of talking points for your beginning, as in the following three instances:

> With the recent improvements on the foot-control hydraulic-power lift on Farmall tractors and the construction of a new implement plant at Poplar Bluff, Missouri, the International Harvester Company of Memphis will no doubt be selling more farm machinery than ever before. As a salesman of Farmall tractors and equipment, I am sure I could help to continue your record of improving sales.
>
> --
>
> The marked increase in General Motors sales for the first two quarters undoubtedly reflects the favorable public reception of the new passenger car models and the new Frigidaire appliances.
>
> These increased sales plus the increased production as announced in your annual report also mean more work for your accounting staff. I can take care of a man-sized share of this extra work, I believe—and with a minimum of training.
>
> --
>
> The regular Saturday night reports your retail dealers submit show consumer trends which I want to help you translate into continued Whirlpool leadership—as an analyst in your sales department.

Each of these candidates continued to talk the terminology peculiar to the job. For example, the sales applicant referred knowingly to farmers and farming activities and to the selling activities of making calls, demonstrating, closing, and—probably most important in selling farm machinery—servicing. Such informed references are highly persuasive in any application letter because they establish in a desirable way the impression that the writer is well aware of the work conditions and requirements.

You want to show such knowledge, of course. But if you state it in independent clauses (flat facts which the reader probably already knows) you'll sound wooden and dull.

The desirability of *emphasizing qualifications instead of analysis* will be clearer to you through comparing the following original letter and the revision. The original is almost painful in its flat, obvious statements. It also uses so much space stating requirements of the job that it fails to establish qualities of the applicant. The revision eliminates the flatness and preachiness through implication or incidental reference.

ORIGINAL

It takes a secretary who is versatile, accurate, reliable and dependable for a firm like the Brown Insurance Company. I realize the importance of your having such a secretary, and I believe I have the necessary qualifications.

Having graduated from the University of Alabama with commercial studies as my major, I am familiar with such machines as the adding machine, Mimeograph, and Comptometer. Since my graduation I have been employed as a secretary with the Reynolds Metal Company. This has given me an opportunity to combine my knowledge with experience.

Insurance takes a lot of time and patience. A large amount of bookkeeping is required because every penny has to be accounted for. My one year of accounting at the University will enable me to keep your books neatly and correctly; and if it is necessary for me to work overtime, I am in good physical health to do so.

REVISED

My year's work as a secretary, four years' thorough college training in commercial studies, and lifetime residence in Tuscumbia should enable me to serve you well as a secretary and further the friendly relations between you and your clients.

Whether you want to send a memo to a salesman, a note to a client, or a letter to the home office, I could have it on your desk for signing within a short time. While earning my degree at Alabama, I developed a dictation rate of 100 words per minute and a transcription rate of 45, which I demonstrated daily during my year's work as secretary with the Reynolds Metal Company.

To help with the varied kinds of record keeping in a large insurance agency, I can use the knowledge and skills from a year's course in accounting and my study of filing systems, office practices, and office machines—all applied during my year of work. You can

ORIGINAL	REVISED
Since the Brown Insurance Company has many customers in different parts of the country, a large amount of business letters and transactions are carried on. As your secretary, I could take dictation at 100 words a minute and transcribe your letters accurately and neatly at 45 words a minute.	trust me to compute premiums accurately, send notices on schedule, and devise and turn out special forms when necessary.
Even though accuracy and speed are important, personality is an important characteristic too. Because of the many kinds of people who are connected with this type of business, it is important to have a secretary who not only can file, take dictation, and type, but who can be a receptionist as well. Since I have lived in Tuscumbia all my life, I will know most of your clients as individuals and can serve them in a friendly manner.	I realize that in an insurance agency everyone from the janitor to the bookkeeper affects the feeling of the public and that all must exercise friendliness and tact in any contact with a client. I anticipate the unexpected, and I meet it calmly; so I am prepared to handle a number of duties and to adjust to the demands of a busy, varied work schedule (including overtime work when it's necessary). I would expect to maintain cordial relations with all your customers quite naturally and easily because most of them are the neighbors and friends I've lived around all my life.
I have enclosed a data sheet for your convenience.	Mr. Bills and the other references I've listed on the enclosed data sheet will be glad to confirm my statements that I can work efficiently and cheerfully for you as a secretary who is able and willing to do more than turn out letters. After you've heard from them, please call me at 374-4726 and name a time that I may come in and talk with you.
Will you please call me at 374-4726 and tell me when I can talk to you?	

Although the revision is a little longer, it accomplishes a good deal more: It establishes qualifications in a good lead; it talks the special language of the reader; it establishes more qualifications. It also has a much better work-for-you interpretation. But the major improvement of the revision over the original is that it eliminates the preachy, flat statements (particularly at the beginnings of paragraphs) that made a smart girl sound dull.

Asking for appropriate action

Whatever action you want your reader to take, identify it as specifically as possible, and ask confidently for it. Ordinarily it is to invite you in for an interview. As a self-respecting human being who has something to offer, you do not need to beg or grovel; but you do need to remember—and to show your realization of the fact—that the reader is under no obligation to see you, that giving you time is doing you a favor, that the time and place of the interview are to be at the reader's convenience, and that you should be grateful for the interview.

The action ending of the sales letter needs to be slightly modified in the application letter, however. You cannot with good grace exert as much pressure. For this reason most employment counselors and employers do not advocate using any reply device (an employer is happy to pay the postage to send a message to a potentially good employee, and writing and mailing a letter are routine actions). But your application action ending still suggests a specific action, tries to minimize the burdensome aspects of that action through careful phrasing, establishes gratitude, and supplies a stimulus to action with a reminder of the contribution the applicant can make to the firm.

You've already seen several action endings in this chapter. But to drive home the point, let's look at the action endings of the four letters with which we started this analysis.

The Red Cross applicant definitely planned a trip to Washington for job-hunting purposes; so she concluded her letter logically and naturally with

When I'm in Washington during the first two weeks in August, I should be grateful for the opportunity to come to your office and discuss further how I may serve in filling your present need for Red Cross club directors. Will you name a convenient time in a letter to me at my Birmingham address?

The industrial-management applicant phrased his ending in this simple fashion:

Please suggest a time when you can conveniently allow me to discuss my qualifications for work in your industrial engineering department.

And the secretarial applicant confidently asked her exporter-reader:

Won't you please call me at 615-5946 and tell me a time when I may come to your office and show you how well my preparation will fit into your firm?

The publisher's-representative applicant was in a slightly atypical situation. He couldn't afford to ask directly for an interview in New York because he had neither the money nor the time right then. So he wrote:

After you've had a chance to verify some of the things I've said about myself in this letter and on the data sheet, will you write me frankly about the possibilities of my working for you?

Possibly I could talk with one of your regional representatives in this area as a preliminary step. And I can plan to come to

> New York sometime this summer to talk with you further about my successfully representing your firm.

(As it turned out, he flew to New York at the expense of the firms on two occasions within two weeks after sending the letters, but that was the result of further correspondence—and it's certainly not anything to count on!)

Such letters as suggested in the preceding pages and in the checklist for applications won't work miracles. They won't make a poor applicant a good one. They won't ordinarily secure a job; usually they can only open the door for an interview and further negotiations, but that is their purpose. To make yours do all it can, you may want to review the list of suggestions on pp. 364–65.

WRITING THE INVITED APPLICATION

Often a firm makes its personnel needs known (especially for middle- and upper-management positions) by running an ad, by listing with an agency (commercial, where they'll charge you a fee, or governmental like the U.S. Employment service offices and state-government equivalents), or simply by word of mouth. As you probably know, most large companies also list their needs for college-graduate personnel with college placement bureaus and have recruiting personnel who regularly visit campuses scouting for talented young men and women.

These situations (where the prospective employer actually goes out searching for new employees) give you one drawback (you'll have more competition because more people will know about the job) and two advantages in writing a letter: (1) you don't need to generate interest at the beginning (you already have it!); and (2) the ad, agency, or talent scout will give you the job requirements or as a bare minimum identify the job category and principal duties.

Even when you hear of the job through other people, they will usually tell you what you'll be expected to do. So matching up your qualifications with the job requirements is easier in the invited situation than in the prospecting because your source will usually identify requirements in some order indicating their relative importance to the employer.

If you are equally strong on all points of preparation, you have no problem. You simply take up the points in the order listed. But such a happy condition you'll rarely find. Most often your best talking point is not the most significant requirement, and usually you'll be deficient in some way. The solution is to employ the same strategy you did in writing the invited sales letter: Tie in your strongest point of preparation with something the reader wants done; take up those points wherein you are weakest in the middle position of the letter and attempt to correlate them with some positive point.

Your analysis of job requirements and compilation of a data sheet are exactly the same procedures as in a prospecting situation. Adaptation is simply easier. And once past the opening, supplying evidence and asking for appropriate action are the same. Since the beginnings in the prospecting and the invited applications do differ somewhat, we need to consider why and to make some suggestions that will help you write good ones.

Whether you learn of the job through an ad, through an agency, or via a third person, your beginning is pretty much the same. The first requirement is that it mention your main qualifications; the second, that it identify the job; the third, that it show a service attitude; and the fourth that it refer to the source of the information (*subordinately* unless it is significant). The reason for naming this fourth function is simply that the reference to the ad, or the bureau, or the person who told you about the job is an automatic attention getter which favorably reinforces the reader's willingness or even eagerness to read your letter. One good sentence can accomplish all four functions and point the trend of the letter.

The opening of the following letter puts emphasis on service through work, clearly identifies the specific kind of work sought, and desirably subordinates the reference to the source. Note that after the opening the letter reads much the same as a prospecting application (indeed, if you omit the lead in the faked address block and the first two lines, it could be a prospecting letter). Note also the adaptation of talking points—the stress on experience rather than on formal training.

I'm "sold
on insurance"

and I believe I can be the aggressive salesman for whom you advertised in Thursday's Express.

Five years of experience in dealing with people very similar to your prospects—in addition to technical training in insurance and salesmanship—would aid me in selling your low-premium accident policy.

As a pipeliner in Louisiana in 1971 I made friends with the kind of men to whom I'd be selling your policies. I had a chance to study people, their hopes and fears and desires for protection and security, while doing casework for the Welfare Society in San Antonio in the summer of 1972. And while working as a waiter both in high school and in college I learned how to work for and with the public.

The most significant thing I learned was to keep right on smiling even though dog-tired at the end of my 6-12 p.m. shift after having been to school most of the day. And I certainly learned the meaning of perseverance when I had to go home after midnight and get on the books for the next day's assignments.

The same perseverance that earned me B's in Insurance and Income Protection, Liability Insurance, and Personal Salesmanship will help me find leads, follow them up, persuade, and close a sale. I know an insurance man makes money for himself and his company only when he sticks to a schedule of calls. But I'm equally aware of the value of patience and the necessity for repeat calls.

Because I'm friendly and apparently easygoing, your prospects would like to see me coming. I was elected a Favorite at Schreiner Institute, and at the University of Texas I was tapped for Silver Spurs, a service-honorary organization. Making these many friends has resulted in my knowing people from all sections of the state.

My build and obvious good health inspire confidence. And since I'm 24 and single, I am free to travel anywhere at any time, as well as to work nights.

Dr. Fitzgerald and the other men I've listed on the enclosed information sheet can help you evaluate me professionally and personally if you'll write or call them.

I should be grateful for your telling me a convenient time and place when I may talk with you further about my qualifications for being the hardworking salesman you want.

Frequently your source—especially an ad—gives you an effective entering cue and provides you with useful reference phrases throughout the letter. From the key phrases you can almost reconstruct the ad the young man answered in the following letter:

Because of my college training in accounting and my work experience, I believe I can be the quick-to-learn junior accountant for whom you advertised in the May Journal of Accountancy.

Having successfully completed down-to-earth studies in tax accounting and auditing while earning my degree in accounting at Alabama, I should be able to catch on to your treatment of these problems quickly.

And while working as assistant ledger clerk for the Grantland Davis firm in Atlanta one semester, I developed a great respect for accuracy as well as an appreciation of the necessity for the conscientious, painstaking labor so essential in public accounting. There, too, I also saw clearly the necessity for absorbing confidential information without divulging it in any manner to others.

My natural aptitude for synthesis and analysis, strengthened by special study of the analysis of financial statements and reinforced with a broad background of economics, law, and statistics, should enable me to handle the recurring tasks of compiling comparative statements of earnings and net worth. And my training in writing reports will help me to tell the story to my seniors as well as to clients.

Realizing that the public accountant must gain the confidence of his clients through long periods of accurate, trustworthy service, I welcome the offer of a long-range advancement program mentioned in your ad. I'm not afraid of hard work. And I enjoy the good health essential in the long, irregular working hours of rush business seasons.

Will you study the diversified list of courses and the description of my internship listed on the attached data sheet?

Note also, please, the wide range of activities I took part in while maintaining an A average. Then will you write the references I've listed as a basis for letting me talk with you further about my qualifications for beginning a career of immediate usefulness to you?

I can start to work any time after graduation on June 4.

A variation of source doesn't affect your procedure—except that you *emphasize a source that would be influential in your getting the job; otherwise, subordinate the source.* If you learn of the work through an agency or a third person, the procedure is still the same. Here are some openings bearing out our statement:

Since I have the qualifications necessary for successful selling that you listed in your recent letter to the dean of students here at the University of Illinois, I believe I could serve you well as a salesman.

--

When I talked with Mr. Hugh Lomer this morning, he assured me that I am qualified by experience and professional training for the duties of a field auditor with your firm.

--

During the four years I worked as a branch-house auditor for the L. B. Price Mercantile Company to put myself through school, I became thoroughly familiar with every phase of accounting work necessary for a branch office of a large installment concern and with the reports required by the home office.

I'd certainly like the chance to prove that my education and personal characteristics parallel the description of the desirable management trainee that you gave to Dr. Morley, head of our placement bureau, when you visited the campus last week.

Two warnings need sounding, however. *The first is to guard carefully against the stupid question, the one with the obvious answer.* It is usually the result of asking a question which is made perfectly clear from the ad or the situation. When a young lady began her application to a legal firm with—

Are you looking for a college-trained secretary who can do the work in your law office efficiently and accurately and who is eager to learn law work? If so, I think I can meet your exacting requirements for a legal secretary.

—she was earnestly trying to highlight the employer's needs. But the reader had made the answer to her question perfectly clear in the ad! And an efficient candidate only looked silly in the eyes of this reader.

You don't need to worry about setting out requirements; they are already clearly established. Even this opening is questionable because the answer is so obvious:

Wouldn't that junior accountant you advertised for in the Tribune be more valuable to your firm if she had a sound understanding of accounting theory and principles and basic training in industrial accounting?

Prospecting Application Checklist

1. The prospecting application must generate interest from the start.
   a) Establish early your central selling point of education or experience or both, in terms of doing something for the reader. You may also cite your research on the company or the field, or tell a human-interest story; but they postpone the real message.
   b) Avoid the preaching or didactic, flat statement.
   c) Avoid implying that your up-to-date techniques are better, or telling the reader how to run the business.
   d) Make clear early that you are seeking work of a specialized nature, not just any job.
   e) Be realistic; talk work and doing, not "forming an association with." Avoid *position, application, vacancy,* and *opportunity.*
   f) You need verve and vigor, not stereotypes like "Please consider my application . . . ," "I should like to apply for . . . ."
   g) Don't let your biography drown out what you can do now.
   h) Don't give the reader an opportunity to shut you off with a negative response.
   i) Mere graduation (rather than the preparation back of it) is a poor lead anywhere, especially at first.
   j) Eliminate selfish-sounding statements or overtones of them.
2. Interpretation and tone are important from the start.
   a) Maintain a consistent, acceptable tone, neither apologizing for what you don't have nor bragging about what you do.
   b) For conviction, back up your assertions of ability with specific points of education or experience as evidence.
   c) Generalizing and editorializing are out of place: "invaluable," "more than qualified," even "excellent."
   d) Avoid needlessly deprecating your good qualifications.
   e) Project your education or experience right to the job.
   f) Use enough "I's" for naturalness, but avoid monotony.
   g) Show the research and thought which have gone into the project. Address the letter to the appropriate individual if at all possible; talk about company operations and trends in the industry; even a deft, tactful reference to a competitor can be a point in your favor.
3. Your education and experience are your conviction elements.
   a) Talk about your experience, schooling, or personal characteristics in terms of accomplishing something. For example, you may register for, take, attend, study, receive credit for, pass, learn, or master a course.
   b) The emphasis should go on a phase of work connected with the job you're applying for.

Prospecting Application Checklist
(continued)

c) Refer to education as work preparation (in lowercase letters) rather than exact course titles (in capitals and lowercase).
d) You need highlights rather than details in the letter.
e) But even highlights need to be specific for conviction.
f) Your data sheet supplies thorough, detailed coverage. Refer to it incidentally, in a sentence establishing some other significant idea, just before asking the reader to take action.
g) A one-page letter may be desirable, but it's more important that you tell all of your story in the most effective way for you.

4. Reflect your personality in both content and style.
   a) Refer to the more significant personal characteristics affecting job performance, preferably with evidence that you have them.
   b) Incorporate phrases which reveal your attitude toward work and your understanding of working conditions.
5. Ask for appropriate action in the close.
   a) Name the action you want; make it specific and plausible.
   b) Don't beg and don't command; just ask. And avoid the aloof, condescending implications of "You may call me at . . . ." Usually you ask for an appointment to talk about the job.
   c) Eliminate references to application, interview, position. Use action references to work and the steps in job getting.
   d) Clearly imply or state that you will be grateful. But "Thank you for . . ." in present tense sounds presumptuous.
   e) Show success consciousness without presumptuousness.
   f) A little sales whip-back at the end will help strengthen the impression of what you can contribute.

FOR WRITING INVITED APPLICATIONS

6. When writing an application in response to an ad or at the suggestion of an agency or friend:
   a) Primary emphasis should be on putting your preparation to work for the reader. But since your reference to the source is an automatic way of securing attention, you should identify it early and emphasize it if it carries an implied recommendation.
   b) Avoid stating what the reader would infer ("I read your ad").
   c) Don't ask questions or phrase assumptions which are clear pushovers: "If you are seeking X, Y, and Z, then I'm your man." "Are you looking for an employee with X, Y, and Z? I have X, Y, and Z."
   d) Postpone salary talk until the interview if you can. If the phrase "State salary required" is included in the description, your reply of "your going rate" or "your usual wage scale" is acceptable to any firm you'd want to work for.

The reader would probably snort, "More? She wouldn't be valuable if she didn't!"

The second warning is against showing signs of selfish glee over having discovered a job possibility of your choice. When you read or hear about the job, you may rightly think, "That's just what I want!"—but don't write this or any variation of it. Resist the impulse and start writing in terms of doing something for the reader: what you can give instead of what you hope to get.

Perhaps a third warning should be sounded against assuming that you don't have much of a selling job to do because the reader is on the asking end. Nothing could be further from the truth. The competition you're up against for an advertised job is keen even in the heyday of prosperity. And because many others will apply, you'll have to write a superior letter to be chosen as one of the final few for interviewing.

In fact, the reader may face such a heap of letters that yours may not even get read. For that reason you may want to do one of several things so that your letter will command attention and thus be selected for reading. Most of these have to do with the physical impression or the mechanics of sending.

A favorite device is sending the letter by special delivery. Few personnel people ever object. If you are in the same town, you can deliver the letter yourself, with the request that it be turned over to the appropriate person.

If you insert the letter in an envelope large enough to accommodate an 8½- by 11-inch page without folding and put a piece of cardboard under it to keep it smooth, the contrast between your letter and all the others that have been folded will call attention to yours.

Cutting out the ad and pasting it neatly at the top of the page may single out your letter for attention. Beginning your message with a faked address block which quotes from the ad is another device. Hanging indention may help to make a rushed reader reach for your letter instead of another. Even appropriate color may cause the employer to read yours rather than another in the stack.

When competition is keen, you'll need to take the time and exert the effort to be sure that your letter is one of the earliest arrivals. This may mean getting up early to get the first edition of the newspaper and having your material in such shape that you can have a complete, well-written letter and data sheet in the hands of the employer hours or even days before less alert candidates get theirs there. Even though you may not get the immediate response you want, your letter (if it is good) becomes better in the eyes of the employer as poorer ones come in through the mail. Remember, too, that people are relieved by the first application that comes in and feel kindly toward it. It relieves the fear of every such advertiser, that maybe no one will answer the ad.

But none of these devices will make much difference if your letter is not written from the viewpoint of contributing to the firm through effective, efficient work.

As you already realize, the items we suggested to you in the prospecting application checklist (p. 364) apply equally when you write an invited letter. Study them again, and review the additional items at the end of that checklist which are peculiar to the invited situation.

CONTINUING THE CAMPAIGN

Regardless of the results from your application, you have some follow-up work to do.

If you get an invitation to an interview, you know how to handle it. Accept promptly, pleasantly, and directly (if that's your decision) as suggested in Chapter 5. Just remember to continue your job campaign by indicating continuing interest in serving. If you decide to turn down the invitation, Chapter 7 has shown you how; but remember, also, the adage about never burning your bridges behind you.

If within a reasonable time you do not hear from the person or firm you've applied to, you'd probably better send a follow-up letter indicating continuing interest.

Follow-up letters

A good salesperson doesn't make one call and drop the matter if that doesn't close the sale. Neither does a sales-minded job applicant. Even if you receive the usual noncommittal letter saying that the firm is glad to have your application and is filing it in case any opening occurs, you need not hesitate to send another letter two, three, or six months after the first one. It should not be another complete application (yours will still be on file); it is just a reminder that you are still interested.

To have a reason for sending a follow-up letter two or three weeks after the original application, some applicants intentionally omit some pertinent but relatively insignificant piece of information in the original.

> I noticed in rereading my copy of the application I sent you three weeks ago that I did not list Mr. Frank Regan, manager, Bell's Supermarket, Anniston, Alabama.
>
> Since I have worked under Mr. Regan's direct supervision for three summers, he is a particularly good man to tell you about my work habits and personality. I hope you will write to him.

Such a subterfuge we cannot commend, if for no other reason than that so many other approaches are available to you. One acceptable one is this:

> I know that many organizations throw away applications over six months old.
>
> Because that much time has elapsed since I sent you mine (dated April 15), I want to assure you that I'm still

interested in working for you, in having you keep my record in your active file, and in hearing from you when you need someone with my qualifications.

Only a lackadaisical applicant would end the letter there, however. Just a few more words could bring the information up to date and perhaps stimulate more interest in the application, like this:

Since graduation I have been doing statistical correlations at the Bureau of Business Research here at the University. I've picked up a few techniques I didn't learn in class, and I've certainly increased my speed on the computer keyboard and calculator.

I still want that job as sales analyst with your firm, however.

Election to an office or an honorary society, an extensive trip that has opened your eyes to bigger and better possibilities of the job, a research paper that has taught you something significant to the job, and certainly another job offer are all avenues of approach for reselling yourself and indicating continuing interest.

Thank-you letters

Following an interview, whether the results seem favorable or unfavorable, your note of appreciation is not only a business courtesy; it helps to single you out from other applicants and to show your reader that you have a good sense of human relations.

Even when you and the interviewer have agreed that the job is not for you, you can profitably invest about two minutes writing something like this:

I surely appreciate the time you spent with me last Friday discussing employment opportunities at Monitor and Wagner.

The suggestions you made will help me find my right place in the business world now.

After I get that experience you suggested, I may be knocking at your door again.

When you are interested in the job discussed and feel that you have a good chance, you're plain foolish not to write a letter expressing appreciation and showing that you learned something from the interview.

Your description of the community relations program of Livania has opened new vistas to me, Mr. Lee.

The functions of the public relations department in your company as you described them made me much more aware of the significance and appeal of this work.

As soon as I returned to the campus, I read Mr. Fields's book that you suggested and the pamphlets describing U.S. Steel's program.

Many thanks for your suggestions and for the time you took with me.

I shall be looking forward to hearing the decision about my application as soon as you can make it.

Job-acceptance letters

When an employer offers you a job and you decide it's the one for you, say so enthusiastically and happily in a direct A–plan letter that keeps you in a favorable light.

I certainly do want to work with Franklin & Franklin——and I didn't need a week to think it over, Mr. Bell, although I appreciate your giving me that much time to come to a decision.

I've filled out the forms you gave me and enclosed them with this letter.

Anything else?

Unless you tell me differently, I'll take off two weeks after graduation. But I'll call you on Friday, June 11, to get report-to-work instructions for Monday, June 14.

Job-refusal letters

Sometime in your life you'll have to tell somebody that you don't want what has been offered. You may feel that it's routine, that it doesn't mean anything one way or the other to a busy person who interviews many applicants and has many other people available. Remember, though, that a human being with pride and ego is going to read the letter. And make yourself think, "I don't want that job *now*," for you may want to reopen negotiations at some future point.

To wind up negotiations pleasantly and leave the way open for you, write a B–plan letter with a pleasant buffer of some favorable comment about the company or the work, some plausible and inoffensive reason, the presentation of the refusal as positively as you can phrase it (possibly with the statement of where you are going to work), and an ending expressing good feeling and appreciation or both. The following letter is a good example:

Meeting you and talking with you about working for Bowen's was one of the more interesting job contacts I have had.

The opportunity to learn the business from the ground up and to grow with an expanding company is a challenging one, one for which I am grateful.

As I told you, however, I am primarily interested in product research. Since I feel that my abilities will best be utilized in that way, I am going to work for (a company) that has offered me such employment.

I shall certainly continue to watch your company's progress with interest, and I shall look forward to reading or hearing about the results of your prepackaging program.

Letters of resignation

Resignation letters, like job-refusal letters, are modified B–plan letters. When you have worked for a firm, you have benefited in some way (in addition to the regular pay you have drawn). Regardless of how you may feel at the time, remember that you can say something complimentary about how things are run, about what you have learned as a result of your experience, or about the people with whom you have associated. By all means, say it! Then announce your plan to leave, giving consideration to the necessity for ample time in which to find a replacement. In some cases no more than two weeks is enough advance notification; sometimes it should be long enough for you to help train the person who will take your place.

Remember, however, that you want to stay in the good graces of the individuals who have assisted you in your career. You will be wise to give ample notification, to give credit where credit is due. The suggestion to "Be kind, courteous, and considerate to the people you pass on the way up the ladder of success; you will likely meet them on your way back down" is good advice to keep in mind when you leave a job.

In many circumstances your resignation can be oral. And in many circumstances it may be better that way. But when you need to write a letter, consider adaptations of the following:

I've certainly learned a great deal about the clothing market from my work as sales analyst at Foley's the past 18 months.

I shall always be grateful to you and the other personnel who have helped me to do the job and to prepare for a more challenging one.

You will perhaps recall that when I had my interviews with you before starting to work, I stressed my interest in working toward a job as a sales coordinator.

Since I now have such an opportunity at Sakowitz, Inc., I am submitting my resignation. Apparently it will be some time before such an opening is available for me in this organization.

I should like to terminate employment in two weeks. But I can make arrangements to work a little longer if this will help to train the person who takes my place.

My thanks and good wishes.

Often when another offer comes your way, you'll feel free to discuss the opportunity with your current employer before making a final decision. Such a conference has many advantages for both employee and employer. Often a counteroffer results, to the mutual satisfaction of both, and the job change doesn't take place. If, despite a counteroffer, you still decide to make the change, you can resign in good grace with a letter somewhat like this:

> Your recent offer is one I appreciate very much, and it made me give serious thought to continuing at Bowen's.
>
> Let me say again how much I have appreciated the cooperation, the friendliness, and helpfulness of everyone with whom I've been associated here.
>
> After considerably more evaluation, however, I believe I can make a greater contribution and be a more successful business manager by accepting the position offered me by Lowen's.
>
> I hope that I can leave with your approval by (specific date); I feel sure that all my current projects will be completed by that time.
>
> You'll hear from me from time to time—if for no other reason than that I'll be interested in how the new credit union works out.
>
> But I'll always want to know how things are going for Bowen's and the many friends I've made here.

When appropriate, a possible talking point is the suggestion of a successor to you; often this is a big help. A constructive suggestion, phrased positively, implies your continuing interest in the organization.

Letters of resignation written by college students who resign after having agreed to work for someone but before actually reporting for work are something we take up with reluctance. Many personnel people regard them as breaches of contract. Certainly a practice of sliding out from under such agreements will soon give you a black eye employmentwise.

We would urge you to give serious thought before definitely accepting a job offer. Don't make the mistake of grabbing the first job offered you, only to have something infinitely more to your liking come along later. We'd further urge you never to let yourself get caught in the position of being committed to two employers at the same time. If you have agreed to go to work for a firm and then you have a later offer which you want to accept, do not accept it until you are released from the first contract. To the second potential employer, reply in some vein like this:

> I certainly would like to accept your offer to come with your firm. As attractive as your proposal is, however, I must delay accepting it until I can secure a release from the Jenkins firm in Blankville. After my interview with you, I accepted this position, which at the time appeared to be the most promising available.
>
> Can you allow me enough time to write the Jenkins personnel manager, explaining my reasons and requesting a release? (I can give him the names of two friends who might be suitable replacements.)
>
> This shouldn't take longer than a week to settle. I appreciate your offer, regardless of how things work out.

If necessary, phone the second potential employer, explain frankly, and get approval to wait. But for your own protection, do it *before* writing a letter like the following:

> As you know, I am now planning to report to work as an executive trainee shortly after the first of June.
>
> Before I made this agreement with you, I had talked with a representative of the Larkin organization in Sometown concerning possibilities of my working there as an analyst in the quality control division, which is the kind of work I have specifically trained for and know I want to do.
>
> I believe I'd be a better adjusted and qualified employee in the Larkin job. That is the main reason I ask that you release me from my commitment with you. The fact that Sometown is a considerably larger city and that the starting salary is somewhat larger are only secondary considerations.
>
> No doubt you have other people you can call on to take my place, but you may be interested to know that Don M. Jones and Peter Lawson are interested in the Jenkins program. You can get portfolios on both of them through the placement bureau here at school.
>
> Since the Larkin people have agreed to postpone a decision until I have heard from you, I should appreciate a quick reply.
>
> You can rest assured that I shall keep my word with you and that if your answer is no, I shall report to work as promised and do all I can to be an efficient, cooperative, and cheerful employee.

Only a Simon Legree would say no to the foregoing letter. If the company releases you, you'd then write the appropriate acceptance letter to the second firm; but you should, as a matter of business courtesy, write a short thank-you letter to the first company.

TWO USEFUL MODIFICATIONS OF APPLICATIONS

The following two letter possibilities for helping you get the job of your choice are *not printed here with the implication that they will take the place of the complete sales presentation* we have suggested to you. Because they may help you sometimes, we simply remind you of them.

The job-anticipating letter

Most personnel people are willing to give advice. And most of them are pleased with a show of interest in their companies and evidence of long-range planning on the part of a student. Several of our students have had successful results from letters like the following, sent in the junior year of college:

A course in the operation of business machines under Mrs. Lora Osmus in the Statistics Department at Alabama gave me skill in their operation and showed me the tremendous possibilities of Burrows equipment for business use.

After comparing Burrows and ABL equipment that was on exhibit on Commerce Day and talking with the Burrows representative in charge of your display, I am coming to you directly and frankly for some help.

Since I have completed practically all of the courses required for the B.S. in commerce, I am free to elect practically all courses I shall study next year before June graduation. On the attached sheet I've listed the courses I've completed and those I'm contemplating. Will you please rank the ones you consider most beneficial for a prospective Burrows representative?

Naturally, I will regard your suggestions as off-the-cuff assistance that implies no commitment. I'm just trying to equip myself as well as I can to meet the competition for the first available job with your company after I graduate.

I shall be most grateful for your comments.

The telescoped application inquiry

We realize that good applications take time. They're worth the time, however.

But we also know that sometime, somewhere, you may need to send some inquiries in a hurry and simply cannot write a complete one. You may be able to make profitable use of the services of your college placement bureau in a letter, as one young man did. He was too busy writing a thesis and sitting for graduate examinations to prepare a thorough application. He sent the following request and a reply card to six firms:

With completion of an M.S. degree in accounting at the University of Alabama and two years of retail merchandise accounting experience, I believe I could make you a good accountant with a minimum of training—and be able to advance more rapidly than the majority of accountants you could hire.

I am not just an accountant: A well-rounded background of finance, transportation, economics, and other related subjects will enable me, in time, to do managerial work as well.

May I have the Placement Bureau here at the University send you a transcript of my college record together with a detailed record of my experience, faculty rating statements, and names and addresses of former employers?

I shall be happy to furnish any additional information you may want and to be available for an interview at your convenience later if you will check and return the enclosed card.

He received replies from all six firms, it's true. But only one resulted in an interview.

This may be a stopgap measure sometime. But this young man's experience simply reconfirms the fact that an applicant must tell a complete story if he expects to get a show of effective interest.

Although letters exchanging information about applicants are a part of the employment routine, applicants themselves do not write them. For that reason, and because you studied them in Chapter 5, we see no point in taking them up here. They are A–plan letters, characterized by directness and conciseness.

Likewise, we do not think you need to study or write the kinds of letters an interviewer or employer writes to an applicant who is accepted for a position (clearly an A–plan good-news letter) or to an applicant who is not accepted (a B–plan disappointing-news letter). With but simple changes of talking points and references, they follow the principles of their basic plan.

LETTER CASES FOR APPLICATIONS

Prospecting applications

1. Assume that you are in your last term of school and graduation is around the corner. Your interest is in finding work which you like, for which you have been preparing, and in which you could support yourself now and a family later as you win promotions.

Newspapers, trade magazines, and placement bureaus list no job of your choice. So you decide to do as any good salesman does: survey the product (yourself); then appraise the market (companies which could use a person who can do what you are prepared to do); then advertise (send the companies a data sheet with an application letter). Such a procedure sometimes creates a job where none existed before; sometimes it establishes a basis for negotiations for the "big job" two, three, or five years after graduation. And very frequently it puts you on the list for the good job which is not filled through advertising or from the company staff.

To analyze the high points of your preparation, you will need to consider the courses you have had and make plausible assumptions (don't go daydreaming and woolgathering; stick to probabilities) about the courses you will have completed on graduation. *This means you'll have to study your college catalog.* It also means that you will have to make a temporary decision about the kind of work you want to do. If you haven't the faintest idea of what you'd like to do, follow the suggestions in Chapter 9.

Distinguish between those courses which actually qualify you to do the type of work you are seeking and those which give you background education. If you've had experience directly related to the job you want as a career, that's fine; but any work you've done means qualifications (military experience—active duty—is in almost the same category as on-the-job experience). With these training and work sections mapped out, complete a tentative data sheet with personal details and some appropriate references.

Then study the market, as suggested under "Analyzing Companies" (p. 331). In actual practice you would compile a list of companies and send them an application. For this assignment, after some preliminary digging around, select one company and plan a letter–data sheet combination addressed to that company. Adapt it as specifically as possible to the one company. You may or may not be able to find out the name of the specific individual to address it to. If not, address it to the personnel department or to the head of the particular department in which you are interested.

You will benefit from this exercise in application letter writing only if you approach it earnestly and seriously. *It should be a job utilizing your college training.* It should be a job geared to what you could reasonably assume will be your level of performance at graduation. Few just-out-of-college folks can expect to be sales managers, chief buyers, senior accountants, copy chiefs, and the like; you'll have to begin at a subordinate level and work up; you'll want to *show in your letter that you realize this fact.* On the other hand, don't waste your time and your instructor's applying for something that you could readily do if you had never gone to college.

You will sometimes hear advice to confine your presentation to a one-page letter and a data sheet. But don't be afraid to go to a two-page or longer letter. As in sales letters, some highly successful ones run to two and sometimes even three pages. What is important is that you make your presentation fully, and in the way that is most favorable for you. Data sheets or résumés seldom fit on one page; and as with the letter, you should take as much space as necessary to present the facts about yourself in the best light.

2. Now that tuition costs and living expenses for next year will increase substantially, the money you saved for your senior year won't be enough to pay your expenses. You'll have to get a part-time job to make up the difference. Before you came to school, you worked for Krooger Foods in Washington, D.C. You liked the work and managed in four years to work your way up from bagger to grocery manager. You also know how to run a cash register. You left Krooger to finish the two years remaining on your degree program at Iowa City, Iowa, after completing your AA degree at Montgomery Community College in Silver Spring, Maryland. You liked the grocery business and might eventually be interested in the manager-trainee program of one of the local supermarkets. Write a letter that with slight changes could be sent along with your data sheet to the personnel directors of the major supermarket chains in Iowa City. In your letter present your qualifications, both schooling and practical experience, and ask for an interview.

3. Write a job-seeking letter for work next summer. It should not only enable you to earn some money to apply on your college expenses; it should also be work which will be good preparation for the career you plan when you finish your degree and/or leave college. Too, consider the prestige value of the company name on data sheets you will prepare later in your life.

This may well be the company to which you would send an application upon graduation; if so, shape your letter presentation accordingly.

4. Look over your local situation for part-time job possibilities, perhaps on your college campus or in the college community (close enough for you to arrange a schedule of classes that would permit you to work in the afternoons). Word the application so the reader will understand about how many hours a week you can work and that between the end of summer school and fall registration you would prefer to work full time. Prepare a data sheet and letter that summarize and interpret your background up to the time of writing.

5. You've decided that you want to earn some money, see some new places, and have some fun this coming summer. So you're going to address an application for summer employment to an inn at a resort (possibly one of the national parks). You'll have to indicate a willingness to do housekeeping duties (including kitchen and dining room duties), although if you have enough maturity and the right kind of experience you may be able to get some kind of clerical or even more specialized assignment. Since college students chosen for such jobs are really hosts and hostesses to the guests, stress poise, dignity, and cheerfulness, as well as any talents for entertaining.

6. Modify the preceding problem to this extent: You want to be a counselor at a summer camp for children at least five years younger than you. Choose a camp with which you are familiar, or find out about one. Address the letter and data sheet to the camp director (by name if you can get it). Note here the importance of understanding and getting along with youngsters, the ability to direct activities, and the emphasis on athletic abilities. Apply to a camp which is not in your home town or your college town; it should be a residence camp, not a day camp.

7. With plausible assumptions and appropriate modifications, write a job-anticipating letter to the company of your choice. Assume that you have one more year of college before graduating.

8. You have heard recently that next year's budget for your school will be cut back extensively. To offset the increased class size that will result from the funding cutbacks, the Board of Regents has authorized departments to use undergraduates who have made A's in survey courses to act as teachers (guiding students through a programmed course) for those courses. The salary will be $2,500 for nine months, enough to cover your tuition and expenses for the academic year. Since you made an *A* in ________ (use your own major), you feel you can qualify. Write a prospecting job letter (you can't reveal your source since the jobs have not yet been announced publicly) to Theodore Riddle, chairman of the ________ department, outlining your qualifications and asking for an interview.

9. Since you will be graduating in June, you feel that now is the time to prospect for a job. You have already spent two months researching likely corporations, and you have asked the campus placement center to keep a file of your transcripts and reference letters. Write a letter to Jonathan Renolds, personnel director of Universal Products, a large conglomerate. Use your own experience and educational background to request an interview at Universal's nearby branch (select a city near you) for a position that your own qualifications best fill. (You will want to do a thorough job now, so you can use this letter for real later on.)

10. Since you will be graduating next June, you decide to send out job-prospecting letters to several large corporations. You will send a data sheet and application letter. Write your job-prospecting letter to Tennet Lee, personnel director of Powell Corporation, a large interamerican conglomerate. In your letter stress your willingness to work and your qualifications for a job (you select the job, based on your own academic major, experience, or both) in one of Powell's subsidiaries. Remember, your best selling point will probably be your educational background, unless you have some experience that relates to the job you want. Stress the work-for-you attitude and (if you have any) special qualifications (linguistic, physical, genetic, sociological—whatever) that might help in an *interamerican conglomerate.*

Invited applications

1. A good starting point in job getting is the want-ad columns of newspapers and magazines (especially trade magazines). Study the ones of your choice and find an ad that describes a job you would like to have, requiring qualifications you could reasonably assume at the time of your graduation (or some other assumed time as affected by your intentions). It should be a job utilizing your college training. And it should indicate clearly that letter—not telephone—answers are wanted. Clip the ad neatly to your letter; or if you find the ad of your choice in a library copy, make an exact copy, with exact reference: name of publication, date of the issue, and page on which you found the ad. You may instead choose one of the ads listed later in this case.

Draw on imagination, experience, and whatever information you can find out to bring the situation as close to reality as you can. Read the ad thoughtfully for what it says, and search mentally for those qualifications which it only implies. Then evaluate your own training and experience in the light of the specific job. You can readily distinguish between courses that actually qualify you to do the job you're considering and those which are only background. You can certainly classify your work experience in an order of applicability to the given job. Further, analyze significant personal factors. And finally, decide upon references. In actual practice you would want to send a data sheet. For this problem assignment you may assume a data sheet much like the one used with the prospecting application and refer to it in your letter.

Submit the letter trying to get the one job for which you are best suited, either from an ad you've found or one of the following (assume the city):

a) Assistant manager—$10,000 salary and up with this national company. Salary increases plus commission after training program. College graduate and retail experience qualifies. Fast promotions, good benefits. Write M. L. Lampkin, Box C–80, c/o *News.*

b) Child development—County Child Development Council has openings for two new staff members. Communications specialist with journalism or writing experience necessary. Educator to work in the areas of health and nutrition. College degree necessary. Reply Box C–77, c/o *Times.*

c) Sales representative—P. Q. Holcomb Manufacturing Company—has a new local opening. A local semi-established high income potential territory will be available within the next 30 days. The individual will call on industrial, institutional, and commercial accounts. The right person for this career opportunity should have successful sales experience and have a keen desire to earn more. In addition to high earning potential we offer an expense-paid training program, no overnight travel, and ample opportunities for advancement. An Equal Opportunity Employer. Write Box T, *Herald.*

d) Credit and adjustment manager of national shirt manufacturer needs assistant. Handle routine correspondence, supervise clerical help. Bright future for right person. College training, business experience, mature judgment necessary. Salary $7,500 to $10,000, depending on qualifications. Box R–88, c/o *Press.*

e) Accountant—expanding national concern. Traveling. Good opportunity for person with ambition, personality, hard-work habits. State training and experience in confidential letter to P–87, c/o *News.*

f) Executive secretary—Outstanding position for friendly and aggressive person. $475. Write Box 987, c/o *Press,* stating training, and experience.

g) Immediate opening—internal auditor. For young college graduate with major in accounting to train as internal auditor with growing national manufacturer in Iowa. Excellent opportunity for person with executive potential, ambition, attractive personality. Experience helpful but not essential. Established concern. Up-to-date employee benefits. Write giving full details of qualifications and salary requirement. All replies will be kept confidential. Write C–90, c/o *News.*

h) Computer programmer—Must have experience in Cobol & Bal languages. Immediate requirements. Competitive starting salary, excellent benefits, fast-growing company. Send résumé to: Central Computer Services, Box D–90, c/o *News.*

i) Insurance manager—American Life Insurance Company. Must be able to hire and train sales personnel. Prefer college graduate with knowledge of insurance and business. Salary override commission and renewal bonuses. Apply with letter and data sheet, Box 98765, *Times.*

j) Office manager. Knowledge of office machines; knowledge of accounting desirable. Must have initiative, ambition, adaptability, eagerness to learn. State full details, salary expected in letter. Large firm with sales-service outlets in key cities of the United States, Europe, Canada, Mexico. Local Box 70.

k) Production manager for small midtown publisher and producer of distinguished and unusual illustrated books. Good experience. Confidence guaranteed. Box 76, *Marketing Communications.*

l) Customer relations—Position open for person with farm background or farm sales experience. Neatness and ability to talk to people essential. College graduate desirable. Person selected will interview farmers and do limited travel in North Carolina. Earnings range from $11–15,000 first year depending on individual selected. Benefits include stock options and substantial yearly increases in income. Write Manager, Box 79, c/o *Herald.*

2. The director of your college placement bureau (use his name) has just told you about the training program of a large corporation. The personnel director indicated in a letter to your placement officer that the company seeks young college graduates between 21 and 25 (this is not ironclad, however) to train for managerial positions throughout the organization. The training program lasts for a year. During that time trainees work in every division under close supervision and attend a series of classes. Assume a specific company, and prepare a letter and data sheet. (If you have already written a data sheet for the prospecting application, you should use that form with only slight modifications; for this assignment, then, you may just assume the modified form. If you have not already prepared your data sheet, do so for this assignment.) As in any application, indicate your particular field of interest, but reflect a receptive attitude toward the various phases of the training program, showing your realization of its benefits regardless of the specific work you'll eventually perform.

3. Your college adviser is head of the department in which you are pursuing your major studies. This morning he tells you that a firm you hold in high regard is seeking a person with substantially your qualifications for a particular job you want—*a job calling for an unusual combination of qualifications that you have.* Fill in with the necessary specific details and write the letter you would send, assuming that your basic data sheet presentation will accompany it.

4. The same college adviser (preceding case) also suggested several other companies as good prospects but stated specifically that he did not know whether there are openings in these companies at present. "They hire a lot of people," he added, "and if there's no opening now, you can be pretty sure there will be one before long." Using his name early in your lead, write the letter (assume the data sheet).

5. This morning, quite unexpectedly, you had an interview with the representative of a firm you'd like to work for. After half an hour of talk which appeared to be mutually satisfactory and during which time you found out a lot about the company, the representative handed you one of the company employment forms for applying, shook your hand, and ushered you out of the room, saying, "Fill this out and return it to me with a letter of application." *Assuming* the form filled in neatly and completely, draft the earnest but enthusiastic letter of application this man invited. Be careful to talk work rather than employee benefits. Assume specific names for the representative and the company. He said he would write you after receiving your letter.

6. Your college adviser (use the name) recently mentioned to you that a good friend, the personnel director of Superior Petroleum (856 Faisel Avenue, Houston 77020), has written to him to steer good prospects his way at the on-campus interviews coming up next month. You like Superior's positive view toward protecting the environment and had thought of writing a prospecting job letter. Now, however, you can write an invited job letter. Your adviser told you that Superior needed people with your qualifications. Write an *invited* job application letter that shows your qualifications for going to work for Superior, and ask for an appointment during the interview period. Assume that your data sheet goes with the letter.

7. When you went past your department bulletin board last week, you noticed that the Nadir Corporation was advertising for a __________ (put in a job for which your experience and training can qualify you). When you spoke to your adviser, he thought you could fill the job. Write a letter to Maxwell Moody (personnel director of Nadir Corporation, 444 Lake Road, Providence, Rhode Island 02905) in which you present your quali-

fications and ask for an interview telling a short span of days you plan to be in the Providence area.

8. As you passed your department bulletin board last week, you noticed (among the job opportunities and openings) one for a(n) ________ (supply a job based on your major and qualifications) with Ladron, Inc., of 909 Wabash, Chicago, Illinois 60696. Assuming you graduate in June, use the information in your data sheet to write an invited job application letter, in which you show your qualifications for doing the job for Ladron. You read about Ladron in *U.S. Business* and *Fortune* and even had a chance to read last year's annual report, from which you got the name George Diament, personnel director in Chicago. The annual report also outlined plans for the next ten years, the construction of branches in Peoria, Cairo, and Bloomington, Illinois. You prefer an Illinois-based corporation since you want to live in the Mid-West. You will be in Chicago the third week in June and would like to talk with Diament about becoming a ________ for Ladron, Inc.

9. Last week the University Placement Office announced that the Campus Police needs 20 students to act as traffic-control personnel at the entrances to the restricted inner campus. The job pays $3,000 for nine months, plus a tuition waiver for those hired. You have to work four hours a day. Write an invited job-application to Arnold Pulver, the director of the Campus Police traffic-control division of your campus, outlining your qualifications for the job (be creative) and requesting an interview. You will want to stress patience and your ability to get along with people. Military service could help in this case.

10. The recent tuition increase and administration talk about increasing the tuition and fees for the coming year mean you must get a job. You will need to attend school full time for a degree next June. The University has advertised for guides, leaders in the Campus-Tour Program—giving prospective students, their parents, and other interested people tours of the University facilities, from classrooms to game rooms—$2.25 an hour, free tuition for the time of your service, and only 20 hours a week; no transportation problems since you work here on the campus. Write Truman Hardy, Director of University Publicity Office, who is in charge of the program. Forthrightly ask for an interview, but only after stressing your qualifications and why you feel you can help this program succeed.

11. Yesterday you noticed an ad in the (title of student newspaper at your school) that the Union Program Office was interviewing for student Staff Assistants. According to the ad, the job entails developing and presenting entertainment programs for students, such programs as movies, concerts, dances, plays, etc. That's right down your alley. You've been social chairman of your fraternity/sorority for two years and responsible for GREEK WEEK, Epsilon Epsilon Kappa's annual week-long spring entertainment program, featuring dancing, contests, movies, skits, etc. You were also a member of last year's committee that sponsored Homecoming festivities, and you have for two years been a coordinator of activities for Student Government Productions. The Union job is part-time, pays $3,000 a year (25 hours a week), and is just what you need to help cover expenses for your last year in school. You graduate next year with a degree in advertising. Write to Shirley Blair, Program Director, presenting your qualifications and asking for an interview.

Follow-ups

1. Not having heard from the application letter you sent in any of the preceding situations, write a fairly short letter reemphasizing your desire to work for the firm. You may want to send it as soon as three weeks after the initial letter; you may prefer to wait longer. Clearly refer to the original application by date and type of work discussed. Include any additional data you think will help sell you. This letter, however, should not be a rehash of what you have already written. It should identify the action you want the reader to take.

2. Assuming that almost a year has passed since you sent your original letter, write a follow-up letter that reassures the firm of your desire to work there. In the meantime a good deal has happened to you (or should have!). Account for the way you have spent the time in such a manner as to show that it is preparation for the job you seek.

3. Assume that you have had an interview as a result of your letter and data sheet. You know the company representative interviewed several other candidates for the job. In a thank-you letter, confirm your interest in employment by the company and add other details to show that you picked up something from the interview. The representative promised to get in touch with you in a week or ten days.

4. As a result of your determined efforts and good showing, you've been offered the job of your choice. The letter so informing you requests you to fill in an employment form and return it and names a starting date that fits in with your plans. Write the acceptance.

5. Although you were offered a job in response to your application, you have decided that you do not want to accept it because it is not in the field of your primary interest and for other plausible reasons—not salary. Write the tactful letter that expresses appreciation for the time spent with you and the interest shown in you and that leaves the way open for you to resume negotiations later if you care to. Comment favorably on some aspect of the company.

6. You have just been informed that you were not chosen for the job you have worked so hard to get—and still want. Remember, however, that you were considered; that someone spent a good deal of time with you; and that, employmentwise, nothing is ever final. Write the letter expressing appreciation for the courtesies extended you, revealing how you have profited from the contact, and showing your determination to reach your intended goal. Above all, the letter should reflect a friendly feeling toward the company and the representative addressed.

7. In response to your application you receive an invitation to come in for an interview at a time and place convenient for you. Write the acceptance confirming the circumstances.

8. Assume that in response to your prospecting application you receive an invitation to come in for an interview at a time which would be convenient if you had the money for traveling to the distant point. Write the letter which reaffirms your interest. Admit your lack of funds and ask if it is possible to see a representative of the firm at a place which is more accessible to you.

chapter 11

Persuasive messages: Requests

SPECIAL REQUESTS

ALTHOUGH letters asking for information about products, services, and people constitute the bulk of business people's inquiries, sometimes they need *special favors from others who have no built-in motivation to reply.* These special requests are more difficult writing problems than direct inquiries—and for a highly understandable reason: Most people, when asked to do something even slightly out of the ordinary, can think of two reasons why they should not for every one reason why they should.

No one ever has enough money or time to give either of them spontaneously and unquestioningly. No one is willing to reveal certain kinds of information without knowing how it will be used and deciding that the purpose is good. To put the question directly in these cases is to get an immediate no. So the special request has to be a persuasive letter. Like the simple inquiry, the effective special request is specific and concise, but it is not direct; and because it usually requires more details in development, it is usually longer.

Favor-seeking letters are C–plan letters, as already discussed in Chapter 2. As explained there, the secret of successful persuasive copy is to (1) offer, suggest, or imply a benefit to the reader—at least talk about something of interest; (2) explain the worth of your proposal to justify it in your reader's eyes; (3) try to foresee and preclude objections; and (4) after giving necessary details, confidently ask the reader to do what you want.

Before we go further in telling you how to write persuasive request letters, however, a point of caution deserves your attention: *You should not be writing such letters unless you cannot get the information or assistance by your own efforts. You should not be asking others to help you until you have done what you can to help yourself.*

Securing interest

If you are going to strike the appropriately persuasive theme, you need to analyze the situation to select the most pertient and applicable *motive* that might cause the reader to do what you want.

Dollars being what they must be in American business thinking, the strongest appeal is one that holds out to the reader the prospect of sales, of saving money, or of promoting goodwill with an audience wherein sales may ultimately materialize. Such potential-dollar themes offer your reader the most concrete form of reader benefit and are responsible for this opening to an advertising manager of a manufacturing company:

```
What would it be worth to Rigate to add some 8,000 potential
customers to its prospect list?
```

and this opening to the circulation manager of a magazine:

```
Who will be your readers ten years from now?
```

If you can apply such reader-benefit themes appropriately and remain within the realm of good taste (avoiding the suggestion of bribery), you undoubtedly have the strongest appeal you can make.

In many instances, however, such dollar-minded talk would arouse indignation (especially from professional people who do not advertise) or would not apply. But you need not despair of finding a talking point which will stress the reader's benefit or interest rather than your own. The letter to the correspondence supervisor (on p. 39) that begins

```
How often have you received—even from well-educated people—
letters that are not worth your attention?
```

clearly holds out a benefit by talking in terms of making the reader's job easier. Many times the basis for a busy person's filling out a time-consuming questionnaire (or one that asks for information ordinarily restricted to the firm) is the realization that a result of the information thus gathered and made available will be improved efficiency.

Indirect benefits may serve too. When you can show how your project (if successful) will promote the welfare of a group in which your reader holds a membership or other interest, you can write a strong letter. On this basis you might write a letter inviting a public accountant to speak to a college accounting club or a correspondence supervisor to address a group of teachers of business writing or an alumnus of a professional fraternity to take on a responsible office in the organization.

Although many special-request letters are written with appeals to altruism,[1] in business situations you will write more successful favor-seeking letters if you select and emphasize direct reader-benefit talking points. The following letter (asking an advertising manager for free samples) stresses reader benefit throughout—so forcefully as to be almost browbeating, in fact:

> How much would it be worth to Rigate to add some 8,000 potential customers to its prospect list?
>
> You can increase the goodwill toward your company of even more people than this—and at a relatively small cost.
>
> Attracting around 300 contestants and 8,000 onlookers, "A" Day each spring at the University is a festival of fun—a program of pie-eating contests, sack races, beauty contests, and other collegiate horsing-around.
>
> Prizes for the winners of these contests come from local merchants who realize the sales-building value of such donations. But if we had some prizes which we could give to each participant—winner and loser alike—they would introduce under most favorable circumstances the donor's product and house.
>
> The loudspeakers would blare out, "And in addition, each participant will receive one tube of Picote tooth paste!" Some 8,000 people would hear this . . . and would laugh . . and would remember your brand name. And 300 would actually receive your product to use and tell their friends about.
>
> The special "A" Day edition of the student paper will carry an account of all prizes given, and the program will also list all contributors.
>
> A man of your experience knows the value of such advertising. Won't you, then, write me (in time for our February planning) that you will send us 300 sample tubes of Picote? You would be getting some low-cost, effective advertising.

If you look back at the letter beginnings quoted in this section, you will note that in addition to highlighting reader benefit (or at least reader interest), these openings are questions. You will note, too, that the questions are rhetorical (not asked to get their answers, as in inquiries, but to start the reader thinking and encourage reading on).

We do not mean to imply that all persuasive requests must begin with a question. In the preceding letter, for example, you could omit the first sentence (a question) and interweave the figure into the second (a state-

---

[1] Letters seeking funds for worthy causes are special-request letters and thus within the scope of this analysis, but we think it best not to take them up here because they are too highly specialized and because of their frequent civic, religious, and fraternal manifestations. When faced with such problems, you can be sure that the fundamental principles we present here will apply; but for more detailed techniques and "tricks of the trade," check some books like Margaret Fellows and Stella Koenig's *Tested Methods of Raising Money for Churches, Colleges, and Health and Welfare Agencies*, Harper & Bros., New York, 1959.

ment). But the question beginning commands greater attention than a declarative statement and more readily leads your reader to a contemplation of your suggestion. Too, a question is never as challenging as some statements are, and it can be subtly flattering.

In phrasing such questions, however, you will be on safer ground if you eliminate the possibility of either a yes or a no answer. To make the reader contemplate the circumstance that will lead up to the request, the following opening employs the strategy:

```
What Ford philosophy of management caused the change from

                "Made in Texas by Texas Labor"

to

                  "Made in Texas by Texans"?
```

We do not mean to imply that to secure interest in favor-seeking letters you must studiously avoid questions that can be answered with either yes or no. The following opening addressed to a retailer of national standing contemplating entering the Texas market is certainly a good one:

```
Wouldn't you consider the respect and attention of some 200
key Texas retailers a valuable opportunity to test the true
business conditions in that state?
```

The mental response to such a question is positive. And as long as you can be fairly sure of a positive reaction, you are probably on safe ground.

The danger lies in getting an irritated answer—whether that answer is a yes or a no or any of the variants of "So what?" The student who invited the head of a large public accounting firm to speak to a college group and began with

```
Do you believe in preparing for the future?
```

apparently gave little thought to the probable snort that would result from such a question. To eliminate the irritating aspects (and get closer to the subject) a supervisor changed the opening to read:

```
What, in your opinion, are the desirable personal
characteristics of the successful public accountant?
```

True, that beginning implies no reader benefit; but it is certainly a subject of practical interest to the reader. Of possibly greater reader-benefit implications is this one:

```
What does it cost you when you have to dismiss a well-grounded
junior accountant because of poor personal characteristics?

The actual cost of additional recruiting and training isn't
the only loss either:  The loss of prestige and possibly of
clients is a greater threat.
```

Careful study of the preceding beginnings will show three other advantages that come from question beginnings implying reader benefits: (1) they are more likely to keep the reader in the picture, (2) they almost prohibit you from making the serious mistake of beginning with explanations or details of circumstances, and (3) they make the transition to the explanation easier.

Justifying the request

Having secured your reader's interest with a beginning which holds some promise of benefit or at least talks of something of interest, you usually need to devote the greater part of your letter to explaining what your project is and what good comes of it. Although, as they start to read, uninvolved readers aren't even faintly interested in

> The National Association of Advertising Teachers of America, which is made up of some 600 teachers in all sections of the country, is planning its annual convention in New York at the Madison Hotel on July 10,11, and 12.

a member of the Association planning to attend the meeting would be.

Even a nonmember would be, after having been almost or completely persuaded to give a talk to the group. Details concerning who, what, when, where, why, how (sometimes how much) always need to be clarified.

A speaker, for instance, needs to know the nature and size of the audience, the time and place, the facilities available, the amount of time allotted, and the topic (if you are assigning one). Sometimes knowing about other speakers who will precede and follow would be helpful. But such details should be incorporated subordinately as much as possible.

Nobody would read with immediate enthusiasm a beginning like this:

> As a Master's candidate at Harwood University, I am planning a thesis on palletization. Professor H.D. Brunham of our marketing department has suggested that I write to you to find out the results of your experience.

Notice in the following copy how the student seeking this information not only changed the opening to an interest-arousing question but also *subordinated* the necessary but uninteresting details of the original opening:

> Just what are the economies of palletization?
>
> Are they as great as my experience in the service led me to believe?
>
> Has palletization been adopted by an increasing number of business firms in recent years?
>
> Regardless of your experience in using pallets, your comments in answering these questions could contribute materially in making a worthwhile, authentic, down-to-earth thesis of the one I am preparing as partial requirement for an M.S. degree at Alabama. Too, the finished thesis may well be of practical interest to all users and potential users of pallets.

Perhaps you have some printed material which you can simply enclose in the stamped, addressed envelope I've included. If not, will you take a few minutes to tell me your experience with pallets, the cost of palletizing (with particular emphasis on warehousing), current uses or ideas in palletization, and/or possible sources?

Although I don't have to, I'd like to be able to quote you; but I'll handle the material with whatever degree of confidence and anonymity you specify. And no part of this correspondence will ever be used for any purposes other than research, I assure you.

Since I have to assemble material and start writing by June 1, I'd be most grateful if you'd let me hear from you before that date.

If you would like to read the finished thesis for a new idea or two that you might be able to put to work, I'll be glad to lend you my personal copy shortly after August 25.

Why—besides the interest-arousing question beginning and the skillfully subordinated facts justifying the request—did seven copies of that letter bring five detailed replies? Did you notice (fifth paragraph) how clear and specific the writer made the requested action and how easy it seems? Did you notice (last paragraph) the reminder of the reader's possible benefits at the end? And how (preceding paragraph) the writer avoided seeming to push the reader around by justifying the request for action by a necessary end date? And did you notice (sixth paragraph) the reassurance against any fears as to how the information might be used? Any one of these points (explained in the rest of this discussion) may make the difference between your getting nothing and getting what you want in a persuasive favor-seeking situation.

Minimizing obstacles

Even though your beginning may have supplied a very good reason which highlights the reader's advantage or interest, in most circumstances some fly is in the ointment: a negative factor you have to overcome. It may be a sum of money you are asking for, which you feel reasonably certain your reader is going to consider out of line; then you break it down into several payments. It may be that you can offer no fee or a smaller fee than a program speaker is accustomed to receiving; then you cite other (perhaps intangible) rewards. It may be that you're asking for secret information. If so, give assurance that you will do all you can to protect the reader's interest. Regardless of the case or the circumstance, you can usually find some positive corollary to the drawback.

As added inducement, you want to make the job sound as easy as possible and as pleasurable as possible. Phrasing can do a lot here. The following letter is a good example of establishing a negative idea in positive language. The fourth paragraph implies, "See, Mr. Philipson, this really won't be much extra work"; and the fifth one implies, "Sorry, there's no pay in this deal."

> Don't you agree, Mr. Philipson, that a business leader who's on the firing line every day can lend real punch to Tau Kappa Rho activities?
>
> Of course, we give TKR's the benefits of brotherhood and a certain amount of social life, but our real reason for being is to get these promising young men realistically oriented to business life while they're still in school.
>
> So that these future business leaders will get superior guidance, will you be TKR's Midwest district supervisor? As you know, the district supervisor, through letters and visits, helps the local chapters develop and expand business-orienting programs.
>
> Frequently you'd be able to combine business and fraternity trips, I'm sure, for the Midwest district of six states and 22 chapters almost corresponds with your sales district. You'd be able to spend many pleasant evenings telling the boys how American does it! And you'd undoubtedly spot a number of promising candidates for work with your company two, three, and four years from now.
>
> Of course, you'd have an expense account for stationery and traveling. But your real pay would come from seeing these young men get a head start in their professional lives.
>
> Won't you therefore write me that I may nominate you to the General Executive Committee when it meets here in Chicago on May 21?

Finally, you should reduce the mechanical aspects of complying with your request to the minimum of detail, time, and money. That is why most questionnaires are fill-in or checkoff forms and why a return-addressed reply device requiring no postage ordinarily accompanies such requests.

Positively anticipating acceptance

After establishing the reader's benefit or contribution, making clear exactly what you want and why, and minimizing obstacles, you should confidently ask the reader to comply with the request. Hesitant, apologetic expressions belittle the request itself and have the disadvantage of suggesting excuses as reasons for refusal. Such expressions as the following hinder rather than help:

> I realize you are a very busy man, but . . . .
>
> I'm sorry to trouble you for such an apparently insignificant matter; however . . . .
>
> I hesitate to bother you with such a request . . . .
>
> If you consider this a worthwhile project, ...

Eliminate such thinking (maybe by rereading the discussion on "Success

Consciousness," p. 48) and forthrightly name the specific action you want the reader to take. Although you may have referred to it earlier, be sure to ask for it or at least refer to it near the end.

In your favor-seeking letters apply the summary of points on page 392.

PERSUASIVE CLAIMS AND POLICY COMPLAINTS

Sometimes you will have good reason to believe that you need to be rather persuasive to get results on your claim. Your reason may be that you know the reader to be rather reluctant to grant claims, that your case is subject to some question and you need to make as good a case as you can within the facts, or (most frequently) that you have already tried a direct claim (pp. 137–42) and have been turned down.

Whatever the cause, you write a C–plan letter (similar to the special request) when you need to be persuasive, and you can appeal to any desire that might motivate the reader. Some of the main appeals (more or less in ascending order of force and objectionable tone) are to the reader's desire for (1) customer satisfaction, goodwill, and favorable publicity; (2) a continued reputation for fair dealing; and (3) legal meeting of a guarantee.

Again your letter is divided rather distinctly into three parts, but their contents are somewhat different from those of the direct claim:

1. You begin by stating and getting agreement on a principle which is the basis of your claim. (In logic, it would be called the "major premise.")
2. You explain all the facts in detail, as in any claim. (The term in logic is the "minor premise.") This part may be several paragraphs long. In it you show clearly the reader's responsibility.
3. You apply the facts or minor premise to the principle or major premise so as to draw a conclusion, as the logician would call it. The conclusion will be that the reader should act in a certain way. You request that action.

Here are two examples of how the system works. The first was an initial claim. It was successful, in spite of the fact that a glance may suggest that the writer had no justified claim. A closer look, however, will make clear that he did. The situation was quite different from a person's just buying something and finding a few days later that the seller has reduced the price. The key difference is the salesman's assurance to the claimant that he would not save money by waiting. The appeal is therefore to the reader's desire for customer confidence.

> If your customers do not trust your sales personnel, going to a lot of trouble and expense in selecting and training them doesn't do much good, does it, Mr. Barnes? That's why I'm writing to you.
>
> On July 5 I was in your store looking at an XXXX suit priced at $97.75. I decided to leave and wait for a late-summer sale, as I frequently do. But your salesman assured me that there

Special-Request Checklist

1. Your opening should be dominated by something of reader interest.
   a) When you can, develop a reader-benefit theme.
   b) A subject line (unsound in any C–plan letter) or unmotivated request is likely to defeat your purpose.
   c) Though a rhetorical question is usually best, one with an obvious yes or no answer stops rather than starts consideration.
   d) Are you promising too much (like total attendance of a group) or so bluntly as to be suspect?
   e) Don't appear to suggest a bribe or depend on obvious flattery to win the reader's help.
   f) Explanations do not arouse interest; put them in the middle.
2. For clear, natural transitions, keep the reader in your explanation.
   a) Give necessary details to prove that your project deserves consideration and to enable informed action on your request.
   b) But subordinate these details to what the reader gets.
   c) Adapt your letter; when you can, personalize it.
   d) If it is long, consider using the reader's name in the second half or referring specifically to the city, work, or . . . .
   e) Don't phrase the exact request until after most of the benefits.
   f) Make the reader's participation sound easy—maybe even fun!
3. The potentially negative element requires careful treatment.
   a) Elimination of the negative element is unethical and wasteful.
   b) Minimize it by positive statement, embedded position, and minimum space.
   c) Maintain a tone of confidence; avoid apologies; but, to avoid presumptuousness, also use the conditional mood in talking about what the reader is to do: *not* "you will be scheduled to speak . . ." but "you would (or could). . . ."
   d) Don't supply excuses for your reader.
   e) Give assurance that you will handle confidential or other restricted material in whatever limited way specified.
4. Introduce any enclosure skillfully:
   a) Not too early; you want the letter read first.
   b) With emphasis on what the reader is to do with or get from it.
5. After justifying it, ask confidently for the reader's action.
   a) Good action endings indicate specifically what to do, how to do it, helps and/or suggestions for ease of action, and reason for prompt action. Make specific and clear the action wanted.
   b) Justify time limits and establish specifically but subordinately.
   c) Establish appreciation cordially in first-person future conditional. Offer to reciprocate if appropriate. Don't "thank in advance."
   d) When you include a return envelope, subordinate it.
   e) Inject a last punch line on reader benefit.

would be no sale on XXXX suits, that the manufacturer had never allowed its suits to be sold at reduced prices and would not do so this year. So, since I wanted the suit, I bought it.

Now I notice that the price has been reduced to $83.95 and that you are selling at that price.

My plan, you see, would have saved me $13.80. Because I was induced to buy through your salesman's assurance that I could not get the suit cheaper by waiting, I believe you will agree that I am entitled to a refund of $13.80.

I am sure that you want me to trust your salesmen. You can renew my faith by standing behind what they say.

The following illustration is a persuasive claim written after a first claim brought a proposal to compromise. It got the money, the full amount without compromise, by appealing to fair-minded analysis of the facts (and hence the injustice of compromise in the case).

Gentlemen:

Subject: Claim No. 070-6289

If a sales representative for the XXXX Casualty Company were trying to sell me a policy and I offered to pay half the premium requested, do you think I would get it? I don't. That would be a compromise.

Compromises are for cases involving doubt about responsibility or about the amount of damage done. In my claim no doubt about either arises.

Analysis of the facts will show that Mr. Hall ran up behind me so fast that he could not control his car and hit the left rear part of the side of my car. Clearly he was responsible.

I got three estimates of the repair job to be sure of having a fair appraisal of the damages. The lowest of the three was $86. So there is no doubt about the damage.

I am therefore returning the Release and Settlement form you sent and asking that you send another based on one of the estimates I formerly sent in. That is the only fair settlement.

I know that your job is to keep your loss ratio down as low as possible while being fair about the obligations the company assumes in insuring clients. The solution is to settle on the basis of one of the estimates submitted.

I look forward to receiving that settlement.

The policy complaint may be like a direct claim or a persuasive one, but it is more likely to be persuasive.

Whereas claims ask restitution for mistakes, damage, or unsatisfactory products, policy complaints request correction of poor service or unsatisfactory policies and practices. The following are two typical situations—and good letters—except that the veiled threat (underscored) in the next-to-last paragraph of the first letter is likely to do more harm than good. The letter would be better without that whole sentence.

> Many people were disappointed last Sunday—<u>and you and we both lost sales</u>—when we received an entire delivery of strawberry instead of the chocolate and vanilla ice cream we ordered.
>
> If you remember last Sunday, you know it was a pretty hot day —a good day to sell ice cream. We sold 2,000 cups but turned away hundreds of tired, hungry swimmers because they insisted on chocolate or vanilla. I believe I could have sold the remaining 1,000 cups had they been those flavors.
>
> Our customers like XXXX ice cream so well that <u>we'd like to continue selling it</u>. Perhaps a little more care in packing, or a little better system of labeling, will assure you of delivering the right flavors for my future orders, and thus increase both our sales.
>
> May I depend on you?

--

> Am I right in thinking that Racine Motors wants its policy on direct-sale commissions and cooperative selling campaigns to promote long-range goodwill and increased sales in this territory?
>
> Because I think so but find the present practice is not working out that way, I think you will want to review your policies in view of my experience.
>
> Recently one of our sales representatives called on a prospect in our territory and found him already enjoying the reliability and efficiency of a 20-hp. Racine motor, which we normally stock. Further investigation revealed that he had bought the motor directly from you at a price below our selling price. Yet we have received no dealer's commission on this sale. This is one of several occasions brought to my attention in the past year which prompt me to ask you for clarification of our agreement.
>
> Admittedly with the helpful assistance of your missionary sales personnel, we have been able to sell a substantial group of the industrial users in this area on the economy and dependability of the Racine electric motor. We want to keep and expand this patronage, but that will be difficult if we are working at cross-purposes with you.
>
> For our mutual good we and you should quote uniform prices and we should get our dealer's commission on any direct sales. You would gain by being relieved of the marketing functions and by having a ready-made market for your motor, and we would gain by getting our just profits and keeping the goodwill of our customers. That, I thought, was the intent of the exclusive-dealership contract you signed with us.
>
> We have been contemplating an expansion of our stock to include your 60-hp. motor, which would play an important part in our sales program. Please give us a definite working policy so we will know where we stand.

PERSUASIVE REQUESTS FOR CREDIT

You can write the application for credit in direct, brief style when you are reasonably sure that you can meet the firm's credit tests (see pp. 131). When you know you are going to have to ask for special concessions, however, a persuasive letter patterned after the special-request, C–plan letter may be in order. The presentation establishes interest by stressing potential profitable business, stresses the capacity of the management, establishes a sensible plan for meeting the obligation, and confidently asks for action. Like all the letters in this chapter, it is a modification of the AICA (attention, interest, conviction, action) of sales letters.

In the following case the young man was asking for 150 days' credit, knowing that 30 days was the usual time allowed by the Long-Shearer Company. *Although the letter is unusually long, detailed, and persuasive for a credit application, it was written for an unusual situation.*

Lots of auto-accessories dollars are floating around in booming Lubbock. Yet the chains sell only a standard line.

An alert independent retailer offering a complete line of parts and accessories could certainly count on the reputation of Long-Shearer accessories to give him a rapid turnover and a good chance to get his share of this increasing market.

Hence my optimism about the store I plan to open on June 24. Right on Main Street, near several garages and body shops, the 50-foot-front store is out of the high-rent district, yet accessible enough to get me my share of the walking trade. The market survey I made last week indicates that conservatively I can expect 300 people in my store every day. And the managers of all the garages and body shops within four blocks of my store have promised me they'll buy from me.

They got to know me while I worked in my father's Ford service shop during and after high school. We became better friends in the year and a half I spent in the parts department after serving in the Navy and before returning to the University of Texas to complete my B.B.A. degree. I made friends with them —and I learned a lot about the business. I also made friends of most of the young businessmen in town through membership in Rotary and serving a term as president of the Jaycees.

I'm willing to put every bit of the $20,000 insurance money my father left me into the new store. My wife and I, having no illusions of getting rich quickly, are fully prepared to plow profits back into our store so that it will get started on the right foot. You can see from the following allocation of the $20,000 that the store will be financially sound.

With $2,000 for store equipment, $3,600 for operating expenses (including six months' rent at $250 per month), and $3,600 plus a small personal fund for six months' personal expenses, about $10,000 will be left to buy an initial inventory. For the sort of stock I'll need to have an edge on my competitors, however, I should have an initial inventory of $20,000. I would therefore like to finance a $10,000 Long-Shearer accessories stock by paying $5,000 now, $2,500 in 120 days, and the other $2,500 30 days after that.

I plan to finance a $10,000 parts stock from the Auto-Life Company in the same manner. With Long-Shearer accessories selling as well as they do, plus living close to my budget with a wife who's able to give me plenty of help, I'm confident that these estimates allow an adequate margin of safety.

An accessories stockturn of 3 and a markup of 50 percent should give me a gross profit on accessories of $10,000 in 120 days. Since I've budgeted my own money for operating expenses for six months, almost all of the $10,000 should be left to pay for the credit stock and to reorder another $10,000 of accessories stock. Look over the enclosed order and see if you don't agree that the accessories I've ordered will sell quickly.

You'll notice that the enclosed list of references is a diversified group of Lubbock businessmen, ranging from Mr. Logan, president of the Lubbock National Bank, to Ed Duffie, manager of the Fix-um Garage. Any one of these men, as well as the Lubbock Retail Credit Bureau, will be glad to write to you about me.

I shall be grateful for your help in starting my new store. With business progressing as it is in Lubbock, and with fast-moving Long-Shearer accessories to sell, I feel certain that the new store will be a success.

CASES FOR SPECIAL REQUESTS, CLAIMS, AND CREDIT

1. Assume you are writing a research paper on whether many small businesses can be served satisfactorily and economically by a strategically-located computer center to which each business is connected by a terminal. In your research, you found that probably 75 percent of the articles and books you read referred to the M.I.T. unpublished M.S. thesis of Professor Leonard Matson, who now works for Cobol, Inc., Warrington Road, Toledo, Ohio 43605, as a systems analyst. You certainly would like to read Professor Matson's whole thesis before you turn in your paper, which will constitute 75 percent of your grade in BA 509, your senior honors seminar in accounting.

Ask Professor Matson to lend you a copy of his thesis. Your professor probably knows about Matson's work and will most likely question you about it.

2. As a direct-mail sales expert for Walter Jay Thompson, a New York based advertising agency, you have been put in charge of the mail division of Senator Alan James' campaign for re-election to the Senate. Senator James is known as a hard-headed political realist, not above wheeling and dealing to get his programs through the Senate (you add appropriate details, but don't get carried away). What you have to do is sound believable. You can't make James into a shining knight; most people are on to him. He does seem to get the job done, however, and has been responsible for some forward-looking legislation, notably on pollution control. Write a letter to be mailed to all the registered members of the Multicrat party in your state, urging them to support James in the March Primary.

3. When you graduated from high school six years ago, at your parents' insistence you went to the University of Michigan, where after a disastrous academic year (*D* average), you left school to take a job in a grocery business in Holland, Michigan. You spent the next four years (you might add military service, if applicable) with World Jitney, a national supermarket chain, during which time you worked your way up from bagger to grocery manager. You recently asked your personnel manager about World Jitney's manager-trainee program, but he told you that you would need a Bachelor's Degree to qualify. That did it! You realize now that you can't advance further in your present job; therefore, you decide to take a three-year leave-of-absence from World Jitney and finish your undergraduate degree at Hope College in Holland. After completing your degree, you can enter the World Jitney manager-trainee program. With your practical experience, you are certain to succeed.

Your application to Hope was turned down because of your below-average performance at Michigan. To be accepted at Hope, a transfer student must have a *C* average in all subjects. According to the catalog, however, you can appeal to the admissions board for a waiver of the *C* requirement. Write Professor Howard L. Felts, chairman of the admissions board, requesting the waiver. Stress your maturity and work record. Admission boards like this. They especially like to hear about a good military record, or any other evidence of responsibility and motivation (e.g., family, church, etc.).

4. Because you usually get along well with animals, you didn't object when the Fox Run Apartments where you live initiated a policy of allowing pets in the complex. When your neighbors moved in two months ago, however, they brought with them a singularly vicious half-beagle, half-German shepherd mongrel that has been terrorizing the other animals and residents in the apartment complex. He has killed several squirrels, two cats, and a cocker puppy and bitten at least two small children that you know of. Last week, however, when he bit you, and the following day bit your three-year-old (requiring five stitches each, not to mention the shots both you and your child had), you had had enough. Either the dog goes or you're moving.

Write Walter Wallbridge, manager of Fox-Run, and persuade him to tell your neighbors to get rid of the dog. You have thought of throwing a strychnine-laced hamburger over the wall, but you want to try a civilized approach first. Use your current address and current date.

5. Your appeal to the Santa Ana, California, public for monies to fund SAEF (Santa Ana Ecology Fund) was successful. Your several mailings drew in about $150,000. Now you need volunteers to help on various projects around town similar to the clean-up campaign of the trailer parks that you organized. In one day 400 people picked up cans, bottles, and paper that picnickers, campers, and travelers had strewn along. There seem to be many ecology-minded people in Santa Ana; 200 of them showed up last week to work on the SAEF project to remove trash from the approaching highways. Rather than rely on public spontaneity, which has a way of suddenly disappearing, SAEF wants to set up a stand-by list of citizen workers who are willing to give one Saturday a month to various clean-up projects.

Write a persuasive request to mail out to your list of contributors that demonstrates the value of community action to clean up Santa Ana and convinces them to pledge one Saturday a month to SAEF clean-up programs.

6. *Letterhead:* University of Hawaii, 1801 University Avenue, Honolulu, Hawaii 96814. *Mailing list:* 10,000 students from the University directory. *Date:* September 15, 19—. *Information:* As a member of the Student Government you have been concerned about the recent rumblings from the state legislature about tuition increases. And these noises come close upon a large increase last year. One legislator, a Senator Paikau, has introduced a bill whereby students will be charged for half the cost of their education. What you and your Concerned Students Committee have in mind is to set up some kind of campus organization (a Student Union) to look after the rights (and some suggest the wrongs too) of students and perhaps, after you have gained support and influence, to ask the administration to give you representation on University committees. It seems logical to you that students ought to have some say in formulating the policies that will affect them for four years, and even longer if they go on to graduate school.

Your immediate problem, however, is organization. How do you overcome traditional student apathy about student government? Write a form letter that can be sent to students inviting them to come to an organizational meeting September 22, 4 P.M., Kaukini Center on the main campus. Dean Oahuan Aipuni has given your organization permission and encouragement to start such an organization. *Signature block:* Sincerely, Pakui Kolopua.

7. When you went home last week end, your family told you that they would not be able to help you pay your tuition costs for the winter and spring quarters. You didn't want to quit school, so you went to talk with Mabel Haring, Director of the Loan Department, First National Bank, about a federally-insured NDEA loan for $600 to help cover your education costs for winter and spring quarters. You didn't expect any difficulty; your family has an excellent credit record. Besides, your *B*-plus average demonstrated your seriousness about getting an education.

Ms. Haring assured you that you would get your loan about a month after she put through the papers. She suggested (and you agreed) a 60-day note for $300 to cover your costs for the winter quarter. You would get the other $300 and pay off the note when your grant came through. That was about two months ago. You got your $300, 60-day note on December 20, 19—.

Although you've been patient about it, your grant hasn't come through. You called Ms. Haring three times and were assured that your money was on its way. During your last phone conversation on February 15, Ms. Haring told you that she had the money and was sending it out to you the next day. It's now February 25, and you still haven't gotten your check; but you have received a due notice and a past-due notice on your $300 note.

Evidently something went wrong with your federal grant. You realize that money is tight and that educational loans are high-risk investments for banks.

Write Ms. Haring asking for the money she promised you and an explanation for the delay. The threat to your credit record is obvious, since the bank will no doubt alert your local credit bureau. Also indicate that you have sent a copy of your letter to Frederick Nichols, the bank president, who is also a good friend of your father.

8. As Rodham T. Delk, Parents Chairman for Funds for the Library of Randolph-Macon, Lynchburg, Virginia 24504, write a form letter to parents of graduates of this fine institution. Facts: Publishers give "educational discount" but by the time a book is catalogued and ready for distribution, it costs an average of $16.25 per book. Every day, 1,000 books are published. Every year, 60 million pages of new scientific and technical data are released. Books are the scholar's tools and the library a workshop. Unless Randolph-Macon continues to acquire books (on a selective basis) the library will be outdated. Scholarly journals as well as books must be purchased. The journals now cost from $22.50 to $35.00 per year. A library also has microfiche, microfilms, and other forms of film so small that an entire newspaper page can be reproduced on an area smaller than a postage stamp—and that requires special "viewers" to enlarge the image until the page can be read. Microforms save money because they consume so little space, but they cost almost as much—sometimes more—than the book itself. The library is an excellent investment because it has helped attract and retain good students and good professors. Ask for a contribution to help the library get new books, periodicals, microforms and viewers.

9. Part of your income for last year was $3,000 from your half-time assistantship at the University of Georgia. After reading the IRS bulletins that explain the tax status of university stipends, you feel that your income can be declared taxable, since it is payment for services rendered. However, your department gave you a letter that stated that your services were required of all candidates for the degree, which seems to indicate that your $3,000 income is nontaxable.

Rather than declare your income taxable or nontaxable—and fix liability—you have decided to take the option that allows the IRS to compute your taxes. Of course, in addition to your W–2 forms, you will send along a copy of the letter you got from your department. What you need now is a persuasive request that presents your situation clearly and tries to get the IRS to declare in your favor (the $3,000 as nontaxable income).

The difference in your refund will be significant. Added to the $8,000 your spouse earned (total income $11,000) the $3,000 as taxable income would put you in a higher bracket and net you a $200 refund (both you and your spouse claimed zero dependents). When your $3,000 is considered tax-exempt, however, your bracket is lowered considerably and your refund would be $700. That's a $500 difference. Besides, even with the $700 refund, you still paid $1,300 in taxes.

Write a persuasive request to accompany your tax forms that will convince the IRS to declare your $3,000 nontaxable income and will get you the $700 refund. Write the Internal Revenue Service, Chamblee, Georgia 30005.

10. As Director of the Youth Work Experience Program for your city, set up a letter to go to major business establishments asking them to cooperate with you in finding work for high school students this summer (particularly by offering jobs if they can). This nationwide program has been helpful in training young people and in keeping down crime. The program introduces students to the world of work, and most young people prefer working to loafing. Work experience helps students develop the job attitudes, job knowledges, and requisite skills. On-the-job work experience in the areas of student's career interest causes education to take on added relevance. For business and industry, the program helps to provide a pool of qualified, potential employees. Students can work at retail outlets, clean up the community, cut lawns, paint and fix up rundown buildings, etc. Assume you are sending a brochure showing how the Youth Work Experience Program has worked in other cities.

11. To Dr. Marybeth Lemmon/Department of Psychology/University of Kansas/Lawrence, Kansas 66042/In a recent issue of the *Kansas City Star*, Dr. Lemmon was quoted as saying: "Once firmly established, a habit pervades so many corners of a person's psychic and physical being that to root it out is equivalent to slaying the Hydra, the mythical nine-headed monster."/As a clinician in a local hospital that treats many patients with emotional and mental problems, you (Mrs. Frank Hepburn) try to keep informed about harmful habits and their causes and cures. You want to obtain a reading list that includes the most recent thinking in this field. Ask Dr. Lemmon for a list of reading references that might be helpful. Your address is 907 University Lane, Iowa City, Iowa 52240.

12. As correspondence secretary for the Missouri Veterans Organization (MVO/2354 Oaktree Street, N.E./Kansas City, Missouri 64118), write a persuasive request to Herschel Morris, the chairman of the House Finance Committee (Rm 22, Capitol Building, Columbia 65201). Rep. Morris has refused to let House Bill 2233 (tuition waiver for Missouri veterans at state educational institutions) out of committee so that the entire House of Representatives can vote on it. What you have to do in your letter is to convince Morris, by sound, logical arguments, that it is to the state's advantage to provide free education for veterans. Begin with a rhetorical question that will get Morris' attention.

13. Back in the years when the American Business Communication Association *Journal of Business Communication*, 317 Kinley Hall, University of Illinois, Urbana, IL 60801, and the Society for Engineering Education *Transactions on Engineering and English*, 999 Arrowhead Drive, Lafayette, Indiana 47904, were young, you were impressed with SEE's information retrieval system. The Society had abstracts at the beginnings of each paper along with index terms under which the papers could be catalogued. You have been trying to install such a system for your *Journal of Business Communication* but are stumped at trying to create a list of index terms to be used in the subject index of the *Journal*. One question that comes to your mind is—did the Society have such a list for the SEE *Transactions*, or did it make up terms as it went along? If the society did have a master list, is there a copy of it anywhere that you might find and look at? You'll be grateful for any advice SEE can give you. (Students: If you don't know it, you might do well to remember that engineers are almost universally proud of their profession but unduly modest about their writing. Many will tell you things like "I always wanted to be a engineer and now I are one so I don't write English so good.")

14. To go to the college of your choice, University of Montevallo, you have to have letters of recommendation from three of your high school teachers. Since graduating two years ago, you have been working out of town at a Mental Health Center in Birmingham. Draft a letter to go to Ms. Sarah Snow, 65 Woodland Hills, Tuscaloosa, Alabama 35401, your teacher of American Literature. Since it has been some time since you were in class, refresh her memory on what you did while in class (special oral interpretation of poems by Langston Hughes) and in high school

(National Honor Society, French Club president, Student Council Representative three years, Glee Club three years). At Montevallo you hope to major in accounting. Ms. Snow writes to Office of Admissions, University of Montevallo, Montevallo, Alabama 35115. Enclose a stamped blank envelope for her use.

15. As president of Beta Gamma Sigma (honorary and professional business fraternity, 760 Office Parkway, Suite 50, St. Louis, Missouri 63141), write a form letter to members asking for voluntary contributions to provide for programs designed to make the honor of being a member of BGS meaningful. The induction fee today ($10) is the same as it was when BGS was founded 63 years ago. Even though the value of ten dollars has declined over the years, BGS has held the price because it did not want the fee to be a barrier to membership. Enclose a return envelope for tax-deductible contributions.

16. Jon Thompson, Business Editor, Plymouth Publishing Company, Inc., Belmont, California 94054, has a questionnaire on a text by Wayne Merideth and Sheila Murphy, *Business Communications: Methods and Principles,* third edition. Help Jon write a covering letter for the questionnaire to teachers of business communication. By answering the questions, the teachers will have a specific voice in the revision of this text, and thereby will help their students and themselves have a better textbook.

17. Over the signature of Valerie Stokes, Professor of Business Communications, Western Michigan University, Kalamazoo, Michigan 49008, write to a selected list of American Business Communication Association leaders asking them to read and evaluate some model letters as part of a research project for an article you are writing. You want the leaders to grade each letter as though it were submitted as student work near the end of the semester with an *A–B–C–D–E* (or *F*) scale. For each letter, the grader is to indicate on a checklist (to be provided) the kinds of deficiencies, if any. You believe that as an active member of ABCA, each leader will want to share Stokes's interest in disseminating (as widely as possible) the principles taught in business communication courses.

18. Public institutions need to periodically review how they serve the public. The needs change and the most effective ways of meeting these needs also change. As a new president of your school, write a letter to full-time faculty members asking them to fill out a form (a detailed questionnaire) that takes about 45 minutes to complete. The questions concern what the school is, is not, and ought to be doing. Also ask them to send specific suggestions regarding the school's goals for the next one or two decades. The survey form will be only the first step in assessing school priorities. Set a realistic deadline for returning the information.

19. Because of the high costs of mailing, the secretary of Delta Kappa Gamma, honorary fraternity for teachers, wants a form letter to all members. Minimum cost to DKG for any change of address plate and for change in office files and records is 50¢. If member tells DKG before a move, it costs only 40¢. The *Journal* is not forwardable; so if it is returned, DKG pays 22¢ and remails for 24¢, making a cost of 96¢. When the member is lost, DKG loses even more. Write the letter to encourage prompt notification of any change of address. Letterhead: Delta Kappa Gamma, 4769 Tippecanoe, Times Corner, Indiana 46804.

20. For a publishable study you are doing, you need to tour Farm Products, Inc., 2447 Tree Lane, Waterloo, Iowa 50705. In a one-day visit you can study the various machines and techniques. The farm product industry at the present time is lacking research on the best processing methods for various farm products. The knowledge of the managers of Farm Products on farm processing can greatly contribute to this much-needed study and give the managers an opportunity to exchange ideas with one of the state's leading farm-product experts. The results of the research could save managers hours of processing time. All information would be strictly confidential and for research purposes only. Since analysis of these results takes a month, and publication is scheduled for eight weeks away, you would want an answer within the next two weeks.

21. From INTERNATIONAL PUBLICATIONS, INC., Leslie I. Combs, Jr., Executive Vice President, writes Mrs. Peter Field, Professional Research Institute, 456 North Wilcox Drive, Rochester, N.Y. 14610, asking her to review Brezhnev Solnevostok's *The World and Deténte* and make a report of approximately 1,800 words for $125. Mrs. Field, a well-respected, sought-after reviewer needs persuasion because so many other publishers want her services. She has had ten years of experience working closely and traveling with Harry Sinnger, U.S. Secretary of State. Also, she is a good friend of Solnevostok and knows a great deal about deténte. Combs would like to mail her the new book and have the review available for publication in June issue of *Publishers' Journal* (need report by March 30). Assume an enclosed sheet giving complete editorial requirements for the report. Ask for her answer as to whether she will review this book for *International Publications,* 171 Newberry Road, Boston, Massachusetts 02139.

22. As a communications consultant (on a retainer basis) who happened to catch it in time, rewrite the following as a form memo for enclosing in pay envelopes of all employees this week:

M. T. Williams Co., 106 East Pecan, San Antonio, Texas 78244. C. W. Miller, president. *Body:* It has become quite noticeable as to the appearance of some of our employees, and I regret to say that in some cases it is not a very pleasing matter.

Each and everyone of you know that the impression we make on our customers or prospective customers is 50 percent of our sales or future sales. In each case that I have noticed it was through pure carelessness and unconcern that made the appearance of some of our employees so bad.

I know that none of us can go dressed like a king, but we can at least be clean. I am not asking you, I am forced to tell you, that a few of you must improve in your appearance.

This memo does not include the majority of our personnel, but just those few who have drifted over to the slouchy side and a reminder to get back on the neat appearing side.

All collectors and salesmen must be neat at all times when on the job, no exception.

Let's all take a look in the mirror before we leave home every morning and ask ourselves: WHAT KIND OF AN IMPRESSION WILL I MAKE ON MY CUSTOMERS TODAY?

23. At Michigan Power and Light, Detroit 48203, your meter readers have been having trouble with biting dogs. In fact, about ten readers sustain dog bite injuries each month, and that doesn't count the near misses. For Clayton Skidmore, Director of Public Relations, set up a form memo that is to go along with the monthly statement asking your customers to please be sure that their animals can't harm MPL meter readers when they come to read the meter. Unless these readers have safe access to the customer's electric meter, MPL has to estimate the electrical usage for the month. This practice is as inconvenient to the customer as to MPL. You do not want to continue the present system (good men are hard to replace, and three have quit in the last three months because of dogs). Still some people have ignored your two former little barks about this situation. See if you can, without really drawing any blood (or even fire in their eyes), convince these people that you too could become a "biter." That is, show some teeth in this bark, but don't bite—at least not yet. Be persuasive but not mean or nasty.

24. Assume that you're a close friend and rewrite this lousy letter written by the student-body president who hasn't had the advantage of taking this course.

Letterhead: Student Body, your school. *Salutation:* Dear Dr. Moeller: *Signature block:* Thank you, Steve Graham, Chairman, Dollars for Scholars. *Date:* Fall, 19—. *Body:* As you might already have heard, the annual Dollars for Scholars fund drive will be November 13th–19th. If you have not heard of our program, "Dollars for Scholars" is the name that students gave to the 1972 fund drive which was set up that year in accord with the National Defense Education Act. Under the Act, each participating school would receive \$9 for every \$1 that is collected. This money was to be used as student loans based upon need which were to be paid back by the graduate beginning one year after graduation at very favorable interest rates. These rates were to be those on E-bonds at the time a loan was taken out. That's usually about half the going rates on personal loans. We have come a long way in Dollars for Scholars since 1972. In that year the fund was able to net only $10,000. Although this year we will be striving to reach a much larger sum of money, our goal is the same. The goal then and our goal now is to provide the means by which our fellow students can continue their education and make this a better nation for ALL of us. Our goal this year is (put in, as dollars, the number of students enrolled in school). This figure was reached by asking each student to give $1. To reach this will be hard, but the cause for which it is given is certainly a worthy one. I have enclosed a return envelope and a blank check made out to (school name). I would like to ask you to help us reach our goal. I would like to ask you to receive some of the same pride and satisfaction that each donating student does. I hope that in the end you will be able to sit back with us and say: "I was but one, but I was one—I was Dollars for Scholars 19—."

25. While attending school, you purchased and put on your National Bank Credit Card a CRA stereo system with an eight-track player recorder for $250 from Newsome Music House, 987 Langdon Street, your city. Three weeks and six weeks later you called Newsome and reported that the stereo refused to work and asked that it be fixed or removed from your apartment. Now that you have the Credit Card bill, write Newsome a letter. The stereo turntable just won't turn. (You'll need to send at least a postcard to NBCC, too—but not for this assignment.)

26. When you bought your fleet of 12 Spiegel motorcycles from Lawrence's Cycle Shop, 900 Broadway, Salem, Oregon 97309, for your pizza delivery service (Zipps Piping Pies, Inc.), Mr. H. D. Lawrence, owner of Lawrence's, was quite talkative about his "quality service" and the Spiegel parts guarantee for one year or 10,000 miles. However, when you reported to Mr. Lawrence that the rims on eight of your bikes were bent, he refused to replace them, even though the one-year/10,000-mile warranty was still in effect. Lawrence claims that your "cowboys," he calls your delivery drivers, were running up curbs which knocked the rims out of shape. You could accept this argument if 1, or maybe 2, of your bikes had bent rims; but 8 out of 12? And besides, five of the eight bikes have bent rims on the rear wheels. Write a persuasive claim to Mr. Lawrence convincing him to honor the terms of the warranty and replace the eight bent rims.

27. You (Claudia Hinton, 1131 S.W. 2d Place, Jackson, Mississippi 39209) bought a $750 Climatrol Central Air unit from Jackson Heating Supply, 940 Bellevue, Jackson, and it was installed five days later. The people who installed the Climatrol explained that they would have to come out the next day and check the Freon level in the unit. When you arrived home from work the next day, you naturally assumed that they had done so, turned the unit on, and it caught fire and almost burned your house down. After much effort, you extinguished the fire and called Jackson Heating Supply. You were told that the Freon had not been put in because no one was able to come to your house today and with the absence of Freon the unit caught fire. Also you learned that the terms of the warranty apply only after the Climatrol has been fully installed and OK'd. If the Jackson Heating Supply is in business to make the citizens of Jackson comfortable, as advertised, you want your money back or a new $750 unit —installed.

28. When you painted the outside of your house with Belmont's Weathereater paint, you thought you had a paint job that would last at least five to ten years. It didn't. Two months later, large strips of paint began peeling off. Now, after four months, your whole house looks like it's recovering from sunburn. Your neighbors first laughed at it, but now there is vague talk of passing around a petition to get the county to force you to clean up what has become a neighborhood eyesore. When the Belmont representative looked, he told you that you probably didn't prepare the surface properly. You carefully prepared the surface, removing all the mildew, dirt, and loose paint before applying the primer coat Belmont recommended as a base for the final coat. You've written several letters asking the Belmont people to make good on their five-year guarantee, but they mumbled vaguely about your not following the directions on the can and gave you no satisfaction at all. One of your neighbors, a chemist, agreed to run some tests on the paint peelings and on paint you had left. He discovered by analyzing the paint that it contained only one third the amount of latex binder that it should have according to Belmont's own specifications. Clearly Belmont sold you a bad lot of paint, and you put out $200 for paint and painting equipment only to be told that you were at fault when Belmont is. Before you blow the whistle, however, you want to give Belmont a last chance to repaint your house. You're right; you now have the evidence. Write a persuasive claim to Harold Yoder, claims processor for Belmont (4798 Airline Highway, Baton Rouge, Louisiana 70808) in which you present the facts and convince him to have your house repainted.

29. Three weeks after you moved into your new apartment at Indian River Apartments, 280 Archer Road, Norman, Oklahoma 73099, you called Bruce Shelton, your State-Ranch insurance agent to have your address changed on your renter's policy. The difference in price was $60 (from $25 to $85 a year) because of the all-wood construction of Indian River Apts. Your check has already cleared the bank. A week after the check

cleared, Indian River burned to the ground. When you called Shelton, he simply mumbled something about making a list of what you lost and sending it to him so he could process your claim. Your total possessions, for which you have the itemized list and most of the sales slips, came to $5,000, which included small appliances, stereo-tape deck, books, clothes, etc. You didn't expect to get the full $5,000 back, but you felt that State-Ranch would pay about $4,000. You could understand about $1,000 depreciation, particularly since some of your appliances and clothes were pretty old. But you were surprised when State-Ranch sent you a check for $1,000 and a release form to sign and return. The letter said usually the refund was about four fifths of the total on complete losses such as yours, but it was hard to believe that a student at the university had $5,000 worth of possessions in an apartment. Although you had offered to let Shelton have copies of your records and sales slips, "I don't feel," he said, "they would be necessary." Your job now is to convince State-Ranch that it should reimburse you the full four-fifths value ($4,000) of the goods you lost. Write direct to State-Ranch, 91 Greenbrier, Dallas, Texas 75206. Include copies of your evidence (assumed).

chapter 12 Persuasive messages: Collections

Defects of old-style collection letters
Attitudes and objectives of modern collection writers
Characteristics of the collection series
Standard collection procedures
- Notification
- Reminder
- Inquiry
- Appeals
  - Basic considerations
  - The resale appeal
  - Pride appeal
  - Fair-play appeal
  - Appeals to economic self-interest
- Urgency
- Ultimatum

Beginnings and endings
Humor in collections
Collecting unearned discounts

THE ONLY SURE WAY to prevent collection problems is to sell strictly for cash. Even with the most careful selection of credit customers, a credit manager will make an occasional mistake and will allow credit sales to somebody who will not pay promptly.

Unfortunately, however, strict cash selling is also an almost sure way to keep sales and profits unnecessarily low. For that reason the old battle among the sales personnel who wanted to sell to everybody, the credit department which would approve sales only to gilt-edged credit risks, and the collection people who insisted on prompt pay regardless of consequences has ended in compromise.

Today the thinking sales representative accepts the fact that you make no profit if you can't collect, does not try to sell without a reasonably good chance of collection, and helps the credit department find out about the chances. The credit manager accepts the fact that every sale turned down for credit reasons is a lost chance for more profit and approves sales to some marginal credit risks. Collectors remember that they not only must collect the money but must retain the goodwill of customers or see them drift away as fast as the sales department can bring them in.

Indeed, modern credit theory stresses selling to marginal risks as a means of increasing sales and profits. If a business firm follows this theory, as most do these days, its collection problems will be numerous—but expected and manageable.

DEFECTS OF OLD-STYLE COLLECTION LETTERS

In the early days of credit sales, things were different. Only the best risks could get credit. When one of them did not pay promptly, the person in business was surprised, disappointed in a trusted customer, and irked because the bookkeeping routine was broken. The letters written to collect the money revealed all these emotions. Combined with stock letter-writing phrases, these emotions led to letters characterized by curt, exasperated, injured, accusing, or self-righteous tone, jargon, strong-arm methods, and ineffective appeals to sympathy, fear of getting one's nose smashed, and fear of legal suit.

Indeed, you still see such letters from people who learned all they know about letter writing years ago only by reading and imitating the poor letters of others. With some exceptions, collection correspondence is still a notorious blind spot in business.

Besides the old faults, all too frequently collectors send obvious form letters to collect long-overdue accounts where a form hardly has a chance, or write many short letters when a good one, only a paragraph or two longer, would do the job. They then defend themselves by claiming that they don't have time or money to spend on individualized letters or long letters, or by saying (without testing to find out) that debtors won't read long letters. Tests have shown that the longer letters nearly always pull better than the shorter ones, and individual-sounding letters always pull better than obvious forms in collecting accounts that are very long overdue. The apparent reason is that in the longer letters you can present enough evidence and reasoning to be persuasive.

The approach of "several poor letters" delays collections and leaves the business to be financed through borrowing instead of through current collections. Thus it loses one of the main values of promptness, an improved cashflow.

The loss, however, is a small consideration in comparison with the main shortcoming of poor collection correspondence—its disposition to drive away customers that the sales department has brought in only at great expense for advertising and sales promotion. Here are two recent examples:

> We are trying to avoid getting impatient over your delay in settling your account amounting to $124.60. The amount is considerably past due, and your failure to answer our letters

(all of which we believe have been polite) has been very annoying as well as discourteous. If you cannot pay the account in full, we should be pleased to be favored with your remittance for part of the amount with approximate date for payment of balance.

Trusting that you will give the above your prompt attention, and with kindest regards, ...

--

You have classified yourself by failure to answer our letter Re: Olympia Clinic Acct., $8. It is therefore our intention to seek other means of collection of this account as we do not intend to let you beat it if at all possible to prevent. We beg to advise that fees for medical services are held by court to be a necessity. So remember, the time to settle a debt is before it gets into court.

It will be to your benefit to communicate with this office at once.

Notice that the only reason given for payment in either of those letters is the implied threat to sue (for $8?) in the second. Such letters increase the difficulty of collecting because they make the reader hate to pay someone so thoroughly disliked and resolve never to do business with the writer again. The results of poor collection correspondence, then, are one or more of these unnecessary losses:

1. A series of costly collection letters, when one good one would do the job.
2. Delayed collection of money needed for operating expenses.
3. Additional purchases which may be added to the account before it is closed (and thus will increase the loss if the account is uncollectible).
4. Loss of sales. Customers with overdue accounts commonly trade elsewhere rather than face the embarrassment of buying where they owe money.
5. Permanent loss of many disgusted customers.
6. The unfavorable attitudes passed on by these customers to other customers and prospects.

These are high prices for any firm to pay for keeping a poor collector—higher than necessary to employ a good one.

ATTITUDES AND OBJECTIVES OF MODERN COLLECTION WRITERS

Modern collection theory and methods are designed to prevent these undesirable consequences. The trained collector takes the attitude that the debtor should pay because of a promise to do so by a certain date—which has come. So a collector need never apologize about asking for money due.

In asking, however, a good letter writer realizes that people pay because of benefits to themselves rather than sympathy or any other reason. The collector therefore not only associates the obligation with the goods through resale talk but, in persuading the debtor, points out the benefits of paying now.

The modern collector's thinking is quite analytical:

I'm not the bookkeeper irked by broken routine. *Avoid a tone of exasperation and self-righteousness.*

A delinquency is no surprise. Most people who do not pay promptly are still honest, and some are in temporary financial difficulty (needing only a little more time). *Avoid a curt tone.*

Feel no hurt or disappointment as if let down by a trusted friend. *Avoid an injured, pouting tone.*

Some delinquents are withholding payment because of dissatisfaction with the goods or charges. *The job is one of adjustment, not collection.* (Since October 28, 1975, federal law has required that sellers cannot even try to collect on customer-disputed goods or billings of $51–up for purchases within the state or 100 miles of home. The law applies equally to a "holder in due course"—that is, somebody like a credit-card company who has bought the original seller's rights in the accounts.)

Some will have to be persuaded to pay. *Use the "you" attitude.*

A few, but only a few, are basically dishonest and will have to be forced to pay or marked off as losses. *Forcing payment does not include even threats of physical violence, extortion, or rumor-mongering (all of which are illegal). Civil court suit, the only legitimate forcing method, is so destructive of goodwill that it should not even be mentioned until you are saying (and meaning) it is the next step.*

Most important of all, the modern collector (unlike predecessors) recognizes the true nature of the job.

The trained writer of collection letters today expects letters to do *two* jobs:

1. They must collect the money, promptly if possible.
2. They must also retain the goodwill of the customer if at all possible.

By adding the second job, the collector retains the customer, prevents the unfavorable publicity inevitably carried by a disgruntled former customer, and makes each letter more likely to succeed in its first job—that of collecting. In many cases the second job is more important than the first. Certainly to collect $4.50 by means that lose the goodwill of a customer who has been buying hundreds of dollars' worth of goods a year is stupid.

If the collector has to sacrifice anything, promptness goes first despite the inherent losses (previously listed).

For effectiveness in both collection and goodwill, the modern collector cooperates with the sales department and may even inject some sales promotion material into *early* collection letters to a good risk when it might be of interest to the customer. It not only promotes future sales, but it shows confidence in the debtor and willingness to sell more on credit. Thus it is a subtle appeal to pride which helps to save the reader's face and goodwill. If used at the end of the letter, it relieves the sting and solves one of the correspondent's touchiest problems—how to provide a pleasant ending for a letter in which some element is displeasing to the customer.

Even when resale is not the basic collection appeal (as discussed later), the collector introduces into letters a few phrases of resale talk to keep the customer convinced of the wise decision in buying *those goods* from *that firm*—and to make the obligation to pay concrete by attaching it to the goods. The following letter includes both resale and sales promotion talk:

> You probably remember your first feeling of pleasure when you saw the dark, gleaming wood and the beautifully proportioned design of the Heppelwaite bedroom suite you bought here a few months ago. The suite was one of the finest we have ever had in our store, and we were well pleased—as we thought you were —when you selected it for your home.
>
> At the time, we were glad to arrange convenient credit terms so that you could have your furniture while paying for it. Now if you will look over your bills, you will notice that those for October, November, and December have not been marked paid. The sooner you take care of them, the more you can enjoy your furniture because each time you use it or even see it you will subconsciously remember that you are up to date on your payments.
>
> When you come to the store to make your payments, be sure to see the home furnishings department as well as the time-payment desk. An entire new line of curtains, slipcovers, bedspreads, and scatter rugs is there for your inspection. You'll find a great variety of colors and fabrics made up in the latest styles. From the wide selection you can choose a beautiful new setting for your Heppelwaite suite.

This letter pretty well exemplifies the attitudes and objectives of modern industrial and retail collection writers: Ask for the money without apology because it is due, persuade by showing the reader benefits, use calm understanding and patience, collect but retain goodwill, and cooperate with the sales department.

CHARACTERISTICS OF THE COLLECTION SERIES

In trying to collect and retain goodwill, the efficient collector classifies delinquent accounts and prescribes the best treatment for each. The method is like a process of repeated siftings or screenings. The procedure is a series of mailings, each of which eliminates some names from the delinquent list and aids in reclassifying and prescribing for those remaining.

To do its two jobs best, the collection series should have the following characteristics:

1. *Promptness.* Credit and collection people know that the sooner they start trying to collect after an account becomes due, the better the chance. The U.S. Department of Commerce has found that a dollar in current accounts is worth only 90 cents after two months, 67 cents after six months, 45 cents after a year, 23 cents at two years, 15 cents at three years, and 1 cent at five years.

2. *Regularity.* Systematic handling of collections increases office efficiency and has a desirable effect on debtors. They see quickly that they are not going to slip through the holes in a haphazard procedure.

3. *Increasing forcefulness.* Wanting to retain the goodwill of the customer as well as collect the money, the collector starts with as weak a letter as is likely to work. Like the doctor who uses stronger and stronger medicine or resorts to surgery only as the need develops, the good collector applies more and more forceful methods and resorts to the court only after weaker methods fail.

4. *Adaptation.* Not all credit and collection workers classify their customers into the clean-cut categories of good, medium, and poor risks suggested by some books; but all competent ones vary their procedures according to the quality of the risk (as well as according to the general bases of adaptation already discussed). Usually the poorer the risk, the more frequent the mailings and the more forceful the messages. Whereas three months might pass before anything stronger than a few statements go to a good risk, much less time might run a poor one through the whole sifting process and to court.

5. *Flexibility.* The collection procedure has to be flexible to take care of unusual circumstances. The collector would look silly to continue sending letters every 15 days to a debtor who had answered an early one with the message of being financially two months behind because of an automobile accident but able to pay the bill by a certain date. After all, you can't get blood out of a turnip.

STANDARD COLLECTION PROCEDURES

Collection plans and procedures vary so much that only a big book could discuss all variations. Also, various collection theorists and practitioners use different terms to mean essentially the same things. The befuddling complexity is more apparent than real, however. Many of the differences are only minor ones of mechanics rather than significant ones of substance. Most well-planned series apply essentially the logic and psychology explained in the next few pages to a screening process somewhat like that shown in Table 12–1 (next page).

Of course, you would send only one mailing at the notification, inquiry, or ultimatum stage. The nature of the letters makes repetition of them illogical. The number and frequency of mailings in the other stages vary from firm to firm, and even within firms according to the class of customer and other circumstances, such as the type of business (retail or industrial) and type of sale (open account, installment).

In general, the better the credit risk, the greater the number of mailings and the longer the intervals between them. Usually, however, you use two to four reminders, two or three appeals, and one urgency letter at 10- to 30-day intervals (which usually become shorter near the end).

The assumption, nature, and gist clearly call for modified A–plan messages in the first two collection stages (where no persuasion seems necessary) and for C–plan letters in the last three. The inquiry stage is middle ground, where one might well use either. B–plan letters would be appro-

TABLE 12–1

Stage	*Assumption*	*Nature*	*Gist*
Notification	Will pay promptly	Usual statement	Amout due, due date, terms
Reminder	Will pay; overlooked	Statement, perhaps with rubber stamp, penned note, or sticker; or form letter or brief reference in other letter	Same as above, perhaps with indication that this is not first notice
Inquiry	Something unusual; needs special consideration	One letter	Asks for payment or explanation and offers consideration and helpfulness
Appeal	Needs to be persuaded	Letters	Selected appropriate and increasingly forceful appeals, well developed
Urgency	May be scared into paying	Letter, sometimes from high executive or special collector	Grave tone of something getting out of hand; may review case; still a chance to come through clean
Ultimatum	Must be squeezed	Letter	Pay by set date or we'll report to credit bureau or sue; may review case to retain goodwill by showing reasonableness

priate in collections only if the debtor had asked for an unapproved concession, such as an unearned discount (discussed later).

Notification (usually a form telling amount, date due, and terms)

On or about the due date, you have no reason to assume anything except prompt payment if the customer knows how much is due, what for, the due date, and the terms. Most people will pay in response to form notices—the first sifting—which give these facts. A personal letter at this stage would insult most people by implying distrust and concern over the account. Instead of a costly letter, then, the notification is almost always a statement (bill) sent on or about the due date. The forms have the advantage of avoiding insults and saving lots of money on the large mailings while reducing the mailing list for the later, more expensive stages.

Reminder (usually forms giving basic information and adding a push)

If the notice brings no response, the collector gives the customer the benefit of the doubt, assumes oversight, and sends one or more reminders (the number and frequency depending on the circumstances, Item 4 below). The collector knows that most of the remaining delinquents will respond at this stage and further reduce the list. Therefore avoiding offense while giving the necessary information (amount, what for, due date, and terms) is an important concern.

Reminders are usually forms, in order to save both money and the customer's face, but they may be of four types:

1. Exact copy of the original notice, or copy plus a penned note or rubber stamp such as "Second Notice" or "Please Remit," or copy with the addition of a colorful gummed sticker carrying a slogan. Effective examples are "Don't delay further; this is long overdue," "Your prompt remittance is requested," "*Now* is the time to take care of this," "Prompt payment insures good credit," "Prompt payments are appreciated," "Don't delay—pay today," "Remember you agreed to pay in 30 days," and "Have you overlooked this?"
Less effective wordings, with the apparent reasons for ineffectiveness in parentheses, are:

    We trusted you in good faith; we hope we were not mistaken
    (undesirable implications and tone, stressing *We*).

    We are counting on you; don't fail us
    (selfish view).

    If there is any reason for nonpayment, write us frankly
    (suggests finding something wrong; lacks success consciousness).

    If this checks up clear, clear it up with a check
    (same criticism as preceding; the word play is questionable).

2. Brief gadget letter (form):

    We enclose a small piece of string, just long enough to tie around your finger to remind you that you should send your check today for $48.50 in payment of . . . .

    --

    The little alarm clock pictured in this letterhead, like any alarm clock, reminds you that it's time to do something you planned to do. This is a friendly remainder that you intended to send your check today for $28.65. . . .

3. Incidental reminder (underscored in the following example) in a personalized letter mainly about something else:

    With fall just around the corner and school starting within a month, no doubt you have been planning to order some more fast-selling Queen candies to have plenty on your shelves before the fall rush begins.

    By this time you have surely realized the advantage of handling Queen products in your new store. You will want to take advantage of our special back-to-school offer too. It includes many delicious assorted candies popular with children.

    <u>When you mail your payment of $126 due July 30, covering our last shipment under our invoice No. 134, dated June 30</u>, won't you include your next order, so we can assure you an early

delivery of factory-fresh candies? Notice the variety in our complete line, as shown in the latest catalog, a copy of which I'm enclosing for your convenience in making your selections.

More of the helpful window and counter displays like those sent with your first shipment are available on request. If in any other way we can help you to sell Queen candies, let us know. We are always glad to be of service.

If we let XXXXX represent collection talk and ——— represent resale or sales promotion talk, the reminder letter may look like either of the following (usually the first, as in the preceding letter):

THIS	or	THIS
———————		
———————		XXXXXXXXXXX
XXXXXXXXXXX		———————
———————		———————

Some collection writers prefer the second version. They feel that most people behind in their accounts expect a collection letter and spot it as such. Better then, they reason, to send it under no such masquerades as the first. In the following letter, after the direct request for payment the sales material reassures the customer that the firm feels no concern over the status of the account.

Now that the end-of-the-year rush has let up, won't you please give your personal attention for a few minutes, Mr. Bowers, to your $95 account for Columbia supplies sent you on December 3?

Personal attention is appropriate here, for you are concerned —more so than are any of your assistants—with the maintenance of your valuable credit reputation among stationery supply houses. You will want to continue this good record, of course, by taking care of your first purchase from us, sent to you with our invoice BB103. Please sit down now and send us your check for $95 covering these supplies.

The $42 worth of supplies ordered on January 26 and shipped with our invoice CB345 brought your account total to $137. Doubtless these Valentine and Washington's Birthday sets enlivened your early February sales. With Easter almost here, the new color books and cutouts shown in the enclosed folder will soon be in demand. May we send you what you need?

Up through the reminder stage in the collection procedure the assumption is that little or no persuasion is necessary. Thus forms or incidental reminders can do the job more cheaply and avoid the sting that personalized, full-length collection messages would carry. You may have noticed that even the incidental reminder in the Queen candies letter is in dependent-clause structure to avoid too much sting.

4. Individual-sounding letter solely about collection. For greater force in the last reminder, or to poor risks, or about large amounts, the collector may, however, decide to write a letter that talks collection all the way and seems to be

individualized. Since most delinquents have so much in common, it still may be a relatively inexpensive fill-in form if the writer watches the tone and content carefully, typing each copy (perhaps made of form paragraphs) or using word processing equipment.

The following letter for a wholesale concern, for example, adapts easily to a large number of customers. With only one fill-in (for the underscored part, conveniently placed at the end of a paragraph) besides the inside address and salutation, it will serve for a large mailing list. It has a touch of pride appeal along with the reminder to reduce the sting of the apparently individualized message.

> As owner of a successful business, you know what a good credit reputation means. You have one.
>
> That's why we immediately extended you 30-day credit on your recent order. We know that the reports of your good credit reputation were correct. And we likewise know that you'll send us payment as soon as this letter recalls the fact that you owe $85 due November 15 for. . . .

Beyond the reminder stage, however, the *obvious* form letters sometimes used can hardly do the job. In the inquiry stage and beyond, the very nature of the collector's working assumptions seems to call for individualized messages.

For the later stages of the collection procedure the collector fortunately has ample information on the credit application form and in the credit records to adapt an individually dictated letter. And earlier mailings have so reduced the list of delinquents that giving some personal attention to each letter late in the collection procedure is both possible and productive.

Inquiry (giving the debtor a chance to pay or explain; offering help)

When the collector has sent enough reminders to decide that oversight is not the cause of delay, another assumption comes into play. With a new customer or a poor risk it may be that persuasion or force is necessary—and lead to skipping a stage or two in the usual procedure.

With an old customer who has paid regularly, however, reason says that unusual circumstances must be the cause. The collector still has confidence in the customer (based on past favorable experience), still wants to retain goodwill, and is always willing to be considerate of a person temporarily in a financial tight spot.

The logical plan, then, is to write *one* letter in a spirit of friendly understanding and helpfulness, asking for the money *or* an explanation. Because the money is the real goal, it (not the explanation of what's wrong, or possible ways to help) deserves the major emphasis. Care not to offend this formerly good customer apparently in a temporary jam, however, is important. So is care not to suggest that something is wrong with the goods or the billing (for reasons explained later). The only persuasion is in frankness, the offer of help, and a considerate attitude. Most people react favorably to requests presented in such a spirit. The letters below illustrate the technique for the inquiry stage. The first (using form paragraphs) is designed to go out over the sales representative's signature.

In the three years I have been calling on you and we have supplied you with truck and trailer parts, Mr. Kingman, we have sincerely appreciated your business. We have also appreciated the way in which you have consistently kept your dealership's account paid up.

To a good customer and a friend, then, can I offer some help? We're sure you want to settle your account; and since some unforeseen circumstances appear to have come up, your agreement to one of these plans will give you an easy way to pay up your account and protect your credit rating:

1. If you can, please send a check today for the full $823.40. This will bring your account up to date and clear the outstanding April and May balances.
2. As an alternative, send a partial payment now for half the full amount and agree to pay the remainder in two equal installments within 30 and 60 days. If this is acceptable, just sign your name next to this paragraph and return it right away with your first check. Your signature will indicate agreement to this contractual arrangement.
3. Third, we can put you on a revolving credit plan, like many of our smaller and less well rated customers. You may continue to keep your open account, subject to a limit of $1,000.00 on your open balance. The finance charge will be 1½ percent per month of your previous balance after deducting current payments, credits, and past-due insurance premiums. This finance charge becomes part of your outstanding balance. The annual interest rate is 18 percent.
4. If for some reason you cannot accept any of these three plans, tell me what the trouble is, what we can do to help you, and how you propose to settle your account.

Please answer as quickly as possible, so I can report your decision to my management.

--

I wish I could sit down and talk with you for a few minutes about the circumstances that leave January and February charges to you on the books.

But because of the distance, I can only study our past experience with you, and various kinds of credit information. Your past record of prompt payment leaves me unconcerned about ultimate collection, but it also leaves me wondering what's wrong now.

Please either make immediate payment of the $157.47 balance due or drop me a note today telling just how you intend to handle the account. You'll find me cooperative in accepting any reasonable proposal for your taking care of it—or better, the $157.47.

You may have noticed that these letters avoid *two common collection-letter errors* that have their first chance to come up in the inquiry stage.

The *first* is that in writing inquiry-stage letters, collectors sometimes ask *questions about the customer's possible dissatisfaction with the goods or charges or both.* The apparent purpose of the questions is to secure some kind of answer—to keep the debtor thinking about the obligation and renew acceptance of it.

But aren't such questions psychologically unsound? If the debtor had found anything wrong with the goods or the billing, would you not have had a claim? Isn't the collector practically suggesting that if the debtor will claim something is wrong, that can gracefully postpone payment and perhaps even produce an unjustified adjustment? Certainly such a suggestion works in the opposite direction from both resale talk and success consciousness.

The *second* common error is *backtracking*—that is, going back to the assumption of an earlier stage in the collection procedure (see Table 12–1, p. 414). Apparently in an effort to save the delinquent's face, a timid collector sometimes grabs back at "oversight" (the assumption of the reminder stage) after starting a letter in the inquiry stage. If oversight is still apparently the reason for the delay, the series should not advance to the inquiry stage.

The same kind of nerveless collector sometimes shows the same tendencies in two other places in the collection procedure. After an inquiry-stage offer of special consideration has been ignored, it sometimes incongruously comes up again in letters of the next stage.

Not many collectors will send an ultimatum and then back down on it —the worst kind of backtracking. Those who do merely spoil customers and lose their respect, just as many parents do with their children by issuing ultimatums and not carrying them out.

Appeals (basically reader benefits, made increasingly forceful)

The delinquent who does not respond to a friendly inquiry evidently is taking the wrong attitude toward the indebtedness. The collector's new assumption is that now the debtor must be persuaded to pay.

Basic considerations. The appeal stage is the collection letter writer's main work. Four important points are guidelines:

1. *For persuasiveness, write individualized messages.* The earlier brief notices, reminders, and inquiries will have collected most of the accounts (the easy ones) as inexpensively as possible in terms of time and goodwill. The remaining few will be harder to collect. Usually they will require individualized (or at least individual-sounding) letters rather than forms, because they have to be persuasive. By using the information in the credit records, the collector can write individualized messages that are specific and therefore persuasive to a degree impossible in a form.

2. *Develop only one or two points.* Scattering shots like a shotgun over several undeveloped appeals weakens the message too much to reach the remaining hard-to-collect-from delinquents. Something like a rifle bullet, with all the powder behind one fully developed central theme, will be more forceful. This usually means longer letters because they must be specific and say enough to make the point emphatic, but they pay off in results.

3. *Retain goodwill as far as possible.* Because they are individualized, pointed, full-length collection messages, appeal-stage letters will necessarily carry some sting. Like doctors and patients, however, collectors and debtors have to accept the fact that the needle carrying strong medicine for advanced stages of a disease often has a sting. Still, the wise collector, like the humane doctor, will minimize the sting as much as possible without weakening the medicine.

You want to be firm without being harsh. Skilfully stimulate the customer's desire to pay and you'll both be happy.

4. *Select a reader-benefit appeal.* Successful collection, like successful selling or any other kind of persuasion, involves showing that the debtor will get something wanted or avoid something not wanted—in other words, the you-attitude.

Appeals to sympathy (variously called the "poor me" appeal or the appeal to cooperation) do not meet the requirement. They are fundamentally selfish.

Though a cleverly and humorously overdrawn picture of the writer's family in need might bring the money (indeed did in one well-known case), it is more likely to bring a wisecrack answer. For instance, one man built a letter around a picture of his wife and 11 children, with the note below: "This is why I *must* have my money." The answer was the picture of a beautiful blonde with the note "This is why I *can't* pay."

Basically, people want

1. To get the service the product supposedly gives.
2. To have self-respect and the approval of others (they have to live with both themselves and others).
3. To avoid loss of what they have and add to those things (money, property, and the credit privilege, for example).

So a collector can be persuasive by reminding debtors of their obligations to pay for what they got and by showing how they benefit in self-respect or in economic self-interest.

The true collector is therefore really a seller of those ideas who makes a careful analysis of the customer, selects the appeal most likely to succeed with the particular individual in the specific situation, and sells the idea of paying by showing the benefits. The resale, pride, and fair-play appeals show the reader how to retain a clear conscience and keep self-respect.

The resale appeal. Touches of resale belong in every collection letter to keep the debtor satisfied and to show what came in exchange for the promise to pay, but resale may be the theme of a whole appeal letter. Essentially it goes back and almost repeats the points a good presentation would make in selling the product. By the time the collector is through reselling, the debtor will see the good value received. Whether you call it integrity, respect for one's word, sense of fair play, or pride, it can motivate payment as the way to a clear conscience.

Although inept phrasing may make any appeal ineffective or kill goodwill, the danger is not great in the resale appeal. Really effective use of it, however, requires imagination enough to paint a vivid, interesting *picture of the product in use*—and willingness to make it complete, detailed, and long enough to be persuasive. The following letter illustrates the type:

> Now that Asbex and Asbar have had time to prove their profit-making ability to you, can you say that we were right? We said that they would be a good selling team for you.
>
> When you followed up your original Asbex order of April 15 with the April 27 order for 20 gallons each of Asbex and Asbar, you showed that you thought the fire-retarding twins would move quickly together. With your good reputation for prompt payment as our guide, we were glad to have such a desirable outlet as your store for this pair of fast sellers. Although your payment of $39 for the first shipment, invoice BT-41198, is now 10 days overdue, you can keep your record intact by sending us a check in the next mail. If you make the check for $273, you can also pay for the second shipment, invoice BT-41390, on its net date.
>
> From all reports on the way business is in Ardmore, you'll be sending us repeat orders before long. We'll be looking forward to serving you now that you have learned that Asbex and Asbar fill a recurring need of your customers. With more and more users and readers of the Architectural Forum, Good Housekeeping, and House Beautiful spreading the good news, you can expect ever-increasing turnover with the twins in your stock.

The following letter from a building and loan collector who made the loan originally and knew the family quite well is even more personal in its resale appeal. The reference to passing pleasures in the second paragraph is a subtle way of telling Barnes, without preaching, that the collector knows where the money went—into expensive parties designed to keep up with the Joneses.

> When you and Mrs. Barnes moved into your new home two years ago, I was very proud that I had something to do with it. If anything contributes to the pleasure of life it is a good place to live—and especially if that place belongs to the occupant. I feel that much more than mere sentiment is behind the words "There's no place like home."
>
> Indeed, so much of comfort, security, and pride comes with home ownership that anyone should forgo passing pleasures that

eat up his income, take the savings, and invest in a home—just as you decided to do.

The importance to you of keeping up your payments on your loan deserves your serious attention. Perhaps by now you are used to your home, and you take it as a matter of course. But take a walk around the lawn. Note the landscaping; note the beautiful architectural lines of the building. Then go inside and think for a minute how comfortable you, Mary, Jim, and Jane are there.

Think where you would be without it. And suppose you were going to build today. Instead of the $38,000 you paid, you would now have to pay about $50,000 because of increased prices. Really, you cannot afford to stop enjoying those comforts.

So will you please come in and take care of your March, April, and May payments as soon as possible?

Pride appeal. Often resale talk joins a subtle appeal to pride, or the appeal to pride may be more or less independent of resale on the goods. In either case the writer uses practical psychology to know when to encourage pride by sincere compliments, when to needle it, and when to challenge it. A bungled approach may get a surprising answer, as did the collector who asked what the neighbors would think if the debtor's new car were repossessed. The answer was that the neighbors all agreed it would be a low-down, dirty trick. The collector had erred in challenging instead of encouraging pride.

One collector succeeded by quoting from a highly favorable credit report on the debtor, asking if the description fit, and encouraging prompt action to retain the good reputation. Others have given percentages of customers who pay at different stages in the collection procedure and said that of course the debtor does not want to be in the minority groups at the end of the list. The essence of success with the pride appeal is to *encourage the debtor toward prideful actions* and to avoid the use of accusations and implications of shame as far as possible.

The following examples show the methods. Note that the first (an early letter) ends with sales promotion, and the last (to a university senior) incorporates a reference that is almost a left hook.

Your choice of the navy-blue suit and the light tan suit with matching shoes, purse, and gloves, for a total of $182.95, shows the care and pride with which you select your clothes.

We feel sure that you want to show the same pride in maintaining your preferred credit rating. Drop your check for $182.95 in the mail today, and your account, due on November 10, will be paid in full.

The next time you are in town, come by and look over our completely new line of Mary Margaret furs. Whether you want to make additions to your wardrobe or merely to see the latest fashions, you will be welcome.

--

Twenty-seven other Lansing residents bought Monora television sets the same week you got yours.

That was just a little over three months ago. Yet 23 of them have already been in to take care of their payments as agreed. We made a note of their prompt payments on their records. And they walked out pleased with themselves, their sets, and us.

When you stop to think about it, the good credit rating you establish by promptly paying as agreed is more than a matter of personal pride. It adds to the value and desirability of your account with any store in Lansing. It's a personal recommendation too, for employers often check the credit record of an applicant for a job.

Take the two minutes now to send us your check. Or bring your payment to the store tomorrow.

Fair-play appeal. By using slightly different wording, you can turn the basic appeal to self-respect into an appeal to fair play. The wording may recall the debtor's sense of respect for a contract, feeling of duty to do as promised, or conscience that commands doing the right thing. It develops the feeling that the debtor should carry out the buyer's part of the bargain, since the creditor has been fair in carrying out the seller's. Integrity or honesty may be as good a name for the appeal. Some people call it a request for cooperation.

Whatever the name, a well-developed, positive presentation (without accusations), showing that the reader should pay to be fair, is an effective appeal. It goes back to the fundamental idea that the debtor promised to pay by a certain time for certain goods or services. Having received the benefits, the debtor knows the fair thing is to pay for them. Almost everybody wants to be fair in dealing with others. Here are two examples of the appeal:

On the basis of your urgent need for drive rivets, and because you supplied us with references, we were happy to fill your order February 6 for eight gross of our "Stellar" ½-inch diameter drive rivets.

When we filled your order, we explained that our terms on open accounts call for payment within 30 days. Our suppliers have faith that we will pay them on time, and we have faith that our customers will pay us on time, enabling us to do so.

You know that your account is now past due more than 30 days.

When we shipped you the drive rivets, we had faith that you would do the fair thing and pay for them promptly. Won't you renew our faith in you, Mr. Spiegel?

Make out a check today for the amount past due—$921.60—and mail it in the enclosed stamped, addressed envelope. That's the fair thing to do, isn't it, Mr. Spiegel?

--

How would you feel next payday if you received no paycheck?

I'm sure you would feel that you had been giving good service and that your employer should pay for it.

When we ask you for the $84.95 for the coat you bought on November 18, we are only asking for what is due us.

At the time we placed your name on our credit list, we made clear that accounts are due on the 10th of the month following purchase. Perhaps more important, you accepted the terms in accepting that becoming coat.

In fairness to us and to yourself, won't you please come in today and give us our paycheck according to our agreement?

Appeals to economic self-interest. Even those who have no sense of obligation to pay for value received (as developed in the resale appeal), or of pride, or of fair play in treating decent people fairly will likely pay if it is clearly to their own economic self-interest to do so. You may therefore write forceful collection appeals to a debtor's desire to retain the valuable credit privilege. In fact this is the main appeal in commercial and industrial credit.

Why is a prompt-pay rating like money in the bank?

Both are able to command goods and services immediately when you want them.

On the basis of your ability to pay and your reputation for meeting payments promptly, we extended credit immediately when you asked for it. Now we ask that you send your check for $898.76 to cover your August shipment of small jewelry, sold to you on credit just as if you had drawn on your bank account for it.

Then look through the enclosed booklet. Notice the color pictures of things you'd like to have in stock for Toledo's Christmas shoppers. The heavy hollow silver plate described on page 3 is a line for moderate budgets. It's durable as well as handsome, since it's triple-plated silver on copper.

Should you care to order on our regular terms, enclose a check covering your balance of $898.76 and order the new stock; use your credit as if it were another check drawn on money in the bank.

Though the following letter speaks of fair play, it is an appeal not to fair play, as explained before, but to the debtor's economic self-interest in enjoying the benefits of the credit privilege:

Are you playing fair—

—playing fair with yourself, I mean?

You want to continue to get what you need promptly by merely mailing orders to your suppliers. Rightfully you can expect the best of service along with good-quality products when you arrange a businesslike transaction. You will agree that your company would not be fair to itself if its actions caused it to lose this privilege.

The Reliable Paint and Varnish Company has continued to honor this privilege because in the past you have always settled your account satisfactorily. At present, however, you owe us $4,723.00, now three months overdue, on invoice 362773 covering a shipment of 575 gallons of Reliable Dual-Coat Zinc Primer.

To treat yourself fairly and to preserve your company's good, businesslike reputation, you will want to get your account balanced promptly. Please use the enclosed envelope to send your check today and put your account in good condition again.

Urgency

When the regular collector is getting nowhere with appeals like those in the preceding letters, the next step may be stronger letters, perhaps from a higher executive taking over for the final few.

When the treasurer, president, company lawyer, credit bureau, or collection agency signs letters, the psychology is to give the reader the feeling that things are getting pretty serious. Although urgency-stage letters are not actually the end of the collection procedure, they should seem close. They therefore answer the question of the customer in the *New Yorker* cartoon who flashed an early-stage collection letter at the collection desk and asked how many more nice letters would come before payment was necessary.

Actually the letter sent over the signature of the higher executive is usually a forceful development of one of the appeals already discussed. It may go a bit further on the economic interests of the debtor and talk about the cost of facing suit (since the debtor would have to pay the bill and court costs), but usually not. Any executive knows that mentioning court suit is a good way to drive customers away—and hence should be postponed as long as possible. Even now the firm is still interested in goodwill. It knows that a chance of retaining the customer remains—if not as a credit customer, as a cash customer who may still speak of the firm favorably. So the executive more frequently plays the role of the good fellow who allows a last chance and still does not turn the screws all the way down by setting an end date. The following letter, signed by the company treasurer, illustrates:

When you began your business, a good reputation in Ardmore made it possible for you to get loans, and your hard work and prompt payments—good reputation again—got you credit on your purchases.

This reputation is more important to you now than ever before, for with the unsettled world conditions causing wide fluctuations in the securities market, credit agencies are becoming more and more strict in their policies—and businesses are learning to be more insistent on their terms.

We have not received your check for the $234 for our invoices 69507, covering our shipment of 10 gallons of Asbex on April 10, and 76305, covering the shipment on April 20 of 10 gallons

```
of Asbex and 20 gallons of Asbar.  Some arrangement for this
settlement is necessary right away.  We are willing to accept
your 90-day note at 8 percent for this amount so that you can
protect your credit rating without lowering your cash balance.

We would of course prefer to have your check; but for the
benefit of your business, your customers, and your creditors,
please settle your account some way with us today.
```

Ultimatum

If the serious mood, the strong appeal, and the bigheartedness of the executive's offer of still another chance do not get the money, the collector will give the screw its last turn—now assuming that the only way is to squeeze the money out of the debtor. Apparently as long as any slack remains, this debtor will move around in it. The collector therefore says calmly and reluctantly but firmly that on a definite date, usually 5–10 days later, the account will go to a collection agency or a lawyer—unless payment comes before that time.

Though the language of the ultimatum is firm, it should not be harsh. To minimize resentment, the collector commonly reviews the case at this point. Carefully worded, this letter may collect and still retain goodwill because of the fair-play appeal in the whole review. Usually it will at least collect.

It is more likely both to collect and to retain goodwill, however, if the writer is careful about these points:

1. Show your reasonableness in the past (without becoming self-righteous), your reluctance to take the present action, and the justice and necessity of it.
2. Word the ultimatum clearly, precisely, and calmly—not as a form of vengeance, penalty, or threat.
3. Stress the positive side (pay and keep all the advantages of your credit) instead of the negative (if you don't pay, you'll get a bad credit record—and lose in court).

As you read the letter below, notice how the writer did all of those things.

```
When we sent your first credit shipment, $95 worth of
Christmas supplies under invoice CA-872 on December 4, we took
the step all stationery wholesalers take when approving
credit:  We verified your good credit reputation with the
National Stationery Manufacturers Guild, of which we are a
member.

The Guild's certification meant that you invariably pay your
bills.  When we received a second order on January 26, we were
happy to serve you again by shipping $42 worth of Valentine
cutouts and art supplies, under invoice CB-345. Since then we
have tried to be both reasonable and considerate in inducing
you to pay by our usual collection procedures.  Now we shall
be compelled by the terms of our membership agreement with the
```

Guild to submit your name as "nonpay" unless we receive your check for $137 by April 15.

I ask you to consider carefully the privileges and conveniences you can retain for yourself by making that payment—the privileges and conveniences you get from your hard-earned and well-thought-of credit rating. You can continue buying from your old suppliers (including us). Credit requests to new supply houses will be approved on the basis of the Guild's favorable reports. You will save the extra costs of a court suit to collect, in which you would pay not only the $137 but the court costs.

All the advantages of an unmarred credit standing among suppliers are yours now, insofar as we know; and we want to help you keep them so that you can continue to stock your shelves on credit. Mail us your check for $137 by the 15th and retain those advantages.

If an ultimatum like that above does not bring the money by the date set, the only remaining letter to write is a courtesy letter, not a collection letter, telling the customer of the action taken. Then the case is out of the collection writer's hands and in the hands of a lawyer.

The trouble with that arrangement is that your public relations went with the case—into the hands of the lawyer—and most lawyers don't seem to understand or believe in public relations. Therefore you should go as far as you can with your own good collection letters.

To make sure that your letters are effective, in both collecting and goodwill, we therefore suggest that you read the preceding letter again; then read it again substituting the following three paragraphs for the last two there. (These three were in the letter when we first saw it.)

You are no doubt aware of the effects of being labeled by the Guild as nonpay. Credit requests to new supply houses would be refused; old sources would be reluctant to continue supplying you on a credit basis. We want to help you maintain your preferred status so that you can continue to stock your shelves on credit.

With the sincerity of a friend, I urge you to weigh carefully the effects of a bad report and the advantages of a favorable one on your hard-earned and well-thought-of-credit rating. I urge you to avoid the necessity of our submitting an unfavorable report. And beyond that, of course, would be a suit in which you would pay not only the bill but the court costs.

All the advantages of an unmarred credit standing among suppliers are yours now. Mail us your check for $137 by the 15th and retain those advantages.

BEGINNINGS AND ENDINGS

For most writers the beginnings and endings of letters, including collection letters, are the trouble spots. Beginnings are more difficult than endings because the background or point of contact varies more than the desired action, and therefore the beginning cannot be well standardized.

This much, however, we can say: You have to capture the reader's attention and interest and hold it through the letter. Identification of the account (the amount due, what for, and when due) should be clear in every case, *but these facts do not make good beginnings for persuasive letters* (those after the notification and reminder stages); the reader has already shown his lack of interest in them.

Neither are references to former attempts to collect good as beginnings. Such references may sound like whining or may suggest that the debtor can again ignore the request with impunity. Since collection letters are basically sales letters—selling the debtor on the benefits of paying—the collector will do well to reapply the principle of reader-benefit beginnings.

Just as the sales writer drives for an order at the end, so does the good collection writer strive to bring in a check or an explanation that will name a payment date. So the standard action ending—telling what to do, making clear how to do it, making action easy, and providing a stimulus to prompt action—is always proper except in the early stages of the series, where it is too forceful. There, resale or sales promotion talk rather than the request for payment usually ends the letter to imply faith, appeal to pride, perhaps promote sales, and remove the sting.

Although the collector always writes with success consciousness expecting each letter to bring results, all except the one serving notice that the account has been placed in the hands of an attorney should leave the way open for more severe action.

Whenever feasible, the collection writer should make response easy for the debtor. An already addressed and stamped envelope does this and also provides a strong stimulus to prompt action. The Direct Mail Advertising Association reported that 798 collection letters sent without reply envelopes brought payments from 42.85 percent and requests for time extensions from 6.78 percent for a total of 49.63 percent answering. A similar mailing of 798 letters which included reply envelopes brought remittances from 45.12 percent and requests for extensions from 16.8 percent for a total of 61.92 percent responding. Even the casual "Don't bother to write a letter; just slip your check into the enclosed envelope . . ." will show the debtor your friendly attitude and will frequently produce the check.

* * *

Because collection letter circumstances vary so much, they have few universal truths suitable for a checklist such as we have provided for some other kinds. The suggestions on p. 433 will be helpful as a partial checklist for collection letters. They, plus your own analysis of the illustrative letters in this chapter (except for the first two), along with the explanations of their circumstances, should provide you with the properly varied checklists you need.

HUMOR IN COLLECTIONS

Generally, past-due accounts are not laughing matters, for either the debtor or the collector. But small amounts early in the collection procedure are not deadly serious matters either. In the early stages, where little or no persuasion seems necessary or even desirable, the main job of the letter is to gain attention and remind the debtor. Under these circumstances a humorous letter may be just the thing. Its sprightliness will supply the attention and memory value needed. The light mood will take the sting out of the letter and make the collector seem like a friendly human being instead of an ogre.

A widely known and highly successful collection letter, the famous "Elmer" letter by Miles Kimball, pictures both kinds of collector. The writer, a friendly human, warns the debtor against the ogre Elmer, treasurer of the company, who sometimes gets out of hand and writes letters that destroy a reader's will to live. The whole thing is a detailed and ridiculous account of the kind of ogre Elmer is and the disastrous effects of the letters, plus a brief warning to pay now before Elmer writes.

Shorter humorous letters are more usual. One merely asks for the name of the best lawyer in the debtor's town, in case the collector has to sue. One collector simply mailed small, live turtles to slow payers. *Time* has long used two humorous letters for people who don't pay for their subscriptions. One, on the back of the front picture cover of the current issue of *Time,* begins "I'm sorry—sorry I can't send you any more than the cover of this week's *Time.*" It then goes into a brief resale appeal. The other begins with the assertion of how much is due, pokes fun at the usual collection letter that breaks into tears in the first paragraph and yells for the law in the second, shows how large numbers of small accounts add up, and ends with the pun that "procrastination is the thief of *Time.*" Still another journal begins a subscription collection with

"CHECKING, JUST CHECKING,"

said the telephone line worker when the lady jumped out of the bathtub to answer. I'm just checking to find out whether you want to continue to receive. . . .

The rest of the letter is the usual resale appeal with a standard action ending.

Another device is that called the one-sided or half-and-half letter. The writer presents what is essentially an inquiry-stage collection letter in a narrow column on the left half of the page and asks the reader to use the right half to attach a check or explain.

Though such letters (usually inexpensive forms) may be effective in collecting small amounts early in the series, they are too flippant for large amounts or late-stage collections. The exception is that they might serve just before an ultimatum to jolt the debtor. But we must not forget that

1. The credit obligation is a serious responsibility, and we can't expect the debtor to take it seriously if we are undignified about it.
2. Written joshing is more likely to offend than oral banter.
3. Gadgeteering and humor in letters of all kinds are likely to be overrated because we probably hear more of the occasional successes than of the numerous failures.

COLLECTING UNEARNED DISCOUNTS

A special problem which does not fit into the regular collection procedure is that of collecting unearned discounts (that is, discounts taken when sending payment *after* the end of the discount period). The fact that the amount is usually small—always small in comparison with the volume of business the collector risks in trying to collect—complicates the problem. Moreover, some large purchasers know the collector would think twice before losing their $200 or $20,000 orders to collect an improper $4 or $400 discount.

Fortunately the collector usually has some advantages too:

1. When the occasion arises, the reader is almost certainly an experienced person who will understand a reasoned business analysis.
2. The sizable purchaser has almost certainly investigated various sources of supply and might be as reluctant to change suppliers as the collector would be to lose a customer.
3. If the collector cannot get the money in early and has to pay interest on money borrowed for financing, the debtor will understand that the end result will be a revised system with no possibility of discount.
4. The fair-play appeal can include playing fair with all the collector's other customers. That is, you cannot well allow one to take the unearned discount while requiring others to pay according to terms.

Armed thus, the collector is ready for the taker of unearned discounts. First, assuming a little misunderstanding of the terms is a reasonable start. Then make the terms clear, and overlook the improper deduction *the first time*.

When no doubt exists, the collector can certainly assume (reasonably enough) that the unjustified deduction comes from failure to check the dates—an unintentional chiseling—and that the additional money will be forthcoming after a little reminder. One writer used an analogy for the reminder by telling the story of the boy who presented nine apples as his mother's offering for the church's harvest festival. When the pastor proposed a call to thank the mother, the boy asked that the thanks be for 10 apples.

If neither misunderstanding of the terms nor failure to check dates is the reason, the collector has a real letter-writing job. Although well armed —with justice, legal advantages, and some psychology on their side—some collectors fear to go ahead. The almost inevitable result is chaos in the collection department, or at least in the discount system. Word gets around.

The bold do better. Their appeals are Item 3 above (the economic justification of discounting practices) and Item 4 (the broadened fair-play appeal). Often a good letter combines both, as in the following illustrations:

From your letter of May 25 we understand why you feel entitled to the 2 percent discount from our invoice X-10 of April 30. If some of our creditors allowed us discounts after the end of the discount period, we too might expect others to do the same.

The discount you get from us when you pay within a definite, specified period is simply our passing on to you the saving our creditors allow us for using the money we collect promptly and paying our bills within 10 days after making purchases. It's certainly true that your discount of $4.57 is small; but large or small, we would have allowed it if we had had your payment in time to use in making a similar saving in paying our own bills. If our creditors gave us a longer time, we'd gladly give you a longer time.

Since they don't, the only solution besides following the terms is stopping all discounts, taking the loss on all our sales, or being unfair to our many other customers by making exceptions and showing favoritism. I don't think you want us to do any of those things, do you, Mr. Griggs?

When you mail us your check for the full invoice amount of $228.57, we know that you will do so with the spirit of good business practice and fairness.

Thank you again for your order. You will find that our merchandise and attractive prices will always assure you of a more-than-average profit.

The letter above did both of its jobs of collecting the money and retaining the customer. Certainly it was not written by the distrusting merchant who told a new employee that if somebody wanted to pay a bill and somebody else yelled "Fire!" to take the money first and then put out the fire.

The problem of unearned discounts becomes particularly difficult after you have allowed one exception, explained the terms carefully, refused to allow a second exception, and received a reply including statements like these:

. . . I thought that an organization such as yours would be above such hair-splitting tactics . . . and I resent your hiding behind a mere technicality to collect an additional $3.69 . . . oversight. . . . If you wish . . . a new check will be mailed, but . . . it will be your last from us.

Here's how one collection writer handled this hot potato—successfully:

I appreciate your letter of December 5 because it gives me an opportunity to explain our request that you mail us a check for $184.50 in place of the returned one for $180.81.

Our sincere desire to be entirely fair to you and all our other customers prompted the request. For years we have allowed a discount of 2 percent to all who pay their bills within 10 days of the invoice date. Such prompt payment enables us to make a similar saving by paying our own bills promptly. Thus we pass on to you and our other customers the savings prompt payments allow us to make.

But if our customers wait longer than the 10 days to pay us, we make no saving to pass on. Of course, an allowance of $3.69 is a small matter; but if we allowed it in one case, we would have to allow similar discounts to all our customers or be unfair to some.

The principle involved is a serious one, since any exception would have to become the rule if we are to be fair to all.

I feel sure that you want us to treat all customers alike, just as you do in your own business. Certainly I do not think you would like it if you found that we were more lenient with somebody else than with you. Our request for the additional $3.69 is necessary if we are to treat all alike.

Thank you again for writing me and giving me this chance to explain. May we have your check—in fairness to all?

This—a letter refusing to allow an unearned discount when forcefully requested—is the only likely kind of situation for B–plan collection letters. But it is not the usual B-situation. Here you're not just refusing to do something for the other person (give a discount). You're refusing to *let* that person *not* do something (send you the extra money). That is, you have to say both "I won't do what you ask" and "Now you do what I ask." It's a combination of the two most difficult kinds of letters—the B–plan and C–plan—and hence an appropriate culmination of your study of letters and end of our treatment of them.

* * *

Because collection letters vary so much, they have few universal truths suitable for a checklist such as we have provided for some other kinds. The suggestions on p. 433, however, will be helpful as a partial checklist. They, plus your own analysis of the illustrative letters in this chapter (except for the first two), along with the explanations of their circumstances, should provide you with the properly varied checklists you need.

COLLECTION CASES

1. Last month your firm (Ryder Rooseter Feed and Grain, 908 Hillcrest, Abercrombie, North Dakota 58001) sold Martin Van Voorhis, a prominent chicken farmer, three tons of Burpee laying mash, total cost $360. The bill is now 25 days past due; and Van Voorhis, who has become a little forgetful since his 70th birthday, has not replied to your notification and reminder. You're not worried about getting your money; Van Voorhis is a millionaire. Although he forgets to pay his bills from time to

Collection Letter Checklist

1. Follow a reasonable philosophy and adapted procedure.
   a) Associate the specific goods with the obligation to pay for them, and show that you expect payment because it is due.
   b) Always identify how much is due and how long overdue.
   c) Except in the first two stages and the ultimatum, the points in b and a are not good beginnings.
   d) Stick to your sequence of assumptions for different collection stages; backtracking shows weakness and loses reader respect.
   e) Try to get the money and keep the customer's goodwill.
2. Fit the tone carefully to the circumstances.
   a) Avoid seeming to tell the reader how to operate.
   b) Nasty, curt, injured, pouting, exasperated, or harsh tone doesn't help; it turns the reader against you instead.
   c) Scolding or holier-than-thou attitude brings resentment too.
   d) To avoid credit platitudes, relate credit principles and regulations to the particular case.
   e) Show confidence that the debtor will pay, by
      1) Avoiding references to past correspondence (except in late-stage reviews).
      2) Stressing positive benefits of payment.
   f) Be sure any humor avoids irritation or distraction.
   g) Avoid (1) accusations, (2) apologies and—except in the reminder and inquiry stages—(3) excuses invented for the reader, including any hint of fault in the goods or billing.
   h) To increase the force, use more collection talk and less sales promotion (good only in early letters to good customers).
   i) To decrease stringency and apparent concern, reverse (h); watch proportions.
3. For persuasiveness (after the first two collection stages):
   a) You have to stress what the reader gains by doing as you ask.
   b) Remember the effectiveness of a developed central theme.
   c) Select an appeal appropriate to the circumstance and reader.
   d) Remember that any kind of antagonizing works against you.
   e) Individualize your message for stronger effect, even in forms.
4. Guard against the legal dangers.
   a) Reporting the delinquent to anybody except those requesting information because of an interest to protect is dangerous.
   b) Don't threaten physical violence, blackmail, or extortion.
   c) Be careful about your facts, and show no malice.
   d) Be sure that only the debtor will read (sealed envelope).
5. Adapt your drive for action to the stage of the collection.
   a) A full-fledged action ending is too strong and stinging early.
   b) But later, anything short of it is too weak.

time, he usually pays—with profuse apologies for forgetting—once you send him a reminder. Since he is a regular customer, who spends about $5,000 annually in your store, you'll want to remind him incidentally but memorably that his bill is past due in a letter that announces your new line of Atmore vitamins and medicines for poultry. Write Martin Van Voorhis at Rt. 12, Box 19, Flaxton, North Dakota 58737.

2. As loans manager of the First National Bank of Durham, North Carolina 27703 (809 Clayton), write an *Inquiry Stage* collection letter to Marvin Harper, owner of Marvin's Motel, 5800 Andrews Chapel Road, Hanover, N.C. 28078. Marvin borrowed $2,000 to remodel the left wing of his motel. His monthly payments are $185. He made the first two payments but missed the third and fourth. Before the fifth payment passes by, you want to find out why he hasn't paid. You sent him two reminders already; and every time you call him, he's not in. You're surprised because Marvin usually pays promptly. He has had at least five loans from your bank in the past that you can recall, and he has paid them all back promptly.

3. As director in charge of collections for Sauer's Tea Company, Boston, Mass. 00138, write the Moon Gate Tea House, 25 Market Street, Knoxville, Tennessee 37986. Alexander Booker owes you $200, now 90 days past due, for 150 pounds of your Sauer #180, a blend of six special Asian teas. Alexander ignored your notification and two reminders, which was strange. You have been doing business with Alexander for ten years, and only once during that time did he fail to take advantage of your 2 percent discount for early payment. That time he paid well before the net period ended. You have to assume that something unusual is keeping Alexander from paying his bill. Ask for your money (preferably) or find out why he hasn't paid his bill.

4. Your company, Benbow Boat Works, 97 Danforth, Portland, Maine 04106, recently sold David Neal, owner, Neal's Boat Dock and Fisherama, 2 Ocean Avenue, Keelhaul, New Jersey 10931, ten plywood flat-bottomed skiffs at $100 each. David rents these boats out by day to fishermen and crabbers. He paid half the cost ($500), and you extended him credit for the remaining $500. He didn't take the 2 percent discount nor did he answer the notification and reminders you sent. Although he did answer your inquiry and promised to pay when the fishing got better, you still haven't got your money, which is now 90 days past due. Write David an appeal-stage collection letter in which you persuade him to pay by using resale talk on the merchandise he got.

5. For Speed-King, 3899 Montague Avenue, Charleston, South Carolina 29407, write an appeal letter to Mildred Selko, owner of the Wash

Cycle, a laundromat located at Hudson Square, Greenville, South Carolina 29609. Mildred bought three of your heavy-duty, commercial-type Speed-King washers ($300 each). When she didn't pay after 30 days, you sent a notification and three reminders. After these didn't work, you sent an inquiry when the bill was 60 days past due. The bill is now 75 days past due, and you haven't heard a peep from her. You must assume that you will have to persuade her to pay. Use as your theme resale on the product —why she got a good buy on the machines.

6. About two months ago Mathew Moore bought a new Wombat ten-speed bicycle from your store on credit. (Your establishment is the Cycle Shop, 440 South Elm Drive, Tempe, Arizona 85281.) The total cost of this precision ten-speed machine was $300. Mathew gave you a $100 down payment and agreed to pay off the other $200 within 30 days. You sent him a notification at the end of 30 days and two reminders (10 and 20 days past due). Five days after the second reminder you sent him an inquiry in which you asked him to call you or write an explanation for the delay. You've heard nothing from him yet. Your assumption now is that he has to be persuaded to pay. You remember how much Mathew liked the Wombat–10 and how he told you he wanted to use the bike as transportation to and from the campus sewage plant where he worked. You have to convince him to pay by reminding him of the reasons he bought the Wombat and reselling the product. Mathew lives at 907 Elm Street, Tempe 85281.

7. When you sent ten Schwannz Wombat–10 bicycles to Philip Adams @ $250 each, terms 2/10, n/30, he sent his check for $2,450, taking the 2 percent discount, 15 days past the date of the invoice. The check was dated 8 days after the invoice date, but the date of the stamp cancellation on the envelope showed that the letter had been mailed 13 days past the invoice date. Clearly Adams is trying to collect an unearned discount, and you can't let him do it. Write Adams a letter (Cycle Shop, 440 South Elm Drive, Tempe, Arizona 85281) in which you reiterate your credit terms, send him back his check for the rest of the net period (15 more days), and collect the full $2,500 by the due date. Your company is the Schwannz Cycle Company, 8422 St. Johns Avenue, Phoenix, Arizona 85012.

8. Five days after your ten-day, 2 percent discount period ended, you received a $294 check from Herman Curtis, owner of the Tap and Keg liquor store and tavern, 426 Ogontz Avenue, Dundalk, Maryland 45628. The full amount due after the discount period ended for the 150 cases of Mallard beer was $300. Herman's check was dated one day before the discount period ended, the postmark stamp was dated three days later, but you didn't get it until five days past the ten-day deadline. Write a letter to Herman in which you explain your discount philosophy and collect the unearned $6 discount. Your firm is Mallard Brewery, Baltimore, Maryland 46734.

9. The AAA Gift Shop, One Locust Street, Reno, Nevada 89502, has an account with Ms. Farley Moody, 1432 Bonita Avenue, Las Vegas, Nevada 89100, for $120.14 now 20 days overdue according to your EOM terms. Ms. Moody is a new customer with good credit references but has ignored your notice and reminders. She purchased a mahogany table for a lamp. Tell her about the *specials you have* on mahogany captain chairs regularly $105.50, now $85.50. *Sign* the letter as Walter P. Jones, Credit Manager.

10. When the account is 50 days overdue, write Ms. Moody (preceding case) a stronger letter than the last one. In the meantime you phoned and found that the bill had "just slipped the mind." Point out the advantages of a good credit rating in these days of tight money and inflation. Assume that you enclose an envelope for payment.

11. Before writing an ultimatum-stage letter, you phoned Ms. Moody (two preceding cases) again. Over the phone she told you about her recent divorce and her adjustment to living on a budget income. She promised payment within a few days. No payment came, however; so you must tell her that she has seven more days in which to pay at least half the past-due amount ($60.07) before you turn her account over to your attorneys, Monroe and Sills. Suggest that if she wants her attorney to handle this action for her, she must send the name and address. Point out how desirable the payment would be versus the costly legal action.

12. You wrote Mr. David Barton (an auto mechanic), 1187 Riverview Drive, Des Moines, Iowa 50300, the following credit letter the second of last month: "We want to be sure to give you credit, but not the kind of credit which is usually given by a credit manager. We mean the kind of credit which is defined by Webster as "praise or approval to which a person is entitled." The way you have handled your account with us during the past year certainly merits our praise. We appreciate the promptness with which you pay your account. So we say thank you, and give credit where credit is due. It is a pleasure to be of service to you." Signed Robert W. Fall, Credit Manager/ Rich's Department Store/ 104 1st Avenue East/ Cedar Rapids, Iowa 52401. A week later Barton charged $1,110.10 for bedroom furniture (queen-size bed with pecan wood headboard, six-drawer dresser, and four-drawer chest). At the end of the month you sent Barton just a statement of his account. About the middle of the next month you called and Barton explained that he had been out of work but hoped to be back on the job in a week. Now it's the end of the month. Follow up your phone call with a friendly letter. The assumption here is that Barton will pay. Add resale about the bedroom furniture. Use the theme that the word credit means believe, entrust.

13. Ten days later (and over two months since the sale) you wrote a stronger letter than the others to Barton (preceding case) trying to persuade him to pay, using the theme of another of Webster's definitions of credit: "time given for payment for goods or services sold on trust." That brought no money but a telephone report that Barton is back on the job and a promise to send $150 the next day. Two weeks later you have not received any money, so you write him an urgency letter with suggested time payment schedule.

14. Now it's a little over three months since the sale and you still have not received any money from Barton (two preceding cases). Write him a last-stage collection letter telling him that you are turning his account over to your lawyers in two weeks. He can keep the lawyers off his back by sending payment for the furniture he bought.

15. When Elmer Bison, a prominent Archer watermelon grower (Rt. 202, Box 12, Archer, Florida 32618) failed to send in his $500 for the five tons of fertilizer you shipped him a month before, you weren't worried about his paying. Elmer is worth several millions; he's the local watermelon king and owns about 1,000 acres of first-rate farm land in the Archer area. He probably forgot to send in the money. He runs a large mechanized farming operation, and your small bill probably got lost in the shuffle. Now, a month later, you still aren't worried; but he ought to pay. Write Elmer a letter in which you tell him that the International-Planter automated watermelon picker he ordered, and paid for, three months ago has arrived. Remind him that it's time to order his watermelon seed for next spring's planting, and at the same time remind him so he will remember to pay the $500 (Invoice 2063) now past due. Your firm is Money and Jamison, 2004 NW Archer Road, Tampa, Florida 33612.

16. As Alvin P. Sellers, Credit Manager, Charles Scooner's Publishers, 597 Fifth Avenue, New York, N.Y. 10017, write an appeal-stage collection letter to Mrs. Esther Loomis, The Book Stall, 42 Green Bay Road, Wichita, Kansas 67216. Enclose a statement that shows The Book Stall owes $375.56 for books purchased 90 days ago. Scooner's terms are net 30 days. Enclose an envelope for Mrs. Loomis' convenience and appeal to her to pay. She has been a faithful customer for three years, has an excellent location, but has been affected by a competing bookstore three doors down and by recession.

17. No word from Mrs. Loomis and The Book Stall, but according to your field representative, John McCann, she said she would pay when business picked up. Point out the value of keeping her good-pay record in time of recession. Her account is 80 days past due.

18. After several phone calls to Mrs. Loomis with no result in collecting the $375.56 (see preceding cases), you must write an urgency collection letter and explain that your past-due accounts are placed with SKD Incorporated, an international collection service since 1913. Urge Mrs. Loomis to pay the 110-day old account and keep you from turning her name and the name of the book store over to SKD.

19. You (Barry T. Hellstrom, House of Lamps, 304 South Phillips, Sioux Falls, South Dakota 57104) received an order for 100 reading lamps from Melvin Johnson, owner of Skyline Motel, 2705 Folsom Avenue, Lincoln, Nebraska 68501, for his new apartment complex to serve the Lincoln student population. The lamps (order No. B–654) were a good buy at $10 apiece. The solid enamel-finished metal construction, not to mention the no-tip weighted base, aluminum shade, and easily adjustable goose-neck assembly made these lamps ideal for the hard wear they would get. Johnson sent along a check for $200 and asked for credit for the remaining $800, which you extended to him. He did not take advantage of your 2 percent discount (2/10, n/30), nor did he send you the $800 at the end of the net period, despite your form notice. You sent him two reminders (September 15, 30). Only because Johnson's credit references were excellent (listed by three credit agencies as a preferred customer), you decide to send him an inquiry stage collection letter today (October 15) to find out if there is some extraordinary reason he can't pay now and ask how he plans to settle the debt.

20. Your inquiry to Johnson went unanswered (see preceding case). You have now (October 30) reached the conclusion that Johnson must be persuaded to pay. Write an initial persuasive appeal stage collection letter.

21. Since your previous letters (two preceding cases) have not budged Mr. Johnson, you now feel that you will have to coerce him into paying the $800 he owes you, which is now 60 days overdue. You checked Johnson's business records with the Lincoln Credit Bureau and have discovered that Johnson has the money ($100,000 tied up in a land speculation west of town). Your bill, strangely enough, is the only account he has past due. You will probably get your money if you send him an urgency-stage letter. Use the approach you think will get him to pay up without losing him as a customer.

22. As collections supervisor for Quartz Mountain Pet Supplies, 1130 Sherman, Denver, Colorado 80204, write a letter to Paul's Pet Parlor, 420 South Oak Street, Colorado Springs, Colorado 80976, in which you try to collect an $8 unearned discount. Paul West, owner of the shop, sent you a check for $392 to cover the pet supplies (leashes, collars, jewelry, cosmetics, and flea powder) he ordered. Although his check was dated on the last day of the discount period, the date the letter was mailed was four days later and two days before you received it. What seems to have happened is that Paul wrote the check but forgot to mail it on time. Write Paul a letter in which you again explain your terms (2/10, n/30), stress your need to stick to them, and collect the unearned discount.

23. As collections coordinator for Kingsgate Furniture (1400 Lockland Avenue, Winston-Salem, North Carolina 27105), write an appeal-stage letter to Mr. and Mrs. Thomas Gladstone (RD 25, Haw River, North Carolina 27258). The Gladstones bought a $1,000 Early-American livingroom suite from your store, put down $200, and financed the remaining $800 on your Budget Payment Plan. The Gladstones made the first two $80 monthly payments but missed the third payment now 40 days past due and the fourth payment now 10 days past due. They ignored your three reminders, but answered your inquiry that they would pay within the week. That was two weeks ago, before they missed payment four. What you have to do now is convince the Gladstones to make the two past-due payments by showing them what a good buy they got on their Ephraim Allen livingroom suite (two chairs, a sofa, two end tables, a coffee table, and two lamps). Base your appeal on product quality and service.

24. When Colby Menninger, proprietor of the Menninger Motel, 1914 Poplar Avenue, Memphis, Tennessee 38128, bought six Coastar innerspring mattresses (invoice 8764, $1,800) from your store, the Sleep Shop, 347 Main Street, Memphis 38104, he seemed pleased with the product and the price. He gave you $1,000 down and was to pay the remaining $800 within 60 days. Just before the end of the net period, you sent him a notice, and later two reminders and an inquiry at 15-day intervals. He responded to none of these, nor did he answer the appeal-stage letter you sent him. The bill is now 60 days past due, and every time you call Menninger, he's out, or just left, or expected at any moment. Write Menninger an urgency-stage collection letter that stresses protecting his credit record. Send it out over the signature of Paul Lyon, your vice-president for finance.

25. Henry Zoellner (Rt. 19, Mountain Peak, Virginia 24599) bought 18 R–90 septic tanks for $1,250 plus $250 shipping charges, total $1,500, from your company, Folrath Septic Tanks Corporation, 109 Acron Street, Lynchburg, Virginia 24508. You extended him credit at 2/10, n/60. At 60 days you automatically sent out a notification; and, when he didn't pay, you followed your notification with two reminders (copies of the bill stamped "past due") at 10-day intervals, which also went unanswered. The bill is now 30 days overdue. You feel there may be some reason why Zoellner hasn't paid. Write him an inquiry-stage letter in which you, with consideration for his position as a big operator and long-time good credit customer, forthrightly ask him to pay or explain why he hasn't paid and make some arrangement to pay.

26. Zoellner didn't respond to your inquiry-stage letter, not even to acknowledge that he heard from you. Your assumption now is that he must be persuaded to pay. Write him an appeal stage letter.

27. Yesterday you (Pine Valley Saw Mill, Pine Valley, Georgia 31823) received a check for $970 from John T. Pearson, owner of Pearson Lumber Co. (9876 Walnut Street in Durham, N.C. 27708), to cover the cost of a shipment of two-by-fours. The cost of the lumber was $1,000, but Pearson took the 3 percent discount (3/10, n/30) even though the check was dated 10 days past the discount date. Write Pearson a letter to collect the unearned discount he took by explaining your terms and your discount philosophy.

28. As credit manager of National Bank Card, Inc. (52000 Olive Road, South Bend, Indiana 46628), you write Ron Mahan (Case 25, p. 405) to collect the $250 charged on his card for a stereo bought two months ago and billed a month ago. You know that (under sections of the Fair Credit Billing Act of 1974, effective 10/28/75) he had 14 days from billing to pay, 60 days to contest a bill for errors or defective goods, and then, unless the selling merchant satisfies customer complaints, you have 90 days to do so, challenge in court, or forfeit the amount in dispute. Nobody (neither Mahan nor the seller, Jerry Newsome) has told you Mahan has any complaints.

29. A month has passed (from preceding case) and you have no word from Mahan. You called Newsome Music House in Madison and Jerry said he fixed Mahan's first CRA stereo but replaced it with a new one when Mahan wouldn't take it back—and hadn't seen Mahan since (too busy with his resort work as a guide for fishing trip to Madison). As far as Newsome knew, Mahan had the new set (sent by UPS) and was happy.

Obviously you have to write Ron Mahan a strong letter pointing out that he must comply with the law by making payment since he has received a new and working CRA stereo. If he refuses, then NBC, Inc. and Newsome Music House will have to settle the dispute with him in court. According to the law and the facts, you can't charge your interest (1.5 percent per month or 18 percent per year) until the time Newsome replaced the original set; since that, however, the interest is running up the bill.

PART THREE

Writing reports

chapter 13

Reports: Importance, nature, classification, and preparation

[Wanting to know is the first big step toward wisdom.]

Why study report writing?
- History, functions, and present need of reports
  - Specific ways reports now serve
  - Questions reports answer
- Help when you're a student and job candidate
- Help when you're on the job

Nature of reports
Classification of reports
Report preparation

WHY STUDY REPORT WRITING?

Two basic facts about report writing, as about letter writing, are that (1) regardless of the work you do (except work for yourself or for wages), your ability to write good reports will be an important consideration in whether you get a good job and how fast you move up on the job; and (2) most people who have not studied how to write reports do it rather poorly.

The basic language of good reports differs little from the standard English used in any good functional writing, it's true; but *good report writing requires the use of certain supplementary communication techniques and devices rarely learned except in report-writing courses.* Though report forms deserve some attention, you can learn them easily. But even the bigger job of learning to phrase the things you want to put on paper is only the last part of the overall problem of writing good reports.

If you consider the meaning of *communicating through reports,* you'll realize that it involves *preparation.* Preparation for report writing means making a plan, getting the facts or evidence (research), organizing for meaning and coherence, analyzing this material to arrive at an interpretation and solution to the problem, and *then* writing up your analysis clearly and concisely.

You'll realize, too, that improving your ability to do all these things is an important part of a liberal education and especially the kind of education needed to cope with today's workaday world. Educated people now usually go into one of the professions (education, medicine, law, engineering, the ministry) or into jobs in government, industry, or business. Today reports serve so many important purposes in all those fields that an educated person needs to know how to write them well to perform effectively—and most educators know that. Study and practice in writing reports *can* therefore help you when you're a student—and they *will* help you when you're a job candidate and when you're on almost any job.

History, functions, and present need of reports

In early history nobody needed reports. Everybody operated a complete one-person business or directed a small group of people under the on-the-spot manager, who had all the facts needed for making decisions. For example, when a shipowner captained a small ship, all the operations were within sight and consequently reports were unnecessary. Personal observation provided all the information needed and thus served the one general function of most reports—*to help the receiver make a decision by providing needed facts and/or ideas.*

Later, as society became more complex, some individuals gained power over large groups as their tribal chiefs, masters, or employers—and found reports essential. When one of these bosses sent an underling to scout an enemy tribe or do some work, the boss wanted a report indicating difficulties encountered or to be encountered and the underling's suggestions on such things as materials, personnel, necessary time, and plans for overcoming the difficulties. For example, when a successful shipowner built a second ship and put a hired captain on it to develop trade along a different route, the owner needed reports to make wise decisions about future operations. Thus the ship's log came into being as one early form of written report.

Specific ways reports now serve. The impossibility of a manager's being in two places at the same time made reports necessary. Overcoming the problem of *distance*, then, is the first specific function reports may serve in achieving their general purpose of helping the receiver make decisions by providing needed facts and ideas.

When organizations grew to where the manager could not find time to oversee all operations (sometimes even under the same roof) and some of the processes became so technical that the manager did not have the knowledge to evaluate all of them, reports became more and more widely used to solve two more specific problems: *time* and *technology*.

With the increasing complexity of society, *records* became more important too; and as their fourth specific function, written reports provided permanent records. Thus they became important in preparing tax returns, in preventing later repetition of the same work, and (through extra copies) in informing interested secondary readers.

As executives became responsible for more and more varied activities, the wiser ones also began to realize that they could not do all the desirable thinking about new products, processes, and procedures. They therefore invited employees with initiative to submit ideas in reports. Hence reports began to serve management in a fifth way as vehicles for *creative ideas.*

As managers became responsible for numerous employees, some of whom they rarely saw, they often found that the written reports submitted were the best indicators they had of how well an employee was doing an assigned job. Thus reports began to serve in a sixth way—as a basis for *evaluating the employees* who wrote them.

You see readily that reports have become essential tools of modern management if you bring these trends up to the present world of large and complex organizations—

—Where top management may be thousands of miles from some operations,

—Where management cannot possibly find time to oversee all the activities (even in one location),

—Where some of the processes are so technical that no one can be competent to decide wisely about all of them without guidance through reports from specialists,

—Where numerous records must be kept and many people informed,

—Where competition pushes a manager to use all the creative brainpower of all employees in developing new ideas, through suggestion boxes and reports,

—And where personnel managers may never see employees they have to evaluate.

Questions reports answer. In helping managers in those six ways, reports help with decision making by answering one or more of three key questions:

1. *Is the project under consideration feasible?* In thinking about any proposed action that is not obviously possible, the decision maker's only logical first question is whether it *can* be done. (Some people do not recognize this feasibility question because they do not interpret the word correctly. *Feasible* does not raise the question of whether something can be done easily, profitably, or practically but whether it *can be done*—whether it is "do-able.") Can you imagine spending time or money considering the other questions about any project until this first question is answered favorably—by prior knowledge or by a report (or the first part of a report)? Michigan could not, in thinking about building the bridge

across the Mackinac Straits; nor could the U.S. government in thinking about trying a landing on the moon.

2. *Should we take a certain proposed action?* With feasibility established, decision makers trying to decide on a proposed new product, plant, or other project will want—in answer to a second question—a report showing whether expected benefits will result in higher profits, better quality or quantity, or less time, material, or effort expended. Particularly in reports for public institutions, at least some of the benefits are likely to be in terms of better service, safety, goodwill (including international relations), law enforcement, ecology, health, or education.

3. *Which is the best (or better) way?* Only with the feasibility and payoff established can one logically consider this third question. Then the study and report may consider a choice between or among proposed ways or it may have to propose and evaluate different ways to lead to a choice. Often the answer is a choice between the present way and a proposed new way. But it may be between or among products: IBM or Royal typewriters for our offices? Chevrolet, Ford, or Plymouth for our fleet? Repair the old or buy a new . . . ?

Any board of directors, president, governor, manager, superintendent, or department head in any organization—public or private—wants satisfactory answers to all three questions before approving substantial expenditures, changes in operations, or new regulations. Many times those questions lead to the assignment of reports. For this reason management today expects all employees (except possibly day laborers) to be able to write reports.

If you need more evidence that learning to write better reports will be a worthwhile activity for you, consider how your study of report writing can help you as a student, as a job candidate, and later as a full-time employee on the job.

Help when you're a student and job candidate

Learning the things necessary to write a good report can help you to earn better grades. The increased familiarity with sources of information—not just published sources and how to find them in libraries, but also methods of securing original data—enables you to do research more efficiently for papers required in other courses. (Reports are certainly not like term papers in objective or in some phases of treatment, but the research behind them is similar.) Documenting—that is, backing up what you say with factual evidence, citing publications you use as authorities or sources of information, and explaining your research methods to assure soundness—are also similar in the two. And certainly you'll profit from the carry-over of organization principles and improved language ability. For these reasons students who have studied and applied report-writing principles usually earn better grades on term papers in advanced courses and hence better grades in the courses.

If you go on to graduate school, you will find that your work in report writing has been your best preparation. When you have to write the many long research papers and a thesis, you will already know how to collect, organize, and interpret data and to write up your findings in good style—using techniques and readability devices learned only in report writing. Indeed, you will probably join the many graduate students we have heard make comments to the effect that "Thanks to my course in report writing, I know how to go about writing course papers and my thesis."

When you apply for a job, you'll find that employers put a premium on the services of people who can write letters and reports well. Because reports play such a prominent role in most businesses (for reasons explained earlier), prospective employers often give preference to those applicants who have learned report writing. They prefer to hire people who can already write reports rather than to spend vast sums of money on company-sponsored report-writing courses (as hundreds of companies do of necessity for people who have not had such preparation for their jobs).

One director of a college employment bureau reports that an increasing number of talent scouts (recruiters) ask, as one of the first questions, what grade a prospective employee earned in report writing. (Note that they assume students have taken the course.) These recruiters apparently regard the report-writing performance of the student in the college reports course as an indication of ability to do something that is important to their organizations.

Help when you're on the job

If you are surprised by the interest of *prospective* employers in your ability to write reports, you may be even more surprised by their interest as employers. The reports a trainee on a new job usually has to submit may not only help to determine assignment to a division of the company but they also often determine whether to retain or drop the employee at the end of the training period. Even after one becomes a full-fledged employee, management studies reports written not only for information and ideas in the solution of problems but also for evidence of the employee's ability to communicate clearly, quickly, and easily. To the immediate superior, an employee will often report orally, but the immediate superior is not usually the one who makes the final decisions about salary increases and promotions. Since those who do may never have met the employee, they often consider equally important the immediate superior's evaluation and the *written* reports of the employee being evaluated. Employers often regard the reports as the best—and sometimes they are the only—indication of how well an employee is doing the job.

Your study of report writing, as you see, can help your grades in school, your chances at a desirable job, and your effectiveness and status in your career. You can hardly find a better set of rungs for the ladder to success than a series of good reports.

NATURE OF REPORTS

In the earlier discussion of the functions of reports—the general and specific ways reports serve—you have seen several implications of their nature. Yet the word *report* is such a broad concept that it cannot be well defined briefly. All known attempts at one-sentence definition are either incomplete, too general to be useful, or not quite true.

Etymology can help in defining *report*. One meaning of *re* as a prefix is "back," as in *recall*. The *port* is from *portare* ("to carry"). Hence the Mountain States Telephone executive who explained a problem and assigned a report-writing job quite properly said "Find the answer, Jim, and bring it back."

From both the etymology and the executive's use, we can derive the best known definition of the term *as we use it here: A report is a presentation of facts and/or ideas to somebody who needs them as a basis for making a decision.* A presentation may be oral or written (as reports may be). "Facts and/or ideas" covers the possibilities of just facts without interpretation, facts *and* interpretation, or just interpretations of already known facts—and that statement fits. You can easily have three reports each falling into a different one of the three categories. Perhaps the most discriminating part of the definition, however, is the last part. As we use the term here, a report *does* go to somebody who faces a problem of making some kind of decision, and the purpose of the report message is to help in making a wise decision. That, you recognize, rules out such things as term papers and write-ups about books read—things often referred to in academic circles as reports. But it does not rule out the kinds of business or technical reports that are our concern here.

Still, the best way to get a clear idea of the meaning of the word *report* —as of many others—is to consider the usual characteristics of reports, along with the special characteristics of different classes. Here and in the next section, therefore, we give you those characteristics.

Usually, but not always—

1. A report is a management tool designed to help an executive in making decisions. Thus it is *functional* writing for the *benefit of the reader.* The important person involved is not the writer but the reader, who wants some useful information which is not already available—quite a different situation from a professor receiving a term paper from a student.
2. A report is an assigned job. Usually the assigner will make clear the kind of report wanted; if not, the writer should find out by asking.
3. A report goes up the chain of command. A few reports go between

people of equal rank, as between department heads, and some (better called directives) go downward from executives (but most reports executives write are to still higher authorities—boards of directors, legislatures, or the people who elected them).

4. A report is written for one reader or a small group of readers unified by a common purpose or problem, and usually having a spokesman who arranges to have the report written, and thus becomes the addressee and primary reader. The primary reader, however, may then send the report on up the chain of command to just a few higher executives or reproduce it and send copies to the whole group. Corporation annual reports, aiming primarily at groups unified as stockholders or employees, have unusually large readership for a report.

5. A report gets more than normal attention to organization. Of course, all good writing is organized; but because reports are usually expositions of complex facts and ideas for practical purposes and for busy readers, report writers work harder at organization than most other writers. Still the most common serious reader criticism of reports is their poor organization.

6. A report makes more than normal use of certain techniques and devices for communicating clearly, quickly, and easily: commonly understood words; short, direct sentences and paragraphs; headings, topic sentences, and brief summaries; itemizations; graphic presentations; and specific, concrete, humanized writing. (Though these techniques and devices can be very useful in almost any kind of writing, good courses in report writing seem to be about the only places they are taught.)

7. A report is expected to be accurate, reliable, and objective. No executive wants to base decisions on a report writer's errors, assumptions, preconceptions, wishful thinking, or any kind of illogicality. Therefore a good report writer strives to be as objective as possible—though nobody can be strictly objective because selection of facts to include and evaluation of them will vary according to who (what kind of person, as a product of background) is doing the selecting and evaluating. And where the reader might otherwise question the validity, the report writer explains sources and methods of collecting data to show the soundness of the facts presented.

8. A report follows the special form, content, and length best suited to its particular functions. That is, reports are of different classes because of adaptation to the varying situations in which they serve.

CLASSIFICATION OF REPORTS

Reports—like buildings, pieces of furniture, or anything else—should be designed according to their functions and conditions of use. When they have been, people who deal with them have naturally given names to the different "designs" and then tried to classify them. There they have run into trouble. We have never seen—and cannot ourselves provide—a strictly logical classification of reports. To remove some of the confusion, however, we give you the following admittedly imperfect classification as the best we know for (*a*) clarification and (*b*) names widely used (though we can't say standard).

From the writer's standpoint the most important classification is on the basis of whether the report includes only facts (an *informational* report) or whether it goes further into interpretation (conclusions and/or recommendations) and becomes an *analytical* report (sometimes called *recommendation* or *improvement* report). A writer can go wrong, and probably be embarrassed, either way. If the person who authorizes a report does not indicate which kind, the writer should therefore ask.

Several kinds of confusion often attend that important two-part classification. Since an *analytical* report has more in it than one giving the bare facts on a subject, it is naturally longer. Hence some people refer to any *long* report as *analytical* and (at least by implication) think of *short* reports as *informational*. They may be wrong in all directions; *long* or *short*, a report may be *analytical* or *informational*.

Similarly, since long reports are more likely to be somewhat formal than are shorter ones, we often see an analytical report on a sizeable subject referred to as a *formal* report and shorter ones as *informal*. In fact, no necessary relation exists between the length of a report and its formality. The only legitimate basis for calling any report *formal* or *informal* is the degree of formality in its style; and that should be a reflection of the relationship between reader and writer—the difference between the familiarity of language and tone in conversation between long-time equal friends and the formality of talk between strangers or people of different status.

Since we deal almost wholly with analytical reports (on the principle that anybody who can write them can leave out the interpretation and make informational reports), the primary basis of classification in our treatment in the following chapters is length. We call them Complete Analytical Reports (or long reports, usually ten or more pages), Short Analytical Reports (usually 6–10 pages), and Short Reports. Admittedly our naming is imperfect (and redundant in the first), but we think it is functional. By "Complete" we mean not only "with interpretations" (redundant with analytical) but also including all the standard parts; hence such reports are usually long. The Short Analytical Report still has interpretations, but it may omit certain standard parts or combine them. Often such a report combines the letter of transmittal and synopsis, skips a table of contents and depends on internal headings, and skips the bibliography, depending on footnotes or internal citations to explain any published sources. Short Reports means only not many pages (but they may be either analytical or informational).

We see no use for classification on the basis of subject matter that produces such names as engineering reports, business reports, or technical reports. After all, report writing is report writing; regardless of the subject matter, the principles don't change. Furthermore, nobody ever completes such a classification (perhaps because doing so would serve no purpose and would require some detailed identification system such as the Library of Congress or Dewey Decimal systems used in libraries).

Other classifications are all cleaner-cut than the foregoing. Perhaps the neatest is that in terms of the issuing schedule. *Periodic* reports (coming out regularly—*daily, weekly, monthly, quarterly,* or *annually*) are the counterparts of *special* reports (written when a special occasion arises). Similarly the names of two other two-part classifications make their meanings clear: *private/public* and *internal/external* reports.

Somewhat similarly, *letter* and *memo* (or *memorandum*) mean that the reports are written in those forms (of any length, though usually short; informational or analytical; and about any kind of subject matter). At that point, however, form as a basis of naming and classifying reports stops—unless you want to consider the *credit* report as a special form. In actual practice it usually is, because the sameness of subject matter and purpose have led to a nearly standard form. But variations are enough that you cannot use the name to mean necessarily a certain form.

Three other often-used names of reports refer to true independents—two of them well identified by name and the other as ambiguous, capricious, and wayward as any bachelor (male or female). *Progress* reports explain what has been done on a project and usually try to predict the future (both in relation to any pre-set schedule). *Justification* reports (usually short and sometimes called *Initiation* reports because the writers usually initiate them) propose certain specific actions and provide evidence to show the wisdom of those actions. As such, the Justification Report is much like a well-prepared suggestion that might be dropped in a firm's suggestion box. The term *Research Report* may mean merely that preparation required some research (as most reports do). Most authorities, however, use the name to mean a report of research done to push back the forefronts of knowledge (often called pure research) and perhaps without any immediate, practical applications in mind. To avoid being misled, you have to know who is talking. (We use the second meaning.)

For the report writer, much more important than knowing the names and classifications of reports (except possibly the distinction between *informational* and *analytical*) is close attention to the characteristics reports should have: *They should be full of useful information that is accurate, reliable, and objective; presented in functional rather than literary style; adapted to the reader(s); carefully organized; and clearly, quickly, and easily readable.* That relates directly to the preparation of reports. To give you a further and more important preview of what is coming, therefore, we give you the highlights of the preparation process.

REPORT PREPARATION

Preparing an analytical report is a five-step process. First the report writer *plans* the attack by getting a sharp concept of the problem, breaking it down into its essential elements, and raising questions to be answered about those elements.

Then the reporter *collects* appropriate facts, using the most suitable of the following methods and checking for reliability: library research (reading), experimentation, observation, and survey (of an adequate sample, by mail questionnaire, personal interview, or telephone interview).

Then comes *organizing* the facts according to the most suitable one of *chronological order, order of importance,* or (more likely) a fast, interesting, and clarifying *deductive order* if the reader is likely to be sympathetic, or a slower, duller, temporarily puzzling but finally more convincing *inductive pattern* if the reader is unsympathetic.

While *interpreting* the facts into logical conclusions and workable recommendations (omitted in informational reports), a good report writer attempts to be objective by avoiding all possible prejudices, preconceptions, wishful thinking, and fallacies.

Finally, the reporter *writes* the report, using all suitable techniques and devices so that it makes clear what the problem is, shows that the information is reliable by explaining the sound research methods, and presents the facts and what they mean. To make the reading clear, quick, and easy, a good report writer—

1. Uses commonly understood words (uneducated, technical, and educated readers all understand them and all appreciate the ease of reading everyday English).
2. Keeps sentences so direct and short (average about 17 words) that they need little punctuation except periods at the ends.
3. Keeps paragraphs direct and short (questioning those of more than eight lines because short ones look easier to read, are easier, and need fewer transitions).
4. Uses headings, topic sentences, and summarizing sentences to show the reader the organization, where the line of thought is going, and where it has been.
5. Itemizes (as here) to call attention to important points and to force concise and precise writing.
6. Uses all kinds of nonverbal means of communication (charts, graphs, tables, pictograms, maps) to assist words in presenting ideas clearly, quickly, and easily.
7. Writes specific, concrete, humanized copy rather than generalizations and abstractions by showing how the facts affect people (preferably the reader), thus making the report both clearer and more interesting, and thus meeting the two requirements for written communication—that the writing be *interesting enough to get read* and *clear when read.*

chapter 14

Preparing complete analytical reports

[To think you know something that isn't so is worse than not to know.]

HAVING SEEN from the preceding chapter what a report *is*—along with the main report uses, characteristics, and classes—you should be ready to learn *how to write one.* You should realize, too, that a good course in report writing is a course in research procedure, a course in the organization of ideas, a course in logic, a course in English composition, a course in supplementary communication devices, a course in organizational behavior and communication, and a course in human relations—all in a current and *practical* setting.

Since we are concerned primarily with analytical reports, because they (if comparatively long ones) involve much learning that others do not, we take up first the Complete Analytical Report—the granddaddy of reports. Then (in Chapter 16) we bring out special points in the preparation of shorter reports of various kinds.

Preparing a complete analytical report, whatever its length, is a five-step process: planning the attack on the problem, collecting the facts, organizing the facts, interpreting the facts, and writing the report in appropriate form and style. Since any or all of these five steps may be necessary in varying degrees in the preparation of a particular report in any form, we present the five steps before explaining and illustrating different forms.

PLANNING THE ATTACK

Planning the attack is a job to be done at the desk—the headwork before the legwork. It involves six procedures, in the following sequence:

1. Get a clear view of what the central problem is. If you can't see the target you're shooting at, you're not likely to hit it.

This procedure requires reflective thinking. It may also require a conference with the person who needs the report. As a check, you can try writing a *concise* and *interesting* title that *clearly indicates the content and scope* (see p. 496). If you can also write in one sentence a precise statement of the purpose, clearly indicating what you intend to cover and what you don't, you have the necessary view of the problem.

2. Consider conditions that influence the report—the attitude, degree of interest, knowledge, and temperament of the reader, the use to be made of it, and its importance.

The reader's temperament and knowledge of the subject have considerable influence on how much background and detailed explanation you need to give, and whether you can use technical terms. Your reputation as an authority and the reader's attitude will influence how persuasive you need to be (whether you use the convincing inductive plan or the faster, more interesting, but possibly less convincing deductive plan). Any known reader biases and special interests may influence what you should stress and whether you must use impersonal style. Your relationship to the primary reader will indicate how formal or informal the style should be.

In considering use, remember that reports commonly go in the files for future reference after they have served their immediate purpose and that therefore they need to be clear to other readers years from now. Also, the immediate superior who asked for the report may have to send it on up the chain of command for approval before anything can happen. So it needs to be intelligible to possible readers other than the immediate one.

Limitations on time, money, or availability of data may affect how thorough you can be and whether you can use costly plates and charts.

3. Divide the central problem (the *text* of your report) into its elements, the main divisions in an outline of the topic. The idea of dividing to conquer applies in report writing as well as in military strategy.

Whatever you do at this stage toward outlining will probably be only tentative and skeletal. You'll probably change it later, after you have the facts. At this point you merely need a starting guide to what kinds of facts to collect. So don't worry too much about form and accuracy; specific instruction on the finished outline comes later (pp. 467–70, at which you might well glance now, to avoid some false steps).

Of course, not all problems divide alike, any more than all jigsaw puzzles do; but the dividing process is a job of finding the natural divisions of the whole. For that purpose you should temporarily ignore the introduction and begin your tentative outline with section II.

If the problem is one of deciding between two or more things, the *criteria* are usually the best major division headings. For example, if you are trying to decide which of several jobs to take, on what bases do you decide? Maybe

II. Kind of work
III. Location
IV. Beginning pay
V. Chances for advancement
VI. Working conditions

Some topics common to many problems are history, disadvantages of present system, advantages of proposed system, costs and means of financing, taxes and tax effects, personnel required, effects on goodwill, transportation, method of installation, utilities available and their costs, materials required, time involved, safety, increases or decreases in quality, market, competition, convenience, and availability of land.

4. Raise specific questions about each element. The questions further divide the problem, lead to subheads in your outline, and point more directly toward collecting data for answers. If cost is one of the elements, for example, you want to ask what the costs are for operating one way and what they would be under a revised system. You would then want to question further about how to find the costs in each instance. And you might do well to break the questions down further into first costs, operating costs, and depreciation; costs for personnel, for upkeep and for power; and the like. Specific questions on goodwill might include those about customers, stockholders, workers, and the general public.

5. Take stock of what you already know. You may pose a hypothesis, but don't let it close your mind to other possible solutions. Don't assume that you know the answer until all the facts are in. You certainly don't want to start out to prove a preconceived notion.

Get a clear concept of the assumptions you are willing to make, and separate those which are to be held without further checking from those which are to be checked and perhaps validated by supporting evidence.

Jot down answers known for the questions raised and the tentative answers to be checked. Clearly indicate information gaps that are to be filled by data to be collected, and jot down what you think tentatively are the best sources and methods for getting the missing data—experts, books and articles, and maybe the person for whom you're writing. Or perhaps you need to plan a survey—kind and size of sample, kind of survey, and the like.

6. Make a working schedule. Assign estimated time blocks for each of the remaining steps in producing the report: collecting remaining data, organizing, interpreting, and writing the final report. If you plan a survey, remember that mail requires time and that people don't always respond to questionnaires immediately. For any except the most routine kind of reports, be sure to allow some time for revising early drafts to put the final report in clear, interesting, and inconspicuous style and form.

The first item on the working schedule is the next step in report preparation—collecting the facts.

COLLECTING THE FACTS

For collecting complete and reliable facts, you may use any or all of the four basic methods of securing information: library research (reading), observation, experimentation, and surveys. The first provides secondary (secondhand) data, and the others provide primary (firsthand or new) facts. In most cases you should use at least two of the methods in such a way as to get at the essential facts and assure their reliability.

Library research

Study of published books, articles, theses, brochures, and speeches is most universally useful and is *usually the best first step.* When you face any problem of consequence, somebody else has probably faced the same or a closely related problem and written something worthwhile about it. And when pertinent data are already written, getting the facts by reading is nearly always easier and quicker than the laborious process the original writer went through to get the information. Besides being the quick and easy way to collect facts, it may also give a bird's-eye view of the whole problem, acquaint you with terminology and methods you may not have thought of, refer to other good sources, show formerly overlooked natural divisions and aspects of the problem, and in general help you to revise your tentative outline and plan of attack.

Fortunately, libraries are pretty well standardized. They nearly always have at least three broad categories of materials—reference books, books in the stacks, and periodicals. Some main ones of the great variety of *regular reference books are:*

Encyclopedias *(Americana, Columbia, Encyclopaedia of the Social Sciences, Encyclopedia of Science and Technology,* and the *Britannica)*

Collections of generally useful, up-to-date statistical and other information, surprising in variety and amount *(The World Almanac* and *Facts on File)*

Census reports (U.S. government censuses of agriculture, business, government housing, manufacturing, population, minerals, and other breakdowns)
Yearbooks of various countries, trades, and professions (commerce, shipping, agriculture, engineering, and others)
Atlases (especially those by Rand McNally, the *Britannica, National Geographic,* and Hammond)
Dictionaries *(American College Dictionary, Standard College Dictionary, Webster's Collegiate Dictionary, Webster's New International Dictionary* [unabridged], and the *Oxford English Dictionary)*
Directories (such as Kelly's for merchants, manufacturers, and shippers; Thomas' for American manufacturers; Ayer's for newspapers and magazines)
Who's who in various fields (including the *Directory of American Scholars, American Men of Science, World Who's Who in Commerce and Industry,* and Poor's *Register of Corporations, Directors and Executives*)
Statistical source books *(Statistical Yearbook, Statistical Abstract of the United States, Survey of Current Business, County and City Data Book*)

These are just a few main examples of the numerous reference books usually placed conveniently on tables or in open shelves in a library. Constance Winchell's *Guide to Reference Books* tells about them and many more.

The standard key to *books in the stacks* is the card catalog, arranged alphabetically by author, subject, and title. But because libraries available to most writers will not have all the books published on their subjects; because it takes months for books to be published, bought by libraries, and cataloged for distribution; and because not all topics are written up in full-book treatment, for reports often the best up-to-date printed sources are periodicals.

Fortunately, one or more of the numerous periodical indexes, both general and specific for almost any field, cover most periodicals. Table 14–1 describes the main current indexes; but if you do not find one for your specific field, look around and/or ask the reference librarian. And if the abbreviations or the system of indexing is not immediately clear to you, the preface always explains.

Whatever library key you use, you need to develop *resourcefulness.* Often when you look under one topic (say "Business Letter Writing" or "Report Writing"), you will find little or nothing. Don't give up. You have to match wits with the indexer and try to think of other possible wordings that might have been used for the topic. "Business Letter Writing" might be under "Business English" or "Commercial Correspondence" and "Report Writing" under "Technical Writing" or something else.

When your resourcefulness brings you to a book or article that seems to be useful, scan it to see what portion (if any) of it is grist for your mill. A look at the table of contents may tell you whether it will be helpful.

If it seems pertinent, check its *reliability.* Remember that no decision-maker wants to base decisions on unsound data, yours or anybody else's. Consider both the textual evidence and the reputation of the publisher

TABLE 14–1 Main current indexes

Title	*Coverage*	*Publication facts (most frequent issue and cumulation)*
Accountants' Index	International; technical books and magazines	Annually
Applied Science and Technology Index	Scientific, engineering and technical American and Canadian magazines	Monthly except August; annually
Biological and Agricultural Index	International; books and magazines	Monthly except August; annually
Business Periodicals Index	Business, industrial, and trade magazines	Monthly; annually
Chemical Abstracts	International; all phases of chemistry	Biweekly; semiannually
Education Index	Professional literature	Monthly except July and August; annually
Engineering Index	Domestic and foreign literature on engineering	Monthly; annually
Index Medicus	International; medicine and related fields	Monthly; annually
New York Times Index	The news in the paper	Semimonthly; annually
Public Affairs Information Service (PAIS)	Periodicals and government documents and pamphlets of general, technical, and economic interest	Weekly except only two in August and three in December; annually, 5 yr.
Readers' Guide to Periodical Literature	General American magazines	Semimonthly; annually and/or biennially
Social Science and Humanities Index	Emphasis on history, international relations, political science, and economics	March, June, September, December; annually
Wall Street Journal Index	Corporate and general business news	Monthly; annually

and of the author for (1) any possible slant or prejudice, (2) the question of whether the author is a recognized authority in the field, (3) the question of whether the material is up to date. Reading a review in a related journal can help in judging the worth of a book. A sound report writer will not be duped by the usual undue worship of the printed word; just realize that something's being in print does not make it true.

If the material meets the tests for reliability, take notes—*a separate card or sheet of paper for each important note*. If you put more than one note to the card, you will have trouble in arranging the cards later because they will not all fit at the same place in your report. To save time later in arranging notes, put a notation at the head of each note card (that is, one that indicates where the information fits in your plan). It may well be the divisional symbol from your outline, say section III(C).

When in doubt, take fuller rather than scantier notes than you think you need; it's easier to omit later than to come back for more.

Some notes you may want to take in verbatim quotations, but usually not. Direct quotation should be used rarely, and then only to gain the impact of the author's authority, to be fair by stating exactly before criticizing, or to take advantage of the conciseness, exactness, or aptness of phrasing. If you do quote, be sure to quote exactly and not change the original meaning by lifting a small part from a context in which it meant something different.

In most cases you can save words and express the idea better for your purposes if you paraphrase. When you paraphrase, however, be sure not to change the original meaning.

In some cases you can save time later by writing your notes as a review of the article or book—that is, from your own point of view, giving the essential content of the article along with your comment on it—because that seems to be the form it will take in the final report. In other cases you will condense, digest, or abstract the article.

Whether you quote, paraphrase, review, or abstract the article or book, list in your bibliography *all* printed sources used directly in the preparation of the report; so you need to take the necessary information while you have the book or magazine in hand. Although bibliography form is not standardized, the usual information is author's name (surname first, for alphabetizing), title of book or article and magazine, publisher and place of publication for books, edition if not the first for books, volume and inclusive page numbers for magazine articles, and the date. For use in citations in the text, record the specific pages used for each note.

What we have suggested here are sound, basic library research procedures. They are as useful and valid in government, business, and industry as in academic work.

Observation

The second method of collecting data—observation—includes not only its usual meanings but also investigation of company records on finances, production, sales, and the like. As such, it is the main method used by accountants and engineers for audit, inspection, and progress reports.

The job of collecting data by observation usually involves no particular problem of getting at the facts. The important part is more likely to be *knowing what facts to consider*. This requires keeping in mind what the purpose is, so as to notice everything relevant and to relate each pertinent fact to the whole situation.

A skilled policeman's investigation of a murder scene or of an automobile accident scene exemplifies the technique. Camera, measuring tape, and note pad are standard equipment for outside observation, just as the accountant's special paper, sharp pencil, and calculator are for inside inspection of the records. Still, the most important pieces of equipment are sharp eyes to see the situation, judgment to evaluate it, and (most important) imagination to see the relevance of a particular observed fact to the whole problem.

Observation has the advantage of being convincing, just as the testimony of an eyewitness convinces a jury more than circumstantial evidence; but it has the disadvantage of not getting at motives. That is, it may answer *what* but not find out *why*. And an observer who is not careful may put too much stress on a few isolated cases or facts.

Experimentation

For the most part, experimentation is useful in the physical sciences rather than in business and the social sciences, and in industrial rather than commercial operations. And of course, the methods used vary almost infinitely according to the particular experiment to be done. Hence some of them are best taught by a specialist in the particular field, in the laboratory with equipment, rather than through a small section in a textbook mainly about something else. Regardless of field, however, an experimenter should be as zealous as a report writer about the reliability of results. The basic requirements for reliability in experimentation are three:

1. Accurate equipment (if used). If a laboratory balance is inaccurate, or if a tachometer or thermometer misrepresents the facts, the results of an experiment using them will be unreliable.
2. Skilled techniques. A technician who doesn't know how to set a microscope won't be able to see an amoeba; and if unable to pipette both accurately and fast, will be no good at Kahn tests. Skilled techniques also include proper selection of specimens for study.
3. Sufficient controls or repetition of results. If an experimenter takes two specimens just alike and treats them exactly alike except in one way (perhaps inoculates one, keeping the other for a control), different results (say one gets a disease and the other does not) make a strong start toward convincing us. If repeating the experiment produces exactly the same thing every time (100 percent), only a few repetitions are thoroughly convincing. For every drop from 100 percent, however, the scientist has to multiply the number of tests many times to produce similar faith in them.

Testing one variable at a time is basic. If soil, seed, and temperature all change in two runs, different results cannot be attributed to any one of them. If you clean your tank and refill with different gasoline, repair your carburetor, and adjust your ignition system all at the same time and your car runs better, you don't know what caused your troubles before.

Experts in certain phases of business can use experimentation that closely parallels laboratory methods if they are careful about their *equipment, techniques,* and *controls.* For example, marketing specialists can test the comparative effects of different advertising campaigns and media, sales promotion devices, prices, and packaging. Their problems of equipment and technique are psychological instead of mechanical and manual, and their controls are difficult to set up to make sure that only one element is changed; but experts can and do manage all three to assure reasonable reliability. (See pp. 303–5 on testing sales campaigns.)

Surveys

Often the quality to be tested is not subject to exact laboratory examination—the sales appeal of a new car, for example. The only place to get an answer to that is from people. In fact, the survey for fact and opinion vies with library research as a method of collecting data for business and social science reports. It is particularly useful in discovering *why* people do certain things and in *forecasting* what will happen (both frequently important jobs of reports).

Regardless of which of the three kinds of surveys you use—mail questionnaire, personal interview, or telephone interview—certain basic problems, principles, and techniques are involved.

The first problem is determining *what people you will survey.* In some cases you may decide that the opinions of a few experts will be worth more than the answers of thousands of the general public, as they will be if the problem is technical or professional (say medical or legal). If the whole group involved (called the "universe" by statisticians) is small, you may decide to ask all of them. But in most cases you take a sample.

For sound results you then have to decide on *how large a sample* is necessary. This will depend on the degree of accuracy required and on the variety of possible answers. For instance, if plus or minus 10 percent is close enough, your sample can be much smaller than if you have to be accurate within a range of 1 percent. And if you have to forecast election returns only in terms of Democratic, Republican, and other votes, your sample can be much smaller than if you have to forecast the purchases of the 50 or more makes and body styles of cars. As an even simpler illustration, you can certainly better predict the fall of a coin (only 2 choices) than of a pair of dice with 11 possibilities.

Although a full treatment of sampling theory would require a complete book, statisticians have provided us with some *simple devices for determining adequate sample size.* The simplest is the split-sample test. You break your sample arbitrarily (that is, to avoid any known differences) into two or more parts. You then compare the results from the various parts. If the results from the partial samples are acceptably close together, the results from the total sample will be acceptably reliable.

Two more precise checks on sample reliability require only a little mathematics.

1. If your survey results are in percentages, you apply the formula

$$N = \frac{pq}{E^2}$$

Suppose you decide that error (E) of plus or minus 5 percent will be close enough for your purposes. When you have enough returns to estimate the apparent division of answers (say 70 percent yes and 30 percent no), you can find N (the number of returns required) by

$$N = \frac{0.7 \times 0.3}{0.05 \times 0.05} = \frac{0.21}{0.0025} = 84$$

2. If your survey results are in terms of the arithmetic mean (average), the formula is

$$\sqrt{N} = \frac{\sigma}{\sigma x}$$

If you don't know how to figure the standard deviation

$$\left(\sigma = \sqrt{\frac{\Sigma x^2}{N}}\right)$$

and the standard error of the mean (σx), any elementary statistics book will explain. But for quick, easy calculations accurate enough for most purposes, use

a) $\sigma = \frac{1}{6}R$ (range of difference between the highest and lowest figures in the sample)

b) $\sigma x =$ allowable error in your result

Thus if you want to find the number of scores necessary on a test to establish an arithmetic mean with allowable error of no more than one point where the highest score is 76 and the lowest is 34, your figures are

$$\sqrt{N} = \frac{42 \div 6}{1} = \frac{7}{1}$$
$$N = 49$$

Even your adequate *sample must be stratified* (sometimes called "representative"), or your results can go wild. That is, each segment of the universe must be represented in the sample by the same percentage as in the universe. According to sampling theory, this will be the result if you take a large enough *random* sample (one in which each item in the universe has an equal chance of getting into the sample). In practice, however, you often have trouble making sure you really have a random sample. Unsuspected selective factors may work to produce a nonrepresentative sample.

To avoid such a possibility, you can use stratified sampling *if you have data showing the proportions of different segments in your universe.* Fortunately, you usually do. Just as a college registrar's office knows the number of students in different classes, majors, age groups, grade-point groups, and the like, the statistical source books provide breakdowns of people in nearly every imaginable way. Whatever group you may want to sample, you probably can find the proportions of the different segments making up the universe. The U.S. Census Bureau breaks its population figures down in almost every imaginable way. Remember, though, that the Bureau's real head count is every ten years (those ending in 0—1970, 1980, 1990, . . .). Figures *between* those years are only estimates—but good ones. If 50 percent of your universe are farmers and 70 percent telephone subscribers, half your sample must be farmers and 70 percent telephone subscribers.

Adequate size and stratification together make a sound sample.

A sound sample can still produce unsound results, however, unless your techniques of getting answers from it are also sound. If you start out by surveying a minimum sound sample but get answers from only half of it, the sample of actual answers is unsound because it is too small. If you survey more than enough and get a large enough sample of answers but 100 percent of one stratification group answers and only half of another group answers, your returns are not stratified and hence are not reliable. You may therefore have to toss out excess returns from some groups to keep returns from all groups in proportion to the original stratification. Of course, the best solution is to get 100 percent returns from all groups—an ideal rarely accomplished.

How can you *induce people to answer survey questions?* Sometimes the respondent is already so much interested, because the benefit is obvious, that you need not point it out. You can therefore begin directly with the request for help, as in the direct inquiry letters discussed on pages 96 ff. At other times you have a selling job to do, as in the persuasive requests discussed on pages 384 ff. Whether you are using a mail questionnaire, a personal interview, or a telephone interview makes little difference in the approach. But to misjudge the situation and make a direct inquiry when you need a persuasive request may result in decreased returns and hence an unreliable sample.

Fundamentally, your persuasive method is the same as in persuading people to do anything, as in sales and collection letters: *Show them a benefit to themselves.* It may be a gift or reward, direct payment of a fee, or less obvious and less material benefits such as appeals to pride and prestige (but not obvious flattery), appeals to their desire for better service or more efficiency in their kind of work, or the possibility of their getting answers to some questions or solutions to problems they encounter in their own work.

The last two are frequently the best (because they avoid suggesting a bribe or being too mercenary, as the first two might), and they are more immediate and tangible than the others. For instance, personnel officers who read lots of poor application letters are likely to answer a textbook writer's or a teacher's questions about preferences in application letters —because of the possibility that they may as a result get more good applications and thereby make their work easier. A frequent method of inducing answers is the offer of a copy or digest of the survey results.

A big point to remember in making persuasive requests is to show a benefit *before* making the request. Then if you explain who is making the survey and why; make answering as easy, quick, and impersonal as possible; assure respondents that you will honor restrictions they put on use of the information; and tell pointedly just what you want them to do, enough people will usually do it to make your results reliable. Skilled approaches, both oral and written, often bring percentages of answers that surprise the untrained who have tried their hands and failed. Chapter 11 explains in detail how to induce reluctant people to respond as you wish.

The approach you use will be a major factor in determining your success in getting returns, but *the questions you ask and how you ask them will affect both the percentage of returns and the worth of the answers.* For that reason, writers of questionnaires and people planning interviews need to keep in mind the following main principles used by professionals:

1. Ask as few questions as you can to get the necessary information. Don't ask other people for information you should have dug up for yourself, possibly in the library. And don't ask a question when you can figure the answer from the answers to others. To avoid unnecessary questions—which reduce returns—write down all you can think of, group them, and then knock out the duplicates. (One kind of duplication is permissible: double-check questions which get at the same information from different approaches as a check on the validity of answers.)

2. Ask only what you might reasonably expect to be answered. Requests for percentages and averages are either too much work or over the heads of many people. Questions requiring long memory may frustrate and bring erroneous results. And most people don't even know *why* they do many things.

3. Make your questions as easy to answer as possible (perhaps by providing for places to check); but provide for all likely answers (at least the "no opinion" answer and perhaps the blank to be filled as the respondent wants to because no one of your suggested answers is suitable).

4. Make your questions perfectly clear. To do so, you may sometimes have to explain a bit of necessary background. If you ask "Why do you use X peanut butter?" you may get "It is cheapest," "A friend recommended it," and "I like its smooth texture and easy spreading" from three respondents. If you really want to know how the customer first learned of X, you should phrase the question in such a way as to get answers parallel to the second. If you are interested in the qualities that users like (as

in the third answer), you should ask that specific question. Questions about *how* cause as many different interpretations as those asking *why* and require the same kind of careful wording. Also, double-barreled questions (Did you see X, and did you like it?) confuse the reader who wants to answer one part one way and the other part another way.

5. Carefully avoid leading questions—questions which suggest a certain answer, such as one to agree with the questioner's obvious view.

6. Insofar as possible, phrase questions to avoid the "prestige" answer —the respondent's answering according to what apparently would make the best impression.

7. Avoid unnecessary personal prying. When your question is necessary to your basic purpose, make it as inoffensive as possible (for instance, by asking which named *income group* the respondent falls in, if that will serve your purpose, rather than the exact income).

8. Arrange questions in an order to encourage response—easier or impersonal ones at first, related ones together in a natural sequence to stimulate interest and aid memory.

9. Insofar as possible, ask for answers that will be easy to tabulate and evaluate statistically; but when they are important, don't sacrifice shades of meaning or intensity of feeling in the answer for easy handling. Often the most helpful answers a survey brings are those to open-end questions; but if you ask many of them, you will reduce your returns. Such questions require time and thought to answer as well as to analyze.

After you have decided on the questions you want answered, your next problem is deciding *which type of survey* (mail questionnaire, personal interview, or telephone interview) will best serve your purposes. No one type is always best. The main *bases for your decision* are as follows:

1. The kind and amount of information requested. People are more willing to *tell* you personal information—and more of it—than they are to put personal facts in writing or to do very much writing. The comparative anonymity of the interviewer and reluctance to talk long over the telephone with strangers are against the telephone method, but generally people consider talk cheaper and less dangerous than written statements. On the other hand, factual information (especially statistics, percentages, and averages) which may not be known at the moment may be dug up and written, because the respondent can take a little time with a mail questionnaire.

2. Costs. Within one telephone exchange, if your group is not large, the telephone is the cheapest method; but if it involves long-distance charges, they become prohibitive unless the group is small. The mail questionnaire has the advantage of wide geographical coverage at no additional cost; and the bigger the group, the greater the advantage, because copies of a good set of questions can be duplicated at little extra cost. The personal interview is almost always the most costly (mainly in interviewer's time) unless the group is small and close together. You need to con-

sider cost per return, however; and since the mail questionnaire usually brings in the lowest percentage, its advantages may not be so great as at first thought unless a good covering letter and set of questions mailed at an opportune time induce a high percentage of answers.

3. Speed in getting results. If you have to have the answers today, you can get some of them by telephone (and by personal interview if your sample is not too large and the people are close together); but you can't get them by mail. Mail answers will flood you in about four days and dribble in for a week or more after that, unless you make clear that you need the information by a certain time (a point which needs careful justifying to avoid the bad manners of rushing a person to do you a favor).

4. Validity of results—all three kinds of survey having advantages and disadvantages. In personal and telephone interviews people may give you offhand answers to get rid of you because the time of the call is inconvenient, and they may answer according to what they think is your view (playing the prestige-answer game). High-pressure selling, obscene phone calls, and other abuses have made many people wary of telephone calls, making telephone surveys increasingly difficult and complicating the job of stratifying samples. In mail questionnaires people can choose the most convenient time and are more likely to answer thoughtfully or not at all. But those who choose not to answer may be a special group (say the less educated who don't like to write) and may thereby unstratify your carefully stratified sample. On the other hand, certain segments of the population have fewer telephones than others and thereby skew a telephone sample. And certain kinds of doors (maybe apartment dwellers') are hard to get into for personal interviews. But everybody has a mailing address where a mail questionnaire can go. On the other hand, the personal interviewer may pick up supplementary information (such as the general look of economic conditions around the home and incidental remarks of the talker) that will provide a check on answers given—an impossibility by telephone and mail. Either the personal or the telephone interview can better clear up any confusion about questions and thereby get appropriate answers. But in view of costs and time, the mail questionnaire is less likely to be limited to a too-small group or one that is geographically or economically limited.

5. Qualifications of the staff. Some people who can talk well and thus get information may not be able to write a good questionnaire and covering letter; and, of course, the opposite may be true. Even some good talkers have poor telephone voices that discourage that method. And others have disfigurations that discourage personal interviews.

If you select an adequate and stratified sample, induce people to answer by showing a benefit, ask good questions, and use the most suitable type of survey, surveys can get you a great variety of valuable information for your reports.

ORGANIZING THE FINDINGS

However you collect the necessary facts for your report, you have to organize them for presentation and, if you're writing an analytical report, for your intepretation. You can't well evaluate a bridge hand until you have grouped the cards into the four suits and arranged the cards in order within the suits—mentally if not physically.

Your problem of organizing is probably easier than you suspect, however, because most of the job will have been done for you by conventional practice or by someone who set up a standard plan of reports where you work. If you have no standard plans to follow, Chapter 16 gives help in organizing the widely varied kinds of short reports. Almost any long analytical report uses something approaching conventional practice (explained in the next chapter) for the overall organization.

Your only problem—and the only one we are talking about here, therefore—is the organization of the *text* of complete analytical reports. The introduction is usually the first major division of your final outline, and the conclusions and recommendations (together or separately) are usually the last one or two.

Because the text—all the report between the introduction and the conclusions—is the essence of the report, *you do not have a section heading for it.* (If you did, it would be the same as the title of the whole report.) The divisions of the text, then, usually constitute sections II, III, IV, and so on—where you present all your facts, explanations, and reasons leading to your conclusions and recommendations.

Basically, organization is the process of putting related things into groups according to common characteristics *and your purpose* (playing poker instead of bridge for example), and then putting the groups into a desirable sequence. In the process you may find that you need to revise your tentative outline because the information classified according to your first plan is not logically or psychologically arranged for good presentation. For instance you will want to *make sure that things the reader needs to compare are close together.*

Certainly you need to check your tentative outline before going further. You may now be able to see enough interpretations of your data to make a sentence outline, as you couldn't earlier, because sentences require you to *say something about* the topics. If you can, it will be easier to follow while writing the report, it will force more careful thinking, and it will give your reader the essence of your report (not just the list of topics discussed but the key statements about those topics). Because of its helpfulness in writing up the report, you may want to make a full-sentence outline (like a lawyer's brief or a précis) for close-knit, logical writing, and then change it to one of the less cumbersome forms (later discussed) for final presentation.

Whether you use full sentences or noun-phrase topics, close adherence to the following principles is necessary for a good outline:

1. Stick to the *one basis of classification* implied in your title and purpose as you break down any topic (such as your text) into its parts. On the basis of credit hours earned, college students can be classified as freshmen, sophomores, juniors, seniors, and graduates. You can't logically classify them as juniors, Protestants, and Democrats. Such a procedure shifts bases in helter-skelter fashion from credit hours earned to religion to politics. You would have overlapping topics, whereas the divisions of an outline should be mutually exclusive.

If your title is "Reasons for (or Why) . . . ," the major divisions of your text can't logically be anything but the list of reasons. If the title is something like "Factors Influencing . . ." or "Ways to . . . ," each major division will have to be one of those factors or ways. The title "Market Factors Indicating Why a Rexwall Drugstore in Savannah Would Sell More Than One in Charleston" commits you to show for each subject—Charleston and Savannah—market factor evidence supporting your thesis. (This does not forbid giving the introduction, conclusions, and recommendations similar major-division status.)

In outlines of comparison leading to a choice, use the criteria (bases on which the choice depends) rather than the subjects (the things between or among which you must choose) as the major divisions. Your criteria are the things on which your choice will stand or fall, and hence they deserve the emphasis. In evaluating a Ford and a Chevrolet, for example, you should use both names frequently in your organization scheme, but neither would be a major heading as such. Your major headings would be the tests you decide to apply: costs (initial and operating—and possibly trade-in value), performance, comfort, and appearance. Under each head you would be obligated to analyze each subject (Ford and Chevrolet).

2. Follow one good system to show the relationship of all the parts. Widely used is roman capitals (I, II, III, etc.) for the major topics (which are logical divisions of your title), subdivided as capital letters (A, B, C, etc.), subdivided as arabic numbers (1, 2, 3, etc.), subdivided as lowercase letters (*a, b, c,* etc.). Various modifications of a decimal system, somewhat like the following, however, are coming into more and more use (note that complicated indentation is unnecessary).

1.0		I.
1.1		A.
1.2		B.
1.3		C.
2.0	instead of	II.
2.1		A.
2.11		1.
2.12		2.
2.2		B.
3.0 (etc.)		III. (etc.)

3. Cover all categories—that is, all the divisions at any level must add up to the whole indicated by your heading over those divisions. All the roman-numeral divisions together must add up to everything covered by the title, and all the capital letters under section II must total the II data. If you classify students according to political affiliation, you would most certainly have Republicans as well as Democrats, in addition to others. If you classify according to religion, you would have to include non-Protestants along with Protestants (or word the title to show the limited coverage).

4. Use no single subdivisions. If you start to divide section I by putting a subhead A, you must logically have at least a subhead B; you can't divide anything into one part.

5. Use parallel grammatical structure for parallel things. All the roman-numeral divisions are parallel things; all the capital-letter divisions under one of them are parallel, but not necessarily parallel with those under another roman-numeral division. They may all be complete sentences, all nouns or noun phrases (probably the best), or all adjectives. In discussing the five sections of the usual application data sheet, for example, you would not list "Heading and Basic Facts," "Education," "Experience," "Personal," and "References." All except "Personal" are nouns, but it is an adjective. "Personal Details" would be all right.

6. Consider the psychological effects (reading ease) of the number of parts in any classification. Three to seven is the optimum range. Of course, the nature of the topic may dictate how many you have. For instance, according to credit hours earned, the classes in a university are just five—from freshmen to graduates—no more and no less. In breaking down some topics, however, you have some choice in the number, depending on how broadly you name the parts. Having too few suggests that you didn't need the breakdown or that you have not completed it; having too many puts a strain on the reader's mind to remember them. In some cases you may be wise to shift to a slightly different basis of classification that will lead to a more suitable number of divisions, and in other cases you can group some of the less important classes together (perhaps as "Others" or "Miscellaneous").

7. Organize for approximate balance. That is, try not to let some of your divisions cover huge blocks of your subject and others almost nothing. You probably need to reorganize on a different basis if you have five major divisions (roman numerals) and any one is more than half of the whole report. Of course, the nature of your subject may force you to some imbalance. If you are writing about American politics, for example, the Democratic and Republican parties will each be bigger parts than all the rest, which you might group under "Others" or "Miscellaneous" for approximate balance.

8. Put the parts of each breakdown into the sequence most appropriate for your purposes and the situation. The *overall sequence or plan of a report* is usually one of the following:

a) Direct (sometimes called "deductive"), giving the big, broad point first and then following with supporting details. This plan arouses more interest than some other plans because it gets to the important things quickly, saves the time of the busy reader who wants only the big idea, and provides a bird's eye view that helps in reading the rest more intelligently. It is therefore desirable if the reader is likely to be sympathetic with the report's conclusion or if the writer is an authority whose unsupported word would be readily accepted, at least tentatively. But it is psychologically unsound where it risks the danger that the reader will raise objections at first and continue to fight the writer all the way through.

b) Inductive (sometimes called "scientific"), giving a succession of facts and ideas leading up to the big conclusions and recommendations at the end. The inductive plan is slow and sometimes puzzling until the conclusion tells where all the detailed facts lead; but it is necessary in some cases for its strong logical conviction, especially when the reader is known to be opposed to the conclusions and recommendations that are coming.

c) Narrative (usually chronological accounts of activities). If no good reason argues against it—but usually one does—the narrative style of report is both the easiest to write and the easiest to read. The main objections are that it doesn't allow you to stress important things (it may have to begin with minor details, and the biggest things may be buried in the middle), and it doesn't allow you to bring together related things that have to be seen together for clear significance. The somewhat similar spatial arrangement (from top to bottom, front to back, left to right, or by geographical area) is usually the obvious choice if it is appropriate for the material at all.

d) Weighted (that is, according to importance). The weighted plan's basic advantage is that it enables you to control emphasis by putting the most important points in the emphatic positions, first and last.

For certain kinds of material and conditions, arrangement according to difficulty or from cause to effect (or the reverse) may be the wise choice. Similarly some kinds of things (for example, proving geometry propositions and facts leading to judicial decisions) almost have to appear in a definite order for the necessary logical sequence.

Whatever the plan of organization, you will need to use meaningful headings and subheads, topic sentences or paragraphs, standard transitional words and sentences, and summarizing sentences to indicate organization, to show the coherence of parts in the organization, and to tell the skimming reader the essence of the sections. The summarizing sentences, however, grow naturally out of your interpretation of the facts.

INTERPRETING THE FACTS

If the report is just informational, you are ready to write it when you have organized the facts; but if it is to be analytical, you have to study the facts and interpret them into conclusions and/or recommendations for the boss, as required. Since the reader wants a sound rather than a prejudiced basis for decisions, your *first consideration* in making the interpretation is objectivity.

Nowhere else in report writing is objectivity more important—or harder to achieve. Since you are a human being, your thinking is influenced by your whole background and personality; but you must strive to be as objective and logical as possible, and to avoid the temptation to stretch the truth a bit for dramatic effect. The following two basic kinds of unobjective attitudes require attention if your report is to be unbiased:

1. *Preconception.* A writer who jumps to conclusions and closes out other possibilities before collecting and evaluating the facts may be influenced by that preconception to overlook or undervalue some facts and overstress others. Such is the danger of working from hypotheses.

2. *Wishful Thinking.* If you have a strong desire that the investigation turn out a certain way (because of a money interest or any other kind), you will find it hard not to manipulate facts (like the referee who has bet on the game) to make them lead to the desired result. Such attitudes can also lead to unintentionally slanted writing, since they will unconsciously affect your choice of words and phrasing as you write.

In addition to these dangerous attitudes to shun if you are to be unprejudiced, you must avoid (as your *second consideration*) the pitfalls to logical thinking (called "fallacies"). Although some of them—like circular argument and shifting the meanings of terms—are not likely to trap an honest report writer, avoiding the following requires constant alertness:

1. Using sources (both books and people) which may be unreliable because of basic prejudice, because they are uninformed, or because they are out of date. Further, your sources may have misquoted or misinterpreted *their* sources —a common occurrence. Although these things would have been checked in collecting your data, they might be examined again in the interpreting process.

2. Making hasty generalizations—that is, drawing conclusions on the basis of too little evidence (maybe too small a sample, too short a trial, too little experience, or just too few facts). The temptation to make hasty generalizations will weaken if you remember that sometimes no logical conclusion can be drawn. Certainly you need to remember that lack of evidence to establish one hypothesis does not prove its opposite.

3. Using false analogies. Although true analogies (comparisons of things that are similar in many ways) are effective devices for explaining, by comparing unknown things to others the reader knows, even at their best they are weak as logical proof. And false analogies (applying principles valid in one case to another case where they don't belong) are tools of shysters and traps to the careless thinker. Essentially the same error results from a false analogy and from a person's putting a thing in the wrong class (say a persuasive request situation misclassified as a direct inquiry) and applying the principles of the wrong class to it.

4. Stating faulty cause-and-effect relationships, such as

   a) Assigning something to one cause when it is the result of several. Comparisons which attribute the differences to one cause need careful controls to be valid. Otherwise, some unseen (or intentionally ignored) cause may deserve much of the credit for the difference.

b) Attributing something to an incapable cause (for instance, one that came later).

c) Calling something a cause when it is merely a concurrent effect—a symptom, a concomitant.

5. Begging the question—just assuming, rather than giving evidence to support, a point that is necessary to the conclusions drawn.

6. Using emotional suasion (usually characterized by strong and numerous adjectives and adverbs, or any kind of emotionally supercharged language like that of a defense attorney pleading with a jury) to influence the reader, instead of depending on logical conviction through marshaling facts.

7. Failing to distinguish, and make clear to the reader, what is substantiated fact, what is opinion, and what is merely assumption.

Your *third consideration* in making your interpretation is discovering the really significant things to point out to the reader. If you avoid basic prejudice prompted by preconception or wishful thinking, avoid the pitfalls of various fallacies, and know what to look for, you should be able to interpret the facts and draw sound conclusions.

When you do, you should be sure they grow out of the facts, state them pointedly, and itemize them if they run to more than three or four. You can then turn them into practical recommendations that are general or concrete and specific, according to instructions when the report was assigned. Itemization will usually help to make the recommendations desirably pointed too.

Some bosses want answers to all of what to do, how to do it, who is to do it, when, and where; others feel that the report writer with so specific a solution to the problem infringes upon their prerogatives of making decisions. But all expect you to show the significance of your facts to the problem. In addition to an organization and presentation of facts that lead to the conclusions, the reader will expect you to point out lesser interpretations along the way. Avoiding doing so is not, as some people (bureaucrats) think, the "safe way." It is failing to do the job properly.

Causes, symptoms, effects, and cures are always important. So (in terms of graphic statistical data) are high points, low points, averages, trends, and abrupt changes (especially if you can explain their causes). Without going into disturbingly technical statistics, you can probably interest your reader in such measures of central tendencies as the mean (call it average), median (midpoint), and mode (most frequent item). Sometimes you might well use indicators of dispersion, such as standard deviation, range, and the *-iles* (percentiles, deciles, quartiles).

Your reader will be interested in comparisons that give significance to otherwise nearly meaningless isolated facts. For instance, the figure $7,123,191 given as profit for the year has little meaning alone. If you say it's 7 percent above last year's profit, you add a revealing comparison; and if you add that it's the highest ever, you add another. If your volume of production is 2 million units, that means less than if you add that you're now fourth in the industry as compared with tenth two years earlier.

Breaking down big figures into little ones also helps to make them meaningful. For instance, you may express capital investment in terms of so much per employee, per share of stock, per stockholder, or per unit of production. The national debt becomes more meaningful if given per citizen; the annual budget makes more sense as a per-day or per-citizen cost; library circulation means more in terms of number of books per student. Often a simple ratio helps, such as "Two fifths (40 percent) of the national budget is for defense."

Whatever the analysis reveals, you need to state it precisely. Guard carefully against stating assumptions and opinions as facts. And select gradations in wording to indicate the degree of solidity of your conclusions. The facts and analyses will sometimes (but rarely) prove a point conclusively. They are more likely to lead to the conclusion that . . . , or indicate, or suggest, or hint, or point to the possibility, or lead one to wonder—and so on down the scale. Usually you can do better than stick your neck out (by claiming to prove things you don't) or draw your neck in too far (with the timorous last three of these expressions).

But phrasing the ideas well is a problem for the fifth and last step in preparing a report—writing it.

WRITING APPROPRIATE REPORT STYLE

Your final writing of the report will not be difficult if you have done well the preceding four steps of preparation. But if your methods of collecting, organizing, and interpreting data have been faulty, you're trapped. Our suggestions for a good report style will help only if you have something worthwhile to write and a pretty good idea of the sequence of points.

You will notice that our suggestions relate more to the *effectiveness* than to the *correctness* of your writing, for two reasons: (1) Correct spelling, grammar, punctuation, and sentence structure do not assure effectiveness. We assume that you have pretty well learned these aspects of writing before studying report writing. And if you haven't, a more basic study of composition—or review of Appendix C (p. 612) or some other good handbook—may be advisable. (2) Effective writing presupposes reasonable correctness but also requires that you help your reader to get your message clearly, quickly, and easily. How to do this is our next concern.

Basics of report style

Because almost everything we say about letter style in Chapter 1 and about communication in Appendix A applies equally to report style—and the few exceptions are obvious—we recommend that you read that material carefully before going on to the special points about report style.

As you have already seen in item 6, page 449, report writers use various techniques and devices for communicating clearly, quickly, and easily: commonly understood words, short sentences so direct that they require little punctuation, short paragraphs so direct that they require few transitional words, itemizations, graphics, and headings.

Even though you have read those other parts of the book, several points of basic style and some of the special techniques deserve a bit fuller treatment for report writers.

Adaptation requires that you consider not only your primary reader but likely secondary readers. Even though some readers may know the background of the problem and the technical terms of the field, others may not. The good report writer must therefore provide the explanations necessary for the least informed of important readers. This includes restricting your vocabulary to words readers will understand readily. If you feel that you must use specialized terms, you had better explain them. Usually a parenthetical explanation right after the first use of a technical term is the best way. But if your report includes many such terms, it should provide a glossary in the introduction or in an appendix—to keep it from being "all Greek" to nontechnical readers.

Coherence becomes a greater problem as the length and variety of points in a paper increase. Hence as a report writer you need to observe carefully the use of transitional words, previewing topic sentences and paragraphs, and summarizing sentences and paragraphs in the illustrations in the next two chapters. **Coh** in Appendix C and items S5–7 in the checklist for complete analytical reports should also prove helpful.

Here is how one writer helped keep readers on the track with good topic statements, summary paragraphs, and transitional ideas. For economy of space, we have quoted only some of the *transitional* parts from various places in the report.

II. NASHVILLE'S LARGER MARKET AREA

Since women often will travel long distances to buy clothes, the secondary area surrounding the metropolitan area is important in determining the location of a Four Cousins retail store. [After this topic lead-in, several paragraphs identifying principal communities and number of people in them for both Nashville and Knoxville followed.]

Even though 370,000 more possible customers live within the market area of Nashville, most of the sales will come from the people within the immediate metropolitan area. [Summarizes II and makes transition to III.]

III. BETTER POPULATION FACTORS IN NASHVILLE

The total population and its rate of growth, number of women, and number of employed women show more clearly the potential buyers of women's clothing. [This topic statement preceded A, B, and C headings of subsections giving the facts about and the interpretation of the topics as announced.]

Even though Knoxville has a larger population and about the same growth rates, Nashville has more women and a significantly larger number of employed women. Thus it furnishes the kind of customer Four Cousins sells to. [Indicates what A, B, and C add up to.]

Potential customers are buyers, however, only when they have sufficient buying power. [Clearly foreshadows a topic coming up and why.]

IV. MORE BUYING POWER IN NASHVILLE

Effective buying income (total and per capita), income groups, home ownership, and automobile ownership give estimates of ability to buy. [The information as presented then follows in four sections.]

[This summary statement comes at the end of the section.] The Nashville shopper has more dollars to spend, even though home- and auto-ownership figures imply more favorable financial positions in Knoxville families. Higher expenditures for homes and cars in Knoxville explain, in part, why Nashville merchants sell more.

V. GREATER RETAIL SALES AND LESS COMPETITION IN NASHVILLE

[The writer continues the use of these coherence devices throughout the report.]

Parallelism is a special pitfall to the unwary report writer because reports so frequently involve series, outlines, and lists. Each is in effect the partition of a whole, the sum of the parts equaling the whole. Hence the law of logic and mathematics—that you sum up, or add, only like things—applies. Thus the breakdown of anything must name all the parts in similar (parallel) grammatical form—usually all nouns or noun phrases, adjectives, or complete sentences. (See Item 5, p. 469, for parallelism in outlines and **Para** in Appendix C.)

Timing of the verbs (tense) in reports also often trips a careless report writer. One simple rule answers most questions of tense: *Use the present tense wherever you can do so logically.* It applies to things that existed in the past, still exist, and apparently will continue to exist for a while (the universal present tense). Otherwise, use the tense indicated by the logic of the situation. Thus in writing about your research activity, you say that you *did* certain things (past tense in terms of the time of writing). But in reporting your findings (which presumably are still true), you say "70 percent answer favorably, and 30 percent are opposed," the universal present tense.

Ten common faults listed in American University Professor William Dow Boutwell's study of government reports (and printed in the *Congressional Record,* Vol. 88, Part IX, p. A1468) occur frequently in business and industry reports too:

1. Sentences are too long. Voted unanimously as one of the worst faults in nearly all writings analyzed. Average sentence length in poor government writing varies from 65 to 80 words per sentence. In exceptionally good government writing (Report to the Nation by Office of Facts and Figures and President's speeches) average length is from 15 to 18 words per sentence.

2. Too much hedging; too many modifications and conditional clauses and phrases. The master writer will say, "A third of a nation ill-clothed, ill-housed,

ill-fed." The amateur will write: "On the whole it may be said that on the basis of available evidence the majority of our population is probably not receiving the proper type of nutriment. . . ." Psychologists say that "conditional clauses cause suspension of judgment as to the outcome of the sentence, and therefore increase reading difficulty."

3. Weak, ineffective verbs. *Point out, indicate,* or *reveal* are the weak reeds upon which many a government sentence leans. Writers overuse parts of the verb *to be*. Hundred-word sentences with *was* or *is* as the principal verb are not uncommon.

4. Too many sentences begin the same way, especially with *The*.

5. An attempt to be impersonal, which forces use of passive and indirect phrases. Example: "To determine whether retail sales have been out of line with expectations based on the past relationship of retail volume to income, estimates of retail sales in the first half of each year . . . have been charted against income payments for the same periods, and a line of estimate fitted to the resulting scatter." The good writer would say: "Our statisticians have charted estimates of retail sales, etc., etc."

6. Overabundance of abstract nouns. Such nouns as *condition, data, situation, development, problem, factor, position, basis, case* dominate the writing of too many government documents. How bright and real writing becomes when picture-bearing nouns take the place of vague ones may be seen from this sentence: "During the lean years when salaries and wages were low and irregular, the people who drifted into the credit-union offices came around because they had dropped behind in their personal and family finances and had to get a loan."

7. Too many prepositioned phrases. In a study of reading difficulty, investigators (Drs. Leary and Gray of Chicago University) found that prepositional phrases ("of the data," "under the circumstances," etc.) add to reading difficulty. Yet, samples of government writing show that many officials use at least one prepositional phrase to every four words. Samples from good writing contain only one prepositional phrase to every 11 words.

8. Overabundance of expletives. "It is" and "there are" and their variants ruin the opening of many good paragraphs.

9. Use of governmentish or federalese. "Shop words" serve a proper purpose for "shop" audiences. But many government writers make the mistake of talking to the public in technical, office terms . . . .

10. Tendency to make ideas the heroes of sentences. People think in terms of people and things for the most part. The government official writes in terms of ideas and phenomena only. Hence, when a writer means "Employers refuse to hire older workers in defense industries," he writes instead: "Refusal of employment of older workers continues." In other words, the writer has substituted "refusal," an idea or phenomenon, for "employers"—living people.[1]

Documentation

Since a report is usually the basis for an executive decision which may be costly if it is wrong, the executive reader rightfully expects the report

[1] An AP Newsfeature, "Gobbledygook; Language of Government," by Richard E. Myer, September 5, 1971, stresses many of the same points.

writer to answer at least two important questions: What are the facts? How do you know? In an analytical report, the writer has to answer two more questions: What do you make of (conclude from) these facts? Then what should I do?

The second question means that the report writer must convince the reader that the information is trustworthy. Usually you do that by explaining your sources and methods of research as a basis for the reader to judge the report's soundness. The only exceptions are in the reports of unquestionable authorities (whose word would be taken at face value) and in cases where the methods and sources are already known or are clearly implied in the presentation of the facts.

In short reports you can best explain the sources and methods in incidental phrases along with the presentation of data, as in the following:

```
Four suppliers of long standing report him as prompt pay
and . . . .

Standard quantitative analysis reveals 17 percent
carbon . . . .

Analysis of the balance sheet reveals . . . .
```

Notice how the illustrative reports in Chapter 16 (the short ones) interweave the references to methodology of research and to published sources —right within the text of the report.

In the complete analytical report the introduction explains methods and mentions printed sources (which are explained more specifically in the bibliography and in footnotes and/or other citations in the text).

At least, any report writer except the recognized authority precludes what one reader expressed as "the distrust I have of those people who write as if they had a private line to God."

Since you usually use some published materials in collecting data for reports, *citing those sources* is an important part of assuring your reader about the soundness of the facts.

Unfortunately, *bibliography* forms are not standardized. For the past 50 years the trend in documentation forms has been toward simplicity and efficiency, especially in business, industry, and the sciences. This does not mean less documentation, but more efficient forms. Some people in the humanities, on the other hand, have tended to hold on to the older forms, especially their punctuation. Others have adopted the library practice of capitalizing only the first word and proper nouns (specific names of people, products, and places) in titles. So unless you are sure that both you and your reader(s) understand and prefer other generally accepted forms used in your field (in the main professional journals, for example), we recommend that you use the following content and form.

Readers generally expect a bibliographical entry to give the author's name, the title (of both an article and the journal), and (for books) the edition (if not the first), the publisher and place of publication, and the volume (if more than one); the volume number (if on the magazine) and all page numbers for magazine articles; and the date of publication for anything (noting n.d. when you can't find it). Preferably the pieces of information are in that order. Some people omit the publisher of a book or put it in parentheses with the place and a colon preceding. The same people (usually in the humanities) use roman numerals for magazine volume numbers and follow immediately with the date in parentheses. In some specialized fields even the date or title may come first.

Usually the several entries in a bibliography appear in alphabetical order by author's name, which is inverted for the purpose. In some specialized fields, however, you will find other arrangements; and in extensive bibliographies (unusual in reports) you often find books and articles alphabetized separately, with headings for each group.

Unless you choose to follow the well-established form of your special field, we suggest that you be up to date and enter books as

Wilkinson, C. W., J. H. Menning, and C. R. Anderson (eds.), Writing for Business, Third Edition, Richard D. Irwin, Inc., Homewood, Illinois, 1970.

In the humanities, however, most authors would enter this book as

. . . , Third Edition (Homewood, Illinois: Richard D. Irwin, Inc.), 1970.

Even in this simple entry, you have three somewhat unusual items:

1. Three people worked on the book, but the name of only the first needs to be inverted for alphabetizing.
2. Since the "authors" were editors rather than writers of the book, you see "(eds.)" right after their names.
3. Because the book is not the first edition, the entry tells which it is. Some writers would add, at the end, 369 pp., $7.95—two pieces of information usual in reviews of new books but not in bibliographies.

The recommended form for magazine articles is

Gallagher, William J., "Technical Writing: In Defense of Obscurity," Management Review, 55:34–36, May, 1975.

Or (often in the humanities):

Arnold, C. K., "How to Summarize a Report," Supervisory Management, VII (July, 1974), 15–17.

If you want to be more helpful to the reader, you may annotate your bibliography with brief notes indicating the content and your evaluation of the book or article:

Darlington, Terry, "Do a Report on It," Business, 94:74, 93, May, 1973.
Good treatment of report functions and short, simple, direct approach for report writing. Especially good on five-point plan for organizing.

You need to note two points here:

1. Titles of parts like magazine articles and book chapters are enclosed in quotes; but titles of whole publications are underscored (italics in printed copy), with the first word and all others except articles (*a, an, the*), prepositions, and conjunctions capitalized.
2. Listings of magazines do not include the publisher and place but do include the volume number (if available) and all page numbers, hyphenated for inclusive pages and separated by commas for jumps in paging.

If no author's or editor's name appears on a book or article, the entry usually appears in the alphabetical list by first word of the title (not counting *a, an,* and *the*). Sometimes, however, a writer chooses to alphabetize by publisher instead—pamphlets, booklets, reports, and the like put out by corporations and governmental agencies. Thus you will see entries like

"Are Your Memos on Target?" Supervisory Management, 9:39–40, August, 1975.

Texaco, Inc., Annual Report of 1975.

U.S. Department of Agriculture Bulletin 1620, Characteristics of New Varieties of Peaches, U.S. Government Printing Office, 1974.

(Note that when a comma and a stronger mark—question mark or exclamation point—need to come at the same place, you simply omit the comma.)

At those points in the report text where you make use of printed sources, you also tell the reader about them by specific references or citations. One way of doing so is *footnoting,* which is decreasing in use because footnotes heckle readers. A better method for most situations, now coming into wider and wider use, is to interweave the minimum essentials of a citation subordinately right into the text, like this:

Wilkinson says ("The History and Present Need of Reports," The ABWA Bulletin, 19:14, April, 1969) that reports . . . .

For other illustrations, see pages 475, 535, and 598.

Still, footnote citations (indicated by raised numbers in the text and matching numbers before the notes) may be necessary in some cases to keep long, interwoven citations from making the reading difficult. Remember, however, that a footnote at the bottom of the page is usually more of an interruption than a parenthetical citation.

The first footnote or interwoven citation, plus whatever bibliographical information may be given in the text, is a complete reproduction of the bibliographical entry with two minor changes: The author's name is in the normal order (given name or initials first), and the page reference is the specific page or pages used for that particular part of the report. Accordingly, first footnote references to a book and a magazine would be as follows:

J. H. Menning and C. W. Wilkinson, <u>Communicating through Letters and Reports</u>, Fifth Edition, Richard D. Irwin, Inc., Homewood, Illinois, 1972, p. 469.

H. R. Jolliffe, "Semantics and Its Implications for Teachers of Business Communication," <u>Journal of Business Communication</u>, 1:17, March, 1964.

Later references to the same work can be shortened forms with the specific page number(s) and just enough information for the reader to identify the source. Usually the author's surname, the title, and the page(s) will do, whether interwoven in the text, put in footnotes, or divided between the two. Thus later references could be as shown below:

Menning and Wilkinson (<u>Communicating</u> . . ., p. 29) discuss letters in three broad categories: . . . .

Jolliffe ("Semantics and Its Implications," p. 18) makes the point that . . . .

The short-form citations of sources, enclosed in parentheses here, could be footnotes if the writer prefers.

The old practice of using Latin abbreviations (such as *op. cit.*, *ibid.*, and *loc. cit.*, to mention only a few), which have long confused many people, is disappearing along with footnotes. Except in scholarly writing for other scholars, the practice is to use English words and a few standard abbreviations like *p.* for *page* and *pp.* for *pages*—preceding page numbers which do not follow volume numbers.

Letters and interviews used as sources of information do not belong in a bibliography but nevertheless are cited by footnoting or by interweaving the information about the giver and the receiver of the information, the form, the date, and any other pertinent facts.

The newest and probably the best citation system—coming into wider use, especially in science and industry, probably because of its efficiency—involves these steps:

1. Numbering the listings in the bibliography after they are arranged in the usual way (alphabetically).
2. Using these numbers and the specific page number(s), usually separated by colons and enclosed in parentheses, at the points in the report requiring documentation—usually just before the periods at the ends of sentences, like this (4:39).
3. Explaining the system at its first use, by footnote or something like "(4:39, meaning p. 39 of Item 4 in the Bibliography)."

Although these are the main points about documentation forms, several large books and many smaller ones, plus numerous pamphlets, deal extensively with this subject. As further illustration of bibliography forms, and as sources of more detailed information about them, footnotes, and other details of form, we list the major publications:

A Manual of Style (Twelfth Edition), University of Chicago Press, Chicago, 1969.

The MLA Style Sheet (Second Edition), Modern Language Association of America, Washington, D.C., 1970.

U.S. Government Printing Office Style Manual (Revised Edition), U.S. Government Printing Office, Washington, D.C., 1973.

Turabian, Kate L., *A Manual for Writers of Term Papers, Theses, and Dissertations* (Fourth Edition), University of Chicago Press, Chicago, 1973.

Objectivity in presentation

Clearly the report reader expects the writer to be as nearly objective as is humanly possible in collecting the facts, in organizing and interpreting them, and finally in writing them.

That does not mean, however, that you must use impersonal style (which is sometimes erroneously called "objective" style). You can be just as objective when saying "I think such and such is true" as when saying "Such and such seems to be true" or even "Such and such is true." The second and third versions mean only that the writer thinks something is true. The only sound objection to the first version is that it wastes two words, not that it is *natural* style.

The only real justification for recommending impersonal style in reports, as many books do, is that methods and results are usually the important things, and therefore they, rather than the person who did the research, deserve emphasis as subjects and objects of active verbs.

But, since most things happen because people make them happen, the most natural and the clearest, easiest, most interesting way to tell about them is to tell who does what. A report about research done by its writer therefore naturally includes *I*'s; and if the writer keeps the reader(s) in mind, it also naturally includes *you*'s. To omit them is unnatural and usually dull, because the writer goes out of the way to avoid the natural subjects of active verbs or uses too many inactive ones and leaves out the most basic element of an interesting, humanized style—*people doing things.*

Because they are professionally trained, constantly practicing, and usually writing about people doing things (although in the third person, which is considered a part of impersonal style), newspaper reporters often write well. An equally trained and practiced report writer (a rarity) *can* by great care write well in impersonal style. But most report writers find it unnatural and difficult. Unless they exercise great care, it usually leads them into awkward, wordy, and weak passive-voice constructions; it gives away the third leg (Frequent Personal References) to Rudolf Flesch's three-legged stool of easy readability, so that the stool falls; and it *does not* gain objectivity.

Strangely, the strongest promoters of impersonal style are people who pride themselves on being scientific. They usually also insist that writing should avoid any kind of exaggeration about the true state of things. But they then argue that impersonal style gives the reader more confidence in their statements. When one of them draws a conclusion, therefore, it comes out as "It was concluded that . . . ," as if some omniscient oracle had drawn the conclusion, when the true meaning is "I conclude that. . . ."

Actually, more destructive to objectivity than the use of a natural style is the use of too many or too strong adjectives and adverbs, or any kind of feverish, high-pressure, hot-under-the-collar writing. Such a heightened style—using emotional connotations, fancy figures of speech, and other techniques of oratory—has its place where the author feels deeply and wants the reader to feel deeply about the subject; but it is often distrusted, and is inappropriate in reports anyway, because both writer and reader are expected to think hard rather than emotionalize.

Simply put, then, our advice on natural versus impersonal style is this: Find out whether your primary reader thinks reports have to be in impersonal style. If so, write it as best you can while

1. Avoiding "It is" and "There are."
2. Putting most of your verbs in the active voice.
3. Picturing people (other than yourself or the reader, of course) taking the action of as many as possible of your verbs.

But any time your primary reader will let you, *write naturally but calmly and reasonably.* Where the natural way to express an idea involves an *I* or a *you,* use it. Don't let anybody talk you into referring to yourself as "the writer."

Except for the fact that letter style allows more use of emotional suasion than report style does, the discussion of style in Chapter 1 applies to reports as well as letters.

In addition, report writers also make more extensive use than letter writers of these other techniques of presenting ideas clearly, quickly, and easily for the reader: using headings and subheads, presenting quantitative data skillfully, and using graphic aids to effective communication.

Headings and subheads

Because they are usually longer than letters, and because the reader may want to recheck certain parts, reports use headings and subheads, in addition to topic and summarizing sentences, to show the reader the organization and coherence. For the same reasons and purposes we have used headings in this book. If you have not thought about them already, for illustration flip back through some parts of the book with which you are well acquainted and see if they don't serve these purposes.

Skill in using heads and subheads can be a valuable technique in your writing, not only of reports but of anything else that is very long—maybe even long letters.

The only reasonable test of how far to go in putting in subheads is this: Will they help the reader? If so, put them in; if not, leave them out.

Despite the fact that headings and subheads are often great helps to readers, no single system of setting them up is in universal use. More important than what system you use is that you use some system consistently and that the reader understand it. Most readers understand and agree on the following principles:

1. A good heading should indicate clearly the content below it, should have reader interest, and should be as brief as possible without sacrificing either of the other two requirements. Trying to keep titles too short, however, frequently leads to sacrifice of exactness. Usually a short heading is too broad (includes more than the discussion below it covers), or it tells nothing about the topic. Note the difference, in examples from annual reports, between "Profits" and "Profits Up 8 Percent from Last Year," and between "Position in the Industry" and "Position in Industry Changes from Eighth to Fourth." In other reports where some readers might only skim, you can help them a lot by making your headings tell the big point about the topic instead of just naming the topic to be discussed. You've already seen some good examples of helpful *informative* headings (as opposed to merely *topical* ones) in the quoted illustration on page 474. The headlines in any newspaper provide others.

2. The form and position of the head must make its relative importance (status in the outline) clear at a glance. That is, headings for all divisions of equal rank (say the roman-numeral heads in an outline) must be in the same form and position on the page, but different from their superiors (of which they are parts) and from their inferiors (their subdivisions). Putting heads of different levels in the same form and position is confusing; it misrepresents the outline.

3. Centered heads are superior to sideheads in the same form (compare second- and third-degree heads in the following illustration); heads in capitals are superior to those in caps and lowercase; and heads above the text are superior to those starting on the same line with the text (compare third- and fourth-degree heads in the illustration).

4. You should not depend on headings as antecedents for pronouns or as transitions. The one word *This* referring to an immediately preceding head is the most frequent offender. Transitions between paragraphs and between bigger subdivisions should be perfectly clear if the headings are removed.

5. In capital-and-lowercase heads capitalize the first word and all others except articles (*a, an,* and *the*), conjunctions (for example, *and, but, for,* and *because*), and prepositions (such as *to, in, of, on,* and *with*).

The following not only illustrates but further explains the principles. Note that *above* second- and third-degree heads the spacing is more than the double spacing of the discussion.

FIRST-DEGREE HEADINGS

The title of your whole report, book, or article is the first-degree heading. Since you have only one title, no other head should be written in the same form. As illustrated here, the title uses the most superior form and position. If you need more than this five-level breakdown for your report, you can type the first heading in spaced C A P I T A L S and move each level of heading up one notch.

Second-Degree Headings

If you use solid capitals centered on the page for the first-degree heading (title), a good choice for the second-degree headings (usually roman numbered in the outline) is caps and lowercase. Preferably, they and any other uncapitalized head should be underscored to make them stand out. If you do not need the five-level breakdown illustrated here, you could start with this form.

Third-degree headings

To distinguish the third-degree headings from their superiors, you may put them at the left margin above the text, underscore them to make them stand out, and write them in initial-cap form (as here) or in cap and lowercase (which would require capitalizing the D in Degree and the H in Heading).

Fourth-degree headings.—For a fourth level, you may place headings at the paragraph indention on the same line with the text and write them as caps and lowercase or as straight lowercase except for capitalizing the first word. These headings definitely need to be underscored and separated from the first sentence, preferably by a period and dash, as here. Some people drop the dash. This form of head saves space.

The fifth-degree headings can be integral parts of the first sentence of the first paragraph about a topic. Underscoring (italic type when printed) will make them stand out sufficiently without further distinctions in form.

Presentation of quantitative data

Most reports make considerable use of quantitative data. Consequently, as a report writer you need to know how to present figures for clear, quick, and easy comprehension. Most readers will want the figures on measurable topics you discuss; and unless they have made clear that they want only the facts, they probably will want your interpretations showing what the figures mean (conclusions) and what you think should be done about them (recommendations). Even if they have the ability to make the interpretations themselves, they likely will want you to make them—for possible ideas they might not see and for economy of their time.

The following brief suggestions are designed to help you present quantitative data the way most report readers want them.

1. Make sure your figures are reliable by checking your sources and derivations of them. And when you present an average, make clear whether it is the mean, the median, or the mode.

2. Write isolated quantities in one of the standard ways explained under **Fig** in Appendix C.

3. Insofar as possible, avoid cluttering your paragraphs with great masses of figures. Tables are better if you have many figures. Ordinarily, however, extensive tables are not necessary to the reader's understanding of the text but are in a report to show that you really have the facts. In that case put tables in the appendix and refer to them specifically in the introduction or text; then follow points 4–7 below for presenting necessary figures in the text.

4. Put necessary statistical information as close as possible to the place in the text where it is most pertinent. The reader will likely refuse to flip pages back and forth to find a table, or at least will resent having to do so.

5. Small tables (usually called spot tables), perhaps using key figures based on extensive data in an appendix, are not only easy to read but can be put close to the relevant discussion. Use them freely.

6. Present key figures as simply as possible. Usually some ratio, rank, or difference is more important than the raw data. Instead of a gross of $2,501,460.70 and expenses of $2,124,101.40, the simple figures $2½ and $2⅛ million tell the story easier. The ratio 1:7 or about 15 percent for the net certainly reads easier than $377,359.30 and is probably the more important figure. Moreover, except in bookkeeping and highly technical research, such rounded and simplified figures are precise enough for most purposes. Indeed, rounded figures in most cases are as accurate as the unrounded ones on which they are based. The means of arriving at most large figures are not accurate enough to make the last few digits anything but a bogus precision and a hindrance to readability.

Another way of increasing readability is to break big figures down into so much per . . . (whatever is an appropriate divider). If the divider is the number of persons involved (employees, students, or citizens, for example), you also gain interest by humanizing the presentation.

7. Help your reader by pointing out highs, lows, averages, trends, ranges, and exceptions or extremes. They are not always readily apparent, especially to the many readers who are not accustomed to analyzing statistical data; but they are usually important, especially if you can also explain their causes and/or effects.

Graphic aids as supplements to words

Since reports so frequently treat quantitative data, designs, organizational plans, and the like, you often almost have to use charts, graphs, pictograms, drawings, and maps as well as tables to present your information well. But in most cases—even for engineers and architects, who have to study drafting—these devices only assist, not replace, words. And since interpretation of graphics is not one of the three *R*'s learned by everybody, most graphics help to explain and/or support the text only *if the text helps them by telling the reader how to look at them and what they mean.* Skillful communication therefore often involves care in interplaying words and graphic aids.

The best procedure begins by introducing the topic; then subordinately referring the reader to the graphic aid at the point where it will be helpful, using the best type of graphic for the purpose; and then further commenting on (interpreting) the graphic device. Note these points:

1. A reader should not run onto a graphic device until *after* an introduction to it; in most cases it would only confuse and break reading continuity.

2. The existence of the graphic aid, or where it is, is *not* the important thing and does *not* deserve the emphasis in your sentence referring to it. So refer to it *subordinately* and use the main clause of your sentence to tell the reader the significant point: "Twice as many men as women like X, as shown in Table 2" is one good way.

3. Insofar as possible, place graphic aids close to the comments on the same point, preferably right before the reader's eyes. Unless the device is staring the reader in the face when you mention it, tell precisely where it is (for example, "As Fig. 1 on the next page shows, X goes up as Y goes down."

4. Carefully label each graphic device (unless obvious) as a whole and by parts, and provide a key if necessary. Variations in color, shading, and kind of line (solid versus broken, for example) are common means for distinguishing the different kinds of data in lines, columns, bars, and the like.

5. Interpret your graphics unless doing so would insult the reader because the meaning is so obvious.

Complete discussion of the uses, advantages, disadvantages, and techniques of preparing different kinds of graphic devices is beyond the scope of this book. And extensive illustrations—which are costly to reproduce and are not very helpful except when accompanied by the relevant text—would quickly run up the size and cost. As an economical, minimum introduction to graphics, however, you should look carefully at the following illustrations of three commonly used types, with just enough text to show how the graphics should be interwoven.[2]

The federal government's share of civilian public employment has less than doubled since 1900, while the shares of state and local governments have increased nearly 9 and 2½ times, respectively, as shown in Table 14–2.

TABLE 14–2 Government employment as a percentage of total employment, United States, 1900–1965*

	1900	*1910*	*1920*	*1930*	*1940*	*1950*	*1960*	*1965*
Federal								
Military	0.5	0.4	0.8	0.5	1.1	2.8	3.6	4.9
Nonmilitary ...	1.1	1.2	1.7	1.4	2.2	3.5	3.3	1.9
State	0.3	0.3	0.5	0.7	1.1	1.8	2.3	2.6
Local	3.1	3.4	4.0	5.4	5.9	5.4	6.7	7.6
Total	5.0	5.3	7.0	8.0	10.3	13.5	15.9	17.0

* Figures through 1940 are adapted from S. Fabricant, *Trend of Government Activity since 1900* (New York: National Bureau of Economic Research, 1952). The 1965 data are from U.S. Department of Labor, *Employment and Earnings,* June, 1965. All school employees are classified as local through 1940. For later years they are distributed between local and state governments in proper proportion. The federal figure for 1940 excludes emergency relief workers.

The commonly heard statements about the burgeoning growth in federal employment are therefore misleading. As the table shows, the great growth in our military establishment (almost a 10-fold increase) is the big factor. It and the big increases in state employment are the main causes all government's share of total employment has increased 2.4 times since 1900. As you see graphically in Figure 1, federal nonmilitary employment is the slowest growing of the four categories of public employment; and it has been shrinking since 1950.

National defense is much the biggest item in the federal budget, as shown by Figure 2, almost three out of five federal expense dollars (58.2%) going there.

If we include the foreign aid and atomic energy programs as part of the defense effort, national defense absorbs about three quarters of the cost of federal services. Everything else has to come out of the remaining quarter.

As a further illustration of the kinds, uses, and techniques of charts, see those illustrated in Figures 3, 4, and 5.

---

[2] The comments are ours, but the graphics are reprinted, by permission of the author and publisher, from Lloyd G. Reynolds, *Economics: A General Introduction,* rev. ed., Richard D. Irwin, Inc., Homewood, Ill. 1966, pp. 459 and 461, respectively.

FIGURE 1 Government employment as a percentage of total employment, United States 1900–1965

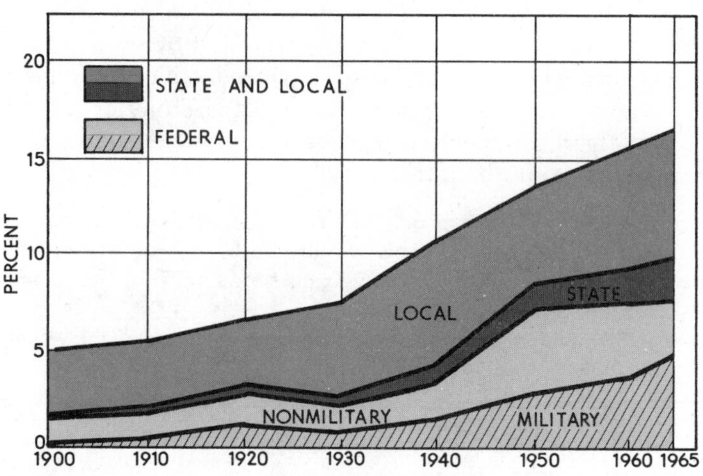

In your reading of other books, newspapers, and especially news magazines like *U.S. News & World Report*, *Newsweek*, and *Time*, notice the numerous good (and some bad) illustrations. Those in *Scientific Ameri-*

FIGURE 2 Cost distribution by level of government and type of service, United States, 1963–1964 (percent)

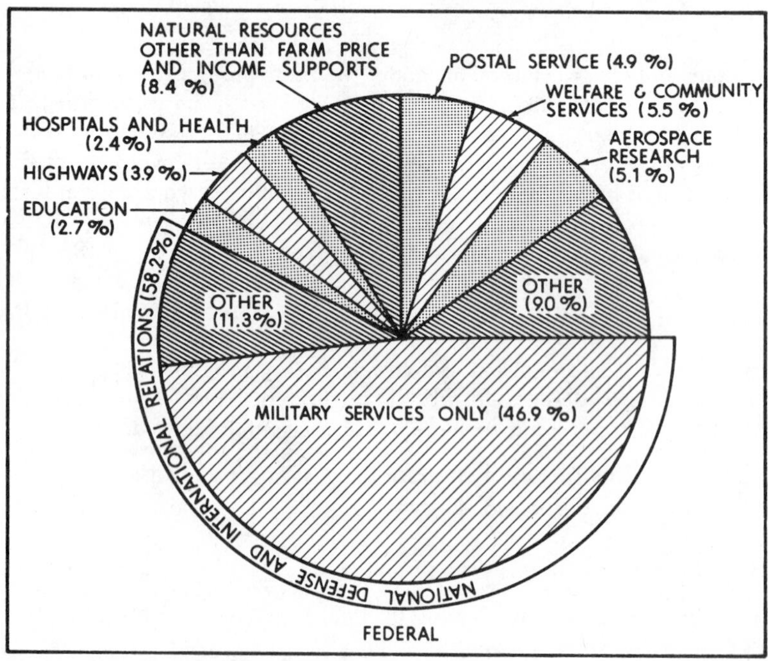

FIGURE 3

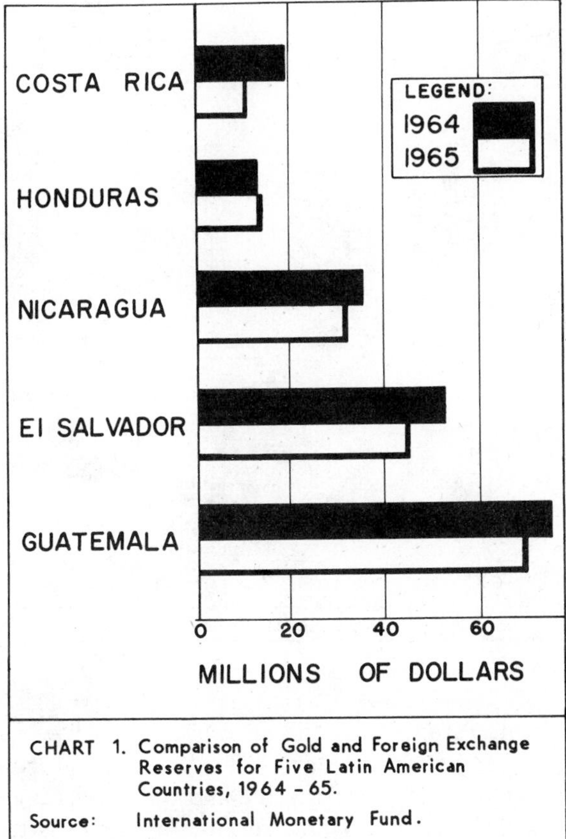

CHART 1. Comparison of Gold and Foreign Exchange Reserves for Five Latin American Countries, 1964 - 65.

Source: International Monetary Fund.

can are particularly good. Look not only at the graphics themselves, but notice what kinds of information call for graphic presentation, whether the graphics really help, and how the authors *interrelate the graphics and words so that each aids the other.*

If you will make those observations, you will probably see how useful graphics can be in your writing and also learn most of what you need to know about using them skillfully. Still we think these suggestions may be helpful:

1. Use line graphs (perhaps marking the tops of columns in a bar chart) to represent trends according to time. Usually the perpendicular axis should represent volume of the subject treated and the base (or horizontal axis) should represent time. Two or more different kinds of lines can show relative quantities as well as the absolute quantities of several subjects at any given time.

Unless you are using several lines or bars (but not so many as to con-

FIGURE 4

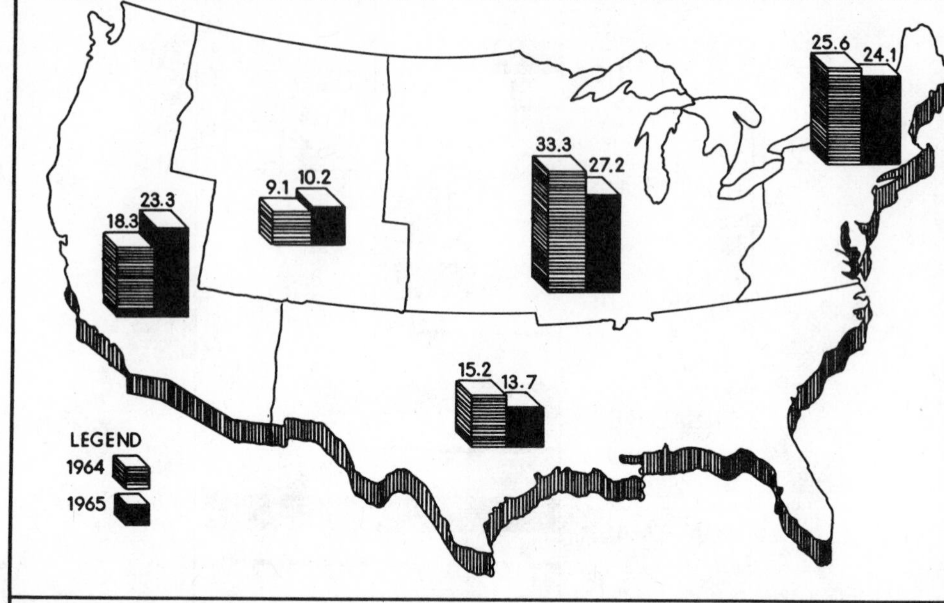

CHART 2. Percentage of Sales by District, Gaylor Manufacturing Co., 1964, 1965. Source: Primary

fuse!) and are interested only in their comparative values rather than their individual changes, be sure to start at 0 as the base. If, for example, you use 40 as the base of the quantity scale and the first year presented has a volume of 50 and the second 60, the second year appears to have doubled the first (20 above the base 40 and thus twice as high on the scale as the preceding year, which was only 10 above the base). But actually it has increased only 20 percent (the 10 points from 50 to 60, a one-fifth or 20 percent increase)—as it would and should look on base 0.

Providing grid lines will help avoid optical illusions and give the reader a quick and precise idea of just where a line is at any given time in the graph.

Remember also to use faired (curved) lines for continuously changing data and straight lines to connect plotted points of data that change by steps, such as enrollments in a university by semesters.

2. Use segmented bars or pie charts moving clockwise from 12:00 to represent the proportions in the breakdown of a whole. Usually the color or shading of sections distinguishes the parts (which should not be confusingly numerous). They should be labeled with both the raw figures for precision and the ratio or percentage of the whole for easy comparison (the ratio is usually the more important point).

3. Use maps for geographical distribution of almost anything; organiza-

FIGURE 5

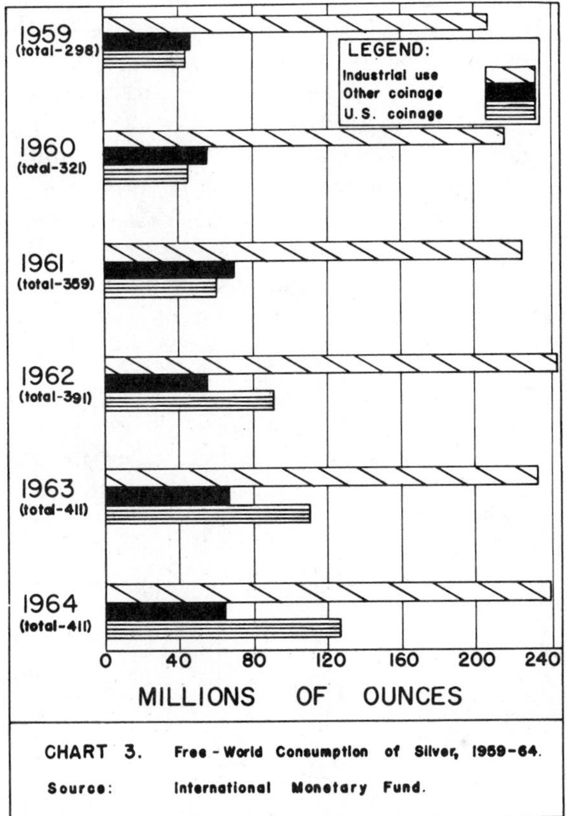

CHART 3. Free-World Consumption of Silver, 1959–64.
Source: International Monetary Fund.

tion charts of rectangles arranged and connected to show lines of authority and communication; flow charts showing movement and stages in processing; blueprints giving precise sizes and relationships; and photographs picturing accurate size, texture, and color. All are useful graphic devices in their places if you keep them simple enough for easy reading and concentrated on the point under discussion.

4. Use symbolic pictograms (like little men representing workers or bags of money representing profits) to add interest, especially for nontechnical readers, when you have the time and money and are preparing a report in enough copies to justify the cost. But *keep all the little characters the same size* (although each may represent any quantity) and vary the *number* of them to represent different total quantities. Otherwise, you mislead because the volume in the pictogram involves a third dimension (depth perspective) not shown in the pictogram. Of two cylinders representing oil production, for example, one actually twice as big as the other looks only slightly bigger because of the unseen third dimension. Even in

the best usage, pictograms are not precise unless you write in the exact quantities. Pictograms should be drawn to avoid prejudicial side messages too—such as the unfavorable and irrelevant suggestion that all welfare cases are diseased, decrepit, or dumb in the drawings of a pictogram designed to represent the changing *number* of welfare cases.

5. If you have to provide multiple copies of your report, consider whether your graphics are reproducible. What may be fine for offset printing may not work in some kinds of Xerographic processes. Computer-generated graphics, increasingly common, often pose problems. A computer print-out or a photograph of a visual display (CRT) may be of such poor quality that you would lose important details in reproduction, necessitating expensive and time-consuming tracing or redrawing.

* * *

Beyond that, the writing of a report depends on the particular form to be used, and the form you choose should be the one best adapted to the situation, as explained along with the illustrations in Chapters 15 and 16. (The cases for reports of different kinds are at the ends of those two chapters.)

chapter 15

Analysis and illustration of complete analytical reports

[The ladder of success must be set on something solid.]

A BIRD'S-EYE VIEW OF REPORT FORMAT

IN PETTY DETAILS the makeup of long analytical reports varies only a little less than the organizations sponsoring the reports. Hence we cannot tell you the details of any report form that will be acceptable universally or specifically to the particular organization for which you may write.

Yet in the larger aspects of report parts and their interrelations, agreement far exceeds disagreement. In this chapter we propose to explain and illustrate report makeup with emphasis on the generally acceptable major points. Since you will also want some guidance on details, however, we will suggest *a* good way to handle them; but we ask you to remember that what we present on details of form is *not the only way.*

Even more important, we do *not* present *the illustrations as perfect reports, and certainly* not as wording *to be followed slavishly or copied parrotlike. At best, they show acceptable content, form, and general style for their particular situations as starters to your thinking—not as solutions to all your problems on these points for your situation.*

Layout and pagination

Most complete analytical reports include three broad categories of several parts each. The parts marked with asterisks in the following list normally do not appear as separate parts except in long, formal reports; but the others are almost universal.

- Preliminaries
  - Cover
  - Title fly*
  - Title page
  - Letter of authorization*
  - Letter of acceptance*
  - Letter of transmittal
  - Table of contents
  - Table of illustrations*
  - Synopsis
- Body
  - Introduction
  - Text
  - Conclusions
  - Recommendations
- Supplements
  - Appendix(es)
  - Bibliography
  - Index*

The following specifics will help in layout and pagination:

1. Generally each of the listed parts except text, conclusions, and recommendations begins a new page; otherwise, only the filling of one page calls for a new one. If used, the table of illustrations may go on the same page with the contents if space allows without crowding. Each appendix begins on a new page.

2. Preliminary pages are counted beginning with the title fly, if used (and pages *after* the title page get lowercase roman numerals). Pages in the body and supplements take arabic numerals. The first page number of any part beginning a new page is centered at the bottom of the page; others appear (preferably) at least three spaces above the end of the first line. No page numbers need adornments such as parentheses, hyphens, periods, and underscores.

3. If the report is to be bound, the "bite" of the binding requires typing with an extra wide margin (usually at the left) so that no writing will be hidden and margins will appear equal when the report is open.

Optional and minor parts

Now, before we present the parts that require full discussion and illustration, let's clear out the no-problem parts and the optional parts marked with asterisks in the preceding list.

The *cover*, much like the cover of a book, is there to hold the report together and protect it. But unless it has an open or cellophane-covered cutout revealing the identifying title page, it needs to carry at least the title (perhaps in shortened form) and the author's name; but it may carry the rest of the title-page information too.

As the name suggests, the *title fly* is a full page carrying only the title. Whatever its use in printed books, it is only excess paper in typewritten reports. If used, it counts as the first of the preliminary pages (lowercase roman numerals), although the page number does not need to appear on it.

Although written by the person who has the problem to be solved and pays for the report rather than the one who prepares it, the *letter of authorization* should be included when the assignment was made by letter. This is most likely to be when the assignment is a big one, especially if it is a public affairs problem or the report writer is an outsider working on a fee basis. By showing what the assigned job was, the letter enables any reader to judge the adequacy of the report. To make sure of getting a suitable report, the writer of the authorization needs to state the problem precisely and make clear the purpose, scope, and limits on time, money, and the like. Asking specific questions and, if known, suggesting sources, methods, or approaches may help further, and also save money.

The letter of acceptance—rarely included—is the answer to the authorization. Together they constitute the working agreement or contract.

Tables of illustrations help only if some of the tables and graphics might be useful to a reader independently of the discussion around them. If used, in table-of-contents form they list separately the tables, charts, and figures in sequence by their identifying numbers and titles, and give the pages on which they appear.

An *index* would serve little purpose in most reports both because they are not long enough to need one and because they are not used the way a reference book is. Ordinarily the table of contents adequately serves the purpose of helping a reader to find a certain point. If, however, you find that you must prepare an index, take some good advice from people who have tried indexing: (1) Hire a professional indexer to do the job or (2) study at least one of the several helpful books on the subject before you start. Indexes done by nonprofessionals are mostly rather poor, including those in most textbooks—too scant and too full of errors.

STANDARD SHORT PRELIMINARIES

Title page

The title page is usually the first of the preliminary pages (counted as lowercase roman numbers down to the introduction), but the page number does not need to appear on it. Four other blocks of information do: the title itself, the name and title of the reader, the name and title of the writer, and the place and date. In many instances the name of the organization with which both writer and reader are connected is desirable information. When needed, a brief abstract, a list of people or departments to receive copies, and project or serial-number identifications may appear also.

Phrasing the title well is usually the main problem. Unfortunately the writing of *functional* titles (as opposed to literary-style titles for stories, poetry, plays, and movies) is something not generally taught in schools. First, a good report title, like any other title or heading in functional writing, should be *precise* in indicating clearly the content and scope to be covered. Frequently, however, first-attempt report titles are too broad, too narrow, or tangential—suggesting more or less than intended or a related rather than the real topic. A good report title narrows the topic and then zeroes in on the real problem. Secondarily, a good report title should be *interesting*—at least to the intended readers. (You cannot reasonably expect to interest everybody in most report topics.) As a third desirable quality, a good report title should be *concise*—have no wasted words like "A Report on . . . ," "A Study of . . . ," or "A Survey of. . . ."

An illustration will make clearer some frequent false steps and final solutions to the problem of writing *precise, concise,* and *interesting* report titles. A student proposed a report on "A Study of the Compensation of Executives." Discussion with the professor quickly led to omitting the first four words, and then changing to "Executive Compensation" for a further 33 percent reduction in words. That adequately solved the problem of *conciseness.*

Further discussion soon revealed, however, that the student never intended to write about all executives but only high-level ones in corporations. The problem of *precision* had come up—in the usual way, pointing to a need for *narrowing the topic* to the intended coverage. But that wasn't even the worst part of imprecision in this case. Despite the emphasis on *compensation,* the student (surprisingly) wasn't even interested in the executives' basic salaries, having already seen evidence that up to $600,000 annually didn't keep executives from leaving jobs. The student revealed that the real topic of interest was evaluation of several new means some corporations are beginning to use to keep their top executives. Long-used means—high salaries, stock options, bonuses, and retirement programs (the things most people would envision from the word *compensation*)—were only tangential to the main topic.

The student felt pride in accomplishment with "New Methods Corporations Use to Retain High-Level Executives"—but almost gave up when the professor said it wouldn't do. The assigned report was to be an *analytical* report, and this title suggests a mere presentation of undigested facts.

Assuming assignment by Pow Chemical Company to study the problem and write a report on what the Corporation might do to reduce executive turnover, the student (with only a little more help) arrived at a satisfactory title: "Pow's Possible Benefits from Applying Some New Means Used by Corporations to Retain High-Level Executives." That title narrows the topic and then zeroes in on the real problem. It says *precisely* what the report was to be about (no more, no less) and implies an analytical rather than informational report. (You might note that it doesn't even—and doesn't need to—contain the key word of the original, *compensation.*) The first three words could not help *interesting* Pow officials, the intended readers. And that title is *concise*—not short, or brief, at 16 words—but concise. If you doubt that, try stating it precisely and interestingly in fewer words.

An analytical report is about a specific problem of an individual or group. As such, its title should indicate that specificness, often to the extent of naming the person or group as well as the problem. You can't answer such a general question as "Should Spot Radio Advertising Be Used?" The answer would be sometimes yes and sometimes no. For that reason, one student phrased a title as "Why the P. L. Lyon Company Should Discontinue Spot Radio Advertising."

That title, however, was a *final* title, written *after* the writer had done the research and made the analysis. Knowing what the decision was, the reporter reasonably chose to tell the reader directly. To have phrased it that way *before* doing the research would have been to act on preconception that could have prevented the writer from facing facts fairly.

With the title well done, you should have no more trouble with the title page. In looking at the accompanying illustration (p. 551),[1] note how the writer grouped information into four parts and used balanced layout (each line centered) for good appearance.

---

[1] To save space—and reading time and extra book costs for you—by slight modifications we have made one report (beginning on p. 551) serve to illustrate both long and short analytical reports.

Letter of transmittal

Following the title page—unless the report is an extensive and formal one, including such things as a copyright notice, title fly, letter of authorization, and letter of acceptance—page ii (counted, but not necessarily numbered) is a letter of transmittal. (In a formal public-affairs report with large numbers of indefinite readers, a typical preface replaces the personalized letter of transmittal.)

Written after the report is completed, in regular letter form (Chapter 4) and a style appropriate to the circumstances, the letter of transmittal must do at least two things: transmit the report and refer to the authorization. In informal situations one sentence can do both: "Here's the report on fish poisoning you asked me to write when we were talking on May 10." Usually it needs to be a little more formal than that, but it needs no bromidic "As per your request, . . ." and rarely such formality as "In accordance with. . . ." Certainly it needs to subordinate the reference to the authorization to avoid a flat and insulting sound—seeming to tell about the request for the report as if the reader were too dumb or forgetful to remember. In the rare cases where no authorization happened, instead of the reference to it the writer tells enough background to arouse interest.

Despite the importance of conciseness and the possibility of doing in the first sentence all it *has* to do, a letter of transmittal will say more, if for no reason than to avoid a curt tone. Some additional things it might talk about (but not all in any one letter) are the appropriate ones of

—A highlight particularly significant in affecting the findings, or a reference to special sections likely to be particularly interesting to the reader.

—A summary of conclusions and recommendations if the reader is likely to be sympathetic and unless a synopsis two or three pages later says the same thing. Even then, the letter can give very briefly the general decision but not supporting data (as on p. 552).

—Side issues or facts irrelevant to the report but supposedly interesting or valuable to the reader.

—Limitations of information, time, and/or money if they are true and not a part of the introduction, where they naturally belong—and provided that they do not sound like lazy excuses.

—Acknowledgments of unusual help given by others not cited later as sources.

The letter may appropriately—almost always should—end with some expression indicating the writer's attitude toward the significance of the report and/or appreciation for having been allowed to work on it. If you are in the business of making such studies, you surely appreciate business. If you're within the company, you certainly should appreciate the opportunity to demonstrate your ability and to learn more about the company. Your superior's giving you an important report assignment is a chance to make a good impression (and be marked for promotion). The value of that chance and a good report could easily be reduced, however, if you do not express your appreciation for the chance.

Table of contents

The next part, usually page iii (with the number centered at the bottom, as always on a page with extra space at the top because of a part heading), is what is commonly called the table of contents or simply contents. It sets out the headings of the report and their beginning page numbers. Thus it quickly shows the organization and serves as a handy guide for the reader, especially the busy reader who may want to check only some parts. In the absence of an index, it needs to be adequately detailed for the purpose.

To list in the table of contents the table itself and those pages that come before it looks a little odd; the reader would already have seen them. Yet conventional practice does condone listing of preceding items. Remember, however, that the *preliminary parts down to the introduction are* not *parts of the outline and do not get outline symbols,* such as *I* and A, but only their names and page numbers (small roman numerals). If a separate synopsis comes after the table of contents, you list it flush left without an outline symbol, usually as the first thing on the list.

Then comes the real outline of the report—the headings and subheads. In most reports you may well give all of them, *reproduced in exactly the same wording as elsewhere* but not necessarily in the same type. Preferably you should put the outline symbols before them—capital roman numerals for the major divisions (including the introduction, conclusions, and recommendations) and capital letters for their subdivisions, according to the system of outlining suggested earlier. (*Remember that roman numerals, like arabics, line up on the right.*) If any heading runs over to a second line, indent it. After each heading is a leader line of *spaced* periods leading to the page number, as in the accompanying illustration. For proper appearance, make *all* those periods while your typewriter carriage is on either even or odd numbers on the scale.

Supplementary parts such as appendixes and the bibliography continue the arabic page numbers of the body copy, but they do not carry roman numerals to the left in the table of contents because they are not logical parts of the discussion being outlined.

The table of contents may be single- or double-spaced, or single-spaced within parts and double-spaced between, whichever makes the best appearance on the page.

Though the illustrative report in the next chapter—see footnote, p. 497—does not have a table of contents, separate synopsis, appendix, or bibliography, as a complete analytical report it would have. In fact, omitting or combining those parts, along with overall length, is the most likely difference between complete analytical reports and short analytical reports. For purposes of illustrating those parts in this chapter, therefore, we made them up or borrowed them from other reports. We made up the table of contents on the next page from the headings in the report on pp. 551–66 by assuming the missing parts were in place.

Synopsis and/or abstract

Written after the report proper has been completed, the synopsis is a condensed version of the whole report (preliminaries, introduction, presentation of facts and the interpretations of them, and conclusions and recommendations). It is the report in a nutshell. Usually it should be somewhere between a 10:1 and 20:1 reduction. In most cases the introduction should be reduced even more, and the conclusions and recommendations less because they deserve the main emphasis as the report's reason for being.

Since a synopsis stresses results, in terms of the psychology of communication you might feel that it should not be used in a report which needs to be strongly convincing because of the reader's likely resistance. In such a situation the condensed presentation of findings might not be adequate to do the necessary convincing before the reader sees the unwelcome or inadequately justified conclusions. The increasing recognition of readers' benefits from having synopses in long reports and the way readers read such reports, however, override the psychological objection. Neither psychologically nor practically can you hold an impatient reader away from the conclusions long enough to read a long report anyway, the way you can on a short one.

So (as in a report which may properly follow the deductive plan because the results are probably welcome to the reader) even in a long report which needs to convince, the synopsis serves several important purposes:

1. It saves time in many cases by giving all a busy reader wants.
2. Even for the reader who goes on through the whole report, the synopsis gives a bird's-eye view which helps in reading the rest more easily and more intelligently because already knowing the final results makes clearer how each fact or explanation fits.
3. Often the synopsis also serves as the basis for a condensed oral presentation to a group of important "readers" such as a board of directors.
4. Sometimes a number of readers who do not get the whole report but need to know the essence of it get what they need from reproduced and distributed copies of the synopsis.

Particularly for the first and last uses, many executives insist that reports coming to their desks have *one-page* synopses up front—an increasing trend started by Sir Winston Churchill while British Prime Minister and given a strong push by General Eisenhower while President of Columbia University. You should therefore try to keep synopses down to one page, even if you have to single-space within paragraphs (but of course double-space between).

The letter of transmittal on p. 552 is also an example of partial, scant synopsizing. In that report the author used no separate synopsis but wove it into the letter. For a more typical example, read the more detailed synopsis below of a different report long enough to make desirable a *sepa-*

Table of Contents

rate, full-fledged synopsis (the better practice in all but comparatively short reports). It specifically and concisely synopsizes a report of six major divisions (besides the introduction and the conclusions and recommendations) running to 27 pages. Desirably, it focuses on a quick presentation of results (the conclusion and implied recommendation) in the first paragraph, while also making clear the purpose, the readers and authorizer, and the writers. Then it summarizes, in a paragraph for each, the six data-filled sections *in the same order and proportionate space given the topics in the full report.* For readers not used to standard kinds of market-research data for choosing favorable locations, we have inserted (in brackets) helpful identifying heads for those six paragraphs.

Synopsis

Savannah people are likely to buy more at a Rexwall Drug Store than Charleston residents are, according to this market evaluation prepared for the Chairman of the Board, Rexwall, Inc., by Factseekers, Inc.

[Population and Buying Units]

Though metropolitan Charleston merchants serve 11,000 more customers from the shopping area, Savannah retailers can expect some trade from almost twice as many out-of-town buyers (340,000 versus 184,000). Savannah's 1,000 more family units more than compensate for the fact that the Charleston family averages 3.62 people while the smaller Savannah family averages 3.4.

[Buying Income]

Savannah individuals average $85 more buying income, but the larger Charleston families average $35 more per family for a total of half a million more annual buying income. With less first-mortgage money to do it, 2,800 more people in Savannah have built homes in the past four years; but 17,000 more Charlestonians own automobiles.

[Retail Sales]

The higher income of the individual Savannah buyer and the larger number of customers from around Savannah explain why $2.5 million more passed through the hands of Savannah retailers last year. Individually, Savannah residents spent $75 more; the small Savannah family, however, spent only $55 more.

[Drugstore Sales]

Though five years ago Charleston druggists outsold those in Savannah by an average of $3,000, last year the 61 Savannah drugstore managers and owners collected about $5 million—$170,000 more than 62 Charleston druggists—for an average of $4,000 more per drugstore in Savannah.

[Overall Business Factors and Stability]

Overall business factors also point to Savannah as the choice. Savannah's estimated business volume of $989 million is almost twice that of Charleston. Since a significant part of this difference is attributable to the 10 million more tons of cargo handled by the Savannah docks, Savannah consumers and retailers will feel the pinch of recessions and strikes more than Charlestonians. The extra $36 million added by Charleston manufacturing, however, is almost as uncertain in the stability of that city as the effects of shipping are on the economy of Savannah. Charlestonians benefit from $35 million more of the relatively stable wholesale business; but $32 million more agricultural income from farms averaging $4,000 more in value helps to bolster the Savannah economy.

[Business Activity]
Certainly Savannah's business activity has been consistently better than Charleston's in the past four years. Though the trend continues up in both cities, construction has averaged $12 million more annually in Savannah. Bankers in Savannah have consistently received about 10 percent more deposits than their Charleston counterparts have—for $150 million more in commercial accounts and $12 million more in savings. In both cities postmasters have collected about 8 percent more each successive year, but Savannah citizens have steadily paid for $200,000 more postage than Charlestonians have.

Since a synopsis derives exclusively from the report itself—which is adequately illustrated and documented—it needs neither graphics nor citations. But you do need to give the main supporting facts. Otherwise the synopsis becomes a nutshell with no meat. This is one reason we use the term *synopsis* rather than *abstract.*

Abstracts are of two kinds—topical, giving *only the points discussed* (shells without meat); and informative, *giving the findings about each topic, with emphasis on conclusions and any recommendations made.* A synopsis is like an *informative* abstract, emphasizing results, but is usually fuller and more helpful.

The best use for informative abstracts seems to be their increasing appearance (usually right under article titles) to give journal readers very briefly the gist of articles. Though chemists swear by *Chemical Abstracts,* a technical journal made up largely of *topical* abstracts, we swear *at* (and see no use for) topical abstracts in connection with report writing. Even good annotations, as in an annotated bibliography, are worth more.

CONTENT AND FORM OF MAJOR PARTS

Introduction

The introduction to a complete analytical report *serves primarily to answer the second of a report reader's two inevitable questions: How do you know?* Rarely does it answer any part of the first question: What are the facts? If that question needs to be answered briefly and early (before the text gives all the facts), the synopsis does the job. Unless a synopsis or informative abstract is a part of the introduction, therefore—as in some forms of reports—the introduction is no place to put your data.

Since the introduction begins the *body* of the report—which also includes the text (the facts and analyses), conclusions, and recommendations if the reader wants them—the *title of the whole report appears at the top of the page.* Remember to set up that title exactly as on the title page, to reign as the superior over all other headings—in content as explained on p. 496 and in form as explained on p. 483. (Number the page 1, centered at the bottom as always on a page with extra space at the top because of a heading there.)

The first real problem in writing an introduction (often best done after the other parts) is selecting a heading for it. The stock term *Introduction,* which fits all but none well, is neither a precise nor interesting preview of the contents. The illustrative report we're using, you'll notice (p. 553), does better. You can too after reading further below about the content of introductions. One of the best we've ever seen was "The WHY and HOW of This Report," but you don't need to use its wording. In fact you should not copy anybody's word patterns in a title or anywhere else, especially if they are unusual. You should look at illustrations for ideas and principles of communication—then express your thoughts in your own way. Regardless of what it says, the heading of the introduction, as the first major division of your outline (usually I or 1), should be in the same grammatical and type form you intend to use for all the other major-division headings. See *parallelism* p. 469 and *headings* p. 482.)

In explaining how you know your forthcoming facts to be reliable, you need to state your *purpose, methods,* and *scope* so that the reader can judge whether the research would produce information that is sound and adequate for the purpose. Clear and explicit statement of the purpose is essential. No reader can judge a report without knowing what the writer set out to accomplish. Similarly, unless the research seems basically sound (in methodology and scope) for the purpose, the reader naturally discredits the whole report. The introduction, then, *is an important part of the conviction in the report and therefore deserves careful attention from both writer and reader.*

The section headed *Purpose* may take several paragraphs for full explanation, especially if it includes history or background of the problem; or it may be short. Long or short, it should contain some *one* sentence which is a pointed, concise statement of the problem you set out to solve. That sentence should come early, too. So, although any necessary background of history is the natural start, to avoid delay if it becomes very long you should state the key purpose sentence early and use the flashback method to follow quickly with clarifying background. As another alternative, you may relegate any very long background story to an appendix and refer the reader to it—especially if it is nonessential for most readers.

Methods and *scope* come under separate headings or (because they are often nearly inseparable) under a combined heading. Your reader does want to know, however, what you intended to cover and how thorough your research was (scope) and how you got and analyzed your information (methods). In a study involving a choice or evaluation, for example, the introduction needs to explain the *criteria* or *standards* used, as a part of method and scope or as a separate part. In fact, since criteria in such a report should become the major subdivisions, explanation and justification of them should be an important duty of the introduction.

How thoroughly you need to explain your methods depends on two major points: (1) how new and questionable your methods and findings are and (2) your reputation as a researcher. On both bases nobody questions the audit report of a reputable auditing firm that says no more on methods than the following: ". . . in accordance with generally accepted auditing standards, and accordingly included such tests of the accounting records and such other auditing procedures as we considered necessary in the circumstances." Most report writers, however, cannot depend so completely on either such well-established procedures or their reputations to convince their readers.

A frequent question is how much methodology to put in the introduction and how much (if any) to relegate to an appendix or to interweave along with the presentation of findings. No simple answer fits all cases and relieves you of thinking. A general answer is that you explain your methods at the best place(s) to show that your facts have a solid basis in valid research. Your reader will want at least a general idea from the introduction. If specific details of research procedure, special materials and apparatus, or technique are too difficult for your reader(s) to remember and associate with the later resultant findings, you had better omit the specifics from the introduction and interweave them with the presentation of findings. (A specific question with its answers from a questionnaire is a good example.)

Like long and unnecessary background, certain details of methodology may sometimes go in an appendix, but only if (1) they would interrupt or unduly slow up the fast movement of the report proper and (2) most readers of the particular report would not want or need them. (Detailed explanations of unusual statistical procedures, such as in the Kinsey reports, are good examples.)

Besides the standard parts (purpose, method, and scope), an introduction may take up one or more (rarely all) of several other possible topics. Some people think that an introduction should start by explaining the *authorization*—who asked for and who wrote the report—leading into or enveloping the purpose. Though the illustrated report (p. 553) does that, we don't think it is usually the best practice. The letter of transmittal will already have given the information. The first paragraph of a synopsis might have, also, because readers of widely distributed synopses would not have the duplicating letter of transmittal.

Unless the letter of transmittal has already done so, the introduction should forewarn the reader of any unavoidable *limitations* that make the report less than might be expected—limitations of time, money, or availability of data, for example. The explanation may be a part of method and scope if it is not so extensive as to need its own heading. But in no case should it be used as an excuse for the writer's own shortcomings.

Sometimes a report uses technical words or certain terms applied in a sense unfamiliar to some likely readers. If so, you may explain them in the introduction or, preferably, in brief parenthetical statements immediately following the first use of each special term. If the list is extensive, the *glossary* may be an appendix.

The important point is for the introduction to answer the big question —How do you know?—*before* the reader asks it.

Then you are ready to present the assuredly reliable facts.

Before asking the reader to go on this mental journey, however, consider whether you can help by giving a final reminder of the route: a concise statement of *plan*. Such a statement should not be long or detailed in its itemization of *all* your headings. It *does* need to remind the reader of the major steps in your organization—usually naming, in order, the topics from II to the conclusions in your table of contents. Usually one effective sentence can chart the way through to the end, like this: "As bases for determining the more favorable market conditions, the report examines—in this order—population characteristics, buying power, retail sales and drugstore sales and the attendant competition, stability of the economy, and the current business outlook." If you compare this statement of plan to the separate synopsis presented earlier (p. 502), you will see that they both reflect the careful organization of the same report.

Text

Even the lazy writer who gets by with *introduction* as the heading for that part cannot get by with *text* as a heading covering the biggest part of the report, where the writer presents the findings and analyses of them. The stock term, fitting all reports and therefore useful in talking about them, fits no one report well.

But more important, the text section of the report is fundamentally the report; so if you try to phrase a suitable title for the section, it will be the same as the title of the whole report. Then the basic elements of your report—the factors or criteria which serve as the basis for the final decision —become third-degree headings with seemingly too little significance.

That is the first of the two major problems confronting the writer in presenting the text: (1) showing the reader the organization carefully worked out as the third step in report preparation and (2) phrasing well the findings of the second step (collection of data) and the interpretations made in the fourth step. Satisfactory solutions to both are necessary if you are to give your reader the reliable information wanted.

Your main methods for showing the overall organization, the relations between parts, and the relation of each part to the whole are headings and subheads, topic sentences, and summary and anticipating statements. (You will find ample illustrations of all in the illustrative report pp. 551 ff.)

The headings and subheadings grow directly out of your attack on the problem, where you broke it down into its elements and further subdivided it by raising questions about each. Now that you are presenting the facts that provide the answers, you need only phrase these elements and questions into headings and subheads. Remember that good headings, like functional titles, are indicative, interesting, concise, and (in some cases preferably) informative to the extent of telling the most important findings about the respective parts. (Notice the heads in the report, pp. 553–66.)

Just as a well-phrased heading may tell the main point about the section over which it stands, a topic sentence can give the essence of a paragraph and clearly foreshadow what the paragraph says. The topic sentence puts the big point across fast, arouses the reader's interest in seeing the supporting details that follow, and makes reading easier because of the preview. Although the resulting deductive paragraph plan is not the only one possible, it is the most useful for most kinds of writing, including report writing.

Reversing the plan produces a paragraph which presents a series of facts and arguments leading to a summarizing and maybe a concluding sentence at the end.

Both plans may apply to larger sections as well as to paragraphs. In fact, both a paragraph's topic sentence and the first part of a larger section may reflect, summarize, or provide a transition from a preceding part, as well as give the essence and preview of what is to follow. And endings of both paragraphs and larger parts commonly summarize them, show the significance of the just-completed part to the whole problem at hand, and foreshadow what is to follow in the next section (as does the ending of the illustrated introduction on p. 553). Although the summaries may imply the advisability of a certain action, they should not go further and steal the thunder of the recommendation section by actually saying that the action should be taken.

Little more need be said about how to put the findings of fact and the interpretation into words. You have already learned in Chapter 14 to use commonly understood words, short and direct sentences and paragraphs, itemizations, summarizing and transitional phrases and sentences, headings and subheads, and graphic aids to words. You know, too, that you need to support your statements of questionable fact with explanations, additional specific and concrete details as evidence, citations of sources, and any meaningful statistics.

But remember that graphic presentations are not complete in themselves, that they only help words to present facts. They cannot interpret. The reader who wants an analytical report will consider your job only half done if you present a mass of undigested data and leave the interpreting undone. But if you put graphics and comments about them close together so that the reader can see both at once, each supplements the other.

References to the carefully chosen, most suitable graphics (about which you learned in Chapter 14) should be *subordinated* to the interpretation of the facts shown. The mere fact that the graph is there, or even the facts shown in the table or graph, are less important than the significance of those facts to the whole problem or the particular point being made at the time. So the emphasis should be on the interpretation. (Note the references to charts throughout the text of the illustrative report p. 551 ff.)

Here's a flat example which is short only because it forces the reader to dig in its Figures 1 and 2 for the information:

> The greatest majority of the students interviewed showed their preference for buying at home in place of buying in the larger cities of Birmingham or Tuscaloosa. The overall percentage for the entire body of male students represented by the sample was 78 percent. The freshmen showed an even greater tendency for home buying by their percentage of 84.
>
> Figure 1, below, gives a picture of the place of purchase of the entire group without regard to the nature of the group. Figure 2 divides the group according to the students' rank.

This rewrite is more informative, emphatic, and readable:

> When University of Alabama men are ready for a new suit, they go home 78 percent of the time. Although 4 out of 100 will buy in Tuscaloosa and 7 in Birmingham, as shown in Figure 1, these 11 atypical cases do not warrant extensive advertising.
>
> The Alabama man, although never weaned in the majority of cases from hometown buying, does slowly shift his clothes-buying sources from home to Birmingham to Tuscaloosa. The gain of only 13 out of every 100 purchasers over a four-year span, however (Figure 2), only confirms the suspicion that Bold Look advertising dollars in Tuscaloosa would be wasted.

Although basically an interpretation may point out trends, high and low points, and significant differences brought out by comparisons and analyses of facts and figures presented, you need not waste words by talking about "a comparison" or "an analysis of" or "a study of." If you state the significances, you imply the comparison, the analysis, or the study. And the comparisons become more quickly clear and significant if you put them in terms of percentages or ratios instead of, or in addition to, giving the raw figures.

To avoid monotony of both sentence pattern and length, especially in a series of similar comparisons, consider different types of sentence beginnings. Nearly always you can do better than use the expletives "It is . . ." and "There are . . . ,"which waste words, delay the idea, and lead you to weak and awkward passive constructions.

And unless the logic of the situation clearly dictates otherwise, you'll do best to use the present tense for both presenting and interpreting the facts. When a reader reads it, your report analyzes, presents, takes up, examines, establishes, and finally concludes (all present tense). Of course, you'll have to use some past and future tenses; but in general, use them for matters of historical record and things not yet done. You have to assume that your most recent information is still applicable; hence, even though last year's sales figures are a historical record of what people bought, you are justified in saying, "People buy . . . ," meaning that they did buy, they are buying, and they will buy.

With the facts and analyses well organized, clearly presented, and sharply summarized at the ends of sections, you have led the reader to your statement of conclusions and (if wanted) recommendations.

Conclusions and recommendations

When you put your conclusions and recommendations into words, they should not be surprising—and they won't be if you have done an adequate job of the preceding part. There you should have presented all the evidence and analysis necessary to support your conclusions. So no new facts or analyses should appear in the conclusions or recommendations.

Whether you separate conclusions and recommendations into two headings makes little difference. Some people prefer separation because, they say, the conclusions are strictly objective, logical results of what has been said, whereas the recommendations are the individual writer's personal suggestions of what to do about the problem. Whichever point of view and plan you use, the important thing is to be as objective as possible in stating both conclusions and recommendations.

As evidence of that objectivity in your conclusions, and as a means of saving the reader the trouble of looking back into the text to see that you *do* have the data, you may well lift basic figures or statements from the earlier presentation and interweave them into the conclusion sentences. The writer of the synopsis illustrated on page 502 knew that the reader could not possibly retain the 200 or more facts and figures given as evidence in 27 pages of analysis. In reminding the reader of the significant evidence affecting the decision in the conclusion, shown below, that writer wisely attached a specific figure to every fact. Note, too, the specific wording of that ending section—as well as the selectivity and brevity.

VII. THE PREFERRED CITY: SAVANNAH

Although a Charleston druggist enjoys the advantages of

—a population with a half million dollars more buying income annually and families with $34 more to spend

—11,000 additional potential customers

a Savannah drugstore would likely sell more because of these advantages:

—$170,000 additional drugstore sales and $4,000 greater sales per drugstore

—$2.5 million uore retail sales and $162 more per person spent in retail stores

—1,000 more families and per capita income $87 higher

—four-year trend increases of 8 to 10% in construction (12 million more), bank deposits ($150 million more), and postal receipts ($200,000 more)

Both conclusions and recommendations need to be as pointed and positive as the facts and the writer's judgment will allow. (Usually itemization will help you to make them so and help the reader to see them as such.) If you toss the problem back to the reader with indefinite conclusions or alternative suggestions, you leave the feeling that the salary or fee paid you for doing the report has been wasted. Still, the reader retains the right of final decision; so even when asked for your recommendations, present them as definite suggestions but certainly not as commands. The example just cited—phrased specifically in terms of the objective of the report, to select the city which will likely be the more profitable scene of operations—avoids indecision on the one hand and its equally undesirable opposite, imperative command.

STANDARD SUPPLEMENTS

Appendix

Although the report reproduced as an illustration in the next chapter needed no appendix, many reports do. The key is this: Use an appendix for material which the reader does not *need* to see to understand the text but which some readers may *want* to see to be sure your textual statements are clear and valid. Frequent uses are for survey questionnaires too extensive for presentation in the introduction and not essential to the reader's understanding; for extensive formulas and statistical calculations; for extensive history, or detailed experimental methodology too long for the introduction; and for large maps, diagrams, or tables of figures that may be the basic data of the whole report but do not belong at any particular place in the text. Often the best way is to put a big table in the appendix and use appropriate figures from it as spot tables at key places in the text.

Bibliography

Most reports of much length or importance have a bibliography. As we said before, on almost any big problem somebody has published something. If your problem is in the same area, finding and reading what others have written is almost certainly the quickest and easiest way to get at least some of the information you need. When you do that, you must tell what your sources are, not only to avoid the accusation of plagiarism but to show that you didn't just dream up the facts and to get the backing of the other writer for what you say—and perhaps to provide your reader with places to get fuller information.

Your footnotes and/or internal citations in the text give the specific references. But at the end you list—in alphabetical order of authors' surnames, or titles if the sources are unsigned—books, magazines, and other printed sources (but not letters and oral communications, which you cite in the text or in footnotes). These include all such sources used for background information or for specific facts, ideas, or direct quotations.

For several reasons the writer of the correspondence-improvement report did not compile a bibliography. The report was fairly short and involved few published sources, which were identified through internal citations. But this is the exception rather than the rule for acceptability in any but very short reports. For that reason (and to illustrate the economy of using numbers only for citing sources as described on p. 480) we took the sources cited in the report and compiled the illustrated bibliography at the end, p. 566.

For another illustration, we present the following bibliography from a 20-page report. After arranging the items alphabetically, this author also provided item numbers for concise, specific citations in the text. The spacing is the preferred form of single within items (except when preparing copy for a printer) and double between them.

PUBLICATIONS CONSULTED

1. "Airlines Will Sacrifice Power to Obtain Lower Jet Noise Level," Aviation Week, 66:34, February 25, 1976.
2. "Boeing Sets Suppressor Flight Test," Aviation Week, 65:41, April 1, 1975.
3. "Portable Jet Engine Muffler Design," Aviation Week, 64:74–75, April 8, 1974.
4. Richards, E. G., Technical Aspects of Sound, Elsevier Publishing Co., New York, 1975.
5. Richards, E. G., "Research on Aerodynamic Noise from Jets and Related Problems," Royal Aeronautical Society Journal, 57:318–42, May, 1975.
6. "Silencing Jet Fleet Will Be Costly," Aviation Week, 64:47–48, May 27, 1974.

* * *

For the feel of report continuity, read straight through the illustrative report interspersed in the next chapter and beginning on p. 551. Selected partly for its shortness (to save pages and reading time), it nevertheless illustrates adequate handling of the standard parts of a complete analytical report. (We feel that the preceding discussion and a little ingenuity will enable you to prepare other possible parts if you need to write them —cover, title fly, letters of authorization and acceptance, table of illustrations, appendix, and index.)

Because the report illustrated here is somewhat short, however, it does not need to make full use of topic and summary statements needed at the beginnings and endings of sections in longer reports. For illustration of how to use them, we refer you again to p. 474 and to Items S6–7 on p. 514.

* * *

Checklist for Complete Analytical Reports

ORGANIZATION/OUTLINING (O)

1. Phrase your title to indicate the nature, purpose, and limits of your study and to provide a basis of classification (see p. 496 and Item 1, p. 468); then make your major divisions on that basis.
2. In making comparisons, distinguish between your *subjects* and *criteria* and between your *criteria* and *methods*. See p. 468.
3. Use no heading for your whole text; your major divisions (usually capital roman numbers) are first the introduction, then the logical divisions of your topic (the text, usually in 2–5 parts), and your conclusions and recommendations.
4. Phrase each heading to include any and all of its subdivisions.
5. In phrasing, placing, and sequencing all division headings at all levels, make clear the relationship of each part to its whole and its function in your interpretation.
6. Maintain parallelism of grammatical form among headings of the same class (p. 469), using synonyms where necessary to avoid monotony of wording.
7. Use no single subheads; they're illogical (p. 469).
8. Try to make your headings informative (not just topical) as well as precisely indicative of what they include (pp. 483 and 496).
9. Use just enough headings to show the reader your organization.
10. Use placement and type variations in setting up headings to show their status in the outline and relations to others (pp. 483–84).

GRAPHICS (GR)

1. Use graphics whenever helpful; but omit useless ones.
2. Choose the best kind, form, and arrangement of graphic for the kind of data (pp. 486–92).
3. For reader convenience, place graphics near the discussion (small ones maybe on graph paper on the same page, larger ones on the next page).
4. Give graphics proper titles, numbers (charts and tables in separate consecutive series), labeled parts, and crediting of published ones as Source: (plus your regular footnote or other citation form).
5. Give reliable dates of graphic information (not always the date of publication), maybe in parentheses after the title.
6. Lead in with discussion of the point and proper introduction of the graphic (see S–8), tell where it is if not in sight, and (usually)

Checklist for Complete Analytical Reports

(continued)

follow with necessary key points of emphasis or interpretation.

7. For easy reading and close relationships, consider small spot tables closely associated with different points though they may all come from one collective source table that buries key points.

INTRODUCTION (I)

N.B.: Clear presentation of the *purpose, method, scope,* and basic plan is the main duty of the introduction, to provide any reader with a basis for judging the report's soundness.

1. Put the exact report title at the top of the first page of the body.
2. Then, for this first major division, try to phrase a more meaningful title than the stock term "Introduction." See p. 504.
3. Focus attention on the nature, purpose, and continuing existence of the report by talking about it in the universal present tense.
4. Use history of the problem only if needed as a lead into *purpose,* putting details in a flashback or the appendix if they become long.
5. Explain your methods of gathering data adequately to show thoroughness and be convincing.
6. As a part of *Scope,* clearly show any limits of coverage not made in the title; but justified (not excuse-making) limits of time or money are more appropriate in the letter of transmittal.
7. You might include a glossary only for a large number of necessary unusual terms; for only a few, preferably explain them parenthetically (or by footnote) as they come up.
8. By careful grouping and phrasing, try to cover the required elements of the introduction without breaking it into too many pieces (especially if the parts are short.)
9. Brief the reader (preferably in a "Basic Plan" section at the end of the introduction) on the sequence of major topics coming.
10. Keep findings, conclusions, and recommendations out of the introduction. If you want to get them to the reader early, a synopsis or even the letter of transmittal is a better place.

STYLE (S)

1. Remember that a natural style is clearer, easier, and more interesting than impersonal style for both writer and reader (pp. 481–82).
2. Enliven your style and increase readability by (*a*) using commonly understood words and short, direct sentences and paragraphs, (*b*) making people (not things) subjects and/or objects

Checklist for Complete Analytical Reports

(continued)

of many if not most sentences, (*c*) using mostly active voice, (*d*) eliminating "It is" and "There are" sentence beginnings, (*e*) using discrete (but not overlisted) itemizations for pointed, concise statements like conclusions and recommendations, and (*f*) presenting quantities (see *Fig* in Appendix C) in easily read and remembered forms (ratios, fractions, rounded numbers, simplified percentages, rankings). Remember that the relative status of something (percent, ratio, or rank—qualitative factors) is often more significant than the absolute value (quantitative).

3. To avoid seeming prejudiced, establish plausible assumptions made, give immediate and specific evidence to support points, give all of the same kind(s) of information about each compared subject, and avoid emotionally persuasive passage and disclaimers like "unbiased," "impersonal," "objective."
4. Use the universal present tense to indicate continuing existence for things and tendencies that existed in the past, exist now, and are likely to continue.
5. Don't use headings as antecedents of pronouns; your text should read coherently if the heads were removed.
6. Make clear, by topic statement at the first of each big section, the topic and any subdivisions (in the order of later treatment). See p. 474.
7. At the end of a sizeable section, sum it up with emphasis on its significance to the overall problem (and preferably with a transitional forward look to the next topic).
8. Interpret key points from graphics in relation to your objective, *emphasizing the message* and (by parenthetical, mid-sentence, or non-subject mention) *subordinating the reference to the graphic and its location.*
9. By evidence, explanation, and logic lead the reader to see likely conclusions and recommendations coming; but (ordinarily) leave the explicit statements of them until the end.

DOCUMENTATION (DOC)

N.B.: When you use others' material, you must give credit. The usual means are a bibliography and specific citations in the text, footnotes, and source indications on graphics.

1. Put in your bibliography an alphabetical listing of publications from which you used ideas, facts (including graphics), or quotations. See pp. 477–81 for forms.

Checklist for Complete Analytical Reports

(continued)

2. Make specific citations (at the points you used others' material) in the simplest way, though long ones almost have to go into footnotes. See pp. 479–81 for explanations, the report (pp. 551–66) for illustrations, and Gr–4 for citing sources of graphics.
3. Avoid repeating a citation (except for different page numbers) as long as you're drawing from the same source.
4. For convenience, start counting footnotes anew on each page.
5. Cite the basic circumstances in the text or a footnote where you use information from interviews, speeches, and letters (without listing in the bibliography); explain questionnaires as sources only in the Method section of the Introduction.
6. Use no source citations for the synopsis, conclusions, or recommendations; they all derive from the text, where needed source citations must appear.

TERMINAL (T)

1. Introduce no new facts in the T section; it derives from, maybe quickly recaps, and interprets information presented before.
2. Put conclusions and recommendations in the order of importance of their main supporting reasons.
3. State conclusions and recommendations pointedly (specifically and concisely, with key supporting facts and figuers), as firmly as your information justifies (rarely involving "prove"), and (preferably) itemized.
4. Take a stand (including "My findings prove nothing," if necessary); being wishy-washy suggests inadequacy or incompetence.
5. Make sure your conclusions and recommendations derive from facts and explanations formerly presented; leave surprise endings to mystery writers.
6. You are to conclude and suggest action but not command.

SYNOPSIS (SY)

1. Make the first paragraph stress the problem solution (or its main part) and subordinately reveal the authorization.
2. Compactly and specifically present (in a paragraph for each major division, in order and preferably in proportion) your main supporting facts and figures, while subordinately interweaving any necessary background, method, and scope.
3. Rely on sequence and only short transitional words for coherence.

Checklist for Complete Analytical Reports

(continued)

4. Include enough about the authorizer, purpose, and preparer for readers who get only circulated extra copies of the synopsis to understand. See Item 1 and p. 500.
5. Emphasize findings, not analysis—preferably in present tense.

TRANSMITTAL LETTER (TL)

1. Start by submitting the report, subordinately and naturally (not too formally or stuffily) referring to the topic and authorization.
2. Though you might reveal briefly the main final decision(s) in any case, don't steal the show from a synopsis (if you have one a few pages later)—or from the introduction by repeating methodology.
3. By implication or outright statement, express appreciation (and perhaps willingness to be further helpful—usually the way to end).
4. Avoid here (as elsewhere) such weak-kneed, disparaging defeaters of success consciousness as "I hope it will be useful." If you feel that way, you'd better rework the report.

AUTHORIZATION LETTER (AU)

You will, of course, never write your own authorization to write a report. When you need to write one, however,

1. Begin directly with an inquiry, request, or order in a tone that fits the writer-reader relationship.
2. To be sure of getting what you want, be as specific as possible about the problem, any known direction the solution should take, how results are to be used, when you want the report, and amount of money you're thinking of spending.
3. Suggest any starting points, procedures, and sources you think might save time and/or money.

MECHANICS (M)

1. Make bottom and side margins of the body 1–1½″, top slightly less, not counting extra space for the bite of any binding used.
2. Start a new page only to (*a*) start a new part (the body is all one —see p. 494), (*b*) leave a bottom margin, or (*c*) allow for at least two lines of copy below a heading.
3. Starting with the title fly, if used, count as preliminary pages down through the synopsis and (beginning with the table of contents) number them in lowercase romans.
4. Give all later pages arabic numbers, *without decorations*, a double space above the right ends of lines (except centered at the bottom on first pages of report parts).
5. Vary placement, spacing above and below, and type form of headings to show different levels. See pp. 483–84.

Checklist for Complete Analytical Reports

(continued)

6. To make it adequately noticeable, underline any typed heading not in solid capitals.
7. Double-space centered headings of more than one line.
8. Set up the title page for pleasant appearance (all lines centered or other neat design) and include at least the information given in four blocks illustrated on p. 551.
9. Since the synopsis is the first report part to follow and is a preliminary one, put it first in the table of contents, use no outline symbol, start at your left margin, and use the appropriate type form and a lowercase roman page number.
10. Likewise (except for their arabic page numbers) at the end show that any appendix(es) and the bibliography are supplements rather than integral parts of the outline.
11. Use lines of spaced dots (vertically aligned) to lead your reader's eyes to page numbers in the table of contents, leaving at least one space before and after the first and last dots.
12. For every section title listed in the table of contents, use exactly the same wording as in the report, though not necessarily the same type form, and give a beginning-of-section-only page number where it can be found.
13. Align (vertically) the right digits of all page and outline-symbol numbers of the same class.
14. Though the body of your report should be double-spaced, for the letters of authorization and transmittal use regular letter form (Chapter 4) or, if appropriate, memo form (Chapter 16), single-spacing within their paragraphs and double-spacing between. You may also (if you want to or need to) single-space within parts of the table of contents and paragraphs of the synopsis; but be sure to double space between headings of different levels in the table of contents and between paragraphs in the synopsis.
15. If you are an untrained typist, take these tips:
    a) Standard within-line spacings are (1) five for paragraph indention; (2) two after a colon or end-of-sentence punctuation (including an enclosing end parenthesis); (3) one after all other punctuation except as explained below; (4) none after an opening parenthesis or before or after a hyphen.
    b) Abbreviations pose a spacing problem: some (like our alphabet soup—HEW, IRS, SEC, CAB, for example) are solid; others (even with the same meaning) go various ways. Learn the main ones; look up the others in your dictionary.
    c) Dashes (not at all the same as hyphens—see P_7 and P_8 in Appendix C) are preferably two hyphens with no spacing.
    d) For quotations of more than two lines, space above and below, indent from each side, single-space, and use no quotation marks.

Although the preceding checklist is primarily for complete analytical reports, many of the items apply to all reports. For greatest usefulness the sections appear in order of preparation of your material, not the order of presentation in the final report. Remember, however, that this is only a checklist. If you need fuller explanation of a point, find it in the appropriate chapter. (The index may help.)

CASES FOR COMPLETE ANALYTICAL REPORTS

(Whether you are going to use Cases 1 and 2 or not, you should read them for points that should apply to nearly any major report-writing project.)

1. Subject to approval by your instructor, choose a topic for your long report. Preferably it should be a real problem actually faced by a company, organization, or individual; if not, it should be a problem likely to be faced by someone somewhere. It should be written for one reader or a very limited group of specific readers. A term-theme topic or something like a textbook chapter will not do because it is not a report. If you can't quickly give the name or title of somebody other than a teacher who might ask for such a report, your topic is unsuitable. It should be an analytical report: the relevant facts plus interpretation and evaluation of the advantages and disadvantages (the pros and cons) of at least two alternatives and the eventual selection of one in your final conclusions and recommendations. In other words, it must be a problem which you help someone to solve.

It should be a topic for which you can get information in the library *and* (not *or*) through either interviews, questionnaires, or your own observation or experimentation.

You should settle on a topic early in the term and should not change topics after midterm for any reason. The kind of problem we're talking about usually takes 10 to 20 pages for the text alone and requires most of the school term.

As your instructor directs, be prepared to submit on one typed page

a) A tentative title (not *now* worded to show a preconception of the outcome, but clear, concise and catching).
b) A one-sentence statement of the purpose of the report.
c) An indication of who the readers are and your relationship (actual or assumed) to them.
d) Sources and/or methods of collecting data, including the titles of five items from your tentative bibliography.
e) Major divisions (with subdivisions, if you like) of the coverage or body of the report.

Be prepared at any time to give your instructor a progress report in memo form, indicating what you have accomplished, what difficulties you've encountered, what remains to be done, and your plans for finishing.

At the time directed by your instructor, submit the report with appropriate cover, title page, letters of authorization and transmittal, contents listing, synopsis, body (including introduction, facts, and interpretations, conclusions, and recommendations), bibliography, and appendix if necessary.

As further clarification and suggestion, here are some of the better topics chosen by students in one class:

—Comparative evaluation of swimming pool (or goldfish pool) disinfectants under specific conditions.
—Comparative evaluation of materials and procedures to reduce black-shank damage to tobacco plants (specific conditions).

2. One of the requests coming to your desk as director of Factseekers, Inc., New York 10032, is from the president of (name of firm supplied by your instructor). The company is a chain of retail (type of store supplied by your instructor) stores with outlets in most major cities. The chain is now contemplating opening a store in either one of two cities (names of two cities supplied by your instructor).

You are asked to make a report evaluating the two as potential locations for the new store.

The letter to you as director, signed by the company president, reads:

Will you please submit in report form your analysis of retail sales possibilities for (specific goods) in (specific cases)?

Before deciding where our next branch will be, we would like the opinion of a firm of your caliber.

Naturally we want to know the story on population, buying power, retail sales—with special emphasis on (specific goods)—competition, and current business. But please include other data which will be helpful to us in making our choice.

Please do not attempt to cover taxes, wage scales, real estate costs, or availability of sites.

Since we plan to have the store in operation within a year's time, will you please confirm that you can submit the report no later than (specific date as assigned), subject to the same rates as on previous studies?

From secondary library sources you can get all the necessary comparative data: *Statistical Abstract of the United States; County and City Data Book; Market Guide of Editor and Publisher;* Rand McNally's *Commercial Atlas and Marketing Guide; Sales Management Survey of Buying Power; Printers' Ink's* special studies like *Sales Planning Guide* and *Major American Markets;* and *Consumer Markets,* published by the Standard Rate and Data Service. The foregoing are some of your more useful sources. But they are not intended to be an exhaustive list. You will of course want to consult the censuses of population, business, and manufacturers for (respectively) breakdowns of populations, influence of wholesaling and retailing on the local economy, and the value added to the economy by manufacturing. In all cases you will want the latest reliable data; recency of information is important.

Your entire analysis should be focused on the answer to the question: Which of the two towns is a better market for selling more of the specific merchandise this store sells? Population is, of course, a factor—size as well as distribution and character. The retail market area always needs examining. Income figures are significant (a person with $4 is in a better position to buy than one with only $2). Retail sales indicate whether people are willing to spend their money (total retail sales, per capita retail sales, and retail sales figures in the particular line you're investigating—if you can find them). Sources of business strength are appropriate considerations (a manufacturing town suffers more than a distribution center during a recession; a community depending primarily upon farming for its sustenance weathers economic storms more readily than one heavily dependent upon shipbuilding, for instance). And the current business picture (as measured by construction, postal figures, employment, and bank deposits) is always examined for its diagnostic value.

The list of topics above is merely to help you start thinking about what to include; it is not intended to be inclusive, orderly, or arbitrary. For instance, no study of this kind would ever omit competitive factors.

This is assigned: Exclude any discussion of banking facilities, communications facilities (newspapers, radio stations, advertising agencies), and transportation facilities. These are adequate in both cities and so would not affect the decision. But when you set out these limitations in the introductory section of the report, indicate in a footnote the sources where the reader can quickly and easily find the information if he wants to check it or tell him frankly that such data are not available if that is the case. Furthermore, the people would have done enough reading themselves to know where the cities are—and the pertinent geographical and climate features.

Although, as an intelligent approach to the analysis, you will want to do some background reading about the cities (in a good encyclopedia, possibly in a chamber of commerce release), *you will not use these sources as documentation (evidence) in your report.*

Once you've made the final decision of what factors to include and—just as important—the order in which to lay them out, the analysis becomes a matter of simply comparing the two cities simultaneously to show which city is the better market—more people with more money to spend, and the apparent willingness to spend it, especially for this kind of merchandise.

Do not attempt to turn out a chamber of commerce root-for-the-home team piece of propaganda. Impersonally, impartially present the facts about the two cities and make your decision on the total evidence.

An analytical report is not just a compilation of tables and labels. Your report must depend on the quotation of facts from other sources; these are incorporated primarily in the wealth of statistical display (graphics primarily, for readability). Without these, your report has no base and, in the reader's mind, no authenticity. But the most significant part of the report is your own expository (analytical) comment which explains the significance of the data you have gathered.

Of course, your report will be graded on physical appearance and mechanical correctness (freedom from errors in spelling, punctuation, and grammar). It will be graded most heavily, however, on

1. Organization (the order of points for logic and emphasis).
2. Readability (stylistic factors).
3. Complete, authentic evidence and its reliability and documentation.

3. Find a recent article giving facts about some significant new findings in your field. Assume that you did the research by assignment while employed by a firm which might well put the new findings to use. Write the research and findings in a report to your boss not only telling about research procedures and results but suggesting applications in the company's operations.

(If your course involves the writing of magazine articles for specialized journals—technical journalism—your instructor may want to make this modification of the assignment: Rewrite the original article with the original and the rewrite in parallel columns on the page; cross-match changes by notations in the two, like footnote numbers in the text and matching ones on the footnotes; and justify, by explanation, every change. The instructor may or may not want you to apply the Robert C. Gunning Fog Index and/or the Rudolf Flesch Readability Formula to both versions as a part of the justification for your changes.)

4. Using a random sample of 460 graduates of the college of business for the past eight years and getting 155 usable returned questionnaires, as assistant dean of the college you have tabulated the results as below. Now you are to present and interpret for the dean and the FEB (Faculty Executive Board) with suggested changes indicated by the findings.

1. Age at graduation

	Number	*Percent*
No response	5	3.2
Below 22	29	18.7
22–25	100	64.5
26–30	15	9.7
Above 30	6	3.8

2. Major area of study

	Number	*Percent*
No response	2	1.3
Accounting	22	14.2
Finance	18	11.6
Economics	0	0.0
Marketing	47	30.3
Industrial relations	9	5.8
Industrial management	15	9.7
Statistics	4	2.6
Business law	4	2.6
General business	34	21.9

3. First job after graduation

	Number	Percent	Current job Number	Current job Percent	
No response	2	1.3	4	2.6	
Accounting	20	12.9	18	11.6	
Military	21	13.5	16	10.3	
Government	10	6.5	11	7.1	
Administrative	15	9.7	8	5.2	
Sales	23	14.8	19	12.3	
Systems analysis and program	9	5.8	10	6.5	
Banking	10	6.5	11	7.1	
Insurance	6	3.9	7	4.5	
Marketing	21	13.5	28	18.1	
Real estate and securities	6	3.9	8	5.2	
Graduate school	4	2.6	7	4.5	
			3	1.9	Self-employed
Labor	7	4.5	2	1.3	
Other	1	0.6	3	1.9	

4. Kind of first employer

	Number	Percent	Present employer Number	Present employer Percent
No response	6	3.9	11	7.1
Contract construction	4	2.6	1	0.6
Manufacturing	33	21.3	33	21.3
Transportation, communication, utilities, sanitary services	10	6.5	8	5.2
Wholesale, retail	23	14.8	21	13.5
Financial, insurance, real estate	21	13.5	29	18.7
Services (including accounting)	29	18.7	29	18.7
Government, including military	28	18.1	22	14.2
Nonclassifiable	1	0.6	1	0.6

5. Location of first job

	Number	Percent	Of current job Number	Of current job Percent
No response	4	2.6	7	4.5
State of graduation	86	55.5	79	51.0
Same region, not state	40	25.8	35	22.6
Other	25	16.1	34	22.0

6. Number of employees at location of present job

	Number	Percent
No response	9	5.8
Fewer than 50	66	42.6
50–100	29	18.7
101–200	4	2.6
201–500	15	9.7
501–1,000	7	4.5
Over 1,000	25	16.1

7. Present annual gross salary (or income if not on salary)

	Number	Percent
No response	9	5.8
Less than $10,000	43	27.7

$10,000–12,500	49	31.6
$12,501–15,000	31	20.0
$15,001–17,500	12	7.7
$17,501–20,000	4	2.6
Above $20,000	7	4.5

8. Number of companies worked for since graduation

			Number of jobs held (all companies)	
	Number	*Percent*	*Number*	*Percent*
No response	7	4.5	12	7.7
1	101	65.2	54	34.8
2	32	20.6	30	23.2
3	9	5.8	35	22.6
4	5	3.2	11	7.1
5	1	0.6	3	1.9
6			2	1.3
7			1	0.6
8			1	0.6

9. Percentage ratings of core program elements on quality of instruction (*A*—good, *B*—fair, *C*—poor, *NO*—no opinion) and frequency of use of the information (*X*—frequently, *Y*—occasionally, *Z*—rarely, *NO*—no opinion)

	A	*B*	*C*	*NO*	*X*	*Y*	*Z*	*NO*
Principles of Accounting	34.2	50.3	9.0	6.5	45.2	33.5	16.1	5.2
Principles of Statistics	31.0	51.0	13.5	4.5	18.7	40.0	37.4	3.9
Principles of Business Law	47.7	39.4	5.8	7.1	29.0	43.2	21.9	5.8
Principles of Economics	23.9	52.3	17.4	6.5	21.9	40.0	32.9	5.2
Principles of Finance	25.8	48.4	19.4	6.5	39.4	44.5	11.6	4.5
Principles of Management	30.3	50.3	13.5	5.8	43.2	39.4	12.9	4.5
Principles of Marketing	36.1	46.5	9.0	8.4	27.9	42.6	23.9	5.8
Labor Economics	17.4	47.1	13.5	21.9	9.0	29.7	45.2	16.1
Business Communication	43.2	38.1	12.3	6.5	62.6	24.5	6.5	6.5
Report Writing	31.0	45.2	18.1	5.8	38.1	34.8	21.3	5.8

10. Percentage ratings of business administration program experiences (*A*—good, *B*—fair, *C*—poor, *NO*—no opinion)

	A	B	C	NO
The level of course difficulty	34.2	57.4	7.7	0.6
The depth of course coverage	24.5	65.8	7.1	2.6
Program fitness for first job	30.3	49.7	12.3	7.7
Program fitness for present job	31.0	47.1	11.0	11.0
The opportunity for general education	43.9	49.0	5.2	1.9
Preparation for further study and research	31.6	58.1	3.9	6.5
The way courses were presented	12.9	73.5	10.3	3.2
The variety of subjects covered	26.5	60.6	9.7	3.2
Availability of faculty for counseling	26.5	47.7	25.2	0.6
The teaching ability of the faculty	33.5	57.4	4.5	4.5
The faculty interest in the student	20.6	51.6	22.6	5.2
The number of credits required in business courses	23.9	67.7	5.2	3.2
The number of credits required in general education	21.3	61.3	11.6	5.8

5. (*Though the following case is about local golf-tournament facilities, a student may—with teacher approval—make the necessary adjustments and write a comparable report on local facilities for any other kind of athletic tournament, or about facilities for a business or professional meeting.*) For the American Golf Association, you are to prepare a report on the golf courses in your area, an early step toward getting a regional pro-am tournament in your area. Your report will not overtly "sell" the A.G.A. but should come up with an honest appraisal of the facilities available. You should consider courses within a 20- or 30-mile radius in your report, but restrict yourself to the number of courses you and your teacher agree you can reasonably inspect.

You will have to go to each golf course. Carefully look over the clubhouse, especially the restaurant or other food service facilities. How many people can they accommodate? At one time? Over a three-hour period? What about a bar? Room for desks and tables for registration, scorekeeping, and officials? A room that could be set up for a press room? Adequate parking spaces available? Area nearby that can be adapted for additional parking? Think of as many items to investigate and report on as you can. Try to imagine a tournament being staged at the course and what activities will take place and what will be needed for them at the clubhouse and clubhouse area.

Play the course if you can, but walk it in any case. Make a sketch of each hole showing tees, fairway, rough, bunkers (sand traps), tree and water hazards, and the greens. If you have watched coverage of golf tournaments on television, you will have an idea of the kind of simple maps of holes you should prepare. Get a scorecard for the course: This will give you the distances and pars, and usually a map of the course you can base yours on.

Through your own observation or interviews with golfers and course personnel, define the most difficult holes on the course. You should include sketches or maps of these in your report that are more detailed, perhaps, than those for less difficult holes.

Pay attention to the condition of the tees, greens, and fairways, especially the greens. If your library has a book on golf course design (there are several), it will give you a wealth of information and some excellent ideas of other things to look for.

Your personal research should result in a wealth of data from which you can describe the courses in your area. Even a single course can provide enough for a long report, if you go into a detailed analysis of it. On the basis of your investigation, recommend which course should hold the tournament, and which others would be suitable as back-up courses and practice courses.

6. (*Though the following case is on scouting a baseball team, teacher and student can agree to adapt it to any other kind of team.*) Assume that

you are a scout for any major-league baseball team and that your team faces any other team in an important game (or series). On the basis of a thorough analysis of the opposing team's and its individual players' past records, recommend specific tactics. You may assume that you scouted the opposing team many times and recorded individual and team records in detail. Since you didn't really, get your data wherever you can—next-day newspaper accounts, special baseball books, or the most recent *World Almanac* (which has a surprising amount of detail on baseball). Obviously, your report will be addressed to the manager. Would your players also read all of it or even the parts that most affect how they should play their positions? This report would not be attempted by anyone who doesn't know baseball well. And of course, it would be restricted information until after the game. (Incidentally, the idea for this assignment came from post-series newspaper accounts of just such a report prepared by the series winner and given credit by the manager for his team's winning. He admitted, however, that the players had a little to do with the win.)

7. Inspect the equipment and/or furniture in a laboratory on your campus where at least some of it needs to be replaced. Write a report which evaluates the equipment and/or furniture and specifically justifies and recommends any replacements and/or additions. To whom should you address the report? What role are you playing—i.e., who do you assume you *are* to be writing the report? What other sources of information will you use to supplement inspection? Should you recommend specific brands, models, and prices of things to be bought? If so, you will need to get acquainted with catalogs and brochures on such things—or with the famous Sweet's File, the architect's bible, available in any architect's office or architectural library.

(As a modification of the situation, write the report proposing and justifying just what equipment and/or furniture to buy for a new laboratory, a whole building, or some other new structure your school is now constructing.)

8. (Parts of this assignment probably should not be taken by a large class in a small community because too many students would be getting in too many businessmen's hair. This danger can be reduced, however, if students work in teams, at least on the data-collecting part of report writing. Also, consider the listed topics, which are *not* report titles, just suggestions to start thinking about what could be an endless list of the same kind of thing.)

For your choice of the following topics, assume that you can and will arrange amicably for access to, observation of, or experimentation with the obviously necessary facts (usually available only in a small local firm). Then write the kind of report (form, tone, and length) which the facts and the situation seem to require (or your instructor assigns). Assume that the appropriate person in the firm has asked you to do the report, and assume an appropriate position for yourself. In most cases you will likely be an employee; but in some, you might reasonably assume that you are a consultant on a fee basis. Each situation is to involve thorough study of existing conditions and application of well-established, up-to-date principles leading to recommendations for betterment of the situation.

—The letter writing done by a small local firm (only students who have studied letter writing should attempt this assignment).
—The public relations of a local firm (limited parts, if necessary).
—The accounting procedures of a local firm (limited aspects, if necessary).
—The advertising program and budget (not copy) of a small local firm.
—The advertising copy (not program and budget) used by a local firm.
—The physical layout (floor plan) of a local store (same problem a housewife works on when she moves the furniture around).
—The hiring and firing and promoting criteria (or just one criterion) and procedures.
—The financing arrangements of . . . .
—The stock control procedures . . . .
—The fringe benefits (or just one) or salary scales of . . . .
—The materials-handling procedures of . . . .
—Pilferage control in . . . .
—A motion-time study of some local processing or manufacturing operation.
—Any other problem of this type which you think of and can get facts on, and which your instructor approves.
—Proposed equipment and procedures for fire prevention and fighting in a certain forest.
—Should a given wood products company devote some of its lands to producing hardwoods?
—Solution to the problem of poor growth and fruiting/flowering of certain plants on a large lot.
—Critical analysis (with suggestions) of the company publications of a comparatively small local firm.
—Possible computer applications in a local library (or company).
—Suggestions for improving appeal and income at a small fee-charging, publicly operated park and lake.
—Would a proposed campground (private, specific location) be a successful business venture?
—Analysis of a local company's employee relations problems, with suggestions for improvement.
—Would a specific large wood products company be wise to set up a sawmill and/or paper mill in a certain locality where it has some landholdings?
—To have or not to have coffee breaks for a given company's employees.
—What the people of a 10,000–100,000 community think of their public schools, with emphasis on suggested improvements.

9. Obtain a copy of the "Business Publications" edition of *Standard Rate and Data Service.* If your library does not have this monthly publication, see if you can get an out-of-date copy from a local advertising agency, or write to Standard Rate and Data Service, Inc., 5201 Old Orchard Road, Skokie, Illinois 60076, for the price on a single copy.

SRDS "Business Publications" lists just about every trade magazine or business publication published in this country, and a good number of foreign ones. Each listing contains a wealth of information about the magazine, including advertising rates, mechanical requirements, editorial policy, circulation, and so forth. Also, many magazines place advertisements in the directory, with further information for potential advertisers.

Choose one of the larger categories, such as "Metalworking" or "Electronics" or "Chemicals." Choose a product common to the field you will work in (lathes for "Metalworking," for instance, testing instruments for "Electronics," or protective clothing for "Chemicals") and assume you work for the advertising agency serving that manufacturer.

Completely analyze the magazines in the category you are working in, on as many points as you can. The listings are comparable, so this is fairly easy. Determine which magazines are the leaders, which are second-best, and which are specialized and not directly comparable to the more general magazines in the field. On the basis of your exhaustive analysis, recommend which eight magazines your client should advertise in, and why. Justify rejecting at least four others.

For an idea of what goes into a media report like this one, check for textbooks and other books and articles on media selection in your library. An interview with a local advertising agency executive or company advertising manager would be very helpful, as would be an interview with an appropriate professor or two.

(By teacher and student agreement, the size of this project can be controlled by limiting the number of publications to be reported on. To enlarge it, say for a group to handle, consider also using SRDS publications on radio and television stations and consumer publications, and preparing a full-scale media plan using a variety of media.)

10. The president of the small company where you work, Marvin Day, is the twin brother of Morton Day (Case 10, p. 572) and is facing the same kind of labor unrest. Hearing from Brother Morton about how his new IRA plan has calmed his workers down, and having read an article that says a Keough plan is sometimes better, Marvin asks you to compare the two for possible use in his company. Take a small real company about which you can get information, assume that Marvin gives you a deadline (the due date your teacher assigns you), and write the complete analytical report your president wants.

chapter 16 Writing short reports

Letter reports
Memorandums
Justification reports
Progress reports
Credit reports
Annual reports
Short analytical reports

THE BEST FORM for a report depends on the situation—mainly who its reader is, its purpose, and its length. This chapter explains and illustrates various kinds of short reports written in the most important forms.

Like all reports, short ones can be classified on various bases. In the case of short reports, the two most common are form and content. To avoid making up new names for short reports, in this chapter we list and discuss them by their common names, although this plan does not provide a strictly logical classification.

Because reports apparently named for their content have become pretty well associated with certain forms, however, the seeming violation of logic in classification is more apparent than real. The primary basis of classification here is therefore form (with the exceptions explained where they apply). Yet the primary emphasis is not on learning the forms themselves but on the uses of different forms and the information, organization, interpretation, and style in the reports.

The illustrations are **not** *presented as perfect reports, and certainly are* **not** *to be followed slavishly or copied parrotlike. At best, they show acceptable content, form, and general style for their particular situations as starters to your thinking on these points for your situation.*

Although we recognize that strictly informational, periodic reports are the most numerous kind, we do not devote our main attention to them because they are mostly printed forms to be filled in with figures and perhaps a little other writing. We therefore treat the commonly used forms which do raise real report-writing problems.

Letter reports

Many short reports, usually one to four pages, are written in regular business letter form. Usually they go between organizations rather than between departments of the same organization, where memorandum form is more likely.

Since the letter report is likely to be longer than the usual letter, however, and since it *is* a report, it may take on the following special features of reports, while otherwise using the form explained in Chapter 4:

1. More than usually careful organization.
2. Objectivity (absence of emotional suasion, viewing both sides of the situation, enough interweaving or implying of methods and sources to assure soundness).
3. Use of appropriate subject lines, subheads, and itemizations where helpful.
4. Use of graphic devices where helpful and economically feasible.

Depending on whether the message will likely meet with reader approval, disappointment, or resistance, the letter report should follow the A–, B–, or (rarely) C–plan, as explained on pp. 36–40 and illustrated thoroughly in Chapters 5, 7, and 8, respectively. More specifically, any of the organizational plans discussed on pp. 469–70 may apply to a letter report.

Although a letter report, like any other, needs to convince the reader that its facts are reliable, it rarely needs a separate section or even a separate paragraph explaining authorization, purpose, methods and sources used in collecting data. Most likely the writer got the assignment because the boss knew that person had the information immediately available. In other words, the writer was already recognized as an expert on the subject. If not, the boss may have said just how to study the problem. Or for the simple problems appropriate to letter reports, the methods and sources are frequently so obvious as to need no explanation.

If any explanations are necessary, usually the best way to give them is in incidental phrases interwoven right along with the information: ". . . seems to be the best solution to our problem of . . ."; "Inspection of . . . reveals . . ."; "Legal precedent in cases like . . . is clearly . . ."; "Microscopic examination shows . . ."; or ". . . , according to such authorities as. . . ."

Indeed, letter reports are like other reports except for the form which gives them their name, the limits of length and hence of topics for which they are suitable, and their usually more familiar style. A letter in impersonal style would be almost a joke. We do not think any kind of report should necessarily be in impersonal style, and even those people who do will almost certainly approve a natural style in letter reports.

Two common types of letter reports are those about job and credit applicants (personnel and credit reports), already discussed on pp. 104 and 105–7, respectively. You should study both the explanations and the illustrations. Notice that both the illustrations use subject lines effectively. Note, too, that both begin immediately with important information because they face no problem of reader disappointment or resistance.

Personnel and credit reports, however, do have the legal problem of avoiding libel suit by referring to the request for information, trying to be fair to both parties, and asking confidential use of the information. Notice how the two illustrations handle that problem.

These two kinds of reports should be informational, in that they should rely on facts and subordinate or entirely eliminate unsupported opinions —and certainly recommendations. But letter reports may be either informational or analytical. In some cases they are more nearly directives than reports, but directives are more likely to be in memo form.

Because the following message is somewhat bad news and the reader may be reluctant to take the suggested action, the report uses the more convincing inductive rather than the faster-moving deductive plan. You will note, too, that it uses no subject line. To do so would defeat the psychological purpose of the inductive plan. As you always should when you have a step-by-step procedure or a series of pointed, emphatic principles, qualities, conclusions, or recommendations to convey, this report uses itemization effectively at the end.

Dear Mr. Rogers:

In our audit of your company's books on January 16, we discovered that for years the total net profit has been added to surplus.

This procedure is usually correct. For the past three years you have had a bond agreement, however, which specifies that a sinking-fund reserve of 3 percent of the par value of the bonds must be set up annually out of surplus. That agreement is legally binding. Moreover, state law requires you to set up the reserve in this situation. The remaining profit, of course, can be added to surplus.

Laws of this type protect investors and brokers who desire a true picture of the financial condition of companies.

The laws also give you protection. Setting up a separate reserve prevents the unlawful declaration of dividends by directors. In other words, the proper presentation of surplus figures is an aid to better management.

We therefore recommend that you

1. Take immediate steps to set up the reserve.
2. Transfer to it now, from surplus, 3 percent of the par value of the bonds for each of the past three years.
3. Regularly each year for the duration of the bond agreement transfer the required amount from surplus to the reserve.

Both the shortness and the nature of the material made divisional headings useless in the preceding illustration. Conversely, both length and content make headings almost mandatory for effective presentation in letter reports of two pages or more, as in the following. It is a reply to a school superintendent's request that recent graduates report on their college expenses for passing on to high-school seniors. (You'll notice that the way of life pictured is not common on college campuses today, but that does not keep the report from showing the helpfulness of carefully classifying information under suitable headings.)

Dear Mr. Loudenslager:

I certainly was glad to receive your letter of January 20. It is nice to know that John is not finding school as hard as he thought it was going to be.

Here is the information you requested. These costs are based on one semester here for the male student. Although I have not kept detailed records, my figures are more realistic than the somewhat outdated ones in the catalog you have.

Being neither plush nor poor, I have spent according to the Typical column, but I have classmates whose expenses more nearly match both the Liberal and the Conservative figures.

Estimated Expenses Table

	Conservative	Typical	Liberal
Course fee	$000	$000	$000
Room and board	000	000	000
Books and supplies	00	00	00
Physical education	00	00	00
R.O.T.C.	00	00	00
Clothing	00	00	00
Laundry and dry cleaning	00	00	00
Transportation	00	00	000
Incidentals	00	00	000

FIXED EXPENSES

Course fee.—Although the regular course fee is $000, certain courses and curricula like music, law, medicine, and veterinary medicine do require extra fees. Insofar as I know, these extra fees have not changed from the catalog you have.

Physical Education.—All students are required to take two years' credit in gym. The $10 fee is for the first semester only.

R.O.T.C.—All able-bodied male students are required to take two years' credit in military science. The fee will be refunded when the equipment is returned after completion of the course.

VARIABLE EXPENSES

Living Expense

College residence halls.—Adequate dormitories are available on the campus. Meals are served in the dining rooms seven days a week. Room and board is $000 a semester. The resident is required to supply linen, toweling, and pillow.

Fraternities.—Room and board in a fraternity may vary from a low of $000 to a high of $000. The average is about $000.

Cooperatives.—If a student desires, he may join a co-op, in which a group may defray part of the cost of living by all helping with the work. Room and board in a co-op usually runs to about $000 a semester.

Individual rooms.—Rooms in approved homes cost about $00–$00 a semester, two men to a room. Food in local restaurants costs about $000–$000. Only graduate students and married students are allowed to have apartments.

Apartments.—Rent for an apartment will run from $00 for the most modest to $000 depending upon whether the student shares it or occupies it alone. Utilities are usually extra and are not included here.

Working for meals.—Male students who want to do so can nearly always find jobs working for their meals in dormitory dining rooms or in local restaurants.

Clothing.—Some students who attend college are forced to buy nearly entirely new wardrobes. Others may get along quite well for some time with what they have. So clothing expense is highly variable, as my figures in the table show. For most students, college clothing costs should be only a little more than for high school clothing.

Laundry and dry cleaning.—Facilities are available for the student to do his own laundry in the dormitories. Several laundromats are also convenient to the area. Dry-cleaning prices are the same as at home. Again, an individual can spend as much or as little as he chooses.

Transportation

At school.—The majority of the activities are located on the campus within walking distance. Bus fare to town is 30 cents a round trip. Taxis are also available. The student who expects to have his own car will find that a jalopy is not the thing here and that keeping a respectable car can hardly cost less than $000 a semester. Depreciation alone could cost that much without anything for insurance, upkeep, and gasoline.

To and from school.—Most students will find it inconvenient as well as expensive to go home more than twice a semester. The round-trip bus fare, the cheapest way, is $00.00.

Incidentals

Necessities.—Students need a small amount of money to spend while out with a group for coffee, cokes, shows, and the like. Also, there is the ever-present emergency of haircuts, shoestrings, razor blades, toothpaste, etc. Normally one may expect to spend $000 a semester on such things.

Dating.—Taking a girl out for an evening can cost a lot of money, or it can be done fairly inexpensively. Some of the larger dances can cost up to $00 for the evening. The item is highly flexible.

```
If anyone in this year's high-school senior class has any
specific questions about this school, I'll try to answer
as best I can.  One thing you can safely tell all who
are thinking about coming here:  They had better learn to
write correctly and to handle simple math, or they will
be in trouble.
```

Except for Item 1 (on form), the checklist for memos on page 538 applies equally to memo and letter reports.

Memorandums

Just as letter reports are more likely for communicating between organizations, memorandums are more appropriate within an organization. Among the supplies of almost any well-run office are printed memo forms (usually half sheets 5½ by 8½ inches turned either way). The printed headings used in the illustrations of memorandums in this section show the main variations (see pp. 534 and 537). Item 1 of the checklist for memos (p. 538) gives further details of form.

Except for the differences in form and use, memorandums follow the instructions already given for letter reports. They are, however, inclined (1) to be ephemeral and hence less formal (often being handwritten without carbon), (2) to make even greater use of itemization (almost characteristically), and (3) to become directives going down the chain of command.

One of the most common and effective techniques is itemization. Numbering each paragraph almost forces the writer into careful organization, precise statement, and conciseness.

Two simple memos showing slightly different forms follow:

January 12, 197–

TO: All Occupants of Business Administration Building, Journalism Building, University College Building, Forestry Building

FROM: R. F. Noonan, Building and Utilities Department

SUBJECT: Interruption of Electrical Service

The electricity will be off in your buildings on Tuesday, January 13, from 8 a.m. to 4 p.m.

Temporary electric service will be provided for lights in main departmental offices only.

All electricity will be off for approximately one-half hour from 8 to 8:30 a.m. and 4 to 4:30 p.m. for connection and removal of the temporary service.

Notice these details in the two memos: One is on an ephemeral topic to one reader; so efficiency pointed to a quick, handwritten memo. The other went to a number of people; so it was a Ditto form. Since some of

UNIVERSITY OF FLORIDA

DATE Jan. 20

MEMO TO: Andrea

FROM: CWW

SUBJECT: Work for today

Since I have an appointment downtown during your working hours, please

1) record the grades of the attached papers in my grade book.

2) check the revised class lists against my rolls and return the lists to the Registrar with proper notations.

3) get the Congressional Record, vol. 88, Part 9, from the Library and copy Congressman Hill's comments on p. A-1486, and

4) make a table showing percentages, by class and major, of students on the E#255 lecture lists (both lists in one table).

its readers would not have known who the writer was, he gave his official title. The other writer would have wasted time even to write out his full name. The subject lines in both are carefully phrased to indicate the content concisely and are underscored to make them stand out. Since itemization seemed helpful in one but would have served no purpose in the other, the writers used it accordingly. Neither needs the kind of authenticating signature a bank requires on your check. Where that is necessary, the usual practice is for the writer to initial by the name in the "From" line.

Probably the biggest user of memos is the biggest business in the world —the United States government. It has its own forms and its own directions for using them, as illustrated and applied in this memo directive (reprinted from *Secretarial Handbook,* Tennessee Valley Authority, rev. ed., 1960, pp. II–10*a,* II–10*c*):

TVA 64 (OS.4.59)
United States Government
MEMORANDUM TENNESSEE VALLEY AUTHORITY

TO : Maybelle Campbell,
Reproduction and Stenographic Unit, 421 Wall Avenue, Knoxville (2)

FROM : Carl Angle, Office Methods Staff, 619 LB, Chattanooga

DATE : June 15, 1960

SUBJECT: STYLE FOR INTEROFFICE MEMORANDUMS

Attention: Yetta Konigsberg

This is an illustration of the office memorandum. Its use is described in the enclosed copy of the Secretarial Handbook. A style sheet for the half-size memorandum is also enclosed.

The items in the heading begin two spaces from the preceding colons, and the body of the memorandum uses the left margin established by the placement of the heading. The right margin should be at least one inch but not more than one and one-half inches.

If two lines are necessary in the "To" or "From" line, the second line is indented two spaces and the break is made between units of the address. But the line should be extended into the margin if that will avoid two lines.

Titles of courtesy, Mr., Mrs., and Miss, are omitted before the names in the heading, but professional titles such as Dr. are used. Job titles are not used when the organization unit provides a satisfactory address. The "To" and "From" lines should be parallel in content. No punctuation is used at the ends of the lines in the heading.

The text begins on the fourth line below the subject. (If additional space is needed on the half-size memorandum, begin on the second line below the subject.) When an attention line is used, it is typed on the fourth line below the subject, with no end punctuation, and the text begins two lines below the attention line.

Block style is used for memorandums; that is, paragraphs are not indented. Single spacing is used within the paragraphs, double spacing between them. If headings are used in a memorandum (as for a progress report), side headings and paragraph headings begin at the left margin. If numbered paragraphs or items appear in the memorandum:

1. The first line begins at the left margin. (Note that in indented style, as for formal reports, the first line—the number—is indented five spaces.)

2. Additional lines are aligned with the first word in the paragraph, as shown in this sample.

2

Maybelle Campbell
June 15, 1960

STYLE FOR INTEROFFICE MEMORANDUMS

This page illustrates the setup for the second and succeeding pages of a memorandum. Each page after the first is numbered with an Arabic numeral on the fourth line from the top of the page, flush with the left margin. The addressee's name is typed two lines below the page number, and the date immediately below the name. The subject is typed two lines below the date, and the text begins on the fourth line below the subject.

No complimentary close is used. No signature line is used since the signer's name appears on the "From" line and his initials or signature in the blank space below the text is sufficient. But if the signer requires a line, it is typed on the fourth line below the text, with the name under the line.

The attachments are identified in the memorandum; therefore, they are not listed in the attachment notation, but the word Attachments is followed by 2 to show how many pieces of material are attached.

Carbon copies of this memo are to go to Billie Burt and Lucy Somerville. Their names appear in alphabetic order. The address must be given for each person listed.

The word Attachments in parentheses after the name and address indicates that attachments (the same as those sent with the original memorandum) are being sent to Mrs. Burt with her copy of the memo. Two copies of the memo without the attachments are being sent to Miss Somerville, as indicated by the number in parentheses following the name. If an extra copy is being sent to the addressee, (2) is typed at the end of the "To" line.

1

2 JF:DG
3 Attachments: 2
3 CC: Billie Burt, 115 AB, Wilson Dam (Attachments)
Lucy Somerville, 1108 Market, Chattanooga (2)

We have given you the TVA report merely to show one widely used form of memos, not to suggest that you adopt it or its rather stiff, heavily passive style. Almost any large organization is likely to establish its own simpler form and style.

The following memo on a company's printed form shows a more usual layout, typical A–plan, and a typical problem:

OFFICE MEMORANDUM—Acme Insurance Company

Date : 2/10/72
To : Mr. J. G. DeWolfe
From : R. R. Fortune
Subject: HOW TO REDUCE ABSENTEEISM CAUSED BY RESPIRATORY DISEASES

1. Conclusion.—Our recent high rate of absenteeism seems to be a result of too low humidity. Absentees reported colds or other respiratory diseases as the causes in 73 percent of the cases.

2. Humidity in relation to respiratory diseases.—According to the U.S. Public Health Service, the higher the humidity in buildings the lower the rate of respiratory diseases. You can see this relationship in Figure 1 on the attached pages. The explanation is that a high humidity prevents excessive cooling from evaporation of skin moisture.

3. Desirable humidity-temperature relationships.—Although our 70 degrees is considered the best temperature, it isn't warm enough for most people unless the humidity is about 40. Ours is 20. As Figure 2 of the USPHS study shows, a humidity above 50 makes most people feel clammy and below 30 causes them to feel a dryness in their noses and throats.

4. Recommended corrective steps.—To reduce absenteeism, improve the health of our personnel, and enhance employee relations, I suggest the following:

   a) Raise the humidity to 40 by making a pan with the necessary evaporation surface for each radiator (to be concealed from view by the radiator covers).

   b) Assign the janitors the job of keeping water in the pans.

   c) Purchase one temperature-humidity guide for each office. Besides providing a constant check on room conditions, these meters will remind the employees that you have done something about their comfort and health.

   Prices range from $2 to $200. The cheapest ones are likely to be inaccurate; but the Wechsler at $4.50 carries the recommendation of Consumer Reports. It looks like a small clock with two red hands pointing to temperature and humidity scales. Hardware, department, mail-order, and specialty stores carry it in varied colors to fit the decor of any office.

Checklist for Memos

1. Form:
   a) Use a neatly arranged heading, including at least the company name (usually in capitals); some wording like Memo, Memorandum, or Interoffice Communication; and a dateline.
   b) Begin To, From, and Subject at the left; preferably, double-space between them; and use colons right after each or align all the colons with the one after Subject. In either case, align the beginnings of what you fill in after the colons.
   c) Use courtesy titles (Mr., Ms., Mrs., Miss) with the names of others (but not yours) if you would in talking with them; do not use official titles unless some readers might not know them.
   d) For emphasis, underscore or capitalize subject lines. End-of-line periods are unnecessary, even undesirable.
   e) Single-space within paragraphs and double-space between.
   f) Use itemizations, headings, tables, and charts where helpful.
   g) For pages after the first, put at least the addressee's name, the date, and the page number on the first line and triple-space below it.
   h) Use no salutation, complimentary close, or typed name of writer at the end; sign only nonroutine memos requiring authentication, unless your firm's practice is otherwise.
   i) When used, file and other references may go under a flush-right date or to the right of the To-From-Subject block. (Carbon-copy lists more commonly appear at the end instead.)
2. Organization and coverage:
   a) Bring in your main point (whether it is a request, conclusion, recommendation, or something else) in the first sentence unless your reader might resist; if so, lead up to it with whatever facts, reasons, or explanations are necessary to convince—especially any reader benefits you can point out.
   b) Be sure to make clear that your information is valid and pertinent by showing what the problem is and how you got your information to solve it; but see 3(b).
   c) Effective dates (for directives)—and when necessary, other time limits, places, and people concerned—are important points.
   d) Consider whether you should mention alternatives to your recommendation.
   e) Should you explain more specifically how to carry out your proposal?
   f) Be sure you have covered all points your reader will need or want covered—especially all steps in your logic.
   g) Check your sequence for coherence, logic, and psychological effect (A–, B–, or C–plan).

Checklist for Memos

(continued)

3. Style:
   a) Make the subject line indicate the content accurately and specifically.
   b) Emphasize the important and avoid undue emphasis on the unimportant. What you found out and the likely effect are more important than how you found out or from whom; so for 2(b), usually you should just imply or interweave in incidental phrases the necessary but unknown parts of purpose and method of the report. Usually the reader will already know the purpose; and if not, it and your method of getting information are usually implied in stating the facts you got. "Sixty-two percent of your employees favor a company snack bar" indicates both the problem and the survey method.
   c) Be sure your terminology, sentence length and structure, and paragraph length and structure make for quick, clear, easy reading. Short words, sentences, and paragraphs usually help; itemizations and tabulations may help further.
   d) Display really significant data, conclusions, and recommendations by such means as increasing white space, decreasing line length, itemizing, and tabulating.
   e) For coherence (and often for conciseness), precede displayed items with an appropriate introductory statement.
   f) Don't develop a fever (with numerous strong adjectives and adverbs, for example).
4. Tone:
   a) Soften commands for acceptable tone; sharp imperatives rankle even in directives. "You will . . ." is too commanding for most situations. Four directives from which you can usually select an appropriate one are (in descending order of sharpness): "Please . . . ," "Will you . . . ," "I ask that you . . . ," and "I would appreciate your. . . ." "If you will . . ." is usually too weak.
   b) Phrase recommendations for acceptable tone (depending on the reader-writer relationship and the firmness of your conviction): "You must . . . ," "I recommend . . . ," "I suggest . . ."; "The only way . . . ," "The best solution is . . . ," and "Probably the wise decision is . . . ."
   c) Accusations are always objectionable.
   d) Positive is better than negative phrasing.
   e) Item 2(a) is an important factor in tone.
   f) Consider whether to write impersonally or (usually better) naturally ("Employees will receive their checks . . ." or "You will receive your checks . . .").

Justification reports

Another kind of short report often using memo form has its own special name. Of course, any analytical report could be called a justification report because it draws conclusions (and makes recommendations if wanted) and presents facts to justify them. But as used in report writing, the justification report is a special kind.

Almost invariably it is an initiating report in which the writer makes an original proposal, rather than a requested study, although it may well be the requested full write-up of a suggestion that has been dropped in a suggestion box.

It is deductive (A–plan) presentation that gives the recommendation immediately, followed by concise statements of the most important considerations and conclusions, before giving detailed explanations and supporting facts. Thus it *quickly* gives all a busy reader needs to know *if the writer is trusted.* Probably this point is the main reason for the increasing popularity of the justification report among executives. But if the reader wants to read the whole explanation, the plan is still good. The reader can follow the details better by having already read the conclusions and recommendations—that is, what the details lead to.

You will provide good organization and coverage if you set up the five standard headings and do the following in this order:

1. State the purpose in one sentence. The first part, in phrase or dependent-clause structure, should mention a benefit. The second part should be the recommendation in an independent clause.
2. State the cost and saving in no more than two sentences. Don't delay the fast movement by explaining.
3. In a third part called "Procedure" or "Method of Installation," cover concisely such things as necessary space, personnel, training, special materials, time, restrictions (rules, regulations), and interruptions of work. Usually one to three sentences will do.
4. Itemize the conclusions, state them pointedly, and keep them to the minimum number that will cover all aspects. One of them has to be on cost and saving. One commonly overlooked is the goodwill of all people concerned. They are not always all benefits; some may point the other way.
5. In a discussion section (sometimes called "Discussion of Conclusions" or "Explanation of Advantages"), give all the details supporting the statements already made. Usually they should be itemized to match the itemized conclusions. Interweave into your explanations enough of your methods to answer the reader's question: "How do you know?" This applies particularly to your method of figuring cost and saving.

The following typical example illustrates both plan and technique:

HOW MECHANICAL PENCILS WOULD SAVE MONEY FOR MORGAN COMPANY

Purpose.—To save the Morgan Company more than $200 in pencil expense each year, I recommend that we purchase mechanical pencils instead of wooden ones for use by employees.

Cost and Savings.—A year's supply of mechanical pencils and refills would cost about $457 as compared with more than $685 for wooden pencils—a yearly saving of well over $200.

Procedure.—A dependable automatic pencil manufacturer—Ray & Company, Rome, Georgia—would supply the yearly need of about 750 pencils with the Morgan name on them at the quantity-discounted price of 40 cents each. The stockroom clerk could distribute them as he does the wooden pencils, and maintain records for control.

Conclusions.—The Morgan Company would enjoy four advantages by using mechanical pencils instead of the present wooden ones:

1. We would save at least $225 a year.
2. The stockroom clerk would have fewer pencils to store and issue—750 as compared with over 13,000.
3. Employees would be more careful about misplacing them.
4. Mechanical pencils stay sharp and thus provide uniform, neat writing without loss of time and patience at the pencil sharpener.

Discussion of Conclusions.—

1. During the past three years pencils have cost us about $1.80 a year per employee, as shown by the following calculations:

	19—	19—	19—	Average
Pencil costs	$ 765	$ 554	$ 731	$ 684
Employees	450	298	395	381
Cost per employee ...	1.70	1.86	1.85	1.80

Converting to mechanical pencils would require, for each employee, an estimated two pencils (at 40 cents each) and 40 cents worth of lead and eraser refills, for a total annual cost of $1.20 per employee.

Cost comparison shows a saving of $228.60 with mechanical pencils:

Cost of wooden pencils, 381 employees, @ $1.80	$685.80
Cost of mechanical pencils, 381 employees, @ $1.20 ..	457.20
Saving	$228.60

2. In the past three years, the clerk in the stockroom has had to allot space for about 1,104 dozen, or 13,248, pencils. Also he has had to take the time (considerable in the aggregate) to distribute each one. With only 762 pencils to store and issue, he could use the relieved space and time for other things.

3. Since mechanical pencils are more valuable and more conspicuous (especially with the Morgan name on them) than wooden ones, I believe employees would be more careful about carrying them home and not bringing them back. Also, if employees had to sign a receipt—which is more feasible with the fewer mechanical pencils—misplacements would occur less frequently. Those misplaced might be worth at least a part of their cost as advertising.

4. The mechanical pencil needs no sharpening and writes with the same neat uniformity throughout its use, instead of becoming blunt and less neat progressively. Moreover, mechanical pencils would avoid the interruptions to thinking and work when employees take their wooden ones to the pencil sharpener (which often annoys by breaking the lead or needing to be emptied).

You might well notice several specifies about the preceding report. The writer who *initiated* this idea—usual for this kind of report—moves fast in presenting the basic idea and facts. The boss, if trusting the reporter, may approve after reading less than the first half; but simply reading further provides details if wanted. The clear, concise, and prominent (by underlining) but easily typed heads serve as guideposts to the reader. And the matched pair of itemizations helps the reader relate pointed conclusions with supporting facts and explanations. The inevitable repetition of cost and saving is justified by deserved emphasis—you make such proposals because benefits outweigh costs (neither of which always has to be in dollars and cents). Perhaps most important of all, notice how the writer *concisely but subordinately interwove* only enough methodology to answer the reader's question: "How do you know?" But the writer wasted no words about tracking down former pencil costs. The answer is obvious.

Although the form of justification reports is commonly memo, it may be letter or some other such as that illustrated. A title page like that of the complete analytical report may precede the form illustrated. If so, the title would be on both pages. In letter or memo form the title would serve as the subject line. Of course, the five division heads may be centered heads or sideheads above the text if you prefer. If you use memo form, Item 1 of the checklist for memos (p. 538) will apply. In any form you can use items 1–5 on page 540 as the subheads under Item 2 of that checklist and have a good checklist for justification reports.

Progress reports

As the name suggests, the progress report is an interim report of how you are getting along on a project. It may be a single, special report or one in a series of required periodic reports. (In the series the last one is called the *completion* report.) As a periodic report, a progress report is usually strictly informational. A special progress report is likely to be analytical, because of the special problem that caused it to be written.

The general purpose of a progress report is to keep the top management informed so that it can act wisely. An owner may want to consider whether to continue as planned, change the plan or methods, or drop the project. A contractor may need to consider such questions as when to order certain materials, whether to increase the people and equipment assigned to the job, and whether to bid on another job.

Basic contents of a progress report are the answers to three questions:

1. Whether the project is on schedule.
2. If the project is not on schedule, why not?
3. What will be done next and what the plans and prospects are for completion on schedule.

Although neither those nor the following are necessarily the subdivision headings, a progress report may cover any or all of the purpose and nature of the project (usually the reader already knows), what has been done, present status, what is now being done, plans and outlook for the future, and unexpected developments. The last may be of major importance if the report is designed to get a decision on a problem that has arisen. In series, each progress report summarizes former work reported but stresses developments since the preceding report. Progress reports on research projects may or may not include tentative findings and conclusions—depending on the writer's confidence in them and the immediate need for them.

No single plan is always best for a progress report. What is best depends upon the whole situation, especially the content, deserved relative emphasis of parts, and the attitudes and wishes of the reader.

One thing can be said: Preferably all the reports in a series should follow the same plan. It may be topical by divisions of the subject (supervision, equipment, materials, and labor; or steps, phases, or divisions of the job); or it may be chronological (by days, weeks, or months; or past, present, and future). One simple plan calls for

1. The transitional elements of background and summary of already reported work.
2. The body giving the details of recent progress.
3. The prophetic or future prospects.

A more specific but somewhat flexible plan is

1. Quick introduction (purpose and nature of the project, unless known; summary of work to date; status, including any significant results).
2. More detailed résumé of earlier progress reported, if any.
3. New progress (work done, methods and personnel, obstacles and what you've done about them) in relation to schedule.
4. Realistic forecast (plans in relation to schedule, and recommendations or requests, if any).

More important than *what* plan, in most cases, is that you have *a* plan—a unifying thread to hang your beads on.

Like the plan, the form of progress reports may vary with the circumstances. Short ones usually are in memo or letter form, longer ones in some adaptation of complete report form.

Since the form, plan, and content of progress reports vary so much and we cannot well illustrate all the possibilities, we think we can help most by illustrating some common weaknesses in progress reports: (1) having nothing to say but trying to pretend that you do, (2) using pompous jargon to cover up, and (3) being nonspecific. The following illustration properly lampoons the main weaknesses.

STANDARD PROGRESS REPORT FOR THOSE WITH NO PROGRESS TO REPORT

During the report period which ends (fill in appropriate date) considerable progress has been made in the preliminary work directed toward the establishment of the initial activities. (Meaning: We are getting ready to start, but we haven't done anything yet.) The background information has been surveyed and the functional structure of the component parts of the cognizant organization has been clarified. (We looked at the assignment and decided that George should do it.)

Considerable difficulty has been encountered in the selection of optimum materials and experimental methods, but this problem is being attacked vigorously and we expect that the development phase will proceed at a satisfactory rate. (George is looking through the handbook.) In order to prevent unnecessary duplication of previous efforts in the same field, it was necessary to establish a survey team which has conducted a rather extensive tour through various facilities in the immediate vicinity of manufacture. (George and Harry had a nice time in New York last week.)

The Steering Committee held its regular meeting and considered rather important policy matters pertaining to the over-all organizational levels of the line and staff responsibilities that devolve on the personnel associated with the specific assignments resulting from the broad functional specifications. (Untranslatable—sorry.) It is believed that the rate of progress will continue to accelerate as necessary personnel are recruited to fill vacant billets. (We'll get some work done as soon as we find someone who knows something.)[1]

The following progress reporters did much better, as a writer usually does on having something to say to somebody for some purpose. Especially if all goes well, as in the first, the report is easy to write. (All these writers used memo form; we'll begin with the subject line.)

SUBJECT: Monthly Progress Report No. 2 on Orangeville Expressway

Present status

1. Work on the 10.8-mile section of expressway running south to Brownville is on schedule. The final surface is 80 percent complete. We have had no delays during the past month and have regained the two days formerly lost and reported.

2. The 18.4-mile section of expressway running north to Malden remains approximately two weeks behind schedule. The right of way has been cleared all the way to Malden, and the roadbed is completed along the first 8.6 miles north of Orangeville.

[1] So widely reprinted in the literature of report writing as to be in the public domain—like many jokes.

3. The overpass for U.S. 1 was completed on December 14, 18 days ahead of schedule.

Expected progress

1. During January the southern link to Brownville should be completed except for the drainage preparation and the approaches. Work on them will most likely have to be fitted in between rains normally expected at this time of year in this area, especially in the valley of Hogtown Creek. Present progress and normal weather expectations suggest that this link will be ready for traffic just before the completion deadline of March 3.

2. During this month the roadbed will be extended along the north section to Malden. The first layer of tar will also be completed along a strip about 5 miles long, beginning at Orangeville and extending north. Additional men are being hired to insure completion of this section before the deadline of June 24.

Sometimes progress reporters must explain their difficulties to defend themselves and to justify requests, as in the following:

SUBJECT: Special Report on Interlocking Plant Installation

Because of a shortage of track cable, I would like to have your permission to advance cutover day to at least January 18. The installation is now about 88 percent complete, as shown by the broken line on the following graph [omitted here] comparing the predicted work schedule and the actual schedule.

If the track cable ordered December 1 arrives within the next few days as promised two weeks ago, and if we have good weather, the future work schedule should appear as the dotted projection line. This points to 100 percent completion on January 18.

Since progress reports often deal with technical work, you need not be surprised if you fail to understand some things in some of them. If you have trouble with the following, for example, remember that it was not written for you but by one technical man to another, who understood perfectly. This report also illustrates a not unusual organization around topics rather than time, while the time sequence and relation to schedule are still clear.

SUBJECT: Progress on Prototype Power Supply for Collins (Job 280)

At the end of three weeks on the two-month schedule for developing a prototype power supply for Collins Radio, the project is two days ahead of the preliminary time estimate. The circuit has been designed and tested for dependability. It is now undergoing final inspection.

1. Results of circuit dependability test.—The test circuit operated within the desired limits of ± 2 percent of the desired voltages and currents. Measured by a thermocouple in the 3' x 3' x 3" base mounting plate of aluminum, the temperature readings (with attendant voltages) ran as follows:

Hour	Transmit Voltage @ 200 Ma.	Receive Voltage @ 110 Ma.	Bias Voltage @ 65 Ma.	Temperature (Degrees Centigrade)

[No use to waste space in this book on the recorded results.]

2. Printed circuit board.—The basic sketch work for the printed board is finished. The component placement and hookup connections were frozen yesterday. Now the enlarged negative is being drawn. It should be ready for the developer on January 13, five days ahead of the final acceptance date.

3. Chassis design.—The chassis drawings went to Alsfab on January 9. The prototype chassis, with finishes of black anodize on the base and gray enamel on the cover, will be ready on January 14. The dimensions are 6" x 4" x 3" or 2 inches smaller than the maximum allowed by Collins.

4. Remaining work.—The printed board has to be etched and built. It will be tested in the small chassis, and the complete unit has to be tested for all conditions, including vibration, moisture, and temperature. Unless now unseen troubles develop, the present rate of progress should continue, and the prototype should be ready for shipment by February 7.

Credit reports

The credit report illustrated as a letter report (p. 106) is typical of those written by individual references about a credit applicant. But various trade associations, credit bureaus, and special credit-reporting agencies have to write so many credit reports that each develops special forms for convenience and the economy of standardization.

Because the purpose of a credit report is always the same and known to the reader, and because the methods and scope are always the same, the credit report omits the introduction. Because the credit report is an informational rather than analytical report, it also omits conclusions and recommendations. And because it is a short-form report, it omits other parts of a complete report—all except the text and perhaps a synopsis.

But because the credit report must protect the writer against libel suit, it includes the necessary legal defenses (in addition to assumed truth in the facts presented) by specifying confidential use for the purpose mentioned when it was requested. Because credit decisions are always made on the basis of the four *C*'s of credit—Capital, Character, Capacity, Conditions (see p. 131)—the report invariably covers these topics (but not under these headings). The information includes anything which might have a significant bearing on the credit worth of the subject (individual or firm) and omits anything else.

The old report on the next page is just one of the many kinds, but it illustrates most of the points. When you notice how the note in fine print at the bottom provides legal protection against libel suit, you will under-

Dun & Bradstreet Report

RATING CHANGE

SIC	NAME & ADDRESS		STARTED	RATING
		CD 26 FEB 2 19-- N		
2 51	SIMPSON HARDWARE CO	HARDWARE & PAINTS	1948	E 2.
	SIMPSON, WILLIAM J., OWNER			Formerly E 2½
	495 N MAIN ST.		TRADE	DISC-PPT
	SPRINGFIELD OHIO		SALES	$89,446
			WORTH	$27,908
			EMPLS	1 + 1 P.T.

UMMARY AN ESTABLISHED BUSINESS CONDUCTING A STEADY AND PROFITABLE VOLUME. FINANCIAL CONDITION IS WELL BALANCED.

RADE

HC	OWE	P DUE	TERMS	Jan 19 19--	SOLD
1551	356		2-10-30	Disc	1948 to date
900	600		2-10	Disc	yrs
400			2-10-30	Disc	1950 to 11-1-6-
1600	300		30	Ppt	Active acct
733	112			Ppt	yrs

INANCE

Statement Dec 31 19--

Cash on hand & bank	$ 4,604	Accts Pay	$ 3,064
Accts Rec	1,315	Accruals	621
Mdse	19,158		
Total Current	25,077	Total Current	3,685
Fixt & Equip	4,008		
Auto	2,113		
Ppd & Def	395	NET WORTH	27,908
Total Assets	31,593	Total	31,593

Net Sales January 1, 19-- to December 31, 19--, $89,446; gross profit $19,551; monthly rent $175; lease expires 19--. Fire insurance on fixtures $4,000; on merchandise $20,000.
Signed Jan 30, 19-- SIMPSON HARDWARE CO. by W.J. Simpson, Owner

-----0-----

When Simpson took over the business in 1948, sales were about $45,000 a year. By working long hours and advertising in the Suburban News he built up volume a little every year. Also there has been an increase in residential building on his side of town. Profits have increased as sales have expanded. Cash withdrawals from the business have been conservative. Merchandise turns satisfactorily and Simpson has been able to improve his financial condition a little each year. Carries good balances at his bank and has not borrowed since 195-.

OPERATION

Retails shelf hardware and tools (65%), S & W Paints (20%) and housewares, cutlery, garden implements, glass, lawn mowers, seeds and sporting equipment (15%). About 90% of sales is for cash; 30 day credit is extended to contractors and householders. Two clerks, one part-time, are employed. LOCATION: Rents a store 25 x 60 in a residential shopping area on the outskirts of town. Premises are well maintained.

HISTORY

Style was registered by Simpson July 17, 1948. Used for buying and advertising. Owner purchased this established business July 1, 1948 from Ralph T. Meyers. Capital was $18,000 of which $10,000 was a loan since repaid.

William J. Simpson, born 190-, is married, a native of Ohio. After graduating from Miami University in 1930, taught school until 1936. 1937-1945 employed by the Wilson Wholesale Hardware Co., Columbus, Ohio, latterly in the accounting department. 1946-48 was a salesman for Davis & Crocker, wholesale builders supplies, Springfield.
2-2 (201 49)

PLEASE NOTE WHETHER NAME, BUSINESS AND STREET ADDRESS CORRESPOND WITH YOUR INQUIRY.

stand that Dun & Bradstreet had to get permission from Simpson to release this report for educational purposes—and why D&B sent an old report.

Annual reports[2]

In accounting to their publics for their management of funds entrusted to them, corporations and governmental units summarize each year's activities in their annual reports.

In the middle of the 19th century, when annual reporting really started, stockholders were the only public considered. Since they were usually wealthy and educated—or advised by investment specialists—early annual reports were little more than financial statements in the formal accounting terms of the day. And the usual attitude of management was to tell as few people as possible as little as possible.

Today all that is changed. Stockholders have increased greatly (now estimated at about a tenth of the U.S. population, many of whom are not acquainted with accounting terminology). Labor has increased its power and become intensely interested in corporate affairs. The changed thinking of the times considers corporations essentially public institutions affecting the public welfare. Management has seen that its publics include stockholders, the financial community, workers, customers, government officials, and the general public. It has realized that many of these people are not educated in accounting and that many of them are interested in more than strictly financial data. They want to know about wages, fringe benefits to workers, products, research and development of new products, and overall policies—for example, company ecological policy.

Annual-report writers today, therefore, try to write so that everyone can understand, and they try to cover topics of interest to all publics. And with the realization that people are inclined to distrust and take a dim view of things they don't know about, management has shifted to the attitude of telling as many people as possible as much as possible (limited only by security regulations and information that might hurt the competitive position of the company).

Indeed, today the annual report is a major part of the public relations programs of most corporations, a means by which they hope to tell their story to all their publics to justify their existence and their way of doing things. They know that any business firm exists, in the long run, only with

---

[2] Although most annual reports are not short, they are largely factual reporting (informational) rather than the analytical studies of problems with conclusions and recommendations discussed in the preceding chapter. They are periodic reports and are something of a special type and form. Certainly they are the most voluminous of reports (many companies distributing more than a million copies annually), and the writings about them are probably the most numerous (we could easily give you a 10-page bibliography). Yet we do not think they deserve extensive treatment here in view of the purposes of this book. Still, you deserve some introduction to them, and it belongs in this chapter more appropriately than elsewhere.

the approval and patronage of a public whose goodwill it has. Most corporations therefore make their reports available to anybody who asks, and some go to considerable expense to make their reports appealing, readable, and informative.

Some have gone so far in telling their stories that the reports seem more like propaganda or advertising brochures than objective reports—and have sometimes thereby lost faith and face. But the usual annual report today is highly informative about the organization it represents. The facts presented are quite reliable. If you read annual reports knowing that they are likely slanted (by not telling everything rather than by misrepresentation), you will be adequately cautious—and well informed.

Usually today's annual reports contain a letter from the highest official as well as financial statements and the auditor's statement of opinion (sometimes called the "certificate"). Often the letter from the president or chairman of the board is only a short introduction to a review of outstanding influences, developments, and trends affecting company operations. Frequently it is both an introduction and a synopsis. And in some cases it is the entire report, running to 10, 12, or more pages.

Either way, most annual-report writers adapt all the devices already mentioned here—readable style, liberal use of meaningful headings, graphic illustrations—to make reading easy and interesting and the reports effective representatives for their organizations.

You can find a tremendous volume of material about annual reports in the library. And as we mentioned in the chapters on application letters, you can get examples by writing to almost any corporation. The annual report of a company is a source of information which anybody should read before investing in a company's stock or applying for a job with that firm.

Short analytical reports

As you have seen, some of the short reports in forms already discussed have been informational while others have been analytical. Yet the name "short analytical report" often has a special meaning in report-writing circles—a meaning indicating a certain form rather than any very definite limits of length. In that sense—the sense used in this section only—a short analytical report is like a complete analytical report which the writer has cut down by (1) omitting certain parts, (2) combining parts where possible, and (3) writing less in the remaining parts simply because their topics require no more. Even so, it is still likely to be longer (maybe up to ten pages) than what is generally called a short report (usually five pages or less).

Since the parts of a short analytical report all have parallels in the complete analytical reports discussed in the preceding chapter, we see no need to explain and illustrate them extensively here. For your study of short analytical reports, therefore, we ask you to keep in mind the following points as you reconsider the preceding chapter.

1. The short analytical report usually omits the cover, the letter of authorization, and the letter of acceptance.
2. It often also combines the letter of transmittal and synopsis, omits the table of contents and depends on headings throughout the report, omits the bibliography and provides the full references as footnotes or interwoven citations, and interweaves the essential parts of possible appendix material right into the text.
3. It may, but rarely does, also put the title-page information at the top of the first page and move right into the next part on that page; combine the essentials of authorization, transmittal, and synopsis as a summary right after the title-page information; and omit the introduction as a separate part and interweave its essentials into the text. It could thus have only three sections—the title-page information, the summary, and the text. This is about as far as it can go. Any report would have these elements, although they might be arranged differently and presented in different forms.

The following report (slightly revised for our purposes) is a good short analytical report. We know additional improvements we could make—and you may see some too—but notice particularly:

1. The exactness of the title, including the general answers to both questions (appropriate in the final title but not in a tentative one, where they would show preconceptions).
2. The telescoping (omitting certain standard parts of longer reports like those discussed in the preceding chapter and combining them with others). In this case you see the letter and synopsis combined, no table of contents but a well-displayed system of heads and subheads, and no bibliography because published sources are interwoven in the text.
3. The use of tables and charts where they help to highlight important quantities (the original contained others, omitted here because we do not think they were worth their space and costs in this book).
4. The smooth continuity and coherence of the whole report, helped by numerous beginning topic sentences and paragraphs and ending summary-transition sentences and paragraphs.

Because the short analytical reports discussed in this chapter are simply cut-down versions of the complete analytical reports discussed in the preceding chapter, you need no checklist for these. You can easily use the applicable parts of the checklist for complete analytical reports (pp. 512–17).

SHORT-REPORT CASES—LETTERS, MEMOS, ETC.

1. As safety engineer for the Illinois Power Company, Chicago 60699, you get the job of writing a memo to all outdoor crew members recommending certain precautions when lightning threatens. Your boss, W. A. Hambright, Director of Safety, wants to see, approve, and distribute; but

HOW A CORRESPONDENCE-IMPROVEMENT PROGRAM
WOULD SAVE MONEY AND BUILD GOODWILL
FOR BURNS, INC.

Prepared for
Mr. C. D. James, President

By Patricia Jean Barksdale
Assistant, Research Department

November 28, 1975

HOW A CORRESPONDENCE-IMPROVEMENT PROGRAM

WOULD SAVE MONEY AND BUILD GOODWILL

FOR BURNS, INC.

I. Authorization, Purposes, and Methods

This report, authorized on October 20, 1975, by Mr. C. D. James, president of Burns, Inc., and submitted by Patricia Jean Barksdale, assistant in the Research Department, was assigned for two purposes: (1) to determine whether Burns really needs to improve its correspondence and (2) to propose and explain any needed action.

Information presented in the report comes from a survey of the quality of correspondence Burns presently puts out, current letter-improvement publications, questionnaires, personal interviews with representatives of local companies which have conducted letter-improvement programs, and an interview with a professional consultant in business letters.

The significant savings in both money and goodwill which would result from instituting a letter-improvement program are evident from the following analysis of the costs of correspondence, the present correspondence conditions at Burns, the success of correspondence-improvement programs, and the costs of methods and plans successfully used by other companies.

Letterhead

RESEARCH DEPARTMENT November 28, 1975

Mr. C. D. James, President
Burns, Inc.
2619 Powell Street
San Francisco, California 81001

Dear Mr. James:

Here is the report you requested on October 20 evaluating the possibilities for improvement and, if needed, the best methods Burns could employ to improve the quality of its correspondence.

The report shows that Burns could both save money and improve goodwill by instituting a correspondence-improvement program.

To achieve the quality that should be maintained in our correspondence, Burns should employ an instructor to conduct classes, issue a correspondence manual, and hire a permanent supervisor to maintain quality correspondence.

In the month given me to prepare this report, I have learned some interesting and useful facts which I believe will help you in establishing a correspondence-improvement program. Please call on me if I can be of further help.

Sincerely yours,

(Miss) Patricia Jean Barksdale
Assistant

II. The High Costs of Correspondence

The average cost of business letters is at least $3 each (according to the article "Cutting Correspondence Expense," by Henry Howard, in the May issue of U.S. Business, p. 29).

On the basis of this figure, Burns's yearly correspondence expense is:

Average number of letters per business year 212,500
Average cost per letter $3.00
Yearly correspondence expense $637,500

This minimum cost, comprising a large part of the firm's total expenditures, consists not merely of supplies expense but more significantly of the valuable time of dictators and typists. The high total expenditures for correspondence seem to offer a vast area for possible savings.

In addition to the possible dollar savings on correspondence, Burns also needs to consider the intangible yet highly significant goodwill value of its correspondence. The impression the company's letters make on the public can either win or lose business. As Mr. Howard says (p. 31), "To get your money's worth, you must be sure that every letter helps to improve public relations."

III. Unfavorable Correspondence Conditions Existing in Burns, Inc.

A survey of current Burns correspondence reveals that it is not creating the best public image. The survey consisted of analyzing 200 letters selected at random from the average 4,250 letters prepared in one week by the 40 typists and 85 dictators.

Many of the company's letters contain outmoded forms, errors in spelling and grammar, poor sentence structure, poor style, and other

undesirable features shown in Chart 1.

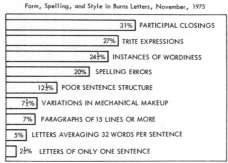

Chart 1

Form, Spelling, and Style in Burns Letters, November, 1975

31%	PARTICIPIAL CLOSINGS
27%	TRITE EXPRESSIONS
24½%	INSTANCES OF WORDINESS
20%	SPELLING ERRORS
12½%	POOR SENTENCE STRUCTURE
7½%	VARIATIONS IN MECHANICAL MAKEUP
7%	PARAGRAPHS OF 15 LINES OR MORE
5%	LETTERS AVERAGING 32 WORDS PER SENTENCE
2½%	LETTERS OF ONLY ONE SENTENCE

A. Layout, Spelling, and Style Improvement Needed.--Since Burns letters are often the only contact readers have with the organization, the impression created by the letters is important. The quality of the typewritten letter creates a picture of the quality of the firm.

Quality correspondence requires accuracy and attractiveness. Spelling errors and poor sentence construction reflect unfavorably on both the company and the company's dictators and typists.

1. Variations in Mechanical Makeup.--Almost one in 12 (7 1/2 percent) of the letters contains variations in mechanical makeup. These variations often result from inconsistency on the part of various typists when the dictator does not specify the form of letter. Such variations are not necessarily errors, since all forms that are consistent are correct; but the outmoded or ultramodern form does characterize the writer and the company. Since the modern trend

is toward simplicity, Burns could save much time and money by adopting a simple form that would suggest that Burns is neither out of date nor frivolously ultramodern.

2. Spelling Errors.--One out of every five letters typed by Burns typists contains one or more misspelled words. To most people a misspelled word is a mark of discredit on the firm on whose letterhead it appears. The typists are responsible for not correctly spelling the words dictated. That 20 percent of the letters sent out each week contain spelling errors certainly indicates the need for study by the typists.

3. Trite Expressions.--About one fourth (27 percent) of the letters sent out by Burns contain trite expressions. These outdated phrases dull reader interest and make the letters sound pompous and unnatural. Use of these expressions is usually due to lack of thinking on the part of the dictators. Triteness, like spelling errors, is not good for public relations.

4. Poor Sentence Structure.--One eighth (12 1/2 percent) of Burns letters contain improper sentence structure. Poorly constructed sentences are often unclear and may convey a meaning different from that intended. More significant than lack of clarity, however, is the fact that poor sentence structure draws attention to the dictator's style rather than to the more important message. Therefore poor sentence structure decreases readability and in turn decreases the quality of Burns, Inc., in the eyes of its readers.

5. Participial Closings.--The survey reveals that the largest percentage of improper phrasings is participial closings--31 percent of

the letters end with outmoded expressions such as "Until such time, I remain, etc." This means that one out of every three letters dictated indicates to customers a lack of up-to-dateness at Burns, Inc.

6. Too Long or Too Short Paragraphs and Sentences, and Instances of Wordiness.--Two out of every five letters contain sentences and paragraphs of considerable length. Five percent of these letters average more than 32 words per sentence. Although an average of 16-20 words is good for readability, sentences of 32 words or more are not improper if necessary for the good presentation of the idea and if easily readable because of direct phrasing that requires no complicating punctuation.

However, 24 percent of the letters contain instances of wordiness. This indicates that the lengthy sentences are probably due to deadwood phrases rather than to good idea presentation. Wordiness indicates lack of careful thought of the dictator.

Also, 7 percent of the letters contain paragraphs of 15 lines or more. These long paragraphs are uninviting and hard to read. If the dictators dictate paragraphing, they should break up their thoughts; but if they leave it to typists, they must learn how to assume the responsibility.

Although short and direct sentences aid clarity, letters that are too short give the reader an unfavorable impression. No one likes to be treated in an abrupt, brush-off manner; but 2 1/2 percent of our letters contain only one sentence and therefore probably sound discourteous.

Burns correspondence leaves a lot of room for improvement. Poor style weakens the impact of the message and also indicates outmodedness or inability of the employees. Much more significant than style, however, is the actual message conveyed to the reader.

B. Offensive Expressions and Duplication Costly.--Approximately two out of five letters leaving Burns offices are probably doing as much harm as good. Yet Burns need not feel that it is exceptional in this way. Professor C. R. Anderson reports that 40 percent of 1,000 carbons he read in a firm where he was consulting represent letters that never should have been sent ("Correspondence Inefficiencies," Journal of Business Communication, 4:13-18, October, 1971). Still, the fact that other firms send out bad letters does not mean that Burns should.

1. Letters Containing Offensive Expressions.--Of the letters that Burns sends to readers, 18 percent contain offensive expressions (Chart 2).

Chart 2

Percentage of Letters Containing Offensive Expressions, Unanswered Questions, and Unnecessary Duplication
November, 1975

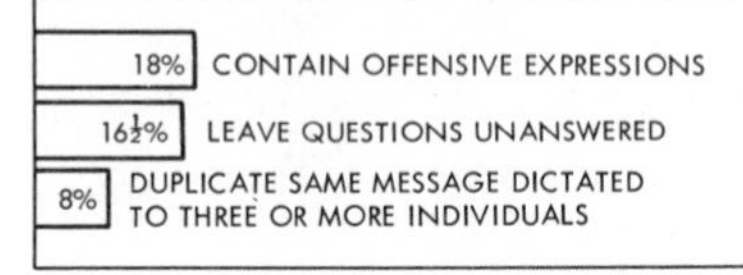

This means that Burns is spending over $100,000 a year to drive business away (0.18 x 212,500 x $3). Accusing the reader ("You failed . . . or neglected . . ."), implying distrust or stupidity ("You say . . . ," "If so, . . . ," "Obviously . . ."), and the like certainly destroy rather than build goodwill. No company can afford this loss of goodwill and waste of money. Burns dictators definitely need instruction in this area.

7

2. <u>Unnecessary Duplication</u>.--About one in six (16 1/2 percent) of Burns letters leave questions unanswered. Not only are customers annoyed by having to write again--unless they decide to drop the subject and go elsewhere with their business--but Burns dictators waste time in preparing letters to answer questions they should have answered in the first letter.

If they have to write again for each letter leaving unanswered questions, a waste of another $100,000 a year results (212,500 x 0.165 x $3). This problem generally occurs because a dictator reads the incoming mail carelessly and dictates before planning carefully to answer what the inquirer asked.

Unnecessary duplication comes also from 8 percent of the letters being essentially the same messages dictated to three or more individuals. Such duplications obviously cost Burns some money. Well-trained dictators and--in many cases--use of a good form letter could save at least part of it.

Spelling errors, poor sentence and paragraph construction and length, offensive expressions, unnecessary duplication, and other faults evidence the unsatisfactory quality of Burns correspondence. Unfavorable correspondence conditions are increasing expenses by thousands of dollars yearly and are also causing a loss of goodwill and business. Only 24 percent, less than one in four, of the letters Burns now sends out are of top quality--clear, correct, complete, and considerate of the reader's feelings.

Correspondence improvement offers Burns a vast area for savings both in money and in goodwill. The results obtained by companies using letter-improvement programs show the success Burns might expect from a program of its own.

IV. The Success of Correspondence-Improvement Programs

The results of companies using letter-improvement programs include improvements in letter quality, in attitudes of correspondents, and in customer relations.

The following excerpt from "Letter Training Program Pays Off," an unsigned feature on page 377 of the January issue of Printers' Week, comments on the improvement received from correspondence instruction: "Bring in an instructor who has had experience in writing letters as well as in teaching. Have him conduct regular classes for several weeks. Require each member of the firm connected with letter writing--from the president to the typist--to attend. Then watch your letters improve!"

The same source lists the names of 57 companies which have carried out letter-improvement programs. The 55 replies to questionnaires sent to these companies indicate favorable results from their programs.

A. Considerable Improvement in Letter Quality.--The first and most important question asked was "What do you believe was the effect of your program on the quality of the company's letters?" Almost three fourths (39 of the 55) say they have received considerable satisfaction with significant improvement in quality. Twenty-seven percent see no noticeable difference, and 2 percent note slight improvement.

B. Favorable Attitude of Correspondents.--More than three fourths of the firms--42 of the 55--report correspondents' favorable attitudes toward their programs. Only 4 percent report unfavorable reactions.

One typical comment is: "On the whole, both correspondents and typists appreciate the constructive criticism of the instructor. Nearly all are enthusiastic when they realize how important their letters are in building goodwill for the company."

Both improvement in letter quality and correspondents' approval indicate that the programs improve the companies' public relations.

C. Improved Customer Relations.--To the inquiry "What do you believe was the effect of the program on your company's customer relations?" more than two-thirds report considerable improvement. Sixty-nine percent report considerable improvement, whereas 20 percent consider the improvement slight and 11 percent notice no apparent change.

A favorable comment states that "Since completion of our training program, we have received fewer complaints than ever before, and many customers have written letters of appreciation."

Improvement in letter quality, correspondents' favorable attitudes, and better customer relations show that other companies' correspondence-improvement programs are successful. The type of program which works best, however, is more difficult to determine.

V. The Costs and Methods Used by Other Companies with Successful Programs

Most companies which have successful correspondence-improvement programs use a correspondence manual, a permanent supervisor, and (to start) a special instructor.

A. Correspondence Manuals Are Effective.--A correspondence manual for reference is an important part of a letter-improvement program. The usual manual contains both instructions and examples of approved styles for company letters to serve as a guide for dictators and transcribers.

Of the 55 companies questioned, only a little more than half (51 percent) said yes when asked "Do you have a correspondence manual?" Those companies which use a manual, however, readily realize its importance and benefits. Of those that report using one, 86 percent answered yes to "Do you believe it has helped to improve letter writing?" Almost 9 out of 10 believe their manuals help, whereas less than 1 out of 10 gives either a doubtful or a negative answer to the question.

Evidently the others (49 percent) do not realize the benefits that users receive from manuals. They serve both as guides to new employees and as reminders and handy references to established employees. In most cases a manual seems to be most beneficial to follow up and answer questions that arise after completion of the course of instruction.

In discussing the benefits of the correspondence manual, one respondent commented, typically, that "The correspondence manual issued at the close of our training period served to crystallize the information presented by the instructor. It is always available for quick reference."

Before a correspondence manual can be justified in a letter-improvement program, however, its benefits must be weighed against its cost.

B. Cost of a Manual Is about $300.--In replies to the question concerning the cost of correspondence manuals, $300 to $500 is the most frequent answer (43 percent). One fourth of the firms (25 percent) paid $400 and over for their manuals, 2 percent less than $200, and only 1 percent spent $200 to $300.

The advantages of the savings in time and money which result from the use of a correspondence manual seem to justify the cost in the thinking of most firms. Evidently, then, a good correspondence-improvement program will provide a manual.

The most successful programs, however, do not depend on a manual alone but also provide a correspondence supervisor.

C. Correspondence Supervisors Maintain Effectiveness.--The correspondence supervisor serves as an adviser to the employees concerning problems and as an inspector to make sure the letters maintain standards of quality. Without the supervisor, dictators and transcribers lapse into their old habits, according to companies which have tried to operate without a supervisor.

The survey reveals that 58 percent of the companies make use of a correspondence supervisor or someone else who assumes the duties under another title. But 42 percent do not have a correspondence supervisor.

A greater percentage (58 percent) of firms make use of a supervisor than make use of a manual (51 percent). And unanimously all 32 companies which have a supervisor agree that a competent one is effective in maintaining letter quality.

The following comment from one firm further illustrates the need for a correspondence supervisor:

> The letter-improvement classes we held five years ago made correspondents conscious of their responsibilities for several months. But since we had no supervisor to encourage consistent effort to make letters effective, correspondents became lax again. Our new program provides for a supervisor who will spot-check outgoing mail and hold regular classes for discussion of letter problems.

Evidently a supervisor helps to keep the letter quality up to par. The most effective letter-improvement program should make use of both a supervisor and a manual.

Still an additional element appears in the most successful programs.

D. <u>All Sources Recommend Instruction to Start</u>.--All articles read, many comments made by interviewees and respondents to the questionnaire, and the advice of a professional letter-writing consultant point to the wisdom of an instructional program as a necessary start to a letter-improvement program.

Dr. R. R. Brawner of Del Monte, the interviewed professional consultant, says that in his varied experience few companies have been successful in greatly improving their correspondence without a definite program of instruction to start. Much of the job, he says, is getting employees to recognize the importance of good letters to their companies and themselves. Although inspiration and exhortation alone will not do much good, some motivating along with good instruction on how to improve usually does produce good results.

Dr. Brawner's statements are in line with specific comments heard or read elsewhere, and he offers a program based on 10 years of successful experience.

Dictators and transcribers would attend 10-week courses in separate groups. Five groups with 17 dictators each and two groups with 20 typists each would include all of the 85 Burns dictators and 40 transcribers while keeping the classes down to effective working groups. Dr. Brawner proposes to analyze letters dictated by each correspondent and to give individual suggestions on the paper (when necessary, in person). Under his professional direction, employees are practically assured of learning the much-needed fundamentals of good letter writing. His fee for each class is $500 or $3,500 for the whole instructional program.

By employing Dr. Brawner to conduct the proposed classes, Burns would be taking a step that everyone with successful experience in attempts at correspondence improvement seems to agree is essential.

VI. The Recommended Program

The high cost of correspondence and the deficiencies in the quality of letters at Burns, Inc., definitely indicate that the company should institute an improvement program as soon as possible.

Published articles, the experiences of firms that have worked at improving their correspondence, and the advice of a professional consultant all suggest that the best plan is a three-pronged attack:

1. Employ a professional teacher to motivate and instruct employees as the first step.

2. Provide a correspondence manual for ready reference.

3. Appoint a permanent correspondence supervisor to keep up the motivation, help with special problems, and spot-check outgoing mail to catch and correct any developing laxness.

As the solution to the problem of poor letters at Burns, Inc., I therefore recommend that the company take these three steps in order as soon as practicable. Specifically, I recommend Dr. R. R. Brawner of Del Monte as the professional consultant and teacher to start the program.

With the recommended program in operation, at a cost of about $4,000 ($3,500 + $300 + overhead), both Professor Anderson's and my estimates suggest that Burns should expect to save at least 50 times that much a year by writing fewer but better letters and by avoiding duplication. But the biggest improvement would be the better company image Burns correspondence would put in the minds of its readers.

14

Bibliography

1. Anderson, C. R., "Correspondence Inefficiencies," Journal of Business Communication, 4:13-18 (October, 1971).

2. Howard, Henry, "Cutting Correspondence Expense," U. S. Business, May, 1971, pp. 29-31.

3. "Letter Training Program Pays Off," Printers' Week, January, 1971, p. 377.

you are to write to the workers, not him. Lightning has killed seven workers this year on the job—one a week ago—and has injured others. Fortunately last month you received from the National Safety Council (of which you are a member) a report of a three-year study on self-protection from lightning. Since that report was for the general public, you'll have to select appropriate points (from your notes below), organize them, and write your memo.

When possible, go indoors, but not in the shower or tub bath. Fireplaces should be avoided as well as radiators, stoves, metal pipes, plumbing fixtures, and electrical appliances such as television sets, radios, lamps, and refrigerators. Stay away from electrical equipment like razors, saws, toothbrushes, mowers, knives. Stay off the telephone and lines outside.

If outdoors avoid the highest object in an area, especially isolated trees. For quick action, crouch down in the open, keeping twice as far away from isolated trees as the trees are high. Get away from hilltops, open spaces, wire fences, power lines, exposed sheds, and metal farm equipment, clotheslines and rails. Drop metal fishing rods or golf clubs and seek refuge in a cave, ditch, or canyon, or under head-high clumps of trees in open forest glades. Get out of the water if swimming, and off small boats. A truck or car offers excellent protection from lightning but don't touch metal parts.

Warning signs are if hair stands on end or skin tingles; if these strike, crouch down immediately.

People hit by lightning may be touched without danger. The victims get a severe electrical shock and may be burned, but they carry no electrical charge. They may appear to be dead but can often be revived by prompt first aid. Until medical help arrives, mouth-to-mouth and cardiopulmonary resuscitation should be used.

2. As the Reserve Book Clerk of your University Library, write a memo to faculty members on the reserve book lists. Ask them to submit their reserve book lists for courses at least two weeks before next-term classes start. Lists arriving later will be given as rapid processing as possible, but with no guarantee that the books will be on reserve on the first day of the term. To speed processing, each form should be submitted in duplicate, and either typed or printed. Lists not submitted in this format cannot be accepted. It is imperative that all requested information be complete and accurate: the call number; the author's name; the type of Reserve desired for the volume; the number of copies desired; the course name and number; the approximate number of students; and the instructor's name and campus address, to include phone extension. Enclose a copy of the *revised* Reserve Book List and ask the faculty member to use it only. Stress the fact that you want to improve library service in every aspect.

3. As Interim Assistant Vice President, write a memo to Dr. Robert Hemp, Dean, X College, with the message that the By-laws of the University Senate stipulate that an evaluation be made of each college at least once every seven years. X College is scheduled for evaluation during the current academic year. The evaluation is made by a team of educators and other specialists. The Office of Academic Affairs will appoint the members of the evaluation committee and reimburse each member of that committee for all expenses incurred in connection with the evaluation plus an appropriate honorarium for their services. You want Hemp to nominate members to the committee and you want nominations from other faculty members of X College. All nominations together with basic biographical information on the nominee should be sent directly to the writer.

4. After a thorough study of sales and profits for Wiggle Piggle grocery chain, Lincoln, Nebraska, you, a management consultant, have the job of recommending technological innovations that might help increase the profits to the Board of Directors. Last year sales at minimarkets increased 22 percent, despite high prices; their pretax profits, as a percentage of sales, averaged 4.8 percent, as opposed to a bare 1.1 percent in supermarkets like Wiggle Piggle. Supermarkets depend on high volume, not high markups, for their profits. Some suggestions you've thought of or heard of include computerized warehouses, automated checkout systems, meat cutting by laser or electronic beam (to reduce waste and labor costs), solar energy to power frozen-food cases, and computer hook-ups with First Federal Savings and Loan Associations.

This last appeals to you, and you have the go-ahead sign from First Federal Savings and Loan and the Nebraska Supreme Court, which ruled that the stores would not be acting as Savings and Loan branches.

Customers are enthusiastic about the system because neither First Federal nor Wiggle Piggle levies a service charge on their transactions, according to the two stores where a pilot study was conducted. The managers of the two pilot stores found that this system attracted more customers to their stores, curtailed time-consuming check-cashing operations, and reduced bad-check losses.

Banks want to put in the same type of system, but they cannot put terminals in locations more than 50 miles away from the bank's main or branch office according to a ruling by U.S. Comptroller of the Currency James Smith (ruling of last December).

A customer of the S and L can present a deposit or withdrawal slip and a coded identification card to a Wiggle Piggle employee, who punches the transaction onto a typewriter-size console tied into First Federal's main computer. Once the central computer approves a withdrawal transaction, funds are transferred from the customer's savings account to Wiggle Piggle's account and the Wiggle Piggle employee hands over the cash. A customer wishing to make a deposit writes a check payable to Wiggle Piggle; the computer credits the customer with the deposit and debits the grocery chain's account.

In your own words write a memo to the store managers of the ten Wiggle Piggle stores in and around Lincoln suggesting that they consider investigating the innovations you have found.

5. Since the present U.S. airport-security program began, has it succeeded? Should it continue? What has worked? What remains? Your responsibility as an employee of Federal Aviation Administration includes writing a report to your immediate superior in FAA. Twenty-five potential hijackings were thwarted by security checks in 1974; 2,663 passengers were denied boarding for various reasons; and 2,450 concealed firearms were detected by baggage and personal inspections; 3,500 persons were arrested at U.S. airports—many for violating antihijacking regulations, others for narcotics smuggling and illegal entry.

Help has been that Cuba, Iraq, Algeria, and other "third world" nations do not offer refuge for the air pirates now. Before the program started, attempted skyjackings in the United States reached a peak of 40; the next year that reduced to only 1. Five hundred U.S. airports handle regularly scheduled airline flights.

All four attempts at skyjacking in the United States last year were unsuccessful. Foreign airliners are still being successfully pirated. Since January 1 last year 212 people have been killed and 140 injured as the result of 104 skyjacking attempts abroad. These involved the airliners and airports of 41 different countries.

Most frequent recent attempts in the United States have been to bring explosives aboard an aircraft as cargo or in a passenger's baggage.

6. Top management people in growing numbers are opting for bigger cash salaries rather than settling for part cash, part deferred compensation. Bonuses tied directly to a company's annual profits are losing allure, at least temporarily, because of declining sales and earnings in some industries. Stock options, under a cloud for the past few years because of the long stockmarket slide, are not satisfying the top executives of big business.

As P. J. Wytmar of Wytmar & Company, Inc., a New York management-consultant firm, help Lester P. Corns, president of a large auto-producing company (Sword of Detroit, Michigan). Suggest in memo form some ways that can be used to keep the executives happy with something more than the average $264,000 salary. (Incidentally pharmaceutical companies who do over a billion dollars worth of business tend to pay their executives more than auto companies—$316,000 according to McKinsey & Company, Inc., annual executive compensation survey.)

Incentive-pay programs or "performance-share plans" are tied to gains in profits over a period of future years. Some of these plans give the hard-working executive an allotment of stock free if the company meets specified goals.

The company could pay the family's medical, dental, and eye-care bills as well as psychiatric consultations and orthodontic work for the executive's children. Company-paid financial-counseling programs that help the executive plan investments could help. Low-cost vacations at company-owned resorts or lodges and expense accounts with generous travel and entertainment allowances might help.

7. As auditor for a nation-wide health insurance company, Protec-O-Shield, you must write a short report showing changing conditions that might affect rates and/or other aspects of operations. Analyze and explain the following facts for the Board of Control of Protect-O-Shield.

Total spending on Health Care in the United States was $17.3 billion in 1955 (1950 population, 150,697,361); $25.9 billion in 1960 (population, 179,323,175); $38.9 billion in 1965; $69.2 billion, 1970 (population, 205,235,298), and $115 billion for 1975; and still going up since the figures have been reported fully. Outlays for health care now equal 8 percent of the nation's total spending for goods and services. The cost per capita is about $530 a year according to U.S. Department of Health, Education and Welfare.

Of the $104.2 billion spent on medical care, $40.9 (or 39 percent) was spent on hospital care; $19.0 billion (18 percent) on physicians' services; $9.7 billion (9 percent) on drugs; $7.5 billion (7 percent) on nursing-home care; $6.2 billion (6 percent) on dentists' services; $4.4 billion (4 percent) construction; $2.7 billion (3 percent) on research; and other things $13.8 billion (13 percent). (Note: details may not add to totals because of rounding.)

Medical costs are rising fastest in operating-room charges (65 percent), followed by hospital room charges (57 percent), physicians' fees (37 percent), laboratory tests (35 percent), dentists' fees (34 percent), eyeglasses (31 percent), over-the-counter drugs (21 percent), and prescription drugs (7 percent).

Nine out of every ten Americans have some form of health insurance, which is one reason given for the high costs (doctors and hospitals are assured of at least partial payments).

8. Speery and Cunningham, consulting firm you work for, has been hired to investigate lowering the decibel count from 90 to 85 or lower for Rand Engineering Company, Cambridge, Mass., by Occupational Safety and Health Administration. Decibels are units of measured noise, with zero representing the threshold of hearing and 130 the threshold of pain. Although the difference of only 5 decibels seems insignificant, the contrast in sounds between 85 and 90 decibels actually is enormous. Every ten-decibel increase in sound approximately doubles the amount of "perceived loudness." For example a medium jet engine has 160, air-raid siren 140, discotheque 120, bulldozer 110, steel-mill blast furnace 100, subway train 90, vacuum cleaner 70, auto traffic near freeway 60, private business office and average home 50, whisper 20.

Approximately 1,500 more Rand manufacturing workers would be saved from hearing impairment if the 85-decibel standard were adapted, rather than the 90-decibel average (about 770,000 for the United States). Workers were not counted in other occupations, such as transportation and construction.

Cost to Rand (and other manufacturing firms) of complying with the 85-decibel average would be $21,497 for each worker saved from a hearing handicap. Cost for compliance with the 90-decibel level would be 13.5 billions—or $19,286 per employee whose hearing remains undamaged.

If Rand continues to operate as it has, probably 2,000 of the workers will incur job-related hearing handicaps by retirement age. Compliance with the 90-decibel standard should reduce this number to 500. Use of 85 decibels as the average noise level would result in only 150 employees with noticeable hearing loss. (A hearing handicap according to the Government is a loss of 25 decibels in hearing ability—or the inability to understand quiet speech in a still room.)

Issuing ear muffs and ear plugs has not been satisfactory in other plants. A survey by Employers Insurance of Wausau of 1,148 plants which issued ear protectors to employees revealed that only 22.5 percent of the programs remained in effect longer than six months.

Your company, too, found that most plants failed to issue ear protection to new employees and that the regular employees felt that they could not work comfortably with the protection coverings.

Other facets of the noise proposal would require regular tests of the hearing of workers subjected to loud noises, and of hearing-conservation measures to protect those found to have impaired hearing because of job noises.

9. Write a memo to Norman Linebaker, Vice President for Sales, from Scott Phelps, Promotion Manager. Use as the subject New Tractor Exhibits. Your company is Paragon Promotions, general promoters of farm equipment to farmers. You are sending color prints of four mock-ups of exhibit designs done by your promotion section. If Linebaker approves the designs this week, you can have finished exhibits ready for use by the first of next month. Ask him to phone you by Monday with any suggestions. To help in making decisions, the following size and cost data may help: Design A, 6′ × 12′ × 9′ (two colors); Design B, 6′ × 9′ × 9′ (three colors); Design C, 6′ × 12′ × 9′ (four colors); Design D, 8′ × 12′ × 9′ (five colors). For most local shows and demonstrations of tractors to farmers either design A or B should be OK. Only for major regional or national shows will design C and D be helpful. Plans call for three major shows this year: Coleman, Texas, two months from now on the 12–15; Macon, Illinois, three months, 20–22; and Blue Mound, Iowa, four months from now. Scheduling of shows is spaced so that one of either Design C or D will be adequate along with enough A's and B's. Ask him to tell you his preference (C or D) unless there's a feeling that both should be used.

10. The employees of your small, independent hardware company (Moore-Bradley) that has six branches in your state have begun to ask about a retirement plan. As comptroller you have been asked by the president, Morton Day, to suggest a plan that will pacify employees but cost little or no money. Trained in finance and keeping up with the subject, you've decided to write a report to the president recommending that your company offer IRA to workers on an individual-option basis. IRA (or Individual Retirement Account), a special tax-deferred savings plan, provides a nest egg for workers who do not benefit from formal company pension plans, and became available under federal law and IRS (Internal Revenue Service) regulations January 1.

As comptroller you can set up the books so that you can help salt away 15 percent of an employee's income up to a maximum of $1,500 annually. The cash deposited in an IRA will be deducted from the worker's pay checks and will not be counted as income at income-tax time on the W–2 forms. And the income earned on IRA deposits (the best current interest rates you can get safely) is not currently reported for tax purposes. All taxes on the funds are deferred until they are withdrawn after the worker retires, when he is usually in a much lower tax bracket. At that point, payments from an IRA can be enjoyed without loss of Social Security benefits, too.

The Frudential Insurance Company is one of the largest insurers entering the IRA field. It plans on 50,000 to 65,000 IRAs this year. Bay View Federal Savings and Loan in San Francisco opened payroll-deductions IRA plans with nine companies during the first 12 days of last month.

Use the following table to explain the tax advantages of an IRA. But remember that your boss (Day) is in hardware, not an income-tax specialist. Furthermore, if he approves, he (or you) will have to explain the plan so that the employees can understand. Better write it that way now.

Taxpayer in 25 percent bracket

Money Invested in—	*IRA*	*Taxable fund*	*Gain in using IRA*
5 years	$ 8,456	$ 6,155	$ 2,301
10 years	19,771	13,824	5,947
15 years	34,914	23,382	11,532
20 years	55,178	35,293	19,885

Taxpayer in 50 percent bracket

Money Invested in—	*IRA*	*Taxable fund*	*Gain in using IRA*
5 years	$ 8,456	$ 3,982	$ 4,474
10 years	19,771	8,598	11,173
15 years	34,914	13,949	20,965
20 years	55,178	20,153	35,025

11. As auditor-consultant (auditing books on student loans) you must write a short report to U.S. Office of Education urging a change in student-loan policy. Nearly one out of five students won't or can't pay back money advanced for an education. Default rate is soaring toward 19 percent. The General Accounting Office predicts an ultimate default rate of 24.3 percent. Since student loans began to mature eight years ago, defaults have cost U.S. tax-payers about $200 million. The money has been paid to banks, educational institutions, and other lenders whose loans to students are insured by the federal government. Student loans were $104 million five years ago with default rate of 9 percent; 11 percent the next year with $255 million; $552 million the next year and 12 percent default; then 14 percent or $952 million. Last year $1,481 million was due, but $266.7 million not paid or 18 percent in default. This year an estimated $2,147 million will go into student loans and $408.1 million or 19 percent will not be paid.

12. As a sociologist-demographer consultant to *Ebony* magazine, you have the job of helping the editors and writers keep informed on the progress of the 24 million blacks the magazine strongly desires to appeal to by careful adaptation. To help *Ebony* serve in this changing society, you collected the following facts from the U.S. Census Bureau's four-year study of the "Social and Economic Status of the Black Population," published last July. Basically the study compares significant figures four years ago (labeled "then") and now. Write a memo using these facts and explain the interesting and significant trends. Though the editors might see the effects these trends should have on the content and style in *Ebony,* you want to go as far as you can in pointing them out—as recommendations.

Median family Income	*Blacks*	*Whites*	*Blacks' income as percentage of whites' income*
Then	$6,279	$10,236	61.3
Now	$7,808	13,356	58.5

Unemployment	*Then*	*Now*	*Increase*
Blacks	8.2%	9.9%	21%
Whites	4.5	5.0	11

Education	*Then*	*Now*
Proportion of blacks in college (age 18–24)	15%	18%
Proportion of blacks with 4 years of college (age 25–34)	6.1	8.1

Migration	*Moving in*	*Moving out*	*Net migration*
West	172,000	49,000	+123,000
South	276,000	241,000	+ 35,000
Northeast	88,000	143,000	− 55,000
North central	96,000	199,000	−103,000

Black demography	*Then*	*Now*	*Change*
Suburbs	3,433,000	4,101,000	Up 19.5%
Central cities	12,909,000	13,777,000	Up 6.7
Small towns, rural areas	5,714,000	5,748,000	Up 0.6

13. Moving across the United States is big business to your Bowe Chemical Company since you pay for the moves of new employees and employees whom you transfer. There's no way to guarantee a perfect move; but from Interstate Commerce Commission (ICC), which requires every moving company to hand it and each potential customer a copy of its performance report for the previous year, you have made a chart of 21 moving companies. From these figures select a company (identified by number—left-hand column) that would be the best carrier for moving your employees' household goods. Your short report in memo form goes from you, the treasurer, to the president, Donald Shellabarger, explaining your choice and your reasons.

		Shipments (percent)			
	Underestimated	*Picked up late*	*Delivered late*	*With damage claim of $50 or more*	*Average time to settle claim (days)*
1	24	5	19	23	42
2	25	16	21	24	54
3	24	5	23	17	40
4	26	4	24	13	46
5	23	6	12	16	18
6	21	21	30	17	24
7	8	5	12	16	52
8	21	2	16	19	37
9	20	8	14	13	46
10	16	18	21	15	45
11	16	11	26	12	20
12	25	1	20	12	26
13	11	7	30	16	63
14	25	1	27	20	44
15	21	1	14	26	28
16	27	13	15	16	50
17	30	2	12	17	67
18	23	1	16	11	32
19	19	10	18	11	43
20	25	16	15	13	31
21	17	3	23	13	46
Average for all 21 Carriers	21%	7%	19%	16%	41 days

14. With rising costs, paper shortage, energy crisis, you, the office manager of Welcome Wagon, 721 Fifth Avenue, New York, N.Y. 10021, write a memo to the office personnel asking cooperation on using the minimum of paper for correspondence to all hostesses and managers of branch offices. You found a great deal of waste paper by the Mimeographing machine also. Encourage the office personnel to turn out lights, to dress warmly for the 68-degree office, and to be more careful at the coffee bar. Coffee prices rose just last month. Several spoonfuls of instant coffee a

day can run up the coffee-bar expense to the point that you might have to remove it.

15. Use a subject line and write to I. B. Stearns, President, from M. K. Stanley, Director of Finance, telling him that the total revenues this year went up to $201.6 million or an 8 percent gain over last year. Your overall tax bill went up to $50.4 million which represented 25 cents of each revenue dollar. Revenues from overseas sales went up 10 percent or $83.5 million while domestic revenues went up 7 percent to $118.1 million. Biggest factor was the high federal taxes. Local taxes increased rapidly too. Local taxes went up from $23.1 million five years ago to $38.6 million this year. This is an annual growth rate of 11 percent a year. Earnings per share of common stock increased 7 cents this fiscal year to $2.08. Income for common stock was $45.8 million. Stanley recommends that of this amount, $32.9 million be paid out in dividends while $12.9 million be reinvested in the business. This will permit a common stock dividend of $1.40 per share.

16. As senior counselor in Peyman Junior High School, Sierra Bonita Avenue, Los Angeles, California 90066, you want to alert all other counselors in junior high schools in the LA district on the rise of births to teen-agers and the rising proportion of out-of-wedlock births among teen-agers. Teen-aged girls account for one of every five births in the United States and one in ten teen-agers has a baby. Four in ten teen-aged mothers are married, three are unmarried, and three marry about time baby is born. Births in past two years to girls under 15 increased from 194,100 to 204,900 (5 percent) in same period. According to Cynthia Green and Susan Lowe in an article in Zero Population Growth's publication *National Reporter* (using HEW and CB statistics), 71 percent of the teen-age girls who did not use contraceptives did not realize they could become pregnant, and 31 percent of the nonusers were unable to get contraceptives.

Besides alerting the counselors with these facts, interpret them, and make suggestions or recommendations.

17. Before you write your application letter and data sheet later in the course, but after reading Chapter 9, you are to think about the job and the company you would like to work for. To avoid loose thinking (and to help your teacher help you too), assume the role and fictitious name of a client adviser in a large employment agency and—1. Get a job description from the Directory of Opportunity. 2. Select a company by reading annual reports, Moody's Series, business periodicals, card catalog. CPA firms like Ernst and Ernst and investment companies like Merrill Lynch, Pierce, Fenner and Smith have helpful pamphlets. 3. Find out what the market is like today from your *Occupational Outlook Handbook* (put out by the U.S. Bureau of Labor) and the *College Placement Annual.* With this information write a letter report (addressed to yourself but turned in to your teacher) on the job (description), the company, and the market or outlook for you and the company. Make your references to the sources subordinate to the information.

18. As Martin Bellinger, Personnel Director of Four-N Company, write a memo report to R. H. Hamilton, Executive Officer, on the progress in Equal Employment Opportunity Program in your company using today's date. Your study included male and female of Caucasians, blacks, Orientals, American Indians, and Spanish, for three years ago and now during which time total employment grew 14 percent. You are reporting on just the blacks and whites because the other groups made up such a small percentage.

Percentage of male, female, and black employees in each job category for three years ago and now

	Male		*Female*		*Black*	
Job category	*3 years ago*	*Now*	*3 years ago*	*Now*	*3 years ago*	*Now*
Officials and managers	99.0%	97.2%	1.0%	2.8%	0.3%	0.9%
Professionals	96.9	92.1	3.1	7.9	0.9	2.0
Technicians	88.1	85.7	11.9	14.3	2.4	4.1
Sales workers	99.7	96.0	0.3	4.0	2.2	3.5
Office and clerical	28.0	19.3	72.0	80.7	2.6	4.1
Craftsmen	98.6	97.2	1.4	2.8	3.2	3.6
Operatives	60.5	58.7	39.5	41.3	6.2	6.9
Laborers	78.1	70.3	21.9	29.7	10.9	12.0
Service workers	77.2	84.6	22.8	15.4	5.4	6.4
All categories	75.4	72.7	24.6	27.3	3.6	4.5

The key word here is *progress*. As a principle and an agreement with EEOC (Equal Employment Opportunity Commission), the 4-N Company is committed to evolutionary (but not revolutionary) employment practices that lead to a work force which reflects the statistical picture of the competent people in the population of the area.

19. Assume that you are Donald R. Samdahl, Tool-Room Foreman, and you want to prepare a justification report for your boss Harvey Mappin, Operations Manager, Robinson Machine Company, New Brunswick, New Jersey 08901. For three years the Robinson Company has been sending tools for numbering to the Revere Electric Company, Patterson, New Jersey, for a cost of $477.50 annually, or 16 cents per tool. Robinson has more than 6,000 items in the tool-room, and Purchasing Department records indicate that annual replacements and additions average 2,980 items. Also, there's added cost of bookkeeping and transportation. And you're getting tired of all the lip (or worse) you have to take from mechanics when they want a tool and it's gone to Patterson for numbering.

An electric pencil with necessary attachments costs $63.85 and is made by the Heinz Products Company. Instruction on its use will be given to the employees of Robinson in an hour's time with no interruption of tool-room operation. Your men spend most of their time on tool maintenance, except during the rush at the first of the shift, and they would have plenty of time to number new tools as they are received. Much of tool maintenance is performed as a "time filler."

20. Andrew Beck, owner of Beck Furniture Company (makers of furniture and built-ins, Austin, Texas), has the problem of high electric bills (jumped from an average $3,500 a month three years ago to $7,500 per month last year and estimated to be $10,000 per month this year). He priced standard modern electrical generating equipment but felt he couldn't afford the one half to three quarters of a million dollar price. To help solve his problem he calls on you, a former electrical engineer for Texas Lone Star Company, Dallas, now doing private consulting, to advise him.

You discover that Beck has been burning wood sawdust for 20 years at the rate of ten tons a day. He even spent $125,000 last year for automatic disposal equipment, including air pollution control. Unbeknown to Beck, a cubic foot of sawdust has the same BTU (British Thermal Unit) value as a cubic foot of lignite coal. Thinking of the sawdust as fuel, when you looked for a steam boiler and electric generators you found that the Navy was decommissioning many of the old ships and for $300,000 you could purchase (from the famous old hospital ship *Hope*) the boiler, three 500 kilowatt steam generators, the coolers, the circulating system, and the switching system (and move them from Brownsville and set them up in Austin, in about six months). By using the generator set-up from *Hope* and sawdust from the furniture manufacturing process, Beck can save money on electricity. In your judgment (based on inspection) all these pieces of equipment should last at least 10 years. Justify the purchase of the equipment.

21. The stenographic work of the Tracey Manufacturing Company, Gadsden, Alabama, is handled by six typists who are paid $120 a 40-hour week. Two of them told the office manager, John B. Green, at the middle of the month that they plan to resign at the next middle of the month. You (assistant office manager) and Mr. Green have both expressed appreciation of their consideration in quitting at the end of a heavy work load and just before an annual half month of light work in the office.

You decided to investigate the advisability of purchasing electric typewriters instead of hiring two new employees. You wonder if the work could be handled by five typists if they had the new machines. You realize, of course, the importance of the typists' feelings concerning such a change.

Cost of new machine: $550 for one; $525 each in groups of four or more from the Electric Machine Company of Birmingham, installed and serviced. With one addition at $15 the electric outlets now in the office can be used.

Present employees' typing rate: between 55 and 65 words a minute.

Statement from Robert O. Smith, director of Smith Business College: When our students who make 60 words a minute on nonelectric machines change to the electric, they must practice for three or four weeks before they can get up to 60 again. However, in another two weeks most of them are making 80 or 90 words a minute without any trouble. Electric machines are so easy to operate that much of the usual strain is avoided.

One dealer in Gadsden offers $240 for your six old manuals.

The head of the stenographic department of the Maxwell Company says, "Since we installed electric typewriters, our typists have not complained of fatigue. I notice that they work more steadily, taking fewer 'breaks' during the day."

One of the four typists who will remain in the department has had experience with electric typewriters. She says, "I like them very much. I can type 60 words a minute on the typewriter I am using here now and 90 words a minute on an electric model." The other three remaining typists have not used electric typewriters, but they are in favor of the change, as they have heard so much about the ease of operation.

Submit your justification report to Mr. Green.

22. As an executive trainee in the Arcola, Mississippi, store of J. P. Taylor and Company, you were somewhat surprised to see that clerks in the piece-goods department used an ordinary yardstick attached to the counter to measure yard goods. They then labored at calculating the charges.

Wondering about the accuracy of the measurements and the calculations, one day you secretly asked customers leaving the store to let you check their purchases of ribbons, lace, elastic, eyelet trim, and dress and drapery materials. On the 50 purchases checked, you found an average of three inches in excess (though the individual discrepancies ranged from one half to eight inches), despite 17 cases of short measurement (none of which exceeded three inches). You also found four errors in the calculations—two for 10 cents and two for $1 in favor of the customer and one a customer had caught (and the clerk had corrected) because it was an overcharge of $1.

You want to suggest the purchase of a Measuregraph, a small cloth-measuring machine which is bolted unobtrusively and easily to the counter with four screws, and costs $90. It measures exactly and also calculates prices automatically, thus making easy and more accurate such calculations as 4⅜ yards at $2.67. The manufacturer guarantees the machine for one year, but information from the manufacturer's salesman and from users' testimonials indicates that it will probably last at least five years.

The piece-goods department employs three clerks, each averaging 24 sales a day for 300 working days a year. The piece goods average $1.98 a yard.

Submit your suggestion as a justification report (memo form) to the General Manager, H. M. Peterson.

23. As city manager in a sizeable city with an excellent three-year old city hall, you want to write a justification report to the five city commissioners recommending two daily 20-minute breaks for employees and an arrangement for an employee snack bar in available space in the hall. Adapting the selected space will cost $1,700, according to a careful estimate made by the contractor who built city hall.

Though breaks have never been approved, your talks with the nine department heads and every tenth name on alphabetical lists of employees reveal that about 67 percent of the 200 employees take one or more anyway (15–40 minutes), conscientious workers resent the liberties taken by others (and many of the guilty feel guilty), and department heads have quit trying to prevent the unapproved breaks.

The city attorney tells you that your proposals are legal, within the power of the city commissioners to authorize.

The proposed breaks are in line with allowed coffee-break time of at least half the business and industrial firms of the city and with the nationwide practices of three fourths of such firms (as reported in a recent survey by the National Office Management Association, *Coffee Breaks in U.S. Business and Industry*, Philadelphia, 1975, p. 17).

Three usual restrictions—which you would want to attach—are that no more than half the employees of a department may be out at any time, breaks longer than 20 minutes will result in deduction of an hour's pay (though with good cause and special permission of the immediate superior, an employee may occasionally combine two breaks for the day), and break time is not to compensate for tardiness or early departure.

The doctoral dissertation—*Efficiency and the Coffee Break*, Harvard Press, Boston, 1973, p. 268—of E. E. Jennings, now assistant professor of personnel management at Harvard, reports that breaks up to 20 minutes increase office-worker efficiency 4 percent in the morning and 6 percent in the afternoon.

From three highly respected restaurant owners who would like the concession, the best offer you could get was from a local man: A five-year lease renewable by mutual agreement, he to pay the city $100 a month plus 2 percent of gross profit.

The hall is three blocks from any presently existing restaurant.

CASES FOR SHORT ANALYTICAL REPORTS

1. As a researcher in the Food and Drug Administration, you made a study for your boss, M. T. Ormand. Using the findings given in the table below, write a report for Ormand, who will in turn make regulations and fix controls along with other administrators in the FDA.

You concentrated on fruits and vegetables. Your shoppers bought at least four samples of every brand (disguised as alphabet letters) and size of food on the list. Each can or package was weighed (solid and liquid) and was checked against the container's net weight declaration. Then you drained each food in accordance with a standard set by the U.S. FDA and weighed what was left.

	Labeled weight	*Average drained weight*		*Average price*	*Cost per lb. of drained weight*
The following fruits were packed in cans, except as noted.					
Fruit cocktail, in heavy syrup					
A	17 oz.	10.1 oz.	59.4%	$ .35	$ .55
B	17	10.7	62.9	.25	.37
C	17	11.9	70.0	.37	.50
D	16	10.9	68.1	.27	.40
Peach halves, yellow cling, in heavy syrup					
E	16	9.8	61.3	.27	.44
	29	17.0	58.6	.37	.35
A	16	9.8	61.3	.28	.46
	29	18.9	65.2	.37	.31
B	16	10.0	62.5	.25	.40
	29	18.6	64.1	.28	.24
D	16	10.5	65.6	.25	.38
	29	18.8	64.8	.33	.28
Pear halves, Bartlett, in heavy syrup					
E	29 oz.	16.2 oz.	55.9%	$ .45	$ .44
A	16	9.4	58.8	.35	.60
	29	16.2	55.9	.57	.56
B	16	9.2	57.5	.33	.57
	29	18.4	63.5	.49	.43
D	16	8.6	53.8	.29	.54
	29	17.2	59.3	.37	.34
Pineapple chunks, in heavy syrup					
E	13¼	8.2	61.9	.27	.53
F	20	13.0	65.0	.43	.53
B	20	13.0	65.0	.39	.48
D	15½	10.9	70.3	.29	.43
Prunes, in heavy syrup (jars)					
A	16	9.2	57.5	.39	.68
G	16	7.8	48.8	.39	.80

	Labeled weight	Average drained weight		Average price	Cost per lb. of drained weight
Strawberries, frozen (cartons)					
E	10	4.7	47.0	.29	.99
H	10	5.5	55.0	.39	1.13
B	10	7.2	72.0	.25	.56
The following frozen vegetables were packed in cartons.					
Asparagus spears					
E	10	10.5	105.0	.69	1.05
I	8	8.2	102.5	.51	1.00
B	10	10.2	102.0	.67	1.05
J	10	10.8	108.0	.73	1.08
Corn, whole kernel					
E	10 oz.	8.9 oz.	89.0%	$ .21	$ .38
H	10	10.2	102.0	.23	.36
B	10	10.2	102.0	.17	.27
D	10	10.3	103.0	.20	.31
Green beans					
E	9	9.1	101.1	.25	.44
H	9	9.1	101.1	.31	.55
B	9	9.1	101.1	.24	.42
D	9	9.2	102.2	.24	.42
Peas					
E	10	10.4	104.0	.21	.32
H	10	9.8	98.0	.35	.57
Spinach, chopped					
E	10	11.3	113.0	.18	.25
H	10	9.3	93.0	.22	.38
B	10	8.0	80.0	.17	.34
D	10	10.1	101.0	.16	.25
The following vegetables were packed in cans.					
Asparagus, spears					
E	15	8.3	55.3	.69	1.33
A	14½	9.1	62.8	.75	1.32
K	15	9.2	61.3	.81	1.41
D	19	11.4	60.0	.79	1.11
Beets, whole					
E	16 oz.	11.2 oz.	70.0%	$ .19	$ .27
B	16	11.3	70.6	.16	.23
D	16	10.8	67.5	.18	.27
Carrots, sliced					
E	16	10.5	65.6	.19	.29
A	16	9.8	61.3	.29	.47
B	16	10.9	68.1	.19	.28
C	11½	10.2	88.7	.21	.33

	Labeled weight	*Average drained weight*		*Average price*	*Cost per lb. of drained weight*
Corn, whole kernel					
K	17	11.6	68.2	.27	.37
C	17	11.0	64.7	.23	.33
Green beans, cut					
E	15½	9.2	59.4	.27	.47
A	16	9.3	58.1	.29	.50
K	16	9.6	60.0	.31	.52
C	16	10.2	63.8	.31	.49
Peas					
E	17	11.5	67.7	.27	.38
A	17	10.6	62.4	.20	.30
K	17	12.0	70.6	.37	.49
C	17	11.7	68.8	.27	.37
Spinach					
E	15	8.8	58.7	.25	.45
A	15	11.2	74.7	.28	.40
B	15	9.1	60.7	.20	.35

2. As the assistant dean referred to in Case 4, p. 521, you have seen that you have a pretty good ex-student evaluation of your college of business, especially in the last two tables in that case (9 and 10). Using only those two tables (and the explanation at the beginning of that case), write a short analytical report to the dean. Make itemized conclusions and recommendations for changes.

3. The biggest chain grocery in your locality is having quite a problem nationally with various forms of larceny—$8 million of losses last year through customer shoplifting, employee theft, etc. The management therefore issued a memo directing the manager of each store to study the situation and institute needed changes. (If you need another memo situation, here's one.)

The local manager, under whom you work, tossed the directive memo (and thus the ball) to you. You are to confer for any information already known, to study the layout and procedures by on-the-spot observation and questioning, and to propose the things to be done to reduce losses.

The job may or may not include a memo or other set of directions to all store employees on just what to do when they know or suspect that larceny or pilferage is going on. This could be a separate memo assignment, requiring a good knowledge of the law and/or law enforcement procedures —perhaps a talk with some police officers.

4. The owners of the Spell-Dees Nursery, Beaumont (Tom Spell and David Dees), have asked you, the office manager, to submit a report analyzing demand over the past few years.

You've gone through the sales records of the past four years to see what sells the best as a guide to what to plant the most of, what to reduce, and maybe even what to discontinue. Classifications are hard to set up; for instance, there's no way to tell what kinds of roses are in most frequent demand—but at average sales of $2, it's a safe bet that not many prize rosebushes are sold. But you've worked out the classifications, the number of bushes sold for the last four years, and the average sale of each variety.

Your records show that you average about 5 percent replacements; that is, about 5 out of every 100 plants sold have to be replaced under the terms of your replacement policy: replacement at one-half price if the plant dies within the first year. Your profit margin is about 50 percent.

Study the figures for what they imply in the way of increasing or decreasing demand for particular types and for the relative profitability of the various items. Then make recommendations about next year's stock.

Submit the report to the owners in attractive, readable form. Use a title page as a cover, a letter of transmittal which is also synopsis, and the analysis.

Gross sales of shrubbery sold by the Spell-Dees Nursery in the last four years

	Four years ago	*Three years ago*	*Two years ago*	*Last year*	*Average sale*
Abelia	2,896	2,980	4,422	4,460	$ 2.25
Ashfodi Juniper	136	144	202	235	3.00
Azalea	2,940	3,672	6,440	8,756	6.00
Berkman Arborvitae	146	105	137	165	3.50
Boxwood	126	262	344	423	18.00
Camellias	2,888	3,070	4,175	5,480	12.00
Cherry Laurel	174	198	234	256	9.00
Dogwood	81	76	143	166	4.00
Gardenia	1,178	1,239	1,897	1,976	9.00
Ilex Bullata	602	875	1,092	1,160	4.50
Ilex Burfordi	247	288	370	406	6.00
Ilex Rotundifolia	1,786	1,930	2,706	2,816	3.00
Irish Juniper	176	189	259	278	3.00
Ligustrum	2,982	2,646	4,562	4,250	4.50
Nandina	3,364	3,544	3,782	3,802	3.00
Pfitzer Juniper	2,078	2,108	2,986	3,208	2.50
Photinia Glabra	472	381	277	199	2.00
Roses	7,271	7,492	8,792	9,879	2.00
Sargent Barberry	601	507	488	462	3.00
Spirea	192	160	107	126	2.50
Spirea Thunbergia	148	164	92	86	3.00
Yellow Jasmine	296	243	203	194	4.00
Total	30,780	32,270	43,710	48,783	

5. In charge of the placement bureau at the University of Oklahoma, Norman, Doris Fields, director, decided to find out what personnel managers prefer in letters of application from college graduates. So she asked you, director of the research bureau, if you would help. After joint consultation with the head of the department of business communications, the head of the vocational guidance department, and the head of statistics, you prepared and sent the following questionnaire to 500 personnel managers in Indiana, Illinois, Ohio, Michigan, and Pennsylvania. The replies of the 324 who returned the questionnaire are tabulated below. From this material prepare a short analytical report for Fields which will help when she talks to applicants. Copies will also be available in school libraries. Submit the report to Fields with cover, title page, letter of transmittal, which is also an epitome, table of contents, the analysis, and conclusions and recommendations.

1. Which of the following do you prefer from an applicant?
   9 Application letter only
   86 Application letter and data sheet
   106 Application letter with placement office credentials sent separately
   123 Application letter and data sheet with placement office credentials separately
2. Which of the following is more important to you in evaluating an applicant:
   55 Application letter
   37 Data sheet
   232 Both equal in importance
3. *a*) Do you object to a duplicated letter of application?
   234 Yes 90 No
   b) When considering several applicants for a job, do you eliminate those who send you a duplicated letter of application?
   103 Yes 221 No
4. *a*) Do you object to a Mimeographed data sheet?
   76 Yes 248 No
   b) Do you object to a commercially printed data sheet?
   48 Yes 276 No
   c) When considering several applicants for a job, do you eliminate those who send you either of the following:
   Mimeographed data sheet 22 Yes 302 No
   Commercially printed data sheet 17 Yes 307 No
5. Which of the following do you prefer?
   123 Applicant's letter addressed to you by name, followed by your title
   85 Applicant's letter addressed to "Personnel Manager"
   116 No preference
6. What is your reaction to the following kinds of enclosures with the application?
   Return-addressed postal card
   29 Favorable 207 Unfavorable 88 Neutral
   Return-addressed stamped envelope
   164 Favorable 21 Unfavorable 139 Neutral
7. *a*) What is your reaction to an applicant's sending you a follow-up letter within a month after the original application?
   252 Good 10 Annoying 62 Neutral

b) If your answer to the above question is "Good," why do you favor a follow-up? (More than one reason allowed.)
73 Shows persistence
178 Indicates interest
220 Lets me know still available

8. In selecting inexperienced employees, which of the following backgrounds do you prefer? Please rank on a 1–2–3–4 basis (highest rank = 1).
   a) Applicant who participated in many extracurricular activities and maintained passing grades
   (1) 37, (2) 74, (3) 114, (4) 99
   b) Applicant who participated in several extracurricular activities and maintained above-average grades
   (1) 102, (2) 124, (3) 79, (4) 19
   c) Applicant who worked to help pay school expenses and maintained above-average grades
   (1) 164, (2) 106, (3) 36, (4) 18
   d) Applicant who participated in no extracurricular activities and maintained honor grades
   (1) 63, (2) 13, (3) 66, (4) 182

9. On many data sheets or application letters the applicant lists several specific references—usually under a caption labeled "References."
   a) When do you check these references?
   187 Before the interview
   120 After the interview
   17 Do not check
   b) Do you want this list of references included on the application?
   260 Yes 16 No 48 Immaterial
   c) If your answer to the above question is yes:
   (1) How many references do you prefer? Please encircle your choice.
   (1) 0, (2) 16, (3) 193, (4) 72, (5) 43
   (2) What types of references do you prefer? (Check as many as you desire.)
   314 Previous employers
   37 High-school teachers
   25 Dean of the college
   252 College teachers of related courses
   193 Former supervisors
   14 Other (banker? doctor? minister? family or fraternity friend?)

10. Many college students have worked. Do you want to know about these jobs

—whether related or not?	304 Yes	20 No
—part-time while attending school	298 Yes	26 No
—full-time during summers	306 Yes	18 No

11. Do you want personal details? (Age, physical condition, organization memberships, hobbies, etc.)
   312 Yes 10 No 2 Immaterial

12. If your answer to 11 is yes, where?
   37 Application letter 256 Data sheet 19 Immaterial

Appendixes

appendix A The communication process and semantic principles

The communication process

WHETHER YOU ARE talking or writing, listening or reading, you are doing one half (sending or receiving) of the two-way process of communication.

Essential to this process are symbols—usually words. (We are not concerned here with smoke signals, smiles, gestures, winks, and other forms of nonverbal communication.) When you have an idea to convey to somebody else, you cannot just hand over the idea; you necessarily use symbols of some kind. In oral communication, these are sounds; written, they become words, figures, charts, and other marks on paper. The first step in communication, then, is the sender's formulating ideas into symbols.

These sounds or written symbols do not communicate, however, until they go through some channel from the sender to the receiver.

Then, to complete the communication process, the receiver has to interpret these symbols back into an idea in essentially the same way the sender had to formulate the idea into symbols.

This simple-sounding three-step process of symbolizing, transmitting, and interpreting nevertheless involves many possibilities of breakdown of communication. If the person with the idea or concept has not learned to talk or is mute, or the would-be receiver is deaf, they obviously cannot communicate orally. But these are problems for the speech and hearing therapists. If the sender does not know how to write, or the receiver to read, they cannot use written symbols. But these are problems for the teachers of young children. Similarly, we leave to the Postal Service and the electrical engineers in telephone, telegraph, radio, and TV companies the manifold problems of transmitting symbols from sender to receiver with a minimum of interference (called "noise" by communications specialists).

But if the person with an idea has not learned the English language (a system of symbols) well enough for the expression of ideas according to the system, or if the receiver cannot interpret according to the system, they cannot communicate effectively—and they are our problem.

These two steps of formulating concepts into meaningful, standard symbols (frequently referred to as encoding) and interpreting the symbols (decoding) are the two major points of communication breakdown. Although many of the causes of communication breakdown involve decoding, we are concerned primarily with writing and hence deal mostly with encoding.

Some basic semantic principles[1]

Fundamental to communication is this general principle: *The symbols used must stand for essentially the same thing in the minds of the sender and the receiver.*

Just as our money is a medium of exchange for goods and services, our language has developed as a medium of exchange for ideas. Although the unit values of both may change with time and circumstances, at a given time and in a given set of circumstances the values of both are pretty well set. You therefore cannot pay a bill for 35 cents by offering a quarter, and you cannot convey the idea of localism by offering the word *colloquialism.* Good diction—choice of the proper word to represent the sender's idea—is thus a minimum essential in oral or written communication.

The diction problem is complicated by the fact that the sender's chosen words must also be in the receiver's vocabulary. You can't use perfectly good Greek to communicate to a person who knows only English. You can't use the highly technical language of medicine, law, engineering, insurance, or accounting to communicate with people who don't know the terms. They're all Greek to the nonspecialist. If you want to communicate, then, you must *estimate your receiver's vocabulary and adapt your own accordingly.* In general, you are justified in using unusual words or the special language of any field only if you're sure all your receivers know the terms or you explain them as you go along.

---

[1] The bibliography of semantics is extensive, and the books vary greatly in difficulty. If you want to read further on the subject, we suggest that you see the following books in the order listed: David K. Berlo, *The Process of Communication: An Introduction,* Holt, Rinehart & Winston, Inc., New York, 1960. William V. Haney, *Communication: Patterns and Incidents,* Richard D. Irwin, Inc., Homewood, Ill., 1960, and *Communication and Organizational Behavior,* 1967. Bess Sondel, *The Humanity of Words: A Primer of Semantics,* World Publishing Co., Cleveland, 1958. Stuart Chase, *Power of Words,* Harcourt, Brace, New York, 1954. Stephen Ullman, *Semantics: An Introduction to the Science of Meaning,* Barnes & Noble, Inc., New York, 1962. Irving J. Lee, *Handling Barriers in Communication,* International Society for General Semantics, 1968. S. I. Hayakawa, *Language in Thought and Action,* Harcourt, Brace, New York, 1972. John L. Austin, *How to Do Things with Words,* Harvard University Press, Cambridge, 1962. Alfred Korzybski, *Science and Sanity,* Institute of General Semantics, Lakeville, Conn., 1948. Ragnar Rommetviet, *Words, Meanings, and Messages,* Academic Press, New York, 1968. Chomsky, Noam, *Studies on Semantics in Generative Grammar,* Mouton, The Hague, 1972.

Even words which properly name a broad group of things for both sender and receiver, however, may still not reproduce in the mind of the receiver the sender's specific concept. If you write *machine* while thinking *typewriter,* your reader is likely to miss your intent by envisioning a calculator, a Mimeograph, or some other machine. To communicate well, then, a sender must *use words specific enough* for the necessary precision.

Even then, words alone are far from the whole of this system of symbols we call the English language; *the way they're put together, punctuated, and sometimes even spelled can make a vast difference.* A bear does not have a bare skin. To a reader who follows the English system of placing modifiers as close as possible to the things they modify, "Only three men passed the first screening" does not mean the same as "Three men passed the first screening only." To the reader who knows anything about the punctuation of essential and nonessential clauses, "The prices which are higher than those last year for the same items are simply too high" does not mean the same as "The prices, which are higher than those last year for the same items, are simply too high." To get the right idea, the reader has to assume that the writer didn't know how to handle participles when writing "Having hung by the heels in the 30-degree temperature overnight, we found the venison made an excellent breakfast." That writer tried to pass a lead nickel in our medium of exchange, the English language. Remember the fundamental principle: *The symbols used must stand for essentially the same thing in the minds of the sender and the receiver.*

Here are eight specific principles that might be considered subheads of the general principle.

1. *A statement is never the whole story.* Even in reporting the simplest event, you omit some details which another reporter might well have told. Usually you report only on the macroscopic level, omitting additional details that could be added if you made microscopic or submicroscopic examinations of all the objects involved. But you also omit much of the macroscopic. Even if you think you cover the standard *who, where, when, why, what,* and *how,* another reporter could easily add more details and more specifics on each of them. By way of illustration, consider how infrequently you see, in other reports, certain details that are standard in police reports of traffic accidents: mental and physical condition of the driver(s), weather conditions, condition of the roadway, etc.

Whether you are sending or receiving the facts and arguments in a court case, you do not have the whole story. Even the witness who takes an oath to tell the truth, the whole truth, and nothing but the truth, never does; additional questions could always bring out more. Even an application letter of ten pages does not tell the whole life story of the applicant.

This concept of inevitable incompleteness—often called "abstracting" and defined as calling attention to some details while neglecting others—is basic in the thinking of semanticists. The International Society for General Semantics has therefore titled its journal *ETC.*, thus stressing Korzybski's suggestion that writers use the abbreviation as a reminder and warning that their statements are incomplete.

The importance of the incompleteness concept stems from the dangers of ignoring it—the "allness" fallacy. If you consider only parts of a whole and judge the whole, you're in danger of the logical fallacy of hasty generalization and unsound conclusions like those of the six blind men who each described an elephant after feeling only one part. If you forget that you do not have all the facts, you are in danger of closing your mind to other facts and points of view. You may think of your way as the only way. You thus act on the basis of preconception and may become unteachable. intolerant, dogmatic, and arrogant. Recognizing that you never have the whole story, on the other hand, helps to keep you open-minded, tolerant, and humble. That's one of the values of travel and of a broad education: to open the mind and replace the provincialism of the person who knows only a small area. The Italians have a proverb which makes the point: *Assai sa chi sa che non sa,* freely translated as "He knows a lot who knows that he doesn't know."

2. *Perception involves both the perceived and the perceiver.* Since you are never telling or considering the whole story, you are *selecting,* from all things that might be or have been said, *those which seem to you important.* What you say about a thing or how you react to it, then, often depends as much on you as on what the thing really is.

Both your judgment of what is important to select and your conclusions based on selected facts are influenced by the kind of person you are. And you are what you are (different from anybody else) because of different inherited traits and different experiences. Your special interests, values, tastes, and attitudes will naturally cause what you say about a thing or how you react to a statement to differ from what anybody else would say or do. In effect, you are a special filter. Another filter (person) with different characteristics would filter out different things. Hence neither of you can be strictly objective. When we claim to be objective, we are deluding ourselves—and others if they believe us. And when we expect others to be objective or to see things exactly as we do, we are simply being unrealistic. Constant recognition of this point will help to keep you reasonably tolerant of people who disagree a bit.

A famous French movie aptly illustrates the point that a person's background influences decisions—sometimes more than the factual evidence. The movie gives a life history (selected, of course) of each juror in an important trial and shows how the different backgrounds produced different votes in the jury room, even though all jurors had heard and seen exactly the same evidence.

Thorough recognition of the point—that in terms of background and point of view the other person may be just as nearly right as you are—can go a long way toward preventing disagreements by making you cautious about using *is* dogmatically. When you use *is* to connect a noun and adjective ("Harry Smith is honest"), you are saying that the quality of honesty belongs to or exists in Smith. This predicate-adjective construction, using what some semanticists call the "*is* of predication," actually misrepresents reality and often seems dogmatic because the receiver either knows different facts about Smith or defines honesty differently. If you remember that your thinking about Smith is influenced by what you know about him (not *all* the facts) *and* by what honesty means to you (probably somewhat different from what it means to the other person), you are more likely to say, less dogmatically, "Harry Smith seems to me . . ."—and to avoid an argument or even a fight.

Two subpoints about the perceiver and the perceived deserve special attention.

a) By the psychological principle of projection, we are inclined to attribute to others our own characteristics and feelings. People who pay their bills are inclined to assume that others will too. The reverse is also true. A credit manager—and anybody else who wants to avoid being duped—needs to realize that views of things depend heavily on the kind of person involved and that others may have different views. The wise credit manager will use the statistician's rather than the psychologist's meaning of *projection:* Get information about a credit applicant's past reputation for paying bills, project the trend line, and decide to approve or disapprove the application according to where the projection points.

b) Psychologists also tell us that we are inclined to resist the unpleasant. Facts and ideas that go contrary to our preconceptions, wishful thinkings, and other selfish interests are among the unpleasant things we must face because they provoke us to change our comfortable old ways. A semantically sound person will therefore try to avoid the comfortable but antisemantic idea in "Don't confuse me with facts; my mind's made up."

3. *Statements or actions based on whims, feelings, imaginings, preconceptions, customs, traditions, and platitudes are questionable.* Although you never get all the relevant facts, and although you can never be strictly objective in evaluating those you do get, you should get what facts you can and evaluate them as objectively as you can. You need not give up and use the excuse "all or nothing." Ignoring observable facts will almost certainly lead you into conflict with reality. And when you go too far "out of touch with reality," as the psychiatrists say, you base action on emotion instead of reason, and you go to the bughouse.

A reasonable approach to problem solving involves two beginning questions: (*a*) What are the facts? (*b*) How do you know? Because of the importance of instantaneous response in some simple situations, we have certain reflex mechanisms (for blinking the eyes, sneezing, etc.) that do not involve thinking. But you are courting real trouble if you make reflex responses to complex situations. Fortunately, as situations become more complex, the allowable time for decision becomes greater, and the reactions become voluntary. A reasonable person will use some of that time to collect and consider at least some of the significant facts—as some semanticists say, will look at the territory before drawing a map; will be extensionally instead of intensionally oriented; will look outside the skin for some facts instead of relying wholly on internal feelings and cogitations. To do otherwise is to act on prejudices, preconceptions, and whims.

While considering the collected data, you need to ask, "How do you know that this information is reliable?" Many platitudes, prejudices, customs, and the like are based on assumptions that simply do not line up with reality. Even "well-established" teachings of science are often discarded after the discovery of new evidence by such researchers as Harvey, Pasteur, and Reed. The atom that could not be split, according to "authoritative" books not many years ago, has been split. More recently, discoveries in outer space are bringing into question many of the "established" principles meteorologists have followed for years.

If scientists—who generally pride themselves on being careful in collecting data and in drawing conclusions, and who usually have good equipment—can be so wrong and so dogmatic as they have been on some of these things, should we all not learn the lesson of humility and caution? Should we not all be careful about the adequacy and the reliability of what appears to be information, and about the validity of our conclusions? Surely we should all see the dangers of accepting information from old books. And the disagreements among "authorities" in almost every field should warn us to question authoritative statements or at least to check them as best we can against our own experience. Even then, reasonable humility would seem to warn that we rarely "prove" anything well enough to justify saying such and such *is true*.

Incidentally, our best modern scientists have just about learned their lessons. They now admit that they usually deal with probabilities rather than certainties.

If the careful research methods and conclusion making of scientists still lead to questionable results and probable truths, what of the statements of people who do not bother to get the facts at all and, without thinking or checking, act on the bases of prejudices, preconceptions, whims, etc.? A semanticist would at least warn you to take what they say with a few grains of semantic salt.

4. *Facts, inferences, and value judgments are not the same thing.* If you have ever heard a court trial, you have probably heard a judge order some testimony stricken from the record because the witness was stating opinions or conclusions (inferences) rather than that seen, heard, felt, etc. (sense data). The fact that our legal procedures do not allow inferences as evidence unless the inferences are made by experts reflects society's faith in sense data and its lack of faith in inferences unless made by people specially qualified to make them. Most of us would do well to be more skeptical of the mouthings of people who have not bothered to get the facts—and especially of nonexperts talking on professional topics.

You see why when you consider the nature of sense data, inferences, and value judgments. Sense data usually approach certainty, inferences vary all the way from near certainty to slight probability (usually depending mainly on how many verifiable facts form the basis for them), and value judgments are nearly always debatable. For example, you see a good friend in a men's store on December 20. She tells you that she wants to buy a tie for her husband Joe and asks your help in selecting a pretty one. After she disapproves three ties you suggest and then you disapprove three she is considering, you leave her to make her own choice because you see that the two of you don't agree on what is a nice tie (value judgments). On December 27 you see Joe wearing a tie that seems to be new and looks like one of the three Jane suggested and you disapproved. More courteously than sincerely, you say, "That is a pretty tie Jane bought you." (Note the dogmatic *is*, discussed in Item 2 above.) Joe says that he hates to be so disagreeable, but he thinks it's ugly and Jane didn't buy it. You see that your value judgment matches Joe's better than Jane's; and when Joe tells you that a friend gave him the tie, you see that you took a calculated risk with your inference—and lost. (Note that to make this decision, you have to assume that Joe is reporting facts.)

Not even the courts rule out inferences completely, however. Judges make them, and jurors' votes are pure inferences. As a matter of practicality, we make and act on inferences all the time. We have to. We cannot always know with the near certainty of sense data; many times we have to act on inferences and thus take calculated risks. Even calculated risks, however, are based on *some* data and are safer than wild guesses or hunches.

The danger in inferences is not in acting on them but in acting on them *as if* they were completely reliable. By recognizing the risks we are taking when acting on inferences, or even on hunches, we can reduce the danger considerably because we will not be so surprised by otherwise unexpected turns of events.

To avoid deluding ourselves and others with whom we communicate, then, we will do well to remind ourselves and forewarn others of the *bases* on which our statements rest. A statement, like a ladder, is no more secure than its foundation. Our readers and listeners have a right to know about the foundations if they are going to risk their necks on our ladders.

Still, we need not make ourselves as ridiculous as the skeptical farmer who remarked, "At least it is black on this side," when asked to observe that black sheep in the pasture. He did seem a bit ridiculous, but he was semantically no sucker.

5. *No two things are exactly alike*. Even things so much alike that they appear identical to the naked eye always reveal differences under close inspection. To be absolutely precise in naming things would require a different word or other symbol for each. Obviously, such precision is impractical—and unnecessary for most purposes.

General words, naming whole groups of things similar in one or more aspects that concern us, help us in classifications. Thus we can save words and time by talking about, or otherwise treating, somewhat similar things collectively instead of individually. If what we say or do with the group applies equally well to all members of the group, we operate efficiently.

Trouble arises quickly, however, when we group things on the basis of a few similarities and then act as if all things in the group were identical in all ways. Such a situation exists when colleges try to treat all freshmen alike because all are first-year students, ignoring the great variety of interests and abilities in the individuals.

Some ugly results of ignoring differences and stressing similarities are faulty categorizing (or labeling or pigeonholing) and faulty analogy making. Thus we get the unsound, unyielding, and prejudicial stereotyping so often seen in fiction. Not all cowboys, politicians, professors, businessmen, delinquent credit customers, Russians, or blacks are alike—although they may have some similarities that justify the grouping *for a particular purpose.*

As a communicator, you can do several things to help solve the problem. For one thing, you can *use symbols (usually words) that are specific enough for your purposes.* When you do mean your statement to apply equally to a number of somewhat similar things (perhaps all new customers), be efficient and use the group name instead of handling each separately; but surely you should not lump together for similar handling as "delinquent accounts" the good customer who got behind because of a temporary misfortune and the marginal risk who tried to skip by moving and leaving no address. And if what you say applies only to typewriters, don't say machines. If it applies only to portables, don't say typewriters. If it applies only to Royal portables, don't just say portables.

Accepting the premise of uniqueness, and recognizing the fallacy of identity, some semanticists recommend using the "which index." To distinguish which individual they are referring to in a group name, they suggest using subscript numbers after the name, typewriter_1 being different from typewriter_2. Carried to extremes, this system is as impractical as the limitless vocabulary necessary to give each individual thing a name; but used in moderation, it can help. In either case a little use of it will remind you of an important point: If significant differences exist in the group named, make clear which members of the group you are talking about. "Businessmen who do such and such things are unethical" is quite different from "Businessmen are unethical."

For another thing, you can *consider significant differences along with similarities.* Analogies, similes, and other metaphors pointing to the similarities between two things help greatly in explanations. Indeed, they become almost necessary, because teaching and learning involve explanation of the unknown in terms of the known. Dictionaries explain words in terms of other words presumably known to the dictionary user. You often hear and read explanations in terms of a football game, which you presumably understand. Because you know English verbs generally go like *stay, stayed, stayed,* you can usually form the past tense and the past participle of a verb you have just learned. But if the new verb is *think*, the analogy misleads you.

That misleading analogy points to three warnings about using analogies to make them helpful rather than harmful.

a) Since no two things are exactly alike, no analogy can be complete. Although *stay* and *think* are both English verbs, they belong to different classes. Although we speak of synonyms, they are alike only in some ways and are not always interchangeable.

b) Because two or more things always have some differences even when they are largely similar, an analogy never proves anything. The truth may slip through one of the holes that make the difference between the two "analogous" things. Stock-market and weather forecasters are often wrong because they have failed to consider significant differences in generally similar background conditions.

c) In using analogies, you must be sure your reader understands the supposedly known side of your analogy. Otherwise, you are in the position of one explaining a Russian word in Chinese terms to a person who knows neither language.

6. *Some either-or, black-white classifications are legitimate, but most are not.* The question is whether your two-part classifications are mutually exclusive. A person is either married or not; no one can be both married and not married at the same time. But you cannot say with equal validity that the same person is tall, intelligent, honest, and the like. Where do you draw the line between intelligent and not intelligent, honest and not honest?

You are being true to reality when you use either-or, black-white, two-valued logic for mutually exclusive things—things that cannot both exist at the same time. But most things are continua, with gradations, shadings, or degrees between the extremes. For them you need a "how-much index." Applying black-white logic to them ignores the gray. It is similar to the false dilemma in logic. And like the false dilemma, it is used especially by the unthinking, the intolerant, and the shysters among us. The results are delusions of self and others, intolerance, and hard feelings if not fights.

As a communicator, you can do several things to avoid the undesirable consequences of two-valued thinking. First, you must recognize the difference between legitimate (mutually exclusive) two-pole classifications and continua. Then you can use the readily available facilities of English to show the proper gradations in continua. English contains not only somewhat similar nouns of varying degrees of specificity and strength but a large supply of adjectives and adverbs with similar variations. Moreover, the adjectives and adverbs have three standard degrees of comparison like *good, better, best* and *speedily, more speedily,* and *most speedily.* If you still feel the need for better indication of the degree of grayness in a continuum, you can always *add* specific details, as in "Quickly (3.2 seconds) the operator turned the heavy (5-ton) crane around and. . . ."

7. *Things change significantly with time.* Nature works as a dynamic process. As part of nature, Joe Smith today is not exactly the same as Joe Smith yesterday, much less 10 years ago. Significant aspects of a present situation may not have existed in the past and may not continue in the future. To be true to reality, you need to consider the date in connection with statements sent or received. Some semanticists refer to this principle as the necessity for the "when index." Ignoring it produces what some call the "frozen evaluation."

Most universities recognize the point in readmitting students, after specified periods of time, who were dropped for poor scholarship or infraction of rules. Most homes would run more smoothly if parents would recognize that their teen-agers are no longer babies. Ex-convicts could readjust to normal living much more easily if their neighbors would at least give them a chance to show whether they have changed instead of pinning permanent labels on them. Many blue laws on statute books should be rescinded. We may as well get used to reinterpretations of the Constitution—and to changed usages and new dictionaries of English. Our language is not static. Fighting new English textbooks and new dictionaries (which do not make but merely record current usage) is more futile than fighting city hall; it's fighting the whole country. Surely a credit manager should know that the facts which force refusal of requested credit may change in a few months—and should hold open the possibility of reconsidering them.

8. *Words are not identical to the objects they represent.* They are symbols of concepts that exist only in the mind. They do not have meanings themselves but only the power to represent or evoke meanings in our minds.

Concrete objects react on our various senses to give us our concepts of those things. We then use words to represent those concepts. Only the physical objects are real; our concepts and the symbols (words) to represent them are the first and second levels of abstraction in the "ladder of abstraction" or "structural differential" which semanticists talk about.

In this scheme, clearly the names we give are not the things themselves—even names that have referents (concrete, tangible objects to which they refer). If you question this statement, try eating the word *pie* the next time you get hungry for something sweet. Or since a word is to its referent as a map is to its territory, just take a walk on your map the next time you want to take a trip. As Korzybski repeatedly explains, our words merely represent the world of events and things outside our skins but are never the real things. Ogden and Richards (*The Meaning of Meaning*) present the symbolic nature of language as a triangle, the three points representing referent, thought, and symbol.

This semantic principle of the symbolic nature of language points to these suggestions for better communication:

a) Insofar as possible, use words with real physical objects or actions as referents, and make them specific enough to call to the receiver's mind the particular referent. If your receiver has seen or touched the kind of thing you are talking about, the concepts you want to convey about it are clearer than if you talk in generalities or talk about abstractions (concepts like loyalty and honesty that do not exist in the physical world but only in the mind). Even when your word has a referent, avoid equating the word with the physical object (for which it is only a symbol) or with some facet of it: "Russia *is* the Berlin Wall" or "Communism *is*. . . ."

b) Especially in reading and listening, try to look behind the words and envision the things and ideas the words represent. You can remember the thought much easier than all the exact words used to represent it. And in taking notes or answering questions about what you've heard or read, present the concepts in your own words except for key words and phrases. If you concentrate on words, you'll likely learn the words and repeat them parrotlike without understanding the thought they were intended to convey. Instead, concentrate on "What does the message sender mean by those words?"

c) Although you cannot avoid the use of some abstract words (which have no referents in the physical world), try to keep them to a minimum. Then consider the context in which they are used. If you have described several actions taken and then you commend the person for *integrity*, the context makes clear what you mean by the otherwise abstract word *integrity*. That's the way abstract words are used best: as summarizing words.

Listening and reading

Speaking and writing are forms of the initiating or encoding phase of communication. Listening and reading are forms of the receiving or decoding phase. Considerable skill in each is vital for a literate individual in today's civilization.

Most training in schools is devoted to writing, reading, and—to a lesser extent—speaking. Yet from the time we start to learn, we spend at least as much communicating time in listening as we do on all the other three. As we advance and become more proficient in and dependent on reading, many of us, unless we consciously strive to do otherwise, steadily deteriorate in listening efficiency.

But how much easier we can make our learning and living if we develop and maintain skill in listening (to TV, radio, lectures, sermons, interviews, conferences, directives, conversations, etc.), which accounts for about three times as much of our communication time as reading does!

The task of listening.[2] Neither good reading nor good listening is easy.

---

[2] See Ralph G. Nichols and Leonard A. Stevens, *Are You Listening?* McGraw-Hill Book Co., Inc., New York, 1957, 235 pp.; Ralph G. Nichols and Thomas R. Lewis, *Speaking and Listening*, William C. Brown Co., Dubuque, 1965, 357 pp. Both these publications contain extensive bibliographies.

Both require training, either supervised or self-disciplined. Of the two activities, listening is the more demanding and the more difficult for most of us. The written word is always there for the reader to go back to. The spoken word, once uttered, is gone unless stored in the reader's mind (a job that most of us do not perform well). The reader can proceed at a self-chosen speed; the listener must adapt to the pace of the speaker.

Although the statement may strike you as obvious, learning to be a good reader does not make you a good listener any more than learning to be a good listener makes you a good reader. Several differences in the two communicating processes help to explain why. Not only are the styles different (greater variety in sentence length and style, much more use of phrases, more personal references, more informality, more repetitions, and more adaptations in oral than in written). The role of the nonverbal is even more significant. A speaker's gestures, facial expressions, pitch of voice, inflections, rhythm and speed, and pronunciation constantly affect the final message received by listeners.

The reader uses eyes alone. The listener uses eyes and ears. This concentration of effort is no easy matter to be taken for granted. It can be immensely rewarding, however.

Although in what we shall term "everyday living" you will listen and learn in interviews, lectures, conferences, and conversation, the following suggestions are concerned primarily with listening to speeches and lectures.

Identify the subject and plan. Most speakers will deliver planned talks organized in the traditional pattern of introduction, thesis, body, and conclusion.

Many excellent speakers will tell a story, or quote from some well-known authority or publication, or say something startling first to secure your favorable attention. Such a beginning may be appropriate, even germane, but rarely is it of the essence. Many excellent lecturers dispense with the irrelevant beginning and start immediately with genuine subject matter, and wisely so.

The essential point for concentration is when the speaker announces the subject, why it is pertinent, and the plan of presentation. If you are not tuned in for this thesis statement, you are going to have difficulty following the rest.

Stay tuned in. The body of the speech (the longest part) includes all the points that support the speaker's fundamental proposition or thesis. The evidence may be statistics, testimony, or stories, to name some.

Major points and the evidence supporting them may come in *deductive* order (usual if the purpose is only to inform). This is, stated very simply, generalization followed by supporting detail. If the purpose is to persuade, an *inductive* order (generalization after evidence) will be better—and more likely if the speaker is a good one.

Obviously, this is the part on which you should exercise your powers of concentration and your critical faculties. The questions of completeness, validity, appropriateness, and recency are significant here.

You will find this part easier to follow (and more interesting to you) if, when possible, you check the speaker's announced plan of presentation against delivery and stay on the alert for transitions—those statements signaling a change of point. The points or principles (the *ideas*) the speaker establishes fill in the blueprint of the plan and establish the final structure. The *facts* supporting the principles are subheads.

If the speaker announces no plan, try to anticipate what is coming. If your guess proves to be right, you'll feel pleasure—and probably reveal it in an empathic circuit response to the speaker. And if you're wrong? Never mind, you'll have concentrated better and benefited from the mental exercise of comparison and contrast.

Good speakers (and good writers) build up their points or principles step by step so that the conclusion suggests itself before it is announced. In an informative speech the conclusion is often very short. It may be no more than a quick recap of the main points and a brief statement of how the thesis (or subject or speech) is significant to the audience. The conclusion of the persuasive speech may be a little longer. The persuasive speaker may not reveal a stand until this time. In addition to establishing the real objective, some speakers may use strong argument. Question. Challenge. But reserve judgment until you've had the time to sift and revaluate —to review and rebuild.

When you're the trapped victim of a speaker who indulges in harangue, cajoling, or bombast, tune out; you're entitled to stop listening.

Be sensible; control your note-taking. The temptation to apply pencil or pen to paper and start to record a speaker's words verbatim is one that is too great for many listeners to overcome—unfortunately. This kind of note-taking causes even the experienced listener to lose many of the significant ideas, to become confused, and eventually to become frustrated and give up on note-taking—and usually on listening also.

Most speakers and lecturers agree that good listeners take good notes. They also agree that those who take good notes *listen a lot and write a little*. Possibly the best piece of advice we can give you is to keep your notes brief and clear during listening (complete thoughts for major points; just words and short phrases for supporting details). You can expand and review later.

Rarely does an introduction merit recording. Even the thesis is better not written down when first stated—although you certainly want to have it clearly in mind when the speaker launches into main points and evidence. (Write it down after the completed speech.) Even the brief outline or plan (if the speaker gives you one) is better recorded point by point as you go along rather than at the time the speaker first announces it, just before going into the first major point.

In listening, try to jot down ideas, not facts and illustrations. The careful distinction between fact and idea leads a listener to one system of note-taking that is economical and efficient. Divide your paper into two columns, one for facts, the other for principles. You'll have difficulty determining which is which sometimes. But the effort will help you to concentrate and will provide enough useful reminders for later review. You'll have more entries in your facts column than in your principles column. If you have to slight the recording of one, slight the facts; concentrate on the principles.

An even less time-consuming system of note-taking is that of précis writing. (The words *abstract* and *summary,* even *synopsis* and *epitome,* mean essentially the same.) Stated very simply, this means to listen extensively, then write rapidly. Most speakers will state a generalization followed by supporting details (or the reverse) and then, by a clearly indicated transition, signal the completion of that point and the approach of another. During this time, jot down a sentence or two stating in your own words the idea or principle the speaker has attempted to establish. Then resume listening until the next generalization.

Certainly, as a good listener, you will always write a précis of the conclusion and of the thesis or fundamental proposition (the latter preferably after the speaker has finished).

The sooner you can review your notes after the speech, the better. Of course, as you listened, you should have mentally questioned for completeness, adequacy and appropriateness, authenticity, recency, and omission of data. An even more fruitful time to do this is shortly after the talk in a review of notes, supplementing and rebuilding, questioning, searching for negative evidence, and finally arriving at an evaluation.

As a good listener, you want to strive to understand each main point made by your speaker. If you're too preoccupied with catching errors, you won't get the message. Withhold your judgments and decisions until after you have reviewed the main ideas and thesis.

Avoid the main stumbling blocks to good listening. Without the wish and the will to, you won't profit from anyone's suggestions. Our pointing out some common failings may help you to improve, however.

To begin with, accept the fact that listening is hard work demanding patience, an open mind, a considerate—even charitable—mind. Most of us much prefer to consider our own individual interests and air what is on our own minds. The temptation to tune out and escape to reverie or daydreaming is ever with us.

And so we are prone to pretend attention when our minds are not receiving any ideas being transmitted. No speaker with much experience is easily fooled by the head nodder, the glassy-eyed starer, the marbleized "thinker." Such audience characters are only fooling themselves. They are no more interested in listening than the foot tapper, the pen flipper, the book slammer, etc. If you fall in one of these classes, wake up—and learn.

Another stumbling block is undue attention to the speaker's appearance, voice, or speech characteristics. A word is only a symbol, not reality; a speaker's appearance is only an outward shell, not an indicator of mind; speech is only the vehicle, not the idea. Although we all like to be personable people and do respond in almost motor fashion more to good-looking people than to those who are not, don't shut yourself off from learning because of a person's physiognomy, size, dress, or voice characteristics. The mind may have a lot to contribute.

All too often we are guilty of abruptly rejecting or dismissing a speaker and subject because we consider them dull or difficult. Very few "uninteresting" speeches are devoid of something useful. Remember that the "dull" speaker is probably doing just what the assignment was—to give you facts and ideas—and refusing to insult your intelligence, or take pay under false pretenses, by entertaining you instead. Be selfish: Take for yourself what is meaningful and useful. As for rejecting the difficult discourse, remember that this can become a pattern of progressive mental deterioration. The more you do it, the flabbier and more superficial your mind becomes. The only suggestions we can make are continually renewed determination to "hear the speaker out" and a planned effort to tackle uninteresting as well as difficult material.

Another stumbling block is the tendency of listeners to let physical surroundings distract them. Airplanes, buses, trains, thunder, and other outside noises are sometimes loud, and rarely can the listener do anything about them. But they are noises that most of us readily ignore when we want to (during a favorite TV program, for instance). Many physical circumstances you can control as an individual. Windows and doors close as well as open. Heating mechanisms turn off as well as on. If you as an individual can't control the distraction, enlist the aid of the speaker. Even if listeners and speakers are trapped and can't move to a more favorable place, at least they will be alerted to the fact that both will have to exert extra effort to concentrate on effective sending and receiving of the message.

One more point, which is a reminder of something already said: In your listening, concentrate on principles, not detailed facts presented in support of principles. Emphasis on facts makes you lose principles, which are the most significant parts of speeches; emphasis on principles makes you not only get the principles or ideas but also helps you remember many of the facts that support them.

Efficient reading. Much of what was said about listening in the preceding section also applies to reading. We shall therefore discuss this form of the receiving phase of communication in much less detail than the listening form just covered.

If you are reading only for pleasure, you can relax and be almost passive as you proceed at whatever pace you please. If you are not satisfied with your reading pace, you may want to enroll for one of the reading-improvement courses offered by many schools and counseling services or clinics.

The aim of these courses is to increase the reader's rate and comprehension. If no such work or counseling is available to you, you may want to read some of the excellent books on the subject.[3]

If you are reading for information and instruction (as opposed to pleasure or entertainment), you can profit even more from such courses and books. The following brief suggestions give you only the main points of some of these books.

When you read an informative publication (book, section, chapter, or article):

1. Understand the scope and limitations of the subject as evidenced in the title and often in a subtitle, the preface, and introductory comments.
2. Determine as closely as you can the primary purpose, which may be only implied. Phrase it in your own words.
3. Take advantage of mechanical aids (indentions, paragraphing, outline symbols, change of type, etc.) and transitions as you read through the first time *rapidly*. Don't ponder over phrases or even whole sentences; don't look up definitions. *Read through and read fast!*
4. When you've finished, try to recall as much as you can. Check the theme or central idea you have formulated against the author's expression of it either in the ending or in the beginning.
5. Reread the material paragraph by paragraph. (The first rapid reading will decrease your reading time at this stage, and much that was foggy the first time will be clear.) If you own the material (but not in library materials, please!), underscore key words and topic sentences, often at the beginning or end.

Then

1. If you are reasonably certain of the meaning of a word from the context, you are probably safe in not looking it up. Otherwise, look it up and pencil the appropriate definition in the margin.

---

[3] We suggest that you start with these books in this order (some of them have bibliographies to direct you further): (*a*) Mortimer J. Adler, *How to Read a Book*, Simon and Schuster, Inc., New York, 1940; (*b*) Walter Hill and William Eller, *Power in Reading Skills,* Wadsworth Publishing Co., Inc., Belmont, Calif., 1964; (*c*) A. L. Raygor and D. M. Wark, *Systems for Study,* McGraw-Hill Book Co., New York, 1970; G. A. Gladstein, *Individualized Study,* Rand McNally, Chicago, 1967; and William W. Farquhar et al., *Learning to Study,* Ronald Press Co., New York, 1960; (*d*) Luella Cole, *Students' Guide to Efficient Study,* Holt, Rinehart & Winston, Inc., New York, 1960; (*e*) Walter Pauk, *How to Study in College,* Houghton Mifflin Co., Boston, 1962; (*f*) Francis P. Robinson, *Effective Study,* Harper & Bros., New York, 1970; (*g*) George D. Spache and Paul C. Berg, *The Art of Efficient Reading,* Macmillan Co., New York, 1966; (*h*) Arthur S. McDonald and George H. Zimny, *The Art of Good Reading,* Bobbs-Merrill Co., Inc., Indianapolis, 1963; (*i*) James I. Brown, *Efficient Reading,* D. C. Heath & Co., Boston, 1962; (*j*) Horace Judson, *The Techniques of Reading,* Harcourt, Brace, New York, 1963; (*k*) Paul D. Leedy, *Read with Speed and Precision,* McGraw-Hill Book Co., Inc., New York, 1963, and *A Key to Better Reading,* 1968; (*l*) M. J. Maxwell, *Skimming and Scanning Improvement,* McGraw-Hill Book Co., New York, 1969; and Paul C. Berg, et al., *Skimming and Scanning,* Educational Developmental Laboratories, Huntington, N.Y., 1962; (*m*) A. L. Raygor and G. B. Schick, *Reading at Efficient Rates,* McGraw-Hill Book Co., New York, 1970.

2. When the article is fairly short and not formally organized, you're probably better off simply to write a short précis.

3. When the article or chapter is formally organized, you may want to write a formal outline. Such outlining is another step in remembering and is a vital necessity if you need to submit an oral or a written report.

These suggestions apply if you want or need to do more than record and possibly transmit what some author write. If you want or need to evaluate, you will have to answer such questions as the following:

1. About the author:
   Who? Position or status? Authority? Biased?
2. About the treatment:
   a) Are generalizations supported by evidence? Ample? Secondary or primary? Based on sound research?
   b) Is coverage of major points adequate? Significant omissions?
   c) What is the announced or apparent intended audience? Is treatment adapted to this audience?

You can add to this list. Certainly it is not intended to be exhaustive.

And remember, no speaker or writer is infallible. A printed statement often means nothing more than that the statement is in print.

Speaking

Speaking is one form of the initiating or transmitting phase of communication (the other, of course, is writing, with which the greatest part of this book is concerned). This treatment of speaking is brief because we have pointed out in the sections on listening some of the basic considerations affecting speakers and speeches and because this book is *not* intended for use in speech development. So many excellent books on the subject are available that we shall not even suggest any.

Certainly successful speeches are characterized by centrality of theme, adequate and reliable facts, coherent and compact organization, clarity and vividness of phrasing, and other stylistic considerations which are also characteristics of good writing.

Although a speaker is relieved of the necessity for observing the conventions of punctuation and spelling, the responsibility for indisputable pronunciation and a greater responsibility for clear, unmistakable labeling of parts (transitions, topic ideas) are there because listeners have no opportunity to ask for repetition of a point—unless in conversation. A writer knows that a reader can, if absolutely necessary, go back and reread passages which are not immediately clear. A listener (except in conversation) must understand the first time or not at all.

Precise pronunciation (necessary in speaking) will help you to eliminate many spelling errors when you write. The principles of good organization you learn in becoming a good speaker will carry over to make you a better writer—and vice versa. And since you talk (not necessarily make a speech) much more frequently than you write, you will write more clearly, effectively, and economically *if you make a constant effort also to speak that way.* Unfortunately, however, most of us merely converse; we do not plan and deliver speeches. And many of us do not practice precision and economy of speech or grammatically acceptable language in our daily conversations. Our bad speech habits, no less than our good, are inclined to show up in our writing too.

But you can plan and even write out an excellent paper which is a miserable speech unless you learn the difference. You will be a better speaker for being a better writer. However, training and practice in writing are no substitute for training and practice in speaking. For the technical details of speaking (articulation, pronunciation, voice control, gestures, audience approach, type of speech), nothing supplants a qualified speech instructor (or coach) and/or a thorough, specialized book.

appendix B

Pointers to good dictation

[To your secretary you may dictate; to your customer, never.]

SINCE MOST business letters are dictated to a secretary or a machine, anybody who needs to send out many letters also needs to learn how to dictate them.[1] Fortunately the learning job is easy and quick—with a little intelligence, a little study, and a little practice—although a person who refuses to give it any study can and usually does make a mess.

To help those willing to learn, we append these pointers—drawn from years of experience on both ends of the dictation job and from the suggestions of various dictating-machine manufacturers.

As with many procedures, getting ready is the biggest and most important part; so don't skip the next section and jump into the fire of the actual dictating.

Before you dictate

1. *Be sure you know how to compose good letters of various kinds.* You won't gain much by learning how to do a good job of dictating unless you first know what a good letter is. Certainly skill in dictating is not going to make a bad message into a good letter. And improved efficiency in getting out bad messages is no virtue. So unless you're sure you know how to compose a good message—with appropriate style, tone, psychology, degree of persuasion, and organization—forget about dictating for the moment and take a good course in letter writing, or at least read Chapters 1–3 in this book.

Once you know how to compose good letters, you can profitably pro-

---

[1] For efficiency in wording, we'll confine our suggestions to dictating letters, the most frequent use of dictation, although most of the pointers apply equally to dictating memos, reports, and other messages.

ceed to learn how to dictate as a means of getting your messages on paper efficiently.

2. *Acquaint yourself thoroughly with your helpers.*

a) If you're going to use a dictating machine, you need to know more about it than where the on-off switch is. You need to know how to change the tape, belt, or disc before it stops recording in the middle of your dictation. Your machine will probably also have volume and tone controls, record and play controls, provision for correcting dictation errors, a paper slip or the like to alert a typist to such corrections and the beginnings and ends of letters.

Each of the many available models has its own peculiarities too. And many dictating machines have great flexibility, a surprising number of conveniences for the person who knows which button to push for what. Trying to use one without learning its ways is like never using your car radio, heater, air conditioner, cigarette lighter, windshield washer, or turn signals because you don't know what all those buttons and knobs are for.

b) Whether you use a machine or not, a secretary (or stenographer or typist, if you like) has to do the transcribing. You two are a team that must learn to work together.[2] You've probably seen the cartoon of the two mules tied together and each trying to get to a different haystack. They got what they wanted only by learning to cooperate. So with you two; you will produce letters better by learning to work in unison, or at least cooperatively.

Most secretaries have some pride (deserved or not) that will be hurt by your dictating things they know well and thus implying that they don't. Some know capitalization, paragraphing, punctuation, and spelling. You aren't being efficient or tactful if you dictate these things to such secretaries. But you're being foolish if you don't dictate them to those who don't know them. Failing to dictate such things when needed also hurts pride.

We don't agree with the wag (or fool) who said you have to keep beating secretaries down to show them you're the boss, their superior. Unless you have given them a chance and found them inept, we don't even think you should dictate every simple little letter. They should be able to handle such things themselves.

If a secretary is capable, recognizing such assets appeals to pride and induces cooperation. Such a person will then gladly meet the challenge, perhaps reducing your dictation load by half—and perhaps doing that half better. We've seen many secretaries frustrated by having to type the poor letters of their bosses and resentful of no chance to make suggestions or write letters themselves.

Cooperation is so important to you that we think you should even size up your secretary's personality and at least to some extent act accordingly.

---

[2] We recognize that the increasing use of network dictating by telephone to pools of machines and typists reduces the significance of some things said here (while raising other problems), but the main principles are the same.

Some are sensitive and jittery. Minimize your boisterousness, impetuousness, and even rafter-rattling throat clearings, which only make things worse. Some secretaries want to be efficient and will resent the inefficiencies of intermittent dictation throughout the day or any hemming and hawing, calling for numerous corrections, long-winded telephone interruptions, or calling for filed information while you should be dictating—and while their work piles up.

Some secretaries are conservative and will resent off-color jokes and stories, flirtations, and facetiousness; others may get distracting ideas. Either way, your dictation efficiency suffers. If efficient dictation is your goal, you need to know your secretary and act accordingly.

3. *Be prepared to start talking* by the time you have turned on a dictating machine or called in your secretary; that is, prepare in advance what you're going to say. Have in your head, or before you, decisions to be given, facts you'll need, and letters to be answered, with at least markings of points to be covered and questions to be answered—and have your thoughts organized. For difficult, long, and important letters, you may need to prepare outlines—maybe even topic sentences for paragraphs. You may enjoy the show of your secretary's bobbing up and down to get things from the files during a dictation session, but the session is inefficient and your secretary won't enjoy the show—unless a show-off.

4. *Stop thinking about other things and get on with the job at hand.* You can best avoid making interruptive appointments and receiving disruptive telephone calls if you set aside a certain time each day for dictation. At best, you will have enough such interruptions, and enough need to get out something on the spur of the moment during the rest of the day, to keep you and your secretary adequately frustrated.

While you dictate

1. *Relax and speak clearly,* piping your voice into the appropriately distanced microphone or directly toward a secretary. Don't slur, don't mumble, don't pace, and don't talk too fast or too slow, too loud or too low, or with great variation in volume or speed. Nervousness is contagious. Sounds are directional. The best distance from machine mikes is about three inches. (The best distance from a secretary will vary depending on factors outside the scope of this book.) Cigars, pipes, cigarettes, and chewing gum are not particularly good megaphones to help your words come out loud and clear. Your smoke screen is more likely to put a haze on your words than to filter out any aberrant sounds. At best, we have enough troubles talking clearly without the help of chewing gum.

2. *Before dictating the copy, dictate the format:* what it is (letter, memo, report), kind of paper and postage, number of copies, and anything else typists need to know to avoid going wrong. Unless you do, they may use letter form on the company's letterhead with one carbon, only to learn

later that it was to have been a memo on plain paper with four carbons. They won't appreciate your misleading them and making them do double duty—maybe half of it after 5 o'clock.

3. *Dictate capitalization, punctuation, paragraphing, and spelling* according to your secretary's needs, erring on the safe side and including the unusual, regardless. You need to spell out all words the sounds of which do not clearly indicate their spelling (confusing pairs like *accept* and *except* and all proper nouns naming people, places, and products unless obvious or well known). A dictated "innuendo" once came out "in your window," caught by the dictator in reading before signing. But this one, not caught because the dictator did not read before signing, caused real trouble for a while before it was cleared up: In replying to sales information about a line of products, a dictator said, "I know your line. When you say XXX . . . , I think a more accurate statement would be. . . ." The typist wrote, "I know you're lying when you say XXX will. . . . I think a more accurate statement would be. . . ."

4. *Try to minimize the need for corrections* (preplanning is the best way), but make necessary ones promptly. Otherwise, you may forget or mislead the typist in going so far wrong as to be beyond correction.

5. *Turn off the recorder during unavoidable interruptions* to keep confusing irrelevancies (which can be embarrassing) from getting into your letters. And if the interruption is a private affair, the recorder here includes the secretary. Some people tattle to the company grapevine.

6. *Keep your equipment in good repair.* Things are tough enough without having to battle malfunctioning dictation or transcribing equipment . . . or a cold in your head or your secretary's. Preventive maintenance is a good idea for machines *and* people.

* * *

Dictators are inclined to become careless. To slap their careless hands, the head of the stenographic department of one firm using network dictation by telephone to a steno pool designed the following form. You might well use it as a kind of checklist for dictation (at least the mechanical part of actual dictation).

Dictator ______________________ Department ____________

We had difficulty in transcribing the attached dictation for the reason(s) checked. We would like to get out your work just the way you want it. Will you help us by attention to these details?

______Number not shown	______Dictation indistinct
______Carbons not marked	______Dictation too ______ fast, ______ slow
______Corrections not marked	______Voice too low, ______ especially at sentence ends
______Length of letters not specified	______No paragraphing indicated
______Stationery not indicated	______Punctuation not clear from context
______Enclosures not indicated	
______Unusual names not spelled	

________Letters needed for names and addresses omitted from dictation
________First words not on cylinder—too short warm-up
________Dictation ran off cylinder (or tape)—watch for warning signal
________Dictated over defective recording device
________Letters sent for addresses not cross-referenced with dictation

Remarks: ____

____

After you dictate

1. *Shut up after dismissing the secretary or turning off the machine.*
2. *Read and sign the letters* that are all right when they come back to you. Remember that you, not your machine or secretary, are responsible for the letters you send out.
3. *Thank your secretary* for good work done, including improvements made. Deserved thanks go a long way in developing cooperation. So do deserved criticisms calmly discussed. Almost any secretary much prefers to be told of dissatisfactions rather than have the boss swallow them (for reasons of goodwill or courtesy) and become dyspeptic.
4. *Ask for corrections* of letters as needed, diplomatically teaching your secretary not to repeat any errors, and consulting about the most efficient way to correct both of yours. Your secretary will appreciate light pencil notations, instead of heavy ink ones that look angry and require retyping the page even though the necessary correction might have been made simply.

appendix C Concise writer's handbook

THIS ALPHABETICAL LIST of short, easy-to-remember symbols will save a teacher's time in marking papers and will help students wanting brief explanations of errors frequently found in business writing.

The symbols (the bold-faced part of each entry) are easy to remember because they are nearly all abbreviations of already familiar grading terms. Even the few abstract, unalphabetized ones at the end are mostly standard proofreader's marks.

The list includes everything teachers and students of business writing are likely to need for correcting the English in their papers. Although it is much more concise than the usual English handbook, it omits only those points college students already know or don't need to know. Selection was based on 30 years of experience in observing the good and the unacceptable in the writing of college students.

The explanations of points of grammar and usage are based solidly on the studies of linguists—the true authorities.

A, an Use *a* as the indefinite article if the following word begins with a consonant sound (including the now pronounced *h* in *hotel* and *historical*—and combined consonant and vowel sounds, as in *European, usage, unit,* and *eulogy*); use *an* if the next word begins with a vowel sound, including words beginning with silent *h* (*hour, honor, honest*).

Ab Before using an abbreviation, make sure it is appropriate, understood, and correct in form (including capitalization, spacing, and punctuation). Ordinarily, dates and states are not abbreviated (except that the Postal Service has a complete system of state abbreviations for envelope addresses—adapting to electronic mail sorting). Mr., Mrs., Dr., A.M., P.M., c.o.d., f.o.b., and e.o.m. are commonly abbreviated. Check your dictionary if in doubt about an abbreviation.

Accuracy Get facts, names, addresses, and statements right. If your statement may be misinterpreted, restate it so that it has only one clear meaning.

Adapt to your reader's interests, reading ability, and experience. A message that seems to be written for somebody else, or for nobody in particular, will be less effective than one which seems to fit the reader. See p. 42.

Agreement of subjects with their verbs and of pronouns with their antecedents is essential to clear, inconspicuous writing. Don't be confused by other words that come between two that are supposed to agree.

1. Notice that the first sentence about agreement is an illustration of the first point: *agreement* (singular) is the subject of the verb *is;* but between them is a prepositional phrase with four plurals. As other illustrations, consider

   —Selection of topics *is* based on the reader's knowledge and interests.

   —Government programs help make more food available to the consumer but *cost* a great deal of money.

   —Lee also tells how important the arrangement of the records offices *is.*

   Part, series, type, and other words usually followed by plural phrases are frequently pitfalls to the unwary writer:

   —The greatest part of their investments *is* in real estate.

   —A series of bank loans *has* enabled the firm to stay in business.

2. *Any, anyone, each, every, everyone, everybody, either,* and *neither* all point to singular verbs (and pronouns)—except that in an either-or situation, with one noun singular and one plural, verbs and pronouns agree with the closer noun.

   —Any of the men in the group *is* expected to give some of *his* time to helping the group when asked.

   —Either board members or the president *has* power to act on the point.

   —Neither the mayor nor the council members *are* allowed to use city-owned automobiles in transacting *their* own business.

3. Two separate singular subjects combined by *and* require a plural verb and pronoun; but when combined by *besides, either-or, together with,* or *as well as,* they take a singular:

   —Mr. Weeks and his secretary *do* the work in the central office.

—The honorary president and leader of this group *is* Mr. Anderson.

—Considerable knowledge, as well as care, *is* necessary in good writing.

4. Be sure your pronouns agree in number and gender with their antecedents (words they stand for).

   —The benefits students get from studying the practical psychology, writing skills, and ways of business in good courses like letter writing and report writing will help *them* throughout life.

   —The company plans to move *its* main operations closer to *its* major source of raw materials.

5. Relative clauses beginning with *who, that,* or *which* require verbs agreeing with the antecedents:

   —The manager is one of those *persons who* expect unquestioning loyalty.

   —The actions in the life of any animal which *interest* a biologist are those concerned with food, shelter, protection from enemies, and procreation.

6. Plural-sounding collective subjects take singular verbs and pronouns when the action is that of the group but plural verbs when the action is that of various individuals:

   —The board *is* having a long meeting.

   —The board *have* been arguing and disagreeing on that point for months.

   —Twenty-five dollars *is* a reasonable price in view of. . . .

   —The faculty *are* allowed almost complete freedom in the conduct of *their* classes while the administration *plays its* part by providing the facilities, general policy, and record keeping (the collective faculty acting as individuals, the administration acting as a group).

7. Beware of letting the complement tempt you to make the verb agree with it instead of the subject:

   —Our main difficulty *was* errors in billing.

   —The biggest cost item *is* employees' salaries and wages.

   (In most such situations, however, rewriting would be better to avoid equating a subject with a predicate noun of different number.)

8. Certain words deserve careful attention because their form is an uncertain or misleading indication of their number:

   —The meaning of the whole context determines the number of *any, all, more, most, some,* and *none.*

—*Acoustics, economics, genetics, linguistics, mathematics, news, physics,* and *semantics* are all singular despite their look and sound; *deer* and *fish* are both singular and plural; and *mice,* like *men,* is a plural word despite the singular smell.

Ambiguous—more than one possible meaning and hence not clear. Usually the temporary confusion can be cleared up (1) by correcting a faulty pronoun reference (see **Ref**) or (2) by rewording to straighten out a modifier so that it can modify only what you intend (see **Mod**).

—He took over the management of the business from his father when he was 55. (When his father reached 55, Carl took over management of the business.)

—We agreed when we signed the papers that you would pay $100. (When we signed the papers, we agreed that you would pay $100 *or* We agreed that you would pay $100 when we signed the papers.)

And is a strong coordinating conjunction—one of the most useful and most troublesome of words.

1. It should be used only to connect (in the sense of addition) things of similar quality and grammatical form. Used otherwise, it produces faulty coordination between an independent and a dependent clause, misparallelism, or sentence disunity. See **Sub, Para,** and **Unit.**

   —The plans call for a new four-story building, and which will cost $4.5 million. (Omit *and;* it can't connect an independent clause to a dependent one.) See **Coh.**

   —In this course you learn the ways of the business world, the principles of practical psychology, and to write better. (The infinitive *to write* is not parallel with the nouns *ways* and *principles.* Make them all the same form before connecting them by *and.*) See **Para.**

   —We feel sure that the saw will serve you well, and we appreciate your order. (The two ideas are not closely enough related to appear in the same sentence—probably not even in the same paragraph.) See **Unit.**

2. *And* is properly the most-used connective, but don't overuse it to connect a series of independent clauses into a long, stringy sentence. If the clauses deserve equal emphasis, they can be made separate sentences. If not, the weaker ones should be subordinated. See **Sub.**

   —The consultant first talked with the executives about their letter-writing problems *and* then took a sample of 1,000 carbon copies *and* classified them into two groups *and* 45 percent of them were for situations that could just as well have been handled by forms. (After talking with the executives about their letter-writing problems, the consultant classified a sample of 1,000 carbon copies from the files. Forty-five percent of them were for situations that could just as well. . . .)

3. *And* may be used as a sentence beginning only if you want to emphasize it.
4. *And* is not proper before *etc.;* the *et* (*et cetera*) means *and.*

Ap The appearance of a letter, as of a person, should be pleasant but unobtrusive and should suggest that the writer is competent, accurate, neat, and alert. It requires a good grade of paper, proper spacing, typing with a reasonably fresh ribbon, and clean type without messy erasures or glaring errors. Check Chapter 4.

Apostrophes (usually considered with punctuation, although they belong with spelling) should be used in

1. Possessives (except *its* and the personal pronouns): before *s* in singulars (*man's*); after the *s* in plurals if the *s* or *z* sound was added to make the word plural (*ladies'* but *women's*).
2. Contractions: to mark the omission of a letter (*isn't, doesn't, it's* —meaning "it is," quite different from the possessive *its*).
3. Plurals of symbols: figures (illegible *8's*), letters of the alphabet (one *o* and two *m's*), and words written about as words (too many *and's* and *but's*).

Appropriateness to the situation is an important test of good English. Is your statement too slangy, colloquial, or formal for the occasion? See **Adap** and p. 27 for a discussion of levels of usage.

Assign Follow the facts and directions in the assignment. Although you are expected to fill in with necessary details of your own invention, you are not to go contrary to the facts or the spirit of the problem; and you are to make only reasonable assumptions.

Capitalization is pretty well standardized (except that newspapers set their own practices and hence are not guides for other writing).

1. Capitalize the names of specific things, including the titles of people, but not general words. For instance, you capitalize the name of any specific college, university, or department; but you write

   —A university education may well cost $12,000, regardless of the department in which one studies.

   —L. W. Wilson, president of the University of. . . .

   —When President Wilson came. . . .

You capitalize any specific course, room, lake, river, building, etc., but not the general words. So you might write that you are

—Taking Economics 215, majoring in engineering, but right now going to a history class in the Liberal Arts Building, after stopping to see a professor in Room 115.

Next summer you may

—Fish mostly in Portage Lake and some in the Ausable River, although you prefer river to lake fishing.

Of course, you capitalize *English, French, German*—all the languages, because they derive from the names of countries.

2. In titles of books and articles capitalize (though library materials don't) the first word and all others except articles (*a, an, the*), prepositions (like *of, to, in, on, for*), and conjunctions (like *and, but, or, nor, although*)—unless you use solid capitals.
3. Capitalize the seasons (spring, summer) only when they are personified (rare except in poetry).
4. Capitalize sections of the country (the South, the East Coast) but not directions (east, west).
5. Capitalize people's titles (*Mr., Mrs., Miss, Dr., Colonel, Professor, Judge, Governor, President*) and terms of family relations (*Uncle Jim*) when used before names but only to show unusual respect when used in place of or after names:

   —Yes, Son, ...
   —The Senator then went. . . .
   —After Mother had seen. . . .

6. Capitalize the first word after a colon only if it starts a complete sentence. (In an itemized listing, you may capitalize the first word of items even though they are incomplete sentences.)

Cardinal numbers (*one, two, three; 6, 7, 9*) are preferable to ordinals (*first, second, third; 1st, 2d, 3d, 4th,* or *2nd, 3rd*) in dates except in very formal invitations and legal documents, or when the day is separated from the month. As a general rule, use the form that would be pronounced if read aloud. Since the simple ordinal forms may be either adjectives or adverbs, they need no *-ly* endings, ever.

—On October 7 . . . ; sometime in November—probably about the 7th.

Choppy, jerky, short sentences are slow and awkward. Usually the trouble is (1) incoherence (the sentences don't follow each other naturally—see **Coh**); (2) poor control of emphasis (all the ideas in independent clauses, although of different importance—see **Sub**); or (3) lack of variety (all the sentences of the same pattern, usually all beginning with the subject or nearly the same length—see

Var). Try combining several of the sentences, subordinating the less important ideas, and stressing the important ones in the independent clauses.

Cl Immediate clearness is a fundamental of good writing. Make sure your reader can get your meaning quickly and easily. Usually a statement that is not immediately clear requires fuller explanation, more exact wording, or recasting of a faulty, ambiguous, or involved construction.

Coherence means clearly showing your reader the relationships between ideas. It comes best from a logical sequence with major emphasis on the important ideas, with less on the related but less important ones, and with any necessary conjunctions to indicate what relationships exist. Incoherence comes from mixing unrelated ideas together in the same sentence or paragraph, but particularly from linking unrelated ideas or ideas of different importance by *and.*

1. Plan ahead—get your ideas in logical sequence *before* you write. You can group seemingly unrelated ideas with a topic sentence such as "Three factors deserve special consideration." Such a sentence will clearly show that the three following sentences or paragraphs are related.
2. Be sure your ideas have proper emphasis (See **Emp** and **Sub**). Important ideas should be in independent clauses or separate sentences. Two closely related and equally important ideas can be together in a compound sentence. Put a less important idea in a dependent clause attached to an independent clause, making a complex sentence.
3. Carefully choose transitional words or phrases if you need them to smooth the natural sequence of ideas (see **Conj** and **Tr**). Consider the following words and phrases as examples:

    —and . . . moreover, besides, in addition, also, furthermore
    —but . . . however, nevertheless, yet, still, although, while
    —either-or . . . neither-nor, else, whether
    —therefore . . . consequently, hence, as a result, accordingly, so, ergo, thus
    —because . . . since, as, for, the reason is
    —then . . . after that, afterward, later, subsequently
    —meanwhile . . . during, simultaneously, concurrently, while
    —before . . . preceding, previously, prior to
    —if . . . provided, assuming, in case, unless

Conciseness (which is not necessarily brevity) depends on leaving out the irrelevant, leaving unsaid what you can adequately imply (see **Imp**), and cutting out deadwood. See pp. 14 ff. for explanation and illustration of techniques.

Conjunctions connect ideas to show the kind of relationship that exists. See **Coh** and **Tr.**

1. Unless the relationship is already clear, put in the necessary conjunction.
2. Be sure the one you use reflects accurately the relationship you intend. (See the list under **Coh** for groups of somewhat similar connectives with different shades of meaning.)
3. Guard particularly against using *but* when no contrast is intended, and against using either *but* or *and* to connect things unless they are of the same grammatical structure (noun with noun, verb with verb, etc.).
4. Before using *therefore, because,* or other similar words, make sure a true cause-and-effect relationship really exists.

Connotations—the overtones or related meanings of words—are often as important as the denotations, or dictionary meanings. Be sure that the words you use are appropriate in connotations as well as in denotations. Consider, for example, the connotations in the following: *cheap, inexpensive, economical; secondhand, used, previously owned; complaint department, customer service department; basement store, thrift store, budget floor.*

Copying from the assignment or from other people produces writing that doesn't sound like you. Put your ideas in your own words. You won't learn much about writing by copying the phrasing of illustrations in the text. Read them for ideas, approaches, and psychology; then express your ideas in your own phrasing.

Cpr Comparisons require special attention to these points:

1. Things compared must be comparable. Usually the trouble is omission of necessary phrases like *that of, that on, other,* or *else.*
   —The markup on Schick shavers is higher than *that on* Remingtons. (You can't omit *that on* or you'll be comparing the height of a Remington—measured in inches—with the markup on Schicks—a percentage.)
   —Frank Mosteller sells more Fuller brushes than any *other* salesman. (Without *other,* the statement is illogical if Frank is a salesman; he can't sell more than he himself sells.)
2. Incomplete comparisons mean nothing; complete them.
   —You get more miles per dollar with XXX. (More than with what?)
   —This material has a higher percentage of wool. (Higher than what?)
3. Be sure to use the correct form of comparison words. Comparisons involving two things usually call for adding *-er* (the com-

parative) to the simple form (*cold, slow*). Those involving more than two usually require the *-est* (or superlative) form (*coldest, slowest, fastest*).

For words of three syllables or more—and for many with two and some with only one—the better form is *more* plus the simple form (for the comparative) or *most* plus the simple form (for the superlative): *more frequently, most hopeful.* Some words may be used either way: *oftener* or *more often; oftenest* or *most often.*

4. Watch these idioms: Complete the *as much as* phrase and use *to* after *compare* when pointing out similarities only, *with* when pointing out any differences:

—Price increases may be worth as much *as*, if not more than, the dividends on a common stock purchase.
—Comparison of X *to* Y shows that they involve the same principles.
—Comparison of sales letters *with* application letters shows that they have minor differences.

CS Comma splice—a serious error. Except when they are in series or are short and parallel, two or more independent clauses must be separated by a period, a comma and a coordinating conjunction, or a semicolon (which may or may not be followed by a transitional phrase like *that is* or by one of the conjunctive adverbs). See **SOS2** and **P2.**

CSP Select a central selling point (in a sales letter) and give it the major emphasis by position and full development. Scattering your shots over too many points leaves the major ones weak. See **Emp** and **Dev.**

Date Date all letters and reports (except possibly ephemera). Any papers worthy of going into files need dates. Dates should be written in the standard form (*November 2, 1976*) unless you have good reason to do otherwise. Your most likely good reasons could be: (1) You are in the armed services, where the form 2 *November 1976* is standard; or (2) you're writing a formal notice, where everything is spelled out; or (3) you're writing an informal note and may well use the form *11/2/76.* Modern business writing usually does not abbreviate months and does not use the ordinal forms. See **Card.**

Deadwood phrases add nothing to the meaning but take writing and reading time. See **Conc** and the list of frequent deadwood expressions on p. 16.

Develop your point more thoroughly with more explanation, definition, specific details, classifications, comparisons, or examples to make it clearer, more interesting, more convincing, or more emphatic. See **Spec.**

Diction Use a more suitable word. The big test, of course, is whether the word, including its connotations, conveys your thought accurately. Consider whether your words will be understood easily; whether they give a sharp, vivid picture by being natural and fresh instead of pompous, jargonistic, or trite; whether they give a specific, concrete meaning instead of a fuzzy or dull concept because they are general or abstract; and whether they are appropriately informal, formal, standard, technical, or nontechnical—according to the topic and reader.

Watch especially the following often-confused pairs: *accept, except; adapt, adopt; affect, effect; almost, most; amount, number; already, all ready; all right, "alright"* (no such word); *altogether, all together; are, our; beside, besides; between, among; capital, capitol; fewer, less; formerly, formally; imply, infer; it's, its; loose, lose; marital, martial; maybe, may be; moral, morale; oral, verbal; personal, personnel; principal, principle; sometime, some time; than, then; there, their, they're; too, to, two; with regards to, in regard to; your, you're.*

Directness saves words, speeds up reading, and makes your ideas clearer. Don't waste words by beginning too far back in the background of the subject, by stating what the reader already knows, or by expressing what will be clearly implied if you begin with the key thought. Write direct, active-voice sentences beginning with the important word as the subject. The expletives "It is . . ." and "There are . . ." are indirect, passive, and wordy (see **Exp**).

Documentation Telling your sources—is necessary when you use the ideas of others—to avoid plagiarism and to convince your reader by showing that you have the backing of cited authorities for what you say. See pp. 476 ff. for discussion and illustrations. Also see reports checklist (p. 514).

Emphasis should be divided among your ideas according to their relative importance.

1. When you state important ideas, give them deserved emphasis by one or more of the following methods: putting them in the emphatic beginning or ending position of your letter or paragraph, putting them in independent clauses, developing them thoroughly (including intentional repetition), phrasing them in active voice, and perhaps underscoring them or writing them in solid capitals (or a different color). See p. 12 for fuller explanation.

2. When you have negative, unimportant, already known, or other ideas that don't deserve emphasis, avoid overemphasizing them. Some useful methods are putting them in unemphatic middle positions, putting them in dependent clauses or phrases, and giving them brief mention or just implying them. Particularly objectionable is overemphasis on things the reader obviously knows and on things that are (or can be) adequately implied. The first insults the reader's intelligence, and both waste words:
   —Spring is just around the corner. You'll be needing. . . . (With spring just around the corner, you'll. . . .)
   —On October 3 you asked me to write a report on. . . . I have finished it and am. . . . (Here is the report requested in your letter of October 3. . . .)
   —I have your letter of April 20 in which you ask for quotations on X. I am glad to give you our prices. Our present prices on X are. . . . (Just omit the first two sentences. They're implied in the third.)

Transitional words like *and, but,* and *however* usually do not deserve the emphasis they would get at the beginning of a sentence; and prepositions usually do not deserve end-of-sentence emphasis. Indeed, this is the only legitimate reason for objection to such words in these positions.

Enclosures See pp. 13, 75, 114, 115(5), 301(5).

Etc., An abbreviation of Latin *et cetera,* meaning *and so forth,* should not be used unless the reader will have a good idea of how to fill out the incomplete list (as in "Please take even-numbered seats 2, 4, 6, etc."). Otherwise, it can mean only "Reader, you guess what else I mean to include," and this does not communicate. Because *etc.* is an abbreviation, it takes a period; but because it is anglicized, it need not be italicized (or underscored in typed copy). In no case should you write "and etc."; *et* means *and.*

Expletives (*it is, there are*) nearly always make your writing unnecessarily wordy, weak, and passive. They often improperly dodge writer responsibility for statements, and they always slow up the reader's getting to significant information.

Expletives usually result from a misguided attempt to write an impersonal style. If you write them in first drafts, revising to remove them will make better sentences at least nine times out of ten. In general, then, you should avoid them, although sometimes they may help to soften a command or avoid presumptuousness in a recommendation, or ease reader acceptance of bad news.

—It was thought that you would prefer. . . . (I thought you would. . . .)

—There are four important factors involved. These are: . . . . (The four important factors are. . . .)

—It will be necessary to have your. . . . ("You must send . . ." might be too commanding.)

Fast movement that gets to the point quickly—without cumbersome detail or explicit statement of ideas that should be implied—is desirable when your message will be accepted readily. But if you need to persuade the reader either to accept an unpleasant decision or to take reluctant action, you have to build up your case adequately before starting the key point. Stating the bad news before adequate justifying reasons, or requesting an action before showing enough reader benefits to motivate that action, is therefore marked **Fast,** meaning "You got here too fast."

Figures are better than words (except at the beginning of a sentence) for serial, telephone, page, chapter, chart, catalog, and street numbers; for money, dimensions, and dates and time (except in formal announcements); for all quantities when several are close together (but not adjoining) in a sentence or paragraph; and for other isolated quantities requiring more than two words. (As an acceptable replacement for the two-word rule, your teacher may authorize usual newspaper practice: Use figures if the quantity is above ten.)

1. If a quantity comes at the first of a sentence, write it in words or recast the sentence.
2. When a sentence involves two different series of quantities, to avoid confusion use figures for one and words for the other; if more than two, use a table.

   —On the qualifying exam, ten percent of the applicants scored 90–100, thirty percent 80–89, ...

   —Please make six 2″ × 3″ and three 5″ × 7″ black-and-white prints.
3. The old longhand practice of stating quantities twice—in figures followed parenthetically by words—is unnecessary and undesirable in type or print, although it is still sometimes used in legal documents, and always in checks, for double certainty and security.
4. Except in dates, street numbers, and serial numbers, use a comma between groups of three digits, counting from the right.
5. Except in tables involving some cents, periods and zeros after money quantities are wasted typing and reading.
6. Two-word quantities between 20 and 100 require the hyphen (twenty-six).
7. Cardinal numbers (*1, 2, 3, 4,* etc.), are preferable to ordinals

(*1st, 2d, 3d, 4th*) in dates except when the day is separated from the month. See **Card** and **Date.**

8. Since ordinals are either adjectives or adverbs, an *-ly* ending is never necessary.

Flattery, especially if obvious, is more likely to hurt than help.

Fragments (phrases or subordinate clauses posing as sentences) are serious errors except when perfectly clear and intentional—as they usually are when used by professional writers for special effects. But they are like dynamite in the hands of the unskilled. Beware! Attach them to the independent clauses to which they belong (see **P3**) or change their wording to make them the complete, independent sentences they pretend to be.

—The latter being the better way. (This is a phrase fragment which should be attached by comma to the preceding sentence. Or you could simply change *being* to *is.*)

—One job in revising any paper is checking for and correcting any fragments. Which is easy to do. (The second "sentence" is a dependent clause and hence a fragment unless attached—by a comma—to the preceding.)

Gobbledygook is big-wordy, roundabout, long-winded, or stuffed-shirt language. Characteristically it shows two or more of those traits and comes in long sentences and paragraphs. Avoid it like poison; it works against both clarity and ease of reading.

Graphic devices of various kinds can often supplement words to make the information clearer, easier, or more interesting. Use them where they will help, but only if they will. Make them big enough and detailed enough (but no bigger or more detailed than necessary) for your purpose. And be sure you use the most appropriate kind (line, bar, or pie chart; drawing, map, or photograph, for example). See pp. 486 and 512.

Gw Goodwill, the fourth basic requirement of a business letter, is lacking or poorly handled here. See Chapter 3.

Idiomatic usage—the natural, customary, accepted way of saying certain things—is correct that way simply because that is the way we say it, although it may defy grammatical analysis and rules. Idioms are so numerous and varied that they cannot be fully explained here. Usually, however, an error in idiom is use of the wrong preposition. Consider *possibility of, possible to, necessity of, need for,* and *ability to.* See **Prep.**

Imply rather than express the idea, to save words or avoid overemphasis. See **Emp** and pp. 12–16.

Italic print, indicated by underscoring in typewritten and handwritten copy, is used to emphasize occasional words; to mark the title of a book or journal; to mark a word, letter, or figure used as an illustration or typographical unit (instead of for its meaning); and to indicate an unanglicized foreign-language expression used in English context.

—Italics are *preferably not* used for titles of *parts,* such as the title of an article in a journal or a chapter in a book. Quotation marks are preferable for that purpose.
—Chapter 1, "The First Test of a Good Letter," stresses clear, natural style and general linguistic *savoir faire.*
—*Convenience* and *questionnaire* are often misspelled.
—Use of fewer *I*'s and more *you*'s would improve many letters.

Jargon is fuzzy or inappropriate writing attributable to pompousness, circumlocution, deadwood, abstractness, big words, technical terms (written to nontechnical readers), or hackneyed expressions. It is the opposite of simple, natural, clear writing. Avoid it.

Juxtapose (put side by side) facts and ideas that the reader needs to consider together. For instance, wholesale and retail prices need to be seen together (with the difference and percentage of markup figured) if they are to mean as much as they should to the retailer being asked to stock the product.

K Awkwardness in expression calls attention to itself, and it may confuse the reader. Reconstruct your sentence or change word order for a more natural flow.

A so-called split infinitive (putting a modifier between *to* and a verb) is usually undesirable because it is usually awkward; but if it is clear and natural, you'll do better to go ahead and split the infinitive rather than write an awkward sentence trying to avoid doing so.

lc Lower case needed here, instead of capital. See **Cap.**

Logic Avoid statements which will not stand the test of logic or for which the logic is not readily clear. Perhaps you need to supply a missing step in the logic. Maybe you need to state your idea more precisely. Or maybe you need to complete a comparison to make it logical. (If the last, see **Cpr** for fuller explanation.)

Mechanics See p. 516.

Modifiers should be placed in the sentence where they fit most naturally and make the meaning clearest. To avoid awkwardness and write clearly, you have to make sure that each modifier relates clearly to the thing it is supposed to modify. As a general rule, the two should be as close together as natural sentence construction will allow.

1. Participles (usually phrases including a verb form ending in *-ing* or *-ed,* and usually at the beginning of a sentence) require careful attention lest you relate them to the wrong word (or nothing at all).

   —Smelling of liquor, I arrested the driver. (The officer did not intend to say that he himself had been drinking.)
   —After soaking in the prepared mixture over night, I set the specimen up to dry for two days. (The scientist didn't really soak.)

   These errors are commonly called "misrelated modifiers" or "dangling participles." Infinitives can dangle the same way:

   —To enjoy the longest, most dependable service, the motor must be tuned up about every 100 hours of operation. (The motor cannot enjoy dependable service.)
   —In order to assist you in collecting for damages, it will be necessary to fill out a company blank. (The two infinitives dangle because they are not related to any doers of the actions indicated.)

   But absolute phrases (a noun plus a participle) and participles, gerunds, and infinitives naming an accepted truth rather than the action of any person or thing do not need to relate to any subject:

   —The sun having set, the fish began to bite.
   —All things considered, Steve is the better man.
   —Counting all costs, the little X is not an inexpensive car.
   —To judge from results, that was an effective method.

2. *Only, almost,* and *nearly* are tricky words. Watch where you put them. Consider the varied meanings from placing *only* at different spots in "I can approve payment of a $30 adjustment."

Monotonous See **Var.**

Natural writing avoids triteness, awkwardness, and pomposity. Clichés, trite and hackneyed expressions, and jargon suggest that a writer is not thinking about the subject and the reader; awkwardness suggests carelessness; and big words and pomposity suggest that the writer is trying to make an impression. Think through what you want to say and put it simply, smoothly, and naturally. Although you cannot write exactly as you talk, you should try to write with the same freedom, ease, simplicity, and smoothness. See p. 19.

Negative in letter writing means anything unpleasant to your reader. Since you want the reader's goodwill, you should avoid the negative when you can, and subordinate it when you can't avoid it. Insofar as possible, stress the positive by telling what you have done, can do, will do, or want done instead of their negative opposites. See p. 46; and for methods of subordinating, see p. 12, **Emp,** and **Sub.**

Objectivity Use of emotional or feverish words (especially if extensive) suggests a prejudiced rather than an objective view of the situation and therefore causes the reader to lose faith in the writer—especially a report writer. See pp. 470 and 481.

Obvious statements—when they are unnecessary as bases for other statements—at least waste words; and when they are put in independent clauses, they show poor control of emphasis and may insult the reader's intelligence. When you need to state an obvious fact as the basis for something else, put it in a dependent clause and use the independent clause for the new idea. (See **Emp** and **Sub.**)

—New York is America's biggest city. Therefore. . . . (Since New York is America's biggest city, ...)

Omission of a word or necessary idea. Make your statements both grammatically and logically complete. See **Tele, Log,** and **Cpr.**

1. Conciseness is certainly a desirable quality in letters and reports, but it should not go so far as to push you into telegraphic style—omission of subjects, connective words, and articles:
   —Please send check $123 for shipment April 1.
2. Unless the same verb form or preposition applies appropriately in a double construction, use the necessary two:
   —His interest *in* and hard work *on* accounting have. . . .
   —He should have *sold* earlier, and perhaps will now *sell,* since the market trend is clearer.
   —The product *is* new and prospective buyers *are* numerous.

Punctuation which follows the conventions of written English (and is therefore understood by most readers) is a helpful device for both *reader and writer in communicating clearly, quickly, and easily.* But when it goes contrary to the understood conventions, it does not help and may even confuse.

You should not try to use even good punctuation, however, as a crutch for bad writing. Heavy punctuation cannot make a bad sentence into a good one; the need for it suggests revising the sentence rather than trying to punctuate the involved statement. The best style is so direct and simple that it requires little punctuation except periods at the ends of sentences. Still, you cannot write much without need for some internal punctuation. Here are the conventions most commonly violated:

P1 Use a comma between two independent clauses connected by *and, but, or,* or *nor* if no other commas are in the sentence; but be sure you are connecting two clauses rather than a compound subject, verb, or object.

—You may buy the regular Whiz mixer at $18.75, but I think you would find the Super Whiz much more satisfactory. (Two clauses.)

—We make two grades of Whiz mixers and sell both at prices lower than those of our competitors' products. (Compound verb; one subject.)

Be sure, too, that you don't use obtrusive commas before the first or after the last item in a series or between a subject and its verb, a verb and its object, or a noun and its adjective. Also, you do not usually need a comma after a transitional word (*and, but, however, therefore*), but you may use one to emphasize.

P2 The semicolon is a pivotal mark; avoid using it between expressions unless they are of equal grammatical structure (usually two independent clauses or two items in a complex series). Use a semicolon between two independent clauses unless connected by *and, but, or,* or *nor;* and even then, use a semicolon if the sentence already has a comma in it (as in this one). Typical weaker connectives requiring the semicolon between two independent clauses are *therefore, so, moreover, hence, still, accordingly, nevertheless, furthermore, consequently,* and *however.* When these words are used as simple connectors not between two independent clauses, however (as right here), they are set off by a pair of commas unless they fit so smoothly into the sentence that they require no marks.

—Jets made airline maintenance men relearn their jobs; the jet manual is twice as thick as the old one for prop planes. (No connective.)

—The preceding sentence could be made into two, of course; but because the ideas are closely related, it is better as one. (Commas elsewhere require semicolon before even a strong conjunction.)

—Good letter writing requires proper punctuation; therefore you must know how to use the semicolon. (Weak connective.)

—The proper style for letters is simpler and less involved than for most other writing, however, and therefore does not require very complex punctuation procedures. (*However* is a simple transition, *not used* between two clauses here and *not* close-knit into the phrasing the way *therefore* is; so it is set off by commas while *therefore* goes unmarked. Note, too, that the weak connective *so* requires the semicolon because it connects two clauses.)

P3 Use a comma after all first-of-sentence dependent clauses, long phrases, or other phrases containing any form of a verb. But when these forms or appositives or transitional words appear elsewhere in a sentence, use commas only with nonrestrictive (nonessential) ones. (Nonrestrictive statements add descriptive detail about an already identified word and are not necessary to the logic or grammatical completeness of the sentence; restrictive ones define, limit, or identify and are necessary to convey the intended meaning or complete the sentence. If, on reading aloud, you naturally pause and inflect your voice, the statement is nonrestrictive and requires the comma(s).

—Because the dependent clause comes at the beginning, we have to use a comma in this sentence.
—We do not need a comma in a complex sentence if the dependent part comes at the end or in the middle and restricts the meaning the way this one does.
—Having illustrated the two points about dependent clauses at the beginning and restrictive clauses elsewhere in the sentence, we now use this sentence to illustrate the use of a comma after a long phrase at the first of a sentence. (Because it includes a verb form, it would require a comma even if it were short, like "Having illustrated the point, we now leave the topic.")
—The three points already illustrated, which are certainly important, are no more important than the point about using commas to set off nonrestrictive clauses anywhere, which this sentence illustrates. (In fact, it illustrates twice: Both the *which* clauses could be omitted; they are nonrestrictive because they merely give added information unnecessary to either the meaning or the grammar of the basic sentence.)

Sometimes you need a comma to prevent misreading—especially after a gerund, participle, or infinitive:

—In the office, files had been emptied all over the floor.
—By shooting, the man attracted the attention of the rescue party.
—Thinking that, he was unwilling to listen to reason.
—Seeing the foreman's unwillingness to help, the men gave up.

P4 Be sure to put in both commas—or dashes or parentheses—around a parenthetical expression in the middle of a structure. Direct addresses ("Yes, Mr. Thomas, you may . . .") and appositives (restatements like this one that follow immediately to explain a term) are typical examples. But, like clauses, some appositives are restrictive or so closely related that they require no punctuation, while others are nonrestrictive or so loosely related that they do.

—His starting point that good punctuation is a matter of following the conventions has not been stressed enough.

—His second point, the importance of writing letters so smoothly and naturally that they require little internal punctuation, would preclude most punctuation problems.

—General Motors opened a new plant in Akron, Ohio, in November, 1965, to produce certain auto parts.

P5 Use commas to separate coordinate adjectives. As two tests for coordinacy, see if you can put *and* between the adjectives or invert their order without producing awkwardness. If so, they are coordinate and require a comma.

—Proper punctuation can help greatly in writing a clear, easy-to-read style.

—Fairly heavy white paper is best for letterheads.

P6 The comma is the usual punctuation between items in a series (preferably including one before the *and* with the last item, because it is sometimes necessary for clearness and is always correct). But if any item except the last has a comma within it, use semicolons at all points between items. (Suggestion: If only one of a series requires an internal comma, consider putting it last and using commas between the items.)

—Make your writing clear, quick, and easy to read.

—Use commas between independent clauses connected by *and, but, or,* or *nor;* semicolons between independent clauses with other connectives or no connecting words; commas for dependent clauses and verbal or long phrases at the beginnings of sentences, for nonrestrictive ones elsewhere, and for simple series; and semicolons for complex series like the one in this sentence.

P7 Dashes, commas, and parentheses are all used in pairs around parenthetical expressions that interrupt the main part of the sentence. The choice depends on the desired emphasis and on the other punctuation. Two dashes (called "bridge dashes") emphasize most, commas less, and parentheses least of all.

If the parenthetical part contains internal parentheses, dashes have to be used around it; if it contains commas, dashes or parentheses have to be used around it. (Of course, only a pair of parentheses can be used around a whole sentence which gives explanations, relatively unimportant additional detail, or side information not germane to the trend of the discussion, as this sentence does. In that case the period comes inside the closing parenthesis, although it comes outside otherwise.)

A single dash—made on the typewriter by two hyphens without spacing before, between, or after—may be used to mark an abrupt change in the trend of a sentence or to precede an added statement summarizing, contrasting, or explaining the first part. In this second function, it is commonly called the "pickup dash."

—Your main weaknesses in writing—misspelling, faulty punctuation, and incoherence—should be corrected before you write letters.

—Errors in spelling, punctuation, or coherence—these all mar an otherwise good letter.

—A letter writer must avoid the common errors in writing—misspelling, bad punctuation, and incoherence. (Of course, the colon could replace the dash here; but ordinarily it should not unless the preceding statement is a formal introduction, usually indicated by the word *following*, or unless it is an introduction to an itemized list.)

P8 Hyphenate two or more words (unless the first ends in *-ly*) used to make a compound adjective modifying a following noun.

—fast-selling product, wrinkle-resistant material, long-wearing soles, never-to-be-forgotten experience

Note that the point usually does not apply when the adjectives follow the noun.

—The material is highly wrinkle resistant and long wearing.

Certainly it does not apply when the adjectives modify the noun separately. See **P5.**

—These slacks are made of a hard, durable material.

The compound-adjective principle does apply, however, to double compounds made with one element in common, where the "suspension hyphen" follows the first: three- and five-pound cans; only light- and middle-weight boxers.

The hyphen also marks the break in a word at the end of a line. See **Syl.**

Other less-frequent uses of the hyphen include (1) spelling of fractions (*three-fourths*) and two-word quantities between 20 and 100, and (2) prefixing words or syllables to names (*post-Hitler* Germany), to other words beginning with the same vowel as the end of the prefix (*re-entry, pre-established*), or to any word that might otherwise be confusing (*re-collect,* not *recollect; re-cover* not *recover*).

P9 Quotation marks are used primarily for short, exact quotations (not paraphrasings) of other people's words and for titles of *parts* of publications, such as magazine and newspaper stories or book chapters. (The titles of journals and books should be italicized—underlined in typed copy—or written in solid capitals. See **Ital** and **Cap.**) If a quotation is more than two or three lines long, you should indent it from each side, single-space it, and omit quotation marks.

When closing quotation marks and other marks seem to come at the same place, the standard *American* practice is as follows: Place commas or periods *inside* the closing quotes; place semicolons or colons *outside;* and place question or exclamation marks inside or outside depending on whether they are part of the quotation.

P10 The colon is either an anticipating or a separating mark. As an anticipator, it is used after introductory lead-ins to explanations or quotations, especially if the lead-in includes such formalizing terms as the word *following* or if the explanation is itemized or lengthy.

—The X Company's ink was even redder: its third-quarter loss of. . . .

—Three main benefits deserve your attention: . . . . (Enumeration follows. Notice that you do not heed—indeed should not use—a browbeating, word-wasting expression like "these benfits are" after the colon!)

—On the use of the colon, Perrin says: . . . . (Long quotation follows.)

Because the colon is also a separating mark, however—used to separate hours from minutes and volume numbers from pages, for example—it should not be used as an anticipating mark when the lead-in phrasing fits well as an integral part of a short, informal statement. Summey calls this misuse the "obtrusive colon."

—The three main advantages are (colon would be obtrusive here) speed, economy, and convenience.

—Perrin reports that (no colon; not even a comma) "*Will* has practically replaced *shall* in. . . ."

Almost invariably words like *namely, that is, for example,* and *as follows* are wasted (and browbeating) when used with a colon. The introductory phrasing and the colon adequately anticipate without these words.

—We have several reasons for changing: namely the . . . (Omit *namely.*)

—We had several reasons for changing. These reasons are: . . . . (This is worse. Omit *These reasons are;* put the colon after *changing.*)

Although practice varies, usually you should capitalize the first word after a colon only if it begins a complete sentence; but if itemizations follow, you may capitalize even though each item depends on the introductory statement for completeness.

The same idea applies to the end punctuation of items following a colon. If the items make complete sentences, put a period after each; but if all are to be considered one sentence, use comma or semicolon at the end of each (except the last, of course) as in other series—or you may use no end punctuation.

P11 Underlining in typed or handwritten copy specifies italic type when printed. Its main uses are to mark titles of books and journals, to emphasize, and to indicate unanglicized words. In copy not to be printed, it should be used also for any heading not written in solid capitals. Otherwise, the heading, which is really a title for the copy over which it stands, does not stand out sufficiently. (A printer would make it stand out by using big or boldface type.)

Type underlining is preferably continuous, rather than broken by individual words, because it is easier both to type and to read that way.

P12 Besides its well-known use at the end of a question, the question mark may be used in parentheses immediately following a statement or spelling about which the writer is uncertain and unable to determine. Obviously, it should not be used as an excuse for laziness; but if you have only heard a difficult name, for example, and have to write to that person, you'd better use the mark than unconcernedly misspell the name.

A question mark should not be used after indirect questions and is unnecessary after commands softened by question form, but some writers feel that it further softens commands.

—We need to know what your decision is. (Indirect question.)

—Will you please ask the secretary in your office to change my mailing address. (Softened command, with or without the question mark.)

P13 Ellipsis (three *spaced* periods) means that something has been left out, and you *must* use this mark when giving an incomplete quotation. Note that if an omission comes at the end of a sentence, you need to add the appropriate end-of-sentence punctuation, usually a fourth dot for the period. Ellipses are also coming into wide use, especially in business, as an additional way to mark parenthetical expressions (see **P7**); but this practice has not yet achieved total acceptance.

—". . . the people of the United States . . . do ordain and establish this Constitution. . . ."

—This rotary dump hopper car . . . like our open-top hopper car . . . comes in a wide range of sizes.

Paragraphs in letters and reports are the same as in other writing—unified and coherent developments of topics—except that they tend to be more compressed and shorter for easier readability. (The symbol ¶ may be used to replace **Par.**)

1. Keep your paragraphs reasonably short. Long ones are discouragingly hard to read. Especially the first and last paragraphs of letters should be short (rarely more than three or four lines). Elsewhere, if a paragraph runs to more than about eight lines, you should consider breaking it up for easier readability. Certainly you should ignore any idea that a paragraph has to be more than one sentence.
2. But develop your paragraphs adequately to clarify and support your points—by explanation, detail, facts and figures, or illustrations and examples.
3. Make each paragraph unified and coherent by taking out elements irrelevant to the topic, by organizing carefully, and by showing the interrelationship of the ideas. Consider beginning with a topic sentence and/or ending with a summary. See **Unit** and pp. 23, 618 for further tips.
4. (**Coh**) Show the relation of the paragraph to the preceding (by following logical sequence, carrying over key ideas, and/or using transitional words) and to the purpose of the whole paper or section (by pointing out the significance and/or by using transitional words or sentences).

   —Paragraph unity also includes. . . . (*Also* means some of the explanation has preceded.)

   —Carrying over key words and using transitional words are both means of providing unity between paragraphs as well as within them. (As *well as* means we've discussed unity *in* paragraphs and now will discuss it *between* them.)
5. **Par** with **No** before it means "No new paragraph needed here because you are still on the same topic and within reasonable paragraph length."

Parallelism means using the same kind of grammatical structure for ideas that are used coordinately, as in pairs, series (including lists), comparisons, and outlines. These structures state or imply relationships usually indicated by *and, but,* or *or* and hence should relate only full sentences to full sentences, nouns to nouns, verbs to verbs, active voice to active voice, plural to plural—indeed *any* grammatical form only to the same grammatical form in the related part. Watch for parallelism with *not only . . . but also, as well as, larger, less expensive,* and the like. (See p. 469, Item 5, for parallelism in outlines.)

—One of the duties of the airline cabin attendant is to offer customers magazines, pillows, and hang their coats. (Two plural nouns and a verb improperly connected by the coordinating conjunction *and.*)

—The No-Skid knee guard is long wearing, washable, and stays in position. (Two adjectives connected by *and* to a verb.)
—John Coleman is 39, married, and a native. (Two adjectives and a noun.)
—If we fair each side of the arc, we produce a more practical airfoil section and an increase in performance is attained. (Active voice related to passive. Rewrite the last part as "increase the performance.")
—The next step is baking or catalyzation ("baking or catalyzing").
—Swimming is better exercise than to walk. (A gerund compared with an infinitive.)

Parallelism in pairs, series, and comparisons is largely a question of logic; you can add together and compare only like things. See **Log.**

Passive voice (in which the subject receives rather than does the action indicated by the verb) is usually wordy, awkward, and weak. Most of your sentences should therefore use the active voice. It makes important words (usually persons or products in letters) the subjects and objects of your verbs, as they should be.

Writers often use passive constructions in a misguided effort to avoid *I* and *We* as the subject. If you feel that you must avoid them to prevent monotony of sentence pattern, you should see p. 20 instead of resorting to the passive. If you feel that you must avoid them to increase objectivity, you are working under a false impression; you can be just as biased without them. But you can avoid the first person and the passive at the same time, as explained in the first illustration below.

Still, you may find appropriate use for passives to meet a thesis director's or company executive's unsound requirement that you write impersonally, to avoid a direct accusation, to put emphasis on something other than the doer of the action, or to weaken an otherwise rankling command or recommendation.

—Your Long-Flight skis were shipped this morning by our mailing department. (Can be made active and impersonal as "Two Long-Flight skis are on their way; they left the mailing department this morning.")
—The subject has been considered from the following viewpoints: . . . . (The requirement of impersonal style may justify the passive here.)
—The mower apparently has not been oiled adequately. (Avoids accusing the user.)
—Careful attention should be given to. . . . (Weakens a possibly rankling command.)
—It is recommended that. . . . (Though this weakens and avoids

egotism in a recommendation, surely you can find a better way. This deserves criticism for both a **pass**ive and an **expl**etive.)

PD Psychological description (interpreting facts and physical features of a product in terms of reader benefits) is the real heart of selling. Unless your reader readily makes the interpretation, pure physical description is ineffective in selling. So when you name a physical feature of a product you're selling, show the reader what it means in terms of benefits. (See p. 111 and pp. 283–85.)

—The Bostonian Sporty shoe has Neolite soles and triple-stitched welt construction. (The Neolite soles and triple-stitched welt construction cause the Bostonian Sporty to last long and keep your feet dry.)

Personalized messages written for and adapted to specific readers are more effective than mass broadcasts. What seems to be for everybody has less interest to anybody. Even form letters should be worded to give the feeling that the message is directed to each reader. Expressions such as "Those of you who . . ." and "If you are one who . . ." give just the opposite impression. (See p. 44.)

Plan your letter more appropriately for the circumstances as an A–, B–, or C–plan. (See p. 36.)

Pompous Try to express the thought simply, not to impress the reader.

Pr Follow more generally acceptable business practice.

PR Personal references (names of people or pronouns referring to them) not only help to keep the reader in the picture and produce the you-attitude (**YA**); they help to avoid the passive (**Pas**), to make your writing specific and concrete instead of general and abstract (**Spec**), and to make your writing easier and more interesting to read. Naming or referring to persons—Flesch suggests at least 6 percent of your words—is an important element in readability.

Prepositions indicate relationships within a sentence.

1. Be sure to use the right one for your construction. Some words require certain prepositions; others vary prepositions for different meanings. See **Id.**

   —ability *to;* agree *to, with,* or *in;* compare *to* (for similarities only) or *with* (for likenesses and differences); different *from.*

2. When you use two words that require different prepositions, use both:

   —Because of your interest *in* and aptitude *for. . . .*

3. Don't use many of the .45-caliber group prepositions (*accord-*

ing to, in regard to, by means of, in connection with, on the part of) for squirrel-size ideas or your prepositions will "bulk too large," as Perrin says.

PV Insofar as possible, keep the same point of view in a sentence, a paragraph, or a whole letter. Make only logically necessary shifts, and let your reader know by providing the necessary transitional words. Watch carefully for shifts in time, location, and those whose eyes you seem to be looking through. For effective you-attitude, look through the reader's eyes whenever possible. See **YA.**

R Bring your reader into the picture early—and don't forget later. The reader is the most important person involved with your letter. See **Per, PR, PV,** and **YA.**

Redundancy includes not only useless repetition but wasting words saying things that are obvious or clearly implied. Avoid it.

Ref The references of your pronouns must be immediately certain and clear to your reader—not ambiguous, too far away, or merely implied. Except for the few indefinite pronouns (*one, everybody, anybody,* and *it* referring to the weather), a pronoun confuses or distracts a reader unless it refers clearly to a preceding noun and agrees with it in number and gender. *Each, every, any,* and their combinations *anybody* and *everybody* are considered singulars requiring singular verbs and pronouns; but see **Agr** for further explanation of agreement.

1. Often the trouble with a pronoun reference is that the antecedent is just too far away. Repeat the antecedent or change the word order so that the reader knows immediately what the antecedent is.
2. Guard particularly against *this, that, which, it,* and *they* making vague reference to ideas of whole preceding clauses instead of clear, one-word antecedents.

   —Dayton adopted the plan in 1914 and has kept it ever since, which is a good example of the success of the council-manager form of government. (What does *which* refer to?)

   —After reading a book about television engineering, the young man wanted to be one of them. (One of what? Only implied.)
3. Don't use the same pronoun with different meanings in the same sentence:

   —The directions say that it is up to the owner to change the filter whenever it needs it.

Repetition of words or ideas seems wordy and monotonous unless it serves a justified purpose. Restatement of important ideas deserving emphasis is often desirable; but even then, the restatement usually should be in somewhat different words to avoid monotony.

Resale material—reassuring a customer that a choice of goods and/or firm was a good one—not only shows your service attitude (**SA**); it helps keep incomplete orders and delayed shipments on the books, rebuilds reader confidence when used in adjustments, and serves as a basic idea in collections. Look it up in the Index and read about it in connection with the particular type of letter involved.

Style See Chapter 1 and (especially for reports) pp. 473–92 and 513.

SA Service attitude—showing a genuine desire to give the kinds and quality of goods and services wanted, favorable prices, and various conveniences, plus unselfish reassurance of appreciation for business—can go a long way toward overcoming any feelings a reader may have that you are indifferent. Your basic techniques are to interweave into your letters some sales promotion material (**SPM**) and resale talk (**Res**). See p. 63.

SC Show more success consciousness. See page 48.

Selfish interest (yours) is assumed by both reader and writer, but it does not help your cause and therefore is best not mentioned. For more interest and persuasion, show what's in the situation for *the reader*. See **YA** and p. 40.

Shifting of tense (time), voice (active-passive), mood (indicative, imperative, subjunctive), or person (first, second, third) should be avoided unless the logic of the situation dictates otherwise.

Simplify Needlessly big words or involved sentences are hard to read.

Sincerity is essential if you are to be believed. Don't pretend or overstate your case. See p. 60.

Slow movement is desirable in a B–plan letter where you must reason calmly with the reader to justify the unpleasant point you are preparing to present (see **Fast**); otherwise, it is objectionable.

1. Don't use too many words before getting to an important point. Starting too far back in the background, giving too many details, or saying things that should be implied are the most frequent faults.
2. Don't use too many short, choppy sentences and thus slow up a message that should move fast.

SOS Serious errors in sentence **o**rganization and **s**tructure justify the distress signal.

1. Don't present a phrase or dependent clause as a sentence. Usually correction requires only attaching the dependent element to the preceding or following sentence (on which it depends). See **Frag.**

   —In answer to your request concerning what the company is like, what has been accomplished, and the future prospects. Here is the information I have been able to acquire. (Replace the period with a comma.)

2. Don't use a comma—or no punctuation at all—between two independent clauses unless a strong conjunction (*and, but, or,* or *nor*) is there. The error is not basically one of punctuation (as discussed in **P1** and **P2**) but the more serious failure to recognize what a sentence is. You need a period if the two statements are not so closely related that they ought to be in the same sentence, or a semicolon if they are.

   —The credit business is big business some people estimate that it is as much as 86 percent of American business. (Period needed before *some*).

   —Running two sentences together without punctuation is about the worst error a writer can make, however it is little worse than using a comma where a semicolon is required, as in this sentence. See **P2.**

3. Don't put words together in unnatural, confusing relationships that the reader has to ponder to get the intended meaning. (See **K** and **Mod.**)

   —Just because you want to sell I don't want right now to buy. (The fact that you want to sell doesn't mean I want to buy.)

4. Don't put ideas together with connectives that falsely represent their relationship. See **Coh, Conj,** and **Unit.**

Spelling error Here are some tips on spelling and a list of words frequently misspelled in business writing.

1. *Ie* or *ei:* When pronounced like *ee,* write *ie* except after *c* or in *either, neither, leisure, seize,* and *weird* (*achieve, believe; receive, deceive, perceive*). When pronounced otherwise, write *ei* (as in *freight, height, forfeit*) except in *die, lie, pie, tie, vie,* and *science.*

2. Double a final single consonant preceded by a single vowel (*a, e, i, o, u*) in an accented syllable when you add a suffix (*-ing, -ed, -er*) beginning with a vowel (*plan, planning; shop, shopping*). Note that if the word already ends in two consonants, or one preceded by two vowels, you do not double the last consonant (*holding, helping; daubing, seeded*). Note, too, that the

consonant usually is not doubled unless in an accented syllable (*benefit, benefited; refer, referred, references*).

3. Drop a final, unpronounced *e* preceded by a consonant when you add a suffix beginning with a vowel (*hope, hoping; owe, owing*); but retain the *e* after *c* or *g* unless the suffix begins with one of the front vowels, *i* or *e* (*noticeable, changeable, changing, reduced*).
4. Change final *y* to *i* and add *es* for the plural if a consonant precedes the *y* (*ally, allies; tally, tallies*); otherwise, just add *s* (*valley, valleys*).
5. Add *'s* for the possessive of all singulars and of plurals which do not end in *s* (*man's, men's, lady's*); add only apostrophe for *s*-ending plurals (*ladies', Davises', students'*).
6. Hyphenate fractions (nine-tenths) and double-word quantities between 20 and 100 (*twenty-one, thirty-two, forty-four, ninety-eight*).
7. Get somebody to pronounce for you while you try to spell the following words commonly misspelled in business. Then study those you miss (along with others which give you trouble, from whatever source) until you are sure of them.

accidentally
accommodate
accurate
achievement
acquaintance
acquire
affect (influence)
all right
among
analyze
apparent
argument
attorneys
beginning
believe
benefited
category
choose (chose)
comparative
conscientious
conscious
consensus
consistent
convenience
decision
definitely

description
disastrous
effect (result)
embarrass
environment
equipped
exaggerate
excellence
existence
experience
explanation
forty
government
grammar
guarantee
height
imagine
immediately
incidentally
interest
interpret
it's (its)
laboratory
led
lose (loose)
maintenance

moral (morale)
mortgage
necessary
noticeable
occasionally
occurrence
offered
omitted
original
paid
passed (past)
perform
personal
personnel
possession
practical
precede
preferred
prejudiced
prepare
principal
principle
privilege
probably
proceed
procedure

prominent	repetition	transferred
psychology	sense	tries
pursue	separate	too (to, two)
quantity	stationary	undoubtedly
questionnaire	stationery	unnecessary
realize	succeed	until
receive	surprise	using (useful)
recommend	than (then)	varies
referent	their (there)	whether (weather)
referring	thorough	writing (written)

Specific wording, like sharpness in a photograph, helps the reader get a clear idea; general words give only a hazy view.

1. If you are inclined to use the general word for a class of things, consider the advantages of giving the specific kind in that class (machine—mower; office equipment—files, desks, chairs, and typewriters; employees—salesclerks, janitors, secretaries, and others).
2. Another kind of specificness is giving supporting details, illustrations, examples, and full explanations for general statements made. If you use generalities to gain conciseness in topic and summarizing statements, be sure to provide necessary supporting explanations or further details; otherwise, your unsupported statements will not be accepted. See **Dev.**
3. Still another important kind of specificness is giving the evidences of abstract qualities you may use. If you are inclined to say that something is a bargain, an outstanding offer, of the highest quality, revolutionary, best, ideal, or economical, give the concrete evidences for these qualities instead of the abstract words. In an application letter, if you want to convey the idea that you are intelligent, industrious, honest, dependable, and sociable, give the evidence and let the reader draw the conclusions. You will sound too cocky if you apply these words to yourself, and your reader will not believe them anyway, unless you give the supporting concrete facts.

SPM Sales promotion material (when appropriate and unselfish) not only shows a service attitude (see **SA**) and produces some additional sales; it helps to take the sting out of early collection letters and provides a pleasant ending for essentially bad-news letters, provided that the situation is not too seriously negative. See p. 65.

Subordinate Don't overstress negative ideas, facts known to the reader, or insignificant points. If you must say them, put them in the middle of the paragraph or letter, devote little space to them, and/or put them in dependent clauses or phrases. Since dependent clauses are particularly useful in subordinating, here are some of the main beginning words that make clauses dependent: *after, although, as, because, before, if, since, though, till, unless, until, when, where, while.*

SW Shall-will; should-would. General usage differs so much from formal usage of *shall* and *will* that formal practice now sounds old-fashioned and stiff in most letters and reports. In general usage (which is usually appropriate for business writing), *will* has almost completely replaced *shall.* Formal usage calls for *shall* with the first person and *will* with other persons to indicate the simple future, and for the reverse to indicate firm promise or determination.

More important for business writers is the distinction between the simple futures and their conditional forms, *should* and *would.* Using the simple future sometimes seems presumptuous.

—I will appreciate your giving me your answer by November 20 so that. . . . (*Would,* in place of *will,* removes the presumption that the reader will answer, by using the conditional mood and saying, in effect, "*If* you will answer . . . I will appreciate it.")

Syl Divide words at the ends of lines only at syllable breaks, and then only if each part has at least two letters and is pronounceable. If in doubt about where to divide a word, check the dictionary.

Tabulate or itemize when you have lots of figures to present or a series of distinct points to make. Itemization will make you think more sharply and state your ideas more precisely and concisely. Thus you produce clearer, quicker reading and more emphasis.

Telegraphic style (omitting subjects, connective words, and articles, as in telegrams and newspaper headlines) is not acceptable practice in letters and reports.

Ten Watch the tense (time indicated by your verbs) for appropriateness in the individual verb and logic in the sequence of verbs. Do not shift tenses unless the logic of the situation requires. Normally you use the present, past, or future according to the time of the action you are reporting; but use the present for statements that were true in the past, are true now, and will be true later. Any statement you might make about what a book *says* fits the conditions. (See p. 514, Item 4, for tense in reports.)

—The law of supply and demand *means.* . . .
—The 1972 edition *says.* . . .

The tense of the key verb in an independent clause governs a sentence. So the tenses of other verbs or verbals indicate time relative to the time of the main verb:

—I will do it as soon as I am able (a future and relative present).

—I had hoped that I would be able to go (a past perfect and relative future).

Tone Watch out for a tone of distrust, indifference, undue humility, flattery, condescension, preachiness, bragging, anger, accusation, sarcasm, curtness, effusiveness, and exaggeration. See p. 52.

Since salutations and complimentary closes are the first and last indications of your feelings about the formality of your relationship to your reader, be sure they represent those feelings accurately. See p. 72.

Transitions between sentences in a paragraph and between paragraphs must show the relationship. Your best method is use of a thread of logic that will hold your thoughts together like beads on a string. When the logical thread does not make the relationship clear, however, you need to do so by repeating a key word or idea from the preceding or by using a connecting word or phrase that shows the relationship. See **Coh** and **Unit.**

Trite expressions (a form of **Jar**gon) are usually overused and hence worn-out figures of speech that dull your writing. The remedy is to state your idea simply in natural, normal English or to use an original figure of speech.

Unity (of sentences, paragraphs, or whole pieces of writing) requires that you show how each statement fits in or belongs (is not irrelevant). Applied to a sentence or paragraph, **Unit** means that the statement seems irrelevant or that the several ideas are not closely enough related to be in the one sentence or paragraph. When applied to a whole letter or report, it means that the content seems so varied as to lack a central theme and should be put in two or more separate papers. Often, however, the writer sees relationships that justify putting things together as they are, and the fault is in not showing the reader the relationships—an error of coherence (see **Coh**).

—Please put your answers in ink and have your signature witnessed by two people. One of our envelopes is enclosed for your convenience. (The envelope is not a convenience in doing what is requested in the first sentence. The two unrelated ideas should not be in the same paragraph. Adding "in returning your answers" would help.)

Usage refers to the appropriateness of the language to the situation. A passage or expression marked with the symbol may be too formal and stiff, literary, flashy, or highbrow; or too slangy, familiar, crude, or lowbrow. The normal, natural English of educated people conducting their everyday affairs is neither formal nor illiterate, but informal and natural. That's what you should use for most letters and reports.

Be on guard against the following illiterate forms (mostly the result of bad pronunciation): "He is prejudice" (*prejudiced*), "He is bias" (*biased*), "usta" or "use to" (*used to*), "had of" (*had*), "would of" (*would have*), "most all" (*almost all*), "a savings of" (*a saving of*).

Variety (of diction and of sentence pattern, type, and length) is necessary to avoid monotony, which puts readers to sleep. Achieving variety should be a part of the revision process, however, and should not distract your thoughts from saying what you want to say in writing a first draft.

In your revision, see that you haven't begun too many successive sentences the same way (especially not with *I* or *we*). If you have repeated yourself, cut out the repetition unless you need it for emphasis, and then change the wording if the two statements of the same idea are close together.

The usual English sentence pattern is subject-verb-complement; in revision, vary the pattern to avoid a dull sameness. (Page 20 lists various kinds of sentence beginnings.)

Good style also requires variety in sentence type. Some of your sentences should be simple (one independent clause); some should be compound (two independent clauses stating two closely related ideas of nearly equal importance); and some should be complex (at least one independent clause and one or more dependent, all expressing related ideas but of unequal importance). Especially to be avoided are too many successive simple sentences for ideas not deserving equal emphasis or too many compound sentences connected by *and.* (See **Sub.**)

Although most of your sentences should be relatively short (averaging 15–20 words for easy readability), you will produce a monotonous choppiness if all your sentences are in that range. See **Sim** and **Chop,** and revise accordingly.

Wordy See pp. 14 ff.

YA You-attitude. The you-attitude is certainly one of the three most important points about letter writing. People do things for their own benefit, not yours. If you want to persuade them to act, you have to show them the advantages to themselves. Both your reader and you know that you're interested in yourself. Trying to deny that fact would be insincere and disbelieved. But you need not put your selfish interests in the letter; the fact that you want something is no reason for the reader to act. The benefits going the other way are. Write about *them.* See **Self** and p. 40.

To show readers what is in the situation for them, you have to visualize their ways of life and show how your proposal fits in. See **Adapt.**

Although using more *you*'s than *I*'s or *we*'s may help, it is no assurance that your letter has the you-attitude.

X Obvious error. Proofread carefully and correct such errors.

∾ Invert the order or sequence of words or ideas.

⊃ Close up the unnecessary space.

¶ New paragraph needed. See **Par.**

Additional space needed here.

ℊ or ℊ Delete (take out); unnecessary.

←↕→ Move in the direction pointed.

INDEX

Index

I

J

K–L

M

N

O

P

Q

R

This book has been set in 10 point and 9 point Caledonia, leaded 2 points. Part numbers are 14 point Helvetica italic and part titles are 24 point (small) Helvetica. Chapter numbers are 12 point Helvetica italic and chapter titles are 18 point Helvetica. The size of the type page is 27 by 46½ picas.